IN SEARCH OF AENEAS

IN SEARCH OF AENEAS

CLASSICAL MYTH OR BRONZE AGE HERO?

ANTHONY ADOLPH

AMBERLEY

For Roy van Trier

Quotation on back of jacket from *The Aeneid*, translator Robert Fitzgerald (1983).

Front of jacket: Aeneas meets the Cumaean sibyl as he proceeds to the Underworld, by Claude Lorrain, from his *Liber Veritatis* 183, based upon *The Aeneid* Book VI, 260-3; see page 233. (Courtesy of the British Museum)

Half-title page: Terracotta statuary group from Pompeii, showing Aeneas escaping from Troy, carrying his father Anchises and leading his son Ascanius by the hand, now at Naples National Archaeological Museum. (Terracotta Aeneas MAN Naples 110338)

First published 2023

Amberley Publishing
The Hill, Stroud
Gloucestershire, GL5 4EP

www.amberley-books.com

Copyright © Anthony Adolph, 2023

The right of Anthony Adolph to be identified as the Author of this work has been asserted in accordance with the Copyright, Designs and Patents Act 1988.

All rights reserved. No part of this book may be reprinted or reproduced or utilised in any form or by any electronic, mechanical or other means, now known or hereafter invented, including photocopying and recording, or in any information storage or retrieval system, without the permission in writing from the Publishers.

British Library Cataloguing in Publication Data.
A catalogue record for this book is available from the British Library.

ISBN 978 1 3981 0536 2 (hardback)
ISBN 978 1 3981 0537 9 (ebook)

1 2 3 4 5 6 7 8 9 10

Typeset in 10pt on 12pt Sabon.
Typesetting by SJmagic DESIGN SERVICES. India.
Printed in the UK.

'You shall have a dear son who shall reign among the Trojans, and his children's children after him, springing up continually. His name shall be Aeneas.'

                Aphrodite to Anchises, Homeric *Hymn to Aphrodite*

'...[Aeneas] had long been aggrieved with Priam because in spite of his brave deeds he did not give him his due share of honour.'

                Homer, *Iliad* 13

'Is it that you hope to reign over the Trojans in the seat of Priam?'

                Achilles to Aeneas, Homer, *Iliad* 20

'It is fated, moreover, that he [Aeneas] should escape, and that the race of Dardanos, whom Zeus loved above all the sons born to him of mortal women, shall not perish utterly without seed or sign.'

                Poseidon to Hera and Athena, *Iliad* 20

'Seek ye your mother of old [Italy]. There the house of Aeneas shall be lord over all.'

                Apollo to Aeneas, Virgil, *Aeneid* 3

'Aeneas came into Italy from the land of the Molossians [Epiros] after Odysseus and became the founder of the city, which he named after Rome, one of the Trojan women.'

                Hellanikos of Lesvos, quoted in Dionysius of Halicarnassus's
                Roman Antiquities, 1.71

'I have given them [Aeneas's Roman descendants] empire without end.'

                Zeus to Aphrodite, *Aeneid* 1

By the Same Author

Tracing Your Family History (Collins, 2004, three editions)
Tracing Your Home's History (Collins, 2006)
Need to Know? Tracing Your Family History (Collins, 2007)
Tracing Your Irish Family History (Collins, 2007 and Firefly, 2009)
Tracing Your Scottish Family History (Collins, 2008 and Firefly, 2008)
Who Am I? The Family Tree Explorer (Quercus, 2009)
The King's Henchman: Henry Jermyn, Stuart Spymaster and Architect of the British Empire (Gibson Square, 2012); revised in paperback as *The King's Henchman: The Commoner and the Royal who saved the Monarchy from Cromwell* (Gibson Square, 2014)
Tracing Your Aristocratic Ancestors (Pen and Sword, 2013)
In Search of Our Ancient Ancestors: from the Big Bang to Modern Britain, in Science and Myth (Pen and Sword, 2015)
Brutus of Troy, and the Quest for the Ancestry of the British (Pen and Sword, 2015)

Contents

	Sketch Maps	9
	Introduction	13

PART ONE: TROY

	Prelude to Part One	17
1	Love Story on Mount Ida	19
2	Anchises' City	25
3	The Great Mother	30
4	Lightning on Rock	36
5	The Sons of Dardanos	42
6	The Hill of Ate	47
7	Searching for Troy	53
8	The Centaur's Cave	59
9	Journey to Sparta	66
10	The Rape of Helen	75
11	The Princes at Large	82
12	The War Begins	90
13	The Blind Poet	96
14	Musters and Raids	105
15	'Men that Strove with Gods'	113
16	Aeneas and Cressida	120
17	The Battle by the Ships	126
18	Aeneas Faces Achilles	131

19	Defender or Traitor?	139
20	The Fall of Troy	147
21	Of Fire and Flood	152
22	Aeneas, King of Troy?	162

PART TWO: ROME

	Prelude to Part Two	169
23	'I Fared Forth to the Deep'	172
24	'Seek ye Your Mother of Old'	180
25	Encounter at Buthrotum	190
26	Via Enea	198
27	Landfall in Africa	206
28	Aeneas and Dido	213
29	Aeneas in Despair	220
30	The Posillipo Hill	227
31	Aeneas in the Underworld	233
32	At Tiber's Mouth	241
33	Aeneas in Latium	249
34	Arrival in Rome	256
35	The Shield of Aeneas	264
36	The Trojan War Replayed	272
37	Aeneas versus Turnus	276
38	The Unresolved Dilemma	282
39	The Marriage of Aeneas and Lavinia	289
40	The Shrine by the Numicius	296
41	Aeneas Indiges	302
42	Apotheosis	308

Aeneas's Family Tree	316
Aeneas and the Rulers of Rome	317
Select Timeline	318
Acknowledgements	321
Endnotes	322
Bibliography	329
Index	337

The western half of Aeneas's world, encompassing modern Italy and Tunisia.

The eastern half of Aeneas's world, encompassing modern Turkey, Greece and Albania.

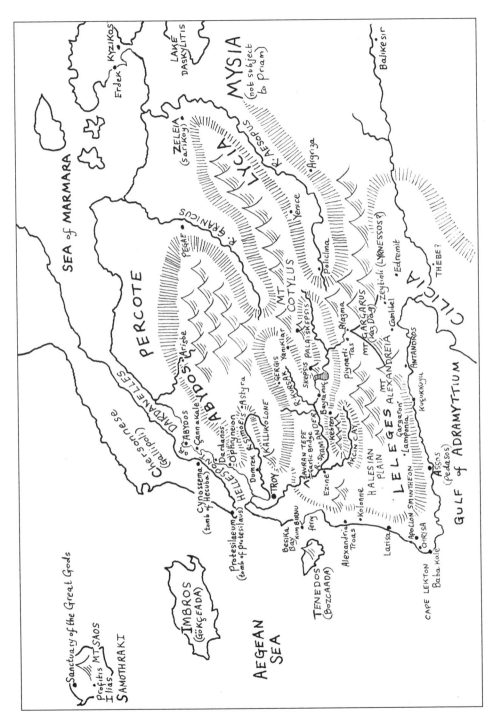

The Troad in Aeneas's time, with the addition of some modern Turkish place names. The kingdom of Dardania was around Palaiskepsis.

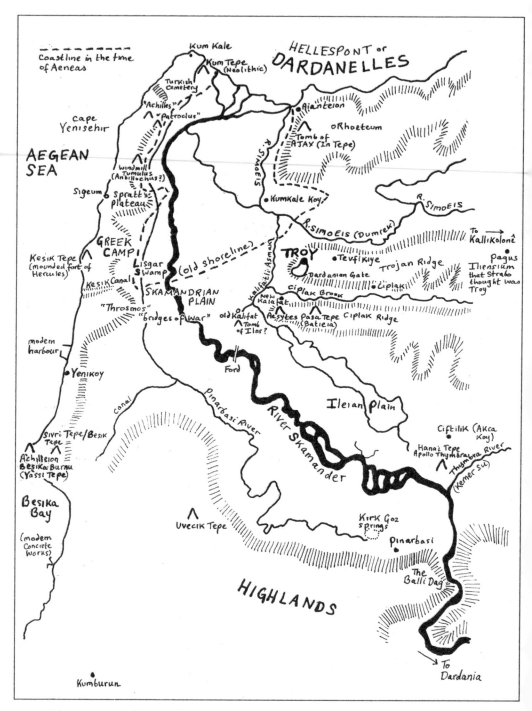

The environs of Troy. The likely coastline of the Hellespont in Aeneas's time, extending almost up to Troy's walls, is shown by a dotted line. Troy's citadel is marked with a black dot, with the outline of its lower city extending south-west down the hillside.

Introduction

The months of July and August commemorate two Roman rulers, Julius Caesar and his heir Augustus Caesar, whose self-image, triumph and calendrical immortality were shaped by their unshakeable belief in their descent from Aeneas, a Bronze Age hero glorified in the Classical mythology of both Greece and Rome.

Aeneas first captured my interest because not only the Caesars but also a number of royal dynasties including some in Dark Age Wales and their royal descendants, down to the Tudors and Stuarts, all regarded him as their ancestor. The current British royal family, much of the aristocracy, the families of most of the American presidents and millions upon millions of ordinary people in and beyond the English-speaking world, all have bloodlines going back to those Welsh monarchs who believed that they were descended from Aeneas. Aeneas was often seen as the forefather of *all* the Romans and Britons, and that increases his role as a mythological ancestor for vast swathes of people across the world today.

Through Aeneas and his mythological mother Aphrodite, all these myriad descendants have a direct genealogical bridge back to the Olympian gods and beyond, to the primeval deities whom the ancient Greeks believed had been born at the start of the world. It is a connection based entirely in myth, of course, but that does not diminish its potency, for in our own history – not least, it could be argued, with the recent storm over Brexit – we humans have acted so often not so much on hard facts, but on what we have wanted to believe was true. Myths of a descent from Aeneas were a major driving force in Rome's rise to pre-eminence as (in its own eyes) a second Troy. Similarly, Medieval and Tudor Londoners, believing the spin-off myth that their city had been founded by Aeneas's great grandson, Brutus of Troy, saw their city as 'Troy Novant', a new Troy in the west, and they justified wars with the Scots on the grounds that Brutus had given Scotland to his second son, but England to his eldest.

In Search of Aeneas

If Aeneas drew breath as a real man, it was in about 1250 BC, as a minor king in Bronze Age western Anatolia, now western Turkey. However inflated his ego may have been by local beliefs that he was the son of a goddess, he would still have been staggered at the way his life was fated to be reimagined so many times, over the centuries ahead, magnifying him into vastly more than he had ever been in real life: a hero beloved of the gods and one of the greatest warriors who fought at Troy; who saved his people and led them west across the sea; who loved and abandoned Dido; who laid the foundations of the Roman Empire – and who became a god, whose apotheosis to Olympia foreshadowed the ascent into Heaven not only of Julius and Augustus Caesar, but also of Jesus Christ himself.

All this made me want to know how such seemingly far-fetched claims were ever justified, and to know everything there was to know about Aeneas; to re-watch Purcell's opera *Dido and Aeneas*; to pick out his fleeting appearances in the 2004 movie *Troy* and the 2018 TV series *Troy: Fall of a City*; and, mainly, to read and seek to understand the venerable works on which they were based – Homer's *Iliad*, which stands at the dawn of all western literature, and Virgil's *Aeneid*, which foreshadowed the close of the Pagan era and the start of the Christian one – and to search out the many other retellings and depictions of Aeneas's life in between and after them both.

In the end, I realised that Aeneas's story was far more than just the complex myth of one man. It is both the product and a driving force of civilisation itself. If we wish to understand properly the civilisation to which we are the heirs today, we must first comprehend Aeneas.

'Where he comes from and where he is going to,' wrote Philip Hardie in his recent study of Aeneas in western literature, 'are in a way, more important than who he is.'[1] True, but Aeneas, both man and mythological hero, remains vitally important, because without him, where he came from – Troy – would be of little relevance now, and where he went – Rome – would be unrecognisable to us without the self-confidence that it derived from him. Perhaps the sheer audacity of Aeneas's myth, above all other factors, was what propelled infant Rome from its early, unfulfilled potential into becoming the predominant city of the whole Mediterranean world and extending its rule into most of Britain.

Aeneas's life is tremendously important to both Western history and culture, but writing it presented some unusual difficulties. Mythological characters can have as many different lives – and deaths – as there were people to invent them. When I wrote my biography of Aeneas's mythological great grandson, Brutus of Troy, I told each version of his story in turn, in chronological order of invention, in order to show how his story had been worked up out of almost nothing. But such an approach made it difficult to compare different re-tellings and re-workings of specific events in his life.

Introduction

In this biography of Aeneas I have taken a different approach, starting with Aeneas's conception, and then working through his life – or lives – step-by-step, comparing at each stage the different versions of his story, as they were told over the centuries, acknowledging along the way his different, alternative fates (as traitor, slave, Trojan king, and travelling hero), and culminating with the grandest Roman stories of his triumph, death, and ascent into the ranks of the Olympian gods. I have also attempted to interweave the necessary historical explanations underpinning the developments of Aeneas's story – and observations on how his myth had a material effect on the unfolding of the history of the western world. The result is certainly complex, but I have tried hard to make it as comprehensible as possible. At the end of the book is a timeline, to make plain the historical events which underpin the story.

Whereas a biographer's task is normally to seek out their subject's individual character, I found multiple personalities reflecting the agendas of the different people who wrote about Aeneas. Though predominantly noble and pious in his actions, we see in these multiple Aeneases plenty of variations, sometimes resentful (of Priam's authority); deceitful (through his alleged plotting with the Greeks); frightened (of Achilles and of the ghost of Creusa); despondent (at sea before Carthage and when his ships were burned at Sicily); angry (at his mother's refusal to meet him in her true form); enraged (with the brutal fury with which Virgil infused him, in order to emphasise his own horror of war) and awestruck (before the glory of the Olympian gods). For all the contradictions, however, there is in our multiple Aeneases a general character progression, from Homer's muscle-bound hero, intent on death or glory, to Virgil's pious pioneer, buffeted by Fate, yet determined to fulfil his destiny: the blue-print on which Roman manhood based itself, but also, thanks to the humanity with which Virgil invested him, a man to whom we can still relate today. As Michael Cunningham wrote in his introduction to R. D. William's *Aeneas and the Roman Hero*: 'The problems of a Trojan prince who lived 3,000 years ago shed light on the perpetual problems of the human race.'

The Romans ended up worshipping pretty much the same gods as the Greeks, but generally used different names for them. This book draws heavily on both Greek and Roman sources, and so, in the original texts, the gods' names appear variously in their Greek or Roman forms, which can cause some confusion, especially to the uninitiated. I have stuck to the original, Greek names throughout. Thus, although Virgil wrote of Aeneas' mother as Venus, she remains for us (as for Homer's Aeneas), Aphrodite.

Where possible, we visited over the decade leading up to the Covid pandemic almost all the places around the Mediterranean to which Aeneas was imagined to have travelled. Time and again, simply being in those places opened our eyes to much that would otherwise have gone unrealised and helped us understand how aspects of his myths had arisen. And because we went to those places with Aeneas's myths as our guide, we saw in our mind's eye so much that we would otherwise have missed: nymphs dancing on the shores of Buthrotum; Cyclopses careering down the side of Etna; Trojan ships gliding silently into the Bay of Naples. Aeneas is the golden thread that connects our culture and mythological genealogy back to the ancient gods and lays bare the psyches of the Greeks and the Romans.

Aeneas is our window, through which we may gaze boldly back into the brilliant dawn of history.

PART ONE

TROY

PRELUDE TO PART ONE

Each morning when he awoke, the rising sun made the inside of his eyelids glow scarlet, as if he was back in his divine mother's womb again. Then, as his blood-flow quickened in the sun's warmth, he gradually opened his eyes, flickering his eyelashes until his pupils adjusted to the brightness, for he did not wish to turn his face away for one moment from the life-giving light.

Before the little boy, the trunks of the pine trees were silhouettes, and so were their branches, bristling with soft needles that disappeared into the blazing aura where the strengthening light shone through them. Warmed by the morning sun, they exuded the pungent smell of resin. Pushing aside the furs that the gentle hands of the nymphs had laid over him, he rose, bursting with joy. Running down to the stream, he cupped his hands to scoop up mouthfuls of ice-clear water. Around him scampered squirrels, their fur as russet as his hair, and the forest echoed with the drumming of woodpeckers.

Now the nymphs came shimmering out of the dark forest like fireflies, even brighter than the light around them. As they approached, they became more corporeal: long-haired, slender, bearing fruit, nuts, a wooden bowl thick with honey, a cup brimming with milk squeezed from the udders of goats up on the mountain pastures. Sitting down in the dewy grass around him, they fed him, each holding out her offerings in turn, and in the chattering of the stream he heard echoes of their voices, laughing as they combed his long, ever-tangled hair, carefully removing the pine needles that were always caught in it.

In Search of Aeneas

He climbed those trees whose nymphs loved him best, branch after branch creating ladders far up towards the vast blue arc of the sky. From the top he gazed out across the treetops, alive with singing birds, up to Mount Ida's peaks, down and away to the distant haze of the Aegean Sea. He explored the mountain's springs, the sources of the youthful river Skamander, following the cascading steams of water down to find rock pools. He lay flat so that the cold steam gurgled all around him, blocking his ears and making the sky above ripple as the water coursed across his eyes. Holding his breath, he waited playfully until the anxious nymphs realised he was missing. The river-god Skamander played along with him, concealing him completely in silvery bubbles so that the poor nymphs were forced to get their diaphanous robes wet, searching about anxiously under the surface for their precious charge.

So his early years passed, until now the morning sun awoke in him something new: an urge to explore further, up to the peak of lofty Ida and down to the salty sea to see its shores for himself; to discover what other mountains, other forests, might lie beyond the silver horizon. He did not think yet of cities, for he had no idea what such things were. He did not know yet the names of Troy, let alone Rome; cities with which his name was destined to be linked, as long as civilisation itself endures.

1

Love Story on Mount Ida

Before Augustus Caesar and Virgil; before Hesiod and Homer; before Priam and Aeneas; before the Olympian gods; before the broad-breasted Earth and the overarching heavens; before even Night had cast her fateful folds across the nascent cosmos, there was, the Ancient Greeks believed, something singular, pure and primal: the divine forebear of all that followed.

The Greek thinkers known as Orphics gave this progenitor many names, including Phanes, Protogonos, 'first-born', and Eros. Sometimes, he was depicted as a dangerously beautiful youth, with cloven hoofs, broad-spreading wings, a lion's head on his chest, a serpent coiled around his lithe body, and flames bursting from his hair. But these were all allegories which attempted to convey the idea that Eros was all things in one; the primal egg that contained the seed of all that was to follow. Eros was something simpler, and greater, than the sum of all his parts. He was the embodiment of that essential, life-giving miracle: Light. Not the brazen light of fire; nor the changing hews of sunlight, that can seem golden at sunset, or buttercup yellow at midday – or blood-red, when seen through closed eyelids. No, Eros's light was as pure and white as the light of a full moon seen against the eternal blackness of the night sky.

And that is why, when the man fated to become Aeneas's father saw an inexplicably pure radiance emanating from the breasts of the girl who stood before him on Mount Ida, inflaming him with desire and making him wonder if she might be a goddess, the poet of the *Hymn to Aphrodite* – who may have been Homer himself – could describe that light in no better terms than being 'like the moon'.

The *Hymn to Aphrodite*, which is among the oldest works in western literature, tells us that as soon as Zeus, king of the immortal gods on Olympus, had filled Aphrodite with insurmountable lust for Anchises, she sped away to her temple in Cyprus. The *Hymn* describes in minute detail how, hastening in, she closed the glittering bronze doors behind her and the three Graces, Euphrosyne, Aglaia and Thalia, bathed the goddess in such heavenly, sweet oil 'as blooms upon the bodies of the eternal gods'. Laughing with delight, Aphrodite was dressed in lovely clothes and golden ornaments. She then dashed away from scented Cyprus, flying high above the clouds, to Anatolia – the land now called Turkey – and to its north-westernmost corner where, Aphrodite knew, lay the land of Troy.

As she flashed through the aether, Aphrodite would have seen the Troad laid out beneath her like a map. Approaching up the Anatolian coast, the Troad's southern border was defined then, as now, by the Gulf of Adramyttium, immediately to the north of which looms the chain of mountains known collectively as Mount Ida. As it runs east along the gulf's northern shore, it rises dramatically. Mid-way on its route, towards the head of the gulf, comes its highest peak, which Homer, in book fourteen of the *Iliad*, calls Mount Gargarus, and which the Turks today know as Kaz Daği, 'goose mountain'. From its eastern end beyond the gulf's head, Ida's range extends northwards, across the eastern end of the upper valley of the Skamander, and it forms an inland massif which the Greeks called Mount Cotylus. A phalanx of lesser mountains then runs right up between the valleys of the Granicus and the Aesopus, towards the Sea of Marmara, thus virtually enclosing what was to become Aeneas's ancestral land from the outside world.

The Sea of Marmara is fed from the east by the Bosporus, at whose neck now sits Istanbul, and thence from the Black Sea, which is filled in turn by the mighty rivers of distant Russia. To the west, as it runs along the northern coast of the Troad, the Sea of Marmara narrows into the straits called the Dardanelles, named after Dardanos, the founder of the family who ruled there. The straits were also called the Hellespont, 'the sea of Helle', after a princess who drowned in its fast-flowing channel (or became a goddess). They separate Troy-land from the Chersonese, or Gallipoli peninsula, to the north, which is part of Europe. Then it flows out into the Aegean, and a low-lying coast sweeps south for 37 miles before turning sharply east into the Gulf of Adramyttium, thus completing our circuit of the Troad's borders.

The Skamander is the Troad's chief river, a name probably dating back to Aeneas's time. The Greeks – and, says Homer, the gods – called this Xanthus, 'the yellow river'; the Turks now call it the Mendere. Skamander rises in the folds of Ida near the Troad's south-eastern corner, fed by many springs, some of which bubble, cold and clear, from the base of mighty Gargarus itself. From its many sources, Skamander flows first west, then north-west, away from the hills, out across the plain towards the north-western corner where the Dardanelles meet the Aegean. Four miles inland from there, airborne Aphrodite would have seen a tiny speck, a tight cluster of houses within high, seemingly impenetrable walls; a city whose name remains to this day loaded with romance, wonder, and doom – Troy.

But just for now, the goddess's desire led her elsewhere, back above Skamander's source, to the highest peaks of Ida around Gargarus. The grey limestone lies exposed to the elements on the very top, but not far below, the mountainsides are clothed with forests of pine trees and further down with planes and beeches. Before Dardanos and his descendants began cultivating the land, these woods tumbled down uninterrupted into the valley of the Skamander. But by now, as Aphrodite descended through the clouds, she would have seen fields and orchards along some of the valley floors and, on the higher slopes, the forest-cover broken occasionally by pastures, where in the summer months grass and bracken was cropped – as it still is today – by horses, cows, sheep and goats, and herdsmen lived, as they still do, in small, seasonal steadings of wooden huts. In such a camp, the *Hymn to Aphrodite* imagines the young Dardanian prince Anchises, playing loudly on his lyre, while his companions were out at work, tending his father's cattle.

Aphrodite avoided the pastures and landed in the wilds. As she walked through the forest, says the *Hymn*, lions, bears and leopards 'fawned' at her feet. Laughing, Aphrodite filled each of them with desire, causing them to hurry away in pairs to copulate beneath the trees, with a passion they had never experienced before. And then she reached the edge of the meadow.

Suddenly, a movement caught Anchises's eye. A girl was standing before him, wearing golden necklaces, bright earrings and intricately twisted broaches, and a dress that outshone fire. Across her breasts shimmered an almost blinding light, 'like the moon'. Anchises guessed she was a goddess, and offered to build her an altar, praying 'let me live long and happily, seeing the light of the sun.' But she claimed she was a mere princess from Phrygia, to the east of the Troad, who had been carried across the farmlands and wilds by Hermes, the messenger-god, to become Anchises's wife and bear him splendid children. She promised that once her father Otreus knew where she was, he would send Anchises a fine dowry.

Anchises was filled by too much 'sweet desire' to question the girl's lies, and he led her at once into his hut. As carefully as she had been dressed, Anchises now removed each of her shining adornments, 'loosened her girdle', and lay the clothes he had stripped from her onto a silver-studded seat. Then, he led her to his bed, piled high with soft blankets, and the pelts of bears and lions that he had hunted and killed on the high peaks of Mount Ida.

There can be few heroes, real or imagined, whose origins and childhood were quite so unusual as Aeneas's. In Homer's *Iliad*, composed in about the 800s BC and the western world's earliest surviving work of literature, we learn that Aeneas's father was Anchises, a descendant of Dardanos and cousin of Priam, king of Troy. Although initially a secret, it became known during Aeneas's lifetime that his mother was golden Aphrodite, the goddess of love, one of the exalted *Dodekatheon* – the 'twelve deities' of Olympus.

The mythological fact of Aeneas's parentage begged more questions than it answered, so a poetic genius, perhaps Homer himself, composed the *Hymn to Aphrodite*, in which the precise circumstances of his conception were imagined. The hymn is one of a collection, often termed 'Homeric hymns', each addressed to an Olympian deity. Each told parts of their stories, and all invoked their blessings. These hymns would often be sung before the recitation of an epic, such as the *Iliad* itself. The attribution of these hymns to Homer is not fanciful, for it was he alone who dared to penetrate the minds and personalities of the gods, giving them the human foibles necessary for them to lust after mortal partners and so conceive heroes – and thus to cause the Trojan War.

Even Homer dared not imagine what it was like to make love to Aphrodite; the *Hymn*'s poet says only that, afterwards, Anchises fell into a deeply contented sleep. But now her ardent desire for Anchises had been satisfied, Aphrodite realised that Zeus had duped her, driving her mad with those same arrows of desire that she had used so often to trick him, and some of the other Olympian deities too, into sleeping with mortals. Only now did she realise quite how humiliating the outcome could feel. Worse, the herdsmen would soon be returning from the pastures with their livestock, and their profane eyes would feast on her naked body.

Quickly, Aphrodite dressed and roused her lover, by invoking the name of his own, god-born ancestor: 'Wake up, son of Dardanos!'

Bleary-eyed, Anchises saw Aphrodite in all her Olympian glory, her head reaching to the rafters. He hid his face in terror below the furs. I knew at once that you were a goddess, he protested, but you did not tell me the truth. Do not leave me alone on Earth now, he pleads; it is well known that mortal men who have lain with goddesses are left permanently sapped of their vitality.

If you could keep your youthful mind and physique, she replied, I'd gladly call you my consort; but soon enough, wearying old age will enfold you. True, she could ask for Anchises to be made immortal, but after Zeus had humiliated her like this, she could not bring herself to beg him for such a favour. In any case, she continued selfishly, things never go well for mortal men who try to pair up with deities. Just think of Anchises's own Trojan relatives, Ganymede, who was abducted by Zeus, and Tithonus, who was beloved of rosy-fingered Dawn. Ganymede was made immortal, so his fate was to remain permanently juvenile. And when Dawn begged Zeus to make Tithonus immortal, she forgot to ask for him not to grow old. Tithonus, according to the myth, was thus doomed to spend eternity as a wizened old man, whose desiccated voice wheezes to this very day, all across the Mediterranean, in the stridulations of cicadas. Immortality, claimed Aphrodite, always comes with a terrible price.

As for the child they had conceived, Aphrodite continued, she would call him Aeneas, which she claimed (incorrectly) came from the Greek *ainon akhos*, 'awful sorrow', an apt reflection of her shame at having been tricked by Zeus. But, sweetening the pill somewhat, she reassured Anchises that their son would one day 'reign among the Trojans, and his children's children after him, springing up continually'. That was a prophecy which, in mythological terms, came true. But, as ever with deities' promises, there was an unspecified price – which we, Homer's audience, know would be the devastation of the Trojan War.

Love Story on Mount Ida

In the meantime, said Aphrodite, 'as soon as he [Aeneas] sees the light of the sun, the deep-breasted mountain nymphs who inhabit this great and holy mountain shall bring him up ... and as soon as he is come to lovely boyhood, [they] will bring him here to you and show you your child.' Anchises would rejoice when he saw his son, 'a scion to delight the eyes ... for he shall be most godlike.' Then, Anchises must take the boy to Troy. If anyone asked who the boy's mother was, Anchises must say it was one of 'the flower-like nymphs who inhabit this forest-clad hill'. And, if you ever brag that you slept with me, she added, Zeus will smite you with his thunderbolt.

That is how the Greeks in Homer's time imagined the conception of Aeneas, high up on Mount Ida, through the union of the Trojan prince Anchises and the immortal goddess Aphrodite. No writers seem to have described his birth, from the womb of a goddess. For Aphrodite, it was presumably a painless experience, attended by the Idaean nymphs and the Greek goddess of childbirth, Eileithyia.

At Aphrodisias, about 200 miles south-east of Troy, stands the Sebasteion, a temple for the worship of Aphrodite and her imperial Roman descendants. It was built in about AD 20-60 by two local brothers, Attalos and Diogenes, keen to curry favour with the Julio-Claudian emperors in Rome who considered Aeneas to be their ancestor. The reliefs on the front include a scene showing a seated, robed young woman, holding a naked baby in her lap. Next to them stands a handsome young man. He is nude as well, save for a cloak, and he gazes lovingly at the woman. Above, the bright moon looks on. The woman is depicted *velificatio*, with her cloak billowing up behind her head, so we know this is Aphrodite. Because this scene is next to one of Aeneas escaping the Fall of Troy, the cloaked man is thought to be Anchises, and the baby Aeneas. Invented to please a Roman emperor, this scene of domestic bliss, witnessed only by the moon, seems never to have been written about in Greek mythology.

We know goddesses could express milk, because Zeus once tricked his wife Hera into suckling his illegitimate son Hercules, and when the boy drew too hard, her milk squirted out to become the Milky Way. But Aphrodite may never have suckled Aeneas, for she seems to have delegated most of his upbringing to the Idaean nymphs. Yet in the British Museum is a bronze mirror from the ancient world, on whose back is engraved two nude women; one is winged, and by the leg of the other stands a little naked boy wearing a Phrygian cap,[1] probably Aeneas. One of the women is probably one of the nymphs who brought Aeneas up; the other could, perhaps, be Aphrodite herself, paying at least a fleeting visit to her little son.

'Of rocks and mountains were you begotten,' Dido says to Aeneas, in the seventh *Heriode* of Ovid (d. AD 18), 'and of the oaks sprung from the lofty cliff.' Flowery pastures aside, Mount Ida could indeed be a harsh place, the home of wolves, bears, *kaplans* or mountain leopards and even lions. They were subject to Aphrodite, as the hymn tells us, but even so the nymphs may have had to be constantly vigilant to stop them eating the young

In Search of Aeneas

Aeneas. Growing up here would have made Aeneas tough and agile, a good preparation for the hard life of warrior and traveller that awaited him.

In Ursula Le Guin's 2008 novel *Lavinia*, Aeneas recalls that he was 'with women in the woods, on the mountain ... they let me run about... I'd get into trouble, and one of them would come and laugh and scoop me up. I was wild as a bear cub.' Aeneas's early childhood world, populated by ethereal spirits, was as magical as the fairyland imagined by Shakespeare in *A Midsummer Night's Dream*. Yet from the nymphs' perspective, looking after Aeneas must have forced them to focus on the material world and human needs. They would have had to learn how to tease milk out of the teats of mountain deer and goats; to gather fruits; to spin wool and weave clothes; and build shelters out of the branches of their own pines. And all in order to tend their precious charge, Aeneas, the son of Aphrodite.

2

Anchises' City

For the Aeneas of the *Hymn to Aphrodite*, life among the ethereal nymphs of Mount Ida would have been reality. The world of men and cities, even Troy, can have been no more than a dream. Yet when Aeneas was five, as Aphrodite had decreed, he was led out of the forest, either by the nymphs or by the goddess herself, depending on which version of the *Hymn to Aphrodite* you read, and across the flowery pasture to the steading where he had been conceived. We may imagine him turning, longing to return to the familiar safety of the woods, only to see his ethereal guardians vanish like mist. In *Lavinia*, he recalls, slightly differently, that Anchises had come to the forest to find him: 'A lame man, in armour. I was afraid of him.' But the result was the same. Aeneas might still be the offspring of a goddess, but from now on he was, primarily, the son of a mortal man.

Anchises would have known, as the *Hymn* tells us, that he must take Aeneas eventually to Troy, but first he probably took him to his own home nearby. Every second of the experience must have assailed Aeneas with new experiences and sensations: the shock of being out in the open pasture; the sweaty smell of his father; the breathiness of human speech; Anchises's shadow long on the short-cropped grass; the odours of livestock; the excited chatter of people as father and son approached the hill-top city with its stone walls; the sight of timber-framed, mud-brick houses, with smoke rising from the fires inside oozing out through the thatched roofs. And Aeneas would have heard for the first time the name of his father's city, the capital of Anchises's kingdom of Dardania: Skepsis.

When Aeneas appears first in Homer's *Iliad*, during the muster in book two, he is introduced as 'brave Aeneas, whom Aphrodite bore to Anchises, when she, goddess though she was, had lain with him upon the mountain slopes of Ida,' and the contingent of men he leads are called Dardanians. In *Iliad* 20, Aeneas himself relates that his ancestor Dardanos founded Dardania 'on the spurs of many-fountained Ida', long before Dardanos's descendants settled on the plain below. Thus, although Greek settlers long after Aeneas's time founded a city called Dardania up by the Hellespont, and this confused some writers into thinking that the realm of Dardania had been on the coast, there is no doubt from Homer's words that Anchises's realm was a mountain one. In book thirteen of his monumental *Geographia* of the Roman Empire, Strabo (d. AD 24) makes this clear, too. Drawing heavily on a now lost 30-book treatise on the Homeric geography of the Troad, written by Demetrius of Skepsis in about the early 100s BC, Strabo asserts that Dardania was 'the country at the foot of Ida', which 'was subject to Aeneas', and before him, by implication, to Anchises. Dardania extended, says Strabo, along the Skamander valley from a point south of Troy, right up to Skepsis, and north-east (along the upper Aesopus Valley) towards the Dardanelles.

Dardania's capital, says Strabo, was Skepsis. There were actually two places of this name: according to Strabo, there was an original city of Skepsis, where Aeneas's family lived, and then, after Aeneas's time, this was abandoned and a new city of the same name was built 60 stades – just over 6½ miles – further down the Skamander valley, after which the original site became known – as we shall call it now – as Palaiskepsis, 'old Skepsis'.

The site of the new Skepsis was identified in 1860 by the local British and American consul, Frank Calvert, at Kurşunlu Tepe, where the Skamander valley broadens out into a fertile upland plain. Calvert proved the identification by finding coins bearing the city's pine-tree emblem, and an inscription referring to Skepsis' temple of Athena. The hilltop there is still littered with broken pottery and we found a few chunks of marble, probably from that same Athena temple, though most of its stone and marble has been reused in the village below and in the modern town of Bayramiç, a couple of miles west along the Skamander. Skepsis's lower city extended across the valley floor, most of which is now covered by a modern reservoir. Strabo places the move to this new city of Skepsis from the older Palaiskepsis in the generation after Aeneas. Modern archaeologists place it more soberly in the 400s BC, but regardless of when the move took place, the story, affirmed by Demetrius of Skepsis, is that Palaiskepsis – and not (new) Skepsis – had been the location of 'the palace of Aeneas' and, by inference, of Anchises, and Anchises's ancestors before him.

Precisely where Palaiskepsis was vexed students of the Troad's geography for a long time. Strabo worked before the invention of modern maps and described everywhere in terms of distances from other places. That makes his descriptions difficult to follow, even when you know where some of the places are, and nigh-on impossible when his points of reference are long-since lost. Three times, Strabo mentions Palaiskepsis as a point of reference when describing other places, and he also provides a description of its location. Professor Cook, the Director of the British School at Athens, concluded that these four descriptions together were 'irreconcilable'; one reference put Palaiskepsis vaguely on the west coast and another in the Aesopus valley near Polichna, a city whose location is itself unclear. The third states that 'higher up [the Skamander] are the Kebrenians, and still higher up ... are the Dardanians, who extend as far as Palaiskepsis and Skepsis itself.'[1] Kebren is an ancient city on the south side of the Skamander valley, south-east of the new Skepsis. This third description accords best with Strabo's direct one: 'Palaiskepsis lies above Kebren near the highest part of Mount Ida, near Polichna; and it was then called Skepsis (whether for another reason or from the fact that the place is visible all round, if it is right to derive from Greek words names then used by barbarians), but later the inhabitants were removed sixty stadia lower down to the present Skepsis.'[2]

Because it was the ancestral home of Aeneas, the location of Palaiskepsis was a matter of interest to explorers. In *Greek Cities and Islands of Asia Minor*, Vaux quotes the claims of a German diplomat, Dr Andreas Mordtmann, to have found 'a most ancient city with its acropolis, towers and walls built of hewn stone, and furnished with four gates [at] Eski Skisepje', somewhere in the upper Aesopus Valley. But it is not at all clear where this was, or whether it really was Palaiskepsis. But tackling the problem afresh in 1967, Professor Cook heard of 'a kale [castle] with walls of cut stones' on the small mountain of Ikizce behind the village of Tongurlu, 6½ miles east up the Skamander from (new) Skepsis. Ikizce belongs to a low chain within the Ida massif, running west from Mount Cotylus. Known locally (we were told) as 'Hera's Mountains', this chain runs west, ultimately, to the hill of (new) Skepsis.

Ikizce is Turkish for 'twins' because it has two peaks, Büyük ('big') and Küçük ('little'). Cook first explored Büyük, the highest one, but his long scramble up availed no evidence of an ancient settlement. But when Cook explored Küçük, which is to the left of Büyük when seen from Tongurlu, he found ruins, part of a black-glazed pot from about the 400s BC, and 'a flattish sherd of red ware',[3] which his colleague James Mellaart, the discoverer of Çatalhöyük, later dated to about 1,000 years *before* Aeneas's time. That makes the site one of the very few settlements in the Troad that might have been flourishing *in* Aeneas's time. Its location fits the third of Strabo's indirect descriptions and answers his direct one very well. The site is indeed 'visible all round', as Strabo had described, and, as Cook wrote, 'The distance from [new] Skepsis at Kurşunlu Tepe fits exactly, and the description harmonizes sufficiently to allow us on the strength of this passage [of Strabo's] to identify Palaiskepsis with Ikizce.'[4]

Armed with Cook's description and a road map which showed Tongurlu as a dot just north of the road along the upper Skamander valley, we approached the village and were relieved to see the two peaks rising up, the left one lower than the right. Despite a few cars, telegraph wires and satellite dishes, Tongurlu seemed immediately to tug us back into the past, for its houses are still largely made with timber frames and mud bricks built over stone bases, a strategy developed long before Aeneas's time, to help withstand earthquakes.

In Search of Aeneas

We drove up the dirt track out of the village, past vegetable patches and hand-hewn wooden sheep pens. Parking at a fork in the dirt track, we continued on foot. The right-hand track curved up and eventually bent sharply right, but a path led off to the left, up between two fences, to an upland pasture, beyond which was a forest, rising up towards the left-hand peak. Once within the pine forest, we could no longer see our destination, so decided simply to keep going up, and it helped when we found a dry stream bed that led us upwards. The sky was blue above the dark green pine branches, and the dried needles on the forest floor were russet-red. A pair of purple emperor butterflies landed on them, coupling, just as Aeneas's parents were said to have done near here, three thousand years earlier.

Finally, we approached the summit and were delighted to find the ground strewn, as Cook had reported, with ancient, broken roof-tiles. In ancient times, most ordinary houses had flat roofs of thatch over wooden beams, so carefully made roof-tiles are often a sign of higher-status buildings. The summit was small, boulder-strewn and overgrown with pines and oaks. For most of its circuit, search though we might, we were disappointed not to find anything resembling masonry. But on the south-western end, at last, we found the remains of walls, about the height of a man. They were made in Cyclopean style, out of large, irregularly shaped boulders, smoothed on one side to give the wall a flattish outer edge. The excitement was enormous. Treasure-hunters had peppered the site with pits, and among what they discarded was an intact pottery loom weight. We left it there but when we later showed pictures of it to a Turkish archaeologist, he thought it dated to any time before 600 BC. Mycenaean loom weights that we have seen subsequently were very similar to this one. In the absence of any more archaeological evidence, all this tends to agree with Cook's identification of Küçük as Palaiskepsis.

Later, exploring the dell below Tongurlu, we met two local farmers. They spoke no English but understood when we said our interest was in 'archaeology'. They pointed immediately to Küçük and said 'Skepsis'. Whether they were recalling an ancient tradition, or simply repeating what Cook had told their fathers, we cannot say. We met the farmers while looking for a row of burial mounds, which Cook had been told were the traditional burial places of the kings of the mountain-top castle. We found instead a recently flattened football pitch, partly bulldozed into the hillside, and the remains of only one mound, two-thirds cut away. The farmers paced out the circumference of where another had been, but then their sons, who spoke English, arrived. They were more suspicious of us, and flatly denied that any such mounds had ever been there. Perhaps these bulldozed mounds had belonged to Aeneas's dynasty.

Although Palaiskepsis was an ancient 'city', it would have been no bigger than a modern Turkish village, its gardens full of parsley, peppermint, basil and bitter mountain herbs, which are said to promote a long life, and teeming with chickens, lambs and the strong, long-legged, golden-furred and black-eared Kazdaği Kangal dogs, which shepherds still use to guard their flocks on Ida today. But with its peak clear of trees, Palaiskepsis's finely built walls would have made an impressive statement, visible from the upper Skamander valley to the south and the valley of the Kursak, a tributary of the Skamander, to the north. Both valleys, we may suppose, were part of Anchises's realm of Dardania. It seems safe enough, therefore, to imagine young Aeneas, exploring his new mountain-top home of Skepsis on what is now Küçük, in the weeks following his arrival, and learning more about who he really was.

3

The Great Mother

The *Hymn to Aphrodite* and the *Iliad* are of course both Greek works, which retell parts of Aeneas's story from a Greek perspective. But Troy, and Aeneas, were Anatolian. To have any hope of understanding the real Aeneas, we must try to see through these Greek works to the Anatolian world that had inspired them.

Humans are not born from goddesses, but some cultures believed this was possible, and ancient Anatolia's may have been one of them. They knew nothing of Aphrodite, who was a Greek goddess, but they did worship goddesses whose origins lay, like hers, in a belief as old as human thought itself and inspired by the fact that women give birth: that a female life-force pervades the world, causing the birth and growth of plants and animals.

This is probably what our ancient ancestors were celebrating when they painted female animals on the walls of caves during the Ice Age. It must surely be what they had in mind when they carved figurines showing mothers with pendulous breasts and bulging wombs. Though they are a world away from the graceful beauty of Classical Greek statues of Aeneas's mother, archaeologists term them 'Venus figurines', after the Roman name for Aphrodite. The oldest Venus figurines date from the start of modern human occupation of Ice-Age Europe, some 42,000 years ago, and they were still being fashioned in Çatalhöyük, the first city built in Anatolia, only 390 miles south-east of Troy, about 9,500 years ago. Whoever they depicted at the beginning, this life-giving female form came to represent Mother Earth or the Great Mother, and she acquired as many names and forms as there were tribes and peoples to imagine them. The name on which the Greeks settled for Mother Earth was Gaia, while other local manifestations of this Great Mother were known as Dione in north-west Greece; Rhea in Crete; Hera in the country around Mycenae; Wanassa in Cyprus; Astarte or Ashtoreth in Phoenicia; and Ishtar or Inanna in Mesopotamia, the land between the Tigris and Euphrates to the east of Anatolia. In Anatolia itself, she was Kuvava or

Kubeleya, a name the Greeks transliterated as Kybele. Each goddess had her own attributes and stories; all had their roots in the ancient reverence for Mother Earth, the Great Mother.

Greek mythology multiplied these goddesses so many times that eventually Olympia was full of them. Athena was seen as Zeus's daughter, the patroness of cities; her half-sisters were Persephone, who caused the rebirth of the land in the spring; Artemis, overseer of hunting and birthing mothers; and Eileithyia, the deity of childbirth itself. Hestia, with care of hearth and home, was seen as Zeus's sister, as was Demeter, goddess of crops. Their roots all go back to the Great Mother, and all were embodiments of the primal female force.

In the Greek pantheon, Aeneas's mother Aphrodite was the goddess of sexual desire, a characteristic she inherited from a re-combination of Wanassa and Astarte/Ishtar, as worshipped on Cyprus. But when the Greek sources speak of Aeneas being conceived on Mount Ida by Anchises and Aphrodite, they imposed the name of one of their pantheon of goddesses onto the local Anatolian one, Kybele, who was in turn a manifestation of Ishtar or Inanna, who was worshipped further to the east. This becomes evident from details in the *Hymn to Aphrodite*. For instance, Kybele is often shown seated on a throne, flanked by sitting lionesses. That is why, when Aphrodite reaches Mount Ida, the lions, bears and leopards worship so willingly at her feet, for in the original myth she was their mistress, Kybele.

The *Hymn to Aphrodite* hints at earlier stories told in Bronze Age Anatolia of Kybele's own sexual exploits; as Kybele's story emerges later on, her lover was called Attis, whose doomed affair with her often led to his emasculation. Of Inanna, Kybele's counterpart further east in Mesopotamia, we know a lot, and Charles Penglase argued that the *Hymn to Aphrodite* showed clear parallels with Inanna's story. In one surviving Mesopotamian text, *Inanna's descent into the nether world*, which is at least 4,000 years old, and probably considerably older, we hear that Inanna was the goddess of love, sex and war. Already queen of Heaven and mistress of the Earth, she was deeply jealous of her sister Ereshkigal, who ruled the Underworld. Much detail is lavished on Inanna's preparations for descent into the Underworld, with adornments including a mascara called 'let a man come', and a pectoral or breastplate called 'come, man, come'. Her preparations are echoed in the *Hymn* by Aphrodite's own preparations on Cyprus, before she set out to seduce Anchises. Once arrayed, we hear that Inanna's breasts shone 'like a moonbeam', just as Anchises saw the light across Aphrodite's breasts shimmering 'like the moon'.

In each case, the goddess's journeys resulted in the loss of their clothes, Aphrodite in Anchises's bed, and Inanna as demons stripped her while she descended into the Underworld. Aphrodite's fate was to fall pregnant by a mortal man: Inanna's was to be killed by Ereshkigal, and her corpse hung up on a hook. The dead Inanna begged the other gods to help her, and her father Ea (Enki) permitted her to return to the world of the living, but only if she sent a substitute to the Underworld to take her place. Inanna hastened up to the living world, to the great apple tree on the plain of Kulaba, where she found her consort 'Dumuzi the shepherd' – whose parallel in the *Hymn*, of course, was Anchises, playing the part of a herdsman. Clothed in magnificent garments and seated on a splendid throne, Dumuzi did not look as if he had missed Inanna very much, so she, annoyed, nominated him to take her place. The demons who had come with her to claim their prize seized him, but a friendly god, Inanna's brother, turned Dumuzi into a snake, and he escaped into the apple tree – all presumably providing the prototype for the story of the serpent in the Hebrew Bible's Garden of Eden, which was composed long after this. Pitying Dumuzi, Inanna negotiated a compromise: he would spend half of each year in the Underworld, and for the other half his place would be taken by his sister Geshtinanna, whose name meant 'vine of Heaven'. Dumuzi's death each autumn was symbolic of the death of the year, when snakes are seen sliding into their holes to hibernate, and his return each spring was heralded by the snakes' return: a metaphor which explained, to the people of ancient Mesopotamia, the death and rebirth of the year.

The details of Dumuzi's fate are not strongly echoed in Anchises's story, save for a probably coincidental incident in *Aeneid 5*, when Anchises's spirit appears briefly in Sicily in the form of a snake. But in general, the result is the same: being a goddess's consort can only end in trouble. In Anchises's case, Aphrodite threatened him with Zeus's thunderbolt if he told anybody about sleeping with her. Presumably, eventually, he did let the truth slip out (for if not, we would not know about it) – and the thunderbolt came. Hyginus (d. AD 17) makes the thunderbolt fatal to Anchises, but Virgil's Anchises says, in *Aeneid* 2, that he was merely crippled by it, and Pseudo-Servius adds that it was Aphrodite herself who deflected the otherwise fatal blow at the last minute. Thus, Joseph of Exeter could write, in his retelling of the Troy story, of Anchises being 'sometimes bent and sometimes straight, unsteady, hates to walk and spares his crippled feet'.[1] So being the lover of the goddess caused both the shepherd Dumuzi and the herdsman Anchises suffering. The Mesopotamian myths make Dumuzi's sacrifice necessary for the renewal of the land in spring; and without Anchises's suffering, we would have no Aeneas. The *Hymn to Aphrodite* is not a straightforward Greek interpretation of *Inanna's descent into the nether world*. But the parallels between the stories do strongly suggest that it was a Greek retelling of an otherwise unrecorded Anatolian version of Inanna's story.

In Mesopotamia, and probably in Anatolia too, such myths were more than pretty stories. Instead, they accompanied and explained actual rituals, enacted by kings and priestesses, intended to ensure the fertility of the land. Again, hard evidence from Anatolia is lacking, but in neighbouring Mesopotamia there is abundant evidence that kings would play the role of Dumuzi by processing to the *eannas*, the temples of Inanna, to climb into a sacred bed with a woman, who was either a priestess or a prostitute (or perhaps both), and who was believed to be inhabited, however temporarily, by the spirit of Inanna. We know this from surviving hymns, including the *Hymn to Inanna*, composed in the Mesopotamian city of Isin in about 1900 BC; the remarkably direct *Plough my Vulva*; and the tenth *Shulgi hymn*. The latter relates how King Shulgi comes to Uruk-Kullab with gifts for the *eanna* temple. Donning a special wig and robes, Shulgi is brought into Inanna's presence, and she recounts the sacred marriage they have contracted, full of detailed descriptions of their sexual exploits. The end result is the fertility of the land.[2]

Another ancient Mesopotamian text, *The King and Inanna*,[3] relates, similarly, how a priest playing the role of Innana's vizir, Ninshubur, would orchestrate the coupling of king and goddess at the city's New Year festival. After this, the king would till the fields like a farmer and tend the flocks like a good shepherd, and the natural world, which was subject to Inanna, would respond with abundance. The king's congress with the goddess-substitute symbolised his people's endeavours to cultivate the land and ensured their success. It also served to elevate the king himself to the status of a goddess's consort. This was no coupling, incidentally, of a powerful king with an unwilling woman. The evidence suggests that high priestesses blessed and controlled the harvest, organised storage and rationing of food, and were therefore people of considerable economic and political power. In fact, their consenting to sleep with kings was probably what bestowed on such men their moral and spiritual authority. Daughters born from such ritual couplings may have become royal consorts or priestesses themselves; sons most likely stood out among all the kings' other sons by wives and concubines – for they may well have been considered to be goddess-born.

Here, then, we have a possible explanation for the Greeks' story that Aeneas was the son of Aphrodite. It may have been true, in the sense that his father, Anchises, might indeed have engaged in a fertility rite with a priestess, whose body was believed to be inhabited at the time by the Anatolian equivalent of Aphrodite, Kybele.

Although such practices had died out by Homer's time, Bettany Hughes argues that myths about Mycenaean Greece, the land that went to war with Troy, conceal plenty of examples of kings gaining their thrones through their marriages to powerful women. Menelaus is said to have become king of Sparta, for instance, not by male-line inheritance, but by marrying Helen, the daughter of the previous king, Tyndareus. The implication is that, at the time, women such as Helen may have been similarly associated with goddesses and might have wielded similar spiritual power.[4]

Oliver Gurney's work on the Hittites shows that the relationship of Anatolia's kings with its goddesses was still a vital one in Aeneas's time. Anatolia's many kings, and those of Cyprus and Syria too, were subject to the Hittite Great Kings, whose capital, Hattusa, near what is now Boğazkale in central Turkey, was 440 miles east of Troy. Gurney quotes the Hittite Great King Hattusilis III (1264-1239 BC), who may actually have been alive during the Trojan War, recording how he was 'dedicated as a young man to the service of the goddess Ishtar of Samuha ... the goddess, my lady, always held me by the hand.' He had been able to overthrow his nephew Urhi-Teshub 'because my lady Ishtar had previously promised me the throne.'[5]

This example catches the tail-end of the close connection between Anatolia's kings and goddesses. It helps confirm that the *Hymn to Aphrodite* and the *Iliad* may have been echoing genuine traditions from the Troad, that Aeneas was a goddess's son. The story added lustre to one of the most prominent Trojan captains in the Trojan War, and seems to have passed down, first in Trojan and later in Greek oral tradition, until it formed the basis of the written Greek texts as we know them now.

That transfer of information, from Anatolian stories to the Greek myths, happened due to an accident of history that helps explain the prominence of the Trojan War, and hence of Aeneas, in our own western tradition. The whole Eastern Mediterranean sits on the join between two tectonic plates, subject to periods of violent disturbance. The Trojan War seems to have coincided with such a period. In its aftermath, mainland Greece, already depleted by the war effort, was struck by a series of earthquakes. Mycenae and its allied strongholds across Greece were shaken to the core, and as they collapsed, roof-beams and ornate wall-hangings were set alight by a myriad displaced oil-lamps, explaining the burnt layers often found in the archaeological record.

It was then, runs the theory, that the age-old faith in protective mother-goddesses was shaken. From then on, they were demoted, becoming subservient wives or daughters to the male deities who had once been their mere consorts. These consorts rose in Greek imagination to pre-eminence, the foremost among them being the brothers Poseidon the sea god, whom Homer calls 'the earthshaker'; Hades, lord of the Underworld, and Zeus, whose lightning and meteors rained down from the heavens, while the (female) Earth heaved subserviently below.

While this physical and psychological turmoil raged, Dorian tribesmen, realising the weakness of once-powerful Mycenae, came ravening down from the Balkans and across the mountains of Epiros to pillage and then settle in mainland Greece. Mycenaean civilisation collapsed so completely that its Linear B script ceased to be used or understood.

In about the 1100s BC, some of the survivors started emigrating east in high-prowed ships. They established new colonies, which dangled down the Anatolian coastline, south from the Troad, like an earring. Ionian Greeks from the Peloponnese settled the lushly wooded islands along the Anatolian coast, such as Chios, and later founded cities along the mainland shore, including Smyrna (Izmir), Ephesus (Selçuk), Miletus (Balat) and Halicarnassus (Bodrum). Meanwhile, Aeolians from Thessaly settled the islands further north, particularly Lesvos, opposite the southern coast of the Troad. In their new havens, these Greeks preserved some of their ancient culture and from their colonies, much later on, there sprung the

The Great Mother

likes of Aristotle, father of natural science; Hippocrates, father of medicine; Herodotus, father of history – and Homer, who sang of Aeneas.

To these Ionians and Aeolians, the Trojan War was no abstract idea. They owed their presence in the east to its aftermath. Lesvos's rulers claimed descent from Penthilus, son of Orestes, son of Agamemnon who had led the Greek attack on Troy. The Lesvians could not only see Mount Ida from their island, but on their north coast are ancient harbours where Agamemnon and Achilles were said to have moored their fleets; we were even shown a stone bollard on the quay at Mithymna which is said to be the very one to which Agamemnon's ship was moored. Furthermore, colonists from Lesvos penetrated the Troad itself, founding, re-founding or taking over cities, at Kebren, Skepsis and even one that they called New Ilion, atop the ruins of Troy itself. This is why so much oral tradition about the Trojan War and the life of Aeneas made its way from Anatolian tales into Greek literature, and why both loom so large in the Greek – and hence the western – imagination.

'In Asia Minor and Greece, as in Italy, the primitive population ... often thought it could see the earthly shape of the Goddess in a mountain, and consequently worshipped the mountain as the Mother.' So wrote Maarten Vermaseren in his masterful study of Kybele.[6] Having explored the likely location of Palaiskepsis on Küçük, we were left pondering an apparent coincidence, not commented upon by Professor Cook, that Küçük and its taller neighbour, Büyük look strikingly like a giant pair of breasts, in just the manner that Vermaseren meant. Many ancient sites do indeed seem to have been chosen because features in the landscape have a human look about them. In this case, the whole of Mount Ida was known to have been sacred to Kybele, so this breast-like pair in Ida's foothills may have suggested to Aeneas's ancestors the particular presence of the goddess, and an appropriate place for her worship. In making his identification of Küçük as Palaiskepsis, Cook drew solely on Strabo and sought only archaeological evidence; he did not consider the landscape's appearance, nor the myths about Aeneas's origins. It is therefore remarkable that Cook's logical identification of Aeneas's ancestral home placed it in a location strongly suggestive of goddess-worship. If Palaiskepsis was on Küçük, then had Kybele, whom the Greeks later identified as Aphrodite, been worshipped up on Büyük?

Cook, of course, had explored Büyük, looking for a city. He commented 'nothing came to light on top. The mountain is rocky and covered with pine forest.'[7] Cook was looking only for man-made structures, so he left disappointed. But there was more than one way to worship a goddess.

4

Lightning on Rock

Forty miles north-west of the Trojan coast lies the island of Samothraki, that westerners call Samothrace. It is a uniquely beautiful island, whose lower slopes are clothed with ferns and ancient plane woods, punctuated by hot thermal springs and cold waterfalls and rock pools, all imbued with a magical atmosphere, enhanced by an annual summer influx of young New Age travellers who frolic naked in its waters.

Samothraki was created by a volcano, now extinct, whose exploded cone forms a towering mountain, anciently called Saos and now known as Fengari, the highest peak of all the Aegean islands. In *Iliad* 13, Homer refers to Poseidon sitting up there to watch the Trojan War. It was once objected that this was impossible because the island of Imbros, that the Turks call Gökçeada, lies in the way. But Professor Luce asserted that Saos's peak can be seen from the Trojan coast, in clear weather, over the top of low-lying Imbros – and we can confirm that this is true.

Samothraki features in Aeneas's myths as the birthplace of his ancestor Dardanos and the original home of the Penantes, which Dardanos was believed to have taken to Italy. The island was first inhabited by Thracians, from the mainland just to the north. Then came Minoan Cretans in about 1800 BC, who settled on the south coast, followed in the 700s BC by Greek colonists from Lesvos. Samothraki is best known today for its Sanctuary of the *Theoi Megaloi* (the 'Great Gods'), a collection of Greek and Roman ruins among which was found the famous statue of winged Nike ('Victory'), now in the Louvre.

The Sanctuary of the Great Gods is easy to find. From the organised chaos of the ferry port at Kamariotissa on the western point of the island, you drive along the peaceful north coast road, past fields and the occasional house and deserted beach bar. After 3½ miles, you approach a spur of Saos that stands above the old harbour, where in ancient times visitors, including Aeneas, would have landed. Just before this is Palaiopoli, a collection of modern houses. You proceed on foot past a little chapel and over a bridge across the stream. It is impossible not to feel excited as the path winds up between the trees, past the archaeological museum, to a ticket kiosk: with relief, we find it open, for you can never really tell in advance with Greek archaeological sites. Then you begin to glimpse between the ancient plane trees the ruined walls of ancient buildings and the five re-erected white marble pillars of the Hieron, two supporting a section of architrave. The bulk of Saos looms behind.

The Hieron is only one of the sanctuary's sacred buildings, and was probably used for some of the mysterious rites conducted here. Among the others is the Rotunda of Arsinoë, the lower parts of its thick, circular stone walls very well preserved. Arsinoë was the wife of Lysimachos, Alexander's general who ended up ruling this region, including Troy. She built her rotunda to emphasise her own piety, and to receive the *theoroi*, the sacred ambassadors who came here from all over the ancient world. Both buildings are Classical adornments to this ancient site, which was far less developed back in Aeneas's time.

Near the foot of the rotunda's outside wall, lacking an explanatory sign and overlooked by most visitors, is something described in Karl Lehman's *Samothrace* that we have come to see in particular: the sacred stone. It is said to be lodestone, in other words, magnetic. It was also believed, probably in consequence of this, to contain the living presence of a deity. Such sacred stones exist across the ancient world: in Palestine, they were called *betyls*, from the Semitic *bet el*, 'house of god'. On Samothraki, the deity present in the sacred stone was believed to be the Great Mother, who was known in Anatolia as Kybele. Images of her appear on Samothrakian coins in Anatolian style, enthroned and flanked by sitting lionesses.

In the 700s BC, and from time immemorial, local rites were performed around this stone in the island's original Thracian dialect. Instead of replacing these rites with Greek ones, the Lesvian settlers encouraged them to continue, retaining the use of Thracian to create an aura of mystery. From this developed the cult of the Great Gods. All the later buildings, whose ruins now dominate the site, came about because of the presence of the stone, and the deity it was believed to embody. In these secret rites of the Great Gods, the goddess's whispered Thracian name was Axieros.

The sacred stone is composed of coloured porphyry, mainly blue-grey, with patches of green and reddish-brown; it is roughly 4 feet high and 7 feet wide. Occasionally, Greek visitors scrambled down to touch or even embrace it; one woman doing so appeared to be in tears. We clamber down, our feet scrunching the dry plane leaves which had drifted there, and try to detect any trace of the stone's ancient power using a magnet. We are disappointed initially, but as we work our way around the rock, suddenly we feel the smallest of tugs, and when we let go of the magnet, it remains attached. Only one small patch of the sacred stone is magnetic but – not at all coincidentally – this part is faced by a rock slab set into the earth, identified by archaeologists as an altar, which had presumably been used for making offerings. Iron rings have been excavated nearby; when placed near the magnetic patch, these would have allowed worshippers to experience the stone's tug, thus enabling them to feel in direct contact with the latent power within the rock.

The pull we felt through our magnet came from a patch of magnetite (Fe_3O_2) in the rock, which had been magnetised to become lodestone (Fe_3O_4). Lodestone is only ever found on the Earth's surface, and never underground. It is believed, therefore, that magnetisation takes place due to the magnetite being struck by lightning, which causes the magnetite's microcrystalline structure to become aligned in one direction. Other ferromagnetic materials such as iron, nickel and cobalt can become magnetised in this way for a while, but only magnetite retains permanently the changes wrought by the lightning. Being magnetised, each lodestone, including the patch we found on Samothraki's sacred stone, has a north and south pole. When we held a small compass next to it, the stone's south pole seemed initially to attract the compass's north pole, but then something rather odd happened, because the compass seemed to flip around. For almost a year thereafter, the compass's 'north' point consistently pointed south, and *vice versa*. Ancient though this lodestone was, it still had the power to realign the tiny compass needle's microcrystalline structure in the opposite direction.

We read so often in ancient writings about the power of the gods and usually dismiss such ideas as make-believe, so it was a moving experience on Samothraki to feel, albeit via a magnet and a compass, the *actual* power of a stone believed by the Greeks to have been inhabited by a goddess. And lest anyone think that this link between magnetic rock and sacred site is a coincidence, we later visited another sacred stone, on the opposite, southern flanks of Samothraki, at Mandal Panaghia above Profitis Ilias. Goddess figurines have been found here, and the rock is faced by the remains of a stone-built altar. And we found, sure enough, that a patch on the rock that was faced directly by the altar was similarly magnetised. And this connection is not unique to Samothraki. Evidence that objects and places struck by lightning were considered sacred, presumably because of the sudden connection they formed between the Earth and the unseen forces of Heaven, comes from elsewhere, too. Recently, the Calanais Virtual Reconstruction Project, studying the Neolithic remains at Calanais on the Isle of Lewis, Scotland, identified a stone circle at Airigh na Beinne Bige ('Site XI') that appears to have been centred on a massive, star-shaped magnetic anomaly in the centre – either the result of a single, large lighting strike or many smaller strikes on the same spot.[1]

Our experiences on Samothraki provided an insight into the way the Great Mother, whether called Kybele, Inanna or Axieros, was worshipped in this part of the Eastern Mediterranean. They gave us the clue we needed as to what we should look for up on Büyük. Perhaps the rocks there, which Cook had stumbled over in his futile quest for man-made walls, could yield evidence of the worship of the Great Mother, who lay at the heart of the myth of Aeneas's origins.

In the spring we returned to the Troad. We approached Büyük. Chaffinches, chiffchaffs and a cuckoo were calling from the leafless oaks around Büyük's base, and the steep woodland floor was peppered with blue wood anemones and grape hyacinths. We pushed our way through budding branches until we found a sort of track, made by the rootlings of wild boars, which led us up through the pines, until at last we reached the rounded hilltop.

Here and there were little outcrops of rock, and stones scattered about, but at the eastern end of the hilltop we found something less jumbled. Two substantial rocks, about 8 feet high and not unlike those used for western European dolmens, stood side by side and at a slight angle to each other, forming a triangular cleft. Students of megaliths, like Alexander Keiler, who devoted his life to the study of Avebury in Wiltshire, often interpret broad dolmen stones as representing females, and thin, phallic ones as representing males; in such an interpretation, this natural arrangement of 'female' rocks could be representative of a vagina. The Bronze Age Dardanians, coming up the hill from the direction of Palaiskepsis, may well have thought the same.

The vaginal cleft does not face Palaiskepsis precisely, but it is in only a few degrees off. Above it is a natural cairn with a clear (or perhaps deliberately cleared) space next to it. Directly below this, and thus behind the two rocks, is a natural rock amphitheatre on the sloping hillside, about 30 feet wide and relatively clear (or possibly cleared) of boulders. This 'amphitheatre' faces directly south across the deep Skamander valley to Gargarus, the highest peak of Ida. Many Neolithic and Bronze Age sites were chosen because they respected prominent features in the landscape: this one, with the rocks facing Palaiskepsis and its amphitheatre facing Gargarus, answers those requirements well.

There was no clear sign of any man-made structures except, just to the north-east of the cairn, a horseshoe of boulders, perhaps natural, but reminiscent of the base of a circular hut. The rest seemed natural. But long after our ancestors started building temples, they also continued to worship in natural 'groves', just like this; places made unusual by nature, and which they believed had been created specially by the deities themselves.

The rocks on top of Büyük are pale grey on their weathered surfaces, but where they had been broken open by frost, they revealed themselves to be deeply ferrous, containing different shades of brown, orange and blood-red, vivid in the sunlight. Patches of bright red thus appeared all over the site, and if this was a site associated with the Great Mother, it would be difficult to dissociate this from the blood of childbirth.

Vermaseren wrote that Kybele's sanctuaries 'were generally situated in a cave or near a rock in accordance with an old tradition'.[2] But our quest, using magnet and compass, to find a rock with a magnetic patch on it proved fruitless. We cannot say there was not one, but we tried our hardest and found nothing.

As we left, I picked up a little piece of rock, almost black, but with patches of blood-red on it. Later, reflecting sadly on our failure to find a magnetic rock similar to those on Samothraki, I was fiddling with it and also, as it happens, with the magnet, when suddenly I felt the slightest tug. To my astonishment, a patch on the tip of it was magnetic. It seemed scarcely credible, but there it was. So, inadvertently, we had found evidence that magnetic rocks exist up on Büyük after all. In Aeneas's time, there could have been a rock, known to the locals, that had been permanently magnetised by a lightning strike; firm proof, to ancient minds, of the goddess's presence in the natural hill-top sanctuary facing Gargarus.

Later, we found more magnetised pieces of rock, one lying near the base of Büyük, and a couple more elsewhere on Ida. Each tells, presumably, of a lightning strike and the consequent realignment of microcrystals of magnetite within. If magnetism was indeed associated with the Great Mother's presence here, as on Samothraki, then it is small wonder that Mount Ida was considered to be sacred to her, in her local persona of Kybele.

A real Dardanian king called Anchises may, therefore, have had ritual sex with a priestess of Kybele, the Great Mother, who was later identified by the Greeks as Aphrodite. If we are right, the goddess's sanctuary was up on Büyük, Palaiskepsis's twin hill, so perhaps it was there that the ritual coupling of Anchises and the priestess took place.

Perhaps, in about 1250 BC, King Anchises of Dardania set out from his palace in the city the Greeks later called Palaiskepsis, on the mountain-top of Küçük. Dressed as Dumuzi, in fine robes and a ceremonial wig of dark, braided hair, Anchises's role was to lead the new year festival. Drums beat and sacred hymns were sung as, led by a priest playing the role of the vizir Ninshubur, Anchises was led down the hill and then up again, through the pine woods, to the top of Büyük, to the *eanna*, or sacred grove, of Kybele. The high priestess of the goddess was already ritually bathed, anointed and arrayed in finery; she was believed to be inhabited by the goddess. She was ceremonially stripped and lay down on the sacred bed, strewn with grasses and flowers. Anchises-Dumuzi was stripped, too, and climbed into bed with her. As the people chanted, the full moon shone bright across the priestess-goddess's breasts, and they made love. The fertility of Dardania was ensured for another year. And, on that occasion, a boy-child was conceived. Perhaps.

The Greek myths speak of Aeneas being brought up on Ida under the goddess's care, and then handed over to his father, so maybe that actually happened. We may imagine Anchises returning to Büyük a year later and, after another great night-time ceremony, being led to the vaginal cleft. Here was the priestess, her hands, arms, breasts and face perhaps drenched in the blood of sacrificed goats. As cymbals crashed and her acolytes chanted, she reached into the cleft and brought forth the baby, naked, his skin painted red, perhaps, using the ground, ferrous rock of the mountain mixed with olive oil. I have tried making such a paste from Büyük's red rock and it colours the skin an orange-red colour, not dissimilar to blood. The baby boy was the biological son of king and priestess but, in the minds of all those present, he was the offspring of king and goddess. The priestess held him aloft, so all could marvel at the prodigy, and then handed him to his waiting father, who kissed him and accepted this gift, from the realm of the immortals, into the world of mortals. And they called him Aeneas.

If we are right, such an event may really have happened, up on Büyük. If not, something similar may have happened elsewhere on Ida. In any event, Aeneas was marked out for posterity as the son of a goddess: an extraordinary origin that destined him for an equally exceptional place in western literature.

5

The Sons of Dardanos

We hear Aeneas's pedigree for the first time from his own mouth, in *Iliad* 20, as he stands facing his arch-foe, Achilles, on the battlefield before Troy.

> 'Learn then my lineage if you will – and it is known to many – in the beginning Dardanos was the son of Zeus, and founded Dardania, for Troy was not yet established on the plain for men to dwell in, and her people still abode on the spurs of many-fountained Ida. Dardanos had a son, king Erichthonius, who was wealthiest of all men living; he had three thousand mares that fed by the water-meadows, they and their foals with them... Erichthonius begat Tros, king of the Trojans, and Tros had three noble sons, Ilos, Assaracus, and Ganymede who was comeliest of mortal men; wherefore the gods carried him off to be Zeus's cupbearer, for his beauty's sake, that he might dwell among the immortals. Ilos begat Laomedon, and Laomedon begat Tithonus, Priam, Lampus, Clytius, and Hiketaon... But Assaracus was father to Capys, and Capys to Anchises, who was my father.'

This is one of the finest, if not the finest, pedigree in the world. It is one to which numerous dynasties have laid claim, by forging ancestral connections back to Aeneas or Priam. The Caesars did so, and later the kings of France and the Holy Roman Emperors. So, too, did the kings of Dark Age Gwynedd in north Wales, via a purely mythological great grandson of Aeneas, invented for them by their own bards and monks, called Brutus of Troy, and the Tudors later forged a link back to it to benefit from its prestige.

This pedigree, that the Homeric Aeneas, at least, may have learned during his time with Anchises at Palaiskepsis (on, as we have argued, the hill of Küçük), linked him back to the very origins of Dardania and placed him in a delicate position that would affect him deeply, in relation to the royal family of Troy.

The Sons of Dardanos

Dardanos's name was invented, like the names of many founding heroes, by Greek etiology. This assumed, incorrectly, that most realms and cities were named after founding heroes. Dardania existed, so there must have been a founding hero called Dardanos. Once the founding hero existed, his story could be embellished with a spouse, siblings and descendants, often all with names derived, etiologically, from local place-names. These lovingly fabricated pedigrees were then brought down to connect with the genuinely remembered ancestors of living rulers.

The founding hero also needed to be given parents. These were often imagined to have been a mortal and a deity, sometimes a mortal man and a goddess, but more often the other way around. All such imagined couplings, which produced the founding heroes of Greece and its neighbours, were collected together in the *Catalogue of Women*. This is often called the *Hesiodic Catalogue*, because it tended to be attributed to the earliest-known genealogist, Hesiod, but Martin West, who reconstructed much of the *Catalogue* from surviving fragments and quotes from it by other authors, dated it convincingly to the 500s BC, about 200 years after Hesiod's time.[1]

In the *Catalogue*, Dardanos gained a mother, Elektra, whom Nonnus, much later, asserted had been Zeus's secret wife. The *Catalogue* adds that besides Dardanos, Elektra bore Zeus a son, Iasion, also called Eetion or Iasios, whose fate was to fall in love with his aunt Demeter.

The name of Dardania is genuinely ancient. It appears as 'Drdny' in an Egyptian text, which lists the Hittites' allies who checked the advance of Ramesses II at the Battle of Kadesh in 1274 BC, not long, probably, before Aeneas was born.[2] While the hero Dardanos might be a later Greek invention, it is possible that the real Aeneas really was a Dardanian, and that he was told of an ancestor whose name echoed that of his kingdom. If so, perhaps this original Anatolian Dardanos was believed to be the son of the Great Mother, conceived up on Büyük. That idea is perhaps echoed in Servius when he says that, among the places where Dardanos was believed to have been born, were 'Troy and Ida'.[3] The Greek story that Dardanos's father was the Greek storm-god, Zeus, could reflect an earlier, local tradition, in which his father was the Anatolian storm-god, Tarhunna or Tešup. Perhaps this original Dardanos's conception was believed to have been caused by a lightning strike that magnetised a rock up in the Great Mother's sanctuary (as we have speculated) on Büyük in the first place.

A later development in the myth of Aeneas's ancestor Dardanos appears in Hellanikos of Lesvos's *Troika*, written in the 400s BC, but perhaps based on a much older tradition. This places Dardanos's birth on Samothraki. Later still, in the 200s BC, Pseudo-Apollodorus's *Bibliotheka* adds that Zeus killed Iasion with a thunderbolt to stop him raping Demeter, and Dardanos's grief at the death of his brother was what caused him to migrate from Samothraki to the Troad.[4]

In Search of Aeneas

This apparent shift in birthplaces may have been due to the Lesvians who, as we have heard, colonised both the Troad and Samothraki. In the process they may have gained local blood and thus had every reason to take to heart any older foundation myths they heard in those places. By asserting that Dardanos, the founder of the earliest kingdom in the Troad, was from Samothraki, the Lesvians created a mythological link between their colonies in those two places. The presence, on both Mount Ida and Samothraki, of magnetic rocks, which were believed to be imbued with the actual presence of the Great Mother, may have helped with this synthesis. If it was believed that a magnetic rock on Ida was the mother of Dardanos, then that belief could be transferred to another magnetic rock, on Samothraki. That may also help explain why, by the time the *Catalogue* was written, Dardanos's mother had gained the name Elektra.

Electricity was given its name by William Gilbert (1544-1603) of Colchester, Essex, who produced static electricity by rubbing amber, whose Greek name is *êlektron*. The Greeks knew of this strange, latent power of amber, and they also knew of the magnetic power of stones like those on Samothraki and Mount Ida. In the 500s BC, Thales of Miletus, a Greek colony 120 miles down the Anatolian coast from Lesvos, gave magnets their name because of magnetic rocks he found at nearby Magnesia. Aristotle, who lived for a time on Lesvos, wrote of Thales's belief that 'a magnet has a soul, because it has the power of moving iron.'[5] We know now that magnetism is caused by rocks that contain certain minerals being subject to a strong electric charge, which can be caused naturally by lightning. While this connection does not appear in early Greek scientific writings, it seems plain enough that in Aeneas's time, a similar connection had been made; both amber (*êlektron*) and rocks struck by lightning contained mysterious yet palpable powers that, in the absence of scientific knowledge, must denote the presence of the Great Mother.

Long ago, let us suppose, a lightning bolt struck a rock up on Büyük, and its electric force magnetised the stone. In the local origin myth, perhaps, the storm god Tarhunna had impregnated the Great Mother, and from their violent union was born the founding hero of Dardania, called something like 'Dardanos'. Much later, finding a magnetic rock being worshipped on Samothraki, the Lesvian colonists transferred the story of Dardanos's conception from Mount Ida to the Sanctuary of the Great Gods. As a consequence, they called his mother Elektra, a name which they associated with rocks that exuded some sort of palpable power.

As the traditions of Samothraki's sanctuary developed, Elektra became separated from the deity of the sacred stone. She gained her own place in Greek mythology, becoming a daughter of Pleione (daughter of the Titan Oceanos) by Atlas, the Titan whose fate was to hold up the heavens to stop them collapsing onto the Earth. Elektra and her sisters, therefore, were the Pleiades, whose fate was to become the little ring of stars that flicker like tiny diamonds, having lost their earlier brilliance, it is said, when they looked down and witnessed the fall of Troy. The goddess of Samothraki's sacred stone, meanwhile, retained her original, Thracian name of Axieros. But it is striking that in the Samothrakian mysteries Axieros had, besides a consort called Kadmilos, two attendant deities, depicted as naked youths and probably sons of hers. They were known as the Kabeiroi and were also identified as Iasion and Dardanos.

We hear more of Aeneas's ancestors coming down from Dardanos, in Pseudo-Apollodorus's *Bibliotheka*.[6] This follows the pedigree recited by Aeneas himself in *Iliad* 20, and which is repeated in the *Catalogue*, but in more detail. It provides the background to the world in which the Aeneas of Greek mythology found himself, as he continued his boyish explorations of Palaiskepsis.

The original Dardanos was probably imagined to have populated a pristine and previously uninhabited Troad with his descendants. But the Greeks had a love of back-stories, so in the *Bibliotheka*, when Dardanos came from Samothraki to the Troad, he found it inhabited already, and ruled by Teucer, or Tewkros, whose daughter Arsiba or Bateia he proceeded to marry. Teucer was either the son of the god of the river Skamander by a nymph of Mount Ida or, according to a later story of Callinus's, as reported in Strabo, he was from Crete.[7] This story – which was later to confuse Virgil's Anchises on Delos – probably arose because there is a Mount Ida on Crete, too, but it may reflect genuine memories of contact between Minoan Crete and the Troad. Cretans definitely settled at Mikro Vouni on Samothraki, and there must have been trading contacts between Crete and Troy. It is because of Teucer that poets sometimes called the Trojans 'Teucrians'.

We learn more about Dardanos from Dionysius of Halicarnassus (c. 54 BC–after 7 BC). Halicarnassus, now called Bodrum, was a Greek city 200 miles south of Troy. Dionysius settled in Rome, where he spent twenty-two years researching and writing his monumental *Roman Antiquities*. As a Greek, Dionysius clearly felt himself better qualified than the Romans to make sense of their history, which they claimed was rooted, via Aeneas, in the eastern Mediterranean. Unlike the Roman poets, and in sharp contrast to most historians before and for a long time after him, Dionysius took the time to state what different sources said about particular subjects, without attempting to synthesise one 'true' story out of them. By doing so, Dionysius preserved many variants of myths which would otherwise have been lost, including a story that Teucer gave Dardanos the land where he built his city (i.e. Palaiskepsis), and that Idaeus, a son of Dardanos by a previous wife, introduced the worship of Kybele into Anatolia.[8]

When Teucer died, Dardanos became ruler of the entire Troad and had by Arsiba a daughter Idaia, who married Phineas, king of Salmydessus on the Black Sea, a marriage which, though mythical, is a fair reflection of the actual reach of Troy's trade-links. Dardanos and Arsiba also had two sons, Ilos, who died childless, and Erichthonius.

Dardanos's heir, Erichthonius, married Astyoche, daughter of the god of the river Simois, which flows just north of Troy, and they had a son, Tros. Erichthonius's name was Greek: another man of the same name founded Athens. Leaf thought that Erichthonius's name had been interpolated into Aeneas's pedigree by Athenian scholars after Homer's time, in order to justify their territorial ambitions in the Troad.[9] So, in Martin West's analysis, Tros may originally have been Dardanos's son, rather than his grandson.

The Greek conceit was that Tros named the land 'the Troad' after himself. He was Aeneas's great great grandfather, and married Callirrhoe, another daughter of the god of the Skamander. Their offspring were Cleopatra, also called Cleomestra; Ilos, the second to bear that name; Ganymede, who was so attractive that Zeus fell in love with him and made him his cupbearer; and Assaracus. Assaracus, who inherited Dardania, married Hieromneme, a daughter of the god of the Simois, and was father of Capys, who was father in turn of Anchises, 'who aroused Aphrodite's amorous desire', as the *Bibliotheka* recalls, and produced Aeneas.[10]

The blood of Olympian gods, river gods and humans intermingled with magical potency in Aeneas's veins, but his pedigree revealed a tension. Although his father Anchises ruled in their ancestral patrimony of Dardania, he belonged to the junior branch of the royal line. For Assaracus's older brother Ilos founded Troy, which was inherited by Laomedon, whose own son Priam was now king there. Troy's kings, as the senior branch of the family, were overlords of the entire Troad, with Aeneas's line in Dardania as their vassals. But if Priam's line died out, Anchises, and then Aeneas, would inherit Troy. The position of Anchises and his son Aeneas was at once privileged and frustrating. They were royal, but were subservient to their cousin Priam and his brood of sons. As Aeneas was soon to discover, this was not destined to be a recipe for family harmony.

6

The Hill of Ate

In the *Hymn to Aphrodite*, the goddess told Anchises that the nymphs would bring Aeneas to him when he had grown into boyhood, and that Anchises must then take him to Troy. We may imagine the pair, therefore, spending some time in the interim at Palaiskepsis, with the young Aeneas gazing out from the ramparts across the woods and valleys, south to the high peak of Gargarus – but with increasing frequency towards the north-west, with youthful curiosity, in the direction of that place which everyone, not least his father, seemed to talk about all the time: Troy. Until, at last, the time came for Anchises to do as Aphrodite had instructed and take their son there. We may assume that by doing so, Anchises would ensure Priam's recognition of Aeneas as the heir of Dardania, and thus his distant, yet still very real, position in the line of succession to Troy.

The route would have been well known to Anchises through numerous earlier visits to Troy, to attend royal councils, feasts and festivals requiring the presence of the extended royal family – or to go to the annual international trading fair which some scholars now believe took place before Troy's walls. The route would have taken them past the royal tombs and through the city's fields in the valley bottom. Today, the whole valley is heavily cultivated with peach, fig and walnut orchards. Then, much of it would still have been virgin forest of plane and poplar, but the land immediately below Palaiskepsis must have been brimming with produce, not least grapes. In his AD 1100s reimagining of the Trojan story, Joseph of Exeter wrote that below Ida's dense pines forests were clearings where 'drunken vines', had plenty of sunlight; the wine produced there was just as good, he claimed, as any from Salerno or Champagne.[1] It was probably akin to the wine still made around Izmir and on Tenedos (which the Turks call Bozcaada), just off the Trojan coast, from a grape called Karasakis or Kuntra. Lean, sweet and tawny-orange, it smells of honey; the locals still drink it and talk long into the night, just as the Dardanians must have done in Aeneas's time.

In Search of Aeneas

Because Anchises was crippled, they probably travelled in a two-wheeled chariot, drawn by two horses, perhaps with a seat for Anchises while his son held the reins. We may imagine them bumping down the ancient trackway, with the river Skamander chattering along companionably beside them, following its stony bed between banks lined with reeds; noisy with frogs, alive with the darting flashes of kingfishers and damsel flies. Soon, the river is joined by another branch, gushing down south from the springs of Ayazma, below the highest peak of Gargarus. Because this branch comes from the highest peak, it is considered to be the river's main source. But it was not for nothing that Homer referred to the mountain in *Iliad* 11 as having many springs, for in reality, Skamander's sources lie all around the valley, each outlet contributing to the river's ever broader course. In Britain, people dedicate park benches to the memory of deceased relatives. On Ida, they dedicate drinking fountains fed by springs,

Soon, the valley broadens and loops north, passing the hill to which, perhaps as much as eight centuries later, the population of Palaiskepsis would move in order to build the new Skepsis. Aeneas and Anchises would have forded the Kursak, whose valley lies to the north of Palaiskepsis, and then the Aidoneus, both of which flow in from the east. Swelled Skamander then turns west again, its banks patrolled by grey herons and white egrets, opening out into the upland plain of Bayramiç, 18 miles in length and 3 or 4 miles wide. Today it is one of the Troad's largest areas of arable, far richer than the land around Troy itself. It is heavily cultivated now, and there may have been some farms among the woods along the riverbank in Aeneas's time.

At what is now Ezine, Skamander meets another branch of itself which flows up from the south, and together they turn north. At some point, Anchises and Aeneas must have crossed the river, perhaps fording it at the place where there is now an old concrete bridge called Garlic Bridge; that bridge was part of the old north-south road, until it was superseded by a dual carriageway that crosses the river via a bridge just to the west.

As their chariot rattled north, they would have seen that the pine-forested mountains which edge the plain were closing in, and Anchises could point out the way into the narrow gorge through which the now broad Skamander snakes its way. Ravens croak overhead in those parts. As they rounded a bend they would have seen the precipitous rocky sides of the hill the Turks now call the Balli Dağ, which means 'honey hill', because wild bees live there. There are barrows nearby, probably from long after Aeneas's time and which were said to contain the bodies of Priam and his sons, Hector and Paris. From the 600s BC onwards, a fortress stood on the Balli Dağ, which some early nineteenth-century archaeologists, particularly Jean Baptiste Lechevalier and Count Choiseul-Gouffier, thought was Troy itself. Perhaps there was a smaller fortress there in Aeneas's time, guarding this rough country, for this is the most likely geographic border between Dardania and Troy.

Leaving the pass and looking back south, Aeneas would have seen that the river had led them through a gap in a wall of high limestone hills. Looking north, a broad plain stretches away to the north and west. To the east are low hills, rising up in the hazy distance towards the northern spur of Ida. Soon they would have encountered some of the famous springs which well up from the base of the limestone hills, at the place now called Kirk Goz, 'forty eyes', near the village of Pinarbaşi, 'place of springs'.

Soon, they would pick up the old waggon road mentioned in *Iliad* 22, and follow it north-west across what Homer, in *Iliad* 21, termed the Ilian Plain. Today it is covered with fruit orchards and fields of wheat, maize, tomatoes and peppers. It was probably only partly cultivated then, but as they grew closer to Troy they would have passed an increasing number of fields of wheat or barley, vines and fruits, and pastures full of herds of horned cattle, and those fleet-hoofed horses for which Troy was famed. In the hedges grow the short, thick-leaved Trojan oaks, home to jays and hoopoes. Always on the track before the traveller are the plain's ubiquitous, pale brown crested larks.

Soon the Skamander, with its rich fauna of emerald frogs, black cormorants and yellow wagtails, is joined from the east by the smaller river Thymbrios, now called the Kemer Su. At their junction, on the low hill later called Hanay Tepe, was, according to Cook, the temple of Apollo Thymbra, which Stephen of Byzantium said had been founded by Dardanos and named after his friend Thymbrus. Aeneas and Anchises may have made a detour across the river to pray there to the sun-god, Apollo, the patron god of Troy, before continuing their journey north.

The mother of Aeneas's great grandfather Assaracus was the nymph Callirrhoe, daughter of the god of the Skamander. In *Iliad* 20, Achilles calls Skamander a son of Zeus, which makes sense, because the river's many springs on Ida are fed, ultimately, by rain from Zeus's thunder clouds. In *Iliad* 21, we learn that the Trojans worshipped Skamander as a god by sacrificing bulls and horses in the river. Imagine, as Anchises took Aeneas further up the river, that they encountered just such a ceremony in progress; how Aeneas would have found the air thick with dust and the smell of dung and seen with astonished eyes the tumult of fine stallions and roaring bulls being dragged into the river by Trojans with long ropes. Then the priests, risking their own lives, plunge into the water and with gleaming swords, slice open the beasts' necks, releasing their fury and fear into the air and causing their blood to gush out in dark clouds, billowing through the turbulent water – transferring the beasts' lifeblood into the living waters of Aeneas's ancestor, Skamander, who in turn bestows his life-giving water, as he still does today, to the entire Trojan plain.

Continuing north across the plain, Aeneas and his father would have drawn close to that city whose name has resonated across the centuries like no other. But if Aeneas had expected Troy to be a towering fortress, like Palaiskepsis or the Balli Dağ, he would have been disappointed. Troy sits on the low Hill of Ate, at the western end of a low ridge, with a stream now called the Ciplak Brook to the south and the Simois, now called the Dumrek

Su, to the north. Today, the Simois makes its own way north to the sea, but in Aeneas's time, it probably flowed into the Skamander below Troy's northwestern bastion. But though the site lacked dramatic height, Aeneas would still have gazed in wonder at the mighty wall which curved down from the ridge to enfold the lower city on the plain below, and the sheer, inward-sloping walls of the citadel upon the ridge's end, painted white to bedazzle all who approached. At regular intervals along the walls, square towers rose up, crowned with battlements and doubtless decorated with brightly coloured flags, flapping in the stiff, cooling breeze which blows down constantly from the north-east, a wind for which Troy was famed.

We may imagine them entering the lower city, weaving their way through shopkeepers haggling with housewives over bread and fish; black-robed grandmothers chatting while they hung washing over the edges of the flat roofs; old men snoozing in the little squares; children scampering around the complaining mules; older boys playing with wooden swords. Among the Trojan voices, Anchises may have pointed out to Aeneas the dialects and tongues of traders and sailors, from the plains of Greece and the mountains of Macedonia; from windswept Thrace and snowy Scythia; from Lydia and Pergamon; Crete and Rhodes; Byblos and Sidon; Hazor and Askalon; Assyria and Babylonia; Philistia and Egypt; Libya and Ethiopia, whose people's skin had been blackened, the Greeks believed, by the relentless blaze of all-seeing Apollo.

Their chariot passes through the Dardanian Gate and clatters up the well-paved street, inset with water channels, towards the Pergamos, Troy's acropolis. Picture Aeneas and Anchises touring the upper city to visit its palaces and the temples of the Trojan gods, including (according to Homer) Apollo and the city's protector, Athena. From the ramparts, Anchises could point out further landmarks. The Trojan War had not yet caused the landscape to become peppered, as it is today, with the burial mounds of fallen heroes. But Anchises could point west to the Sigeum ridge, which runs north along the Aegean coast towards the settlement of Kum Kale at the north-western tip of the Troad, where the Dardanelles flow out into the sea.

Today, low-lying, fertile, efficiently drained farmland stretches east along the Dardanelles' shore, from Kum Kale to the hills north-east of Troy. But Yüksel Ergen, owner of the Iris Hotel in Guzelyali, drew our attention to his book, in which he writes that even in his childhood winters, 'the entire Trojan plain was flooded by waters of the overflowing rivers and it looked like a gulf opening to the mouth of the Dardanelles ... and stayed without any change for months on end.' Even in summer, Mr Ergen told us, the land was a *batak* or swamp, teeming with wildfowl, and was not drained until 1953. The swamp is the result of the felling of forests and the cultivation of fields from the Neolithic period onwards, which caused soil to be loosened and then washed into the Skamander and Simois, causing their mouths to silt up, a problem widespread throughout the Mediterranean. In the 1970s, bore holes sunk across the plain north and north-west of Troy confirmed that when Anchises and Aeneas stood on the ramparts, that process was in its infancy. They would have seen a great bay stretching down from the Dardanelles, between them and the Sigeum Ridge, and almost up to the walls of Troy itself. The bay's shoreline below the city would have been crowded with huts, animal pens and warehouses, and the quayside would have bristled with pitch-black ships from all over the eastern Mediterranean, the Sea of Marmara and the Black Sea, all acquiring or disgorging cargoes.

The Uluburun shipwreck, on the south-west corner of Anatolia and dating from the 1300s BC, revealed to archaeologists a cargo including ostrich eggs, pine nuts, almonds, pomegranates and turpentine resin, used for preserving wine. No less exotic or varied commodities must have assailed Aeneas's eyes and nose now, for before him lay one of the most important stops on one of the ancient world's busiest trade-routes. Any ships plying that route had no choice but to put in here for provisions; to wait for the winds to change; to trade at the great market before Troy's walls; and to pay their dues for customs and safe passage. Troy's kings were harked back to as the very paragons of magisterial power by the rulers of Medieval and early modern Europe. Yet the Trojan kings, Aeneas's cousins, owed their magnificence not to prowess in war and conquest, but to being tariff-collecting middlemen in the long-distance trade between the Black Sea and the Aegean. But, for all that, their mercantile, city-based wealth was real. It probably made Aeneas feel that he and his father were country bumpkins, kings of nothing more than a few mountain goat pens. And it was wealth that made the Mycenaean Greeks, who lived far away in the west across the Aegean, hollow with jealousy.

This, then, was Troy; Aeneas's patrimony, renowned across the ancient world. The city from which Aeneas and Anchises would eventually be lucky to escape with their lives.

This is the story of Troy's origins, as related in the *Bibliotheka*. While Anchises's grandfather Assaracus remained up in Dardania, Assaracus's older brother Ilos went travelling east, and ended up in Phrygia, where he won a wrestling match. The prize was fifty boys, fifty girls and a dappled cow. The cow began to wander, and Ilos set off in pursuit, determined to build a city wherever it stopped. Greek mythology is full of stories of animals showing heroes where to found cities. They may date back to when our hunter-gatherer ancestors fixed their campsites according to the movements of the wild animals that they hunted. The cow's route took Ilos back west, through Mysia, across the Aesopus and the Granicus, past the northern spur of Ida and back into the Troad, to the north of Dardania. At last the cow collapsed, exhausted, on the Hill of Ate, and refused to go any further. Ilos probably sacrificed the cow there and he built the city of Troy, which he named after his father Tros.[2] But the city was also called Ilios, after Ilos himself – which is why Homer's tale of Troy is called the *Iliad*.

Ilos's choice, however, was unfortunate, for Ate was the deity of rash decisions. When Ilos prayed to Zeus for confirmation that his city was to be built here, a statue, the Palladium, suddenly appeared. Ilos took this to be divine confirmation that he had made the right choice, but he was mistaken: Zeus had flung the Palladium there for a completely different reason, as we shall see. So, right from the start, Troy was doomed. But for many years, it flourished; even Ilos's brother Assaracus, king of Dardania, had a palace there, as mentioned in passing in book nine of Lucan's *Civil War*. Ilos himself married Eurydice, daughter of Adrastos, who was presumably king of Adrasteia, a realm in the north-eastern Troad. Ilos and Eurydice had a daughter Themiste, who married her cousin Capys and was mother of Anchises, so Ilos was Aeneas's great grandfather as well as his great great uncle. Ilos and Eurydice also had a son Laomedon, who ruled ill-fated Troy and had sons including Tithonus – he who was transformed into a cicada – and Priam, who was king of Troy in Aeneas's time.

Discussing the rise of civilisation in his *Laws*, Plato reasoned that human society must have developed in stages, from primitive life in the wilds, followed by basic farming settlements and finally civilised cities.[3] As evidence, Plato cited Aeneas's pedigree. Teucer's primitive people lived in the wilds; Dardanos's kingdom was a simple farming community, and Troy was a fully-fledged, modern city. Our archaeological understanding agrees with Plato, positing a progression from Ice Age and Mesolithic hunter-gathering to Neolithic farming and settled communities, and then to the fully-fledged city states of the Bronze and Iron Ages. The analogy between Aeneas's pedigree and our modern understanding of the world works further back, too, if the reign of Dardanos's grandfather Kronos accounts for the long history of primitive humanity, and the reign of Kronos's father Uranos for the period when life was evolving. Before that, in both narratives, comes the birth of Earth, and before that, in the Greek version, the primal Chasm and a blaze of light, while modern science speaks of the Big Bang. Science may have reworked the story of our origins in remarkable detail, but it has not deviated too far from the Greeks' simpler ideas about how things might have developed, as embodied in the pedigree of Aeneas.

7

Searching for Troy

Aeneas's new, ill-fated home of Troy, on its Hill of Ate, survived its own destruction in the Trojan War and lingered on as Greek Ilion and Roman Ilium until early Byzantine times. But from about AD 1200 onwards, nature undid what Aeneas's great grandfather Ilos had begun, and by the time European travellers, such as Pierre Bellonius in 1548, started to explore the Troad, the city's remains had vanished below the stony earth.

Their imaginations fired by the Dark Age myths, which traced Europe's origins back to Trojan refugees including Aeneas, these European visitors, who came either deliberately or in the course of other journeys, poked about the tumuli and ruins along the coast. They were particularly excited by the ruins of Alexandria Troas, built by two of Alexander the Great's generals and still impressive today, and having visited the site many travellers left hoping that they had walked there in the footsteps of Aeneas and Priam. Few visitors penetrated far inland, and those who did missed the real Troy, hidden beneath bushes on the unassuming Hill of Ate.

As the Enlightenment gripped Europe, mainstream interest in Troy's myths waned in favour of science. In 1795 and 1796, responding to Lechevalier's published claim that he had found Troy on the Balli Dağ, Jacob Bryant of King's College, Cambridge, published two dissertations arguing that Homer was pure fiction, and Troy with all its heroes, including Aeneas, were mere fables. Yet the power of myths continued to draw at least the curious. When Lord Byron and John Cam Hobhouse were travelling along the Anatolian coast in 1810, their ship anchored off the Trojan shore to wait, like countless ships throughout history, for the weather to change. In the fourth canto of *Don Juan*, composed in 1819-20, Byron recalled that:

> ...where I sought for Ilion's walls,
> The quiet sheep feeds, and the tortoise crawls;
> Troops of untended horses; here and there

In Search of Aeneas

Some little hamlets, with new names uncouth;
Some shepherds (unlike Paris) led to stare

As a poet, Byron was enraged by Bryant's view that Troy was make-believe, writing in the same canto:

...I've stood upon Achilles' tomb,
And heard Troy doubted; time will doubt of Rome.

'We *do* care for the authenticity of the tale of Troy,' Byron wrote in 1821. 'I have stood upon that plain *daily* for more than a month, in 1810, and if anything diminished my pleasure, it was that the blackguard Bryant had impugned its veracity.' Yes, he had read Bryant's argument, but 'I still venerated the grand original [the *Iliad*] as the truth of *history* (in the material *facts*) and of *place*.'[1]

Up to then, searches for Troy had relied heavily on Strabo and were misled by his incorrect belief that the Greek and Roman city of Ilium had not stood on the site of the Homeric Troy. But Byron's confidence in Homer was prophetic because, in 1822, Charles Maclaren (1782-1866), the founding editor of *The Scotsman*, published a dissertation drawing on the topographical details found in the *Iliad*, and concluding that Classical Ilium, and Homer's Troy, must have been in the same place after all. Maclaren visited the Troad in 1847 and explored the area immediately west of the tiny Turkish settlement of Hişarlik, whose name, as the Troy guide Mustafa Aşkin told us, means 'where there was once a fortress'. In 1863, Maclaren published his belief that the site next to Hişarlik matched Homer's descriptions: it was at the end of a ridge, and at the confluence of the Skamander and the Simois, just as Homer describes in *Iliad* 5, while Aeneas himself says in *Iliad* 20 that Troy was built 'on the plain' (and not in the hills, like the Balli Dağ). That same year, Frank Calvert, who acted as the local consul for both Britain and America, was so convinced by Maclaren's ideas that he bought some land at Hişarlik. An experimental dig revealed enough to confirm at last that this was the site, at least, of the Greco-Roman city of Ilium. Calvert then appealed to the British Museum to fund more extensive investigations, to prove his growing belief that this was also Homer's Troy. But the British Museum declined.

There things may have rested, were it not for Heinrich Schliemann (1822-1890). Schliemann may never have come to the Troad at all had he not, as a child in Germany, seen a picture-book about the Greek myths, which included Aeneas carrying his father Anchises away from Troy's burning ruins. The image filled Schliemann's young mind with wonder, but he later recalled that his father, evidently influenced by Bryant's still popular views, told him Troy was make-believe. 'But I don't believe that!' exclaimed the boy: 'When I am big, I shall go myself and find Troy and the King's treasure.'

Fired with determination, Schliemann educated himself in Greek and Turkish and amassed a fortune supplying provisions to the Russians during the Crimean War and bankrolling the California gold rush. At last, in 1868, he was able to visit the Troad. Schliemann found little at the Balli Dağ to match Homer's descriptions but was convinced by Calvert's enthusiasm for Hişarlik. In 1870-1, Schliemann's workmen's spades cut down through dry earth until they clanged against Bronze Age palace walls. In 1872, they dug the great 55-foot trench that still scars the site today, and found walls and a magnificent stone ramp, and a hoard of gold.

Schliemann thought he had found Aeneas's Troy. Forgetting Maclaren and Calvert, he announced his discovery and claimed all the glory for it himself. But over time, the smallness of the ancient citadel Schliemann had discovered began to worry him. In 1884-5, he and his new advisor, Wilhelm Dorpfeld, excavated Mycenae and gained a greater understanding of the styles of building and pottery prevalent at the time of the Trojan War. Returning to Hişarlik in 1890, Dorpfeld realised that, in Schliemann's earlier enthusiasm to reach Aeneas's Troy, he had sliced straight through it and reached a layer, with its ramp and gold, a thousand years older. Based on that, Schliemann and Dorpfeld started excavating the correct layer and announced that, at last, the true Troy of Aeneas's time had been found. Following Schliemann's death in 1890, his widow Sophia and Dorpfeld continued the work. In 1893-4, they excavated the great, inward-slanting citadel walls which greet visitors as we approach today, and which would have greeted Aeneas himself, that first time he saw Troy when he was a boy.

Calvert's enthusiasm, Schliemann's money and Dorpfeld's scientific care changed the way the world thought about Troy. Instead of theoretical debates on whether Homer's *Iliad* and its heroes, including Aeneas, might be true or not, scholars could see pictures of the exposed ruins of a city which undoubtedly matched many of Homer's details. That did not end the debate: Homer could still have based a fictional story upon a real place. But at least now physical, archaeological facts could be brought into the mix.

In the early twentieth century, Walter Leaf undertook important work trying to match the geography of the Troad to Homer's descriptions, and this work was perfected by Professor John Luce during his visits to the Troad in the 1990s. Meanwhile, further archaeological investigations on the citadel of Troy recommenced in 1934 but were halted by the war. Digging resumed in 1988 under the Troia Projekt, a joint venture by the universities of Cincinnati and Tübingen. Excavation of the Homeric layers was directed by Manfred Korfmann (1942-2005), who loved Turkey so much that he adopted the middle name Osman. Thanks to the Troia Projekt, Troy and its immediate environs became a national park in 1996 and a UNESCO Cultural Heritage of the World site in 1998.

Today, you drive along the dusty road past the village of Tevfikiye and see, on the right, a replica of Schliemann's original hut, standing next to Mustafa Aşkin's characterful Hişarlik Hotel. On the left of the road is the strange, modernist cube that opened in 2018 as the Troy Museum. Then comes a long driveway, lined with oleanders, until you reach the car park. Next, you

In Search of Aeneas

see a life-sized replica of the wooden horse from the 2004 movie *Troy*, a film which brought a great surge of tourist visits to the site. Finally, the modern world recedes, and you approach the exposed walls of the city that became so familiar to Aeneas.

What you see now is a mixture of all of Troy's history, and all its excavations. There are sections of walls; archaeologists' trenches; exposed pediments and pillars; bases of buildings and temples; paved streets and ramps. The ground is littered with potsherds from all the city's many periods. It takes a few visits, and a fair bit of reading, to even begin understanding everything you are seeing; but it is a site that amply repays the effort. It is also one of the best places in the world to simply wander and imagine the world of Aeneas.

Just like Aeneas's pedigree, as interpreted by Plato, excavated Troy is a metaphor for the development of civilisation. Around 11,000 BC, the last phase of the Ice Age locked up so much water in the ice caps that the formerly lush eastern Mediterranean coastal regions dried out, forcing the hunter gatherers who lived there to settle in places where fruits, large-grained grasses and pistachio nuts could still be found. Hard-pressed to survive, these people, the ancestors both of Aeneas and of all Europeans, encouraged the plants they preferred, cleared away less useful ones, started herding animals instead of just hunting them: and thus began the development of farming.

Those first farming people are termed 'Natufians', after the Wadi Al Natuf in Palestine, where archaeologists in the generations after Schliemann first found their remains. People started living in permanent villages, and then in embryonic cities, like Jericho in Palestine, which has been inhabited continuously for over 10,000 years. This cultural revolution is termed Neolithic (the 'new stone age') and its farmers and their settled lifestyle spread south into Egypt, east into Mesopotamia and north-west into Anatolia, to the Troad. There were Neolithic villages at Beşik Tepe and Kum Tepe, both by the sea in the Troad's north-western corner. From the Troad, Neolithic farming crossed the Dardanelles and started spreading through Europe, reaching Britain by about 4,500 BC.

City-dwelling was perfected in Mesopotamia where, copying the harvesting instincts of the black ants common to the region, the Sumerians piled up grain surpluses in granaries attached to their great temples, and rationed it out carefully. This stimulated the development of pottery, tool making, bureaucracy and castes of priests, warriors, and kings. This way of life spread, too, and when it reached the Troad the results were Troy itself, and probably, Palaiskepsis, though it has yet to be properly excavated. At Troy, a real-life precursor of the mythological Ilos established a settlement on the Hill of Ate in about 3,500 BC, roughly 2,000 years before Aeneas's time.

It was Dorpfeld who made sense of Troy's different archaeological layers, assigning to each a Roman numeral, and his system has been refined since. The first layer, established in about 3,500 BC, is labelled Troy 0. Then came

Troy I (c. 2920 BC), the first level known to Dorpfeld. This comprised a small, walled city next to the hill's steep northern scarp, the only part of the hill that matches *Iliad* 22's description of Troy's citadel as 'beetling'. Troy I's houses had stone foundations and mud-brick walls, just like those that can still be seen in the local villages. Today you see at Troy replica bricks protecting the excavated remains, but up to a few years ago the original bricks were exposed, just as they had been unearthed, some with bits of Neolithic straw still sticking out of them.

Over this proto-city was built Troy II, from about 2550 BC onwards, a larger walled city with the famous stone ramp found by Schliemann. There were further changes and enlargements until the start of Troy VI, about 1730 BC. These included a new set of citadel walls encircling two-thirds more of the hilltop than had been enclosed before, about 5 acres in all. These are the walls that still defended Troy's citadel in Aeneas's time. They survive best in the eastern gateway. The gateway is constructed in such a way as to force us in between an outer and inner wall, which form a channel that is impressive today, and would have been fatal for any invading soldiers, who could easily be trapped in the narrow passageway and stoned from above.

It is a shame that later generations wrought so many changes. Alexander the Great's successor Lysimachos, for instance, razed much of the upper city, the Pergamos, to create his huge marble temple to Athena. If we set this vandalism aside, we may still imagine the hilltop as it was in Aeneas's time, surrounded by its high, slightly inward sloping walls. The southern, Dardanian gate is easy to see, with its paved roadway edged by drainage channels leading up the hill. On the western side is the Scaean Gate, looking out across the much later Sanctuary area, with some more remains from Troy VI exposed nearby.

Troy's citadel was an imposing one, but for decades this was all that was exposed. It was an impressive fortress, yet it did not amount to the great city which Homer described. But Korfmann kept his faith in Homer and, in 1992, magnetometer readings began to reveal what had been missing: a lower city, extending out south-west from the acropolis. Its main defences were two great ditches, 300 feet apart, cut into the bedrock and designed to block chariot attacks. A bowshot back from the inner ditch was a mile-long wall, stone-footed, with mud brick sides and a wooden palisade on top, encircling a lower city of about 45 acres. Troy's size, its defensive towers, mud brickwork and Minyan ware pottery all compare well to other great Anatolian cities of the period. The combined upper and lower cities make Agamemnon's Mycenae look like the mere brigand's fortress that it really was.

Archaeology has now confirmed Homer's claims that Troy had broad streets, strong walls and towers, and stone-built mansions. These match the era in which he claimed they had existed, but not Homer's own time, when fine masonry was reserved for temples. All this suggests that Homer was repeating genuine details from an earlier, grander period than his own.

In Search of Aeneas

Despite everything, doubting voices remain. A few years ago, I sat in the office of a London businessman whose family tree I was tracing, as he pontificated that Homer was all made up. When I told him I had been standing amidst Troy's ruins less than a month earlier, he looked disconcerted, but seemed ignorant of, and determined to ignore, the mounting evidence that the archaeological site at Hişarlik is Homer's Troy. Academia is largely won over now, and so are most people who have studied the evidence. And if Hişarlik really is Troy, in contradiction to Jacob Bryant's theories, Homer's story of Troy, and of Aeneas, seems more likely than ever before to be based in truth.

8

The Centaur's Cave

Soon after his arrival in Troy, Aeneas would have been brought into the presence of his father's cousin, Priam. In Greek art, Priam is usually depicted as a rather frail, elderly man in Greek-style robes. But in book twelve of Dares Phrygius's *History of the Fall of Troy* we find a somewhat different account. Dares's work is one of the odder sources for the Trojan story. It purports to be an eye-witness account of the war, written by a Phrygian called Dares, who fought on the Trojan side; perhaps he was intended to be 'Dares, priest of Hephaestus', who is mentioned in *Iliad* 5. We first hear of this work in the first century AD, and it had probably been composed not long before then, most likely in Athens, but that does not preclude the remote possibility that its author drew on older, now lost sources. Dares's description of Priam, at any rate, is that he 'had a handsome face and a pleasant voice. He was large and swarthy.'

While we have no depictions of Trojans contemporary to Aeneas's time, we do have some of Troy's neighbours. Not far from Izmir, 120 miles south-east of Troy, an old road, originally Hittite, runs through the Karabel gorge below a massive stone relief carved into the rock, which is believed to depict Tarkasnawa, King of Mira around the time of the Trojan War. He wears a tall, pointed hat and knee-length tunic, and has a bow slung over one shoulder and a spear in his left hand. Elsewhere in Turkey are reliefs of the nominal overlords of both the Trojans and the Mirans, the Hittite Great Kings, with almond eyes, long beards and braided hair. Often, they are depicted with bows drawn, standing tall and proud in two-wheeled chariots pulled by pairs of plumed horses, beneath whose pounding hooves their hapless enemies are being trampled to death. Such a king was, as Gurney described him, 'at the same time supreme commander of the army, supreme judicial authority, and chief priest'.[1] And indeed, they are sometimes depicted pouring libations to their storm-god, Tarhunna, whom the Greeks called Zeus, or standing with hands raised before bulls,

In Search of Aeneas

representing the god on Earth, all just as Priam himself may have done in the Troad.

Priam and Anchises were cousins twice over; both were royal descendants of Dardanos; both were kings in their own right. They probably addressed each other as 'brother' and had shared memories from boyhood onwards. Yet Priam was Anchises's overlord, and there may have been a certain amount of abasing necessary on the parts of Anchises and his son as they entered the royal presence, for Priam's court would have been heavy with protocol, swarming with slaves and eunuchs, a place of complex ceremony and lavish display. Anchises's aim would have been to present Aeneas as his son, and for Priam to acknowledge this, so that Aeneas's eventual right of succession to the Dardanian throne would be secure.

Thus would have begun Aeneas's introductions to his kindred. In the *Iliad*, we hear of Hecuba, Priam's queen and principal wife, their eldest son Hector, and Priam's other children by Hecuba and his many other wives and concubines. Homer's Priam had fifty sons in all, including Deiphobus, Helenus, Polydorus and Polites, and twelve daughters including Cassandra and Creusa: a lot of names to remember. Priam's family, for their part, would probably have been curious to see Anchises's nymph-born son, for that was the story everyone was presumably told. Such an origin did not make Aeneas exceptional, though; Hecuba's mother Eunoë was said to have been a nymph too, as was Priam's mother Strymo, daughter of Skamander. For his part, faced with so many fascinating faces, Aeneas's memories of the diaphanous pine nymphs of Ida who had raised him would probably have begun to fade, until, amidst the sweaty rough-and-tumble of the palace yard, they evaporated altogether.

Aeneas's more immediate family circle is harder to fathom. Although the *Hymn to Aphrodite* states that Anchises was Aphrodite's lover only once, the *Bibliotheka* claims that 'besides Aeneas, Aphrodite bore Anchises a son Lyros who died without offspring.'[2] Unless this Lyros was a twin of Aeneas's, which the *Hymn* rules out, this suggests that Aphrodite had visited Anchises again – but we never hear any more of Lyros. *Iliad* 23 refers to Echepolus 'son of Anchises', who lived in great wealth in Sicyon, Greece, and who payed off Agamemnon with a horse to avoid fighting at Troy. This Echepolus's father may have been a different Anchises, but as we shall see the Greek sources suggest that our Anchises had travelled in Greece as a young man: perhaps having a Trojan father was what made Echepolus unwilling to fight against Troy. But, as with Lyros, we hear no more of this potential half-brother of Aeneas's.

In *Iliad* 13, however, we discover that Anchises definitely had a daughter Hippodameia, 'the darling of her father and mother, the pride of their halls', who 'excelled all her generation in beauty, the art of the loom and good sense'. Both the *Scholia* on *Iliad* 13, and Hesychius of Alexandria, identify Hippodameia's mother as Eriopis. We hear nothing else about Eriopis; she may have died long before Aeneas was conceived. Hippodameia was married to Alcathous who, as Deiphobus reminds Aeneas in *Iliad* 13, 'being husband to your sister, brought you up when you were a child in his house'.

Alcathous, who was therefore Aeneas's brother-in-law and guardian, was son to 'noble Aesytes' (*Iliad* 13). The tomb of Aesytes was such a prominent feature of the Trojan plain that it was used as a lookout point in *Iliad* 2. Luce argued that Aesytes' tomb was probably the mound at the very end of the Ciplak ridge, just south-east of Troy.[3] Strabo said it was 5 stades from Troy on the way to Alexandria Troas (which was on the coast, south-west of Troy). While the precise length of a stade remains a vexed question, it was probably between 515 and 606 feet – or between a tenth and eighth of a mile. So, if Strabo was measuring from the wall of Troy's lower city, the distance works. This, and a reference in *Iliad* 12 to Alcathous fighting in a battalion led by Priam's son Paris, all suggest that Aesytes and his son Alcathous lived in Troy – which suggests, in turn, that when Alcathous brought Aeneas up, it was in Troy itself.

Some later additions were made to Alcathous's genealogy in the *Chronicle of the Trojan War* by Dictys Cretensis. Mirroring Dares's pro-Trojan account of the Trojan War, this work claimed to be by Dictys, a follower of Prince Idomeneus of Crete, one of the leading Greeks commanders in the war. It is known from Latin copies of a Greek manuscript dated AD 66, whose author claimed he had discovered and copied something much more ancient. Such claims, however, were often literary conceits that provided thin excuses for literary creativeness. As with Dares's, account, therefore, we are left unsure as to whether any of its details were drawn from genuinely old material; but some of them might. In book three of his history, Dictys stitches together some genealogical loose ends, making Alcathous a cousin of Anchises and Priam by claiming that his mother was Cleopatra (or Cleomestra), daughter of Tros, King of Dardania. Dictys also makes Antenor, an elderly Dardanian nobleman mentioned in the *Iliad*, into Alcathous's brother.

It appears, then, that Homer's Anchises had been a young widower by the time Aeneas was conceived, and that he entrusted Aeneas into the care of his older daughter Hippodameia, and her husband, Alcathous, who may have been a cousin of theirs, so that the boy could grow up in close proximity to his royal cousins in Troy. Not far from the Scaean Gate, within the walls, we can still see some houses from Aeneas's time. Schliemann identified one of these houses as Priam's megaron, or palace, but it is too close to the gate for this to be considered plausible now. Perhaps this was the townhouse of Alcathous and Hippodameia, where Aeneas grew up.

Some of Aeneas's education probably took place there, learning his family's and country's history, its political and religious protocols and ceremonies, and the geography of the surrounding world, with perhaps some music and dancing too. Much of his education would have been outdoors, learning to fight and hunt: spearing boars, deer and perhaps bears, wolves and even lions up in the hills east of Troy, and shooting wildfowl with bow and arrows in the reedy marshes on the Trojan plain.

The true Aeneas is grounded in the Troad. But his life is the common property of western civilisation, and over the centuries his story has been embellished many times, so he lived many lives, in multiple ways. Once the Romans had enshrined him as the founder of their empire, Aeneas required a more exalted education. Book one of Pseudo-Xenophon's treatise *Cynegeticus* ('On Hunting') provides a list of the heroes who were tutored in boyhood by the centaur Chiron. They include Nestor, Odysseus, Diomedes, all leading figures in the Greek attack on Troy – and also Aeneas.

Half man, half horse, Chiron was said to have been fathered on the nymph Philyra by Zeus's father Kronos, while in the form of a horse. Chiron was entirely different to the rest of the centaurs, who were a riotous herd of drunks. He lived, instead, in great simplicity on Mount Pelion, on the east coast of Greece, until the famous war between the Centaurs and the Lapiths caused him to move far south, to Cape Maleas on the south-easternmost tip of the Peloponnese.

Pseudo-Xenophon's Anchises must have taken Aeneas there by sea from Troy, west across the Aegean. While this probably never happened to the real Aeneas, the notion of such a journey is not inconsistent with the archaeological evidence that points to Troy's considerable commercial contact with the Greek world. Ships must have been coming and going between the Peloponnese and Troy all the time; the young Aeneas could, conceivably, have gone to Cape Maleas and back.

The limestone mountains of Cape Maleas are riddled with caves, but none today seem to have a particular association with Chiron. Some, such as the recently discovered Kastania cave, lead down to measureless chambers decorated with wondrous natural sculptures created by millions of years of dripping, calciferous water, in whose shapes you can imagine people, birds, beasts – or even centaurs. Other caves pepper the south-eastern shore, and if Chiron had lived in one of these, Aeneas may have gazed out each day at the pale outline of the island of Kythera, which lies to the south of Cape Maleas, and which was sacred to his mother, Aphrodite.

Even for a boy brought up by nymphs, meeting a centaur must have come as a surprise, but familiarity would soon have taken over. A wall painting found at Herculaneum shows Chiron sitting on his haunches, a lionskin around his neck and his brow crowned with laurels befitting a poet, tenderly instructing a naked – and slightly bored-looking – youth to play the lyre.[4] It was a homoerotic theme often found in Greek and Roman art: the naked man-horse with the unabashedly nude youth, usually in some form of innocent physical contact as Chiron shows the boy how to string a bow, wield a sword, or ride on his back. Such scenes are usually identified as Chiron educating his final pupil, his own great grandson Achilles, whose heroic career was destined to mirror Aeneas's own. But it is possible that some of the youths depicted were supposed to be Aeneas himself.

The Centaur's Cave

The backbone of the education that Chiron gave his pupils was how to hunt with hounds. From the skills required to accomplish this successfully, claimed Pseudo-Xenophon, flowed all other heroic qualities, including piety towards Apollo and Artemis, the gods of the chase: and piety was certainly a virtue later attributed to Aeneas. Pseudo-Xenophon's original treatise is from the 200s BC, but the addition of Aeneas to this list of Chiron's pupils, and the centaurs' emphasis on piety, are thought to be later Roman additions. But though a blatant addition to Aeneas's myth, it was scarcely an inappropriate one for a son of Aphrodite.

Although isolated in Chiron's cave from the outside world, Aeneas cannot have failed to notice that he was in Mycenaean Greece. Its city-based civilisation had some cultural influence from Anatolia, but its strongest roots lay in Crete, about 70 miles south-east of Cape Maleas. Crete's Minoan civilisation arose about 2700 BC, with its own cultural roots in Egypt and the Levant. All such roots, like Troy's own, go back ultimately to the inception of farming by the Natufians in the Middle East. On Crete, civilisation and power were based in a string of red-walled palaces, the foremost of which was Knossos, in the middle of the island's north coast. Excavated by Sir Arthur Evans in the wave of enthusiasm for archaeology which followed Schliemann's discovery of Troy, Knossos's complex architecture was immortalised in the myth of the Labyrinth, home to the bull-headed Minotaur. Crete exercised considerable power over the Peloponnese and Attika, whose people were civilised through trading with, and being colonised by, the Minoans.

This Cretan power on mainland Greece was recalled in the story of the tributes of boys and girls, whom the Athenians were obliged to send to Knossos to be devoured by the Minotaur. The myth tells of the young Athenian prince, Theseus, who was an early pupil of Chiron's, travelling to Crete with the captive youths, and slaying the beast. That was a metaphor for the eventual rise of Mycenaean power, which took place after Minoan civilisation was shaken by a terrible earthquake about 1750 BC, and then destroyed when the volcano of Mount Thera erupted about 1400 BC, sending a tsunami surging across the sea to devastate Crete's northern coast. By then, Greece was dominated by Achaean warlords, who had come south from the Balkans after 1750 BC, and whom the later Minoans probably employed as mercenaries. After 1400 BC, these Achaeans established a new civilisation of their own in Greece, based not in Minoan-style palaces, but in heavily fortified cities, such as Tiryns, Gla, Orchomenos, Pylos and Mycenae, in the north-eastern Peloponnese, and which came to dominate the rest. Chiron's cave lay on the periphery of this Mycenaean world: a world that would later – and partly due to Aeneas's own involvement in the abduction of Helen – come storming up to the very walls of Troy itself.

After Aeneas returned to Troy, Chiron educated Achilles. Then, the centaur, who was half-brother to Zeus himself, was struck accidentally by a poisoned arrow belonging to Hercules, and died – a portent that the Trojan War, which heralded the end of the Age of Heroes, would not be long in coming.

Whether he had been tutored only by Alcathous in Troy, or also by Chiron on Cape Maleas, or both, Aeneas was a boy no longer. Back in the streets of Troy, heads must have started turning as the accomplished young man strode along, the sweat glinting on his maturing muscles, and an indefinable whiff of divinity about his demeanour.

Classical sources seldom provide physical descriptions of people, so for a written account of what Aeneas looked like, we have to wait until book twelve of Dares's *History of the Fall of* Troy: 'Aeneas was auburn haired, stocky, eloquent, courteous, prudent, pious and charming. His eyes were black and twinkling.' If so, maybe Aeneas's red hair was imagined as having resulted from the mixing of Anchises's dark brown hair with Aphrodite's fair locks, just as later combinations of Turkish dark hair and European blonde hair, whether from Crusading Franks or Christian slaves in Ottoman times, resulted in the redheads you still sometimes see around the Troad today. The idea that Aeneas had an unusual hair colour that set him apart from the crowd is appealing. Later, Joseph of Exeter wrote of him having 'menace in his hair' but being otherwise 'calm-faced and serene in speech, and easy in his words'.[5] Recalling Dares, Joseph imagined him being 'attractive with black eyes, pious in counsel, balanced in his stance, Aeneas stands, his shoulders spread, his gaze on high.'

Traditionally, northern European pictures made Aeneas fair skinned. In the 2004 *Troy* movie, he was played by the white actor Frankie Fitzgerald, better known as Nick Cotton in BBC1's soap opera, *EastEnders*. Later, BBC 1's 2018 drama *Troy: Fall of a City* cast mixed race Alfred Enoch as Aeneas. Surviving Roman wall paintings show Aeneas with the sun-browned skin, deep brown eyes and dark brown hair that was typical of the Mediterranean peoples. Aeneas died before he grew old, but there are countless depictions of him as a lithe young man, and as a muscular middle-aged one. Henry Gibb's 1654 painting of him in London's Tate Gallery, which shows him fleeing Troy with his family, makes him likewise well built, but with a long nose, wispy moustache and downcast eyes, surely an attempt to cast him as a defeated, turn-tail Charles I, who had been executed by Cromwell in 1649. But Gibb was an exception: virtually every other depiction of Aeneas makes him extremely handsome. Virgil in particular made Aeneas as good-looking as possible, even before Aphrodite 'breathed on her son', prior to his encounter with Dido in *Aeneid* 1, 'and his locks were beautiful; he was clad in the rosy light of youth, and his eyes were lustrous and glad – as when the artist-hand lends loveliness to the ivory, or when silver, or Parian stone [white marble], is enchased in the yellow of gold.'

In her 1983 novel *Cassandra*, written in the repressive atmosphere of East Germany before the fall of Communism, Christa Wolf imagined Aeneas encountering Priam's daughter Cassandra at Athena's temple in Troy. A ritual imagined by Wolf was taking place, whereby the Trojan girls who had just passed puberty were selected, and effectively raped, by whichever Trojan man chose to deflower them. Gradually, the precinct emptied, until at noon Aeneas appeared and Cassandra realised she had been noticing him in every crowd for some time. Although they had never been formally introduced, Aeneas asked Cassandra's forgiveness for his being late, and led her to a secluded spot in the temple grounds. Instead of the hurried intercourse expected of them, they simply touched, and kissed, and fell in love. 'I would have done whatever he wanted,' Cassandra recalls, 'but he seemed to want nothing.' Cassandra's burden, in myth as well as in Wolf's novel, was that she could see into the future, but nobody would ever believe her prophecies. As she lay dozing in Aeneas's arms, she dreamed of him sailing away, and the sea between them bursting into flames. She awoke screaming, so Aeneas carried her home to her mother Hecuba who, mistakenly, thanked him for having disposed of her daughter's virginity. But Aeneas and Cassandra did not marry, for she was destined to be a priestess: 'Aeneas vanished from my view, the first instance of what became a pattern,' she says. 'Aeneas remained a glowing point inside me; his name a sharp stab that I inflicted on myself as often as I could.'

According to Pausanias,[6] Lesches's *Little Iliad* and the *Cypria*, Aeneas married a woman called Eurydice. She shared her name with the wife of Ilos of Troy, and also the wife of the poet Orpheus, who came from Thrace to the north-west of Troy. But Virgil identifies Aeneas's bride as Creusa, a daughter of Priam and thus a sister of Cassandra; perhaps Aeneas's Eurydice was also imagined to have been a daughter of Priam, and thus a great granddaughter of that earlier Eurydice, the wife of Ilos.

No description survives of the marriage of Aeneas – to Creusa, if we follow Virgil – when he would have known that all the eyes of Troy, and probably of Mount Olympus too, were fixed on him and his bride; when he appeared, probably long-haired and clean-shaven, a lion-skin thrown over his shoulders, adorned in the finest jewels that the coffers of his father and Alcathous could muster; when numerous fattened cows and sheep from the Dardanian uplands were sacrificed and roasted; when Trojan wine flowed in a seemingly unceasing river from pithoi brought up from Priam's cellars; when the robes and flowers were bright; when the drums boomed and songs were sung of the sexual encounters of the Great Mother and the fertility of the land. When nobody, least of all Aeneas, would have given a thought to another wedding that had taken place some years earlier, far away on Mount Pelion in Greece, the repercussions of which were about to overwhelm them all.

9

Journey to Sparta

Today, Homer's *Iliad* is the most famous retelling of the story of Troy. But in Homer's time, the story of Achilles' battles against Aeneas and his compatriots before the walls of Troy was merely a part of a much wider cycle of epic poetry about the Trojan War; and the Trojan Cycle was but one planet in a dazzling solar system of epic cycles lying at the heart of Greece's self-awareness, recalling, mythologising and moralising the events of the Mycenaean era.

Their performers, like Homer, were creative poets but also custodians of the Greek psyche, acting as historians, theologians and genealogists in an age before such subjects were considered separate from one another. Their primary job was the performance of the different cycles. The Iolkos Cycle included the tale of the Argonauts who, led by Jason of Iolkos, sailed off to the Black Sea in their quest for the Golden Fleece. The Aetolian-Elean-Pylian Cycle included the famous hunt for the Calydonian boar by Theseus, Hercules and the other great heroes of their generation. The Theban cycle included the cautionary tale of Oedipus, who mistakenly slept with his mother and killed his father. Finally, at the culmination of events flowing from these other cycles, came the Trojan Cycle, of which the *Iliad* tells a small part. This is the cycle in which Aeneas is one of the foremost of the Trojan heroes, and which ends with the struggles of the Greek heroes, particularly Odysseus, to return to their homes after the destruction of Troy; and it begins with a fated wedding.

Lesches's *Little Iliad* and the *Cypria*, which survive now only in fragments quoted mainly in Proclus's *Chrestomathy* and Pseudo-Apollodorus's *Bibliotheka* – as collected together in West's *Epic Fragments* – are both retellings of the Trojan cycle which are either contemporary with, or a little later than, the *Iliad*. Indeed, Aelian, in his *Historical Miscellany*, asserted that Homer wrote the *Cypria* himself, as a dowry for his daughter.[1]

The *Cypria* relates how, when Chiron was still living on Mount Pelion, half-way up the east coast of Greece, the gods and heroes gathered at his cave for the marriage of Peleus, a mortal prince from the island of Aegina, and the sea nymph Thetys, the couple destined to be the parents of Achilles. Several caves around Pelion claim to be Chiron's; one, in a steep, wooded gorge near Milies, below the Taxiarhis chapel, is a good contender, with its ledge along the overhanging cliff like the top row of a Greek theatre, along which the myriad guests, mortal and immortal alike, could have sat, arrayed in splendour.

But compiling guest-lists for weddings can be fraught with pitfalls, and in this case one guest who did not receive an invitation was Erys, goddess of discord. Erys was so incensed that, as Colluthus, a Greek poet living in Egypt in the AD 400s, wrote in his *Rape of Helen*, 'she fain would unbar the bolts of darksome hollows and rouse the Titans from the nether pit and destroy the Heaven, the seat of Zeus.'

In the end, though, she adopted a more subtle approach. Appearing outside Chiron's cave, Erys threw into the wedding feast a golden apple, declared that it was a prize for the fairest goddess of all, and invited Zeus to choose the winner. Zeus picked out the three main contenders: his wife Hera; his daughter Athena; and Aeneas's mother, Aphrodite. But having to choose a winner would incur the wrath of two losers, so Zeus sagely side-stepped the task and nominated in his place the shepherd-boy Paris, who, he said, was to be found far away on the slopes of Mount Ida.

Earlier, when Hecuba was pregnant with Priam's son Paris, she dreamed that her womb burst into flames, and fire from it engulfed the entire palace, until all of Troy was destroyed. Recognising this as a terrible omen, Priam sent the new-born baby away to be left to die on the slopes of Mount Ida. But a she-bear suckled baby Paris, and then a shepherd took him in and raised him. In the wilds, Paris married Oenone, a nymph-daughter of the river Kebren, a tributary of Skamander, and because of his fierceness in defending herdsmen from the wolves, he gained the extra name Alexandros, 'defender of men'.

Now, hurrying east from the abandoned wedding feast, Hera, Athena and Aphrodite found Paris-Alexandros tending his flock on Ida; specifically, says Strabo, on Mount Alexandreia, the spur of Ida directly above the harbour of Antandros, facing the Adramyttium Gulf. Each attempted to bribe him: Athena with victory in battle, Hera with the kingship of the world and Aphrodite, says Colluthus, vowed 'in place of manly prowess, I will give thee a lovely bride, and, instead of kingship, enter thou the bed of Helen.' Forgetting Oenone, Paris chose love, and handed Erys's golden apple to Aphrodite. Thus, as Homer writes in *Iliad* 24, Paris earned the hatred of Hera and Athena for himself and for 'sacred Ilium and Priam and his people'.

Soon after this, Paris's identity was discovered in Troy. Mistaking his survival against all the odds as a positive omen, Priam and Hecuba welcomed him back. Aeneas would have met his long-lost cousin almost at once, and their early experiences growing up away from Troy, and on different parts of Mount Ida, gave them something in common. To fulfil her promise of making

Helen into Paris's bride, Aphrodite engineered a journey to Greece for him. To her surprise, Hera and Athena offered to help. Little did Aphrodite realise that their motivation, far from securing Paris's marital bliss, was to destroy both Paris and the city of his birth.

There was a story, well-known in Homer's Troy, that Homer's Aeneas would have heard sung at feasts by bards: how, long ago, Poseidon and Apollo tried to overthrow Zeus. They failed and as punishment were forced to work for a time as hired labourers for Priam's father Laomedon, building new walls for Troy. Laomedon (whose sister Themiste was Anchises's mother), was a venal man, and held back Poseidon's wages, so the god sent a sea monster to terrorise the coast of the Troad. Later, the Argonauts came to Troy on their way to the Black Sea, in search of the Golden Fleece. They discovered that to placate the monster, Laomedon had exposed his own daughter Hesione on the rocky shoreline below the Sigeum Ridge, due west of Troy.

Hercules, who was one of the Argonauts, volunteered chivalrously to fight the monster and save Hesione, so the Trojans and Athena built him what Homer described in *Iliad* 20 as a 'mounded and lofty fort' to use as his base, and which features later in the story of the Trojan War. Professor Luce identified this 'fort' as Kesik Tepe, a natural limestone outcrop, with artificial earthen additions, on the coast immediately south of Sigeum.

From this vantage point, Hercules killed the monster. The grateful Laomedon gave him some horses, promising to look after them until the completion of the Argonauts' mission. But when Hercules returned to claim his prize, Laomedon changed his mind and refused to hand the horses over. This caused the first great Trojan War: Hercules raised an army in Greece and returned to lay siege to the city, reducing it to rubble and taking prisoner Hesione and Laomedon's youngest son Podarces.

It was a shameful part of Troy's history. As Cassandra comments in Christa Wolf's novel, it was part of a chain of ruinous events stretching back into antiquity: 'destruction, rebuilding, destruction again, under the sovereignty of a shifting succession of kings, most of them luckless' – ample justification for regarding the Hill of Ate, on which Troy stood, as cursed.

Having regained Hesione, Hercules gave her, derisively, to his friend Telamon. Hesione begged successfully for her brother Podarces to be set free, and Hercules agreed. The boy was known ever after as Priam, which the Greeks thought meant 'ransomed'. Priam rebuilt Troy as a more splendid city than it had ever been before – with those very walls, now labelled 'Troy VI', which were known to Aeneas.

As for Hesione, Telamon took her to the Greek island of Salamis, just off the southern coast of Attika, as his captive and concubine – never, it seems, as his wife and queen – and she was mother of his two of his sons, Teucer and Trambelus. In *Aeneid* 8, Virgil made a curious addition to this story, saying that when Priam was a young king, he and his equally young cousin Anchises travelled to Salamis to visit Hesione; presumably they really wanted to secure her release, though Virgil does not say as much; but on Salamis she remained.

Now, in order facilitate Paris going to Greece to meet Helen, says Dares, Aphrodite filled Priam's mind with a renewed desire to liberate his sister. Hercules was long-since dead, so Priam decided to send an embassy to Greece, led by Aeneas's cousin Antenor, to negotiate Hesione's return. We learn this in book five of Dares's Trojan history; in book thirty-eight we hear, after the event, that Aeneas had gone, too. It was not unusual to choose young noblemen to attend diplomats. If Aeneas had indeed been educated by Chiron, as the Romans believed, he would now be able to put his knowledge of Greece and its heroes to good use.

Their voyage would have taken them across the Aegean to the east coast of Greece. Once they were under the shadow of Mount Pelion, they would have turned south-west through the straits between the island of Skiathos and the end of the Pelion peninsula, which coils like a scorpion's tail into the Pagasitikos Gulf. From the Gulf's shore, they would have made their way to the court of elderly king Peleus – for it was he, says Dares, that the embassy visited first – to seek his help in persuading his brother Telamon to return Hesione to Troy.

The brothers Peleus and Telamon were believed to have come from Aegina in the Saronic Gulf, the island of which their father, Aiacos, was made king by his own father, Zeus, who turned the island's *myrmidons* (ants) into people, the Myrmidons, for him to rule. When Telamon accidentally killed their half-brother Phocus, he was exiled to the island of Salamis, which lies between Aegina and mainland Attika. Peleus, who had helped cover up the crime, was also expelled, travelling north with his Myrmidon followers, through Attika and Locris, to Phthia.

Phthia was an ancient name for a wide region of central-eastern Greece, probably dating back to the mysterious Pelasgians, of whom Herodotus wrote so often, who lived there long before the arrival of Mycenaean warlords – arrivals of the sort recalled, in myth, by the appearance there of Peleus and his Myrmidons. The *Iliad* refers to Peleus, and also his northern and north-eastern neighbours, Protesilaus and Philoctetes, ruling parts of Phthia. The northern part of Phthia was known in Classical times as Magnesia, and by the 400s BC, the Magnesian city of Pharsalos, 25 miles west of the Pagasitikos Gulf, was laying claim to having been Peleus's capital. Euripides helped promote this claim in his play *Andromache*, by giving a speech to Andromache, who had been enslaved by Peleus's grandson Neoptolemus at the end of the Trojan War: 'Phthia is my home now, these fields surrounding the city of Pharsalos.' This influenced Dares, who tells us that the Trojan embassy visited Peleus 'in Magnesia'; clearly, he had Pharsalos in mind. The claim lives on, and modern Farsala (as it is now spelled) has a fine new statue of Peleus's son Achilles in its main square and calls its football team 'The Myrmidons'. Immediately south of the city is a wooded hill haunted by merlins and crowned with a magnificent acropolis, whose surviving walls and gates are Byzantine, but with Classical bases. It is a fine enough place to imagine Peleus receiving the Trojan ambassadors. However, although one Mycenaean tomb has been found down in the town, evidence of Mycenaean occupation of the hill itself so far is lacking.

It appears, in fact, that the Pharsalans had laid claim to someone else's glory, for Peleus's own realm is defined in *Iliad* 2, without any reference to Pharsalos. The fifty ships that Peleus's son Achilles brought to the Trojan War, says Homer, were drawn from 'Pelasgic Argos, Alos, Alope, and Trachi [within the lands of] Phthia and Hellas, the land of fair women', and Achilles himself referred several times in the *Iliad* to the river Sperchios, to which he had dedicated a lock of his hair, and which flows into the head of the Malian Gulf just north of Trachis. This suggests that Peleus's realm was based not in the plain around Pharsalos, but further south, around the Sperchios Valley and the Malian Gulf, where remains of all the cities named by Homer can be found. Pelasgic Argos, which Homer names first, was presumably Peleus's true capital.

If Dares was right about the ambassadors visiting Peleus, but anachronistic about his capital being 'in Magnesia', then Antenor and Aeneas's first destination was presumably Pelasgic Argos.

In 1959, Hope-Simpson and Lazenby identified Pelasgic Argos with Larissa Kremaste, which Strabo said was also called Pelasgia.[2] Its modern name means 'hanging city', because it sits (or 'hangs') on a hill on the south-eastern flanks of Mount Orthrys – the mountain, incidentally, which had been the stronghold of the Titans in ancient times, during their war with the Olympian gods. Along the road 2 miles north out of the modern village of Pelasgia, we spotted an old wooden sign, marked '*kastro*' ('castle'), that sent us rattling up a rutted track for just under a mile, until we reached open grassland and walked to the hilltop. Potsherds, especially roof tiles, abounded, and a narrow path led up through prickly holm oak bushes to sections of the ancient walls and gateways.

This all happened on a late summer afternoon, when the sinking sun cast diagonal shafts of golden light across the dark flanks of Mount Orthrys, and over the hills and valleys leading down to the Malian Gulf. We could see not only across most of the gulf that was the heart of Peleus's realm but also south-west to Trachis and then the mountains leading south to Mount Parnassos that stands above Delphi; south-east to the silvery-pink straits between the mountains of Euboea and the mainland of Locris; and north-east to the Pagasitikos Gulf and the distant peak of Pelion. To see so much, bathed in such majesty, seemed extraordinary. It was a fitting home for the Homeric Peleus and his son Achilles – and a fine place to imagine the Trojan ambassadors visiting the elderly king.

Peleus entertained his visitors, says Dares, for three days. Here, Dares diverges from *Iliad* 20, in which Aeneas comments that he has never seen either of Achilles' parents, Thetys and Peleus. The Greek myths thrived on contradictions and inconsistencies, and here is one of them – unless Aeneas accompanied Antenor as far as Peleus's palace, but for some reason never set eyes on the elderly king in the flesh.

When Antenor asked for Peleus's help in securing Hesione's release, the king became 'deeply upset', and ordered them to leave. Aeneas and Antenor sailed away, south-east down the coasts of Locris and Attika, round Cape Sounion, anciently sacred to Poseidon, where later there arose the magnificent Classical temple to the god that still dominates its cliffs today. Entering the Saronic Gulf, they would have passed Athens, which Homer describes in *Iliad* 2 as being ruled by Menestheus, and which would later send fifty ships to the Trojan War. The ambassadors did not stop there, however, for Athens was not yet a place of great consequence; they sailed, instead, to the island of Salamis, which lies just off the Attikan coast beyond Athens' port of Piraeus. It was in the narrow straits between Salamis and the Attikan coast, hemmed in by the island's needle-like promontory called the Kynosaura, 'dog's tooth', that the Athenian navy would later lure and dismember the vastly larger Persian fleet in the famous sea battle of 480 BC. But now, back in Aeneas's time, Salamis was home to the aged Telamon.

For a long time, the location of Telamon's palace was a mystery, but in 1999 a plausible site was found by Yiannis Lolos, an archaeologist from the University of Ioannina, which has since sponsored extensive excavations there. The site is on the south-western end of Salamis, on a hill just south of the modern village of Karakiani. The site has yielded numerous finds from Mycenaean times, suggesting trade from as far afield as Crete and Egypt, and it appears to have been abandoned soon after the time of the Trojan War. Below the site, on either side, are valleys opening down to two natural harbours. So, whereas we crossed by ferry from the mainland to the north-east of the island – with a ticket issued, Greek-style, in triplicate – the ship of Antenor and Aeneas could easily have come to anchor right below Telamon's city.

Ascending through the pine woods and garrigue to the hill top, with its views down to the broad northern valley, which would doubtless have contained Telamon's herds of cattle, Antenor and Aeneas would have found in flourishing splendour what we saw in excavated ruination; a lower city on the lower slopes of the hill and above it, a saddle of land between a rocky outcrop facing the sea, and a higher outcrop backing the scrubby inland hills. The whole site was curiously lacking in defensive walls, but it brimmed with Mycenaean buildings with stone bases and brick walls, doubtless once several stories high, the greatest of which must have been the palace of old Telamon himself. The wall bases remain, and embedded in the soil all around were numerous sherds of pale grey Mycenaean pottery.

Telamon is said to have come here as a young man from Aegina, which is visible from Salamis's southern coast (but not from the palace), after his accidental murder of Phocus. Newly landed in Salamis, Telamon ravished and later married Glauce, the daughter of the king, Cychreus son of Poseidon, and eventually inherited the island and palace for himself – a story probably echoing the practice of Mycenaean men gaining the right to land through their wives. During his visit, Aeneas would have met Telamon and Glauce's son Ajax, destined to become one of the greatest Greek heroes in the Trojan War.

Although there can be no certainty that Dares's story of the Trojans' visit here was drawn from genuine tradition, let alone actual events, the site itself is real and adds to the swelling body of evidence that Homer's *Iliad* was based in reality. Homer said Ajax was from Salamis, implying a Mycenaean city somewhere on the island, and now one has indeed been found.

Dares does not mention whether Aeneas and Antenor ever met, or even just glimpsed, Hesione herself, she whose fate had been to while away most of her adult life on Salamis. In any event, they had now to explain to Telamon why they had been sent. The audacity of the request must have left the former Argonaut and boon-companion of Hercules open-mouthed. Hesione was a legitimate prize of war, Telamon told them, so he would not return her. Had it not been for the Greek taboo on killing guests, he would doubtless have had these two presumptuous Trojans flung straight off the rocky height of his acropolis.

From Telamon's megaron, you can see a small island – once home, one suspects, to a Poseidon shrine – and also the pale blue outline of the northern Peloponnese. That is the way the ambassadors sailed next, making for the land of Achaea, where, says Dares, they hoped that the semi-divine twins Pollux and Castor would help tip the scales in their favour. Achaeia (Aegialea) was the ancient name for the northern coastal strip of the Peloponnese, facing the Gulf of Corinth.

Dares did not specify where in Achaea they met the twins, who were known collectively as the Dioscuri, 'Zeus's boys'. Maybe it was at Keryneia, perched up on the hills between Mount Erymanthus and the Corinthian Gulf, some of whose archaic foundations can still be seen amidst ruins from later periods. But Dares here is at odds with conventional mythology, which makes Pollux and Castor kings, not of Achaea, but of Sparta, before the accession of Menelaus. Regardless of where the meeting took place, the Dioscuri refused to help.

Finally, Aeneas and Antenor sailed right round the southern end of the Peloponnese, that same Cape Maleas where, according to Pseudo-Xenophon, Aeneas had been tutored by Chiron. They reached rocky Pylos on Greece's south-west coast, the home of Nestor. This is another example of a Mycenaean palace, alluded to in the *Iliad* and described in the *Odyssey*, that has been discovered and confirmed by modern archaeology. The site was discovered and first excavated in 1939 by Carl Blegen, who also worked on Troy and hoped now to work on an undisturbed Mycenaean site on mainland Greece, for comparison. He found the site by combing the land around modern Pilos, which is in Navarino Bay, and seeking help, as Michael Wood describes in his excellent *In Search of the Trojan War*, from locals. Blegen's efforts were rewarded when, digging into the Ano Englianos hill, 6 miles inland from the bay but commanding fine views of it, he found 'substantial stone walls, more than one metre thick [and] fragments of plaster retaining vestiges of painted decoration'.³ The ruins transpired to be the remains of two palaces, side by side, one older, the other, newer one perhaps that of Nestor himself. 'There was the same megaron (royal hall)' wrote Wood, 'as at Tiryns and Mycenae, its central hearth still in place with its painted decoration; there were storerooms full of the crockery of a Bronze-Age palace [and] frescoes bore scenes of chariots, warriors in boar's tusk helmets fighting roughly clad mountain people... There was even a painting of a bard playing the lyre.'⁴ Nearby they excavated an archive of 600 Linear B tablets. Mycenaean Tholos tombs nearby may even include the last resting place of Nestor himself.

Nestor was destined to be the oldest and wisest of the kings who fought at Troy. Now, he told the ambassadors that Laomedon should never have insulted Hercules in the first place, and that by losing Hesione, the Trojans had had their just desserts. The embassy then sailed all the way back home to Troy, for Antenor to explain his failure to the royal council.

Priam's response was to try again, this time choosing his son Paris to lead an embassy to Sparta. That is what Dares reports; in most other versions of the story, Antenor's mission never took place and there was only ever one embassy to Greece, with Paris at its head. This is why Aphrodite had inspired Priam to long so much for his sister's return, because the embassy afforded Paris the perfect opportunity to go to Greece, where he was destined to meet Helen.

To speed Paris over the seas, Aphrodite inspired Phereclus to build ships. Though well-constructed, they were destined, as Homer commented in *Iliad* 5, to bring 'disaster on the Trojans and on Paris'. Priam's daughter Cassandra and her twin brother Helenus, who could both see into the future, prophesied as much, but of course nobody listened. The *Cypria* confirms that 'Aphrodite tells Aeneas to sail with Paris.'

Colluthus's *Rape of Helen* tells how Paris and his companions made sacrifices to Aphrodite and departed, but even as they left the shelter of the Dardanelles, 'the dark sea leapt aloft' in a waterspout; rain poured down 'from the murky air, and the sea was turmoiled as the oarsmen rowed'. They toiled along the Thracian coast, past the mouth of the Ismarian Lake, which is now called Lake Mitrikou, and then south, past 'flowery Phthia' and Attika, and right down the east coast of the Peloponnese. Then, doubling Cape Maleas, they headed north-west up the eastern shore of the Laconian Gulf. Aeneas and Paris would have seen the dramatic outline of the broad Eurotas Valley becoming clearer through the haze: on the east side, the distant bulk of Mount Parnonas and its foothills that surge south to form Cape Maleas; and on the west, the astonishing snow-capped pentadactyls or 'five fingers' of Mount Taygetus. Towering 7,887 feet high, Taygetus's peaks are a full 2,000 feet higher than Aeneas's own Mount Ida, with vast foothills running south to form the Mani Peninsula, its serrated peaks defining the gulf's western shore.

At the head of the gulf, the river Eurotas forms a swampy estuary. So much silt has been carried down the Eurotas since Aeneas's time that the coastline then was a good 3 miles further north than it is now, so it was probably near Skala – now 3 miles inland – that the Trojans 'cast the hawsers of the ship upon the shores', as Colluthus put it.

As the boys raced up the Eurotas Valley, they would have seen Taygetus looming ever closer to the north-west. Closer to hand, their attention would have become focussed on the hill of Amykles among the broad valley's olive trees, 18 miles north of the gulf's head, and 1½ miles west of the river. On its bluff sat the stone tomb of Hyacinthos: later, from about the 600s BC onwards, a colossal statue of Apollo, golden-faced, would tower above it. Amykles was the capital of Lacedaemonia, also called Laconia, and Colluthus relates how Paris and his companions 'surveyed the splendour of the city' with its 'high-built houses' and temples. Archaeology confirms that Amykles did indeed flourish in Aeneas's day, and besides many finds at the site, there are the remains of a splendid tholos tomb nearby at Yaphio, confirming the area's importance in Mycenaean times.

Amykles was said to have been founded by Amyclas, son of Lacedaemon, whose parents were Zeus and Taygete, one of the Pleiades. Taygete's sisters included Elektra the mother of Dardanos, the ancestor of the Trojans, so Aeneas must have felt at home here. The boys would have heard, too, how Lacedaemon's son Hyacinthos was killed by mistake by his divine lover (who, by Classical times, was identified as Apollo) who, grieving, transformed the boy's dead body into the hyacinth that blooms and dies each spring. That story would have accompanied the fertility rites that doubtless took place at Amykles, not unlike those of Dumuzi further east, which attempted to explain the endless cycle of birth and death – of which we are all a part.

On the hill of Amykles, the boys were brought into the presence of Sparta's king, Menelaus, to explain their mission to recover Hesione. Menelaus would not help them, but showing hospitality to guests was such an ingrained convention in Bronze Age society that he invited Aeneas and Paris to his palace at Therapne. Menelaus thus made one of the greatest mistakes in history, for his wife was Helen, the only mortal woman whose beauty rivalled goddesses; the woman whose love had been promised, by Aphrodite, to Paris.

10

The Rape of Helen

The eastern side of the Eurotas Valley is marked by a line of low, red-earthed hills that rise up steeply from the plain, backing onto a scrubby hinterland that stretches further east to the mountains. On the bluff of one of these hills, some 7 miles north-east of Amykles, stand the substantial remains of a small, stepped pyramid, constructed from monumental stone blocks over a natural rock outcrop. Built about the 700s BC and remodelled three hundred years later, it commands expansive views out across the Eurotas valley towards snow-capped Taygetus to the west. It was surely to this pyramid that Herodotus referred, when he wrote of a temple to Helen hereabouts,[1] but by Roman times, placing more emphasis on husband than wife, it was being called the Menelaion. Visiting the site in his epic tour of ancient sites in the AD 100s, the Greek antiquarian Pausanias was assured that it was the tomb of Menelaus and Helen.[2]

Three hundred feet north-east are the ruins of the Mycenaean palace of Therapne. What survives best is part of the basement storage area; you can see the base of a staircase that once led up to the palace proper, where Menelaus would have entertained the Trojan boys. During the cataclysmic aftermath of the Trojan War that Aeneas and Paris were about to start, the palace was burned and destroyed, and over the ensuing centuries much of it crumbled away down the steep earthen cliff on the bluff's southern flank. Maybe an earthquake caused the initial fire, but after the Trojan War the area was taken over by Dorian invaders from the north, and the discovery of skeletons of two children and a young woman with her legs drawn up to her chin suggest, as Bettany Hughes thought, that Therapne was sacked. The Dorians abandoned the site and built a new city, Sparta, 2 miles to the north-west. Lacedaemonia then became known for its harsh, 'Spartan' militarism, but back in Aeneas's time Therapne was splendidly luxurious, and the Trojan boys would have been entertained in the most unspartan manner imaginable by Helen herself.

In Search of Aeneas

Although some retellings of the story, such as Colluthus's, do not mention Aeneas being present at all, he is usually included in scenes from it in Greek art, as the work of Lilly Ghali-Kahil has shown. A red-figure cup found at Nola, near Naples, shows Aphrodite and Eros helping Helen to beautify herself, while youthful Paris and Aeneas, dressed in travellers' robes, sandals and broad-brimmed hats and holding spears, are being received by bearded Menelaus.[3] The boys are exchanging a glance: Aeneas seems keen to leave, but Paris, who is naked below his robe, is about to push past Menelaus to reach Helen.

A Pontic *oenochoe* or wine cup from Etruria in central Italy shows Paris approaching Helen, shading his eyes as if blinded by her beauty: behind them is Aphrodite and a lion, and beyond them, Aeneas.[4] Unaware of his mother's presence, Aeneas holds a marriage diadem destined for Helen's head, but hangs back: 'Whereas Paris is completely entranced by Helen,' commented Hampe and Simon, 'Aeneas has to keep a cool head.'[5] Below the same scene sits Nereus, the Old Man of the Sea. That is a foreshadowing, perhaps, as Galinsky suggested, of Horace's first *Ode*, in which Nereus commands the winds to sleep, so all can hear his dire prediction: that Paris's actions will be 'the death-knell of his race'.

Aeneas cannot have helped being almost as smitten by Helen's beauty as Paris was. She was, after all, the most beautiful mortal woman in history, and Aphrodite was at hand to make her as gorgeous as possible. In act 4 of Shakespeare's *Troilus and Cressida*, Aeneas lets slip his true feelings: 'Had I so good occasion to lie long [with Helen] as you, Prince Paris, nothing but heavenly business should rob my bed-mate of my company.'

As the breeze wafted the resiny smell of pines across the porticos and terraces of Therapne, Paris and Aeneas, marvelling at Helen's beauty, may have recalled the myths whispered about her origins: how Zeus, enflamed by Aphrodite's arrows of desire, became a great white swan and pursued Night's daughter Nemesis, she who punished those guilty of hubris. Nemesis took the form of a black goose and fled from Zeus across the entire world, until she sank down exhausted, either just here, by the Euratos, or on the scrubby hillside at Rhamnous on the Attikan coast. There, they copulated, poultry-style. His lust sated, Zeus flapped away, and Nemesis laid a great egg. On the base of Nemesis's temple at Rhamnous was a frieze showing her giving the egg to Leda, wife of Tyndareus, King of Amykles (a great grandson of Amyclas). From it hatched the twins, Pollux and Castor, and Helen. When Helen came of age, Tyndareus invited the forty-one most eligible young men in Greece to Amykles, to compete for Helen's hand. Menelaus, the younger brother of the king of Mycenae won, and eventually succeeded to his wife's father's throne – a suggestion, as Bettany Hughes writes, that Bronze Age Mycenaean society still operated a form of matriarchy.

Now, due to Aphrodite's intervention, Menelaus was called away to a funeral in Crete. Generously, he bade Aeneas and Paris stay on in Helen's care. Helen's fidelity to her husband did not stand a chance against these lads, who had come up the Eurotas valley like the white gulls from the sea, brimming with the promise of adventure. We learn in *Iliad* 24 that Aphrodite gave Paris *machlosýne*, an aura of irresistibility. Colluthus imagines Paris boasting to Helen of his descent, via Dardanos, from Zeus; how Poseidon and Apollo built shining walls for his grandfather's city; how he had sat in judgement over the beauty of goddesses. In the sixteenth of Ovid's *Heroides*, Paris promises Helen, 'You will make your progress through the Dardanian towns like a great queen, and the common folk will think a new goddess has come down to Earth.' Soon, says Colluthus, Helen found herself longing to see Troy's great walls and pastures, by Paris's side. And thus Fate, thanks to the will of Zeus, the machinations of Aphrodite, and the unknowing assistance of Aeneas, followed its inexorable course.

At the start the *Hymn to Aphrodite*, we hear how Aphrodite used to walk through the halls of Olympus, laughing with delight at having tricked so many of the gods, especially Zeus himself, into sleeping with mortals and producing the Greek heroes. Zeus resented this mockery so much that he engineered her encounter with Anchises, which produced Aeneas. That may have evened the score on a personal level, but the problem was far greater. At the very start of the *Cypria*, we hear of Zeus visiting Themis, a member of that very ancient race of Titans who had ruled the world before the Olympian Gods, and who stood for natural order. This natural order had become unbalanced because, as the *Cypria* explains, the countless races of men had multiplied so much that Earth herself was being weighed down. Zeus resolved to relieve this burden by starting the Trojan War, in which vast numbers of men and god-born heroes would die.

Zeus's specific strategy for engineering this would be the marriage of Thetys and Peleus (that produced Achilles) and the birth of Helen. Similarly, in his play *Orestes*, Euripides wrote that Zeus made Helen beautiful in order to cause the Trojan War and thus to cleanse the overburdened Earth of its excess human population. The *Catalogue of Women* relates, likewise, how Zeus planned to mingle 'storm and strife' to exterminate humanity altogether, but then slightly contradicts itself by saying that Zeus's purpose was to destroy only the heroes, those born from the unions of deities and mortals, and that henceforth – after the Trojan War – gods and men would dwell utterly apart. It is ironic, then, that Aeneas's conception, as engineered by Zeus, had resulted from Zeus's anger at the begetting of heroes. But now, Zeus planned a clean sweep; the destruction of the products of all such unnatural unions – including, presumably, Aeneas himself.

But things did not work out that way. Aeneas, along with a handful of others, was destined to survive by a power even greater than Zeus. All of Zeus's work in engineering the Trojan War was in obedience to the will of Fate, but Aeneas's survival, too, was Fate's will. To understand why Fate was more powerful even than the lord of Olympus, we must understand the true nature of the universe itself, as comprehended by the

Greeks. And the key to that, they believed, lay in the origins of Aeneas's ancestor, Zeus himself.

Hesiod was a shepherd-poet from Ascra, at the foot of Mount Helicon in Boetia, north of the Gulf of Corinth in Greece, who lived about 700 BC. He is the second earliest Greek poet, after Homer himself, whose work has survived, and he is the world's earliest named genealogist. Hesiod's *Theogony* traces all the immortal denizens of the world back to a single starting point. He was inspired, I think, by the way Helicon itself seems to touch the heavens with its pinnacle, and then spills downwards, and outwards, to the Earth below, like an ever-broadening family tree. 'At the first, Chaos [or 'Chasm'] came to be,' sang Hesiod, and out of it was born 'wide-bosomed Gaia [Earth] ... dim Tartarus in the depth of the wide-pathed Earth, and Eros [Love], fairest among the deathless gods'. Gaia gave birth to Uranos, the god of the starry heavens, 'equal to herself, to cover her on every side, and to be an ever-sure abiding-place for the blessed gods', and she also 'brought forth long hills, graceful haunts of the goddess-nymphs', and the deep sea. From the couplings of these and their innumerable descendants came all the generations of Titans, Olympian gods, nymphs and monsters with which the Greek imagination populated the world.

Hesiod described how, in the early aeons of the world, the perpetual intercourse of Uranos with Gaia made her pregnant with innumerable beings, including the Titans and Cyclopses. But Uranos lay so heavily on Gaia that their children remained imprisoned inside her groaning caverns. To end her son-husband Uranos's tyranny, Gaia made 'the element of grey flint and shaped a great sickle' and handed it to the Titan Kronos, the eldest of her sons by Uranos. The next time Uranos descended onto the Earth, bringing dark night with him, Kronos 'from his ambush stretched forth his left hand, and in his right took the great long sickle with jagged teeth, and swiftly lopped off his own father's members and cast them away to fall behind him'. Kronos's brother, the Titan Atlas, stepped in quickly to hold up the heavens, so that they would never crush the Earth again, and the children of Earth were set free.

As his father's emasculator, Kronos became king of the world and married his own sister, Rhea. Anxious to avoid being overthrown by his own children, Kronos swallowed them on Mount Cotylus in the Troad, but Rhea gave him a rock to swallow instead of the baby Zeus, and thus Kronos was deceived. Zeus grew up in secret in a cave, either the Idaean Cave on Crete, or one on Mount Mainalo, anciently called Mount Thaumasion, in Arcadia. When Zeus grew up, he rebelled against Kronos and forced him to disgorge the other children he had swallowed; these become the other Olympian gods. Zeus imprisoned Kronos, either down in Tartarus, or far out in the Ocean which encircles the world. Zeus and his disgorged brothers divided the universe between them, Poseidon taking the seas and Hades the underworld. Zeus took the Earth and heavens and became king of the gods, seated on his throne on Mount Olympus. Zeus's sister Hera became his wife, and he had by her Ares the war-god, Hebe (youth) and Eileithyia, goddess of childbirth. Zeus was also goaded by Aphrodite's arrows of desire into sleeping with other deities, and even mortals, and fathered a host of children – Persephone by his sister Demeter; Athena by Metis; Apollo and Artemis by Leto; Hermes by Maia; Hercules by Alcmene; Dionysos by Semele, and so on. And by Atlas's daughter Elektra, Zeus fathered Dardanos, the ancestor of Aeneas.

Hesiod's pedigree takes Zeus's ancestry back to the primal Chaos, and he thought that was enough. But in the centuries following Hesiod, Greek mystic thinkers termed Orphics, who claimed inspiration from the Thracian shaman-poet Orpheus, wanted to explain the origin and fate of our souls. To this end, they pushed Hesiod's genealogy further back. No single, complete Orphic theogony survives, and it is clear that there were several different versions, but a broad outline, based on Professor Guthrie's reconstructions, is as follows.

The prime mover was Chronos (Time). From Time came Aither (a formless moistness); Chaos (the yawning gulf); Erebos (darkness over all), and Adrasteia or Ananke (Fate or Necessity). Aither filled Chaos, and from the union of Time and Fate there appeared in this dark, swirling moistness an egg. From this egg was born Eros, whose other names include Phanes, 'shining light' and Protogonos, 'first-born'. Eros was imagined as a marvellously beautiful figure of shining light, with golden wings on his shoulders. Sometimes he had four eyes, or even multiple heads – of ram, bull, lion and snake – symbolising the way he contained within him the seeds of all life. He was the embodiment of the sexual urge, and when he copulated for the first time, with himself, Eros produced a daughter, Night (darkness, his opposite). Night became Eros's consort and succeeded him as ruler of the universe. Together, they were the parents of Nemesis, the mother of Helen. And whereas Hesiod thought Gaia, Mother Earth, was born out of Chaos, and that she was the mother of Uranos, the Orphics believed that both Gaia and Uranos were children of Night and Eros, and that Night willingly yielded to her son Uranos her power over the universe.

Thus, Eros, the child of Time and Fate, was ancestor of the world; everything in it, from the planets to the smallest creatures; all beings, including Aeneas, and you and me, trace our origins back, ultimately, in this world-view, to him: 'Everything comes to be out of One,' said Orpheus's pupil Musaios, adding, equally importantly, 'and [all] is resolved into One.'[6] It is therefore to the radiant light of Eros, with which the universe began, that our souls must ultimately return.

In some versions of the Orphic theology, once Zeus became king of Olympus, he swallowed his ancestor Eros, and became his own ancestor; that very light from which the entire universe, and even he, was descended. But even after so profound an achievement, Zeus remained a mere descendant of those colossal powers that shaped our universe: despite all his power and ability to shape events on Earth, he was ultimately just as subject as everyone else to Eros's progenitors, Time and Fate. In conceiving Helen, and Dardanos;

in causing Aphrodite to conceive Aeneas; in engineering the enslavement of Hesione; in causing the wedding of Peleus and Thetys that produced Achilles and so enraged Erys; in commanding Paris to judge the beauty contest on Ida that led to Aphrodite causing Helen's love for Paris – in all these acts, great Zeus was merely, it seems, following Fate's bidding.

Secretly, perhaps, the Olympian gods knew this. As Roberto Calasso pointed out in his inspired reinterpretation of the Greek Myths, *The Marriage of Cadmus and Harmony*, the gods were descendants of both Eros (sexual desire) and his mother, Ananke (Fate), and 'of the two, they prefer to submit to Eros rather than Ananke, even though they know that Eros is just a dazzling cover for Ananke.'[7] The Olympians could have chosen to present themselves as solemn, grey-clad instruments of Fate; but instead they bathed themselves in Eros's light to make themselves as physically gorgeous as possible. They chose to enact Fate's will not soberly, from high thrones, but gloriously naked, in bed. And all this helps to explain why Aeneas suspended his usually serious nature and aided, with such apparent willingness, in his cousin's sexual conquest of Helen.

Night came, and, says Colluthus, 'opened the two gates of dreams', one of truth, the other of deceit. Paris and Aeneas carried off Helen, along with her slaves and plenty of Menelaus's treasure, back the way they came, down the Euratos valley to their ship. In about the 480s BC, Makron, one of the most prolific of Athens' identifiable vase painters, decorated a skyphos, or two-handled wine cup, which was later exported to Etruria, Italy.[8] It shows Paris pulling Helen along by the arm, while Eros and Aphrodite crown her with a bridal diadem; Aeneas, with a shield and a spear over his shoulder, leads the way, turning his head back 'as if to admonish them not to tarry'.[9] Another Attik cup found in Etruria, also by Makron, shows Paris leading Helen away while behind him, centre-stage, Aeneas fends off Helen's half-sister Timandra, who is presumably trying to stop them.[10] An Etruscan funerary urn from Volterra shows Aeneas and Paris back at their ship. Helen is being dragged aboard by two Trojans. Paris sits by, fully clothed and sporting a Phrygian cap; Aeneas is naked apart from his cloak.[11] 'He is every bit Paris's accomplice', commented Galinsky: 'Confidently he has placed his right hand on Paris's shoulder while his left carefully rests on the grip of his sword. He watches Helen intently...'[12]

They set sail to avoid capture. Aeneas had colluded in Paris's abduction of Helen, but in the movie *Troy* (2004), Paris's companion (whom the script writer changed from Aeneas to Hector), does not find out what has happened until Helen has been smuggled abroad. Foreseeing the consequences, he is duly furious.

The wind was probably from the north-east, because their first destination was some 9 miles south-west along the shore of the Laconian Gulf, near Gythio, the main port of Sparta. Avoiding the port itself, they landed on the islet of Cranae, just off the coast; 'I snatched you from lovely Lacedaemon,'

Paris recalled to Helen in *Iliad* 3, 'and sailed with thee on my seafaring ships, and on the isle of Cranae had dalliance with thee on the couch of love.' Bettany Hughes imagines Paris violating Helen there 'while Aeneas and his men took a break from cataloguing their loot, to watch'.[13]

Potsherds have been found on Cranae, proving that ships had indeed visited the island in Mycenaean times. A causeway now connects Cranae to the mainland, but instead of a romantic bower we found only a lighthouse, a deserted tower, rotting boats and a lot of scrub. As we sat in one of Gythio's waterfront tavernas that evening, we noticed the youth of the town coming and going from the islet, perhaps to re-enact Paris and Helen's first passionate encounter. The Greek antiquarian Pausanias saw a shrine on the shore closest to Cranae, said to have been dedicated by Paris to Aphrodite Migonitis, 'the joiner' (hence the coast south-west of Gythio being called Migonium), in grateful thanks to the goddess for making good her promise of Helen.[14] Tavernas and the coastal road have now obliterated any trace of this shrine. But that is the least of the destruction that resulted from Paris's desire for Helen, in which Aeneas had been so naively complicit.

11

The Princes at Large

What shocked Classical writers most about Paris and Aeneas's abduction of Helen was not the violation of a woman, but their betrayal of her husband's hospitality. So, penning books 9 and 10 of his pro-Trojan account of the Trojan War, Dares claimed that the abduction had taken place under quite different circumstances. When Aeneas and Paris entered the Laconian Gulf on their way to petition Menelaus for Hesione's return, they saw the king sailing east to visit Pylos, so they diverted their own course to Kythera. The boys heard that Helen had landed on Kythera too, intending to while away her husband's absence at the island's famous temple of Aphrodite, so they set off, eager to gaze on her fabled beauty for themselves.

Kythera lies 34 miles south of the head of the Laconian Gulf. The island was colonised first by the Minoans, so its main settlements were along the shore that looks south towards Crete. Dares says Helen was supposed to have landed at Helea, which is thought generally to be Avlemonas, a rocky cove and fishing village on the south-east coast. Aeneas and Paris may have landed at the island's main settlement, Skandeia, which is now known as Paleopolis, just over a mile west of Avlemonas. Here was a harbour, formed by the mouth of the River Vothonos, which is now silted up. A small town, of Minoan origin, stretched along the back of the beach, west of the river mouth, and up onto a rocky promontory called Kastri. Some remains of walls are still there, and the low earthen cliff along the back of the beach bristles with potsherds.

The harbour settlement fell into sharp decline after the Trojan War, but inland, to the north-west, a city was founded on a steep rocky hillside in the 700s BC by Peloponnesian Greeks, at a site now called Palaikastro. The hillside there is littered with potsherds, some black-glazed, and there are numerous rubble walls among the prickly garrigue.

Herodotus confirms that there was a temple of Aphrodite on the island and says it had been founded by the Phoenicians,[1] a Bronze Age race of seafaring traders from what is now the Lebanon, on the coast of the Levant. It could have existed, therefore, in Aeneas's time. The truth of Herodotus's statement is suggested by Xenophon's *Hellenika*, which calls one of Kythera's harbours (probably 'Helea' or Avlemonas), 'Phoinikous',[2] and the Kastri area is covered with murex shells, of the sort from which the Phoenicians made their famous purple dye. Despite hard archaeological evidence to support Herodotus's assertion, therefore, a Phoenician presence on Kythera is possible. If so, they may well have established a sanctuary to their goddess Astarte, who was later Hellenised, here, as on Cyprus, into the Greek Aphrodite. That may help explain in turn why Hesiod claimed, by the 700s BC, that Aphrodite had been born in the sea off Kythera.

Nobody knows where Aphrodite's famous Kytheran temple was. In 1808, Castellan drew a Classical temple on the coast near Skandeia and labelled it as Aphrodite's temple, but all trace of this building is lost and no further evidence links it to the goddess. There was a dramatic Minoan sanctuary up on the mountain behind Avlemonas, from which you can see Crete, but no trace of the worship of Aphrodite (or Astarte) has been found there. But when Pausanias visited Kythera in the AD 100s, he mentioned Skandeia, followed by Palaikastro, and wrote that Aphrodite's temple on the island was 'the most ancient of all the sanctuaries of Aphrodite among the Greeks'.[3] Archaeologists from Schliemann onwards, therefore, have sought Aphrodite's temple up on Palaikastro – and so did we. Even though the bulk of Palaikastro was built long after Mycenaean times, there is no reason why a Classical temple of Aphrodite should not have been built there over a far more ancient sanctuary, and such a Classical temple would probably have been the place where Dares imagined Aeneas and Paris seeking out Helen.

Schliemann's favoured site for the temple of Aphrodite at Palaikastro was below the chapel of Agios Anargyroi – Saints Kosmas and Damien. Papa Giorgios showed us the way, using a shepherd's crook to clear the narrow path of thorny branches and the webs of enormous orb spiders. Not far from the chapel, we passed a semi-excavated wall, which included a piece of Classical pillar. The chapel itself is on a lower spur of the hill, looking south-east towards Skandeia and Crete. The long, low, stone building dates from the AD 500s and is entirely unremarkable outside. But in its cave-like interior, as a startled bat fluttered about, we passed through three successive chambers, reminiscent of the layout of a Classical temple. The first (the narthex) contained four half-height fluted Doric columns, built into the chapel walls. Entering the central chamber (the naos) below a piece of ancient architrave, reused upside down as a lintel, we found four full-height Doric columns of poros stone. The furthest chamber, the church's altar area (and perhaps the temple's *opisthodomos* or rear-chamber), contained four truncated pieces of column, and we noticed at least one piece of column built into the chapel's walls. If the four full-height columns represent the original height of the temple then they compare well, according to Plommer, to other Doric temples from the 500s BC, including those at Amykles.

Schliemann was convinced that two of the Doric columns in this chapel were in their original positions. While later archaeologists agree that the columns are from a Classical temple that stood somewhere on the hill, they have questioned whether it was really where the chapel is now, because the area around was not levelled. Such a levelled site exists 1,000 feet to the west-south-west, close to three ancient wells and a water basin. Another possible site, proposed by G. L. Huxley, is further up the hill, at a spot backed by a wall of rough polygonal blocks. In addition, by following a goat-track through the site of the ancient city and scrambling up through the jagged limestone rocks, we reached the chapel of Agios Giorgios on the very top of the hill. Here, quite recently, archaeologists found the foundations of a long, narrow building covering 531 square feet, made of local stone, with a few dressed stone blocks and a hexagonal pillar lying down. The earliest parts date from the 700s BC, but they may have been built over an earlier sanctuary.

Any of these sites may have been Kythera's famous temple of Aphrodite. Against the Agios Giorgios site being Aphrodite's is the discovery there of a stone base for a votive offering, inscribed AΘANAIAI ANEΘHKE, 'dedicated to Athena', and finds here include a clay plaque depicting Medusa, whose head appears on Athena's shield and also several heads of goddesses, one helmeted, which have been identified as Athena. But Pausanias says that on Kythera, Aphrodite was depicted here fully armed (because she had been the lover of the war god, Ares). They also found two small carved heads with a hairstyle like Aphrodite's – so maybe this hill-top site was after all the location of Aphrodite's temple where, in Dares's version of the story, Aeneas and Paris encountered Helen.

'Confident in his own good looks,' writes Dares of Paris at Aphrodite's temple on Kythera, 'he began to walk within sight of her ... thus they met and spent some time just staring, struck by each other's beauty.' An Italian chest panel from the AD 1400s shows Paris and Aeneas at the neo-Classical temple, with their retinues, all in Renaissance finery:[4] Aeneas must be one of the noblemen standing outside, waiting for his cousin. A late AD 1400s painting by the school of Antonio Vivarini shows the two cousins dressed as stylish Venetian bucks.[5] Paris leads Helen away from a neo-Classical temple by the arm, gallantly but firmly; while Aeneas, equally gallant, stands behind, guiding her other arm, just in case she might try to escape.

These are elegant, courtly scenes, but Dares tells us that Paris waited for nightfall and then invaded the temple to carry off Helen, her women and belongings, and, later, in book thirty-eight of Dares, we hear that Aeneas helped him. A maiolica dish from Urbino, based on a drawing of Raphael's, shows pandemonium erupting as naked, bearded Paris, aided by a satyr representing lust, carries off a terrified, bare-breasted Helen from a Renaissance-style temple of Aphrodite, while the armed townsmen try to stop them; on the right is a naked young man, perhaps Aeneas, drawing his sword, hurrying to aid his cousin.[6] This follows Dares's account, in which the townsmen intervened to try to prevent the abduction. A battle ensued – the first of Aeneas's life – in which many Kytherans were killed. Heady with blood and testosterone, Paris then despoiled the temple.

Was Aeneas really involved in this shocking act? Perhaps, for he was young, and probably easily led by his charismatic cousin, and maybe he did not yet know he was Aphrodite's son. Yet, had Aeneas been involved, we should surely hear of him suffering some dire consequences from the gods, like those that befell Paris – and because we don't, perhaps he was not involved in the temple's desecration.

Kythera's devotion to Aphrodite was revived in Roman times, when the goddess was depicted on coins there. These may have been minted to elicit Roman support for the islanders' efforts to free themselves from Spartan domination, by reminding Rome of the island's close association with the goddess, the mother of the Romans' founding hero, Aeneas.

Whether Aeneas and his cousin had abducted Helen from Sparta, or from Kythera, it was time now for Paris 'to carry to Ilios [Troy]', as Colluthus put it, 'his freight of war'. But Proclus relates how a storm swept their ships east, straight across the Mediterranean as far as Sidon. This was one of the greatest, and perhaps the oldest of the Phoenician cities on the Levantine coast, in what is now Lebanon, 20 miles south down the coast from Beirut. This was the land that the Old Testament calls Canaan, and indeed the cousins were entering Biblical territory now, for they were only 120 miles north of Urušalimum, Jerusalem. A thousand years later, Jerusalem would become the capital of King David's kingdom of Israel and Judah. Much later still, Jerusalem would supplant Troy, in the western imagination, as the most significant ancient city in the world.

Sidon, where the cousins came ashore, was a trading city, famous for its glass, purple dyes and embroidery, and had strong trade links to Troy. Still heady from his dreadful conduct in Greece, Paris sacked it. The boys' eastern adventures are enlarged upon in book one of Dictys's anti-Trojan account of the Trojan War. This describes Paris being received hospitably by the Sidonian king, but then treacherously slaughtering his host, ransacking the palace and carrying off as much loot as he could. This was Aeneas's second conflict, and again a shameful one, but he would learn better. The Sidonians mounted a counter-attack; two of the Trojan ships were set ablaze, but the rest escaped, with most of the loot aboard. *Iliad* 6 refers to the multi-coloured robes from Sidon that Paris had brought back 'over the broad sea' to Troy, along with 'high-born Helen'.

According to pseudo-Apollodorus's *Bibliotheka*, Paris was careful not to return too quickly to Troy, lest Menelaus pursue him, so he lingered 'a long time in Phoenicia and Cyprus'.[7] This statement, therefore, brings Aeneas to the home of his mother, Aphrodite.

There was never a single, orthodox version of Greek mythology, or of the origins of Aphrodite. Homer's *Iliad* presents her as the daughter of Zeus and the Titaness Dione (either a daughter, or granddaughter, of Gaia, Mother Earth, but really, like Gaia and Aphrodite, yet another manifestation of the Great Mother). But Hesiod's *Theogony* relates how, when Uranos's genitals were cut off by his son Kronos, they fell into the foaming ocean and there emerged 'an awful and lovely goddess, and grass grew up about her beneath her shapely feet ... gods and men call her Aphrodite ... and with her went Eros, and comely Desire followed her at her birth.' Both versions feature in retellings of Aeneas's life and, as with Aeneas himself, their contradictions encouraged rather than stifled the development of new myths. Whichever myth about Aphrodite's origins one prefers, she was in many ways an outpouring of Eros; a manifestation of that primal, sexual urge which animates the entire universe – whether Eros was later swallowed by Zeus or not. Later, Aphrodite gave birth to a new Eros, whom the Romans called Cupid. A half-brother, therefore, of Aeneas, this new Eros embodied erotic desire all over again, but this time in the form of a winged boy. Some Athenians traced Aphrodite's origins back even further to the beginning of the world, seeing her as one of the triple personifications of Fate. But it was for love, not destiny, that Aphrodite is best known.

Of Aphrodite's possible origins, it is Hesiod's which most excites the imagination. It was visualised most notably in Sandro Botticelli's *Birth of Venus*, a picture that still draws crowds daily in Florence's Uffizi Gallery. This shows the golden-haired goddess being blown ashore in a cockleshell, having travelled far over the flower-spangled sea. Both Kythera and Cyprus, the sites of the earliest and most famous temples to Aphrodite, claimed that their seas were the site of her foaming birthplace. The story on Kythera now is that she was born close to the rock of Avgo, in the sea off the island's southern tip. 'Avgo' means 'egg', but the name might be a corruption of *afros*, 'foam', which lies at the root of Aphrodite's name. Homer calls Aphrodite 'Kythereia', and a generation later, Hesiod reconciled the conflicting claims by saying she was born in the sea near Kythera and was then wafted to Cyprus.

To understand Aphrodite's origins, we travelled, like Aeneas, to Cyprus. Aphrodite's temple-home there was, in the Homeric *Hymn to Aphrodite*, the place where she prepared herself before travelling to Mount Ida for her encounter with Anchises. Paphos, on the south-western coast of Cyprus, is a fried breakfast tourist resort, but 9 miles north-west, close to the village of Kouklia, is the broad hilltop of Palaipaphos, where the ruins of Aphrodite's temple lie bare below the glaring sun. The sea is about a mile from the hill now, but it probably came much closer in the Bronze Age. Little of the temple remains, save for the bases of walls and a few scraps of Classical pillars.

The Cypriot goddess worshipped there in the Neolithic and Copper Age was originally called Wanassa and is exemplified by the stone figurine found there known as the 'Lady of Lemba', with its prominent sexual features and, somewhat surprisingly, a high phallic neck – a more primitive expression of the deity than Botticelli's Venus, though the common Indo-European root of 'Venus' and 'Wanassa' is evident. Herodotus believed that the worship of Aphrodite had been brought to Cyprus by Phoenicians from Askalon in Syria.[8] More correctly, the Phoenicians introduced the worship of Astarte (or Ishtar, or Ashtoreth), who was herself a version of the Mesopotamian Innana, and her fusion on Cyprus with the native deity Wanassa resulted in Aphrodite.

As with Elektra's cult on Samothraki, Aphrodite-Wanassa's worship at Palaipaphos seems to go back to a rock. In this case, it was a bluish-grey stone, streaked with pale grey like lightning, almost 6 feet high, and worn smooth by generations of adoring hands. We found it standing, forlorn and unlabelled, in a neglected ante-chamber of the archaeological site's museum. It is a meteorite and, taking into account the myths it generated, it was probably seen by the ancient Cypriots plunging into the sea below these cliffs and sending up a momentous plume of steaming foam, similar to the waterspouts caused by wind and wave that have been seen nearby at the white-rocked beach of Petra Tou Romiou, 4 miles to the south-east. Backed by gleaming limestone cliffs, this beach is said to be the place where the goddess came ashore, as in Botticelli's painting, and the waterspouts there have been likened to girls with waving hair. Presumably, Cypriots hauled the phallic meteorite out of the sea, set it up on the hill of Palaipaphos and enshrined in their mythology how it had appeared so suddenly from the sky, and how its dramatic union with the sea produced a foaming apparition of their goddess, Wanassa. This is surely why they gave the goddess a new name, 'foam-born'. Later, when Mycenaeans settled in Cyprus, they presumably translated her name into Greek, and because *afros* is Greek for 'foam', they called the Cypriot goddess Aphrodite, which means 'foam-bright' or 'foam-traveller'.

Thanks to the Mycenaeans' repeated contact with Cyprus, Aphrodite became incorporated into the Olympian pantheon. She was a firm fixture by Homer's time, but she retained her Cypriot temple and the Greeks imagined her marrying Hephaestus, the lame god of metal-workers, precisely because Cyprus, with its reserves of copper, had been a centre of Mediterranean metal-working. As Bettany Hughes remarked, Aphrodite 'was brazen in a number of ways'.[9] Although Virgil, much later, followed the more conservative story of Aphrodite being Zeus's daughter, he, too, acknowledged Cyprus as her home and place of origin.

The meteorite which plunged down from Heaven, and which has resided ever since at Palaipaphos, and whose first appearance caused the myth of the foamy birth of Wanassa-Aphrodite, found its place in the succession battles of the different generations of immortals, which were characteristic of Middle and Near Eastern origin-myths. The stone became identified with – or perhaps was the inspiration for – the story of the severed penis of Uranos, which was sliced off by his son Kronos with a sickle. In *Travelling Heroes*, Robin Lane Fox suggests that this story, which we encounter first in Hesiod, may have been Hesiod's own idea. Visiting Delphi, 35 miles south-east of his home in Ascra, Hesiod may have heard eastern stories of the succession battles of the gods, and of the foamy, Cypriot origins of Aphrodite, from merchant-pilgrims who had visited both Cyprus and the Near East. He may then have synthesised these with Greece's more home-spun tales of the gods, to create Aphrodite's story as we know it now.

After emasculating his father, Kronos threw his bloodied sickle away. Some Greek travellers identified it as sickle-shaped Corfu; others, later, as the Drepanum peninsula (now called Trapani) off the western coast of Sicily, the name derived from the Greek for sickle, *drepane*. There seems to be no tradition of the sickle's fate on Kythera, unless it was Cape Maleas, on the Greek mainland and visible from the island's north-eastern coast. But in Cyprus, the ultimate justification for the story was found just up the coast from Palaipaphos, in a sickle-shaped peninsula – which of course they called Drepanum. This, said the Cypriots, was the true sickle of Kronos.

We may pause to imagine Aeneas visiting his mother's temple at Palaipaphos, and the other sites around the island associated with her, such as the Baths of Aphrodite, below a breast-shaped mountain on the north-west coast near Polis, where she is believed to have cavorted with her Cypriot lover Adonis. But now, it is time to set sail again.

The boys' next port of call is suggested by Herodotus,[10] so we may imagine the stormy Mediterranean carrying the Trojan ships south from Cyprus until they docked at Heracleum, amidst the salt-pans at mouth of the Nile. Paris and Aeneas would have been confronted by all the glories of Nineteenth Dynasty Egypt, with its gilded, monumental statuary, sacred cows and strange, animal-headed gods.

Egypt's civilisation was as ancient as Anatolia's. The Mycenaeans knew secretly that their own civilisation was junior to Egypt's, yet in their myths they claimed that Egypt had been founded by Epaphos, whose mother Io had arrived there, in the form of a cow, from the Peloponnese. But that would not have diminished the magnificence which Aeneas and Paris encountered in Egypt. In the late nineteenth century, André Castaigne depicted Alexander the Great at the temple of Apis in Memphis, but the picture may as well show Paris, who was also called Alexander. He stands at the foot of a huge set of steps leading up to a vast altar, with colossal pillars towering up into darkness, and on the altar stands the Apis bull, an embodiment of Zeus, flanked by its attendants, all adorned in restrained grandeur. Though a great man in his time, whose shadow casts itself far across history, Egypt's magnificence dwarfs him.

All that is left of Heracleum now is the port of Abu Qir (or Aboukir, anciently called Canup), 11 miles north-east of Alexandria, at the eastern edge of the Nile Delta. Once the main port of entry for foreign ships coming to the delta, most of the city has been submerged, and only recently have underwater archaeologists begun to rediscover its riches, dating mainly to the centuries following Aeneas and Paris's time. Herodotus visited Heracleum in 400s BC and wrote of a temple to Hercules there.[11] It was probably originally dedicated to Khonsou, son of Amun, who was seen as the Egyptian version of Hercules, but as Greek culture pervaded Egypt, a stronger equation was made between the two heroes and eventually the city even took Hercules's name as its own. When the Earl of Sandwich visited this area in the 1730s, he saw a

Turkish castle nearby 'built out of the ruins of some ancient edifice, as appears from several pieces of granite pillars inserted in them, and many fragments of marble inscribed with hieroglyphics'. He thought it 'not improbable that they once belonged to the temple of Hercules at Herculeum'.[12] Herodotus heard that the temple of Hercules offered sanctuary to escaped slaves, and reports a story that Paris's slaves, wishing to escape their bonds, had fled thence.

The slaves, in Herodotus's story, told the local governor, Thonis, how their master had robbed his host, Menelaus, and raped his host's wife, Helen. *Odyssey* 4 seems in part to corroborate this story, by mentioning that Helen later possessed medicines given her by Thonis's wife, though of course the story Herodotus heard may have grown out of this Homeric detail.

Before long, says Herodotus, Paris found himself being summoned to Memphis to answer for his behaviour before the king. Aeneas, we may assume, would have accompanied Paris on the journey, 121 miles south-east as the crow flies, travelling slowly by barque or barge up the now extinct Canupian branch of the Nile, until they joined the mother-river itself. Their journey would have taken them past reed-fringed riverbanks punctuated with irrigation channels leading into patchwork cornfields, peppered with reed-thatched villages, white-housed towns, and temples. On the horizon beyond the date palms, where the fields meet the Sahara Desert, the pyramids of Giza would have appeared, growing impossibly huge as the boys approached Memphis. This was the Greek name for the city the ancient Egyptians called Inbu-Hedj, 'the white-walled city', and called today Mit-Rahineh, 12 miles south of Cairo. Commanding the head of the Nile delta, Memphis was one of Egypt's major naval bases and capitals. As old as Troy, it was in the process of being restored and rebuilt by Ramesses II.

Herodotus calls the king they met 'Proteus', but Egypt had no such king and that was clearly a Greek name applied to an Egyptian ruler. For most of the 1200s BC, from 1279 to 1213, Egypt was ruled by one man, Ramesses II, so we may say with confidence that he was Herodotus's Proteus. It was Ramesses II who built the magnificent temple 500 miles further south along the Nile at Abu Simbel, the frontage carved with colossal statues of himself; and who had fought the Battle of Kadesh, in the Levant, about 90 miles north-east of Sidon, against the Hittites, in 1274 BC. Proclaiming his victory, Ramesses II listed the 'Drdny' or Dardanians among the Hittites' allies. Small wonder, then, that Ramesses had little sympathy for these two young hoodlums now.

In his interview with the king, as reported by Herodotus, Paris tried to lie about his abduction of Helen, but he became confused and his ex-slaves contradicted him. Ramesses said that, were it not for the Egyptian custom of never killing guests, he would slay Paris for his wife-stealing misdemeanours. Instead, he declared, 'For thyself and thy companions [including, presumably, Aeneas], I command thee to begone from my land within the space of three days – and I warn you, that otherwise at the end of that time you will be treated as enemies.'[13] Worse, he commanded, Helen and the stolen treasure must remain behind, until Menelaus reclaimed them, in Egypt.

12

The War Begins

Now Paris and Aeneas sailed home. In some versions, Helen remained in Egypt. In others, she reached Troy in the same ship as her lover. Works such as Pseudo-Apollodorus's *Bibliotheka* and Stesichorus's *Palinodia* report an ingenious attempt to reconcile this contradiction, by claiming that the real Helen remained in Egypt, as the king had ordered, but an *eidolon* or phantom of her, fashioned out of clouds by Hermes, travelled back to Troy with Paris and Aeneas. Thus, in some versions of the story, the Trojans told the Greeks repeatedly that she was not in Troy, and the truth of this was only discovered after the city had been sacked, and the real Helen was found by Menelaus in Egypt.

Wolf's novel *Cassandra* describes the fleet returning at night, and Paris slipping into Troy without Helen. The shameful truth that he had abducted Helen, only to lose her in Egypt, needed to be covered up. As Priam's police-state intensified its grip on the people, the party line was that mighty Priam was standing up to Greek demands for the return of the woman whom Paris had so boldly abducted. The Trojan people never knew they were fighting for a woman whose presence there was no more than what the modern Greek poet Giorgos Seferis characterised as 'a bit of cloud', and an 'empty tunic'.[1]

But in other versions of the story, the real Helen lived in Troy throughout the siege, and walked and talked as Homer described. Phantom or not, she ceased now to be called Helen of Sparta. She became Helen of Troy.

In Dares's account, Paris, Aeneas and the real Helen made landfall on the island of Tenedos, just off the Troad's west coast. Paris sent news of his arrival to his father, who decided to use Helen as a bargaining counter in his ongoing efforts to secure Hesione's return. That is the last we hear of efforts to repatriate poor Hesione; in the kerfuffle which followed, she seems to have been forgotten completely, either living on as Telamon's slave or, according to Tzetzes's *ad Lycophron*,[2] escaping to Miletus with Trambelus, her son by Telamon, who was later killed in one of Achilles' raids. But, as Calasso and others have observed, women in Greek myths seem so often to be interchangeable, one merging into another. Conflict between Troy and Greece was always going to be over a woman, and once Helen had stepped into her shoes as the focus for discord, Hesione was surplus to requirements. That is why, in Colluthus's version of the story, when Cassandra saw Paris and Aeneas's expedition returning to Troy, she tore her hair in grief at the very sight of Helen. Not heeding Cassandra, continues Colluthus, the Trojans 'unbarred the bolts of the high-built gates and received ... the source of their woe'.

According to Dictys, Paris and Aeneas found Menelaus already in Troy, angrily demanding his wife's return. The majority of Trojans led by Antenor wanted peace, but Priam's sons, 'being barbarians in language and morals ... driven astray by greed and lust' voted to keep Helen, along with Menelaus's riches and her female attendants, with whom they had fallen in love. Helen wished to remain, too, and argued her right to stay on the grounds of genealogy. She claimed descent, albeit via her foster-mother Leda, from Agenor, King of Tyre, whose nephew Danaus of Argos was father of an earlier Hesione, the mother of Dardanos's mother Elektra – Dardanos of course being the ancestor of the Trojans. But Helen – or Dictys – had their genealogy muddled, because Elektra's mother was not Hesione, but Pleione, daughter of Oceanos. Nonetheless, this faux genealogy seems to have swung the Trojan assembly, who decided to allow Helen to stay, and it was only with Antenor's assistance that Menelaus managed to escape with his life.

It was clear now to the older Trojans, particularly Antenor and probably Anchises too, that the abduction of Helen had been a terrible mistake, but the younger generation, Aeneas included, were unrepentant. For them, what was coming seemed to promise the greatest adventure of their lives.

The modern view is that, if the Trojan War really happened, its real motivation was probably Mycenaean Greece's desire to end Troy's stranglehold on the lucrative trade route, up the Dardanelles and Sea of Marmara, with the Baltic. But such venal motives are unlikely, ever, to have been the war's stated reason. Paris's theft of Menelaus's treasure was hardly sufficient justification for so great an expedition, but his abduction of Helen would have provided an excellent and emotive *casus belli*, to rouse the indignation of the Greeks.

When Menelaus triumphed over the other suitors in winning the hand of fair Helen, the rest, we hear, led by clever Odysseus, king of the island-realm of Ithaka off the west coast of Greece, swore to defend the couple against anyone who tried to separate them. Now, cuckolded Menelaus ran to his older brother Agamemnon, king of Mycenae, and together they called in these promises from all over Greece, assembling an invasion force at Aulis, 30 miles north of Athens.

The Greeks' first voyage to Anatolia took them too far south, to Teuthrania, between modern Bergama and Izmir, in the kingdom of Mysia, from which they were repelled by its king, Telephus, son of Hercules. The fleet was dispersed by a storm, but while Aeneas and his relatives celebrated prematurely in Troy, the Greek ships reassembled at Aulis. Here they were detained by storms caused by Artemis's fury at Agamemnon, so, at the advice of Calchas the seer, the king tried to appease her by sacrificing his own daughter, Iphigeneia. At the last moment, Artemis relented, saved Iphigeneia, and allowed the wind to change. In his play *Iphigeneia at Aulis*, Euripides reflects not only on the immediate drama at hand, but also on its cause, Paris's abduction of Helen, writing of the way love's arrows bring pleasure and pain in equal measure. Wherever Eros walks, wrote Euripides, Erys, the goddess of discord, follows: and the play's chorus is vocal in blaming Aphrodite for having stirred up all this trouble in the first place.

In his play *Faustus*, Christopher Marlowe (1564-1593) wrote memorably of Helen having the 'face that launched a thousand ships', but Classical sources number the fleet that darkened the Aegean at 1,186 vessels (which, admittedly, wouldn't have the same ring to it). This angry swarm settled on Tenedos, where Achilles slew the king, Tennes, son of Apollo, thus drawing upon himself the wrath of the god, which would lead eventually to his death. Then, the Greeks sailed across the narrow strait. Achilles longed to be the first ashore, but his goddess-mother, Thetys, warned him to hold back, so Protesilaus, leader of the Thessalians from Phylace, was the first to set foot on the Troad.

On hearing that the Greeks were on Tenedos, Aeneas and his companions would have sallied forth from Troy, led by Priam's eldest son, Hector, and hastened over the Skamander's ford, which still exists south-west of Kalafat, then south-west across the Trojan plain. We may imagine the dust rising as they drove their chariots, or ran: this was only the first of many such races, to and fro across the plain, that over ten years would turn the once-fertile fields into a desert in summer and a slippery mire in winter. Once the Trojans had reached Beşika Bay, they could have watched for the Greeks and positioned themselves to oppose the landing.

As Protesilaus stormed through the surf, weapons ready, he would have seen Trojan spears aimed at him by warriors whose breastplates and helmets flashed in the sun. Protesilaus knew not the names of these warriors, especially not that of the man whose spear struck home. Nor are we certain who it was: Proclus says it was Hector, but in book two of his Trojan history, Dictys claims that Protesilaus 'fell among those who were fighting up front, struck by Aeneas's weapon'. This is Aeneas's first recorded kill, though probably he had drawn blood already at Sidon and perhaps on Kythera as well. Right from the war's start, Aeneas was marked out as a warrior; as the hero his semi-divine birth had destined him to become. Countless more such kills would follow.

Now Achilles and his army of Thessalian Myrmidons pounded through the waves, with the rest of the Greeks behind them. Like a fierce tide, they broke the Trojan line. Bravado turned to fear, brave resistance to panicked

The War Begins

retreat, sending Hector, Aeneas and all the rest careering back across the plain in disorganised bands, confused and angry. And, behind them thundered the Greeks.

The fields before Troy, where Priam's horses grazed so recently, were transformed. As Aeneas, Hector and his comrades stared down from the walls, they would have seen only a bristling sea of Greek spears and helms, glinting in the sun – before the next wave of Greek arrows came whirring through the air, forcing them to duck down behind the battlements for cover.

For an interminable time, the Greeks remained on the plain before Troy. But eventually they realised that its broad ditches and well-built walls, all defended by fierce counter-waves of Trojan arrows and spears, were too much for them. They became aware that, once Priam's allies arrived, their own position would be vulnerable. So, as the stalemate became apparent, the Greeks withdrew to establish a camp nearby.

Three times in the *Iliad*, the Greeks cry in retreat 'to the ships and the Hellespont!'[3] so everyone from Strabo to Schliemann imagined the Greek camp being north of Troy, somewhere along the southern shore of the Dardanelles, which is also called the Hellespont. But Homer also stated that the Skamander, with its ford, lay between Troy and the Greek camp. To make this fit with the idea that the Greeks camped on the Dardanelles' southern shore, Schliemann argued that the Skamander must once have flowed along the channel of the Azmak, which passes much closer Troy, but this was a contrived and unprovable theory. In addition, we know now that in Aeneas's time, most of the land north of Troy was underwater, so there could have been no camp there at all.

In 1912, both Alfred Brückner and Oscar Mey proposed, independently, that the Greek camp was at Beşika Bay, on the western coast of the Troad, just to the north-east of Tenedos, a location which was indeed separated from Troy by the Skamander and its ford. The north end of Beşika Bay is dominated by the mound of Beşika Burnu (also called Yassi Tepe). Excavations at Beşika Burnu revealed some Mycenaean pottery; nearby was a Mycenaean cemetery with about two hundred graves of men, women and at least two children, all from about the time of Aeneas and surely related to the Greek occupation of the area. But the trouble with the idea of the Greek camp being there is that the site would have been difficult to defend, and the cry 'to the ships and the Hellespont!' would have made no sense.

However, when much of the northern plain of Troy was underwater, the Sigeum Ridge, north of Beşika Burnu, was a peninsula. The Aegean was on the western side, as it is today, and on the other was the ancient bay in the Dardanelles, or Hellespont, covering what is now dry land. In 1998, Professor Luce suggested that the Greeks may have established their semi-permanent camp on this peninsula, on the shore that looked across the Hellespont bay towards Troy; from which, in fact, they could see fires burning before Troy, as described in *Iliad* 10. Luce thought that the camp was probably between Kesik Tepe, which stands on the top of the ridge, next to the cliff above the

Aegean, and the strange, deep trench, known as the 'Kesik Canal', 1,800 feet south of the tepe. The Kesik Canal cuts through the ridge and cliff, forming an easy route between the fields on the lower part of the ridge to the east and the otherwise unreachable beach. Luce considered the Kesik Canal to be 'a natural depression that appears to have been enlarged by human agency' forming 'an impassable barrier for any chariot' coming from the south.[4] We found it wider and deeper than we expected, and wondered whether, besides defending the Greek camp, its digging out may have been Agamemnon's way of keeping bored Greek soldiers busy during quiet spells in the long years of the war. The 'canal' was also wide enough for ships to be dragged up from the beach to the camp, or even across to the camp's eastern shore.

One objection to this identification of the camp might be that *Iliad* 7 describes the camp having not only a ditch, but also a great earthen wall, whereas Luce's proposed site has only the ditch and no wall. However, Luce argued that Homer's description of the walls matches what is now known of Troy's lower city walls, so the poet may imaginatively have relocated these to the Greek camp, to add drama to the battle there. Indeed, Homer virtually admits that the walls there were thanks to his imagination, because in *Iliad* 7 we hear that once the war is over, Poseidon will obliterate them – a way for Homer to have his dramatic walls, and also to forestall objections from contemporaries who knew that no trace of them existed. The real camp, if it was there, was presumably protected by the Kesik Canal and perhaps by a modest stockade, but not by high earthen walls at all.

Unable to capture the city, the Greeks began ravaging the Troad and the lands of Priam's allies, capturing Priam's son Polydorus in the process. Proclus relates how Menelaus and Odysseus went on an embassy to Troy, seeking the return of Helen and everything else Paris stole from Therapne, to end the war. This sort of embassy was entirely in keeping with practices at the time for, as Hughes points out, Hittite sources are full of details of diplomatic negotiations between the great powers.[5] Dictys describes, or imagines, these particular negotiations in detail; how the majority of the Trojan nobles longed to be rid of both Helen and the Greeks, but Aeneas, with Priam's son Hector and other members of the royal family, arrived and interrupted proceedings. Hector explained that returning Helen was out of the question but, in compensation, he offered Menelaus one of his sisters, Cassandra, or Polyxena (a girl not mentioned by Homer, and who appears first in Apollodorus).

Menelaus, says Dictys, reacted furiously: first the Trojans stole my wife, and now they offer me a different wife I don't want! In response to his tirade, Aeneas leapt to his feet in fury and told Menelaus that the favour of marrying one of Priam's daughters, an idea which he and Paris's other friends had always opposed anyway, was now off the table.

'Fortunately,' Aeneas proclaimed, 'there are, and always will be, those who safeguard the house and kingdom of Priam.' Priam's son Polydorus may have fallen into Greek hands, but the king had many more sons, eager to fight. Aeneas claimed that Paris's abduction of Helen was fair compensation for the number of Asians abducted, over the generations, by Greeks. Aeneas did not, oddly, mention Hesione, but he cited the way Zeus abducted both his great-great uncle Ganymede from Troy, and Europa from (he says) Sidon, and how the Argonauts had abducted Medea from Colchis, too. Finally, Aeneas made the extraordinary claim that Io was stolen from Sidon and taken to Argos by Zeus. The Greek myth was that, although she ended up in Egypt, Io began life as a priestess of Argos. Aeneas was effectively turning the pretension that Egyptian civilisation started in Greece on its head and claiming that honour for Asia instead.

'Up to now,' concluded Dictys' Aeneas, 'we have merely been bandying words. But now, unless you and your fleet leave our land, you will taste Trojan valour and courage. Troy has more than enough young men who are ready for battle, and every day new allies are coming.'

Aeneas's strutting argument was countered by level-headed Odysseus. Famed for his cunning and quick-wittedness, Odysseus argued that history lessons are all very well, but you Trojans, Aeneas, started this conflict by abducting Helen, and you're welcome to start the fighting as well. With that the council broke up and Menelaus and Odysseus returned to their camp. Then the Greeks reappeared before Troy's walls with their captive, Polydorus, and stoned him to death, before resuming their raids, says Dictys, across the Troad.

Aeneas's unconciliatory attitude towards the Greeks may have pleased Priam's family, but it went down badly, says Dictys, in the rest of Troy, where the people raised 'a huge tumult'. Aeneas, they thought, was 'without doubt a diplomat of the very worst sort; he was the reason why Priam's kingdom was hated and Priam's whole house was headed for ruin.'

13

The Blind Poet

Each version of Aeneas's story was written with a different agenda. Dares was pro-Trojan, while anti-Roman Dictys sought to cast Aeneas and his fellow Trojans in the worst light possible. Wolf's Aeneas, an unwilling subject of a totalitarian state, grew less enamoured with Priam's rule as the conflict developed. As Troy was warped by fear both of the Greeks and of its own rulers, Cassandra saw ever less of her lover. People said, disapprovingly, that Aeneas was away in the mountains: yet she felt herself to be 'with him with every fibre of my body and soul'.

With the possible exception of Proclus's quotes from the *Cypria*, which may in turn have been written by Homer and are certainly drawn from the same epic tradition in which Homer worked, all these views of young Aeneas come after Homer's *Iliad* and build on the information that Homer supplies. The *Iliad* says nothing of Aeneas assisting Paris in abducting Helen; or arrogantly advocating war; or being blamed for the consequences; nor of him opposing the Greeks so bravely when they first came ashore and slaying Protesilaus. Instead, aside from references to his goddess-mother Aphrodite, his origins in Dardania and his upbringing by his brother-in-law Alcathous, Aeneas appears in the *Iliad* with a clean slate, tending his family's herds back in his native mountains, where we – and Achilles – will find him soon. But as we enter the world of the *Iliad*, we must ask: what is this poem, that stands at the head of all western literature, and what is known of its poet? To what extent might Homer have been retelling real stories about a real-life of Aeneas?

His original name, the Greeks believed, was Melesigines. Martin West's collection of Homeric lives and apocrypha include stories that Homer was descended from Odysseus; or from Orpheus; or that his mother bathed in the River Meles at Smyrna (modern Izmir), 115 miles south of Troy, and was impregnated by the river god; or that he was conceived by a human father on Chios, the island due west of Smyrna; or that his conception was on the mainland just north of Smyrna, at Kyme (which was also, coincidentally or not, the birthplace of Hesiod's father). Modern studies of Homer's writing suggest that he had an Ionian dialect, consistent with origins in the Smyrna area.

The Greek for 'the blind one' is *Homeros*, hence the nickname by which we know him now. The consensus is that Homer went blind in middle age, after he had been able to observe the Troad with his own eyes. One story is that he caught an eye infection while visiting Ithaka, the erstwhile home of Odysseus; another relates how he approached Achilles' tumulus in the Troad and prayed to Apollo for a glimpse of the hero. His wish was granted, but the sun flashed so brightly on the apparition's armour that Homer's eyes were burnt out. In *Odyssey* 8, Homer writes of a blind bard, Demodokos, who claims that the Muses have deprived him of sight so as to enhance the sweetness of his singing. Some scholars believe that this was Homer writing about himself.

Many places around Greece claimed that Homer had lived in or visited them, and as he was a travelling bard, many of them might be correct. The island of Chios, in particular, claims him as a resident, for the Homeric *Hymn to Apollo* refers to 'the blind man who dwells in rocky Chios'. On the east coast of Chios, facing Smyrna, is a sanctuary of Kybele, where part of an enormous rock was hewn away to leave a block called the Daskalopetra, on which Homer was said to have sat, singing and teaching epic poetry. Meanwhile, in the north of Ithaka, near Stavros, is an archaeological site that was almost certainly the palace of Odysseus, and which includes another stone block, where Homer may have done the same, hence the site's name, 'the School of Homer'. I have sat on both blocks, and can confirm that they are almost identical. They probably date back far beyond Homer's time, and the similarity of the Ithakan one to the Chiote one may have given rise to the story that Homer taught in Ithaka too; but maybe he really did.

Homer was certainly the poet of the *Iliad* and the *Odyssey*; and very likely of the 'Homeric hymns', including the *Hymn to Aphrodite*, and perhaps also of the *Cypria*, all of which provide valuable information about Aeneas. Herodotus dated the *Iliad* to about 850 BC, but Luce thought Homer lived around 750-700 BC and Janko's respected analysis places the *Iliad*'s composition in about 735 BC, while some scholars date it to as late as 670 BC.

Under any of these dates, Homer's work, like Hesiod's, stands on the boundary between oral tradition and written literature. Writing originated 1,000 miles south-east of Troy, in Uruk, the oldest Mesopotamian city, where temple priests recording sheep and bushels of grain scratched simple pictures of what they were counting onto clay tablets. In time, these symbols evolved into ever simpler, more abstract, hieroglyphic symbols. By about 3100 BC, they had developed further into cuneiform, in which symbols no longer stood for things but for syllables, and these sound-symbols started being combined to record all the words in the language, as they sounded, and their users soon found that they could record information not just about things but also about thoughts and ideas.

Offshoots of this original idea gave rise, later, to the syllabic scripts of the Cretans and then of the Mycenaeans, called Linear A and Linear B respectively, but the use of these was lost when their civilisations collapsed. Meanwhile, the Phoenicians went further, breaking down syllables into the individual sounds from which they are composed, with a simple symbol for each consonant. Greek mythology asserts that this new 'fly's feet' alphabet was introduced to Greece by Kadmos, who came to Greece from Phoenicia. It was more likely introduced to Greek traders by Phoenician ones, about the 700s or 600s BC, perhaps, as Lane Fox argues, at the trading port of Amathous on Cyprus. Crucially, as he also suggests, the Greeks misunderstood what they were being shown and introduced vowels where the Phoenicians had represented only consonants; and thus emerged the Greek alphabet which, for the first time, could convey thought with as much subtlety as speech.

Lane Fox and others believe that the work of Homer and Hesiod lived fresh in oral tradition for a few generations before the Greek alphabet appeared and their works were recorded; it is true that in Volissos, on the west coast of Chios, there lived the Homeridae, 'the sons of Homer', who earned their living reciting his work long after it had been committed to writing, right down to the 300s BC. However, Jachim Latacz (a colleague of Korfmann's), along with Professor Luce and others, argue that Homer and Hesiod lived at the very time when the Greek alphabet was invented, and their work was written down straight from their own mouths. Either way, it was writing that immortalised both Homer and Hesiod, placing their work at the head of European literature. Writing is the means by which Aeneas's deeds have remained known to each generation from Homer down to us – and through which the core of our civilisation lives on.

Back in Mycenaean times, Greece's old, Linear B script was good for recording bureaucratic lists, but it was less adept than the much older Mesopotamian cuneiform symbols at conveying stories. The Mycenaeans therefore had a class of *aoidoi*, 'bards', who composed, learned and passed on epic poetry orally, from one generation to the next. In the turbulent gap between the collapse of the Mycenaean world and consequent loss of the Linear B script, and the appearance of the Greek alphabet in the 700s or 600s BC, these bards flourished as pretty much the only conduit for their people's civilisation. They composed in very strict metre, using hexameters of six dactyls per line, each dactyl being composed of one long syllable followed by two shorter ones, whose regular pattern aided their recollection.

Homer's *Iliad* was composed in this traditional manner, with 15,693 lines of strictly metred dactylic hexameters. It seems plausible that Homer's story of Troy and Aeneas was his retelling of tales drawn from the oral tradition to which he belonged, as opposed to an original work of imagination that was composed in traditional style. And remarkably, it is possible to mine the *Iliad* itself for evidence that this was indeed the case.

Homer's *Iliad* concerns fifty-one days in the last year of the Trojan War. Its focus is not the war itself, but the quarrel between Achilles and Agamemnon. As a result, the background story of how the war began and what had happened in the intervening nine years is mentioned here and there, in passing, where it is relevant to the plot at hand, but not in such a way as to make it readily comprehensible in itself. As Latacz argued, it is apparent that Homer was drawing on a well-established story which was already well known enough for his listeners not to require detailed explanations. For example, the opening lines refer to the quarrel of Achilles with 'the Atreid', without explaining who this was. It was expected that everyone listening already knew that Agamemnon and Menelaus were the sons of Atreus, and that Achilles' quarrel was with the former in particular. To give another example among many, Helen's abduction, the primary cause of the war, is not explained in the *Iliad* at all, and Aphrodite's gift of *machlosýne*, which allows Paris to succeed in seducing Helen, is not mentioned until the *Iliad*'s final book, and again with the assumption that the listener would know exactly what Homer was referring to.

Homer appears, therefore, to have taken the well-known story of the Trojan War as related in existing epics and used it as the background and context for his own epic, which was a psychological study of the quarrel of two men, Achilles and Agamemnon, and its far-reaching consequences. This suggests that the story of Troy was well established in Greek culture by the 700s BC and that it had been conveyed, through the epic poetry of the Trojan Cycle, for several centuries. 'Those fragments of information from the larger story which he does convey,' wrote Latacz, 'may therefore be taken to be fundamentally authentic elements, until proved otherwise, of the original structural framework.'[1] This ties in with very ancient views of Homer. Thucydides in the 400s BC believed that Homer 'was born much later than the time of the Trojan War' and that he had heard the true story of it from others. Homer himself says as much in *Odyssey* 8, when Odysseus tells his bard Demodokos to 'sing the tale of the Achaeans' [the Greeks'] venture ... as if you had been there yourself, or heard it from one who was.'

The Trojan story was an old one, therefore. But did it recall real events and people, including Aeneas, or had it simply been made up in Mycenaean times, out of thin air? The *Iliad* contains plenty of evidence that the former is more likely. For instance, Homer uses three terms, interchangeably, for the Greeks: Achaeans, Danaans and Argives. Two of these terms have been found in sources contemporary to the Trojan War. Latacz cites Hittite letters written in cuneiform (that they had inherited from the older civilisation of Mesopotamia) referring to a land called *Ahhijawa*. This lay across the Aegean from western Anatolia, so most scholars agree that this was Mycenaean Greece, which Homer calls Achaea. An inscription in the funerary temple of Amenhotep III of Egypt (*c.* 1390-1353 BC) lists foreign lands including

In Search of Aeneas

Danaja, encompassing *Kutira* (Kythera), *Mukanu* (Mycene); *Thegwais* (Thebes); *Misane* (Messana); *Nuplija* (Naplion), *Waleja* (Elis) and *Amukla* (Amykles, the old capital of Lacedaemonia). This *Danaja*, surely, was the land of Homer's Danaans. Homer's term 'Argives' has yet to be found in such ancient sources, but it must refer to Argos ('flat plain'), the ancient city from whose kings the Mycenae rulers had claimed descent.

Homer's use of different names for the same things was due to the demands of hexameter poetry. Having interchangeable names of different lengths made the composing of such lines easier. It was for this reason that Homer used two names, Ilios (with three syllables) and Troia (with only two), interchangeably, for Troy. Sometimes, and for the same reason, he called the Trojans 'Dardanians', even though it is clear that Dardania was Anchises's realm up in the mountains, and not the area around the city on the plain.

All three names are attested in Hittite sources contemporary to the Trojan War. We have seen already that the Egyptians recorded, in hieroglyphics, that a contingent of 'Drdny' were part of the Hittite forces at Kadesh in 1274 BC. The Hittite Great Kings ruled by asserting their dominion over other local kings (in the same way that, in the *Iliad*, Priam was overlord of a number of lesser rulers, including Anchises of Dardania). A letter written in about 1300 BC by one of these local kings, Manatabarhunta of Seha (which was Homer's Maeonia, around modern Bergama), to his overlord the Hittite Great King Muwatalli II, talks about the island of Lazba (Lesbos) lying within sight of both Seha and 'the land of Wilusa'. As Professor Starke of Tübingen argued successfully in 1996, 'Wilusa' could only refer to the Troad. The name Wilusa is probably from *wellu*, meaning 'meadow' in Luwian, an ancient Anatolian language used in parts of the Hittite empire – including Troy – as a diplomatic language, just as Latin was used in Medieval and early modern Europe.

It seems highly likely that Wilusa was the root of one of Homer's names for Troy, Ilios. The city of Wilusa is mentioned in the *Alaksandu Treaty*, a Hittite document from about 1290-1272 BC, and the similarities to Troy are striking. It attests to the worship of *Apaliunas* in Wilusa, which ties in with Homer's assertion that Troy's patron deity was Apollo. The treaty also refers to *Kaskalkur*, the god of Wilusa's 'underground watercourse'. Few cities had such watercourses, but Korfmann excavated one next to Troy. You can walk down from the Sanctuary area to a sort of cave mouth, and peer through a barred gate into its four dark channels, leading to a deep reservoir – an enormous and unusual advantage for any city to possess, and one plausible reason why Troy held out against the Greeks for ten years.

Then, in about 1410 BC, the annals of the Hittite Great King Tudhalija I refer to his quelling of a rebellion by some of his vassals in the 'Assuwa lands' including 'the land of Wilusija, the land of Taruisa'. The 'Assuwa' lands probably refer to Assos, a city on the southern coast of the Troad, facing Lesvos. The similarity between the linked place names Wilusija and Taruisa,

The Blind Poet

and Homer's two names for the same city, Ilios and Troy, is striking. Homer's three names for Troy, therefore, can all be attested by sources dating, not to Homer's time, but to the Bronze Age, the period in which his story was set. That suggests that the story-material on which Homer was drawing was genuinely old.

Detailed analysis of ancient linguistics makes this case even stronger. As Latacz shows, the Ionian dialect tended to drop many initial 'w's from older Mycenaean words. That explains why Homer or his immediate predecessors, whose dialect was Ionian, had dropped the 'W' of the Luwian word Wilusa, to end up with 'Ilusa', and from Ilusa it is a short jump to Ilos, who Homer said founded Troy, and to Homer's Ilios (hence, later, Greek Ilion and Roman Ilium). Strikingly, in forty-eight out of Homer's 106 references to Ilios, the lines only fit the exacting requirements of hexameters if the initial 'w' is restored. This suggests that in these forty-eight instances, Homer was recycling stock phrases or even whole lines about the Trojan War from poetry dating back to Mycenaean times. Through being spoken in Ionian, they had lost a syllable, but the lines were otherwise so canonical that their use was acceptable, despite their not scanning properly any more.

Latacz gives a number of similar examples from the *Iliad*, such as 'Meriones, like to Enyalios, the killer of men'. Homer's Ionian word for 'men' is *andrei*, and the line is just too long to scan correctly. However, the Mycenaean word was *a-nr*, and if that is substituted for *andrei*, the metre works perfectly. We hear, too, that Meriones had a boar's tooth helmet. Such a helmet, made from a framework of boars' tusks, was actually found in excavations at Mycenae; it appears that the story of Meriones, along with a reference to his characteristic helmet, had been passed down, from bard to bard, word for word, from Mycenaean times.

Indeed, it appears that the epic tradition was full of stock phrases, which poets could use to fill out their lines. For example, Hera could be 'Hera', or 'lady Hera', or 'ox-eyed lady Hera', as the metrical requirements of the line required. Similarly, Aeneas could be 'brave Aeneas', 'the hero Aeneas', 'Aeneas, king of men', 'Aeneas son of Anchises', 'Aeneas, prince among the Trojans', 'Aeneas, counsellor of the Trojans', 'Aeneas the valiant son of Anchises', or 'Aeneas, counsellor of the mail-clad Trojans', according to how much space in the line Homer wished to fill. These additions to the names of Hera and Aeneas do not jar, but others do and thus better reveal their ancient origins. For example, in *Iliad* 8, Homer refers to stars being visible around a 'brightly shining' moon, but this makes no sense, as bright moons make it impossible to see the stars around them. 'Brightly shining' was a stock phrase, filling out the line correctly, so Homer used it, even though it did not make sense in context.

Far from proving that Homer had simply made the *Iliad* up out of thin air, such close, scholarly analysis of Homer's text suggests, increasingly, that it includes genuinely old material which survived down through the Dark Ages from Mycenaean times, thanks to the highly structured tradition of

In Search of Aeneas

oral epic poetry. So, besides seeing Homer as the starting point for western written literature, we may also recognise him as a bridge to an oral tradition reaching back to the Trojan War. That does not, and cannot, prove that every event, speech and character in the *Iliad* is historically true; but it offers us the hope that in Homer's Aeneas we may be glimpsing the shadow, at least, of a real prince who fought at a real siege of Troy.

No written archive has yet been found in Troy to provide contemporary witness to Aeneas and his relatives in their own words. Perhaps, when Schliemann sliced down through the city, eagerly seeking its golden treasures, he unwittingly destroyed its vastly more important written records. But other cities across the Hittite Empire have yielded cuneiform writings that bring Aeneas's world to life, with its palaces brimming with office holders, from priestesses and bureaucrats down to barbers and cymbal players. These records sometimes touch on the Troad, and even on places and people described by Homer.

There is, for instance, a treaty between Great King Muwatalli II of the Hittites, who ruled from 1290 to 1272 BC, and King Alaksandu of Wilusa. The name Alaksandu must be a local version of the Greek Alexandros ('defender of men'). This was Homer's sometime name for Paris, so the treaty provides a direct connection between the *Iliad* and an attested historical source, albeit that the Alaksandu concerned seems to have lived a generation or so before Homer's Paris. The treaty starts by relating previous diplomatic relations between overlord and vassal; how, long ago, the Arzawa lands, including Wilusa, had become client kingdoms of the Hittite Empire. Wilusa was then embroiled in a rebellion by the other Arzawa lands – probably the one mentioned in Tudhalija I's annals for about 1410 BC mentioned above. Wilusa's king at the time managed to remain on friendly terms with his Hittite overlord, so after the rebellion was quashed, good terms were restored. The treaty then skips forward to another conflict in the region during the reign of the Hittite Great King Suppiluliuma I (1344-1322 BC), but again the friendship of Suppiluliuma with the Wilusan king, Kukkunni, ensured peace between the two. Later, Kukkunni was succeeded by Alaksandu, and Suppiluliuma by his son Mursili II, who ruled 1321-1295 BC. Mursili aided Wilusa in a war against its eastern neighbour, Masa (Mysia). Once Mursili 'became a god' (i.e., died), his son Muwatalli II became King of the Hittites. It was to Muwatalli II that Alaksandu of Wilusa now professed loyalty, and the two agreed to collaborate in the crushing of rebellious Masa. Muwatalli agreed, further, to support Alaksandu and his descendants, whether by his wife or his concubines, against any possible challenge from Alaksandu's relatives.

It was this same Muwatalli II who checked the expansionist advance of Ramesses II of Egypt at the battle of Kadesh in 1274 BC, with Dardanians, and perhaps Alaksandu, too, among the Hittite forces. Muwatalli II had also to deal with Pijamaradu, probably a deposed Arzawa king who was given asylum in Ahhijawa, which most scholars agree was Achaea – Mycenaean Greece. Pijamaradu started raiding Lazba (Lesbos) and Wilusa, so Muwatalli II's brother and successor, Hattusili III, who ruled from about 1265 to 1240 BC, wrote the 'Tawagalawa Letter' to the King of Ahhijawa, asking him not to allow Pijamaradu to use Ahhijawa as his base for raids.

In the letter, Hattusili refers to an unspecified incident regarding 'Wilusa' over which, he wrote, he and the Ahhijawan king had quarrelled. The middle of the word 'Wilusa' is missing, so the translation cannot be certain, but some scholars wonder if this 'incident' could have been the Trojan War. In Homer, and Greek history, the Trojan War was one of the most momentous events in world history. Seen through the eyes of the Hittite Great King, however, a Greek raid on the western extremity of Anatolia was simply an incident, a mosquito stinging an ox. But perhaps it stirred the imaginations of the Hittites as well as the Greeks, nonetheless, for there exists a fragment of late Hittite poetry, *ahh=ata=ta alati awienta Wilušati*, which could, possibly, be translated 'When they came down from steep Wilusa' – a Hittite version, perhaps, of the story the Trojan War.

Priam's name seems genuinely Hittite too. It could be from the Luwian *priimuua*, 'highly courageous', or a variant of the name *Pariya-muwasi*, found recorded at Kizzuwatna in southern Anatolia; either way, it is clearly not a name that Homer simply made up. Besides the names of Alaksandu and Priam, however, there is no miraculous match between the surviving cuneiform fragments and the Trojan pedigree given in the *Iliad*. The names of kings Tros and Ilos, for instance, are derived from the place names Troy and Ilios. Although Alaksandu matches Alexander, Homer's Paris, he seems to have lived a generation earlier, and we do not encounter in Aeneas's Homeric pedigree a king called Kukkunni at all. True, the Greeks had a habit of applying their own names to people and things: they called Skamander 'Xanthus' ('yellow river'), for example, and alleged that Priam had previously been called Podarces. One might argue that Laomedon and Ilos, Priam's father and grandfather, were Greek names for Alaksandu and Kukkunni – but that can never be more than a suggestion.

While the names of Aeneas, his father Anchises, his grandfather Capys and great grandfather Assaracus have yet to be found in Hittite texts, they are, however, among those Homeric names which von Kamptz thought were not Greek and could, therefore, have been of genuine Anatolian origin. The *Hymn to Aphrodite* suggests that Aeneas's name meant 'awful sorrow' in Greek, but this was simply a Greek interpretation of an Anatolian name, just as they thought Priam's name meant 'ransomed', because it sounded like a similar word in Greek. We do not know what Aeneas's name meant in his own language, but we hear of another 'Ainos/Aineus', son of Apollo, who founded the city of Ainos, north of Troy, and whose son, Kyzikos, founded the city of that name on the Sea of Marmara, east of Troy.[2] That suggests, at least, that Aeneas's name may have been a genuinely local one. The assertion that Aeneas was believed to be a goddess's son is plausible, as we have seen, in the context of contemporary beliefs in the region as to the close relationships between rulers and goddesses.

Therefore, although the names in the pedigree that connect Aeneas to Priam may be a partly Greek invention, this does not rule out the likelihood that Anchises and his son Aeneas, and Priam with his sons Hector, Paris (also called Alexander), and so on, along with at least some of their purported ancestors, were genuinely remembered in the oral tradition. Nor does it rule out the possibility that Anchises and Priam were cousins, to a degree similar to that suggested by the Homeric pedigree, even if the real, connecting names were different. The name of Aeneas's country, Dardania, is confirmed, as we have seen, as 'Drdny', in an Egyptian source. Anchises and Priam may well have claimed descent from a founding hero of their country, whose Luwian name could have been something like Dardanos; a son, perhaps, of the Dardanian versions of the storm-god and the Great Mother, as recalled, again, through the distorting mirror of Greek mythology.

Through the translated cuneiform fragments, we can see Troy operating as a client state of the Hittite Empire, just as, in Homer, Priam had his own vassal states, including Dardania. We see in the fragments Troy sending troops to fight in the Great Kings' wars in the Levant, just as Priam's allies gathered, as we shall see, to help him fight off the Greeks. We see in the Hittite sources the Trojan kings variously rebelling against, or seeking closer alliances with, their overlords, and facing the possibility of overthrow from their relatives, just as in the course of the war tension grew between Priam's family and their cousin Aeneas. Crucially, we see in the Hittite texts Troy facing raids from Mycenaean Greece, which may have included Homer's Trojan War itself.

As more ruins are unearthed and Hittite records are translated, the evidence that Homer was reusing epic material which recalled elements of genuine history grows stronger. 'There is an immense amount of circumstantial evidence,' wrote Michael Wood, 'which suggests that a kernel of the tale of Troy goes back to a real event in the Bronze Age.'[3] It would still be absurd, as Wood cautions, to argue that every detail Homer gives about the war, and indeed about Aeneas and his family, must be accurate. But it would be harder today than it was a few generations ago to argue that Homer's stories contain no historical truth at all. In Aeneas's story we can hear and glimpse, though Homer's words, echoes and shadows, at least, of real people, real events and real beliefs from ancient Anatolia, over three thousand years ago.

14

Musters and Raids

In *Iliad* 2 the Greeks surged across the plain. The Trojans and their allies, including Aeneas himself, were within Troy's walls, but Zeus sent Iris, disguised as Priam's son Polites, to report having spotted the Greek approach from his look-out point on Aesytes' tomb. Thus inspired, Priam's eldest son Hector ordered a general muster out by the *Batieia*, 'thicket hill', which the immortals called 'the mounded tomb of the leaping Amazon Myrine', or 'Skipping Myrine's Tump', depending on translation.

Troy's lower city extended south-west down from the citadel's hill, towards the Çiplak brook. On the other side of the brook, the ground rises to a low ridge, running east to west, parallel to Troy's own. Halfway along this ridge, to the south-east of Troy, is a mound, Paşa Tepe, where Schliemann found remains from Aeneas's time, and which Luce identified as the Batieia. It stands today in the middle of fields and has recently been planted with olive trees. Soon, the growing trees will obscure the view, but we can confirm that the mound affords clear views right across the plain. Though the Greek camp was due west of Troy, water prevented the Greeks from charging due east; they had instead to go south, round what was then the southern shore of the Hellespont, down the Skamander to its ford and then up, north-east, across the plain. The Çiplak ridge would therefore have blocked their route to Troy, so the Batieia is exactly where an intelligent Trojan general might have mustered his forces.

Here, Homer provides us with a nice problem of chronology, for he seems to present Aeneas's next two appearances in the wrong order. The *Iliad* relates events in the tenth year of the Trojan War, but it also looks back to what had taken place during the preceding nine years, including a cattle raid on Mount Ida, referred to in *Iliad* 20, in which Achilles surprised Aeneas. In *Iliad* 2, meanwhile, Homer catalogues the Greek forces and the Trojan foes who mustered against them at the Batieia, and whose fighting takes up the rest of his epic. Homer implies that this catalogue reflects the state of play in the tenth year and after the cattle raid. But the *Iliad*'s internal, textual evidence suggests that in the older epic tradition from which it was borrowed, it actually applies to the start of the war, before the cattle raid.

The clue comes from Homer providing the Greek catalogue in terms not of who marched across the plain, but of the ships in which they had arrived from Aulis. As Kirk and others have pointed out, the catalogue even includes characters who had been in the invasion fleet but who were no longer at Troy in year ten, such as Philoctetes, who had led the Meliboeans but who, by the tenth year, was ill on Lemnos, and Protesilaus, who, as we know, was killed in the first landing.

The catalogue of the Greek forces thus appears to have been a list of the contingents which came to Troy by ship at the beginning of the war, that belonged to the epic tradition and which Homer inserted into his epic unedited. The ships were drawn from cities all over Greece, and the catalogue's 178 place names offer us further compelling evidence that it derives from historical tradition. Working without the aid of maps or reference books, a poet inventing a story from scratch would most likely have listed places he knew in his own time, not least to earn the favour of those locations' rulers. But Homer has never been caught out by modern scholars or archaeologists for being anachronistic. A quarter of the places he names were otherwise unknown to Greek scholars in the centuries immediately after Homer, suggesting that they had been abandoned long since, presumably due to the collapse of the Mycenaean world. All the cities which Homer names that did exist in his day have been found through archaeology to have flourished, also, in Mycenaean times, so he was not being anachronistic in mentioning them. Some of the places he named had fallen by Homer's time into ruin and obscurity. 'The importance of the great fortresses, such as Mycenae' commented the philologist Denys L. Page, 'might have been conjectured from visible remains: but how [apart from the epic tradition] could the poet learn about Dorion, abandoned at the close of the Mycenaean era and never reoccupied?'

Homer's catalogue refers, under Boetia, to 'Eleon, Hyle and Peteon'. A Mycenaean Linear B tablet excavated at Thebes in Boetia refers to three Boetian cities which were important in Mycenaean times: 'Eleon, Peteon and Hyle'.[1] The similarity to Homer's catalogue is remarkable. In fact, it has been commented that the entire catalogue, like the tablet, has the character of the sort of bureaucratic lists favoured by Mycenaean scribes. Like the Trojan muster which follows, the catalogue opens an astonishing window onto the real Mycenaean Greek world that came storming up to Aeneas's door.

Homer's description of the Trojan forces mustering at the Batieia parallels the catalogue of Greek ships it follows. First came the Trojans themselves, led by Hector. Straight after him marched the Dardanians led, says Homer, by 'brave Aeneas, the offspring of Aphrodite's amorous encounter with Anchises on the slopes of Ida'. Aeneas's officers were Archelochus and Acamas, sons of Antenor, both experienced warriors and, we may infer, hardy mountain-men like Aeneas himself.

Aeneas's bronze chariot was drawn by magnificent horses who, we learn from *Iliad* 6, were a gift from his father. Years before, when Zeus abducted beautiful Ganymede from Troy, he had compensated his father Tros with the finest horses 'that live and move under the sun'. These were inherited by Tros's son Ilos, and then by Ilos's son Laomedon, the father of Priam. Anchises, who was the grandson of Tros's son Assaracus, managed to steal some of this exalted blood-stock – doubtless with a twinkle in his eye as he did so – by putting some of his mares to Laomedon's stallions in secret. Six foals were born as a result, four of which Anchises kept and two he gave to Aeneas. They were naturally skilled in drawing chariots; as Diomedes commented admiringly in *Iliad* 8, they could dart cleverly here and there, both in charge and retreat. Anchises had probably given them to Aeneas as much to enable him to escape danger as to win glory.

Homer's story reflects a truth, for Troy VI's excavated remains are full of horse bones. A cuneiform text from the 1300s BC called *The Horse Book of Kikkuli* shows that the Hittites were ahead of all other civilisations in their knowledge of rearing, breaking and training horses. When horse-tack was found in a grave in Mycenae, it was of Anatolian style. Archaeologists now believe that the Trojans imported horses from the northern shore of the Black Sea and bred them for chariot warfare, hence this story of Aeneas's horses, and Homer's description of Hector as a 'tamer of horses'.

Back to the muster now, and after Aeneas and his Dardanians came the other armies sent by kings of the Troad who were subject to Priam. First marched the Lycians from Zeleia, 'beneath the lowest spurs of Mount Ida', men of Trojan blood, led by Pandarus son of Lycaon, who had been taught archery by Apollo. Zeleia is on a low hill near the modern town of Sarikoy, just south of the Sea of Marmara; the mountains behind it are indeed part of a chain leading down south to the heights of Ida. The hill of Zeleia is strewn with potsherds and parts of the city's outer walls can be seen along the road below. There were Lycians much further south, too; Leaf wondered if the name was a Greek term for any peoples who worshipped Apollo Lykios, the wolf-god.

Next in the muster were the men of Adresteia, Apaesus, Pityeia, and Mount Tereia, places along the Marmaran coast west of Zeleia, around the mouth of the Granicus. They were led by Adrastos and Amphius, sons of King Merops of Percote. Merops had foreseen doom for his sons, but they had defied him and come to fight anyway. After them came the fifth contingent, the men of Percote itself, and of Practius, Sestos, Abydos (near modern Çanakkale) and Arisbe; the lands, that is, between Adresteia and Troy itself. Their leader was Asius son of Hyrtacus, owner of fiery stallions. Sixth came the Pelasgian spearmen of Larisa. Cook identified them with Liman Tepe in the south-western corner of the Troad; they were led by Hippothous and Pylaeus, sons of Lethus.

Later, Strabo conjectured on the basis of this catalogue and also other indicators scattered through the rest of the *Iliad* that the Troad was 'divided into nine dynasties', including Troy, all of which were subject to Priam.[2] Leaf analysed both Strabo and Homer and concluded that the sixth item in the catalogue lumped together Strabo's final four:[3] the Leleges, led by Altes, whose daughter Laothoe was one of Priam's minor wives, who came from Pedasos, which became Assos and is now Behramkale, on the southern coast of the Troad; the two realms of the Cilicians, who lived around the head of the Gulf of Adramyttium (Edremit), centred on Lyrnessos and Thebe; and finally the land ruled by Eurypylus, to the south east of the Cilicians. As with the Greek catalogue, modern archaeology has yet to show that any of Homer's references to the Troad in Aeneas's time are anachronistic.

Homer's muster now enumerated Priam's allies from further afield. Far from the jumble of names which it first appears to be, Leaf showed that 'the tribes named are all along [four] lines converging upon Troy; the extremity of each radius is marked by the words "far away"... these four lines I take to represent the four trade routes which converged on Troy as a common emporium.'[4]

First came the Thracians from the northern side of the Dardanelles, led by Acamas and Peirous, who, in *Iliad* 4, was identified as king of the port of Ainos, 52 miles north of Troy; then the Kikonian spearmen from the long tract of Thrace which stretches east towards Greece, led by Euphemus son of Troezenus; and then the Paeonian archers led by Pyraechmes, from 'far away' Amydon by the river Axius, which Leaf thought was near Thessaloniki, at the western end of Thrace.

The second group comprised the Paphlagonians, the land of wild mules, led by stout-hearted Pylaemanes from Enetae on the southern shore of the Black Sea near Sinop; and then the Halizonians from 'far away' Alybe, led by Odius and Epistrophus. Leaf thought Alybe was Tirebolu, further east along the Black Sea shore and, together, these races were crucial to 'the Euxine [Black Sea] trade, that very trade which Troy commanded by the control of the mouth of the Hellespont.'

The next group started with the Mysians, led by Chromis and the augur Ennomus, who lived immediately east of the Troad (though later we hear of other Mysians, ruled by Telephus, living down south near Bergama); after them came the Phrygians, the race of Priam's wife Hecuba, from 'far away' Ascania, led by Phorcys and noble Ascanius (not to be confused with a later Ascanius, son of Aeneas himself). Although 'Phrygia' was used later as a synonym for Troy, the Phrygians in fact lived to the east of the Mysians (and south-west of the Paphlagonians) in the region later called Bithynia, around the Ascanian Lake, which is now called Lake Iznik, where Nicea stands.

Finally came the southerners, starting with the Maeonians from Mount Tmolus, led by Mesthles and Antiphus; this was the land later occupied by the Lydians, east of modern Izmir. Then came the Carians from Miletus, led by Nastes and Amphimachus, whose land was further down the coast where Bodrum and Marmaris are now; and finally, the men of 'far away' Lycia, which is the bulge in the coast beyond Caria, west of modern Antalya. They were led by Sarpedon and Glaucus. It was through this region, thought Leaf, that trade was conducted between Troy and great kingdoms of the Levant.

The part of the catalogue covering Anatolia does not compare too badly with what is now known from Hittite sources. East of Taruisa/Wilusa (Troy) lay Masa (Homer's Mysia), extending along the Sea of Marmara, and then along the Black Sea coast were Pla and Tumanna (presumably, Homer's Paphlagonia). South of Wilusa, Seha corresponds with Homer's Meonia, Mira with Caria and Lukka with Lycia. Wilusa, Seha and Mira (together with an inland realm called Haballa, south of Mysia) comprised what the Hittites called the Arzawan lands; all were self-governing components of the Hittite Empire.

This, then, was Aeneas's world, as described by Homer and represented by a magnificent array of Anatolians and Thracians at the Batieia on the ridge before Troy, with Hector and Aeneas at their heart.

As explained above, Homer placed this muster in *Iliad* 2, in the tenth year of the war, but in the original epic it had surely come much closer to the start of the conflict, once the Greeks had landed in the Troad and made their camp on the Sigeum ridge, and their threat to the trade-based prosperity of the whole region had become apparent. In real life, many of the Asian and Thracian forces listed by Homer might have been sent by the Hittite Great King, but in the *Iliad*, as perhaps in Greek eyes at the time, they are presented as allies or vassals of all-powerful Priam himself.

Between that first muster and the war's tenth year, there must have been many battles with indecisive outcomes. But there were probably also long periods of stalemate, with the Greeks idling in their camp and the Trojans in their city, not under siege but simply menaced by the Greek presence. The Trojans and Dardanians probably went on farming and trading as best they could, and the Greeks made occasional raids inland. This provides the context for our next sighting of Aeneas. *Iliad* 20 relates how, during the course of the long stand-off, Aeneas was tending his family's herds on Mount Ida when they were raided by Achilles. Some commentators thought that Achilles' raid was what first brought Aeneas into the war, but this cannot be so if the grand muster, which includes Aeneas, had in fact come at the start of the conflict. Thus, while Dictys was probably being fanciful in imagining Aeneas standing up hot-headedly to Menelaus and Odysseus, as we heard earlier, he may have been closer to the mark in asserting that Aeneas had been among those brave Trojans who fought the Greeks and slew Protesilaus when they first landed on Trojan soil. But as the war went on, when the Greeks were not actively attacking Troy, Aeneas was not needed there. And tending herds back in Dardania remained an essential job, war or no war, for without the animals they would all starve.

Walter Leaf wrote in 1912:

> As the lower pastures get dried up in the heat of mid-summer, fresh grass is springing up round the melting snows which commonly lie on the heights well into June. Towards the end of May the semi-nomad tribes, who now

pass their winters in the villages of the plain, start to drive their flocks and herds up the hillside; and by the middle of July there is a great collection of sheep, goats, and cattle up to the very top of Ida, the highest point of which [Gargarus] is, in fact, marked by a rough fold of stones. Natural conditions make it certain that this custom must have endured from all time, ever since there was a population subsisting on pasture in the Troad. The flocks of Aeneas must unquestionably have been taken up these highest ridges.[5]

In 1973, Cook reported, similarly, that 'shepherds come up on the high ridge [of Ida] in June or July from villages as far away as the west coast. By the Sarikiz spring we met a group of young men from Balabanli who might have been the companions of Anchises in modern dress; their music was not of pipes but of transistor radios.'[6] Although the slopes of Ida are generally forested, there are patches of pasture and it is true that the uppermost ridge of Gargarus, now called Kaz Dağ – the highest part of Ida, that can be seen from Palaiskepsis – is treeless. Even halfway up, by the Edremit to Yenice road, there are places where the forest gives way to boulder-strewn pastures of grass and ferns, which are the summer home of cattle, sheep, goats and horses, still attended by brightly clad semi-nomadic herders, who live in a seasonal roadside camp of huts and sheds, some of which, like English shepherds' huts, are on wheels.

So, Aeneas would have gone up the soft tracks beneath his childhood planes and pines, the paths that his and his animals' ancestors had trodden since the time of Dardanos, until they came out onto the upland pastures.

It may have seemed far removed from the trouble at Troy, but the Greeks were bored and hungry. Unbeknown to Aeneas, Achilles and his army of Myrmidons had already embarked on a raid. References to it appear throughout the *Iliad*, prompting Leaf to speculate that Homer knew of an epic poem within the Trojan cycle that he termed, speculatively, 'the Great Foray'. Now that we know more about Hittite history, it has been suggested that this raid, like the Trojan fleet's first and apparently abortive landing in Mysia, may have been part of a wider campaign by Mycenaean Greece against the 'Assuwa lands' on the west coast of Anatolia – but that can only be speculation.

Achilles' fleet would have sailed south from the Greek camp and then east up the Adramyttium Gulf to the furthest point he intended to plunder – Thebe, which sits on a hill a few miles inland from the gulf's head, near modern Kizikli (though Leaf thought it was underneath Edremit itself). Thebe's king, Eetion, whose daughter Andromache was married to Priam's eldest son Hector, was killed. Thebe was sacked, and Achilles carried off Andromache's mother, as referred to in passing in *Iliad* 6, and Chryseis, the daughter of a priest of Apollo, as mentioned in *Iliad* 1. Achilles acquired so much plunder that items from it – a horse, a lyre with a silver bridge, and a great lump of iron, all from Thebe – are mentioned throughout the *Iliad*.[7]

Now, Achilles wished to raid the region's livestock, so he led his men up Mount Ida, perhaps by what is now the Edremit-Yenice road, or, as Leaf thought, 'by the long but easy path which runs north-westward from the modern village of Zeitünlü [Zeytinli]... Achilles finds, to his great satisfaction, that the herdsmen have collected there from all parts. There are the cattle, not only of Thebe and Lyrnessos, but of Dardania; Aeneas himself has led them up from his home in the north, and, never dreaming of such a great flank move, has neglected to bring any guard with him.'[8]

When faced with the prospect of fighting Achilles in *Iliad* 20, Aeneas says, 'his spear has already put me to flight from Ida, when he attacked our cattle and sacked Lyrnessos and Pesados; Zeus indeed saved me in that he vouchsafed me strength to fly, else [I would have] ... fallen by the hands of Achilles and Athena, who went before him to protect him and urged him to fall upon the Lelegae and Trojans.' Later, also in *Iliad* 20, Achilles himself taunts Aeneas: 'Have you forgotten how, when you were alone, I chased you from your herds helter-skelter down the slopes of Ida? You did not turn round to look behind you.'

While exploring the upland pastures off the Edremit-Yenice road, we sat on a rock to enjoy the view. It was a lovely, soft September day, with the late afternoon sun edging the dry grasses and flower heads with bronze, shedding a gentle golden light across Ida's peaks above, and glittering on the distant waters of the Adramyttium Gulf below. We tried imagining Achilles' Myrmidons appearing suddenly out of the pines with their flashing helms, spears and swords glinting, and the herds stampeding. Then, it suddenly happened – a boy shouting; frenzied barking of dogs, and horses and cows stampeding before a modern-day Achilles, a herdsman's son on a quad bike hurtling fearlessly over the uneven ground to herd the livestock downhill. Cows kicked and reared to avoid the dogs – descendants, no doubt, of Aeneas's dogs that snapped at the Myrmidons' heels – as the whole chaotic raid careered downhill. It took very little imagination to see Aeneas in the midst of it all, trying to avoid being speared or trampled to death.

Aeneas was not alone. We know from *Iliad* 11 that with him were Priam's younger sons Antiphos and Isos, whom Achilles caught, bound with willow-ropes, and later ransomed back to their father. Also with them, as we hear in *Iliad* 6, were the seven sons of King Eetion of Thebe, all of whom Achilles slaughtered. But Aeneas escaped the massacre by fleeing south down through the mountain's pine forest, and below it groves of fig, arbutus, acacia and olives that grow closer to the sea.

'You took refuge in Lyrnessos,' Achilles later reminds Aeneas. This was somewhere near the head of the Adramyttium Gulf; nobody knows exactly where. Strabo says of 'Thebe and Lyrnessos, a strong place', that one was 'sixty stadia from Adramyttium on one side, and the other was eighty eight stadia on the other side'.[9] That was 'an apparent exactitude', as Leaf commented, 'which leaves us entirely in the dark as to what he meant'.[10] Leaf thought that 'the other side' did not necessarily mean a full 180 degrees, and that Lyrnessos was probably somewhere up in the olive groves on the southern flanks of Gargarus, most likely near Zeytinli, which has a track leading straight up to the pastures. Wherever Lyrnessos was, Aeneas's flight led to its gates, and the king, 'the divine Mynes', gave him shelter. But Aeneas's flight to Lyrnessos led to its destruction, because, as Achilles continues, 'I attacked the city, and with the help of Athena and father Zeus I sacked it and carried its women into captivity.' Among Achilles' captives, as we learn in *Iliad* 19, was Briseis, who may actually have been King Mynes's wife. Leaf says, 'She is driven off to the ships to mingle her tears with those of the unhappy Chryseis.' As for Aeneas, 'Zeus and the other gods rescued you,' recalls Achilles, which means that he got away and made it back, eventually, to Dardania.

Having raided Lyrnessos, Achilles packed his cattle, female slaves and loot into his ships and began his homeward voyage, stopping to sack Pesados (Assos), which sits on a hilltop further west along the gulf's coast. Then he sailed across to sack northern Lesvos, capturing seven women 'skilled in excellent handiwork', referred to in *Iliad* 9. On the hillside near Mithymna in northern Lesvos are the remains of a harbour attributed to Achilles, complete with holes bored in the squared-off rocks. The site is far above sea-level now. This, we were assured, was due to volcanic activity, and there was certainly evidence of sea-erosion on some of the rocks nearby, though probably far more ancient than Achilles' time, and the holes were probably made for other purposes than mooring ships.

The story of the 'Great Foray' probably ended with Achilles' return to the Greek camp on the Sigeum ridge, and the division of the spoils. As we hear in the *Iliad*, Agamemnon, as the over-king of all the Greeks, claimed Chryseis, whom Achilles had captured at Thebe, and the pick of the Lesvian spoils. To Achilles, he granted Briseis, who had been captured at Lyrnessos. It was an arrangement that was not destined to end well.

15

'Men that Strove with Gods'

Christa Wolf was one of those who believed, incorrectly, that Achilles' raid had somehow galvanised an otherwise unwilling Aeneas into joining the war. Her Cassandra relates how Troy rejoiced when Aeneas and his men came marching down from Dardania to join them, but he admonished them solemnly for celebrating when he had come only because of the disaster which was unfolding. He and Cassandra met in secret, whispering each other's names in the darkness, made love with animal passion. Then, already disillusioned with the war and Priam, Aeneas left on a trading mission to the Black Sea, but when he returned he was drawn into the war completely. He told Cassandra that Priam would employ 'delaying tactics' in the form of single combats with Greek champions, which would be no more than 'athletic contests fought by rules acceptable to the Greeks'. But Wolf's scepticism reflects her Cold War upbringing: it was not shared by Homer's Aeneas.

Homer's story fast-forwards us from the raid across weeks, months, perhaps years of stalemate between the Greeks and Trojans, to the tenth year of the Trojan War, and the fifty-one days covered by the narrative-proper of the *Iliad*. *Iliad* 1 covers the twenty-one days in this tenth year during which a terrible argument erupted between Agamemnon and Achilles due to the arrival of Chryseis's father, Chryses. Chryses was a priest of Apollo, probably from a place called Chrysa on the south-west coast of the Troad. Chrysa is where the ruins of the later, Classical temple of Apollon Smintheion can be seen today. Perhaps as far back as Aeneas's time, Apollo was worshipped there as the god of mice, which were fed daily and thus inhabited the place in vast swarms; Strabo says that this unusual cult was introduced by Dardanos's father-in-law Teucer, whose camp was invaded by mice when he first came ashore nearby.[1]

Chryses begged Agamemnon to return his daughter. The king refused, but as the priest wandered disconsolately home, he prayed to Apollo, who inflicted plague upon the Greek camp – whether it was carried by rodents or not, Homer does not say. After ten days, as the corpses started piling up, Agamemnon called an assembly. His seer, Calchas, believed that the only way of appeasing Apollo was to return Chryseis to her father. Agamemnon agreed, but as he was losing one girl, he demanded another, Briseis, back from Achilles. When Achilles refused, Agamemnon seized Briseis from his tent anyway. The relationship between the powerful king and his most charismatic warrior was doomed from the start: 'Agamemnon is a fool to offer to command Achilles,' as Thersites comments in Shakespeare's *Troilus and Cressida* – adding that Achilles was equally unwise to allow Agamemnon to command him.

Achilles refused to fight for Agamemnon any more, and retired to his tent in the most monumental sulk in western literature. Achilles' mother Thetys, equally offended by the king's behaviour, sought redress from Zeus. Long ago, Hera, Poseidon and Athena had rebelled against Zeus by trying to chain him down, but Thetys had brought the hundred-armed monster Briareus up to Olympus to stop them. Now, Zeus agreed to repay his debt to Thetys. He would appear to favour the Trojans, making the Greeks suffer, but only enough to force Agamemnon to beg Achilles for help and return Briseus to him. Thus, he would make Achilles' ultimate glory all the greater – and thus, too, Zeus set his face against Aeneas's Troy.

Iliad 2 concerns day twenty-two of the epic and the mustering of the forces on each side, the Greeks in their camp and the Trojans at the Batieia to the south-east of Troy, as if for the first time. Regardless of where the muster belonged in the original story, Homer placed it here for a dramatic purpose. Matters had clearly been drawing to a head for some time, and Aeneas was back in Troy with his father's Dardanians, ready to defend the city; Anchises was crippled, and old; it was Aeneas, as we have seen, who led their men in the muster.

The Greek and Trojan armies almost clashed, but, in *Iliad* 3, conflict was delayed when Paris offered to fight a Greek champion in order to settle the question of who should keep Helen. Menelaus himself took up the challenge. Paris's courage failed him, but Hector goaded him to fulfil his promise. From the top of the Scaean Gate, Helen pointed the Greek leaders out to Priam. Scaean means 'on the left' in Greek, so Luce identified this with Troy's eastern gate, near the later Sanctuary area. Its excavated remains show that it was filled hastily with rubble, perhaps to prevent the Greeks from breaking in on this very occasion. Helen and Priam watched while Menelaus quickly overpowered Paris, dragging him through the dust by his helmet. But Aphrodite, who favoured Paris because he had judged her the most beautiful goddess of all, spirited him invisibly back to safety behind Troy's walls.

By the terms of the agreement, Paris had lost and Helen must be handed back, but jealous Hera and Athena were desperate to see Troy destroyed, so they prolonged the fighting. Athena tricked Pandarus, the leader of the Lycians, into firing an arrow which wounded Menelaus. This broke the truce and a fierce battle began. These are 'the ringing plains of windy Troy' which

Tennyson evoked in his poem *Ulysses* – ringing with the clash of bronze swords and spears, as the fight raged to and fro across the fields below Troy's walls, with Athena encouraging the Greeks, Apollo goading on the Trojans, and Aeneas in the thick of it.

In *Iliad* 5, within this first day of fighting, Athena enflamed the heart of Diomedes, son of Tydeus, King of Argos. Like a lion killing heifers, Diomedes slew Echemmon and Chromius, two younger sons of Priam. Seeing this, Aeneas dodged the spears and arrows of the battlefield to find Pandarus. Their kingdoms bordered each other, and they were at least friends, if not relatives. 'Pandarus,' cried Aeneas, 'where is now your bow, your winged arrows?' Nobody in Lycia can rival your skills in archery, continued Aeneas, so pray to Zeus and fire an arrow at that man, whoever he is, who is killing so many Trojans.

It was Pandarus's arrow that broke the earlier truce, but, commented Professor Galinsky, 'Aeneas has no scruples to avail himself of Pandarus' talents.'[2]

Aeneas added, perceptively, that a deity might be using Diomedes to punish the Trojans for neglecting to make the proper sacrifices to the holy ones of Olympus. This comment is sometimes taken to herald Homer's characterisation of Aeneas as a pious Trojan, and so it is; yet Aeneas's view also encapsulates, as Galinsky wrote, a 'pragmatic realisation' within the world of the *Iliad* of the very tangible power of the gods.[3]

Pandarus agreed, acknowledging Aeneas as 'the counsellor of the Trojans'; Homer uses this term for other Trojans too, but it is applied most often to Aeneas. But, continued Pandarus, arrows seem to have no effect on Diomedes, who must indeed be under the protection of a deity. As with Menelaus, Pandarus's arrows seemed only to sting Diomedes into greater rage. Aeneas resolved, pragmatically, that he and Pandarus must act together. 'Things will not mend till we two go against this man with chariot and horses and bring him to a trial of arms.' Aeneas's horses were exceptionally fleet-footed, he reminded Pandarus, so if it turned out that Diomedes did indeed have divine protection, they still stood a good chance of escaping back to Troy. Aeneas would drive, because he knew his own horses, and Pandarus would be ready with his spear.

Diomedes' second-in-command Sthenelus saw them coming, 'both of them men of might, the one a skilful archer, Pandarus son of Lycaon, the other, Aeneas, whose sire is Anchises, while his mother is Aphrodite'. So, by now, Aeneas's semi-divine birth was a matter of common knowledge. Climb into your chariot and flee, Sthenelus cried, but Diomedes declared he would kill both the young heroes, and urged his side-kick to remain at hand to seize Aeneas's famous horses before they stampeded back to Troy. Aeneas's chariot bore down on Diomedes. Pandarus threw his spear, anticipating glorious victory as the shaft's bronze smashed through Diomedes's shield and pierced his breastplate. But the point stopped short of piercing flesh. Then, Diomedes threw his spear; Athena guided it so that it struck Pandarus's face, 'crashing in among his white teeth'. The spear's bronze point cut 'through the root of his tongue, coming out under his chin, and his glistening armour rang rattling round him as he fell heavily to the ground'.

Anxious to prevent the Greeks from capturing Pandarus's body and armour, Aeneas sprung out of his chariot and bestrode his fallen comrade's body 'like a lion'. Brandishing his spear and shield, Aeneas roared challenges at anyone who dared come near. To his anguish, Aeneas saw Sthenelus stealing his precious horses (and in *Iliad* 23, we hear of Diomedes using them in battle). But Aeneas's problems were more immediate, for, seizing a rock, Diomedes hurled it straight at him.

Visiting Olympia in the Peloponnese in the AD 100s, the ever-questing Pausanias noted that the battle of Diomedes and Aeneas was one of a series of scenes showing Greeks fighting foreigners depicted by the Classical sculptor Lycius on a semi-circular stone pedestal near the Hippodamium.[4] Their epic combat was a popular scene, too, on Greek vases. A red-figure kylix-krater by Oltos shows Aeneas and Diomedes, both black-bearded and bare-legged, wearing short tunics, high-crested Greek helmets and vests made (anachronistically, for it had not been invented by Aeneas's time) from chain-mail. Their shields are turned away from us so we can see how the oxhide coverings were stretched and fastened at the back, with two straps, one for the arm, the other for the hand. Aeneas brandishes his sword. Diomedes impales Aeneas's thigh with a spear.[5]

But that is not how Homer described the scene: the rock thrown by Diomedes smashed into Aeneas's groin, 'where the hip turns in the joint that is called the cup-bone'. It crushed the joint, breaking the sinews and tearing away the flesh. Aeneas sunk to his knees in a mixture of shock and agony, propping himself up with one hand. And the darkness of impending death hurtled towards 'Aeneas, king of men'.

That Aeneas was the son of Aphrodite was stated first in *Iliad* 2. Now, we hear again of Aphrodite, 'who had conceived him by Anchises when he was herding cattle'. However ashamed she may have been after she was tricked into sleeping with the mortal Anchises, the goddess seems to have developed a genuine, maternal love for Aeneas, for it emerges that she had been keeping close watch on him throughout the battle. As death threatened to engulf her son, Aphrodite protected Aeneas with her white arms and a fold of her robe, so that no wayward Greek spear could harm him further and made to bear him swiftly away from the fight.

A black-figure amphora from Vulci, Etruria, captures the exact moment in the melee of battle when wounded Aeneas sinks to his knees. Diomedes's sword (as opposed to a rock or spear) is about to come slicing down, but winged Aphrodite spreads her cloak over her son to save him from death.[6] The Tabula Iliaca in the Bibliothèque Nationale in Paris shows Aphrodite trying to carry Aeneas away, while Diomedes stands with his foot on Pandarus's body.[7] Oltos's kylix-krater, mentioned above, shows Aphrodite in the midst of the battle, supporting Aeneas's shoulders as he sinks back. To balance the scene, Oltos adds helmeted Athena at Diomedes's back, her hand just touching his spear-arm, suggesting that it was she who had guided the blow that struck poor Aeneas. The British Museum has a print by Joseph Hogarth, after John Gibson, showing nude Diomedes thrusting forward from the right, his spear aimed at Aphrodite, whose left arm is outstretched to stop him; she is levitating and holding in her other arm wounded Aeneas, whose rise into the air seems like a direct result of Diomedes' onrush.[8] An Attik cup by the Kleophrades Painter, found at Kameiros on Rhodes, shows an almost identical scene: blood streams from Aeneas's wound,[9] but Galinsky commented that 'his fighting spirit has not deserted him: with his right hand he still is struggling feebly to raise his sword.'[10]

And with good reason, for although Aeneas was protected by Aphrodite, he was not yet safe. Athena had allowed Diomedes to see the gods, warning him not to risk attacking any of them, save perhaps for Aphrodite, who was unlikely to strike back. This is the time recalled in Tennyson's *Ulysses*, of the 'men that strove with gods', and what follows must have shocked Homer's god-fearing listeners to the core. Leave war to us men, Diomedes yelled at Aphrodite, and stick to beguiling foolish women! Diomedes thrust his spear at the goddess, ripping the robe which the Graces had woven for her, piercing Aphrodite's skin between the wrist and palm of her hand, and drawing ichor, the immortal gods' equivalent of blood. Poor Aphrodite found out – as perhaps humanity first found out, through Homer's imagination – that deities could feel pain. She screamed aloud, and Aeneas tumbled from her arms.

Dazed, the goddess was spirited away by the rainbow goddess Iris. Then Aphrodite's lover, the war-god Ares, sped her up to Olympus in his chariot, where she flung herself into her mother Dione's lap. Diomedes has wounded me, Aphrodite cried, 'because I was bearing my dear son Aeneas, whom I love best of all mankind, out of the fight'. The Greeks have forgotten their quarrel with the Trojans, she complained, and are at war now with the gods! Dione urged her daughter to be strong, and she healed her. Her father Zeus advised her to keep out of the war from now on. So all was well with Aphrodite. But what about poor Aeneas?

Besides the kylix-krater mentioned above, Oltos also painted a cup showing the battle of Aeneas and Diomedes. Oltos captures the moment when Aphrodite, alarmed at Diomedes' onslaught, turns to flee. In this version, Aeneas crouches, naked save for his grand helmet and shield, but although he is losing one deity's protection, he is gaining another because, from the right, an archer is hurrying to his rescue.[11] That echoes Homer, who relates how, as Aeneas fell from his mother's arms and death threatened to snatch him, Apollo, the archer-god and patron-god of Troy, who had been watching from his temple in the upper city of Troy, swept down, caught Aeneas just in time, and wrapped him in darkness.

But Diomedes's courage knew no bounds. Determined to strip Aeneas of his armour, he now assaulted Apollo himself. Three times the god beat him back. As Diomedes made his fourth onslaught, he heard Apollo's awful voice, warning him not to match himself against gods. At last, the battle-madness which Athena had inspired in Diomedes abated and he drew back. Apollo fashioned a wraith in the form of Aeneas, complete with phantom armour, and flung it down on the battlefield for Diomedes and the Trojans to fight over. Simultaneously, Ares took the guise of Acamas of Thrace, and goaded the Trojan chiefs: Aeneas, whom you hold in as much honour as Priam's son Hector, lies wounded and helpless in the battlefield! Inspired, Hector and Sarpedon, the leader of the Lycians from the south, led a fresh charge.

Meanwhile, Apollo bore Aeneas's real body into Troy's upper city, which Homer also calls the Pergamos, to his own temple there. There Aeneas lay with his shattered pelvis, a mangled wreck of a young man, sure to die; but quickly Apollo's sister Artemis and their mother, the Titaness Leto, came to his aid. Their ministerings made Aeneas's broken bones whole again, and his flesh and groin as healthy as they had been before Diomedes's rock struck home.

What does it mean, this groin wound, healed by goddesses associated with childbirth? Later, Homer relates how great things were destined for Aeneas's descendants. Here, Aeneas's production of any offspring at all is gravely jeopardised, until it is restored by the hands of goddesses. Did those of Homer's listeners who believed themselves to be Aeneas's descendants gasp in shock at the news of the wound, only to be relieved, not to say complimented, by this divine intervention? What Aeneas remembered of these encounters with gods, is not indicated. Small wonder, all the same, that Aeneas would become ever more pious as he grew older. Restored to strength, Aeneas was carried back into the heat of battle by Apollo. He was 'glorious to behold'; it was almost, though Homer does not say so, as if he had been resurrected from the dead.

Agamemnon, urging his Greeks to victory, killed Aeneas's comrade Deicoon. Raging forth with renewed vigour, Aeneas slew the Peloponnesian brothers Crethon and Orsilochus, who tumbled before him like felled pines. Ares mades sure Menelaus saw this, for he wished them to fight so Aeneas could slay him. So, Aeneas found himself face-to-face, again, with the cuckolded husband of Helen, and saw the enraged king's face darken with a purposeful desire to kill him. Unlike Paris, Aeneas did not waver. The two men brandished their spears, preparing to fight to the death – and if Aeneas had succeeded, perhaps the Greeks might have lost heart and the war would have ended. But wise Nestor's son Antilochus, fearing exactly this, stood by Menelaus's side. Aeneas, 'bold though he was', knew he could not fight two heroes at once, so he drew back. Instead, Menelaus and Antilochus fell upon Pylaemanes, the leader of the wild Paphlagonians from the Black Sea coast, and slaughtered him.

This episode establishes Aeneas as one of the foremost Trojan heroes. He was equal in bravery to the Greek kings; held in as much honour as Hector by the Trojans; and unusually favoured by the gods, both on account of his mother and (as we will hear later) his particular destiny. It was for this reason that the Greek sophist Philostratus (who died *c.* AD 250) wrote of Aeneas, in the thirteenth book of his *Heroicus* ('On Heroes'), that he was

> ... somewhat less of a fighter than [Hector], but ... in intelligence and sagacity he was the best of the Trojans. He was esteemed as much as Hector. He was very much aware of the divine prophecy concerning his fate after the fall of Troy. He was not stricken with any fear, and he never ceased reasoning and calculating even in the most frightful circumstances. The Greeks thus called Hector the arm of the Trojans, but Aeneas, their soul [or mind], and they put greater stock in Aeneas' wisdom than in Hector's raging.

Brave enough to face the enraged Menelaus, Aeneas was also intelligent enough to withdraw from an unequal fight against two heroes that he knew he could not possibly win. Whether Aeneas was really a lesser warrior than Hector is hard to gauge. He certainly experienced fear, and good for him, because fear is closely linked to survival. That Aeneas knew of 'the divine prophecy concerning his fate' is Philostratus's assertion and is not supported by Homer; in the *Iliad*, Aeneas was, like most other men, entirely unaware of his destiny. As far as Aeneas was concerned at the time, the battle to drive the Greeks from his homeland was the all-consuming purpose of his life.

16

Aeneas and Cressida

With Aeneas and Hector at their head, and Apollo and Ares spurring them on, the Trojans forced the Greeks back across the plain. But this was only because Zeus was holding Hera and Athena in check; his plan, remember, was to make the Greeks think they were losing, so that Agamemnon would relent and beg Achilles to return to the battle. But Homer was fond of depicting Zeus as a hen-pecked husband, and at length his wife and daughter's complaints became too much, and he allowed them to intervene again. With Athena at his side once more, Diomedes attacked and wounded Ares himself and the tide turned again, so that towards the end of the day, in *Iliad* 6, Aeneas and his compatriots had their backs to Troy's walls and were planning to retreat within its well-built gates.

In the midst of the melee, Priam's son Helenus, the seer of Troy, sought out Aeneas and Hector, whom Homer describes as Troy's foremost leaders in council and on the battlefield. Rally the men in front of the gates, Helenus urged them – do not let them retreat back inside. Aeneas and Hector did so, and despite the raging attacks of Diomedes the Greeks could not break through to attack Troy itself. Then, and also at Helenus's advice, Hector left Aeneas in charge of the battle and hurried back into the city to urge his mother Hecuba to pray to Athena to stop wishing ill upon Troy.

Hector found Paris skulking about the palace, no longer participating in the war he had caused; a more dismal contrast to Aeneas's unquestioning bravery could not be imagined. Hector then visited his own wife Andromache and their little son Astyanax. Andromache begged Hector not to return to certain death on the battlefield; but return he must, and he forced Paris to accompany him.

As he fought on into *Iliad* 7, Aeneas may have glanced up see two vultures landing in the great oak that stood outside the Scaean Gate. These, says Homer, were Athena and Apollo in disguise, conferring and agreeing that the day's fighting should be concluded by a duel between Hector and a Greek hero, chosen by lot. Ajax son of Telamon won, and everyone, including Aeneas, stopped fighting to watch the clash. The duel ended in stalemate, night fell and Zeus made the heralds call an end to the day's combat.

It was within these heated, bloody days that William Shakespeare chose to set his play about the Trojan War, *Troilus and Cressida*. It was based, via its retellings in Chaucer's *Troilus and Criseyde* (c. 1385) and Benoit de Saint-Marie's *Le Roman de Troie* (c. 1155-60), on Dares' Trojan history, which introduced the story of Priam's son Troilus and a girl whom Dares calls Briseida, whose name is derived from Homer's Briseis. Shakespeare had a peculiarly ambivalent attitude towards the Trojan myth. Elizabeth I claimed direct descent from Aeneas via the Welsh princes and the mythological Brutus of Troy, whom the Welsh monks claimed was Aeneas's great grandson. One might expect Shakespeare to have made Aeneas the play's hero; but instead, his role was to do little more than move the plot along.

'Hark what good sport is out of town to-day!' said Aeneas, trying to shake Troilus out of his love-induced torpor and send him back to battle. The object of Troilus's desire, Cressida, was under the control of her uncle Pandarus, a Trojan lord (and a completely different man to the noble Lycian whom Diomedes had killed in *Iliad* 5). 'That's Aeneas.' Pandarus told her and continued, with a nod, perhaps, to Elizabeth I herself; 'Is not that a brave man? He's one of the flowers of Troy.'

When Hector decided to offer single combat to a Greek champion, Aeneas was the one who delivered the challenge to the Greek camp. He asked a Greek where Agamemnon was and how will 'a stranger to those most imperial looks know them from eyes of other mortals?' Why do you want to know? asked the Greek. Aeneas replied that he wanted to know so that, once in the king's presence, he could 'waken reverence, and bid the cheek be ready with a blush' and ask, 'which is that god in office, guiding men?'

The comedy here is that the unremarkable Greek whom Aeneas was addressing was in fact Agamemnon himself. Like us, Agamemnon was not sure whether Aeneas was being sarcastic, or demonstrating a genuine Trojan instinct for ceremony in its due place, but after some banter he revealed his true identity. Aeneas immediately rose to the situation, fitted his manner to the king to whom he was speaking, and delivered his challenge. Overall, Agamemnon was impressed by Aeneas's conduct: 'Fair Lord Aeneas, let me touch your hand,' he said, and invited him to dinner before he returned to Troy.

Meanwhile, the Trojans agreed to hand Cressida over to the Greeks in exchange for Antenor, whom Agamemnon's men had captured. When Aeneas returned to Troy, Diomedes accompanied him to effect the exchange. Though bitter enemies on the battlefield, Shakespeare makes them courtly and friendly to each other now, though both promised, in knightly fashion, to return to being the blackest of enemies once the fighting resumed. Having agreed this, Aeneas exclaimed to Diomedes 'now, by Anchises' life, welcome indeed! By Venus' [Aphrodite's] hand I swear no man alive can love in such a sort the thing he means to kill.' Such cordiality between sworn enemies was not entirely Shakespeare's invention: much later, as we shall see, Virgil imagined them communicating on magnanimous terms once they were both exiles in Italy.

'With a bridegroom's fresh alacrity', as Aeneas put it, he and Diomedes accomplished their mission of delivering Cressida to the Greek camp. Already heartbroken that Cressida had been snatched away from him, Troilus then saw Cressida yielding, apparently willingly, to the advances of Diomedes himself. All Cressida's pledges of true love, Troilus realised in this bleak, unhappy play of Shakespeare's, had been false.

At the end of the play, fighting resumed. Achilles killed Hector, and Ajax almost killed Aeneas, but Troilus exclaimed 'Shall it be? No, by the flame of yonder glorious Heaven.' Troilus was sure that, with Hector dead, Troy would fall. But Aeneas reprimanded him: 'You do discomfort all the host.' Assuming Hector's role, Aeneas rallied the men of Troy: 'Stand, ho! yet are we masters of the field. Never go home; here starve we out the night.'

Shakespeare's play ends before Troilus's death. In the *Cypria*, Troilus died before the action in the *Iliad* even begins. Dictys, on the other hand, says that Troilus died after the *Iliad*'s events were over. All agree, however, that Troilus died at Achilles' hand, and the *Cypria* places Troilus's death at the temple of Apollo Thymbrus, just to the south of Troy.

The scene was depicted frequently in Greek art, and Aeneas was often shown being present. A cup made in the 500s BC by Oltos shows the boy collapsing under Achilles' spear-thrust, while Aeneas, his shield painted with a snake, tries to defend him.[1] A black-figure amphora from Vulci in Etruria shows Aeneas and Deiphobus, with helms and undecorated shields, hurrying to aid Hector as he fights Achilles over Troilus's naked corpse, while the boy's severed head streams blood from the end of Achilles' spear.[2] A black-figured hydria (a three-handled water jug) from Etruria in the British Museum shows two fully armed warriors, thought to be Aeneas and Hector, defending Troilus's headless body, which is lying on an altar; one of them has on his shield an ivy wreath, the other a lion's maned head, shoulders and forepaw.[3] And a black-figure amphora from Etruria shows Achilles holding Troilus's severed head and Aeneas, this time accompanied by Agenor, is there to back Hector up.[4] The story was clearly popular in Etruria, where Aeneas appears to have been recognised as one of the foremost, and bravest, of Troy's defenders.

Back now to *Iliad* 7 and the end of day twenty-two, the day of that great battle in which Aeneas would have died, had not the gods intervened to save him. As dusk fell, the exhausted Trojans held council up in the Pergamos, the upper city of Troy. Antenor – Aeneas's Dardanian compatriot and, according to Dictys, his cousin – argued that they had no right to keep Helen and

Menelaus's treasures; if they returned them to the Greeks now, they might yet be left in peace. Paris refused but offered to pay off the Greeks with his own riches and Priam, of course, supported his wayward son.

The next day (day twenty-three of the *Iliad*), the herald Idaeus visited the Greek camp with this offer, but revealed that he, like most Trojans, was fed up with the king's support of Paris. If only Paris had drowned on his way back from Greece, he exclaimed. Most Trojans would gladly return Helen. Perhaps Aeneas thought the same; here is the background to the dissent within Troy imagined by Dictys and Dares, and which also maybe contributed to Aeneas's own grievance with Priam's family, about which we will hear in *Iliad* 13.

In *Iliad* 7, Idaeus negotiated a truce, so that both sides might collect, wash and burn their dead. Aeneas must have sought out the body of his gallant Lycian comrade Pandarus, even if it was by now stripped of its armour. On day twenty-four, as the fires died down, the Greeks built a high tumulus over the ashes of their dead, and then continued it as a high earthen rampart, with a ditch in front, to protect their ships in case of a Trojan counter-attack. As we discussed earlier, traces of the ditch seem to survive in the form of the 'Kesik Canal', while the walls are from Homer's imagination; they are destined, he writes, to be obliterated by Poseidon after the war.

At dawn on day twenty-five in *Iliad* 8, Zeus ordered the gods to let the war take its own course, and not to interfere in the fighting any more. He settled down on Gargarus, where he had a 'precinct and fragrant altar', to watch the fighting resume. In *Iliad* 14, Homer states clearly that Gargarus was the highest peak of Ida (the modern Kaz Dağ), but there is no obvious sign of an altar up there. Much lower down Ida, at Ada Tepe above Küçukkuyu, there is a very impressive rock-cut sanctuary. Schliemann found this and wanted it to be Zeus's altar, and indeed it is still signposted 'Zeus Altari' as a result. It commands a very impressive view of the Troad's southern coast, but it would have been impossible even for Zeus to watch the war from there. In Homer's time, when the Greeks were colonising the Troad, they built a city called Gargara, not on the highest peak but on the rocky pinnacle of Koca Kaya ('great rock') near Yesilyurt, at the low, western end of the Idean range. Cook confirmed this as the location of the city of Gargara, and because it has a clear sight-line to Troy, Luce thought this was where Homer envisaged Zeus sitting. But none of these considerations change Homer's clear statement in *Iliad* 14 that Gargarus was the name of Ida's highest peak so that, surely – and surviving altar or not – is where Zeus took his seat.

Aeneas must have participated in the battle that Zeus watched, but in *Iliad* 8 his deeds are overshadowed by others. Dares, however, describes a battle which fits in here,[5] as it comes shortly before the capture of Dolon, whom we shall meet shortly. Menelaus and Ajax of Locris (who was distinct from Ajax, son of Telamon) pursued Paris, whom they wounded in the heel, but Hector and Aeneas came to his aid. 'While Aeneas, using his shield, provided protection, Hector led Paris out of the fighting.' Dares tells us that Aeneas then fought and killed Amphimachus and Nireus. Both are mentioned in *Iliad* 2; Nireus was from the island of Symi, 'the handsomest man who ever came to Troy', and Homer does not account for his fate, but in *Iliad* 13 he says that Amphimachus, a grandson of Poseidon, was killed by Hector, not Aeneas.

Back in *Iliad* 8, the Trojans drove the Greeks right back over the Skamander's ford, across the plain and behind the Greek camp's newly built walls. Hera and Athena, who were under strict instructions from Zeus not to intervene, knew (as Zeus planned) that only Achilles' return to the battlefield could save the Greeks from destruction. Night fell and the Trojans made their camp on the west bank of the Skamander, the side closest to the Greek camp, upon what Homer calls the *ptolemoio gephurai*, the 'bridges of war'. Luce suggested that these were 'elevated parts of the plain, natural rises or even artificial embankments, where chariots could run without fear of getting bogged down in waterlogged ground.'[6]

During the long night, as they allowed their chariot horses to rest and made optimistic sacrifices to the gods, unaware that Zeus's face was still turned against them, Aeneas and his compatriots kept their watch-fires bright. Homer's attention in *Iliad* 9 focusses on the Greek camp, where the leaders begged Achilles to agree to fight the following day. Even Agamemnon, in despair, heeded wise old Nestor's advice and offered Achilles a wealth of treasure if he would take up arms again. But Achilles' resentment against Agamemnon was so engrained that he still refused. In *Iliad* 10, Diomedes and Odysseus set out in the darkness, pretending to be a peace embassy, but really to spy out the Trojan forces. They encountered Dolon, a Trojan spy, going their other way, and forced information out of him about the Trojans' positions.

They, and we, learned from Dolon that Hector and his chiefs, who would have included Aeneas, had withdrawn a short way from the main camp back across the Skamander towards Troy and were holding council on Ilos's barrow. In *Iliad* 24, we learn that this barrow was near Skamander's right bank, not far from the ford. In the 1800s, Charles Newton found a small mound in this area, near Old Kalafat, which Luce thought was a good candidate for Ilos's tomb.[7] Cook looked for it in vain and we could not find it either, but a spot in this approximate area would have been a good place for a council of war, set back from the army.

Dolon then divulged the arrangement of the Trojan forces, ranged along the western bank of Skamander. The wing 'towards the sea' (i.e. stretching north-west) comprised the Carians, Paeonians, Leleges, Pelasgians and 'Kaukones' (Kikones). The wing 'towards Thymbra' (stretching south-east) consisted of the Lycians, Mysians, Phrygians and Maeonians. More Thracians had arrived recently, added Dolon, and were camped in a vulnerable position on one of the flanks, so Diomedes and Odysseus crept there, killed their king and stole his chariot, in a passage which Luce thought was from 'a very ancient piece of saga material deriving from the actual Trojan War'.[8]

In the past, some scholars, like Agathe Thornton, have argued that 'Homer's Trojan plain is a poetic construction.'[9] Even Schliemann, who only found Troy due to Homer's descriptions, wrote that Homer 'writes with poetical licence, not with the minute accuracy of a geographer'.[10] But most scholars who have been to Troy have generally been deeply impressed with the accuracy of Homer's descriptions. In 1912, Leaf concluded that 'so far as I can judge, no case of ... a local inconsistency ... can be brought home to the *Iliad*.'[11] In fact, Leaf did not solve all the difficulties, but in 1998 Luce, with the exception of the confusion over Gargarus/Gargara, managed to iron out those Leaf could not – so Leaf's view, though unproven by him, holds true.

While Homer's historical details were drawn, we think, from the epic tradition, and, ultimately, we hope, from actual events, his geographical descriptions were surely based on personal experience. Homer's sight probably only failed him in middle age. As a young man, he drank in all he saw and then conveyed this to us in his work. He came from the Smyrna area, only 120 miles to the south-east of Troy, and as a bard he would have travelled; in *Odyssey* 17 he refers to bards, as well as seers and doctors, being 'welcome visitors in men's houses over the wide surface of the Earth'. The Greek city perched on the ruins of Priam's Troy, with its prominent temple of Athena, was 'in all probability', as Leaf thought, 'an object of patriotic pilgrimage from early days'. In *Iliad* 7, Hector predicts that 'a man as yet unborn might come sailing over the wine dark seas' to be awed by the burial mounds of the heroes who fought there, and it is tempting to think that Homer was referring to himself. In *Iliad* 12, Homer writes about tons of oxhide shields and horned helmets lying in the silt between the Skamander and Simois, reminders of the race of heroes. Luce wondered whether Homer wrote this because he had seen such archaeological relics of the Trojan War himself.

It would have been extraordinary if Homer had not visited the city about which he rhapsodised. Indeed, he may well have recited the *Iliad* there in person – and, even if Homer did not revisit Troy after his epic was completed, any geographical errors he may have made could easily have been corrected by other travellers. Luce wrote that Homer's 'eagle eye and well-stocked mind gave him an accurate and comprehensive grasp of the landscapes in which his epics are set'.[12] Having retraced most of his steps through the land of Aeneas, we agree.

17

The Battle by the Ships

The long night ends and in *Iliad* 11, at the dawn of day twenty-six of the epic, the Trojans advance to the *throsmos*, the 'rising slope of the plain', which Luce thought was where the plain begins to rise westward towards the Sigeum Ridge; there is also a very low hill to the east of the Kesik Canal which seems to swell up out of the flatness around, which could be this place. At the army's heart were 'great Hector, noble Polydamas [a Trojan commander not mentioned before], Aeneas who was honoured by the Trojans like an immortal, and the three sons of Antenor, Polybus, Agenor, and young Acamas, beauteous as a god'.

But as the sun rose, the goddess of Strife appeared by the beached hulls of the Greek ships and raised 'a cry both loud and shrill' to fill the Greeks with courage. Agamemnon, resplendent in his horned helmet, led the Greek charge against the Trojans, who responded in kind, each side felling their enemies like reapers among barley. The Trojans were forced inexorably back until Hector was obliged to lead a speedy retreat across the plain, past Ilos's barrow, and a wild fig tree which was also a landmark, towards Troy's gates. Agamemnon killed Antenor's son Iphidamas but was wounded by another of Antenor's sons, Coon.

Now the tide turned, and the Trojans battled the Greeks right the way back across the plain. In *Iliad* 12, the Trojan onslaught was halted only by the camp's defensive ditch, presumably the Kesik Canal. Leaping down from their chariots, the Trojans prepared to storm the earthen wall. They formed five parties, the first (and, says Homer, the bravest) led by Hector and Polydamas; the second by Paris; the third by Priam's sons Helenus and Deiphobus; the fourth by Sarpedon and Glaucus; and the fifth by Aeneas, 'the valiant son of Anchises', accompanied by Antenor's sons Archelochus and Acamas, both 'well-versed in all the arts of war'.

Raising their oxhide shields against the rain of arrows, the Trojan heroes charged forward, longing to destroy the Greek ships, slay their foes and end the war for good. Telamonian Ajax and his half-brother Teucer, whose mother was that same Hesione whose abduction from Troy lay at the root of the whole war, led the Greek defence of the wall. The Trojans saw the ill omen of an eagle dropping a serpent into their midst, but eventually Sarpedon made a breach, Hector's men smashed down one of the gates, and the Trojan army poured into the Greek camp.

The ensuing battle occupies a line in the Capitoline Museum's *Tabula Iliaca*, which depicts fighting warriors surging around a beached ship, while Hector and Aeneas, armed with bows, stand up above, probably on the wall.[1] In *Iliad* 13, Hector killed Amphimachus, grandson of Poseidon, and in revenge the sea-god sent the Cretan prince Idomeneus on a rampage of slaughter through the Trojan ranks. Among those whom Idomeneus encountered was Alcathous, 'the bravest man in all Troy', who was married to Aeneas's half-sister Hippodameia. Poseidon blinded and paralysed Alcathous, so Idomeneus could cut him down easily. Seeing this, Deiphobus hurried to alert Aeneas to the tragedy.

Now comes something shocking. Up to now, Aeneas has been an exemplary Trojan commander. But Deiphobus finds Aeneas 'standing in the rear, for he had long been aggrieved with Priam because, in spite of his brave deeds, he did not give him his due share of honour.' This disaffectedness of Aeneas's resurfaces in book four of Dictys's anti-Trojan history, at a different stage in the story (when Eurypylus is leading the Trojans) and for a different reason: 'Aeneas stayed behind in the city [along with Anchises and Antenor] and, for the first time, refused to fight' because, in this case, Paris had violated the temple of Thymbrian Apollo by committing murder there. In Homer's story, although we have heard of other Trojans being disaffected with Priam and his support for Paris, Aeneas's attitude seems to come out of nowhere. But throughout the *Iliad*, Homer makes Aeneas to a certain extent a parallel of Achilles. Both had goddesses for mothers; both had superb and intelligent horses; both were young, golden heroes serving older, ungrateful masters. Now, we learn, Aeneas resents Priam's intransigence almost as much as Achilles loathes Agamemnon's – and so, like Achilles, he is holding back, refusing to fight. Maybe there had been an earlier tale of Troy focussed more tightly on this pair, in which both were disaffected with their masters, and both refused to fight until their fated time.

Deiphobus appealed to him: 'Aeneas, prince among the Trojans, if you know any ties of kinship, help me now to defend the body of your sister's husband [who] brought you up when you were a child in his house.' Just as, later, Patroclus's death would bring Achilles back to the war, so now news of Alcathous's death goads Aeneas to action. That Aeneas must have loved Alcathous as much as Achilles loved Patroclus is unstated. But the affection must have been deep, and with it Aeneas's grief at the news of Alcathous's death.

'Big with great deeds of valour', and eager again for battle, Aeneas sought out Idomeneus. The Cretan prince, a grandson of the legendary king Minos, called on his friends for help: I go in great fear of swift-footed Aeneas, he said, who 'is a redoubtable dispenser of death in battle. Moreover, he is in the flower of youth when a man's strength is greatest.' For his part, Aeneas called for help to Deiphobus, Paris, and Agenor, 'who were leaders of the Trojans along with himself', and his heart was gladdened when he saw many ordinary soldiers gathering around him as well.

The two sides fought furiously over Alcathous's corpse, 'wielding their long spears; and the bronze armour about their bodies rang fearfully as they took aim at one another in the press of the fight.' Aeneas and Idomeneus, 'peers of Ares', were fiercest of all. Aeneas cast his spear first, but the Cretan dodged aside and it landed quivering in the ground. Idomeneus smote a Trojan called Oenomaus, making his guts spill out onto the battlefield, but now his strength began to fail and he retreated. Deiphobus threw his spear at Idomeneus. It missed, but killed Idomeneus's friend Ascalaphus, son of Ares, and a fight ensued over his armour, in which Aeneas sprung upon Aphareus. That scene is also shown on the Capitoline Museum's *Tabula Iliaca*: stricken in the throat with Aeneas's spear, Aphareus's head lolls and his helmet falls off.[2] We do not hear whether or not Aeneas ever succeeded in recovering Alcathous's body.

In *Iliad* 14, Hera tricked Aphrodite into loaning her her famous girdle, which inspired passionate love. Approaching Zeus up on Gargarus, where we left him earlier, Hera seduced him into making love to her, and then lulled him to sleep, so that Poseidon could further disobey his brother's command not to interfere in the war. Poseidon inspired the Greeks to regroup for a fierce counter-attack. Hector was struck on the neck with a rock by Telamonian Ajax and fell, like an oak struck by lightning. Aeneas, Polydamas, Agenor, Sarpedon and Glaucus hastened to surround Hector. Homer calls these men the Trojan *aristoi*, 'the best'. These aristocrats protected Hector with their shields; a black-figure hydria from Caere, Italy, shows Ajax bearing down on Hector, while Aeneas, his spear held aloft, his white shield blank except for a small X in the middle, hastens to Hector's aid.[3]

Homer describes how Aeneas and his companions bore Hector safely to his chariot and transported him away, as far as the ford in the Skamander. Here, Hector vomited dark clots of blood. Meanwhile, the sight of this retreat of the Trojan chiefs inspired the Greeks to rout the remaining Trojan forces out of the camp.

Zeus awakens in *Iliad* 15. Looking down from Gargarus, he chastised Hera furiously for her deception. If only she and Poseidon had allowed the Trojans to continue ravaging the Greek camp, then eventually Agamemnon would have been forced to beg Achilles again to join the fight. Thus, Zeus's promise to Tethys, and his obligation to Fate, would have been fulfilled, and Hera would have had the satisfaction of watching Troy burn. But her meddling had ruined the plan. Poseidon was now ordered to stop helping the Greeks. Then Apollo, who was genuinely on the Trojans' side, inspired Hector, who had recovered from his injury, to lead the Trojans in a fresh assault on the Greek camp. Hector, Polydamas, Agenor and Paris all made kills; Aeneas's triumphs were the slaying of Iasus, an Athenian leader, and Medon, an illegitimate brother of the Locrian Ajax. These combats are not described in detail.

The Trojans reached the Greek ships again, and in *Iliad* 16 one of them was set ablaze. Despite this, Achilles continued to sulk in his tent, refusing to lead his army of Myrmidons into battle because of his feud with Agamemnon. But Achilles' beloved companion Patroclus, seeing the rest of the ships in peril, persuaded him to lend him his armour. Dressed as Achilles, Patroclus led the Myrmidons in a rout of the Trojans, driving many of them into the defensive ditch and slaying Sarpedon, the leader of the southern Lycians.

Sarpedon's second-in-command, Glaucus, hurried to find the other Trojan leaders, first Polydamas and Agenor, and then Aeneas and Hector, named in that order. You have forgotten your allies, protested Glaucus. The Greeks are about to strip Sarpedon of his armour, and you stand here doing nothing! Overcome with grief at the news, the lords of Troy began a mighty struggle with the Greeks to recover Sarpedon's body, all under a dark cloud summoned by Zeus, for Sarpedon was one of his mortal sons. Galinsky thought this was the scene depicted in the east frieze of the Siphnian Treasury at Delphi, showing Menelaus, probably backed by Ajax, attacking from the right, and Hector, backed by Aeneas, coming from the left, shields at the ready and long, braided hair hanging below their Greek-style helmets.[4]

The charging Trojans were forced back by Patroclus, but then Glaucus led a counter-attack. Meriones, son of Molus, one of the Cretan commanders, slew Laogonus, a highly honoured Trojan warrior, whose father Onetor was a priest of Zeus on Mount Ida. Laogonus was therefore presumably a Dardanian, so it was Aeneas who retaliated. He threw his spear at Meriones, but the Cretan ducked and the weapon landed in the earth, its butt-end quivering until Ares the war god robbed it of its energy. 'You are a good dancer, Meriones,' cried Aeneas angrily, 'but if I'd hit you, my spear would have been the end of you.'

You may be brave, retorted the Cretan, but you cannot kill everyone who comes against you; if I hit you with my spear then, strong and self-confident as you are, you'll yield your life to Hades. But Patroclus rebuked Meriones. His taunting would only provoke the Trojans into fighting harder for Sarpedon's body, he warned: 'Blows for battle, and words for council; fight, therefore, and say nothing.'

By killing Zeus's son Sarpedon, Patroclus had doomed himself. Zeus pretended to give Patroclus the advantage, instilling such fear in Hector's heart that he led the Trojans in a full-scale retreat back across the plain to Troy. Only Apollo's intervention stopped Patroclus from storming the city, but now, below the walls, he was confronted by Hector. Patroclus killed Hector's charioteer, and was only prevented from slaying Hector by Apollo, who wounded him. Thus weakened, Patroclus was then slain by Hector. In *Iliad* 17, jubilant Hector stripped Patroclus of Achilles' armour and donned it himself, unaware that, by doing so, he in turn guaranteed his own doom.

The Greeks pressed forward, desperate to recover Patroclus's corpse. The battle is shown on a red-figure cup by Oltos, found at Vulci. Oltos painted Aeneas, backed by a Trojan called Hippasus, pitted against one of the Ajaxes: both wear greaves (shin protectors); short tunics with sword belts, and crested Greek helmets. Both carry spears and shields, Aeneas's showing a crouching lion.[5] An early Corinthian bowl depicts the same scene. Aeneas, naked save for his crested helmet, with a snake painted on his shield, fights a similarly attired Ajax, whose shield faces away from us. They brandish spears while the other Ajax waits behind, on horseback (which is an anachronism, for riding horses, as opposed to using them to pull chariots, had not become commonplace by then). This scene is matched on the other side of the bowl by the combat of Hector and Achilles, whose shield depicts a falcon or eagle. Aeneas and Achilles occupy identical positions in these parallel scenes, suggesting that the Greek painter held the two heroes in equal esteem.[6]

The Greeks' charge threatened to drive the Trojans back within the city gates, so Apollo assumed the form of Periphas, whose father Epytus had grown old serving as herald to Aeneas's 'aged father', Anchises. 'Aeneas,' cried Apollo in Periphas's voice, 'can you not manage, even though Heaven be against us, to save high Ilium? I have known men, whose numbers, courage, and self-reliance have saved their people in spite of Zeus, whereas in this case he would much rather give victory to us than to the Greeks, if you would only fight instead of being so terribly afraid.' Oh, fickle gods; yes, Zeus will give the Trojans the semblance of victory – but only to lure Achilles out of his sulking. But Aeneas, realising that Periphas was voicing Apollo's advice, took the god at his word. To Hector and the other Trojan leaders, Aeneas cried, 'Shame on us if we are beaten by the Greeks and driven back to Ilium through our own cowardice. A god has just told me that Zeus, the supreme disposer, will be with us. Therefore let us make for the Greeks, and make things hard for them if they want to bear Patroclus back to their ships!'

So speaking, Aeneas sprang out far ahead of the others, spearing and killing an Achaean warrior called Leiocritus as he did so, and the rest of the Trojans surged forth behind him. Hector saw Achilles' chariot, which had borne Patroclus into battle, being driven by the Myrmidon Alcimedon and his comrade, Automedon. Turning to Aeneas, Hector pointed out the horses, which were immortal, and had been presented by Zeus to Achilles' father Peleus. 'I am sure,' Hector said to Aeneas, 'if you think well, that we might take them: they will not dare face us if we both attack them.'

Aeneas agreed, 'and the pair went right on, with their shoulders covered under shields of tough dry ox-hide, overlaid with much bronze,' accompanied by Chromius and Aretus. But Automedon, seeing them approach, was filled with courage by Zeus and called to the Ajaxes and Menelaus to leave the guarding of Patroclus's body to others. Come instead, Automedon cried, and rescue the living from Hector and Aeneas, 'who are the two best men among the Trojans [and who] are pressing us hard in the full tide of war'.

Automedon's spear pierced Aretus's shield, penetrating his belly. Hector flung his spear at Automedon, who ducked aside. The Ajaxes forced the Trojans back, so that victorious Automedon might strip Aretus of his armour. But the Ajaxes could not stem the tide: the Trojans surged forward again, with Hector and Aeneas at their head, scattering the Greeks, says Homer, like a flock of starlings before a falcon.

18

Aeneas Faces Achilles

The great charge of the men of Troy seemed like a prelude to victory; but it helped fulfil the promise that Zeus had made long ago to Thetys, to glorify her son Achilles. Just as in *Iliad* 13 Aeneas was stung into returning to the fray by the death of his brother-in-law Alcathous, now in *Iliad* 18, the news of Patroclus's death brought Achilles hurtling back, at last, onto the battlefield. The Trojans drew back, quaking at Achilles' grief-stricken bellows, allowing him to reclaim Patroclus's body and take it back to the Greek camp to be washed and laid out. Meanwhile, Athena robbed the Trojans of their wits: instead of retreating now that Achilles was back in the war, they resolved to attack the Greek camp the following day.

At dawn on day twenty-seven in *Iliad* 19, Achilles donned new armour and a new shield, made at Thetys's behest by Hephaestus, the gods' blacksmith, and his mother fed him ambrosia, the gods' food. Agamemnon handed over all the gifts he had promised Achilles and finally returned Briseis, the original object of their quarrel. Up on Olympus in *Iliad* 20, Zeus acknowledged that Achilles' rage might cause Troy to fall before its fated time, so he allowed the gods free rein to interfere again on their chosen sides. Poseidon shook the earth and Zeus's thunder made Mount Ida tremble.

Apollo, in the guise of Priam's son Lykaon, said to Aeneas: 'Aeneas, counsellor of the Trojans, where are now the brave words with which you vaunted over your wine before the Trojan princes, saying that you would fight Achilles son of Peleus in single combat?' Perhaps one night in Priam's palace, where the princes caroused over their roasted meats, Aeneas imagined himself as immortal as his mother, and bragged that he could fight anybody; yes, even Achilles. But now, sober, on the battlefield, Aeneas replied 'Why do you thus bid me fight the proud son of Peleus, when I am in no mind to do so?' Aeneas related how, with Zeus's help, he had survived Achilles' cattle raid on Mount Ida. Achilles' weapons always flew straight and never failed to pierce his enemies' flesh, but what made him no match for any mortal was that Athena protected him and ensured him victory. But 'if Heaven would let me fight him on *even* terms,' Aeneas added, 'he should not soon overcome me, though he boasts that he is made of bronze.'

Pray to the gods for victory, advised disingenuous Apollo, still in his disguise as Lykaon, for after all, 'men say that you were born of Zeus's daughter Aphrodite.' He reminded Aeneas that Achilles' mother Thetys, though a goddess, was merely the daughter of the Old Man of the Sea, and thus (he opined) of 'inferior rank' to Aphrodite, an Olympian. 'Bring your spear to bear upon him,' Apollo goaded Aeneas, 'and let him not scare you with his taunts and menaces.'

Fey, beautiful, untrustworthy Apollo, exalting Aeneas to greatness – but to what end? To triumph over Achilles or to die in glory on the battlefield? But Apollo's words 'put courage into the heart of the shepherd of his people', and Aeneas 'strode in full armour among the ranks of the foremost fighters'. He was so heroically impressive that white-armed Hera called to Poseidon and Athena, 'Apollo is sending Aeneas clad in full armour to fight Achilles. Shall we turn him back at once, or shall one of us stand by Achilles and endow him with strength so that his heart fail not' and make sure he suffers 'no hurt at the hands of the Trojans'. But Poseidon counselled against such an approach, which would bring them into conflict with the pro-Trojan gods.

So, concealed by dark clouds, Poseidon, Hera and Athena settled down on Hercules's 'mounded and lofty fort' on the Sigeum ridge, to watch the fight. This was probably Kesik Tepe, though Cook thought it was Spratt's Plateau, adding, in a rare moment of levity, that it was 'better placed for viewing and much more comfortable to sit on'.[1] Meanwhile, Apollo, Ares and the other gods who favoured Troy, respecting the truce, settled themselves upon Kallicolonê, which means 'beautiful hill'. Luce identified Kallicolonê as Kara Tepe, a wooded hill on the south side of the Simois valley, 9 miles due east of Kara Tepe and 5 miles east of Troy; this agrees with Homer's description, also in *Iliad* 20, of Hermes running from Kallicolonê along the Simois to Troy. From Kallicolonê, Apollo and his colleagues saw the plain seething 'with men and horses and blazing with the gleam of armour'. It is true that Troy can be seen in the hazy distance, through the pines on Kara Tepe's summit. And the gods, whose hearing, as well as sight, was more acute than ours, could hear the earth resound with the tramp of feet, as the Greeks and Trojans rushed towards each other. At their heads were their two opposing champions, Achilles and Aeneas.

The whole *Iliad* so far has led to this, the clash of two goddess-born heroes, so finely balanced. Aeneas strode forward, the horse-hair plume on his helmet tossing defiantly. He held his shield before his breast and brandished his bronze spear. Achilles faced him like a lion, burning to leap upon and kill his assailant. Already, we know he will not be killed by Aeneas; in *Iliad* 5, Aeneas was described as being like a lion, but here Homer grants the lion metaphor to Achilles – so how will things go for Aeneas?

Aeneas Faces Achilles

Before deeds come words. 'Aeneas,' cried Achilles, 'why do you stand thus out before the host to fight me? Is it that you hope to reign over the Trojans in the seat of Priam? Even if you kill me, Priam will not hand his kingdom over to you. He is a man of sound judgement, and he has sons of his own. Or have the Trojans promised you a rich estate, full of orchards and corn lands, if you should slay me?' These are taunts: back in *Iliad* 13, we heard of Aeneas hanging back because he was aggrieved with Priam: this is the first we have heard of him coveting his ancestors' throne of Troy – but if he felt discontented in his role as a junior cousin of great king Priam, we should not be too surprised. Achilles' aim, however, was merely to rile his enemy; next, he reminded Aeneas of their encounter on Mount Ida, and of Aeneas's humiliating escape down to Lyrnessos. Zeus protected you that time, taunted Achilles, but the gods won't do so now, so return to your men. 'Even a fool may be wise after the event,' Achilles continued, so be wise now, and don't become embroiled in a fight you're sure to regret.

Few heroes, Greek or Trojan, could have failed to rise to such baiting, but with Aeneas, the future lies in different hands – heroic, for sure, but not blindly so. Here, like Odysseus, the most god-fearing of the Greeks, is a hero of undoubted courage, but who was willing to give ground if necessary, even to flee, if it served a greater purpose. So instead of being needled into rash action, Aeneas replied calmly, 'Son of Peleus, think not that your words can scare me as though I were a child. I too can brag if I feel like it ... we know one another's race and parentage as matters of common fame, though you have never seen my parents, nor I yours. Men say that you are son to noble Peleus, and that your mother is Thetys, fair-haired daughter of the sea. I have noble Anchises for my father, and Aphrodite for my mother.' One of these sets of parents, said Aeneas, would soon be mourning a dead son, for it is not idle talk, but hard fighting which will settle things.

Aeneas was doing what Apollo had suggested, subtly putting Achilles down, because it was obvious that Olympian Aphrodite outranked Thetys. Aeneas followed this by reciting his father's entire genealogy back to Dardanos, son of Zeus. 'Such do I declare my blood and lineage,' Aeneas concluded, but as for valour, Zeus bestows or withdraws it as his pleasure, for he is lord of all. Aeneas's comment is important; while he is often characterised as being pious, he did not revere the gods just for the sake of it. In his world, Zeus's favour, or his ire, had a tangible effect on Earth.

Let's stop this childish prattling, Aeneas continued, for we could fling each other so many taunts that a hundred-oared galley would not hold them. People can say anything and mean nothing, so why should we stand here like women quarrelling in the streets, when I am determined to fight you, brazen spear to brazen spear?

So saying, Aeneas hurled his spear, and it struck Achilles' shield with a deadly clang. Achilles feared the spear would pierce through the shield and strike him, but Hephaestus's craftsmanship held strong: Aeneas's spear-tip only penetrated the shield's golden surface and one of the tin layers, but a further layer of tin and two of bronze remained, protecting Achilles from harm.

A Pontic black-figure amphora from Vulci depicts the combat: Aeneas, wearing a short tunic, greaves and helmet, is centre-stage, spear in one hand, with his shield raised against Achilles. Achilles, naked apart from greaves, helmet and shield, his muscular chest defined by white lines, aims a spear at Aeneas. Behind Aeneas, a tunic-wearing Paris is ready with bow and arrow, anticipating the way Achilles himself will eventually die. The scene is matched on the other side of the vase by a depiction of Achilles killing Hector, and we must remember that of all the heroes shown here, the only one who survived was Aeneas.[2] Hence Galinsky's view that the whole scene 'borders on hero worship' of Aeneas.[3]

Achilles cast his spear back. It struck Aeneas's round shield at the upper edge, where the bronze and bull's hide was thinnest. The shield rung under the blow, and Aeneas, also fearful, crouched down and raised his shield so that, as the spear shattered through, it struck only the air above his bent back and then plunged into the earth behind him. Aeneas had survived but found himself 'blinded with fear and grief because the weapon had gone so near him'.

Achilles seized the advantage, springing forward 'with a cry as of death and with his keen blade drawn'. Recovering quickly, Aeneas grasped a great stone, too heavy for two normal men to lift together, and raised it. But had Aeneas struck Achilles with it, says Homer, the divinely wrought helmet or shield would have deflected the blow, and then nothing would have stopped Achilles from hacking Aeneas to death with his bronze sword.

And there the story might have ended, with Aeneas half-remembered as one of those many obscure Trojans in an old poem called the *Iliad* and listed in the glossary to modern editions as 'son of Anchises and Aphrodite, one of the leaders of the Trojan forces; killed by Achilles'. That would have been that; within the internal logic of the world of myth, there would have been no Rome, no Caesars, and no line of British kings descending from Trojan Brutus.

Instead, as time stood still, Poseidon turned to his companions up on Kallicolonê and said, 'I am sorry for great Aeneas, who will now go down to the house of Hades, vanquished by the son of Peleus. He was foolish to listen to Apollo, who will never save him from destruction.' So Apollo, the friend of Troy, had almost sent Aeneas to his death, yet Poseidon, Troy's foe, argued that Aeneas – though deeply embroiled in the quarrel between Menelaus and Paris – was guiltless. Aeneas had always made pious offerings to the gods, argued Poseidon. And besides, if Achilles slew Aeneas, he would doom himself by incurring Zeus's anger.

But there was another reason for saving Aeneas: 'It is fated, moreover, that he should escape,' prophesied Poseidon, 'and that the race of Dardanos, whom Zeus loved above all the sons born to him of mortal women, shall not perish utterly without seed or sign.' Zeus had grown to loathe the family of

Priam, 'so Aeneas shall reign over the Trojans, he and his children's children that shall be born hereafter.'

Faced with Poseidon's prophecy, Hera relented. Athena and I, she said, have sworn not to help any Trojans, even if Troy itself is in flames, but you may do as you please. So Poseidon hurtled down into the fury of battle and cast a dark cloud in front of Achilles' eyes. This scene was illustrated on some of the surviving *Tabula Iliacae*, but it appears most dramatically in a mural in the 'Homeric House' in Pompeii. Achilles bears down on Aeneas, who collapses backwards, but Poseidon surges between them using his shield to protect the Trojan[4] – a happy reminder, of course, to the Roman viewers, of the far-reaching consequences of the rescue.

Poseidon wrenched the spear out of Aeneas's shield, says Homer, and laid it next to Achilles, so that he could fight on. Then he lifted Aeneas up and hurled him into the air, so that he flew high over the battlefield and landed (we must assume, unharmed) where the Kaukones were arming themselves for battle.

Achilles, his clear sight restored, exclaimed angrily: 'What miracle has just happened? My spear is lying by me and Aeneas has vanished. I thought his boasting was idle, but the gods must be protecting him after all. Well, good luck to him: he will never dare fight me again.' So saying, Achilles led the Greeks in a renewed onslaught on the Trojans.

Meanwhile, Aeneas, lying stunned on the earth, heard Poseidon's voice next to him: 'Aeneas, what god has egged you on to be so foolish as to fight Achilles, who is stronger and better protected by the gods than you? Yield to him [Achilles] always, for the alternative is death: only after he is dead can you fight without fear, for there is no other Greek who can defeat you.' Aeneas knew not of the prophecy Poseidon had just uttered to Hera and Athena; but he knew now, for sure, that the gods were watching him.

In Orphic philosophy, Fate and Time existed at the very start of everything, predating their child, first-born Eros, light. Their descendants, the Olympian gods, were subject to them, so if Fate decreed Aeneas would survive, so he should. As we shall see later, it is highly likely that in Homer's time the rulers of Skepsis, at least, claimed descent from Aeneas. 'Not for him,' as Scherer wrote, 'was the immortality of a glorious death, but rather the establishment of an enduring state'[5] because, as Reinhardt wrote, 'ancestors have to survive.'[6] Both are partially wrong: Homer could perfectly easily have killed Aeneas off at this point, provided he left behind him a surviving son. Indeed, the Iliupersis krater in the British Museum, which was found in southern Italy, shows Aeneas's father Anchises leading Aeneas's son Ascanius away from the sack of Troy, without Aeneas's help at all.[7] But maybe Homer felt that the claims of his Skepsian patron – if such a patron really existed – would be more convincing if Aeneas himself survived the war. Hild put it well, arguing that Homer chose 'to give prominence to the hero, who is reserved for the future, if not by the splendour of an illustrious victory... at least by the glory of a noble attempt'.[8]

One of Poseidon's reasons for saving Aeneas was his piety. Virgil and Augustus later emphasised this as his greatest virtue, so much so that (as W. B. Yeats told Ezra Pound) an Irish sailor, reading Virgil's *Aeneid*, commented of Aeneas, 'Ach, a hero, him a hero? Bigob, I t'ought he waz a priest.' But Galinsky, after careful deconstruction of the evidence, pointed out that in Homer, piety was only one of Aeneas's traits, and not his most defining characteristic. Aeneas might be 'dear to the gods' in *Iliad* 20, but not quite as much as Achilles thirteen lines earlier, and Hector in *Iliad* 24 was 'dearest' of all; while, in *Iliad* 1, Zeus says that Odysseus has made more sacrifices to the gods than any other man. Indeed, Odysseus is so pious that, despite all his sufferings in *The Odyssey*, we never hear him cursing Heaven. For Homer, Aeneas's courage in battle and his sagacity are just as important, if not more so, than his personal piety. But what really matters about Aeneas is that he survives.

This is the last we hear of Aeneas in the *Iliad*, but what follows in the remaining books concerns his story deeply. Hector emulated Aeneas, recklessly, by fighting Achilles, but was unequal to the task and had to be rescued by Apollo. In *Iliad* 21, Achilles' rampage extended to attacking the god of the Skamander. The river – Aeneas's ancestor – rose in rage, clearing his bed of the corpses that were choking him, bringing the full forces of his watery anger down on the hero, who had to cling to an elm's root to survive. Hera sent her son Hephaestus to subdue the river with his smithy's fire, burning the elms, willows and tamarisks – whose descendants all still grow along Skamander's banks to this day – and boiling the water, until the river god retreated. Even the gods now came to blows, Athena against Ares and Aphrodite; Hera against Artemis; and Apollo, nearly, with Poseidon. Meanwhile, the Trojans, including presumably Aeneas, fled back behind Troy's walls. Achilles, pursuing, them, was challenged first by Antenor's son Agenor, whom Apollo protected from death, and then by the god himself, who barred the hero's way.

Only Hector remained outside Troy's gates, refusing to come in to safety. When Achilles confronted him in *Iliad* 22, Hector fled and was chased around Troy four times, while the Trojans, including presumably Aeneas, watched helplessly from the walls. Here arises the knottiest problem in Homeric geography, because the chase took Achilles and Hector four times past twin springs of the Skamander, one of which flowed hot, and the other cold. There are no such springs near Troy's walls, and most commentators thought that Homer had abandoned here his usual geographical precision in favour of imagination. But Luce argued, brilliantly, that the common assumption that the race took place only below the city walls was incorrect. What Homer actually describes is a much broader circuit, from the Scaean Gate, 'along the waggon-road ... past the lookout station, and past the weather-beaten wild fig-tree' to the springs. Waggon routes tend, Luce argued, to lead away from cities, not around them, and the lookout post past which this road led was presumably Aesytes's tomb, which Polites had used for that purpose in *Iliad* 2.

The route taken by Hector and the pursuing Achilles appears therefore to have led to the ford in the Skamander and then south along its bank to the springs at the southern edge of the Trojan plain, at what is now Pinarbaşi – the way, in fact, that led to Dardania. The springs at Pinarbaşi no longer flow into Skamander, but nineteenth-century maps show that there used to be streams leading from the springs into the river, so they were indeed among the many sources of Skamander's northern reaches. No amount of testing has shown that these springs, or any others in the Troad, run hot and cold, but they are tepid, so they could seem cold in summer but warm in winter. Homer says that the Trojan women used to wash clothes there (as local women still do now) before the war. Had the springs really been below Troy's walls, women could have continued to wash clothes there during most of the war; it was precisely their situation right across the plain which made them unsafe once the Greeks arrived. Even the sceptical Cook wrote that 'if we are disposed to look for a natural feature that could have inspired poetic description [of the springs], only inveterate prejudice can deny that honour to these springs [at Pinarbaşi].'[9]

Thus, instead of the relatively short sprint around Troy itself, which so many scholars imagined, Achilles and Hector's chase entailed a more heroic marathon which took them on a long, elliptical route, with a sharp turn at Pinarbaşi. Homer even uses the simile here of race horses wheeling around turning posts. Each time Hector almost reached the safety of Troy, Achilles' hound-like pursuit forced him out again 'towards the plain'. Luce's interpretation solves an age-old problem and enforces the idea that Homer's story – including what he says of Aeneas – contains elements of remembered historical truth.

The fourth time the heroes reached the springs, Zeus observed from the golden scales of Fate that Hector's time had come. As the heroes reached Troy's walls again, Hector's brother Deiphobus appeared at his side and filled him with courage to turn and fight Achilles. Hector did so: too late, he realised that he had been duped by a phantom sent by Athena. The ensuing fight reminds us acutely of Achilles' clash with Aeneas, but this time there was no god to intervene to save Hector. He was wearing Achilles' original armour, which he had stripped from Patroclus's body, and Achilles, knowing its weaknesses, stabbed Hector deftly in the throat. Then Achilles reclaimed his armour, tied Hector's naked body to his chariot, and dragged it up and down before Troy's walls for all to see.

In *Iliad* 23, on day twenty-eight, Achilles cremated Patroclus's body and the Greeks built a tumulus over the burnt-out pyre. In *Iliad* 24, the Trojans remained confined inside Troy, and for ten days (days thirty to forty) Achilles continued to drag Hector's body about outside until, on day forty-one, Apollo persuaded Zeus to allow it to be ransomed. Priam entered the Greek

In Search of Aeneas

camp in secret and knelt before Achilles, begging him for Hector's corpse, reminding him how his own father Peleus would feel in the same situation. Finally, Achilles wept for both Peleus and Patroclus, agreed to return Hector's corpse, and allowed a truce until the body was buried. Priam returned with Hector's corpse, and all of Troy, including even Helen, and surely Aeneas too, mourned their greatest hero. Alleged tumuli for Hector exist at the Balli Dağ and up on the coast at In Tepe. 'And thus', on day fifty-one,[10] after elaborate preparations, 'they busied themselves with the funeral of Hector, tamer of horses.' So ends Homer's *Iliad*.

19

Defender or Traitor?

Aeneas's cousin Hector, Priam's eldest son, was dead at the hands of a seemingly invincible hero. We know what happens next from surviving fragments of the Trojan cycle from which Homer had drawn his inspiration for his tale about the quarrel between Achilles and Agamemnon. According to West, Proclus's *Chrestomathy*, for example, includes a summary of Arctinus of Miletus's otherwise lost *Aethiopis*, which was probably composed in the 7th century BC. Arctinus tells how the Amazons, led by the warrior queen Penthesilea, came out of the wilds of Thrace in support of Troy, forcing the Greeks back from Troy's walls. The 2018 BBC drama *Troy: Fall of a City* adds an unexpected layer to this story with a scene in which Aeneas empathises with Penthesilea over the death of her female lover, and then indicates his own attraction for her. 'Men and me,' Penthesilea responds: 'it doesn't happen.' When Aeneas moves away, she adds, 'it's a shame. You're quite a picture.'

The Trojans, presumably including Aeneas, were able to come back out of Troy until Penthesilea was slain by Achilles. Then arrived the Ethiopians, led by Memnon, whose father Tithonus was Priam's brother. Memnon slew Nestor's son Antilochus, whose burial mound is perhaps Windmill Tumulus, on the coast north-west of Troy. Achilles slew Memnon too, and the Trojans were driven back once more within their walls.

When Achilles was a baby, his mother Thetys immersed him in the River Styx, making him invulnerable to wounds, except for the heel by which she held him. Now, recounts Arctinus, an arrow shot by Paris and guided by Apollo pierced Achilles' heel, and he died outside the Scaean Gate. That is one version of how Achilles died. Dictys and Dares tell another; that he was lured to the temple of Thymbrian Apollo by his love for Priam's daughter Polyxena, and he was murdered there in cold blood by Paris.

A black-figure amphora from Etruria shows the battle over the naked body of Achilles, who has braids of hair dangling down over his lifeless face. Paris and Aeneas have tried to take the body, but Menelaus engages Paris in fierce combat while Ajax carries away the corpse. Aeneas is engaged, meanwhile, in combat with another Greek, identified as Achilles' son Neoptolemus, but here the vase-painter has anticipated too much, for in the literary sources this boy has yet to appear on the scene.[1] A Chalcidian amphora from Vulci shows Achilles' helmeted body lying prone, with blood pouring from the arrow wound in his ankle. Ajax charges forward to defend the corpse; his spear pierces one Trojan, while Paris aims another arrow at him. Aeneas, with a vortex of stripes whirling out from a central point on his shield, charges up to help.[2]

The Greeks burned Achilles' body and his ashes were buried with those of Patroclus. Despite this, later antiquarians were determined to find *two* adjacent tumuli for Achilles and Patroclus, like the pair on either side of the track at the northern end of the Sigeum Peninsula, north-west of Troy. But Cook thought that Kesik Tepe, further south, was more likely to be the one which the Greeks attributed to Patroclus, with nearby Beşik (or Sivri) Tepe, which is actually a Neolithic site, much enlarged in Greek times using limestone boulders covered with earth, as the one honoured as Achilles' tomb.

The next tumulus to be erected was for Telamonian Ajax, who killed himself in shame when Achilles' armour was awarded, not to him for courage, but to Odysseus for cunning. Ajax's burial mound was on the north coast of the Troad; the sea washed it away but someone, probably the Emperor Hadrian, built a replacement further inland, and this can still be seen to the north of Troy.

Achilles was dead, but the Greeks battled on. Lesches's *Little Iliad* tells how the beleaguered Trojans were relieved by Eurypylus, son of Telephus, who arrived from the south with a great force of Mysians. Quintus Smyrnaeus's *The Fall of Troy*, written in the late AD 300s, but probably drawing, in part, at least, on ancient stories from the Trojan Cycle, takes up the tale. In book six we hear how Eurypylus chose his champions: Paris; 'fiery-souled' Aeneas; Polydamas; Pammon; Deiphobus, and Aethicus from Paphlagonia. These heroes swarmed out of Troy like bees, and 'the thunder-tramp of men and steeds, and clang of armour, rang to Heaven.' In book eight, Quintus relates how Aeneas fought the Greek Aristolochus, using a boulder to crush his helmet and the skull within.

Eurypylus led Paris and 'stout-hearted' Aeneas in a fresh charge against the Greeks. Aeneas hurled a rock, which sent the surviving Ajax tumbling down onto the dusty ground, but Fate has not ordained he should die that day. The Trojans surrounded Agamemnon and Menelaus, who fought like cornered lions until Teucer and Idomeneus staged a counter-attack. Teucer smote Aeneas's shield with his spear, and though Aeneas recoiled in sudden fear, the four layers of his shield held firm, so he was unharmed. In the ensuing battle, Aeneas slew two Cretans, Antimachus and Pheres.

Defender or Traitor?

The war went on. Both Achilles and Hector were dead, so the armies were too well balanced for one to gain the advantage. Odysseus therefore sailed to the island of Skyros, which lies in the Aegean between Troy and Greece, to fetch Achilles' son Neoptolemus. Though still a young boy, Neoptolemus had inherited his father's ferocity; clad in his father's armour, a gift from Odysseus, Neoptolemus slew Eurypylus, and the Trojans were again driven back behind their gates. Christa Wolf likened Troy at this time to a city of gravediggers waiting to bury themselves. She imagined Aeneas coming again to visit his former lover Cassandra, stroking the air above her head, and watching with her the way everything glows just before the end of the sunset. For Cassandra, the world seemed to be letting out its light before submitting willingly to the oncoming cold; but Aeneas told her that the glow was the world making its last valiant stand, as the darkness surged forth.

We see this same fortitude again in book ten of Quintus, in which Aeneas chided his colleague Polydamas. 'They call you wise,' said Aeneas,

> 'but you want us to suffer endless miseries cooped up in these walls. The Greeks will not lose heart, however long they tarry here, but when they see us skulking about they will attack with even greater fury. So more fool us if we stay hiding like this. Thebe will send no food, Maeonia no wine, and though our walls will not fall, we shall all surely starve within them. Let's not die through famine, but don our armour and fight for our sons and grey fathers! We are of Zeus's blood, and he may aid us yet; and if he turns his back on us, it's still better to die in the glory of the field than to starve agonisingly within these walls.'

This piece of stoic oratory anticipates the man Aeneas will become in Roman eyes; everyone who heard him cheered. Suddenly the men of Troy were mustered in their gleaming helms, with shields and spears – and Zeus, seeing them to ready for battle, awakened yet more courage within their hearts.

Bloodstained Fury loomed over the battlefield, with fire blasting from her mouth. The plain of Troy quaked as the armies clashed. Aeneas was the first to kill a Greek – Harpalion from Boetia, whom he stabbed below the waist. Then Aeneas plunged his barbed javelin into the throat of Hyllus, son of Thersander. Aeneas's friend Eurymenes rampaged through the Greek lines before being cut down; when the Greeks tried to strip him of his armour, Aeneas beat them off, like a vineyard tender, says Quintus, swatting wasps away from ripening grapes.

The Greeks were aided by another new arrival: Lesches's *Little Iliad* relates how Helenus, having been captured by Odysseus, prophesied that Troy could only be taken using Philoctetes's bow and arrows. Philoctetes ruled near Mount Pelion. He was the hero who ignited Hercules's funeral pyre on Mount Oeta and was given in reward the hero's massive bow and Hydra-poisoned arrows. Philoctetes sailed to Troy with the Greeks, but when they first landed on Tenedos he was bitten by a water snake sent by Apollo.

In Search of Aeneas

The wound became so foul-smelling that Philoctetes was sent to Lemnos. But now, hearing Helenus's prophecy, Diomedes hastened there to fetch him back and the Greeks' physician, Machaon, healed the wound.

Lesches (who places these events before the arrival and death of Eurypylus), relates how Philoctetes fired one of his poisoned arrows at Paris. At last the culprit who caused the entire Trojan War, but who was also Aeneas's cousin and friend, was killed. Menelaus mutilated Paris's body, but the Trojans recovered and buried it. A tumulus near the Balli Dağ used to be identified as Paris's, but it is too far from Troy to be plausible. Paris's brother Deiphobus, adds Lesches, married Paris's widow Helen, as a matter of principle. The Trojan War had been fought to keep her in the family, and in the family she remained.

Quintus now describes the last battles in the war. Hector, Paris and many of Priam's sons were dead by now, and others such as Helenus were in Greek hands, so Aeneas's star shone so much the brighter. In book eleven, Quintus describes Aeneas encountering two Cretans, Bremon from Knossos and Andromachus from Lyctus. Aeneas dragged them both down from their chariots, spearing one and striking the other with a rock, while his men seized their horses and chariots as Aeneas's prizes.

The struggle continued, and later we encounter Aeneas fighting shoulder to shoulder beside Antenor's son Eurymachus, who was the same age as him. They were flagging, so Apollo assumed the guise of Polymestor and roused them to greater efforts: 'Eurymachus, Aeneas, seed of Gods, do not flinch from the Greeks; you would daunt even Ares, were he to encounter you in battle, because Fate has spun long threads of destiny for you both.' Again, Quintus reveals his Roman bias, for by his day both Aeneas and members of Antenor's family were believed to have travelled to Italy. In book three of his own history, Dictys asserted Antenor's descent, via Cleomestra, from Zeus.

Apollo's words flooded Aeneas and Eurymachus's hearts with boundless courage and maddened their spirits, so they leapt upon the Greeks like wasps attacking bees. The Fates were overjoyed, Ares laughed and Enyo, the battle goddess, 'yelled horribly'. 'Loud their glancing armour clanged,' wrote Quintus, 'they stabbed, they hewed down hosts of foes untold with irresistible hands,' cutting through the Greeks like reapers harvesting corn or lions chasing sheep, smiting the backs of their fleeing foes. Aeneas's spear pierced the navel of Anthalus's son, pushing the innards out the other side and the young man fell, his teeth tearing at the earth in agony.

At last the tide seemed to have turned. The Greeks were ready to escape to their ships, but Achilles' son Neoptolemus rallied them. You remind me of starlings fleeing before a hawk, the boy scolded, stand and die, don't flee like women. Neoptolemus charged, his spear like lightning, with the Myrmidons behind him. Alone among the Trojans, Aeneas's doughty spirit persuaded him to hold his ground. Enyo held up the scales of Aeneas's fate, but saw that, unlike with Hector at the end of the *Iliad*, they were evenly balanced. Neoptolemus charged at Aeneas, but then something strange happened.

Defender or Traitor?

Thetys herself, the goddess-mother of Achilles, turned her grandson aside, so that he encountered and killed other Trojans, leaving Aeneas surprised, but unharmed. Why had Thetys acted so? Because of her reverence, claims Quintus, for Aeneas's mother, Aphrodite.

As the battle continued, Aeneas killed many Greeks. In the dusty confusion, men killed members of their own side by accident, and 'over the battle-slain the vultures joyed'. Now Athena emboldened the Greeks to make one final push, and the final siege began. Aphrodite, watching the rout, worried that Athena would ignore what Fate has decreed for Aeneas and kill him. So Aphrodite poured a thick mist about her son and snatched him away from the field: no more, says Quintus, would Aeneas fight the Greeks upon the plain of Troy.

Within Troy's walls, Aeneas mustered the city's defenders as the Greeks surged about below, 'From wall and tower with huge stones brave Aeneas made defence,' wrote Quintus. Looking down from the battlements, Aeneas saw the Greeks attacking the very walls themselves and trying to prise away the gates' hinges. He raised 'a stone like a thunderbolt, hurled it with uttermost strength, and dashed to death all whom it caught beneath the shields, as when a mountain's precipice-edge breaks off and falls on pasturing goats'. Rock after rock Aeneas hurled; he was like Zeus hurling lightning bolts, and the Greeks below quailed 'because a god gave [him] more than human strength'. The Greeks dared not even look up at Aeneas because the armour around 'his sinewy limbs flashed like the Heaven-born lightnings'. Beside Aeneas stood his mother's lover Ares, guiding each of Aeneas's boulders to strike fresh targets. Aeneas threw down anything he could find lying about on the walls, sending countless Greeks to their deaths, and never stopped encouraging his fellow Trojans to fight, 'for home, for wives, and their own souls, with a good heart'.

Pitted against Aeneas's 'giant might', however, was the unstoppable Neoptolemus, urging the Greeks to raise ladders against the walls. Brave Alcimedon from Locris reached the parapet first, but Aeneas dashed out his brains with a rock and then peppered his body with arrows as it fell back among his comrades below.

Amidst the chaos, Philoctetes marked the Trojan hero storming about the walls and aimed at Aeneas one of those swift arrows which, in ancient days, Hercules had dipped in the Hydra's poison. The Hydra was a multi-headed monster that lived in the swamp at Lerna, on the shore of the Argos gulf, 13 miles south-west of Mycenae. Killing it was the second of Hercules's twelve labours, and was thus among the earliest of his complex myths, almost certainly dating back to Mycenaean times. So the arrow, as related by the Roman Quintus in the AD 300s, flew at Aeneas straight out of the ancient kernel of Greek mythology.

Only divine intervention could save Aeneas. At the last instant, his mother Aphrodite deflected the poisoned arrow's path. It grazed the edge of Aeneas's shield, and struck a Trojan called Medon instead. In surprised wrath,

In Search of Aeneas

Aeneas flung another boulder down, but it narrowly missed Philoctetes and shattered the helmet of Toxaechmes instead. Philoctetes shouted up: 'Aeneas, you think you are a mighty champion fighting up there from the safety of a tower, like a woman, but why don't you come down here and test my prowess with spear and arrow like a man?' Valiant Aeneas made no reply; there was no time for duelling when the city was so badly beset by the Greek onslaught. It was thanks to Aeneas alone that the enemy could not break in. For a while at least, Troy was safe.

Quintus's stout-hearted Aeneas fought with a pure soul, but Dictys, in book four of his Trojan history, paints a different picture of what might have been going on within Troy's walls, as the Greeks clamoured beyond the gates and the madness of keeping Helen, despite everything, continued. Some Trojan nobles launched a plot to return her and the stolen valuables to Menelaus, and recruited Aeneas and Antenor's sons to their cause. It was only when Priam's son Deiphobus heard of this plot that he married Helen, to make sure she remained in Troy.

Matters came to a head at the next council meeting. We hear from Dictys of Aeneas 'heaping insults upon [Priam]' and the weary king giving way, enough to allow Antenor to open peace talks with the Greeks. Antenor was greeted warmly in the Greek camp and was promised great rewards if he would help them overcome the royal family's stubbornness concerning Helen. Antenor agreed: Priam's father Laomedon, he said, was well known for breaking his promises (to Hercules, for one) and this war had made Priam and his remaining sons similarly vindictive and mean. But the agreement they reached went way beyond Antenor's brief. He and Aeneas would help the Greeks enter Troy, so they could sack it and kill the remaining members of Priam's family. Antenor would receive half of Priam's wealth and one of his own sons would be the new king of Troy; Aeneas and his people would be offered a share in the spoils, and his house in Troy would be spared.

Antenor returned to Troy and the council reconvened. Dictys describes how Aeneas was the second last to appear, followed by Priam himself. Antenor made a long speech, lying to the council that the Greeks would go away if the Trojans handed over Helen and some gold. In return, the Greeks would send the gift of a wooden horse for Athena, to place in her temple on Troy's acropolis.

Priam broke down, tearing his hair, protesting that everyone was against him: do whatever you see fit, he sobbed, to end the war. When Antenor returned to the Greek camp at dawn the next day, Aeneas was with him, now fully conversant with the plot, and Priam's fate was sealed. Antenor and Aeneas returned to Troy with Odysseus and Diomedes. Locrian Ajax wanted to go too, but Aeneas forbade this, saying the Trojans were as afraid of him as they had been of Achilles. After some heated discussion over the amount of gold to be paid, a sham peace treaty was finalised. Aeneas and

Antenor oversaw the collection of the agreed sum in the temple of Apollo up on the acropolis. Aeneas's part in all this, says Dictys, had been prophesied by Helenus 'from an oracle of Anchises'.

This sorry portrayal of Aeneas as *proditor*, 'traitor', plotting with the Greeks for Priam's downfall, builds on Homer's hints at bad feeling between Aeneas and Priam's family in *Iliad* 13 and *Iliad* 20. Dionysius of Halicarnassus reports Menecrates of Xanthus (also known as Hegasianax of Alexandria), who probably lived in the 300s BC, as being the first writer to allege that Aeneas betrayed Troy to the Greeks, because he had been 'scorned by Paris and excluded from his prerogatives'.[3] By Menecrates's time, Aeneas was believed, from the writings of Hellanikos of Lesvos, to have founded Rome, so maybe this allegation of Aeneas's treachery was a Greek reproval born of Rome's fledgling power. Aeneas's treachery is not known in Greek or Roman art, but an AD 1400s Franco-Flemish tapestry in Madrid shows Odysseus pretending to parley with Priam, while in the background stands Aeneas, his hat pulled down over his eyes, whispering to Diomedes about the traitorous plot that is already afoot.[4]

The pro-Trojan Dares, probably writing to rebut Dictys, tells of a similar plot in books thirty-seven to forty, but spins it in a manner more favourable to Aeneas. With the Greeks at the gates, Antenor, Polydamas and Aeneas begged Priam to call a council. Retelling the story, Joseph of Exeter added that Polydamas was more eloquent than Antenor, but Aeneas had a voice that persuaded 'most gently of them all'.[5] Kings have fallen, Aeneas said; the army is ever more depleted, and the land itself laments so destructive a war. Antenor proposed returning Helen and her valuables to Menelaus, says Dares. Priam's son Amphimachus opposed Antenor with curses, but then 'Aeneas arose and tried to refute him. Speaking calmly and gently, but with persistence, he urged the Trojans to sue for peace with the Greeks' and Polydamas gave in. But Priam rose and hurled curses at Antenor and Aeneas: all this is your fault, he spat, because you failed in the mission to bring Hesione back from Greece, and you, Aeneas, helped Paris carry off Helen and the booty. You started the war, Priam concluded irrationally, so I will not listen to your peace plans now. Joseph of Exeter, likewise, imagined Priam ranting that Antenor had urged war and now wanted peace, while *impious* Aeneas had gone off cheerfully with Paris to raid Lacedaemonia, but now hoped to curry favour with the Greeks by handing Helen back to them.[6]

Later that day, says Dares, Antenor, Polydamas, Ucalegon (a Trojan elder mentioned in *Iliad* 3) and Dolon met in secret (Dares had forgotten that Dolon died in *Iliad* 10). They were appalled by the king's stubbornness when Troy was in such peril. They sent for Aeneas and together they hatched a plan to 'betray their country, and in such a way that they might safeguard themselves and their families'; later, they brought Anchises into the plot, too. Polydamas was despatched to inform Agamemnon of their plans, and he told the Greeks the Trojan watchword. The Greeks swore not to harm the plotters, their families or property. Polydamas told the Greeks to come

In Search of Aeneas

at night to the Scaean Gate: 'Antenor and Aeneas would be in charge of the guard at this point, and they would open the bolt and raise a torch as the sign for attack.'

Hero, villain or pragmatist, these stories by Menecrates of Xanthus, Quintus, Dictys and Dares are all portraits of how a Trojan aristocrat might have acted under the extreme stress of a seemingly endless siege. Both Dictys and Dares involve Aeneas in plots to end the war. It seems shocking, even though Priam and his remaining sons' irrational refusal to make terms seemed set to bring destruction on them all. Yet in these accounts, Aeneas had a higher purpose: by sacrificing Priam's family and Troy itself, Aeneas might save the Dardanian people from destruction – and of course his own family.

But all this plotting seems to have been a late invention, starting with Menecrates of Xanthus, expanded by the anti-Trojan (and anti-Roman) Dictys, and then somewhat ameliorated, or justified, by Dares. In the earliest versions, however, Aeneas was innocent of plotting and the deception was entirely on the Greek side. In *Odyssey* 8, Odysseus takes credit for the idea of filling Epeios's wooden horse with heroes and tricking the Trojans into taking it inside the walls and says nothing of any compliance with Trojan plotters.

However Aeneas really acted, the outcome was the same.

20

The Fall of Troy

Dares claims that the Scaean Gate's exterior was carved with a horse's head. But in all other versions, the Greeks' means of ingress into Troy was within the famous wooden horse. According to Lesches, Epeios, the Greek who built the horse, was inspired to do so by Athena. A life-size replica of the horse stands at the entrance of Troy to this day, and a miniature version, one of millions sold at Troy to visitors, stands on my desk as I write this.

Dictys relates how the Greeks hauled the wooden horse up to Troy's walls, set fire to their camp and pretended to sail away. They hid their ships, adds Lesches, behind the island of Tenedos. The Trojans, believing Aeneas and Antenor's story that the horse was an innocent offering for Athena, tore down a section of wall to pull it into the city. On the east side of the upper city of Troy, the usual, regular masonry of wall gives way to a ten-foot section filled with rubble. Some guides mischievously point to this as the very place where the horse was brought in; but Luce, as reported earlier, thinks this was the Scaean Gate itself, which the Trojans blocked up when Patroclus assaulted the city in *Iliad* 16.

Lesches describes the Trojans holding council around the horse and eventually deciding to keep it. Arctinus, like Lesches, drawing on the same ancient material as Homer, relates the debate in detail. Some wanted to push the horse off 'the cliff' (presumably, the steep northern scarp of Troy's hill); or to set fire to it. But finally it was agreed that the horse was sacred to Athena, so the Trojans began feasting and celebrating around it. Cassandra foresaw what would follow, and spoke up, but it was fated that her prophecies would never be believed, and the Trojans ignored her. The Trojan priest Laocoön, likewise, foresaw doom and believed that the horse was full of soldiers. Nobody believed him either, so Apollo sent two serpents swimming across the sea from 'nearby islands', including, presumably, Tenedos. These serpents attacked Laocoön and his two sons and strangled them to death. The scene is depicted in the famous Hellenistic sculpture unearthed in Rome in 1506, now on display in the Vatican Museum, with numerous copies elsewhere, showing the three men writhing in agony as the serpent constricts them. But still, nobody heeded the warnings.

The Trojan horse remains a by-word for deceitful entry, used most commonly nowadays in the context of 'Trojan' computer viruses, which people are tricked into downloading, and which then wreak havoc within computers. The original version was more destructive still. It was not for nothing that, in *Aeneid* 2, Aeneas so famously repeated Laocoön's warning: to be fearful of Greeks bearing gifts.

As torches flared and drunken Trojans staggered about, ecstatic that the war appeared to be over, a god filled Helen and Deiphobus with suspicion. They circled the horse thrice, as Menelaus recalls in *Odyssey* 4, with Helen whispering the names of the heroes inside in voices resembling their own wives. The heroes longed to answer her; Anticlus almost did so, but clever Odysseus clapped his hand over his mouth – and the Greeks' deceit remained secret.

'Mythological figures live many lives, die many deaths, but in each of these lives and deaths all the others are present, and we can hear their echo.'[1] So wrote Roberto Calasso. In this instance, Aeneas cannot oppose Fate by preventing Troy's destruction, but in no version of the story does he perish with the city. He is always – as Poseidon prophesised in *Iliad* 20 – destined to survive. But the manner in which he does so varies enormously in the different sources. So, like a river nearing its delta, Aeneas's life now divides into a number of different branches, flowing towards several widely different futures for him and, by implication, for the wider world. And the contradictions between these different lives and deaths creates, for us, a dissonance not incompatible with the chaos of a city under destruction.

Arctinus relates how the Trojans, drunk with joy, ignored all the warning signs, but Aeneas and his people recognised the dire omen of Laocoön's death and slipped away safely to Dardania while the others were still carousing. Aeneas's disaffection with Priam's family is plain from the *Iliad*: in these tales of Aeneas's early escape from Troy lie, perhaps, the roots of those later stories of plots found in Dictys and Dares.

Here, too, lie the roots of Wolf's Aeneas, who also leaves before Troy falls. He was desperate to take Cassandra with him, 'to found a new Troy somewhere else. Begin again from the beginning'. But Cassandra knew, just as Wolf always knew, that her destiny was to die as a result of Troy's fall, while Aeneas's fate was to survive. Their love stood no chance against 'a time that needs heroes... I saw by your eyes that you had understood me' said Cassandra, as they parted. 'I cannot love a hero. I do not want to see you being transformed into a statue.' And so Aeneas and Cassandra watched the final glow of sunset together for the last time, and bade each other farewell.

These stories, in which Aeneas left Troy before the massacre began, are exceptions; most assert that he was still there, as the revelry abated and

The Fall of Troy

the Trojans sank into a drunken torpor. Sinon, a Greek who had gained admission to Troy by pretending to be a defector, used a flaming torch to alert the Greek fleet that the time had come. The Greek army crept up to the city walls, and in the meantime the heroes inside the horse climbed out and opened the gates. And so began the sack of Troy.

Hellanikos of Lesbos's *Troika*, written in the 400s BC, but perhaps retelling a story from the old Trojan Cycle, relates how Aeneas tried to defend Troy's acropolis, through whose high walls and ruined gates we can still walk today, imagining the flames, screams and bloodshed of that momentous night that changed the world. Varro (116-27 BC) related, in book two of his *Histories*, how Aeneas 'occupied the citadel with a large number of persons after Troy had been captured'.[2] Dionysius of Halicarnassus reports, likewise, how, as the Greeks destroyed the lower city, Aeneas withdrew his Dardanians and also the Ophrynians (the men of Ophryneion on the north coast of the Troad), into Troy's acropolis. Here, brave Aeneas made his last stand.[3]

Menecrates of Xanthus (alias Hegasianax of Alexandria), who alleged that Aeneas had sided with the Greeks, says that Aeneas used the sack of Troy as a means of overthrowing Priam and 'became one of the Greeks'. That ambiguous statement perhaps helped inspire later stories, to which we shall return later, of Aeneas settling in Arcadia in the central Peloponnese. But earlier, Lesches's *Little Iliad* says that having fought bravely to defend Troy, Aeneas was captured by the Greeks. When Neoptolemus sailed back to 'Pharsalia, Achilles' homeland', his ship was laden with slaves, including Hector's widow Andromache, and 'Aeneas himself, the famous son of Anchises, the horse-tamer'.[4]

It is not just mythology that speaks of slaves being taken back to Greece from Troy. Linear B tablets from Pylos and Thebes include 'Tros' and 'Troia' in lists of slaves, and there were probably Trojan slaves elsewhere in Greece. We may imagine a broken Aeneas, toiling in Neoptolemus's fields in Phthia or Epiros, longing in vain for his native Dardania, full of regrets that he had not met a glorious death in battle. In that alternative future, Aeneas never sailed to Italy and so, within the world of mythology, there was never any Rome – and therefore no Roman Britain either.

In most other versions, Aeneas realised that his efforts to defend Troy were hopeless, and managed to escape with his family. Hellanikos of Lesvos reported how Aeneas, realising his efforts to defend the upper city were futile, fled to Mount Ida. A fragment of Ennius's Roman *Annales*, quoted by Festus, reads 'but be sure to do what your father pleads for in prayers with you.' It has been suggested that the voice here was Aphrodite's, urging Aeneas to obey his father Anchises's prayers for him to abandon his heroic defence of the citadel, and escape. And 'reasoning that he could not hold out [in the citadel] indefinitely', wrote Dionysius, Aeneas evacuated the women, children and elderly, along with Troy's sacred treasures, sending them out under armed guard, presumably via the citadel's steep northern side, and away to the Dardanian mountains. Then, when Neoptolemus finally broke through the citadel's gates, Aeneas organised an ordered retreat of his army, guarding his father's best chariots, the statues of Troy's gods, and his own wife and children – all of which was possible because the Greeks were so intent on plunder that they let the people go.[5]

But how was it really possible for Aeneas to escape with his father and son, and his household gods, and so many of his people? The *Origo Gentis Romanae* in the Bodleian Library's *Codex Oxoniensis*, dated to about AD 380, tried to fashion a clear narrative out of the many contradictory stories of Rome's origins and Aeneas's myth, and in doing so it quoted, or misquoted, from many old and now otherwise lost sources. One of these is Alexander of Ephesus's *Marsic War*, written about the first century BC. This tells, allegedly, how Aeneas tried to leave Troy by night 'carrying his household gods before him and his father Anchises on his shoulders and dragging his little son by the hand' because the city 'had been betrayed to the Achaeans by Antenor and other leaders'. When dawn broke, Aeneas was apprehended, but Agamemnon allowed him to leave 'because he [Aeneas] had been so greatly weighed down by a burden of piety'.

In Varro, as reported by the Veronese scholiast on the *Aeneid*, we find a similar idea of Greek complicity in Aeneas's escape: 'by great [good will] of the enemy [Aeneas obtained] the right to leave... Aeneas [carried] his father on his neck, and the Achaeans [looking in amazement] on his devotion, granted him the opportunity of returning to Troy.' As a result, Aeneas returned and rescued their household gods, 'consisting of images made of wood or stone, and also of teracotta'.[6] This story was repeated in the *Varia Historia* of Aelian (AD *c.* 175-*c.* 235).[7] The Greeks allowed each Trojan to rescue a single possession, so Aeneas took his household gods. The Greeks were so impressed by Aeneas's piety that they allowed him a second possession, whereupon he carried out his father, and this amazed the Greeks so much that they let him to go back and take everything he owned – proving, Aelian moralised, that even mortal enemies could be made mild when faced with sufficient evidence of piety.

In similar vein, Pseudo-Xenophon's *Cynegeticus* asserted that, due to the virtues instilled in him by Chiron the centaur, Aeneas 'saved the gods of his father's and his mother's family, and withal his father himself; wherefore he bore away fame for his piety, so that to him alone, among all the vanquished at Troy, even the enemy granted not to be despoiled'. This was either a Roman view, or one that was inspired, at least, by the Romans' reverence for him; they wished to believe that if the Greeks spared Aeneas, it was not because of any shady deals he had struck with them, but because of his piety. The Vatican *Epitome* to Pseudo-Apollodorus's *Bibliotheka* asserts, likewise, that Aeneas escaped with his family because the Greeks respected his piety; again, this was probably a Roman interpolation into the older work.[8]

For some writers, recalling Aeneas's earlier disputes with Priam over the justice of the war, this was all too good to be true. For them, Aeneas's escape proved that he had been a *proditor*, a traitor reaping his reward for betraying the king. Thus, the *Origo*'s writer added that 'in truth', Lutatius Catulus, who was a Roman consul in 102 BC, had written that Aeneas joined Antenor in being 'a traitor to his fatherland'. The anti-Roman Dictys wrote that the Greeks placed guards outside the houses of Aeneas and Antenor to stop them being pillaged.[9] In that version, we can only imagine Aeneas and Antenor, who had aided the Greeks, cowered cravenly inside their houses, listening to the sounds of their city being burned and of their countrymen being slaughtered.

In most versions, Aeneas escaped the city, and in dramatic fashion. The sack of Troy, and Aeneas's escape, have inspired artists ever since to create night-time scenes in which lurid flames stand out sharp against the smoke-blackened sky as fires consume magnificent Classical temples or Gothic towers; fantastic cities which helped inspire Tolkien's Gondor and countless cityscapes imagined in modern computer games. Here and there, Greeks in high-plumed helmets slaughter cowering Trojans; Adam Elsheimer's *The Burning of Troy* (*c.* 1602) seems to draw on Hieronymus Bosch's visions of Hell, filling burning Troy with writhing, naked bodies.[10] Somewhere in these scenes there is always Aeneas, carrying his father Anchises, leading his son Ascanius by the hand, and accompanied by Aphrodite, or his wife Creusa, the daughter of Priam; or Creusa can be seen already lost, about to meet her fate as the Greeks destroy Troy and massacre its inhabitants. Sometimes, Aeneas and his family are placed prominently in the foreground. Other times, they can be spotted in the distance, tiny figures attempting to flee the destruction around them.

At the nexus between this comparatively recent art and the ancient, written accounts of Arctinus, Dionysius and the rest, stands Virgil's *Aeneid*. Virgil's retelling of Aeneas's escape inspired most of the paintings that followed, and it drew selectively on all the tradition that came before. Virgil's words, like purifying fire, expunged any notion of Aeneas's treachery, or of Greek complicity in Aeneas's departure. They confirmed Aeneas's flight as an act of heroism. And thus, now, we enter into the same, willing pact with Virgil with which Western minds have been engaged – for marginally longer than they have been influenced by Christianity – in his reworking of the myth of Aeneas.

21

Of Fire and Flood

'What tongue shall unfold that night's havoc, that night's slaughter? What eye match our disasters with tears? An ancient city was falling, a queenly city for many years, and helpless frames lay without number, scattered in streets and homes and the hallowed precincts' of the temples on Troy's acropolis.

Thus, in the second book of Virgil's *Aeneid*, Aeneas recounted to Dido the dreadful night when his world changed for ever. In Virgil's version, Aeneas was no different to the rest of the Trojans who, presented with the Trojan horse, failed to heed Laocoön or Cassandra, and festooned the city's temples joyfully with festal boughs. But after the celebration, as Aeneas slept in his father's house, Hector appeared in his dreams. 'Flee, goddess-born', Hector told him. You have done all you could for Troy and Priam: now, 'Troy bequeaths to thy keeping her holy things and gods of her homes: these take, that they may share thy destiny.' Go, bids Hector, and dwell in the city you are destined to establish, far across the seas.

Then noise awakened Aeneas. He recalled to Dido how he stood on the roof and saw Troy burning like a cornfield around him. He is in Virgil's hands now, and is about to 'step out of Homer's world and become the first Roman', as R. D. Williams wrote, but he 'has not yet begun to learn that his mission must preclude the glorious death' of a hero, or that 'his life is not his own to give away'.[1] So, like a pure, Homeric hero, Aeneas ignored Hector's prophecy and resolved to die in this last battle. Rallying his friends Rhipeus, Epytus, Hypanis and Dymas, and brave young Coroebus, he led them into the midst of the fighting.

They were like frenzied wolves; like Achilles. Encountering a band of Greeks, they slaughtered them and donned their armour, so they could move about the city unsuspected, killing enemies at will. They saw Cassandra being dragged from Athena's temple by the hair and fell upon her captors, but they were assailed by fellow Trojans on the temple roof above them who, fooled by their Greek helms, flung spears down at them. Then a party of

Greeks, led by Ajax himself, attacked. Most of Aeneas's companions were killed; he could not prevent Cassandra's enslavement. Later, Wolf imagines her as a prisoner, watching Aeneas escaping, and being secretly glad that she would live on, in some small way, through his memories of her. Cassandra's fate, in most versions, was slavery and then death in Mycenae, but there was a family of Molossian consuls almost a thousand years later who claimed descent from her, so maybe her prophetic blood lived on in Greece after all.[2]

Having failed to rescue Cassandra, says Virgil, Aeneas and his remaining men saw Priam's palace under siege and tried to save it. Entering by a secret doorway, they hurried to the roof and toppled its high tower, so that it crashed down upon the Greeks below. But they were too late: Neoptolemus, like a 'serpent fed on poisonous herbage ... drunken from blood' led an unstoppable charge, like 'the foaming river, when, barriers burst, it goes forth', slaughtering all before him.

Old Priam, recalled Virgil's Aeneas, had donned the armour of his youth and clutched his sword in his palsied hand. At the altar of Troy's household gods, by the bay tree in the palace's central courtyard, the old king found Hecuba and his daughters; they witnessed his son Polites, mortally wounded by Neoptolemus, collapse and die before their eyes. Proud Priam berated Neoptolemus for dishonouring Achilles, who treated him with more respect, but was dragged bodily to the altar. In Shakespeare's *Hamlet*, Hamlet and one of his players expand on the story, describing how Pyrrhus (Neoptolemus) seemed to hesitate; as his sword swept down it 'seem'd i[n]' the air to stick', leaving him 'like a neutral to his will and matter'. But then, as a breaking storm seems to pause before the first clap of thunder, resolution returned and the sword fell on Priam 'like the Cyclops' hammers',[3] and Neoptolemus slashed off king Priam's head.

Suddenly, Virgil's Aeneas had a warning vision of his own family being put to the sword as well, and realised he must save them. As he turned to go, he spotted Helen, 'crouching mute' in the shrine of Hestia. Tears of fear and remorse trickled down her lovely face and glistened in the lurid glare of the flames. Aeneas imagined her sailing home to Greece, attended by a throng of enslaved Trojan women. Filled with fury, he resolved to slaughter her. An AD 1400s manuscript of the *Aeneid* in the British Library includes a vignette of Aeneas cornering Helen, his sword raised high, ready to terminate her destructive life.[4] Servius tells us that Virgil's literary executors, Varius and Tucca, cut this event out of the *Aeneid*, as they thought it shameful that pious Aeneas should even have considered killing a woman; but by quoting these same edited lines, Servius saved them. Robert Fagles, for one, thought them genuine,[5] and they appear in his excellent modern translation of the *Aeneid*.

Aeneas told Dido how, as he made to kill Helen, 'my gracious mother, never erst so bright to my eyes, offered herself to view, and in pure radiance flashed through the night – goddess confessed, in beauty and stature.' Virgil implies that Aeneas had seen Aphrodite before, but this is the first time we hear for sure of him setting eyes on his mother's radiance. Aphrodite urged him not to waste his anger on 'the loathed beauty of Spartan Helen'. Heaven itself decreed that Troy should be laid waste in this way, Aphrodite explained, and she removed the clouds which obscured mortal sight, so that Aeneas could see Poseidon shaking the walls with his trident, and Hera, Athena, and even Zeus himself, urging on the Greeks. You can do nothing here, Aphrodite told Aeneas; if it were not for me, your family would be dead already. Hasten to rescue them while you still can.

Aphrodite did not add what dire consequences would have befallen Aeneas if he had killed Helen, for she was Zeus's daughter. Had Helen died at Aeneas's hand, Zeus would surely have doomed him, regardless of what Fate had in store. But such a caution was unnecessary. Aeneas's shock at seeing the gods tearing Troy apart was immense, and that alchemy which Virgil performed on Aeneas begins to work. Reason, and obedience to Fate, started to override Aeneas's Homeric rawness; he lowered his sword and let Helen live.

Virgil imagined Anchises's palace being in a tucked-away part of the acropolis. Here, Aeneas found his wife Creusa; their little son Ascanius, and his crippled father Anchises. Leave me behind, urged old Anchises, for since I was smitten long ago by Zeus's thunderbolt, I have been old and useless. Aeneas despaired that they would all die and, see-sawing back to his Homeric persona, he resolved to gather his remaining men and re-join the battle; at least his family's deaths would not be unavenged. An etching after Caracci shows their home in turmoil; Anchises sits woefully on a couch draped in cloth and little Ascanius looks bewildered, while Creusa kneels, begging restraint on Aeneas who, in full armour, is hurrying out.[6]

Suddenly, a heavenly flame blazed around their son Ascanius's head. Aeneas and Creusa panicked and tried to quench it with water, but Anchises recognised it as a sign and beseeched Zeus to confirm this. Thunder boomed and a falling star shot through the sky. It sunk, resplendent, onto the distant slopes of Mount Ida – a sign from Heaven that the family must indeed abandon the burning city.

Aeneas's resolve to leave was now firm, and Anchises abandoned his own determination to remain behind. Aeneas draped a lion skin over his shoulders; later, Virgil emphasises Aeneas's piety, but in this emergency he bestows on Aeneas the emblematic costume of Hercules, the paragon of fighters. And then, onto his heroic shoulders, Aeneas hoisted Anchises and bade him carry the images of the household gods of Troy which, conveniently, had been brought to their house earlier in the chapter. Aeneas took little Ascanius's hand and bade Creusa follow close behind. While he owed his and his family's survival to his obedience to his mother Aphrodite, it is Aeneas's filial piety in shouldering of the burden of his father Anchises that will define him for ever more. Aeneas is usually depicted thus, 'not in the splendid isolation of a Hercules or Achilles', as Hardie wrote,[7] but carrying his father, a metaphor for his transmission of culture from east to west. On artefacts from all across the ancient world, when we see one man stooping under the burden of another, it is invariably Aeneas, carrying Anchises out of burning Troy.

The flight of Aeneas and his family was depicted countless times in Greek art, with many subtle variations, from at least the 500s BC onwards. The Iliupersis kalyx-krater (wine bowl) shows Aeneas carrying his father Anchises (who holds a crutch), with his wife Creusa behind him, all following a man (perhaps Antenor) whose shield depicts a snake.[8] A cup by the Pythocles painter shows a chaotic scene of fighting, amidst which a soldier, whether Greek or Trojan we cannot tell, leads a robed woman – Creusa, perhaps; then comes armed Aeneas, stooping under the weight of Anchises; and behind him an outlandishly dressed Phrygian archer, who tries to ward off a pursuing Greek warrior.[9]

Similarly, a white lekythos (oil jar) from Gela, Sicily, shows a young Aeneas in full armour, leading his robed father (again with a crutch) by the wrist, in a kindly manner, a scene that seems to emphasise the contrast between youth and age.[10] On another lekythos from Gela, helmeted Aeneas strides along with Anchises on his shoulders; no warriors interfere, and Aphrodite goes before them, leading the way, while Creusa hurries along behind.[11] A black-figured amphora from Vulci shows helmeted Aeneas bearing two spears, carrying Anchises with his crutch and led by Aphrodite, while behind them an archer runs in the opposite direction.[12] Another black-figure amphora from Gela, Sicily, shows Aeneas carrying white-bearded Anchises, again in very similar style, but without any accompanying figures this time. As Anchises looks back, we may imagine that he sees the burning city of his ancestors behind him.[13] An Attik hydria (a three-handled pitcher) shows Aeneas and Anchises, both looking back anxiously. They are accompanied by Aeneas's little son Ascanius and two women, and are leaving the city. Two soldiers with high-crested helms and an archer escort them to safety.[14]

Aeneas's flight from Troy was even depicted on the Acropolis in Athens, on the twenty-eighth metope on the north side of the Parthenon. Created in the 400s BC, and now badly worn, this metope shows Aeneas with sword drawn, naked save for his cloak, crested helmet and shield, which he holds protectively behind his nude son, with his father leaning on his shoulder and Creusa following along behind.[15]

Depictions of this sort were familiar to all Romans from childhood; they were engrained in their minds, even more so than members of our generations know the characters from *Star Wars* or *Harry Potter*. They were the stuff on which Virgil drew, as he reimagined that fateful night as Troy burned. Instead of seeking out the battle, Aeneas had now to skulk fearfully down its darkest paths. When he looked back, it was too late: Creusa had vanished. Hastily, Aeneas ushered his father and son to the safety of a temple of Demeter, which Virgil imagined standing in a secluded place outside the city walls. Demeter was the deity of the fertile plough-lands, so it was reasonable to imagine her being worshipped where the city met the fields. The site of such a temple has not been identified and may have existed only in Virgil's imagination, but there are a few fragments from a temple in the graveyard at New Kalafat, just south of Troy, and Mr Ergen of the Iris Hotel, for one, is convinced that these came from that very same temple of Demeter.

It was thus that Virgil defined Aeneas's flight. As Tiberius Claudius Donatus wrote in about AD 430, Virgil 'eliminates the accusation [of treason and cowardice], and then turns it [the flight] into praise', making fleeing Aeneas 'a worthy parent and ancestor of Augustus' and 'founder of the imperium Romanum ... free of all blame ... the worthy object of great praise'.[16]

Retelling the story about 300 years after Virgil, and deeply influenced by him, Quintus, in book thirteen of his *The Fall of Troy*, likens Aeneas to a helmsman in a storm who, realising his ship is sinking and he can do no more to save it, seeks a rowing boat in which to escape. Aeneas had spent the night fighting in the streets to save Troy but could do no more. He raised his aged father onto his shoulders and took his young son Ascanius's soft hand, trampling over dead bodies to escape the carnage, while Aphrodite helped by cleaving walls of flame asunder and deflecting Greek arrows and javelins. The Greek soothsayer Calchas saw them go, and he urged the Greeks not to shoot at Aeneas's noble head. Calchas told them:

> Fated he is by the high gods' decree to pass from Xanthus [Skamander], and by Tiber's flood to found a city holy and glorious through all time, and to rule o'er tribes of men far-sundered. Of his seed shall lords of Earth rule from the rising to the setting sun. Yea, with the Immortals ever shall he dwell, who is son of Aphrodite lovely-tressed. From him too is it meet we hold our hands because he hath preferred his father and son to gold, to all things that might profit a man who fleeth exiled to an alien land. This one night hath revealed to us a man faithful to death to his father and his child.

Through Calchas's words, Quintus here endorses centuries of myth-making which had elapsed since Homer's time; he justifies his own decision to praise Aeneas as the paragon of pious heroes.

Quintus makes no mention of Creusa, but back in *Aeneid* 2, having left Anchises and Ascanius at the temple of Demeter outside the city walls, Aeneas hurried back into Troy and searched for her everywhere. Their home was in flames, and on the acropolis he saw the Greeks mustering captured boys and women into lines. Time and again Aeneas cried Creusa's name, but then her shade appeared before him, making his hair rise in fright. A print of 1781 by Valentine Green, after Maria Cosway, shows Aeneas, dark and armoured against the blackness of night, running forward to try to embrace Creusa, but she floats away, nude and seductive below her billowing veil, brighter in death than even burning Troy beyond.[17]

Do not grieve for me, she says; I was fortunate indeed to have been 'a daughter [i.e., descendant, via her father Priam] of Dardanos, who was wedded to the seed of Aphrodite'; her death is the will of Zeus.

Virgil drew on tradition here: while Creusa is often shown in Greek art in the act of escaping with Aeneas, it is hard to tell whether she will remain with him or be lost before the family reaches safety. An Attik lekythos from Villa Pace al Piombo in Camarina, Sicily, shows Aeneas stooping under Anchises's weight while Aphrodite raises her arm, as if urging him to hurry, and white-bearded Anchises looks back to where Creusa has already turned, waving farewell to the men she knows she is fated not to follow.[18] A virtually identical scene is on a black-figured amphora in the British Museum, said to be from Vulci.[19] Once separated, Creusa either died or was enslaved along with many of the other Trojan women. Pausanias reports that Polygnotos's painting at Delphi, which showed the enslaved Trojan women, included Creusa. But Pausanias adds that 'the story is told that the mother of the gods [the Great Mother] and Aphrodite rescued her from slavery among the Greeks, as she was, of course, the wife of Aeneas.'[20] What became of her then is not clear, unless his implication is that they spirited her up to Olympus.

For Virgil, Creusa's death was important because, as her shade told him, 'queenly bride' (Lavinia) awaited him at his journey's end, 'where the Tiber flows through fertile fields'. So, like Aphrodite and Hector's ghost, Creusa's ghost also urged Aeneas on towards his destiny in the west. Just before dawn, therefore, Aeneas escaped for the second time from the burning city of Troy.

Troy lay smouldering in ruins, and the fertile earth of the Troad groaned under the weight of dead bodies – but for what? Everything, the Greeks believed, from the abductions of Hesione and Helen, right down to Aeneas's escape, had been dictated by Fate, with Zeus as the complicit puppet-master of the entire chain of events. In *Iliad* 6, Helen herself told Hector what was clearly Homer's own view, that Zeus had doomed both him and Paris, and by inference all those who died at Troy, 'to be a theme of song among those that shall be born hereafter'. Thus did Homer glorify his own profession.

Echoing this, the great Cretan novelist Nikos Kazantzakis wrote in his 1961 novel *Report to Greco*: 'What does it matter if Troy was reduced to ashes and Priam and his sons killed? In what way would the world have benefited, and how much poorer man's soul would be, if Troy had continued to live in happiness and if Homer had not come along to convert the slaughter into immortal hexameters? A statue, a verse, a tragedy, a painting – these are the supreme memorials man has erected on Earth.'[21]

By falling, Troy became vastly more than it ever was when it stood; a fixed point, blazing bright in the past, to the extent that, as Plato reported in *The Apology*, when Socrates faced the Athenian judges who wished to sentence him to death, he said he would welcome his early passage down to Hades, for 'what would not a man give, O judges, to be able to examine [in Hades] the leader of the great Trojan expedition.'

For Roberto Calasso, it was not just that Troy would be remembered in song, but that such songs would recall the glory of the heroes who had died there, especially that of Achilles. 'Zeus's plan seems appalling, but the

In Search of Aeneas

extermination of a whole race turns out to be a necessary step in exalting the glory of a single person, Achilles ... [and] to bestow glory on a hero means to bestow it on all the heroes.' Yet, Calasso explained, Homer and his successors, in singing of Troy, were benefiting themselves:

> Thanks to the death of the heroes, men would win themselves a bond with time... Zeus wanted the death of the heroes to be a new death. What had death meant until now? Being covered once again by the earth. But, with the heroes, death coincided with the evocation of glory. Glory was something you could breathe now. The men of the iron age would not be composed in body and mind as the heroes had been, but they moved in an air that was drenched with glory.[22]

Everyone who lived in Homer's time and beyond, including us, might fear death, but we can look back to Troy and try to draw down to ourselves some of that immortal glory which mankind willingly conjured up and bestowed on Troy's heroes. And nobody sought to clothe themselves in that hand-me-down immortality from a bygone age more than those who claimed descent from the heroes who fell there – not least from Troy's greatest survivor: Aeneas.

That drenching of the future in glory may have been the effect of the Trojan War, but it was not the war's true purpose. In the end, because Aeneas's descendants were the only ones who benefited from the fall of Troy, the logographer Akusilaus asserted in the 500s BC that Aphrodite had engineered the entire conflict, solely to establish Aeneas in power in the Troad.[23]

That is not a view we hear repeated very often. But there was a much more prevalent opinion, found across Greek literature from the *Catalogue of Women* to Euripides and beyond, and which touches a nerve with us now in our era of population increase: that the 'storm and strife' of the Trojan War was engineered by Zeus to cleanse the world of excess population, not least of the race of heroes, born through the shameful unions of deities and mortals. For the Greeks, the Trojan War was a defining event in the history of their world. The Greek colonisation of the Anatolian islands and coast, which created Homer's world, was a direct result of the collapse of the Mycenaean world, which at least coincided with, and may actually have been caused by, the Trojan War. The Greek myths told of a shining race of heroes, born of deities and mortals, who by Homer's time were remembered only in song, so some explanation was needed for what had happened to them. The Trojan War, again, was the answer.

There is a confusion in the sources as to whether Zeus intended to cleanse the world of just the heroes, or of almost everyone. This is because, besides seeking to answer their own immediate questions, the Greeks spun their myths out of a variety of traditions from Greece and the Near East. The Hebrews in Palestine, 700 miles to the south-east of Troy, had similar tales, repeated in *Genesis*, about the sinfulness of ancient times, when 'the sons of [the Hebrew God] Yahweh' took 'the daughters of men' as their wives, resulting in 'the Gibborim who were of old, the men of renown', presumably their equivalent of the Greek heroes.[24] In his desire to end this sinfulness, and also the general sinfulness of humanity, Yahweh engineered not the Trojan War, but the Great Flood, which only pious Noah and his family survived.

The stories of the Trojan War and the Great Flood existed in parallel and influenced each other. The genealogical structure of *Genesis*, which includes the flood story, may in part have been influenced by the *Catalogue of Women*; and the *Catalogue*, in turn, echoes the flood story with Zeus's 'storm and strife'. The flood story itself, however, is much older than the Trojan cycle, for it appears in the Mesopotamian tale of *Gilgamesh*. The earliest surviving version of *Gilgamesh*, found on cuneiform tablets at Babylon, dates from about the same century as the Trojan War, but it clearly relates a much older tradition. It tells of Gilgamesh, king of Uruk, who undertook a pilgrimage to find his ancestor, Uta-napishtim who, long ago, survived a flood sent by the gods to wipe out humanity. Uta-napishtim explained to Gilgamesh that the first humans had been created by the gods out of clay, but they had bred and become far too numerous. The noise of human cities kept the gods awake at night, so the flood was sent to destroy them. The supreme god, Ea, took pity on Uta-napishtim and his followers and allowed them to survive in a boat. But Ea decreed that, henceforth, humanity's numbers would be kept in check by infant mortality, infertility, and religious celibacy. There was no Biblical sinfulness here, and no interbreeding of gods and men to bring to an end; this older story simply relates how the gods dealt with overpopulation by engineering a cataclysm in the form of a flood. Gilgamesh's story comforted its listeners by assuring them that death was a necessary part of the natural order; without it, humanity's weight would indeed burden the Earth intolerably. Death, therefore, served a higher purpose.

Before the Trojan War, both Aeneas's Troad and Mycenaean Greece probably had their own versions of this same, very ancient flood story. But while it took on new life as a moral tale in *Genesis* and set the tone for the entire Old Testament, the flood story's impact and importance in Greece had dissipated by Homer's time. We hear about it in the Greek myths, but not as a world-changing event. Dardanos was said to have survived such a flood, as we shall see presently. Elsewhere in Greek mythology, the flood covered all of Greece and was survived only by Deucalion, who, coincidentally or not, was a first cousin of Dardanos's mother Elektra. Deucalion's 'ark' eventually settled on the peak of Mount Parnassos above Delphi, and from the seeds sown by him and his wife sprung up an ancient people called the Leleges. But in these Greek versions, the flood was not the single most important defining event in the ancient past as it was in *Gilgamesh*, or *Genesis*.

In his *Olympiai*, Pindar (d. 443 BC) tried to re-synchronise Greek mythology with eastern tradition by claiming that not just the Leleges, but *all* modern humanity derived from Deucalion's seeds, but by then Greek mythology had grown too complex for this to be widely accepted. Dardanos and his descendants, who existed independently of Deucalion and his seeds, could not be fitted into this scheme and nor could many other mythological genealogies, such as that of the Inachid kings of Argos, whose earliest ancestors had clearly lived long before Deucalion's time. Similarly, the world chronology on the Parian Marble, now in Oxford's Ashmolean Museum, places 'Deucalion's Flood' fifty-three years *after* Cecrops founded Athens.

In Greece, then, the flood had lost its place as the most cataclysmic and all-encompassing event of the distant past. And this was partly because that place had been taken over by the Trojan War, in which vast numbers of people and heroes died, and from whose survivors the Greeks of Homer's time believed both they, and their Anatolian neighbours, were descended.

All this mythmaking was intended to portion up time to make is manageable, dividing it into 'Now', our own time, and 'Then', in which things came to be. Whether we start our reckoning with the Big Bang, or Yahweh's seven-day creation of the world, or Hesiod's chasm, we need to imagine some fixed points in the past, so as to steady ourselves against the giddying onrush of Time; to provide some rationale for our lives, and a little consolation in the face of the inevitability of death. For the ancient Greeks in Homer's time, the Trojan War was just such a fixed point. Vastly more than just any old ancient conflict, the Trojan War was *the* archetypal war, which for the Greeks filled the role that the Great Flood played in other cultures. It marked the moment when the Golden Age of heroes ended, and our present era commenced.

Neither the Great Flood, nor the Trojan War, succeed completely in destroying humanity. If either had, we would not be here now to remember them. There always have to be survivors to populate the world as we know it now. In any case, while the Trojan War was supposed to have exterminated all the heroes, the Greeks could not bear to lose them all at once, so they clung on to a handful, long enough, at least, for them to lay the foundations of the modern world. Thus, some of the Greek heroes survived the war and sailed home, and, for as long as they lived, the gods continued their close involvement in worldly affairs.

The last part of the Trojan Cycle, and indeed the closing chapter of the Greek myths altogether, comprised the *nostoi* ('returns'), which told how the surviving Greek heroes made it home – how Agamemnon was murdered on his return to Mycenae; and how Menelaus, having killed Deiphobus and rescued Helen from burning Troy, was forced to wander through the eastern Mediterranean before finally reaching Therapne, his old home. In *Odyssey* 4, Homer tells us that Helen returned with Menelaus to live out her life at Therapne, as if nothing had happened – and yet everything imaginable had altered. In many ways, her return was the most direct outcome of the Trojan War: Paris and Aeneas stole Helen away from Therapne, but to Therapne Helen returned. Seen from the Menelaion, on its bluff above the Eurotas Valley, with the wind sighing gently in the pines and the sweeping views across to Mount Taygetus in the west, the fate of Troy and the entire story of Aeneas, and even the rise of Rome, seemed like side-shows to a more domestic tale of marital disorder, which ended with a happy reconciliation of a husband and wife, Menelaus and Helen.

When it came to *nostoi* stories, Homer's attention focussed most sharply on Odysseus. Homer's other great poem, the *Odyssey*, describes Odysseus's voyage, opposed by Poseidon but aided by Athena, before he finally made it home to Ithaka. But for the kings of Skepsis in Homer's time, as later for the Romans, Troy's destruction, that dividing line between 'Then' and 'Now', required a figure like Uta-napishtim, Noah or Deucalion; someone who would survive and lay the foundations of the new world order. And that is why Homer made Poseidon foretell, in *Iliad* 20, the survival of Aeneas.

For the Romans in particular, Aeneas was required to survive, in order to relay the baton of civilisation from Troy to Rome. Rome had inherited flood myths too, just like everyone else; Virgil's near contemporary, Ovid, placed a flood story, complete with Deucalion surviving through personal piety, near the start of his *Metamorphoses*. But, as with the Greeks, Troy remained the greatest dividing line between the ancient past and the modern era. In his fourth *Eclogue*, Virgil prophesied that before Augustus's Golden Age could begin in earnest, the most important events in world history would need to be replayed. Floods are not mentioned here, but the Trojan War looms large.

Aeneas' story, especially as re-imagined by Virgil, is the last which concerns close, personal dealings between gods and men. Thereafter, the gods' withdrawal up into the clouds of Mount Olympus is painfully obvious. They reappear and interfere in human affairs again from time to time, and even break the taboo occasionally by interbreeding with them; Ares (Mars), was believed to have raped Aeneas's descendant Rhea Silvia and fathered Romulus, while Alexander the Great claimed that his real father had been Zeus himself. But these rare visitations were grubby and furtive, entirely incomparable with the heady relations between gods and mortals in Aeneas's time. When, in Geoffrey of Monmouth's *History of the Kings of Britain*, Aeneas's great grandson Brutus needed the gods' guidance in order to find Britain, he had to go out of his way to seek it and was rewarded with nothing better than a vision sent in a dream by Diana (Artemis). That was vastly more than most people could expect, but it was scarcely the intimate sort of relationship between Earth and Heaven which had seemed fairly normal, back when Aeneas had been a lad. Ultimately, it was Aeneas alone who carried that connection between gods and men forward. It was Aeneas whose survival would allow our own murky world to be illuminated by a chink of light, streaming down from the very end of the Golden Age.

22

Aeneas, King of Troy?

Towards dawn on that first, ashen-grey day of our own era, Virgil's Aeneas, convinced by Creusa's ghost that his fate lay 'where the Tiber flows through fertile fields', returned to the temple of Demeter beyond the city walls, and found his father and son where he had left them, along with a great crowd of homeless, dispossessed Trojans.

In the *Aeneid*, Aeneas's leadership of the survivors was immediate and required no justification. Priam and his sons were dead or enslaved, and any surviving grandsons were too young to assume the mantle of leadership. In Aeneas's branch of the family, Anchises was too old. Only Aeneas was fit to lead, so lead he did. The *Excidium Troiae*, 'the destruction of Troy', a Medieval text which retells the Trojan myth from Homer, via Virgil, down to the life of Romulus, goes into slightly more detail. It imagines Aeneas arriving at Demeter's temple and finding 'a great multitude of Trojan nobles' together with their riches. 'When they saw Aeneas, they all started to plea to him falling on their knees with great tears. To him thus they said: "We confirm you from this day as a duke for us, and wherever your fortune will be, we will follow." And with this saying, Aeneas was confirmed as a duke by them.' 'Duke' here is simply the Latin *dux*, 'leader'.

As the new day began, Virgil imagined Venus, Aphrodite's morning star, shining over Ida and beckoning them to safety. 'I yielded the struggle,' Aeneas recalled later to Dido, 'took up my sire, and journeyed to the mountains' – the source of our expression 'to head for the hills'. The scene was painted by Anton von Maron on the ceiling of the Villa Borghese in Rome. He imagined Ida being much closer to Troy than it really is and depicted Aeneas struggling to carry his crippled father up the steep mountainside, with smouldering Troy in the background. Behind them, Trojans toiled under their own heavy loads. It is a grim exodus and yet, as they ascend into the clear mountain air, the picture also brims with hope for the future.

The final scene of the 2004 *Troy* movie ends similarly. The film introduces Aeneas only towards the end when, as Troy burns, Paris hands him 'the sword of Troy' – the film's secular substitute for the household gods. Paris asserts that as long as a Trojan wields the sword, 'our people have a future' and he bids Aeneas lead the surviving Trojans to a new home. Thus, in the final scene, we see the Trojans trudging away up Mount Ida, among them Paris and Helen, which does not accord with the myths at all. We also glimpse Aeneas helping Anchises. It is left to the educated viewer to know that Aeneas will indeed provide his people with a glorious future, as foretold.

If this exodus really happened, we may wonder what Aeneas must have thought, as he led his people over the devastated plain, below the Balli Dağ, along the upper Skamander valley and into the folds of Ida, back home to Palaiskepsis. Did he recall so many earlier journeys, and that first time when his father led him down this way, out of the mountains, when Troy was for him a city of dreams and anticipation? Now, as Aeneas glanced behind to make sure his people were following, Troy, smouldering in its own ashes, was only too grimly real.

Arctinus of Miletus, writing in the 700s BC and probably working in the same epic tradition as Homer, says that Aeneas escaped with the survivors of Troy to Dardania. Strabo refers twice to a city in Dardania, whose precise location is unknown, called Aenea. Maybe this had been founded by Aeneas, after his escape from Troy. An alternative possibility is that it was founded by later Greek colonists who simply named it after him.

In book five of his Trojan history, Dictys says that before the Greeks left the Troad, they made Antenor king of Troy. They offered Aeneas lands in Greece, but he chose to remain behind and then 'tried to drive Antenor out of the kingdom'. Leaving Troy, Aeneas 'approached all those who were inhabitants of Dardania and the peninsula nearby [the Chersonese, now called Gallipoli], and begged them to help him': Dictys was fooled here by the establishment, much later on, of a Greek city called Dardania by the Dardanelles, so he thought, erroneously, that this was where Aeneas had lived. Expanding on Dictys, Joseph of Exeter wrote of Aeneas daring to risk war, and even seeking the help of Menelaus and 'the towns of Thebes' in his attempt to drive Antenor from the Trojan throne – but all in vain. Aeneas 'was unsuccessful', continued Dictys, 'and when he tried to return to Troy, Antenor, who had learned what was happening, refused him admittance.'[1]

That is one version of the story. Another is provided by Strabo who, having cited Poseidon's prophecy in *Iliad* 20 that Aeneas would rule over the Trojans, asserted that Aeneas 'remained in Troy and succeeded to the empire and bequeathed the succession thereto to his sons'.[2]

Similarly, Dionysius, in his collection of conflicting stories about Aeneas's destiny, wrote that some unspecified sources claimed Aeneas settled his Trojan followers in Italy and then returned home, 'reigned over Troy, and dying, left his kingdom to Ascanius, his son, whose posterity possessed it for a long time'.[3] Dionysius commented that the people who asserted this may have supposed that Homer knew of Aeneas and Ascanius ruling in the region. And maybe it was so.

Thanks to these stories, we may enjoy, briefly, the image of Aeneas enthroned in his rebuilt megaron in the reconstructed citadel of Troy, growing old on the throne of Ilos, the founding king of Troy (whose daughter Themiste had been the mother of Anchises, making him Aeneas's own great-grandfather).

The television series *Troy: Fall of a City* also leaves Aeneas in possession of Troy. As the city burns, Paris, who in this version has survived this long but is about to be hunted down by the Greeks, urges Aeneas, 'hide yourself ... you're wounded, you can't help me. You have to live, for all of us.' Having hidden among the corpses, Aeneas emerges once the Greeks have left and collects together the last few Trojans – presumably, to start again.

The archaeological layer labelled Troy VI, which seems to correspond to Aeneas's time, culminates in a phase identified as Troy VIh, which has been dated, through its pottery, to about 1250 BC. Troy VIh flourished until some catastrophe befell it, during which bricks in the outer walls were burned. The cause may have been an earthquake, or a siege. But many modern scholars, including Luce, believe that this disastrous event could have been the Trojan War.

After this disaster in around 1250 BC, the city appears to have been repaired and life went on into the next phase, Troy VIIa, which ended in about 1140 BC. But Troy VIIa operated on a much-reduced scale to its predecessor. There was less monumental architecture. Where there had been open spaces within the citadel walls, these were now filled with small, hastily built houses, with storage jars sunk into the floors. The general sense, as the archaeologist Carl Blegen concluded, was of a city of insecure inhabitants, crowding inside the walls for protection. This limited revival chimes with the myths of the re-founding of the city, by either Antenor or Aeneas, after the war.

Of Troy's history in this phase, the 'Millawanda letter', written from the Hittite king Tudhalija IV (*c*. 1240-1215) to an unknown recipient, refers to Walmu, king of Wilusa (Troy) being overthrown. 'Send me Walmu, who is in exile with you,' writes Tudhalija, 'so that I can restore him in the land of Wilusa to the throne. Just as he was previously king of the land of Wilusa, so shall he be again!'[4] Walmu does not feature in the myths, but perhaps these events underlie the story of Aeneas trying to overthrow Antenor, or of rivalries between the families of Ascanius and Skamandrios, whom we shall encounter soon, in the post-war Troad.

About 1170 BC came the general collapse of civilisation in the eastern Mediterranean. It used to be thought this followed immediately after the Trojan War, and that is probably what Homer believed. It is now considered more likely that about eighty years elapsed between the two events, during a prolonged period of drought, but the collapse must have had its roots in the rot that set in during those long years when the bulk of Greece's warriors were away at Troy. Even after the Trojan War ended, Mycenae seems to have remained obsessed with its efforts to dominate western Anatolia's coastal trade routes: we know, for instance, that Tudhalija IV managed to regain control of Milawata (Miletus) from the Greeks, and further conflict there may have ensued. But while Mycenae's eyes were turned eastward, Dorian tribesmen were massing on Greece's northern borders. They surged south in about 1170 BC, overwhelming the once mighty citadels of Mycenaean Greece and causing its civilisation to crumble. About the same time, Syria and Egypt were beset by the mysterious 'Sea People', who may in part have been Greeks displaced by the Dorians.

Meanwhile, in the Hittite world, we hear of Tudhalija's son Suppiluliuma II struggling to retain control of Cyprus. In about 1175 BC, his royal capital of Hattusa was sacked, most likely by the *habiru*, the growing outlaw population excluded from the empire's wealth. The Hittite Empire disintegrated, and cuneiform records come to an abrupt stop.

Though seemingly independent, these great fortress-controlled beacons of civilisation in Anatolia, Greece, Syria and Egypt were all dependent on the same diplomatic and trading networks. Once one fell, the rest were destabilised and eventually collapsed as well. Troy seems to have survived these upheavals for a generation, but Blegen and Korfmann detected evidence of a great fire in about 1140 BC which destroyed Troy VIIa, and in the sanctuary area they found many arrow points, some unmistakeably of Greek origin, along with piles of sling stones, skull fragments and a girl's skeleton, hastily interred. These were not traces of *the* Trojan War, but of some other, later conflict, linked to this general collapse.

Troy's ruins were later reoccupied, not by Anatolians, but by people from further west, possibly from the Balkans. Under their tenure, the city dwindled away and the site was finally abandoned between about 1020 BC and 950 BC. Troy lay desolate, until it was revived again by Aeolian Greek colonists, probably from Lesvos, around Homer's time. It was this new city, perched upon the mighty ruins of Priam's city, that Homer probably visited, and where, doubtless, he sung his tales of Achilles and Aeneas in the glorious days of old.

Linked to stories of Aeneas ruling Troy after the Greeks had departed is Stephen of Byzantium's claim that Arisbe, which was some 25 miles north-east of Troy, was founded by Aeneas's son Ascanius and Hector's son Skamandrios.[5] Skamandrios was the byname of Astaynax, so this story contradicts Lesches and others, who relate how Neoptolemus dashed out little Astyanax's brains during the fall of Troy, but it is not entirely at odds with Homer, who allows Andromache in *Iliad* 24 to anticipate death *or* slavery for her son, whilst Dionysius affirms that the boy had been enslaved but later freed by Neoptolemus.[6]

Hellanikos of Lesbos told a related story, that the people of Daskylitis invited Aeneas's son Ascanius to be their king, and they named the Ascanian

Lake there after him. Dascylitis is either Daskyleion, a ruined city on the southern shore of Lake Aphnitis (Kuş Gölü), 92 miles north-east of Troy, or Dascylium, another archaeological site on the coast of the Sea of Marmara, 37 miles to the north-east of Daskyleion. Dionysius of Halicarnassus, repeating this story, adds that Aeneas sent Ascanius 'with some of his allies, chiefly Phrygians' to Dascylitis, because the inhabitants had invited the young man to rule there. He added that Ascanius later returned to Troy itself, where he and Skamandrios re-founded the city.[7]

Perhaps Ascanius's name was inspired by the Ascanian Lake, which may in turn have come from the old name for the Black or Euxine Sea, *Pontos Axeinos*. But it is always possible that these tales stem from genuine traditions of the survival of Aeneas and his family in the Troad.

Connected to these stories, Strabo, repeating what he had learned from Demetrius of Skepsis, wrote that the new Skepsis, in the heart of Dardania, had been founded 'by Skamandrios, the son of Hector, and by Ascanius, the son of Aeneas: these two families reigned, it is said, a long time at Skepsis. They changed the form of government to an oligarchy.'[8]

Later, under Greek influence, Skepsis became a democracy, but, Strabo continues, 'the descendants of these families had nevertheless the name of kings and held certain dignities' down to the time of Alexander the Great. Some supporting evidence for this comes from Dionysios of Chalkis, who wrote in about the 300s BC that, in the aftermath of the Trojan War, Akamas of Athens founded a number of cities in the Troad, including Skepsis, and allowed Ascanius and Skamandrios to be regarded as the city's founders.[9] That claim was clearly Athenian propaganda, but it had been framed, presumably, to modify an existing tradition – that Skepsis's rulers claimed descent from Aeneas's son Ascanius, and Hector's son Skamandrios.

Archaeology suggests that the new Skepsis dates back only to the 400s BC, but the tradition that it was founded from Palaiskepsis, at some point in the past, seems reasonable, as the two are not far apart. The existence of a ruling dynasty that transferred the city from the old to the new site, and which claimed descent from Aeneas, seems plausible enough. Whether they really were Aeneas's descendants, or simply laid claim to him as an ancestor to bolster their prestige, may not have been known for sure at the time, and certainly cannot be proved or disproved now.

Many Homeric scholars, from Enno von Wilamowitz-Moellendorff to Felix Jacoby, accepted that such a dynasty, which they dubbed 'the Aeneidae', existed in Homer's time. Robert Wood in 1769 proposed that Poseidon's prophecy of the survival of Aeneas's line in *Iliad* 20 was written specifically to praise these Aeneidae. In 1800, August Matthiae thought the same of the Homeric *Hymn to Aphrodite*, in which Aphrodite prophesied that Aeneas would 'reign among the Trojans, and [his] children's children after him, springing up continually'.

It has even been speculated that the Aeneidae were Homer's patrons, whom he wished to honour and humour. It is interesting in this context that

Aeneas, King of Troy?

we hear the Trojan dynasty's genealogy, not early on in the *Iliad*, from the mouths of Priam, Hector or Paris, who were all fated to die, but much later, in *Iliad* 20, from Aeneas himself. The pedigree coming down from Dardanos was important because it led to Aeneas and his descendants.

In 1981, Peter M. Smith launched a spirited onslaught on the idea of the Aeneidae. The prophecies in *Iliad* 20 and the *Hymn* were literary devices, he argued, the former as a dramatic foil to the death of Hector, and the latter as an amelioration of Aphrodite's refusal to petition Zeus for Anchises' immortality. And if he was trying to humour a real Aeneid king, why did the *Hymn*'s writer make Aphrodite bemoan so loudly her conceiving of Aeneas? Those are interesting arguments, but Aphrodite's complaints scarcely overshadow her prophecy of the future glory of Aeneas's descendants. Smith also objected that historical evidence, aside from Strabo, was lacking, but overlooked Dionysios of Chalkis and despite quoting Dionysius of Halicarnassus, seems to have discounted his testimony, too. Smith objected that archaeological evidence, such as Aeneas or Aphrodite shrines, or coins depicting Aeneas, were lacking at Skepsis, but so much at Palaiskepsis and Skepsis has not been excavated: who knows what new evidence some fresh digging at either site might produce? Smith was also concerned that 'any notion that the founders of the [Skepsian ruling] clan might be identified among the heroes of Greek epic will not have preceded the arrival of Greek settlers,'[10] but he was surely wrong here. The Trojan War was known to the Greeks through the Greek epic cycle, but if it was based on real events, then the Trojan heroes could also have been remembered perfectly well by the native people of the Troad – indeed, how could they have been forgotten?

None of Smith's points negate the positive statements of the ancient writers, and indeed it is unlikely that Strabo quoted all of what Demetrius of Skepsis had to say about the Aeneidae. Nor do Smith's objections remove the fact that, when it comes to looking forward to the future in which Homer lived, both the *Iliad* and the Homeric *Hymn to Aphrodite* focus the spotlight firmly on Aeneas. And how odd would it have been if the newly composed *Iliad* and *Hymn*, with their promises of the survival of Aeneas's line, were recited in the Troad to audiences who knew of no such survivors? The simplest solution is that, in Homer's time, there really was a dynasty ruling in Skepsis who claimed descent from Aeneas and Hector, just as the ancient writers claimed, and Homer implied. And, for all we know, their claims could even have been true.

If Aeneas ruled in the Troad, then he was surely buried there. Professor Cook relates how Choiseul-Gouffier and Fellows both identified 'Enea's Tomb' near Ezine, the modern town in the broad Skamander valley at the western end of Dardania. Cook tried to find it and saw a mound in a military compound which he could not investigate. But about 3 miles north of Ezine, Cook also found Ebe Tepe or Savran Tepe, a natural hillock surmounted by a 'flattish mound', next to where Garlic Bridge crosses the Skamander. Cook found a rubble wall and fragments of 'grey and micaceous buff ware', porary with pottery found in Troy from Aeneas's time, and heard ᴊcals that this was indeed reputed to be Aeneas's burial mound.[11]

ᴇ mound is still there, though its western side has been sliced away ᴊesident Erdoğan's modern highway between Çanakkale and the south. ᴊis really was Aeneas' tomb, its location would be significant, mid-way ᴊween his ancestral realm of Dardania and the land of Troy, over which he ᴊy have ruled in later life. But stories of Aeneas being buried there cannot ave survived orally over 3,000 years. Far more likely, the stories reported ɔy Cook had started with eager travellers imposing their desire to find Aeneas's tomb on local burial mounds, and with locals who were keen to show them mounds that answered their wishes. 'Savran', incidentally, might sound temptingly like 'sovereign', as some have thought, but it appears to be a local term for men who kept camels for camel wrestling.

We heard in Guzelyali that each year the Alevis, whose villages are on the southern slopes of Ida, go up onto the mountain to honour Aeneas as their ancestor. I was not able to get to the bottom of that story, but even if it is partly true, then Aeneas has perhaps become conflated with a tribal forebear of the Alevis, whose ancestors were woodcutters who came from the Taurus mountains barely 500 years ago, to work as shipbuilders. But these rumours of tombs and ancestors show that Aeneas's story, however lately revived, remains a living presence in the land of his birth.

At the end of the Trojan War, the Greeks sailed home. There is no reason why a surviving Dardanian prince should have chosen to abandon the region. If Aeneas ever existed, therefore, the tales of him and his progeny remaining in the Troad are probably closest to the truth. The real Aeneas, maybe the son of Anchises and a priestess of Kybele, may well have ruled in Troy and been buried beneath a great mound somewhere in the Troad, perhaps even Savran Tepe. Aeneas's descendants through his son Ascanius, the 'Aeneidae', may have ruled for a time in Troy, and at Palaiskepsis down to Homer's time, and in the new Skepsis down to the time of Alexander the Great, and their existence may have influenced what Homer wrote of Aeneas in the *Iliad*. None of it is impossible, and the scant evidence available even hints at this being true. Thereafter, traces of the Aeneidae vanish for ever.

As time went by, however, traditions of Aeneas remaining in the Troad were outnumbered by stories of him sailing west. These stories are clearly not based on genuinely remembered tradition but on the imagination of mythmakers, who desired to attribute western civilisation to Troy, with Aeneas as the means of transmission. But the more we delve into this mythmaking process, the more something singular becomes apparent. Western civilisation did not just develop and then happen to co-opt Aeneas's myth along the way. In a very real sense, western civilisation developed as it did *because*, in part, of the imaginings of those mythmakers. And, at those mythmakers' forefront, stands Virgil.

PART TWO

ROME

PRELUDE TO PART TWO

Two thousand years ago, a visitor to Rome feels his pulse quicken as he approaches the greatest city in the world. Gliding up the broad-flowing Tiber, between the lower slopes of the Janiculum Hill to the left and the Aventine Hill on the right, the merchant ship, on which he has made the last stage of his journey, noses up against the newly built limestone quayside of the Forum Boarium, and sailors and dockside slaves scramble to secure the ship against the river's powerful current.

Jumping ashore, the visitor pushes through the merchants haggling over the herds of penned cattle which give the Forum Boarium its name. Keen to explore this famous new Troy which had risen in Italy, about 750 miles west of the old one, he follows the wide, shop-lined thoroughfare uphill between the Palatine and Capitoline Hills. The odour of cow dung is soon replaced with the fishy smell of oysters, which are for sale everywhere, and of garum, the fish sauce ubiquitous in Roman cuisine.

Suddenly, the atmosphere changes and the visitor sees the gleaming columns of the Temple of Saturn rising above him. Nearby he finds the Basilica Julia, built by the lately assassinated Julius Caesar, whom the Romans say is now a god. At the foot of the Capitoline Hill, he crosses the Via Sacra and pauses amidst the jostling crowds to gaze past the numerous forum buildings and away south-east towards the Alban Mount, the Romans' sacred mountain, whose snow-capped peak he can just make out in the distance.

In Search of Aeneas

Then he approaches the newest and greatest of the forum buildings, the Forum of Augustus. He ascends the broad stairway and passes below the portico; its marble pillars seem as broad as the oldest trees in his native land. Inside, and dominating the broad, white courtyard, towers a massive statue of the Emperor Augustus himself, a stocky young man, well-built, fresh-faced, with a wreath of gold leaves glinting upon his marble head; half man and half god. Augustus's statue stands proudly in a chariot, gazing serenely out over the rearing horses. All around the chariot are stacked strange-looking weapons and standards which, a guide is explaining, were captured by the Roman army in the recent victory over the Parthians in the east.

Beyond the statue stands a fine Classical temple. The shining brass doors are adorned with images of swords, spears and axes, the emblems of Mars, the god of war, whom the Greeks called Ares. Within the temple stands a statue of Mars Ultor, 'the Avenger', who brought Augustus victory in his wars against Rome's enemies, both foreign powers and also traitors within, not least Mark Antony, the last lover of Cleopatra.

By Mars's side stands a statue of Julius Caesar himself. After his murder, the gods apotheosed Caesar into a blazing star, and now he feasts with the immortals on Olympus. On the other side stands Venus Genetrix, 'Mother Aphrodite', the lover of Mars, a counterpoint to the god's warlike nature. She is the ancestress of both Caesar and Augustus. One marble hand coyly covers her marble breasts, the other reaches down to conceal that which lies below the delicate curve of her waist. Her face, once so animated with life on Mount Ida and during the Trojan War, is now fixed in unmoving marble, and her painted eyes give away nothing of what she might be thinking.

On either side of the temple are two sweeping, semi-circular bays lined with statues. In the right-hand one are some of the luminaries of Rome's past, clustered around Romulus, founder of Rome, whose father was Mars and whose mother, Rhea Silvia, was descended, via the red-booted Alban kings, from Aeneas. In the other bay, flanked by statues of those same kings and the leading members of the Gens Julii, is Aeneas himself.

The visitor approaches reverently and gazes up. Oil lamps suspended on brass chains from the high ceiling cast flickering light across the muscular torso of Aeneas as he strains forward, one leg planted firmly in front of the other. With one strong arm, Aeneas clasps the withered legs of the old man he is carrying, ancient Anchises, one-time lover of Venus. In his bony arms, Anchises clasps the precious Penantes, the household gods of Troy, which he and his son have rescued together from their burning city.

Aeneas's other arm reaches down and in his strong, sinewy hand, which had so often grasped a spear or sword in battle, he clasps the hand of a little boy, who hurries along by his side, his head turned up, anxiously seeking reassurance. This is Ascanius, whom Julius Caesar's family claimed was also called Iulus or Julius. So much energy is captured in their marble forms that they almost seem alive, caught in one dramatic second of their flight from Troy. Aeneas's bearded head strains forward, his painted eyes penetrating

Prelude to Part Two

through space and time, towards Rome, and destiny. Yet, as the light flickers across his face, the visitor notices that a thin layer of dust has settled across the bridge of Aeneas's nose, and on the curling, stylised hairs of his beard.

Here is a man being forced to flee his own home; a man from a junior branch of a dynasty that once ruled an Asian city, that had been destroyed long ago by Greeks. How is it, the visitor wonders, that such an unlikely character is commemorated here in the heart of Rome and in Rome's dreams about its own ancient and bedazzlingly complex past? And did such a man ever journey so far from Troy, and under so great a burden? How, the visitor wonders, did it all begin?

23

'I Fared Forth to the Deep'

'We built our fleet fast beneath Antandros,' Aeneas tells Dido, recounting his travels in book 2 of Virgil's *Aeneid*. And, when the first blush of summer came, 'I quitted the shores and harbours of my country, and those plains where Troy was once a city. An outcast I fared forth to the deep.'

When the place from which Aeneas set sail is specified, it is usually Antandros, on the southern coast of the Troad. As his fleet ploughed through the waves, Aeneas would have looked back to see the beach from which they had departed, with Antandros sitting on the low hill of Devren, and above it the towering massif of Mount Alexandreia. Part of the saddle-backed chain of Ida, Alexandreia was where Paris had judged that fatal beauty contest between the goddesses, which precipitated the Trojan War. Now, he would have seen it fading from dark purple to pale blue as the ships sped away.

The Devren Hill, between modern Avilcar and Altinoluk on the southern coast of the Troad, is now covered with olive trees. When we visited, archaeologists were excavating the remains of a Roman villa. Below this, where the hillside slopes down to the modern road and then to the shore of the Edremit Gulf, they have exposed remains of graves dating from Homer's time. The site's identification as Antandros was confirmed by an ancient Greek inscription including the word 'Antandros', found built into the wall of a nearby mosque. Due south of Dardania, Antandros lay within the kingdom of the Leleges. The city which flourished here in Roman times celebrated its status as Aeneas's point of embarkation. A coin minted in the reign of the Roman emperor Severus Alexander (AD 222-235), inscribed with the city's name, depicts Aeneas boarding his ship, leading Ascanius by the hand and carrying Anchises, who is holding the Palladium.[1]

By the time that coin was minted, other retellings of Aeneas's story had faded into obscurity and Virgil's *Aeneid*, which had been written some 250 years earlier, held sway. Antandros held the same place in Rome's origin myths as Plymouth does for America: it was from here that their founding fathers were believed to have embarked on their epic voyage west.

Despite that, those older, contradictory stories remained. As with the stories of Aeneas remaining in the Troad, there are multiple versions of his voyage west. Dio Chrysostom's eleventh discourse, written c. 71-80 AD, set out to prove that Homer's account of the Trojan War was a lie; the city never fell to the Greeks, he wrote. Hector and Priam survived, so Aeneas sailed west, not to escape a ruined city but to conquer Italy. But this was mere oratory, written simply to show how opposites could be argued, and not something, we assume, that Dio Chrysostom, or anyone else, really believed.

In one of the many contradictory stories related by Dionysius, Aeneas missed the fall of Troy altogether, because Priam had sent him on a military expedition to Phrygia, and he was thus free to sail west. In another, Aeneas happened to be near the Trojan ships when the Greeks started sacking Troy, and he escaped by sea. Yet another of Dionysius's collected stories relates how, once the Greeks had sacked Troy and the lowlands, they prepared to march into mountainous Dardania to attack the survivors. Aeneas sued for peace and, in return for abandoning his realm, the Greeks granted safe conduct for Aeneas's people and valuables by land or sea, so he sailed away.[2]

Book five of Dictys's history relates how, after his failed bid to seize the Trojan throne from Antenor, Aeneas was forced to set sail. 'Taking all of his patrimony, he departed from Troy and eventually arrived in the Adriatic Sea, after passing many barbarous peoples. Here he and those who were with him founded a city, which they called Kerkyra Melaena [Black Corfu].' That is Korcula, an island off the coast of Croatia about 55 miles northwest of Dubrovnik. It is a curious place for him to have ended up; perhaps, having so severely besmirched Aeneas's character, Dictys dared not make him the founder of mighty Rome, so he exiled him to somewhere completely inconsequential instead. Retelling the same story, Joseph of Exeter says that Aeneas ended up in Corcyra 'and there he reigned content within a narrow land.' Joseph adds that 'he was foretold as founder of the walls of Rome,' but leaves it at that.[3]

In book forty-three of Dares's history of Troy, in which Aeneas and Antenor sided with the Greeks because of Priam's stubborn refusal to make peace, we read how, in the smouldering ruins of Priam's palace, on the day after the sack of Troy, the Greeks agreed unanimously to spare Aeneas and Antenor's lives. But then it emerged that the night before, 'Hecuba, fleeing with [her daughter] Polyxena, met with Aeneas and entrusted her daughter to him. He had her concealed at the home of his father, Anchises.' After Hesione and Helen, it was now Polyxena's turn to become the source of animosity between Greece and Troy, for in Dares's story, she had been instrumental in the death of Achilles. Neoptolemus, therefore, demanded vengeance. Antenor was sent to Aeneas 'and earnestly begged him to hand over Polyxena, so that the Greeks would set sail'. Either Aeneas gave in, or

In Search of Aeneas

Antenor discovered Polyxena hiding in Aeneas's house himself, for Antenor handed her over to Neoptolemus, who cut her throat over Achilles' grave.

Polyxena's death, though not the means of her capture, is part of the older epic tradition. So, too, is Hecuba's grief over this and the deaths of so many of her other children, which sent her mad, howling like a dog. Already a prisoner of the Greeks, Hecuba was stoned to death at Abydos and buried on the other side of the Dardanelles at Kalidbahir, which was called Cynossema, 'the tomb of the bitch'. Later, Ovid's *Metamorphoses* describes Hecuba actually turning into a hound and roaming the wilds of Thrace, where her howls of grief could be heard ever afterwards.

Meanwhile, Aeneas's concealment of Polyxena earned him Agamemnon's wrath. Antenor was made king of Troy, and 'Aeneas set sail with the twenty-two ships that Paris had used when going to Greece. He had about 3,400 followers, people of all different ages.' With that, Dares's history of Troy ends.

The *Aeneid* does not tell the story of Aeneas's seven-year journey west in strictly chronological order. It probably did originally, but Virgil realised that he could achieve greater dramatic impact by starting with Aeneas reaching Carthage (*Aeneid* 1), and recounting to Dido the story of the fall of Troy (*Aeneid* 2), followed by the tale of his voyage. Thus, at the start of *Aeneid* 3, Aeneas tells Dido how he and the other Trojans he had led away from Troy spent the spring at Antandros, labouring hard to build their fleet, and how he then disembarked with his father, son and companions, taking with him not only 'the gods of hearth and home', including the Palladium, but also 'the Great Gods', that is, the images of the Great Gods of Samothraki, which his ancestor Dardanos was believed to have brought to the Troad, and which, Virgil believed, were destined to become the Penantes of Rome.

The fire of Virgil's poetry, written once the Trojan myth was well-established in Rome, purged away any suggestion of jealousy towards Priam, or collaboration with the Greeks, on Aeneas's part. What was left was Homer's hero, tempered by Virgil's own view of a near-perfect paragon of Roman manhood, struggling at times to adapt to our own, not so heroic age. Virgil's Aeneas was 'the first Roman', as R. D. Williams called him, forced by his mythological status 'to step out of one world (the world of Troy, finally destroyed by Greek fire) into another' in which the pursuit of individual glory had to be subordinated to piety and duty towards those around him.[4] 'We must not judge Aeneas adversely because we think he ought to be like Achilles,' continued Williams. 'It is the human experience and problems of Aeneas as a human person (not a super-human person) which are emphasised in the *Aeneid*.'[5]

Before and long after the Trojan War, Antandros's busy shoreline was where timbers from the stout oaks and flexible pines of Mount Ida were shaped into sleek, narrow ships and made watertight with black resin from the same pines. They had no keels, so they could be hauled up onto beaches.

'I Fared Forth to the Deep'

Their insides were hollow, just as Homer described ships in the *Iliad*, with platforms in the bow and stern below which goods could be stored and passengers could shelter from sun and storm. They had a single linen or papyrus sail, hoisted on a removable pine mast. When the wind dropped, oarsmen would seat themselves along each side, and power the ship with oars held over the gunwales by leather thongs. Many of the ships' bows were painted, like so many Anatolian vessels to this day, with *oculi*, 'eyes', derived perhaps from the all-seeing eye of the Egyptian sun god, Ra. Thus were the Bronze Age ships built at Antandros; thus the ships of Aeneas's own fleet.

Aeneas's fleet comprised twenty ships, says Virgil in *Aeneid* 1. Their captains included old Ilioneus; Achates; Abas; old Aletes; Antheus; Capys; Caicus; Amycus; Lycus; Gyas; giant Cloanthus; Sergestus; Serestus, and Orontes with a crew of Lycians. We also hear elsewhere in the *Aeneid* of Mnestheus, Nautes and Thymbraeus,[6] who may have been captains, too. Aboard Aeneas's own ship, besides his son Ascanius and father Anchises, was Misenus, his trumpeter, and Palinurus, his helmsman, a descendant, Virgil suggests in *Aeneid* 5, of Dardanos's brother Iasion.

We hear in *Aeneid* 10 that Aeneas's own ship's bows were adorned with Phrygian lions, presumably one on each side. Virgil drew here on the ancient Anatolian cultic sculptures of the Great Mother in her guise of Kybele, the goddess of Mount Ida; a majestic woman seated on a throne, with lionesses sitting on their haunches on either side. She was also worshipped at Ephesus, 150 miles south of Troy, where the Greeks identified her with Artemis, so Artemis of Ephesus was depicted, similarly, standing between two seated lions. The Homeric *Hymn to Aphrodite* makes clear Aphrodite's identification with Kybele; when Aphrodite appeared on Mount Ida to find and make love to Anchises, fierce-eyed lions came fawning to her side. While Aeneas's donning of a lion skin before leaving Troy and (later) setting out from Evander's city made him seem Herculean, this adorning of his ship with images of lions alludes to his goddess mother.

Most Greek and Roman shields carried simple designs, some geometric, some figurative, that were not necessarily particular to the owner or his family. In Greek art, Aeneas appears with shields decorated with a variety of designs: an 'X'; a serpent; an Ethiopian with a spear; a whirling spiral.[7] These images may be purely decorative, or perhaps they had particular meanings for the painters. But Oltos's red-figure cup found at Vulci, which shows Aeneas fighting Ajax,[8] and also Makron's skyphos, likewise from Etruria,[9] show his shield emblazoned with a lion. Both lions are in exactly the same posture, crouching with their hind legs straight but their forelegs bent to bring their roaring, maned heads closer to the ground, a posture they share with a lion shown in obeisance behind Aphrodite on a Pontic oenochoe, which depicts Aeneas participating in Helen's abduction.[10] This lion appears to be an emblem of Aphrodite, so perhaps the lions on Aeneas's shield identified him as her son. It is possible that such depictions were an additional encouragement to Virgil to decorate the prow of Aeneas's ship with lions.

175

In Search of Aeneas

This connection between Aeneas and lions was perpetuated by the *Aeneid*. Therefore, when heraldry developed in western Europe in the AD 1100s, as a means of identifying armoured warriors by use of hereditary shield emblems, Heinrich von Veldecke's *Eneide* gave Aeneas a lion for his coat of arms, and an illustrated *Aeneid* from about 1200 shows Aeneas in full Medieval armour, riding a horse, and on his shield and banners are rearing lions.[11]

Small wonder that several western European royal houses opted for lions as the main feature of their hereditary coats of arms. Lions were not only seen as kings of beasts, they were also closely associated with Hercules and Aeneas. The lions in the English royal arms, which remain there to this day and appear on British coins and passports, owe their origins to the lion-shield granted to Henry II's father Geoffrey Plantagenet by his own father-in-law, Henry I. It was during Henry's reign that Geoffrey of Monmouth wrote his *History of the Kings of Britain*, which traced the British monarchy back to Brutus of Troy, a great grandson of Aeneas. When later Medieval heraldists attributed arms to Brutus, they gave him a lion, too. The Plantagenets' adoption of lions as their hereditary emblem may well have been inspired by its association with Aeneas, as highlighted by their appearance on the prow of Aeneas's ship in the *Aeneid*.

In about AD 1560, Luca Cambiaso of Genoa sketched the moment of Aeneas's embarkation,[12] reminding us how much of Aeneas's story from now on will be concerned with greetings and farewells, arrivals and departures. It is a sketch full of movement as a phalanx of Trojans crowd down a flight of steps that leads diagonally across the page. Centre-stage is Aeneas, a bulky figure due to his cloak, shield and magnificently plumed helmet, yet he shows his humanity by allowing himself to be assisted into his waiting ship by a muscular sailor, who holds his right hand, and by his leg we see naked Ascanius. To the left, we see some of his fleet, already at sea.

Their journey would have taken them west down the Adramyttium Gulf, along the straits between the south-western Troad and Lesvos. Then they would have turned north up the Troad's west coast, the other ships following close behind. They would have passed Tenedos on their left, and on their right the low cliffs of the Sigeum ridge, beyond which, they knew, lay the ruins of Troy. Then they would have passed the mouth of the Dardanelles and the end of the Gallipoli peninsula, the start of the region the Greeks called Thrace. To the north-west across the sea lay Imbros, and beyond it the high peak of Samothraki.

Until the Second World War, many scholars hoped that Aeneas's journey was based either on genuine events; on racial memories of similar migrations from the east; or, as L. T. Farnell posited, on the diffusion of a cult of Aphrodite Aeneias – Aphrodite, mother of Aeneas. This, Farnell theorised, originated with the Aeneidae, the priest-kings of Skepsis, who believed that their ancestor, the Aeneas of the *Iliad*, was the 'emanation of a divinity'. The cult spread west, and a belief arose that different sanctuaries dedicated to

Aphrodite Aeneias had been founded by Aeneas himself on the course of his journey. So theorised Farnell.

The modern view is that the story of Aeneas's journey was worked up by mythmakers as a purely literary activity, stitching together a route out of ports-of-call whose fortuitous names invited their being woven into the fabric of the tale, or which had some historical, religious or political significance to the myth's tellers.

The foremost collector of the myths surrounding Aeneas's journey was Virgil's near contemporary, Dionysius of Halicarnassus. Where Virgil forged one single, elegant narrative, Dionysius reported each story individually, however contradictory they all were when put together, and always cited his sources. Both Dionysius and Virgil make Aeneas's first port of call a place in Thrace called Aeneia. However, there are other stories which take Aeneas's fleet, first, to Samothraki.

Perhaps this was not our mythological Aeneas's first visit to Samothraki. Perhaps Anchises had taken him, earlier in life, to visit the sacred, magnetic stone there that the islanders believed represented the Great Mother. Or maybe this was Aeneas's first time, stepping ashore at what is now the largely submerged ancient harbour and walking up the little gorge between the island's bracken and ancient plane trees; drinking from the stream's cold, clear waters; feeling the extraordinary energy of the island; and entering the wider valley in which the sacred stone lies.

The Greek philosopher Critolaus (d. 118 BC) wrote of 'Saon from Samothraki, who brought over [to Italy] the household deities with Aeneas'.[13] Saon's name echoes Saos, the great peak of Samothraki. Cicero's friend Attikus (d. 32 BC), meanwhile, wrote that the household gods Aeneas brought to Italy had come, not from Troy, but direct from Samothraki itself.[14] These stories imply – but do not state specifically – that Aeneas landed on Samothraki to collect the statues of the gods. But in his commentary on the *Aeneid*, written about the early AD 400s, Servius wrote that after leaving Troy, 'Aeneas sought Italy, went to Thrace and Samothraki, and took up and carried the deities with him for the sake of his ancestral mother [i.e, his ancestress Elektra].'[15] Servius referred separately to these deities 'whom Aeneas carried from Samothraki',[16] adding that Aeneas consecrated a shield on Samothraki, presumably in the Sanctuary of the Great Gods.[17] Based on these references, Perret suggested that there may have been a Samothrakian legend of Aeneas stopping there.[18] He may well be right.

The desire to bring Aeneas to Samothraki was obvious. Having been embraced by the early Greek colonists from Lesvos, Samothraki's ancient, native Sanctuary of the Great Gods had flourished. It offered its initiates the gods' protection at sea, and also the promise of a happy afterlife. It was therefore an extremely appropriate place for Aeneas to visit at the start of his epic voyage. In Classical times, Samothraki's sanctuary attracted pilgrims and would-be initiates from all over the civilised world, particularly during its summer festival, which was attended by *theoroi*, sacred ambassadors, from all over Greece. The island was beloved of the Macedonian kings, who endowed it with several magnificent buildings; Alexander the Great's parents are said to have met at the festival there, and even to have conceived their son in the magically charged atmosphere of the island. Samothraki attracted pilgrims from Rome even before it fell under Roman control in 190 BC and its formal adoption into the Empire fifty years later; thereafter, the number of Roman pilgrims increased even more.

One reason for Rome's fascination with Samothraki was the myth (albeit by then contradicted by other ones) that Dardanos, the ancestor of Aeneas, and therefore of themselves, had been born there. The islanders, in turn, curried favour with the rising super-power of Rome by talking up their Dardanian links. In 200 BC, Dymas of Isos was awarded a golden crown by Samothraki's chief magistrate for a drama about Dardanos, which was doubtless performed before the assembled *theoroi* in the theatre within the Sanctuary of the Great Gods. Later, Herodes of Priene wrote an epic about Dardanos and his family, and Hegemon of Alexandria Troas wrote *Ta Dardanika*. These plays are all lost, but they probably talked up the island's ties to Rome through Dardanos and, as Rutherford suggests, they surely supported the Roman idea that their revered Penantes had come from Samothraki.

Ilion, the Greek city built on the site of Priam's Troy, probably joined in this game, especially after Rome conquered the area in 85 BC. Ilion's citizens enlarged the tumuli that pepper the Troad with layers of earth and potsherds to make them more impressive for Roman pilgrims. They also reminded the Romans of their links to Aeneas by producing votive clay plaques depicting a cloaked, mounted man, who, Korfmann theorised, was Dardanos. These plaques were excavated in the Sanctuary area, the part of Troy which, probably not coincidentally, faces towards distant Samothraki.

Rome's belief in its Trojan origins kept the story of Dardanos and Samothraki alive to the end of the Classical world. In the AD 400s, in book three of his *Dionysica,* Nonnus wrote of Kadmos visiting Samothraki to beg Elektra for the hand of her daughter Harmony. When Elektra became pregnant by Zeus with Dardanos, 'the Seasons came running to her house' bearing Jupiter's [Zeus's] sceptre, Time's robe and Olympus's staff, all symbols prophesying 'the indissoluble dominion of the Ausonian [i.e, Roman] race'. When Kadmos stood before Elektra on Samothraki, he hailed her: 'Good be with you ... bedfellow of Jupiter! Most blessed of all women that shall be hereafter, because Kronion [Zeus] keeps the lordship of the world for your children, and your stock shall steer all the cities of the Earth! This is the dower of your love.' This was a prophecy that Nonnus knew would be fulfilled through Aeneas and his Roman progeny.

Nonnus then provides some fascinating detail about the life of Aeneas's ancestor. When Aeneas's ancestor Dardanos was 'in the bloom of his youth', with down on his cheeks, he was swept away from Samothraki in a terrible flood which deposited his ship atop Mount Ida. When the waters receded,

Dardanos 'scored the dust of Ida with a plough-furrow, and marked the limits of Dardania, the fortified city which bore his name'.

Nonnus's story draws on, or at least echoes, two sources. Back in the first century BC, Dionysius of Halicarnassus asserted that instead of being born on Samothraki, Dardanos had actually been born in Arcadia in Greece, but was swept to Samothraki by a flood.[19] About the same time, Diodorus Siculus recorded this remarkable story: 'Before the floods which befell other peoples', the Black Sea, swollen by river water, burst violently into the Dardanelles. It flooded much of Asia and drowned the lower parts of Samothraki, so 'in later times fishermen have now and then brought up in their nets the stone capitals of columns, since even cities were covered by the inundation.' The inhabitants of Samothraki survived by retreating up Mount Saos, and when the gods spared them by halting the rising waters, 'they set up boundary stones about the entire circuit of the island.'[20] These stones presumably included the island's two known, magnetic, sacred stones, even though they are in fact at considerably different heights above the present sea level.

Diodorus's tale is remarkable because modern geology suggests the Black Sea was once a freshwater lake that became swollen with meltwater as the Russian steppes thawed out after the end of the Ice Age. In about 5800 BC, it burst through a land-bridge that had connected Europe with Asia, carving out the Bosporus, filling the Sea of Marmara and pouring through the Dardanelles. This could well have caused a *tsunami* surge that affected Samothraki. It seems beyond credibility that the Samothrakians could have preserved an accurate memory of such an event for over six thousand years; but the story does seem to match the geological evidence; and in Samothraki, anything seems possible.

The flood stories of Dionysius and Nonnus turn Aeneas's ancestor Dardanos into a hero like Uta-napishtim, Deucalion or Noah; a flood-survivor whose progeny repopulated, in this case, the Troad. It is tempting to speculate that these stories also drew on older traditions from Aeneas's time, which accounted for Dardanos's movements between Samothraki and the Troad. If, as we speculated earlier, Dardanos was believed originally to have been born on Ida, there may even have been earlier stories of his having been swept *to* Samothraki from Ida, and maybe even back again, by the great flood or its backwash. But on this we can only speculate.

Dardanos's changing birthplaces helped define Aeneas for different generations. And Aeneas's destiny caused Dardanos's place of origin to continue shifting – from the Troad to Samothraki, Samothraki to Arcadia – and then even further west. That is why, despite the potent appeal of Samothraki, Virgil ignores it in his story of Aeneas's voyage. Virgil wished to promote a different myth about Dardanos's origins, as we will discover soon: that Dardanos's place of birth lay at the *end* of Aeneas's journey – 'where the Tiber flows through fertile fields'[21] – in Italy.

24

'Seek ye Your Mother of Old'

After Samothraki, our mythological Trojans put to sea again, but which way they headed is controversial, for Aeneas's next stop was 'Aeneia', a place for which there are two contenders. Some commentators have identified Aeneia as Ainos, on the Thracian coast, 28 miles north-east of Samothraki. Commanding the mouth of the River Hebros, which is now the Greek-Turkish border, the Turks call this place Enez. Its Lesvian founders claimed that its mythological founder was 'Ainos/Aineus', son of Apollo. It was probably only when this name became confused with Aeneas that the myth arose of Aeneas founding the city during his voyage.

Dionysius and Virgil, however, are clear that Aeneas's Aeneia was not here, but a place much further west. As the peak of Samothraki receded into the eastern sky, the Trojans' fleet would have hugged the Thracian coast as it headed west towards the first of the triple prongs of the Chalkidiki Peninsula, on the south-eastern tip of which there now perches the monastery of Mount Athos. They would have passed the second prong too, and then sailed up the western coast of the third one, the Pallenê Peninsula, and into the Thermaic Gulf.

Near the top of the gulf, before the bay of Thessaloniki and just north of Nea Michaniona, is a low-lying promontory backed by a prominent bluff. A sign identifies the site as 'Aeneia'. It was an easily defensible location, and indeed it is dominated today by the ruins of twentieth-century military defences, overgrown with fig trees, out of which we startled two nightjars. The real Greek founders of this city of Aeneia came from Corinth, but the name suggested Trojan origins. Therefore, a story arose, as evidenced by a fragment of Hellanikos's *Troika*,[1] that having escaped from Troy to Mount Ida, Aeneas left the Troad altogether and founded this city of Aeneia.

It may be that the people of this outlying and semi-Asian city found themselves in conflict with the cities on the Greek mainland opposite, and identified themselves with Aeneas, who stood up so bravely to Greek

Achilles. From the 400s BC onwards, the Aeneians started minting coins, proudly depicted Aeneas carrying Anchises on his back. One shows Aeneas following Creusa, who holds above her head the *dolium*, the clay vessel believed to contain the gods of Troy.[2] Other coins from Aeneia show a quartered square, representing the city, with the letters A I N E A S written around it, and a helmeted head of Aeneas on the other side.[3] This interest in Aeneas is probably why, once the belief had arisen that Aeneas had gone to Italy and scholars started seeking out the precise route, Aeneia became an obvious choice for a stop-over. Thus, Dionysius, probably following Varro, wrote that Aeneas overwintered on the Pallenê Peninsula and founded a temple of Aphrodite 'and also a city called Aeneia'.[4] Virgil is less explicit, thus allowing Ainos/Enez to make its rival claim to be Aeneia. But Virgil's details do in fact point to this Aeneia, on the Pallenê Peninsula.

Looking south-west across the Thermaic Gulf from Aeneia by day, you can see only a hazy blue horizon. But as evening approaches, the outlines of mountains emerge centred on a mighty tower of peaks. Each time you think you have seen the highest, a greater one emerges beyond, as if you were looking at an endless succession of pinnacles, reaching into the heavens. And so they do, in myth at least, for you are looking at Olympus, seat of the eternal gods, whose highest peak, snow-capped and bathed in gold by the setting sun, is called *Thronos Dios*, 'the throne of Zeus'. Out of the eastern clefts of Olympus, the river Baphyras cascades down onto the plain, where it flows, lined with silver-leaved poplars and alive with dragon flies, past the ancient shrine of Dion. There is a great stone altar at Dion, looking back across the plain towards towering Olympus, where, in 336 BC Alexander sacrificed white bulls to Zeus before beginning his campaign against Persia. And by the Baphyras at Dion is also a shrine to Aphrodite Hypolympidia, 'she who dances on Olympus'. One evening in the village of Litochoro on the eastern slopes of Olympus, as the purple darkness gathered, we saw Aphrodite Hypolympidia herself, in the form of the planet Venus. Gently, she lowered herself down, until her shining form brushed the pines on the black slope of Olympus. As she seemed to settle in her couch, her light blazed bright for an instant, and then was gone.

The sacrifice of bulls and the dancing of Aphrodite, both evidenced at Olympus, chime fortuitously with Aeneas's words in *Aeneid* 3, when he recalls his founding of Aeneia: 'I was praying the holy rites to my mother, Dione's child, and the rest of Heaven, that they might watch over the work begun, and was standing on the beach in act of slaying a shining bull to the high king of gods.' Where else could Virgil have imagined him, but on the shore of Aeneia, facing Mount Olympus?

Dionysius reports stories of Hegesippus and Cephalon of Gergis that Aeneas died in Thrace, but emphasises his own belief that he merely overwintered there.[5] The Pallenê Peninsula is a harsh, rocky place, littered in places with mammoth bones. The Greeks said it was the graveyard of the giants killed in their failed bid to oust the gods from Olympus. It was as unpropitious a location for a city as Ilos's choice of the Hill of Ate had been for Troy. Virgil's Aeneas tried to uproot a cornel tree from a mound on the crest of the bluff, but blood came oozing out of the earth. As fear gripped Aeneas, he heard the disembodied voice of Priam's son Polydorus, telling him that he lay buried below. Myth accords several fates to Polydorus; in this version, he had been sent to Thrace with Priam's gold, to keep it safe during the war, but when the Thracian king heard of Troy's fall, he stole the treasure, murdered the boy and hid his body here.

That was the last straw for Aeneas. Wearing wreaths of dark cypress – a tree that we noticed growing all around Aeneia – Aeneas and his men reburied Polydorus under a proper funeral mound and made offerings to him of milk and sacrificial blood. Then, with the agreement of Anchises and the other Trojan elders, Aeneas waited for the spring, abandoned Aeneia, and led his fleet away south.

Their route would have taken them down the east coast of Thessaly, along the length of Euboea, and then south, foam flying high as the ships' dark prows cleaved the blue water of the Aegean. Past the lace-fringed shores of Andros and Tinos, they would have sailed into the heart of the Cyclades, the archipelago whose countless tiny islands cluster protectively around the sacred island of Ortygia, or Delos, which many scholars, right down to Medieval times, believed was the centre of the world.

Virgil writes that Delos used to drift freely in the seas until Apollo fixed it in its current position. Earlier myths explain why: when Zeus wished to rape the Titaness Leto, they each turned into a quail, *ortykio*. Jealous Hera forbade any dry land to allow Leto to land and give birth, so the Titaness-quail flapped hopelessly over the Aegean until her sister Asteria turned herself into two floating islands, Delos and Rheneia. These do look, from a distance, like a recumbent Titaness, with Rheneia as the head and breast, and Delos's Mount Kynthos as a bent knee. Leto gave birth to Artemis on Rheneia, and then flew across to Delos to give birth to Apollo by the tiny lake of Inopus, while Zeus sat watching from the peak of Kynthos. It was only later that Apollo fixed his birthplace to the sea floor with rocky pillars, a detail perhaps inspired by Greek knowledge of undersea volcanic activity. The name Delos signifies the 'bright glory' which appeared there when Apollo was born; it was an island of great sanctity, adorned with rich sanctuaries and altars. Their excavated remains, rasped by the constant, warm breeze from the sea, still pepper the desiccated landscape.

Aeneas's fleet would have entered the calm of the Kato Rematiaris, the strait between Rheneia and Delos and, weary from their voyage, moored in Ortygia's harbour, close to the walls of Artemis's sanctuary, near where tourist boats dock today. From among the stones appeared old King Anius, who served his father Apollo as a priest. Engraving the scene for an edition of Ovid's *Metamorphoses* in 1659, J. W. Baur imagined Anius wearing an eastern turban, but it is more likely that he resembled an archaeologist we met there, one of the island's few modern inhabitants save for the crested larks and hooded crows; he wore no hat at all, and his wind-strafed hair and beard had been bleached almost gold, in contrast to his skin, darkened by Apollo's ever-blazing sun.

Baur shows Anius and Anchises embracing fondly because, says Virgil, they had met many years before. The king led Aeneas to Apollo's temple 'and its venerable stone'. That was either the Temple of Apollo, or the nearby Keraton, the hoary altar said to have been built by Apollo for himself: both are near his sister Artemis's sanctuary and face Zeus's throne of Mount Kynthos. Aeneas prayed to the 'god of Thymbra', referring back fondly to Apollo's temple, to the south of Troy. 'Grant us a home that shall endure,' Aeneas cried, 'grant the weary their walls, a nation, and an abiding city!'

The earth shook, and a voice reverberated through the bronze tripod which stood before the altar: 'Ye stout sons of Dardanos, the land that first bore you from the stock of your sires – that land shall receive your returning feet on its fruitful soil. Seek ye your mother of old. There the house of Aeneas shall be lord over all climes.'

Virgil's inspiration for those words was Poseidon's prophecy in *Iliad* 20, that 'Aeneas shall reign over the Trojans, he and his children's children that shall be born hereafter.' Strabo quotes Homer accurately, but adds 'some write, "the family of Aeneas will rule over all, and his sons' sons", meaning the Romans.'[6] Thus, as Conington and Nettleship wrote, Poseidon's prophecy was 'converted', by the substitution of 'Trojans' with 'all', from something quite parochial, concerning nothing more than the Troad, into 'the promise of the Roman empire'.

Throughout Aeneas's journey, we shall see him trying, not always successfully, to subjugate his own desires to the fulfilment of Fate's plan. But on Delos, at least, the two coincided and Apollo's prophecy overjoyed him. But where, specifically, was Aeneas to go? As with all his prophecies, Apollo was frustratingly vague, although Anchises thought he knew: Teucer, the father-in-law of their male-line ancestor Dardanos, was said in some versions of the myths to have come from Crete. Rumour had reached Delos that Prince Idomeneus had abandoned Crete, so this seemed like the perfect destination, and they sacrificed bulls to Apollo and Poseidon in gratitude.

A retelling of Aeneas's story appears in the *Metamorphoses* of Ovid (43 BC-AD 18). Effectively a compendium of Greek mythology with an emphasis on changes of form, it starts with the birth of the world and a great flood and culminates with the Trojan War and a 'mini *Aeneid*', as it has been described, about Aeneas's journey, following broadly the story told by Virgil and the tale of Rome to the apotheosis of Aeneas's supposed descendant, Julius Caesar. Ovid imagined the Trojans on Delos feasting in Anius's palace and resting, anachronistically, on high couches in Roman style, while Anius related how during the war, his daughters, having nobody like Aeneas to protect them, fell into Agamemnon's hands and were saved from rape only when the wine god Dionysos metamorphosed them into white doves. *Origo Gentis Romanae* relates, differently, that Anius gave Aeneas his daughter

Lavinia as his wife and she travelled with him to Italy. Though in most versions, particularly in the *Aeneid*, Lavinia was Latinus's daughter, whom Aeneas met and married after he reached Italy.

Parting, they exchanged gifts; little Ascanius received a cloak and quiver; Aeneas a bowl for mixing water and wine, crafted with images of the Greek city of Thebes and Orion's daughters, who sacrificed themselves to save their city from plague; and Anchises was given a wooden staff to lean on, the gift of one old man to another. Dionysius says there were 'many evidences of the presence of Aeneas' on Delos.[7] One of these might be the sanctuary of Aphrodite, which is on the rocky slopes of Mount Kynthos. Perhaps this was one of the factors which inspired Virgil to take Aeneas to Delos in the first place.

They sailed joyfully south, the foaming spray doubtless cooling their sweating bodies, past 'Naxos and its bacchante-haunted peaks', as Virgil wrote. Dionysos (Bacchus) had visited Naxos on his own travels and encountered Ariadne there, lately abandoned by Theseus. There is a ruined temple to him at Yria, just south of Naxos town. Fanari is the highest peak and presumably the god had left behind there some of his noisy followers, the bacchantes. After Naxos, they passed 'green Donysa, Olearos, glittering Paros, and the Cyclades strewn along the deep, and threaded those seas, gemmed with so many an isle. The cry of Aeneas's sailors rang clear... "Onward to Crete and our forefathers!"'

Crete is long and thin, with its own Mount Ida forming its central spine. The Trojans settled about halfway along the island, on the northern slopes of Cretan Ida, at a place they called Pergamea after the name of Troy's acropolis, Pergamos; Virgil probably had the idea of placing them there because of the coincidence of these names. The village is now called Perama. Only 13 miles north-west of the Idean Cave where Zeus is said to have spent his childhood and 25 miles west of the magnificent Minoan palace of Knossos, Perama is an uninspiring village, now as, apparently, then. Aeneas's first harvest there failed and Anchises wanted to return to Delos to ask Apollo for clarification. But Troy's household gods intervened, appearing to Aeneas in a dream. Apollo's instructions to 'seek ye your mother of old ... the land that first bore you from the stock of your sires' did not refer to Teucer, they explained, but to Dardanos himself. And Dardanos, they announced, was in fact born, not in the Troad, Samothraki or Arcadia, but in Italy. 'Seek Corythus,' the household gods urged, 'and the Ausonian shore.' Ausonia was a place in Latium, not far from Rome. Virgil does not explain Corythus until *Aeneid* 7, as we shall see. In Italy, continued the household gods, Aeneas's descendants would rule a mighty empire and be 'raised to the stars'.

Thus, on Crete, the focus of Aeneas's myth changes. Until now, he has been journeying away from Troy. But after Crete, Aeneas's story becomes a *nostos*, a story of home-coming, as he travels towards Italy, the place, we now learn, where his ancestor Dardanos had originated. In the *Aeneid*, Troy had only ever been a temporary seat for the glory of cities and the centre of empire. The true home of the archetypal Earthly metropolis would be – as it always had been, in the new Roman conceit – the city which, as Virgil wrote in his first *Eclogue*, 'reared her head as high among all other cities as cypresses oft do among the bending osiers'. That city was Rome.

From Crete, the fleet embarked again. Dionysius sends them to Kythera, a fifty-seven-mile voyage north-west, passing the islet of Antikythera as they went. On Kythera, Dionysius continues, Aeneas founded the temple there to his mother Aphrodite.[8] This was the famous sanctuary of Aphrodite about which we heard earlier, that Herodotus said was of Phoenician origin and which we tried to find on the scrubby slopes of Palaikastro. Dares claimed that Aeneas visited Kythera with Paris and asserted that the temple was there already, and Paris sacked it. If one wished to reconcile these contradictory strands of myth, one might suggest that Dionysius's Aeneas now piously *re*-founded his mother's temple, which had been sacked by Paris on their earlier, fateful visit to the island.

According to Pausanias, storms then drove Aeneas's fleet north into the Gulf of Boiai (pronounced 'Véa'), to the south of Lacedaemonia (modern Sparta).[9] On the gulf's long, sweeping shoreline, Aeneas founded Aphrodisias and Etias, which he named after his mother and an otherwise unknown daughter of his.

Before catching the ferry to Kythera, we stayed in Neapolis, which sits on top of ancient Boiai itself, and explored the gulf's coast, in search of these rumoured cities of Aeneas's. Neither city existed in Pausanias's time, their inhabitants (along with those of a third city, Side, not of Trojan origin), having been 'expelled' for an unstated reason and relocated long-since to Boiai itself. Pausanias wrote that the ruins of Etias were 7 stades from Boiai. About 1½ miles south of Neapoli is the rocky promontory of Paleokastro, with a few ancient walls visible; it could possibly have been Etias, except the distance is about half as far again as Pausanias suggested. As to Aphrodisias, a journey around the gulf brought us to the sunken city now called Pavlopetri, 5 miles west from Neapoli and immediately to the east of the jetty for the ferry to Elafonisos. Backing onto salt pans, this city was occupied from about 2800 BC until it was half-submerged *c.* 1100 BC. We explored the rock-cut graves cut into soft rocks along the shore, and paddled in the warm, pale blue water among the bases of ancient, submerged walls. This city existed in Aeneas's time and its inhabitants were certainly 'expelled' by the land sinking below the sea. Maybe Pavlopetri was Aphrodisias, and was so-called because it faces Aphrodite's island of Kythera. It is possible that, between 1100 BC and Pausanias's time, and despite it having existed for over a millennium and a half before the Trojan War, a story had arisen that this city, named after Aphrodite, had been founded by her son Aeneas.

In Dionysius's account, Aeneas's companion Cinaethus died at sea and was buried on a promontory of the Peloponnese, called Cinaethion after him, but he does not provide enough detail for us to locate this place. Then, says Dionysius, Aeneas visited Arcadia.[10] If Aeneas made this improbable diversion from his journey to Italy, he would have retraced the earlier journey he made with Paris, up the Eurotas valley to Therapne and the site where Sparta later rose, and would then have continued north, over the broom-covered hills that are sparsely inhabited even today, until he came down into fertile Arcadia in the central Peloponnese. Dionysius quotes from Agathyllus of Arcadia, who claimed that at Nesos, which he said was on an island in marshes or in a river, Aeneas left behind two daughters, 'fruit of his love for Anthemonê fair and for lovely Codonê'.[11] Dionysius also quotes Ariaethus's *On the Early History of Arcadia* (only fragments of which survive), which asserted that Aeneas founded Caphiae, named after Anchises's father Capys, near the Arcadian Orchomenos. Pausanias in turn believed that Aeneas and Anchises had come to this region 'for some reason or other'.[12] As Pausanias travelled south-east from Orchomenos to Maera (modern Artemisio), he passed Mount Anchisia, which he said was named after Anchises, and found at its foot a sanctuary to Aphrodite, and the tomb where Aeneas buried his father.

These places are not randomly scattered about Arcadia but form a tight cluster some 43 miles north of Sparta, and 24 miles due west of Mycenae. Nesos, where Aeneas fathered two daughters, has not been identified precisely, but is believed to lie in the Tragos valley, probably not far from the modern village of Panagitsa. The wide and now largely dry valley contains several low hills that were probably once islands in a marsh, and on one of these, presumably, was Nesos.

Aeneas's city of Caphiae was the location of a famous battle between the Aetolians and Achaeans in 200 BC and has been studied thoroughly. Its ruins lie in the fields immediately south-east of the small village of Choutousa, which is only 3 miles west, over Mount Kastania, from Panagitsa. Walking through the fields we found some dressed stone blocks and traces of Caphiae's walls. Below the poppies and flowering grasses, the earth was littered with potsherds, including one black-glazed piece. It is a land of towering mountains surrounding broad valleys, once full of marshes or lakes, partly drained in ancient times and then neglected, but almost entirely re-drained now. As a result, the agricultural plains run, almost perfectly flat, up to the scrubby edges of the uncultivated, rocky hills. Caphiae is in the corner of such a plain, with its back to the foothills of Mount Kastania. It looks south over the fields, across a huge ditch built in ancient times to protect it from seasonal flooding, towards the looming bulk of Mount Mainalo, anciently called Mount Thaumasion, which means 'wonderful'.

As to Mount Anchisia, at whose foot Aeneas founded a sanctuary to his mother and – most surprisingly of all – buried his father, we followed Pausanias's directions perfectly easily to a spot 5½ miles south-east of Caphiae, on the opposite edge of the same agricultural plain. Here, where a turning leads off north-east to Palaiopyrgos, is Mount Anchisia, a spur of the massif of Mounts Trachi and Lyrkio that form the eastern side of the valley.

At the foot of this spur is a spring and the excavated remains of a Mycenaean sanctuary spreading from the valley floor up the spur's lowest slope. There was no sign of the burial mound we were expecting, but climbing up among the ruins we were delighted to find an oblong grave, 4 feet by 7 feet, cut into the sloping rock, containing many reddish-brown potsherds. The story of Anchises's death here is out of sync with the rest of the myths, in which Anchises remained alive throughout the voyage to Italy. Nonetheless, as thunder rumbled above, we could easily imagine old Anchises lying here, his body stricken by old age and by Zeus's lightning bolt, his lifeless eyes gazing out across the plain to Mount Thaumasion, before his dead body was covered over.

Thaumasion is linked to Aeneas' genealogy twice more. When his ancestor Dardanos's father Zeus was a baby, his own father Kronos, fearing Zeus would grow up to overthrow him, decided to devour him. Zeus's mother Rhea therefore hid him in a cave, either in Crete or, as Pausanias heard locally, on Mount Thaumasion, 'into which no human beings may enter save only the women who are sacred to the goddess'.[13] A road rises up Mount Thaumasion from near Vytina, reaching almost the mountain's highest peaks and coming down eventually in Levidi. A track off the highest part of the road leads south to a cave, signposted fancifully *Edo drakotrypia*, 'here's a dragon'. The entrance had a barred door, but luckily it was unlocked, so – and despite not being women, sacred to the goddess or otherwise – we went down into a magnificent underground chamber full of stalactites and stalagmites, where one could easily imagine the Titaness concealing her son. (Rhea concealed Zeus's brother Poseidon, incidentally, in the fountain of Arne at Mantineia, south-east of and in sight of Thaumasion, though with less success, because Kronos eventually found and swallowed him).

Dionysius also relates that Aeneas's ancestor Atlas was the first king of Arcadia and 'lived near the mountain called Thaumasion'.[14] In Arcadia, the gaps between mountains always reveal other peaks, receding into an endless, silvery light and creating a giant landscape, a suitable landscape for Titans. The idea of Atlas ruling here was easy to believe on a grey morning, when the mountains appeared to be the only things stopping the clouds from smothering the Earth. Dionysius tells how Atlas's daughter Elektra married Zeus and gave birth to Dardanos and Iasion. Contradicting the older myths that said Dardanos was from Samothraki, Dionysius implies, though does not say explicitly, that Dardanos and Iasion were born here, in Arcadia. Dardanos married Chryse and had sons Idaeus and Deimas. Then came a great flood, which left all but the mountain peaks under water. Some of the survivors remained, with Deimas as their king. The rest, under Idaeus, and with Dardanos in company, sailed away. They settled on Samothraki and later, Dardanos continued on to the Troad.

Altogether, these stories seem to provide Aeneas, Anchises and their ancestor Dardanos with alternative homes in Arcadia. Perhaps this story was linked to the idea, in Menecrates of Xanthus and others, that Aeneas had sided with the Greeks and become one of them. Galinsky, for one, thought the whole business was the 'fictitious product of fertile minds'.[15] Perhaps those minds, inspired perhaps by the coincidence of the names Anchises and Mount Anchisia, belonged to the Iamid dynasty of Peloponnesian seers and bards mentioned by Pausanias, at least one of whom was named after Aeneas.[16] Maybe Ariaethus and Agathyllus, whose reports are quoted above, were members of this family. These stories may all post-date Rome's successful takeover of Greece and have been invented in Arcadia, in the hope that Rome would grant privileges to the region, just as it did to Samothraki and the Troad, because of its alleged connections with Aeneas.

After this peculiar detour in Arcadia, Dionysius speeds Aeneas's fleet up the west coast of Greece to the wooded island of Zakynthos. The Trojans received a warm welcome here, for the hero Zakynthos had been a son of Aeneas's ancestor Dardanos. Games were held in Zakynthos in Dionysius's time, which were said to commemorate the first games there, held between the Trojans and the islanders. The games known to Dionysius were presided over by statues of Aeneas and Aphrodite; being wooden, it is hardly surprising that they appear not to have survived, and indeed, archaeological evidence of occupation in Aeneas's time is scant altogether.

On the Greek coast east of Zakynthos is the city of Patras. Pausanias refers to a chest there which contained an image of the wine god Dionysos, made by Hephaestus and given by Zeus to Dardanos, which drove anyone who looked in it mad; Aeneas was said to have left it behind there during his journey up the coast.[17]

Virgil, meanwhile, says that after the Trojans abandoned Crete, a storm drove them to the Strophades, a set of tiny islands south-east of Zakynthos. Finding plentiful herds there, they killed some animals and began feasting, but were ambushed by Harpies. These hideous creatures had birds' bodies and the faces and breasts of girls. These 'fellest of abominations', as Aeneas called them when he recounted the story to Dido, 'plundered our banquet, befouled all with unclean touch'. Aeneas set an ambush for the Harpies but found them immune to weapons. Then Celaeno, the greatest of the Furies, appeared on the cliff above them. She had heard from Zeus, via Apollo, that the Trojans were destined to reach Italy and their promised city, but not until 'hunger and the sin of your onslaught on us shall constrain you to grind with your teeth your half-eaten boards': to eat their own tables.

Virgil's Aeneas then sailed straight past wooded Zakynthos, Dulichium, Sâme, craggy Neritus and the little island of Ithaka, cursing 'the region which fostered pitiless Ulysses [Odysseus]'. Next came the 'cloud-capped peaks' of Leucata, which is now called Lefkada – and which do often seem to attract clouds. The brilliant white limestone cliffs of Lefkada's south-western tip slice through the waves like a jagged serpent's tail, and on their tip you can see the impressive ruins of the famed shrine of Apollo, 'god of mariners', which Virgil mentions the fleet passing. In Classical times, the shrine's beacon warned vessels away from the dragon's teeth rocks below.

Lefkada used to be linked to the mainland by a natural causeway, which the Greeks cut through to create a sea route down the protected eastern side of the island. Dionysius says that 'on the little island between Dioryctus' ('dug-through') and the town of Lefkada, Aeneas dedicated a temple to Aphrodite Aeneias ('Aphrodite the mother of Aeneas').[18] This temple was, therefore, on the causeway. It is not there now; perhaps its remains are below the Venetian castle of Santa Maura, which stands midway along the causeway.

Later, in Dionysius's account of the voyage, Aeneas dedicated other temples to Aphrodite Aeneias at Actium, Ambracia and Eryx. This prompted theories that the voyage of Aeneas had been imagined by linking up actual sanctuaries of Aphrodite Aeneias. But Jean Perret thought it was the other way around: as Rome's power increased, these towns added the appellation Aeneias to existing temples of Aphrodite, in order to endear themselves to the Romans – and he was probably right.

In such ways, the imaginary journey of Aeneas was traced, embellished and enforced, so that for many, it became – and for some people even now, it remains – a matter of irrefutable fact.

25

Encounter at Buthrotum

Travelling up the north-west coast of Greece, just beyond the island of Lefkada, the Trojan fleet altered its course and turned west into the straits of Actium that lead into the Ambracian Gulf. Here, says Dionysius, Aeneas founded another Aphrodite Aeneias temple, which, along with a temple there to the Great Gods of Samothraki, 'existed even to my time'.[1]

For thirteen years after the assassination of Julius Caesar in 44 BC, the eventual triumph of his great-nephew and heir, Augustus, over his rivals, was far from certain; and had Augustus not come to power, he would never have commissioned the *Aeneid*, enshrining Aeneas and his family's own fabled descent from him in the heart of the Roman psyche. And without the *Aeneid*, Aeneas might be remembered now not as the heroic founder of Rome, but merely as a footnote in history, a broken-spirited slave in the household of Neoptolemus, on this very coastline of Epiros. But Augustus did triumph – and Aeneas's myth along with him; and that triumph took place here, at Actium.

Gaius Octavius Thurinus, known as Octavian, was born on 23 September 63 BC. His grandmother Julia's brother, the great Julius Caesar, left him both his fortune and also his name, so Octavian became Gaius Julius Caesar. It was four years after the Battle of Actium that the Senate granted him new names: 'father of his fatherland', as if he was indeed a new Aeneas, and Augustus, 'the illustrious one'. And we have called our summer months July and August after Julius Caesar and his adopted son Augustus ever since.

Julius Caesar possessed an unshakable belief in his descent from Aeneas, and thus from Aphrodite. Because of what he believed was his semi-divine blood, Caesar wanted the senate to declare him a god after his death. They refused, but while Caesar's funeral games were being played in Rome, thirteen years before the Battle of Actium, a comet blazed – quite coincidentally – through the heavens. Augustus, probably genuinely astonished at such apparently divine confirmation of all he had been brought up to believe, declared the comet to be the *Sidus Iulium*, 'the Julian Star'. It was, Augustus asserted, visible evidence that Caesar had ascended into Heaven. Ovid related at the end of his *Metamorphoses* how Aphrodite, unable to save Caesar from Fate, had gathered the atoms of his soul as they left his murdered body. As she bore them aloft, they ignited and blazed, to become a star. And in his first *Georgic*, Virgil wrote: 'We know not yet what mansion of the skies shall hold thee soon,' nor whether Caesar would become a god of cities, of mariners or, as Virgil hoped, of farmers; but that he had become a god was beyond question. So, Augustus took on a new title – *Divi filius*, the 'son of god'.

So grand a title did not deter his rivals for power, who included Sextus Pompey (son of Caesar's great rival, Pompey the Great) and Mark Antony, from challenging him. Indeed, they played Augustus at his own game, Pompey declaring himself to be *Neptuni filius*, 'son of Neptune (Poseidon)', while Mark Antony's genealogists decided that his family's progenitor, Anton, was a son of Hercules. Thus, Appian relates in his *Civil Wars* how Augustus once chided Pompey for siding with Mark Antony: Caesar might have adopted Pompey, too, he said, 'if he had known that you would accept kinship with the family of Aeneas in exchange for that of Hercules'.[2]

Pompey was executed in 35 BC, leaving Antony as Augustus's sole rival for power in Rome; and by Antony's side was his lover, Cleopatra, Queen of Egypt. Together, Antony and Cleopatra mustered five hundred ships, including two hundred and thirty quinqueremes, here in the Ambracian Gulf. Against them Augustus could raise only two hundred and fifty lesser warships, which waited nervously outside the Straits of Actium that led into the gulf.

In *Aeneid* 8, Virgil allows Aeneas to see into the future, when Hephaestus depicted the battle of Actium on his new shield. 'The eye might see all Leucate [Lefkada] aswarm with the array of war, and the waves ablaze with gold. Here on the tall poop stood Caesar Augustus, leading his Italy to the fray, with senate and people and gods of home and of Heaven, while from his auspicious brows twin flames shot, and his [adopted] father's star beamed over his crest.'

The reality was less glorious. Antony and Cleopatra's sailors were weak and depleted by malaria, so on the blustery morning of 2 September 31 BC, they ordered their ships to return to Egypt. Augustus, aware of his own numerical weakness, wanted to let them go, but his admiral, Agrippa, persuaded him to give battle.

Antony's quinquerimes were armed with massive bronze rams. Powered by their five banks of oars, they could potentially smash into the sides of Augustus's ships with a splintering of pine timbers, sending them quickly down into the depths. But thanks to the malaria, few of Antony's ships had sufficient manpower to deliver such deadly blows. Instead, they floated helplessly while Augustus's lighter vessels blanketed them in a storm of darts, sling-shots and firebrands. Seeing the carnage, Cleopatra ordered her ships to slip out behind Antony's and head for Egypt. Believing a general retreat had begun, Antony's ship broke through Augustus's line, not to fight, but to follow his lover. Panic spread through Antony's fleet – and thus Augustus won his great victory. Both the doomed lovers committed suicide in Egypt the next year. There would be no *Herakliad* composed by a Roman poet to laud the triumph of Mark Antony; it was the myth of Augustus's ancestor Aeneas, instead, that was apotheosized so gloriously in Virgil's *Aeneid*.

Though it has a beautiful setting, Actium itself is an unremarkable place; the temple of Aphrodite Aeneias that Aeneas is said to have founded here was nowhere to be found among the seafront houses and boatyards that spill across the strait from the town of Preveza on the northern shore. But one boatyard's name stands out for its perfect irony: the Cleopatra Marina.

The Trojans came ashore on what Virgil calls 'the Actian strand' where, he says, there was a shrine of Apollo. The latter was not actually at Actium itself, but on the Michalitsi hill, 6 miles up from the straits and above the western shore of the Ambracian Gulf, commanding the narrow strip of land, barely 2 miles wide, between it and the Ionian Sea. During his fight with Antony, Augustus had his camp on this hill. After the battle, he consecrated the site to Poseidon, Ares and (mainly) Apollo Aktios, and built a substantial monument there commemorating his victory, facing south over the gulf and straits, its base decorated with thirty-six of the bronze prows from Antony's quinqueremes. The earth there has subsided badly, but some of the blocks proclaiming Augustus's victory, including one bearing the monumental letters 'VICT', remain, and along the base you can see the bell-shaped holes that once held the bronze rams. In the site's museum nearby is the last surviving chunk of bronze, barely a foot long; a single, tangible survivor of that pivotal day in history.

In Dionysius's account of Aeneas's voyage, he mentioned celebratory games held by the Trojans on Zakynthos. Virgil made no mention of these because he transferred these games to Actium. Here, on the beach, he imagined the wrestling Trojans 'stripped and sleek with oil' and described Aeneas nailing a shield won from the Greek Abas during the Trojan War to the door of a temple. The games, says Virgil, were to celebrate Aeneas's progress so far, but by writing this he invented a Trojan origin for real games that had been held by the local Akarnanians at Actium for hundreds of years, and whose real origins are forgotten. After his victory at Actium, Augustus reorganised these Actian Games, decreeing that they should be held every four years, with crowns as prizes, placing them on a par with those held at Olympia. They comprised equestrian and naval games, athletics, and also arts competitions, particularly, of course, in poetry. They were held first, probably, at Actium itself in 27 BC, but Augustus quickly built a magnificent stadium and theatre for them at the foot of the Michalitsi hill, below his victory monument, and with a theatre nearby; most of the theatre is still just about standing. The stadium, still largely unexcavated, forms a scrubby dent in the landscape next to it.

Above: Dardania, the homeland of Aeneas – the Middle Skamander valley, looking towards the heights of Gargarus, the highest peak of Mount Ida. In the foreground is a lake created by recent damming of the river. New Skepsis's ruins are on the dark green conical hill just left of centre. The Palaiskepsis site is up the valley leading off left, behind the conical hill.

Right: Smallholding in Yaniklar, with buildings little changed from Aeneas's day. Behind rises Mount Ikizce, with its twin peaks, Büyük (left) and Küçük (right), the latter being, we believe, the site of Palaiskepsis, the city of Anchises.

Below right: Walls on Küçük, the likely site of Anchises's city of Palaiskepsis.

Above left: Ancient loom weight found on Küçük/Palaiskepsis.

Above right: This stone sculpture of Kybele was found on the beach at Tenedos and is now set into the wall of the 'Café at Lisa's' in Tenedos town. It shows the goddess as she was worshipped in the Troad in Classical times, plump and enrobed, sitting on a throne flanked by two sitting lions, one of which is visible at the lower left. This is the 'Great Mother of Mount Ida', the local equivalent of Aphrodite – the mother of Aeneas.

Below: Partly bulldozed tumuli below the village of Tongurlu, at the foot of Küçük. These are the tombs of the ancient lords of the fastness up on Küçük – the real family, perhaps, of Aeneas. Photographed in 2015.

The Great Goddess's Sacred Stone, in the Sanctuary of the Great Gods, Samothraki. Behind rise the pillars of the Classical Hieron, and the slope of Mount Saos. The flat stone to the bottom left appears to have been an 'altar' for offerings to the goddess, and it faces the part of the rock that is magnetised.

Above left: The 'vaginal cleft' on Büyük, perhaps an ancient cult site of Kybele and hence the birth-place of Aeneas.

Above right: One of the many rocks on Büyük that, when broken into by frost, as here, reveal an astonishing, blood-red interior and lend circumstantial support to the idea that there was a cult-sanctuary of Kybele here.

Above: The River Skamander, looking south towards the Balli Dağ (hidden by the trees). The trackway here is part of the ancient route between the plain of Troy and the Upper Skamander valley. It was along this track that Aeneas and Anchises would have travelled from Dardania to reach Troy.

Left: The author examining the inward-sloping, eastern double gateway of the upper city (or Pergamos) of Troy, an impressive excavated survival from Aeneas's time.

Below left: The 'Kesik Canal' on the west coast of the Troad, probably dug to protect the southern edge of the Greek camp from attacks by chariots driven by Aeneas and his comrades during the Trojan War.

Seasonal herdsmen's camp on the higher slopes of Mount Ida, near the road that leads up from Edremit, with some of Ida's peaks looming above. It was in such a place as this that Aeneas and the Trojan herds were attacked by Achilles.

The Menelaion, near Sparta. This heroön or hero-shrine to Helen and Menelaus stands on a bluff dominating the broad Eurotas valley, with sweeping views across to the 'pentadactyls', or 'five fingers', of Mount Taygetus. The ruins of Therapne, where Helen entertained Aeneas and Paris, are immediately behind the photographer.

Two of the ancient columns inside the church of Agios Kosmas and Damien on Palaikastro, Kythera, thought to have been from the temple of Aphrodite where Paris, abetted by Aeneas, courted – or abducted – Helen.

Above: A tumultuous abduction of Helen by Paris and Aeneas, depicted in a fifteenth-century engraving after Luca Penni.

Left: Aeneas carrying his father Anchises and leading his son Ascanius out of burning Troy, depicted on a Limoges enamel from the sixteenth century. (Metropolitan Museum of Art)

Right: Aeneas strides boldly out of Troy, carrying Anchises and Troy's sacred Palladium (a statue of Athena), depicted on a silver denarius, ¾" wide, minted by Julius Caesar.

Above: The Sanctuary of Apollo on the island of Delos, at the heart of the Cyclades, with Mount Kynthos looming beyond. It was here that Aeneas came and received Apollo's prophecy to hasten on to 'the land [Italy] where the house of Aeneas shall be lord over all...'

Right: Part of the Mycenaean sanctuary near Palaiopyrgos, Arcadia, with Mount Thaumasion in the distance. In the foreground is the stone outline of a grave, probably the very one that Pausanias was told belonged to Aeneas's father Anchises.

The view north-east from Lefkada, across the narrow isthmus (on which was a sanctuary of Aphrodite Aeneia) that connects it to the mainland; then across the stretch of sea in which Augustus won the Battle of Actium against Antony and Cleopatra in 31 BC; then a narrow strip of mainland Epirus with the entrance to the Ambrakian Gulf – and the mountains of Epiros in the distance.

Left: Part of the monumental inscription that once ran along the now badly subsided front of the Monument of Augustus at Nikopolis, proclaiming that he, 'son of the divine Julius, following the VICTory in the war which he waged on behalf of the Republic... after peace had been secured on the land and sea, consecrated to Neptune and Mars the camp from which he set forth to attack the enemy, which is ornamented with naval spoils'.

Below left: The buildings next to the little theatre in Arta (Ambrakia), Epiros. This was almost certainly the hero shrine of Aeneas, described by Dionysius of Halicarnassus, and which Virgil claimed Aeneas himself had founded during his westward journey.

Part of the walls of the 'new Troy' that was Buthrotum (Butrint, Albania), facing the Vrina Channel, with the hill of Kalivo to the right. Aeneas longed to remain here, but knew his destiny lay further west, in Italy.

Roman ruins on the shore of Sarandë, Albania, that Dionysius called the 'Harbour of Anchises', where Aeneas's fleet rested before crossing to Italy. Behind looms the conical hill of Lëkursit, a likely ancient site of a temple of Aphrodite.

Aeneas's fleet enters the perilous Straits of Messina, between Charybdis and Scylla, prior to their first landfall in Sicily, as imagined on a sixteenth-century Limoges enamel. (Metropolitan Museum of Art)

Above: Virgil's 'joyless strand' of Drepanum (Tripani), Sicily, facing the sea and with Mount Eryx looming behind. To the left is a 1930s monument erected by Mussolini, quoting Virgil's lines about Aeneas burying his father Anchises below a mound here. The only mounds we could find were those in the foreground, which seemed more modern than ancient.

Left: The castle of Eryx, Sicily, built over what Virgil described as the 'star-pointing fane [temple] to Idalian Venus [Aphrodite]', which he claimed Aeneas had founded. (Tristan Ferne)

Below left: An ocean of clouds at sunset, stretching across the sea as far as the Egadi Islands, viewed from the site of Aphrodite's temple on Mount Eryx, Sicily.

Above: The great Elymian temple at Segesta, the city said to have been founded by Aeneas before he left Sicily, surrounded by springtime flowers.

Below: Claude Lorrain's *The Trojan Women Setting Fire to Their Fleet*, depicting the women, tired of wandering and stirred up by Iris, beginning to burn the Trojan ships so as to remain in Sicily. (Metropolitan Museum of Art)

Tiepolo's imagining of 'Aeneas recognising Venus as she disappears in a cloud' on the coast of Carthage. Fresco at Villa Valmarana ai Nani.

Aeneas and Dido as lovers, depicted in a sensuous fresco in the House of Citharist, Pompeii. (Stefano Bolognini)

Manetti's seventeenth-century painting *Dido and Aeneas* captures the couple's parting, shortly before Dido's suicide. The two women behind anticipate that things will not end well. (Los Angeles County Museum of Art)

Cape Misenum, where Aeneas's herald Misenus was said to have been buried. Cumae is out of sight in the distance to the left, and to the right the coast of the Bay of Naples stretches towards the Posilippo Hill, where Virgil lived, and the outskirts of Naples.

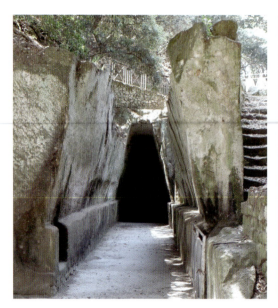

Above left: Entrance to the sibyl's cavern at Cumae, which Virgil's Aeneas visited prior to his journey to the Underworld.

Above right: The Etruscan necropolis of Banditaccia, Caere (Cerveteri), Italy. Caere is where Virgil's Aeneas received his armour from Aphrodite and joined forces with the Etruscans.

Aphrodite in her chariot is presented with the arms made by Hephaestus (seated, centre) for her son Aeneas. (Metropolitan Museum of Art)

Salvator Rosa's seventeenth-century depiction of the god of the Tiber appearing to Aeneas in a dream, directing him to visit Evander in what will become Rome. (Metropolitan Museum of Art)

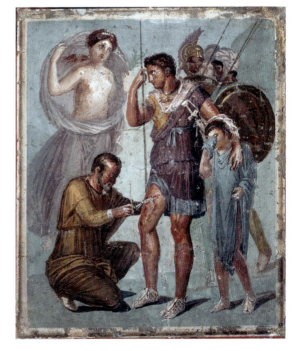

Aeneas waits stalwartly whilst Iapyx removes the arrow from his thigh during a lull in the climactic war with Turnus, whilst Ascanius covers his eyes and Aphrodite looks on lovingly, as depicted in a Roman fresco at Pompeii. (Carole Raddato)

The Ara Pacis Augustae, Augustus's enigmatic altar to the Pax Romana. The figure sacrificing in the top-right panel is widely believed to be Aeneas. (Rabax63)

Mount Olympos in northern Greece, the throne of Zeus and home of the gods, whither Aeneas and his descendants Julius Caesar and Augustus were believed, throughout the ancient world, to have been apotheosed.

Encounter at Buthrotum

Between this area, all of which was declared to be sacred to Apollo, and the sea, 2 miles to the west, Augustus built the city of Nikopolis, 'victory city', as the new Roman capital for this turbulent region, forcing the inhabitants of several local Akarnanian and Epirote cities to abandon their homes and come to live here instead. Even Cassope, up in the hills to the northwest and anciently sacred to Aphrodite, was forcibly abandoned in order to populate Augustus's city. Nikopolis's walls that we see now were built by the Byzantines and seem vast; but then you realise that they encompass only a small portion of the original, Roman metropolis. If one ever feels in doubt of the scale of Augustus's confidence and ambition, Nikopolis serves as an indelible reminder. Its size and grandeur, even after so long, are truly staggering. And when Nikopolis was still being built, Virgil turned Aeneas's sojourn there into the city's poetic genesis.

After Actium, says Dionysius, Aeneas made a detour to Ambracia, simply to found a temple of Aphrodite Aeneias, which Dionysius knew was there. Ambracia is now called Arta, and the journey would have entailed crossing the northern part of the Ambracian gulf and then rowing up the river Arakthos for 7 miles. Dionysius says that Aeneas's visit to Ambracia was also commemorated by a hero-shrine 'near the little theatre'.[3] The shrine contained 'a small archaic wooden statue of wood', said – by Roman times, at least – to be of Aeneas, which was attended, with sacrifices, by priestesses called *amphipoloi*, 'handmaidens'. A local archaeologist, Dr Konstantina Zidrou, kindly confirmed to us that the whereabouts of the Aphrodite Aeneias temple is unknown, but the little theatre has been excavated and next to it there was, sure enough, 'a rectangular building of public character'. We found the site down an alleyway off Agiou Konstantinou Street, a big hole in the ground surrounded by modern buildings. In it is the base of the small theatre and, next to it, the stone footprint of a building, about 20' by 10', with the less substantial foundations of two smaller adjacent rooms between it and the theatre. As Dr Zidrou agreed, this could well be the hero-shrine of Aeneas of which Dionysius wrote.

After these sojourns, as imagined by Virgil and Dionysius, the Trojan fleet would have returned through the straits of Actium, out of the Ambracian Gulf and into the Ionian Sea again. 'Icy Winter began to ruffle the waves under his northern blasts', says Virgil, and the Trojans would have strained at their oars to row up the coast of Epiros. They would have passed the mouth of the river Acheron, which the Greeks believed had its source down in Hades. Their route would then have taken them past steep limestone mountains, peppered with dark green oaks, as they passed what is now the border between Greece and Albania. Then they would have found the Vrina Channel, an opening in the otherwise hostile coastline, opposite the northern promontory of Kerkyra, that we call Corfu. The Vrina Channel curves inland, around the base of a wooded spur, and then almost doubles back on itself before entering the lake of Pelodes, 'the lake of the Nymphs'. Virgil calls all this 'the Chaonian harbour'.

In Search of Aeneas

Aeneas was amazed to see upon the wooded spur 'a little Troy, a Pergamos mimicking the great, and a waterless brook styled Xanthus' and 'the portals of a Scaean Gate'. Aeneas had reached the city of Buthrotum, which the Albanians call Butrint. On the shore of the Vrina Channel, which Virgil calls 'a counterfeit Simois' after one of Troy's rivers, Aeneas saw a lone figure, praying by an empty burial mound. It was Andromache, who had built the mound in memory of her late husband Hector. Amazed to encounter a fellow survivor of the Fall of Troy, Aeneas embraced her joyfully.

Andromache's presence so far from Troy resulted from a myth-making process scarcely less complex than Aeneas's own. In the 400s BC, as Classical culture seeped north into Epiros, its kings learned how their southern neighbours used mythology as propaganda, so they started to manipulate myths and etiology to prove themselves to be proper, full-blooded Greeks rather than northern barbarians. Thus, in his seventh *Nemean Ode*, probably written in 467 or 462 BC, Pindar, who appears to have been the *proxenos* or representative of Epiros in the Greek city of Thebes, claimed on behalf of his paymasters that on their way back from Troy, Achilles' son Neoptolemus and his men 'wandered till they came to Ephyra [Epiros]. Neoptolemus ruled in Molossia for a brief time [and afterwards left for Delphi]; and his race always bore this honour of this.' Achilles was from Phthia in Thessaly, but his mythological blood was now transplanted to Molossia in Epiros, and the story caught on.

In about 425 BC, the Athenian playwright Euripides wrote *Andromache*. Andromache, having been taken captive by Neoptolemus, became his concubine and had a son by him. At the end of the play, Thetys, the goddess-mother of Achilles, said that Andromache must marry Priam's son Helenus, who was also a slave of Neoptolemus's, and go to live in Molossia, taking with her the baby later sources call Molossos. From this child, Thetys foretells, would descend a line of Molossian kings, who would live in prosperity – for although Troy had fallen, the Trojan race was not destined to be erased. There was some poetic licence here, for although Andromache had been the wife of two of Priam's sons in turn, she was not herself a Trojan *per se*, for her father was king of Thebe, to the south-east of Troy. But he owed allegiance to Priam, and perhaps Andromache's family had some Trojan blood through intermarriage with the Trojan royal family. Euripides' aim in this was clear, for Athens wanted to bolster its alliance with Epiros in its war with Sparta, so confirming the upstart Epirotes' belief in their descent from Achilles was the least they could do.

In composing the *Aeneid*, Virgil altered this story only slightly. Andromache told Aeneas that she had been Neoptolemus's concubine, but when he got married (to Hermione), she was given in marriage to Helenus, 'slave mated with slave'. When Neoptolemus died, she says, he left part of his realm to Helenus, 'who named these plains Chaonian ... from Chaon in Troy; and Pergamos is this Ilian tower'.

Encounter at Buthrotum

The sight of Aeneas's son Ascanius reduced Andromache to tears. He was a surviving grandson, through his mother, Creusa, of Priam, and he reminded Andromache of her own son Astyanax (also called Skamandrios) – likewise a grandson of Priam's – who, in Virgil's version of the myth, had had his brains dashed out by the Greeks against the walls of Troy. Now Helenus appeared and escorted his cousin Aeneas into the new Troy, where he 'gave them welcome in his ample colonnades; goblet in hand, they made libation of wine in the central hall, and the feast was set on gold.'

Dionysius tells the story slightly differently. Anchises and the fleet sailed from Actium to Buthrotum, but Aeneas himself ventured inland from Actium to the ancient oracle of Dodona – a two-day match north-east, barely 50 miles as the crow flies, but over difficult, mountainous terrain. Ovid sends Aeneas to Dodona too, to 'the grove of the talking oaks'. Dodona was the most ancient oracle in Greece. Its deities were Dione, the local version of the Great Mother, and her consort Dias, identified with Zeus. Together, they whispered prophecies that could be heard when the breeze rustled the leaves of an ancient oak. The sanctuary remains, in a beautiful valley among the soaring mountains, and a new oak has been planted there, through whose leaves the constant breeze blows; but with no priests to interpret them any more, the prophecies it whispers are no longer decipherable. It is here at Dodona, says Dionysius, that Aeneas met Helenus, and they travelled down together for four days to Buthrotum – a 60-mile journey to the north-west.

Dionysius adds that 'the presence of the Trojans at Buthrotum is proved by a hill called Troy, where they encamped at that time.' This was probably the hill now called Kalivo, which is an hour's walk east of Buthrotum along the opposite bank of the Vrina Channel. In 1930-1, Benito Mussolini, the Fascist ruler of Italy from 1930 to 1945, commemorated the bimillennial of Virgil's birth in order to draw attention to Rome's former grandeur. As part of this, he organised the *Crociera Virgiliana*, a Mediterranean cruise by prominent archaeologists retracing the voyage of Aeneas, which included a stop at Buthrotum. Mussolini was particularly keen to prove the truth of Aeneas's presence in Buthrotum, in order to add a mythological lustre to his alliance with Albania, so he founded an Italian Archaeological Mission in Albania and told them to start excavations at Buthrotum and Kalivo. The excavation's director, Manfred Ugolini, dug hopefully at Kalivo, as at Buthrotum itself, hoping to find hard evidence of Aeneas's presence there. While Ugolini unearthed later Iron Age fortifications at Kalivo, which can still be seen now, the only thing he found from approximately Aeneas's time was a handful of crude stone tools, patently of local, not Trojan, origin.

The prosaic reality was that the Trojan presence at Buthrotum was a myth, probably going no further back than the 400s BC. It probably arose as a side-effect of the Epirote kings' claim to have Achilles as their ancestor. It became in useful in its own right when Alcetas II of Epiros (313-307 BC) wrested control of Buthrotum from Corfu. In opposition to the Corfiots' occupation of Chaonia, Alcetas may have asserted the myth that the Buthrotans were

In Search of Aeneas

of Trojan stock, so he, as a descendant of Andromache, could be seen as their just ruler and protector. The Buthrotans became proud of their Trojan ancestry, minting coins showing a bull's head in commemoration of a story that Helenus had wounded a bull in sacrifice, and it had swum to the promontory of Buthrotum as a sign that he should build his new city there.

When the Romans invaded Epiros in 167 BC, they razed seventy Epirote cities and enslaved all the inhabitants, but Buthrotum was spared, almost certainly because of the citizens' well-established claims to Trojan ancestry, which made them kinsmen to the Romans. The story pleased Caesar, because of his own family's claim to be descended from Aeneas, and he wanted to send Romans to live in Buthrotum. Augustus enlarged Buthrotum and his building work is still apparent there now. Buthrotum's place in Virgil's *Aeneid* was therefore assured. Virgil probably went there himself, for the 'Scaean Gate' he describes there exists: it so excited Ugolini when he discovered it, in the tangled woods down by the Vrina Channel, that he did not hesitate in applying that explicitly Trojan name to it, and so it is labelled now.

Buthrotum is a beautiful and evocative place to visit, with its ruins rising up among the trees beside the serenely lapping waters of the Vrina Channel. It was easy for us to imagine that Aeneas, Helenus and Andromache were still there, feasting from gold plates in the high halls, reminiscing about Troy. Virgil's Aeneas longed to remain there, but Helenus, gifted with foresight, reaffirmed that his destiny lay in Italy. Only there would Aeneas make the name of Troy mighty again through his deeds. 'With welling tears', Aeneas bade farewell to Helenus and Andromache. A favourable wind was blowing, and it was time to go. 'Live and be happy,' Aeneas told them: 'you have won your peace.'

The wind sped the Trojan fleet north along a coastline dominated by the Ceraunian Mountains. Dionysius says they stopped next at 'the Harbour of Anchises'.[4] This is the Albanian port of Sarandë, 8 miles north of Buthrotum, and it is here that you can come by ferry from Corfu, if you want to visit Butrint. Sarandë was anciently called Onchesmus, so Dionysius thought it was named after Anchises. Dionysius says Aeneas built a temple to Aphrodite there. There is no evidence of it now, but the harbour is dominated by a conical hill, the top of which is completely covered by the Ottoman castle of Lëkursit. The hill gazes out to the double peaked, or breasted, mountain of Pantokrator on the northern coast of Corfu. Corfu is sickle-shaped and as previously mentioned was one of the imagined locations of the sickle which had castrated Uranos, so it was thus associated with the foamy birth of Aphrodite. It would make sense for there to have been an Aphrodite sanctuary on the Lëkursit hill, and if Dionysius knew of such a temple, we can understand why he imagined Aeneas and old Anchises struggling up the hill to found it, and thus to enlist the goddess's protection ahead of their potentially dangerous crossing to Italy.

The narrowest point in the Straits of Otranto, between Albania and Italy, is a little further north of Sarandë, where the north-western end of

Encounter at Buthrotum

the Ceraunian Mountains forms the Karaburun Peninsula. This marks the dividing line between the Ionian Sea to the south and the Adriatic to the north. At dawn and dusk you can see the distant Italian coastline opposite. Virgil imagines the Trojans reaching a place where they beached their ships at sunset, when the shadows darkened on the hills. Maybe he was thinking of Sarandë itself, or of somewhere on the Karaburun Peninsula. The Trojans lay down, and 'the dew of sleep sprinkled the limbs of the weary.' Only Aeneas's helmsman Palinurus remained awake, studying the stars: 'Arcturus, the rainy Hyads, and the twin Bears – and he gazed on Orion in his panoply of gold.' Only when the sky was clear did Palinurus sound his horn to wake the Trojans.

If they left from Karaburun, they struck out across the open sea; if they departed from Sarandë, then they would have skirted the north coast of Corfu, black against the dawn-blushed sky and then passed the tiny islands of Ereikoussa and Othonoi, before heading west. At last, Aeneas saw, amidst the silvery haze, 'distant hills and lowly coast'. Full of joy, they cried out the blessed name of Italy, and Anchises 'wreathed a mighty bowl in a chaplet, filled it with wine, and called upon Heaven' to grant them safe landfall. In answer to Anchises's prayer, the breeze freshened and the Trojans landed, at last, on Italian soil.

26

Via Enea

Some of the Trojan ships, says Dionysius, made landfall at 'the Promontory of Iapygia, which was then called the Salentine Promontory'.[1] The Iapygians were the native people of the heel of Italy, part of the region now called Apulia or Puglia, and Strabo clarifies that the Promontory of Iapygia was the southernmost tip of the larger Salentine Peninsula. Aeneas himself, continues Dionysius, came ashore at 'a place named after Minerva'.[2]

Strabo is noncommittal about where this was, but Virgil's description of the landing-place is so detailed as to suggest he had visited it, probably by land. But he imagined what it was like for Aeneas, approaching by sea:

> 'Closer now, open to our gaze, and we saw a shrine to Minerva on the cliff. The mariners furled sail and turned their sterns to the strand. There a roadstead [a stretch of calm water just outside a harbour] sweeps curving from the eastern wave in semblance of a bow: invisible itself, before it stand rocks foaming with salt spray, while turreted crags stretch arms of stone like a double wall to the beach, and the temple recedes from the sea.'

On the shore they saw four white steeds. These could be harnessed for war, Anchises observed, or yoked to the plough: a prophecy of war, therefore, followed by peace. A Limoges enamel of about 1530-35, based on a woodcut of Grüninger's 1502 edition of Virgil, shows the fleet, guided by Palinurus, approaching the rocky coast; Athena's temple rises behind like a Byzantine basilica, and a turbanned Anchises watches four (incorrectly, brown) horses grazing on the shore.[3]

Several harbours along the Salentine shore, such as Porto Badisco, have laid claim to be Aeneas's landing place, but the most convincing is Castro Marina, due west of Sarandë. Anciently called *Castrum vel Arx Minervae*, 'the castle of the fortress of Athena', it has a rocky bay in which two arms of rock protect an inner roadstead of calmer water; set back from this is a high, rocky outcrop, now dominated by an Aragonese castle, around whose base can be seen ancient walls attributed to the local Messapian people of the 300s BC. According to an article in *La Repubblica* entitled 'Castrum, ecco il porto che accolse Enea', ('Castrum, the port that welcomed Aeneas'), excavations at the castle by Francesco d'Andria of Lecce University revealed fragments of a temple, the statue of a goddess, and votive offerings including arrowheads, speartips and other iron weapons.[4] These suggested that there had indeed been a sanctuary there to the warrior-goddess Minerva and, when we visited, we heard that the mayor of Castro Marina was considering changing the town's name back to Castrum Minervae for this reason. Down by the harbour, we found a colourful modern signboard depicting the arrival of Aeneas and his joyful people there. It included four white horses grazing on the headland, just as Virgil described.

Virgil's Trojans made their way up to Minerva's temple on the hilltop. Veiling their heads with their Phrygian cloaks, they sacrificed to Athena-Minerva. Remembering Helenus's advice, Aeneas sacrificed to Hera, too, hoping thus to palliate her hatred of Trojans, caused, as we have heard, by Paris's choice of Aphrodite over her and Athena in the beauty contest on Mount Ida.

The close proximity of the heel of Italy to Albania and Greece led to many real crossings of immigrants from the east, and some of these were mythologised as being survivors of the Trojan War. Prince Idomeneus of Crete is said to have founded this same temple to Athena at Castro Marina on his roundabout return from the Trojan War. Aeneas's old adversary Diomedes was believed to have landed further north and settled at Aecae, near Foggia. When Aecae was rebuilt by a Byzantine general in AD 1018, it was renamed Troia, and the myth spread that Diomedes had named it (though somewhat irrationally) after the city he had helped to destroy. It was also said that the local Neolithic dolmens were blocks of stone that Diomedes had removed from Troy's walls; and that the local wine grape, which produces a dark, spicy wine, gained its name, Nero (or Uva) di Troia, because Diomedes had brought it with him from the Troad. With so many reminders of Greeks and the sack of Troy around them, it would not be surprising if the Trojans felt uneasy here. They set sail again, rounding the base of the Salentine Peninsula where the port of Leuca is now. In honour of the myth, modern Leuca has roads named Via Enea and Via Virgilio.

Rather than striking out across the Gulf of Taranto, they hugged the shore, up the western side of Italy's heel, to Taranto. This was 'Hercules's town, if Fame speaks truth', according to Virgil. The city was actually founded long after Aeneas's time by Spartan colonists in 706 BC. It was one of the cities of Magna Graecia, the name given to those parts of southern Italy and Sicily which were colonised by Greeks. Taranto's mythological founder was said to have been Taras, who was son either of Hercules, from whom the Spartan kings claimed descent, or of Poseidon. Two impressive pillars of the Classical temple to Poseidon can still be seen at Taranto, next to the Medieval castle.

In Search of Aeneas

Along the north-western rim of the Gulf of Taranto, low-lying plains stretch north towards the blue outline of the Lucanian Apennines. Dionysius wrote that Aeneas left 'some traces' along this otherwise dull coast, particularly a bronze patera (a mixing bowl for libations) bearing his name, which he dedicated in one of Hera's temples. Dionysius does not say which temple; maybe it was the temple of Hera at Metaponto, the next major Magna Graecian city along the gulf after Taranto. Metaponto's origins were attributed to Nestor, on his own circuitous return from Troy to Pylos, but it was actually founded by the Magna Graecian city of Sybaris as a buffer against Taranto. The remains of Metaponto's walls and civic temples are impressive; on a hillock to the north-west is its outlying temple of Hera, known later as the Tavole Palatinum. Fifteen of its squat Doric columns are still standing. This was where Pythagoras used to teach his pupils, and perhaps where that bronze mixing bowl, attributed to Aeneas, was shown to curious visitors.

Next along the coast is the mouth of the River Aciris, which the Greek colonists thought was another branch of the Acheron that flowed up from Hades. Then comes modern Policoro and, on a low hill just behind it are the ruins of the Magna Graecian city of Heraclea. Heraclea was founded in 433 BC in place of an earlier city called Siris, which was destroyed in the internecine wars between the Magna Graecian cities. The archaeological museum next to the Heraclea site claims that Siris lies below, but Strabo said that the two places were distinct, and about 24 stades apart. An alternative possible site for Siris would be somewhere between Heraclea and the modern coastal settlement called Nova Siri. At any rate, Strabo says that when Aeneas's fleet reached Siris, the Trojan women were so fed up with the seemingly endless quest for Aeneas's promised land that they set fire to the ships, so as to force the men to settle down here. Dionysius does not mention this story in relation to Siris; Virgil, as we shall see, saves the ship-burning story until Aeneas reaches Sicily. The people of Siris had a wooden statue of Trojan Athena, which they claimed had been set up by the Trojans when the city was founded, and which is said to have closed its eyes when Greek colonists took it over from the descendants of its purported Trojan founders, a claim which – along with the claims of Rome and Lavinium to have items of Trojan provenance – Strabo found rather far-fetched.[5]

Further down the western side of the Gulf of Taranto are the ruins of Sybaris, one of the earliest of all the Magna Graecian cities, founded in 720 BC and later destroyed by its southern neighbour, Crotone. The low coastline is dominated by high, grassy dunes, with the Calabrian Apennines dark blue in the distance; as we drove along, the ominous purple sky above them was shot through with forks of lightning. Next comes the mouth of the River Neto, anciently called the Neaethus, a name derived from 'burnt ships'. Strabo says a fleet of Greek ships returning from the Trojan War had Trojan slave-women aboard, and these women burnt the boats, in similar fashion to those at Siris, to end the voyage. Crotone, which was actually founded in 710 BC, used this story as its origin myth, so its people claimed to be of mixed Greek and Trojan race.[6]

Below Crotone, the bay sweeps back south-east into the long, low promontory of Lacinium. This is the next landmark after Taranto that Virgil mentions. The Trojans must have been extremely glad that they had made offerings to Hera, because Lacinium was sacred to her. The rocks around it could be fatal to shipping, but Aeneas's fleet sailed around it without incident. The temple of Hera Lacinia, as Virgil calls it, was actually built by the Crotonians in the 400s BC, both to worship Hera and to act as a visual warning for shipping. For many centuries, the promontory was called Capo Nau, from the Greek *naos*, 'temple', until one of Crotone's bishops stole all but one of the temple's columns for his palace. The one column which he left behind still stands proud on the headland. The place is now named Capo Colonna, 'the cape of the column'. Swallows and bee-eaters soared past through the air, and it was easy to imagine Aeneas's fleet sailing past.

The coastline now turns back south-west, out of the gulf and along the bottom of the toe of Italy. The Trojan fleet passed Virgil's 'hills of Caulon', the Magna Graecian city of Caulon, already ruined by Virgil's time, near Monasterace. The modern town called Caulonia is 10 miles further south; it was called Castelvetere, but changed its name in 1863, in the mistaken belief that it stood on the site of the ancient settlement that Virgil had mentioned. Next, Virgil mentions 'Scylaceum, the home of shipwreck', that is, Squillace; Virgil's geography lets him down here, because this actually comes just before Caulon. Scylaceum's mythological founder was either Odysseus or Menestheus of Athens, one of Helen of Troy's suitors; it lacks a proper port and its coast remains as dangerous for shipping now as it was then. The next danger would have been Cape Larme, at the southernmost point of Italy, but Aeneas's ships must have rounded this successfully and entered the Straits of Messina between the toe of Italy and Sicily.

Aeneas would have wanted to sail north between Italy and Sicily, but both nature and Homer were against him, for the straits' strong, south-flowing current makes this one of the few places in the Mediterranean where the tides are strong. This posed great dangers for Bronze Age ships, and there is wide agreement that the Straits of Messina were the ones described in Homer's *Odyssey*, where Odysseus tried to negotiate a safe course between the terrible whirlpool of Charybdis on one side, and a rock on the other, on which perched the Scylla, with six writhing necks and slavering dog-like heads. Circe had warned Odysseus about this, and back in Buthrotum, Helenus had foreseen similar difficulties for Aeneas. Scylla's rock is identified now as one on the western Italian coast, on which perches the Castello Ruffo di Scilla. In book 13 of Ovid's *Metamorphoses*, Scylla was turned to stone after Odysseus had been there. By skirting next to her rock, says Ovid, and keeping well away from the whirlpool opposite, Aeneas's fleet reached the Tyrrhenian Sea, only to be swept back down through the straits again by a storm. Virgil's Aeneas, mindful of Helenus' warnings, entered the straits between Scylla and Charybdis but encountered terrifyingly turbulent seas. Later, in *Aeneid* 1, he recalled hearing the baying of Scylla's hounds, but maybe this was just the roar of the waves. Quickly, the fleet altered its course to the south-west, planning to avoid the perilous straits by sailing right around Sicily instead.

As Aeneas's ships approached the Sicilian coast, the menacing bulk of Mount Etna would have loomed ever closer. The volcano is still alive and volatile today, puffing smoke and venting spurts of lava. We climbed part of it, an unforgiving struggle up its shifting, ashen slopes, as far as a café; the following year, we saw a newspaper report that this 'refuge' had been destroyed by a minor eruption. The Greeks reasoned that Etna's volcanic activity was due to Typhon being imprisoned below it. This dreadful monster was sent by Kronos to punish Zeus for overthrowing him, but Typhon failed; Etna's molten lava was believed to be his bile as he lay below, imprisoned for eternity. The Greeks also believed that Etna's fiery depths contained the forge of lame Hephaestus, the Olympian consort of Aphrodite. Besides armour for the heroes, Hephaestus fashioned Zeus's thunderbolts, assisted in his work by the hideous Earth-born Cyclopses. When Odysseus landed below Etna, he and his men were trapped in the cave of the Cyclops Polyphemus. Cunning Odysseus plied the Cyclops with Maroneian wine and blinded his single eye with a pointed stake. As Odysseus and his men fled back to their ship, the Cyclopses flung jagged rocks at them. These became the Isole Ciclopi, the basaltic rocky islands along the shoreline at Aci Trezza.

This was one of the landing places in the Allied invasion of Sicily in the Second World War; by uncanny coincidence, an old army map of Sicily, in my grandfather's papers, had a single, pencil arrow pointing straight at Aci Trezza, and an Italian war memorial on the shore attests to fierce fighting here. It seems that my grandfather, who was a major in the Royal Artillery, made landfall in Sicily in the precise place where both Odysseus and Aeneas were said to have landed before him. Aeneas's landing there allowed Virgil to create a perfect link between his *Aeneid* and Homer's *Odyssey* – for on the shore, Aeneas encountered Achaemenides, one of Odysseus's sailors who had been left behind in the rout and who was now emaciated and half-deranged with fear.

Even as Achaemenides recounted his sorry tale, the Trojans saw monstrous Polyphemus himself, using an uprooted tree trunk as a blind-man's cane, groping his way down the hillside to bathe his still-inflamed eye socket in the salty waves. In the Casa de Laocoonte in Pompeii was a painting, now lost but known from a drawing, showing a strapping, youthful Aeneas, naked below his cloak, with his men freshly landed from their high-prowed ship, gazing at coarse Polyphemus. He has a ragged skin tied round his neck and is leaning on a tree trunk, with his sheep flock around him;[7] a fine metaphor, as Galinsky suggested, for civilisation encountering barbarism.[8]

Terrified, the Trojans crept down to their ships, taking poor Achaemenides with them, and cast off. But Polyphemus heard them and raised a blood-curdling cry that shook the waves and moaned through Etna's caverns. The other Cyclopses appeared, 'a conclave of fear' as Aeneas described them. But, just in time, a brisk breeze filled the sails and sent the Trojans speeding safely away.

As they travelled south, Achaemenides pointed out the sights – 'Pantagia's mouth and its living rock' and then 'the Megarian gulf and lowly Thapsus'. The Gulf of Megara, now called the Gulf of Augusta, gained its name in the 700s BC, long after Aeneas's time, when Greek colonists from Megara in Attika founded Megara Hyblaea there. Just to the south of Megara Hyblaea is Thapsos, on the Magnisi Peninsula. Thapsos was a Bronze-Age trading port, whose inhabitants gouged their burial chambers out of the soft rock of the low peninsula next to the sea, as can still be seen now; pots, daggers and beads from Aeneas's time have been found within them.

Next came Ortygia, 'quail island', facing across the Sicanian bay, says Virgil, towards the promontory of Plemmyrium. Today, Plemmyrium is Plemmirio, while Ortygia is covered by the city of Syracusa, which Corinthians founded in 733 BC. Their temple to Athena still stands, the spaces between the columns in-filled to create the walls of what is now the city's cathedral. Ortygia was also another name for Delos, the birthplace of Apollo, so, because of the coincidence, the Greeks venerated both him and his sister Artemis at Syracusa.

Aeneas stopped on this Ortygia's shore to visit the fountain of Arethusa, where two springs, of Alpheus and Arethusa, bubble out of the volcanic rock and cascade down together into the waves. The nymph Arethusa, says the myth, once bathed in the river Alpheus, which flows past Olympia in Arcadia. The river god tried to ravish her, but aided by Artemis, Arethusa fled to Ortygia. Undeterred, Alpheus flowed under the sea and burst up here as a spring. Artemis tried to conceal Arethusa as a second spring, but as her waters mingled in the fountain with Alpheus's, her attempts to evade him were finally thwarted. The springs and their pool are now enclosed by a circular wall built by the Emperor Charles V. It is home to tall, exotic papyrus plants which the emperor imported from the Nile, and it is marked by a plaque quoting the relevant lines from the *Aeneid*. The plaque is one of several erected at sites connected with Aeneas's journey as part of Mussolini's commemoration of the two thousandth anniversary of Virgil's birth. In Aeneas's time, it was all much simpler, just rock and springs, and he paid homage to 'the high powers of the place', presumably including Artemis herself.

They put to sea again, passing 'the bountiful soil of stagnant Helorus', now called the river Tellaro, which floods its delta each spring. One of its tributaries rises far up in the Sicilian mountains, below Akrai, which is now called Palazzola Acreide. Akrai's hilltop is dominated by the ruins of a temple of Aphrodite, gazing out towards her husband's forge within Etna. It raises the possibility that Aeneas may once have been imagined venturing up here, hunting for food, perhaps, and founding a shrine to his mother – but Virgil does not mention this.

Next, Aeneas's fleet passed 'the tall cliffs and beetling rocks of Pachynus', which is Cape Passero, the south-eastern tip of Sicily, and it began traversing the island's southern coast, past Camarina. This was founded from Syracusa, long after Aeneas's time, in 599 BC. Camarina was famous for the stupidity of its inhabitants, who had purposefully drained the great marsh that surrounded them, thus opening themselves up to attack by the Carthaginians, who killed them all in 405 BC. Further up the coast was Gela; this was colonised in 688 BC from Rhodes and Crete, and was named, as Virgil tells us correctly, after the river there. Then 'the steep of Acragas – sire of gallant steeds in the years to come! –revealed its steely walls in the distance.' Now called Agrigento, Acragas was founded from Gela in about 581 BC. When we went in the spring, its Valle dei Templi was carpeted with knee-high marigolds growing around a sanctuary to Asclepios, the healing god. The valley is so-called because of the row of Classical temples that still stand in crumbling majesty along the ridge – Virgil's 'steep' – above it. The oldest temple is labelled the Temple of Hera, but it faces a breast-shaped mountain and nobody really knows which of the Great Mother's manifestations was in the minds of the people who first worshipped there; maybe the temple was originally Aphrodite's.

After Acragas, Aeneas's fleet passed 'palm-crowned Selinus', modern Selinunte. This was originally a settlement of the local Elymian people and was probably named Manuzza after their version of the Great Mother. In the mid-600s BC, it was taken over by Greeks from Megara Hyblea, and renamed Selinus, because of the *sélinon* or wild celery that still grows here. Selinus's great catastrophe was in 409 BC, when Carthage attacked it before reinforcements could come from Agrigento and Syracusa. One of its surviving temples, on the city's eastern hill, now labelled 'Temple E', may have been dedicated to Hera or Aphrodite.

At the western end of Sicily, the Trojan fleet skirted 'the Lilybaean shallows and the perils of their ambushed reefs'. Lilybaeum was founded in 396 BC by the Carthaginian navigator Himilco. Much later, invading Arabs renamed it *Marsa Allah*, 'port of Allah', hence its modern name, Marsala. It is famous now for its sweet wine, which the Sicilians use best as a sauce for fried veal and sage. Rounding this westernmost point of Sicily, Aeneas would have looked north from the prow of his ship to see the nipple-shaped peak of Eryx, now called Erice, rising above Sicily's west coastline – the coastline of the Elymians.

The dramatic escape from the Cyclopses must have proved too much for poor old Anchises. During his long life, he had experienced an unimaginably passionate encounter with Aphrodite; been lamed by Zeus's lightning bolt; seen Troy burnt to ashes and endured six years as a refugee. Some considered he died in Arcadia or Latium, but not Virgil. We may imagine Anchises lying in his ship's stern, ever frailer and less substantial, only his eyes still quick in his shrunken face. They landed below Mount Eryx, on the 'joyless strand' of Drepanum (Trapani) and, as Aeneas tells Dido in *Aeneid* 3, 'buffeted by so many a tempest of ocean, I lost, alas, my father Anchises, my stay in all sorrow and calamity. This was the crown of my sorrows.'

Via Enea

Aeneas buried Anchises below a tumulus on the strand. There are some low mounds just set back from the gritty beach between Trapani and Pizzolungo, but whether any go back beyond Virgil's time and were his inspiration for placing Anchises' burial mound there, is impossible to tell. Near the mounds stands the Stele Virgiliana, a monument to Aeneas's landing erected by Mussolini. In Pizzolungo, each street name echoes parts of the *Aeneid*, including the Via Anchise. The main road is called the Via Enea.

27

Landfall in Africa

The western spread of Aeneas's myth was linked closely to the western spread of the Greeks themselves. In and just after Homer's time, Greeks started trading, and later establishing colonies, along both the northern coast of Africa and the southern shore of Europe, particularly in Sicily and southern Italy. With them travelled their myths, especially the story of Troy. Both the siege, in which the Greeks proved themselves more cunning than foreigners, and the connected *nostos* stories of the Greek heroes' attempts to return home, resonated with the Greek traders and colonists, echoing the many perils they had experienced and helping them explain the origins of the races which they encountered.

Some of these new races were identified as descendants of Trojans. Any scholarly notions that any of them actually were Trojans have long been discounted, for want of any compelling archaeological or linguistic evidence. It appears far more likely that labelling newly encountered foreigners as Trojans was simply a convenient way for the Greek settlers to fit them into their world-view, or, as Knight summarised Mommsen's view, 'to adorn the history of their new homes by connecting it with the poetry of their old'.

What criteria they used in applying the label 'Trojan' to a newly encountered people is disputed. Some scholars, such as Wilamowitz-Moellendorff, argued that the Greeks tended to label hostile natives as Trojans. Galinsky tested out the opposite argument.[1] True, he wrote, during the Persian wars in the 400s BC, the tragedies of Aeschylus (d. 456/5 BC), who had fought in the conflict, equated the Persians with Trojans, so from then on Trojans started being depicted in Greek art as louche, deceitful easterners. But before the Persian wars, when Aeneas and Hector were depicted in Greek art, they look just the same as Achilles or Ajax (whereas the Trojans' own neighbours, the Cimmerians and Scythians, were often depicted as savages). On those grounds, argued Galinsky, the Trojans, with their descent through Dardanos from Zeus, were seen as a branch of the extended Greek family. Labelling a foreigner as a Trojan, Galinsky suggested, was therefore 'not political enmity, but a cultural distinction'.[2]

Galinsky weakened his argument, however, by claiming that the Greeks chose 'Trojan' as a positive label in preference to negative ones, such as 'Phoenician'. But the Greek genealogical system accounted for the origins of all known Mediterranean peoples within the same overarching pedigree: the Phoenicians' progenitor was Phoenix, descended from Io who came from Argos; the Egyptians, similarly, were descendants of Io's great grandson, Belos. If even their greatest commercial rivals, the Phoenicians, were seen by the Greeks as having Greek origin, then assigning Greek origins to the Trojans did not make them automatically into equals.

In general, the model proposed by Wilamowitz-Moellendorff seems to work better. Peoples who were friendly to the incoming Greek traders and colonists were hailed as descendants of Greek heroes who had been swept off course on the way home from Troy. Those peoples who were cultured, yet opposed to the incoming Greeks, could conveniently be labelled as 'others' and thus as Trojans.

Having acknowledged all this, we may speculate for a moment that one early step in the western spread of the Trojan myth may have been made without the help of Greek imagination. In *Timaeus*, Plato relates how the priests at Saïs, in the Nile Delta, told his ancestral uncle Solon of Athens (638-558 BC) that their city's founding goddess, Neïth, was identical with Athena, and that the Saïsans were descended from survivors of the destruction of Atlantis. Atlantis was of course a mythological city, yet, as Zangger suggested, some elements of its myth may have been based on Troy. Both cities had Athena as their patron goddess; their kings both had sub-kings ruling under them; both citadels were famously well defended, albeit in different ways; both fell; both falls were instigated by Zeus, and the destruction of both heralded a general collapse in world civilisation. If the nine thousand 'years' which had elapsed since Atlantis's fall were actually lunar cycles – for that was the chief unit by which the Egyptians measured time – then this would place its destruction in about 1300 BC. That is not much earlier than 1250 BC, which is, roughly, when the Trojan War is thought to have taken place. So, maybe the people of Saïs had believed, once, that their ancestors were survivors of the Fall of Troy – or it could even be true.

About 600 miles west along the north African coast from Saïs is Cyrene, now called Shahhat, in modern Libya. Cyrene was founded by Greek colonists in about 630 BC and its kings claimed descent from Odysseus. Yet Pindar (d. 443 BC), in his *Pythian Odes*, relates the myth that Cyrene had been founded, before any Greeks reached there, by the sons of Aeneas's cousin, Antenor.[3] Cyrene founded a colony yet further along the coast, named Teukria; this may, perhaps, have been named after Teucer, the Trojan father-in-law of Dardanos.

Beyond Teukria lie the stony lands known as the Maghreb, that stretch west across western Libya, Tunisia, Algeria and Morocco. The Maghreb's people were called Libyans by the Greeks, and Meshwesh by the Egyptians. The Maghreb tribes included the Massyli, who later founded Numidia. Herodotus called these north Africans 'Maxyans', who 'say that they are descended from the men of Troy'.[4] In 1937, Knight thought 'this may well be true, because their peculiar way of dressing their hair is likely to have been learnt in Troy.' That is an almost entirely unsupportable argument, as we do not know how the Trojans of Aeneas's time styled their hair. How many of the non-Greek-speaking Massyli really claimed Trojan ancestry is open to question. Perhaps this was a myth imposed on them by the Greeks, although it is always possible that their ancestors, like those of the Saïsians, Cyrenians and Teukrians, really had migrated there from the east in the chaotic period after the Trojan War.

Besides establishing colonies along the north African coast, the Greeks also spread west along the southern coast of Europe. They founded their Magna Graecian cities around the heel and toe of Italy and then, by 750 BC, they started to colonise Sicily. Initially, they confined themselves to eastern Sicily, partially displacing the native Sicels. But over the decades, like strawberry plants sending out runners that grow into new plants and issue runners of their own, these Greek colonies spread west through the lands of the Sicanians. Then, by the 600s BC, Magna Graecia started intruding into western Sicily, the land of the Elymians.

The Elymians emerged in western Sicily in about 1000 BC. Their origins are hotly disputed. Hellanikos, as reported by Dionysius, thought they came from Italy,[5] but it has been suggested that they came instead from Anatolia, just as their later myths asserted, having travelled thence via North Africa – perhaps via that fragmentary trail of Trojan origin tales stretching west from Saïs to the Maghreb. Thucydides (c. 460-395 BC), asserted, slightly differently, that some refugees from the fall of Troy sailed direct to Sicily, mixed with the native Sicels and became the Elymians. They founded Eryx and Segesta, Thucydides added, and were joined by men from Fokia in central Greece, who had been driven off course by a storm on their return from Troy.[6] Archaeological studies of Elymian culture suggests influences from both the Phoenicians and the Mycenaeans, probably via trade. Galinsky wondered whether Thucydides and his predecessors knew of some sort of eastern Mediterranean influence and chose to label this as 'Trojan'; perhaps the Elymians accepted the label because, through Dardanos, it gave them a shared ancestry with the Greeks.[7] This idea may have started through contact with the Greek settlers of Selinus on the south-eastern borders of the Elymians' part of Sicily. The 'Trojan' label, Galinsky thought, may have been a compliment paid by the Selinians; a way of saying 'you are like us and almost our cultural equals.'

However, the Elymians' Trojan origin myth could have arisen just as easily through false etymology. The term 'Elymian' was coined by the Greeks themselves, because the western Sicilians grew an old strain of grain called foxtail millet, or *elymos*. The name sounds a bit like 'Ilios', and this may have enforced, or spawned, the idea that they came from Troy. It may have pleased the Greeks to imagine that this was true, for the Elymians were peculiarly skilful in several areas considered to be particular preserves of high civilisation, particularly masonry, and the colonists needed to reassure themselves that these skills were, ultimately, of respectable, eastern Mediterranean origin. They even imagined Daedalus escaping from King Minos on Crete and flapping on his artificially feathered arms all the way to Sicily, so as to seed this technological advancement in western Sicily. To make the Elymians worthy recipients of such skills, the Greeks decided that they must have been descendants of the men of Ilion, the Trojans, who had come all this way in their beaked ships after their city had fallen.

Regardless of their real origins, once the Elymians had heard from the Greeks of the tales of the *Iliad*, and how the Trojans had withstood their enemies so heroically, they appear to have embraced the notion of being Trojan, with a particular emphasis, as evidenced by their coins, on Aeneas. This fascination with Aeneas may have been influenced in part by the local goddess cult up on the craggy peak of Mount Eryx at the western end of Sicily. The people living here in Neolithic times may have called this goddess Manuzza. Phoenician merchants reimagined the Eryx goddess as their own Astarte, whose cult they had also established on Cyprus in synthesis with its native female deity, Wanassa. Once Greek merchants reached both Cyprus and Eryx, they reinterpreted these cults of Astarte as cults of Aphrodite. As a result, a strong connection existed between the Cyprus and Eryx cults; both their goddesses, in Cyprus and Sicily, had special care of mariners, and both Theocritus and Calpurnius associated the Eryx goddess, specifically, with *Cyprian* Aphrodite.

Both cults had strong connections, too, with prostitution and fertility. We read in Eryx that every spring, in Classical times, Aphrodite's priests and *ierodules* or 'sacred prostitutes' who resided at Eryx, would gather to celebrate the *katagóghia*, when a cloud of white doves would emerge out of the southern haze of the blue sky and come winging across the broad plain below, to settle down gracefully on the temple rock. When the vegetation browned and the fruits had been gathered in the autumn, the reverse ceremony, the departure of the goddess, was celebrated. This was the *anagóghia*, when the doves flew away south over the salt pans, past the little island of Motya, their white wings vanishing in the direction of Africa.

The landscape, too, enforced the link between the Eryx goddess and the Cyprian Aphrodite. The sickle-shaped peninsula just north of Aphrodite's temple at Palaipaphos on Cyprus was called Drepanum, because it was said to have been the sickle used by Kronos to castrate his father Uranos, and which thus, inadvertently, caused the birth of Aphrodite. As we have noted earlier, a similar, sickle-shaped peninsula exists on the Sicilian coast only 4 miles south-west of Eryx, helping to form the harbour which the Greeks, therefore, called Drepanum – hence the town's modern name, Trapani.

In Search of Aeneas

Just to the south of Drepanum the Phoenicians had a trading base on Motya, which is now called Mozia, or Isola San Pantaleo. This looks north to Drepanum, with Mount Eryx rising steeply behind. Seen from Motya, Mount Eryx looks very similar to Mount Vikles, which rises behind Amathous, a city on Cyprus's southern coast that had a mixed Greek and Phoenician population. Both mounts have a similarly breast-like appearance. On Amathous's mount was a shrine to Aphrodite (and, earlier, probably, to Wanassa-Astarte). Perhaps these similarities helped enforce the idea in the minds of merchants, Phoenician and Greek alike, that the deity of Mount Eryx was identical with the Cyprian goddess.

Once the Greeks had convinced themselves that Eryx's goddess was Aphrodite, her presence invited the notion that her son Aeneas had come here and that he, of all Trojans, had established her shrine on top of Mount Eryx. Once Rome had adopted the Trojan myth, the Elymians saw the political value of talking up their connection with Aeneas. They even started minting coins in commemoration of the myth, which exalted their Trojan origins by showing Anchises being carried to safety by Aeneas.

The Greeks in Sicily, particularly perhaps those in Selinus, turned to Trojan myths, too, to invent eponymous founders for the Elymian people and their cities of Eryx, Segesta and Entella. The oldest of these founders was Eryx, who they said was killed in a wrestling match with Hercules, and whose story we will hear later. Egesta is the eponym of Segesta, who was imagined as the daughter of a Trojan nobleman who had been exiled to Sicily by Priam's father Laomedon. Her son Acestes or Aegestus travelled to Troy to fight for Priam, survived the city's fall, and returned to Sicily before Aeneas arrived. He brought with him to Sicily a hitherto unheard-of cousin of Priam's called Helymus or Elimo, the eponym of the Elymians. Finally there was Entella, originally Acestes' wife, whom Virgil turns into Acestes' male friend.

Although Virgil does not say so when describing Aeneas's arrival on the Elymian shore, Aeneas must have met this trio of Elymian heroes then. This is because when he left Sicily for Carthage he had with him Sicilian wine given him by Acestes (as related in *Aeneid* 1), and also, when he went back to Sicily, the trio welcomed him back (in *Aeneid* 5), so knew him already.

The Trojan myth was destined, thanks to the Greek merchant adventurers in the time of Homer, to make its way to Rome. And so it was time now for Aeneas to continue his voyage towards the city his descendants were destined to found. But before Aeneas reached Rome, a very peculiar diversion took place.

Having buried Anchises, the Trojan fleet embarked, intending to sail up around the coast of Sicily and away north-east to Italy. But Hera, determined to prevent Aeneas from fulfilling his destiny, stirred up a furious storm which swept them in the opposite direction and scattered his fleet. Remember that the story of Aeneas escaping from Troy and his journey up to this point is related as a back-story told by Aeneas to Dido in Carthage in books 2 and 3 of the *Aeneid*. But Virgil chose to begin book 1 of his *Aeneid* now, in the dramatic chaos of Hera's storm. Orontes' ship was gulped down by a whirlpool; some ships were split apart by the waves; others were dashed onto the Syrtes reefs off the Libyan coast or wrecked on 'the Altars', the real shoals and shifting islands between Sicily and Tunisia, caused by the underwater volcano Empedocles.

Bereft of his father, Aeneas was at his lowest ebb, his limbs 'loosened in the chill of fear'. Happy were those who died at Troy, he groaned; if only Diomedes had slain me there, so I would not have to endure this. Aeneas's character is far removed from the standard Homeric hero, and a long way, too, from the paradigm of Roman stoicism which he never fully became. In the introduction to his 1668 translation of the *Aeneid*, Jean Renaud de Segrais criticised Aeneas for being 'timid ... ungrateful ... too often with tears in his eyes'. The turmoil of Aeneas's mind matched the raging of the seas that were about to destroy him. But Poseidon, indignant that another deity had stirred up his seas, calmed the waves, like a skilled orator calming a mob – Virgil's metaphor for the way good Romans should overcome their surging human emotions.

Aeneas made it to the Tunisian coast with only seven of his twenty ships intact. Virgil describes their landfall precisely: a deep bay, mostly sheltered from the sea by an island, surrounded by forested cliffs and crags. The Tunisian coastline is pitted with salt lakes. One, Ghar el Melh, on whose shore stood the Roman town of Rusuca, has an island across its opening. The northern channel is still open and the southern one is silted up, but it may well have been navigable in Virgil's time. There is a hill behind; not quite the dramatic crags Virgil described, but he had probably never been there in person. Under the fronting crags, wrote Virgil, was a nymphs' cave, containing sweet water and seats carved out of rock. Servius thought Virgil's description of the cave was a *topothesia*, a description of an imaginary place: 'We can tell already,' Peter Levi commented, 'that there is something tricky about this nymph-haunted place.'[8] But stretches of rock around Ghar el Melh are undercut by the waves and maybe someone found a cave there and told Virgil about it. At 20 miles north of Carthage, Ghar el Melh is an appropriate distance from the city for what follows.

The bay was so calm that the ships did not need to be moored. The brine-drenched Trojans collapsed exhausted on the beach. Achates started a fire and they tried to dry their damp grain and grind some flour to make bread. Aeneas was too distracted to join in; he and Achates climbed the hill, looking in vain for the missing ships. Instead, they saw and shot three stags and four does; one carcass for each remaining vessel.

A 1672 drawing by Claude Lorrain shows the high, craggy cliffs, just as Virgil imagined, enclosing and shadowing a bay in which the Trojan ships lie peacefully; these, and luxurious trees to the right, frame the bay's opening and allow the evening light to pour across the closer rocks, on which are silhouetted Achates, holding a spear, and Aeneas, his bow drawn, shooting deer in the shaded pasture to the right.[9] The Trojans revived themselves with venison, washed down with wine given them in Sicily by Acestes. They lay down to sleep in the marram grass, but Aeneas's grief over his lost comrades kept him awake all night. At dawn, he was filled with fresh resolve to scout out this new land.

Armed with steel-tipped javelins, he and Achates set out through the wilderness. They encountered a girl-huntress, who explained where they were, and whom they would soon be meeting. Aeneas was wise enough to recognise her as some sort of deity, but only as she left did he smell ambrosia in her hair and see a light flash from her rosy neck that could emanate only from a great goddess. This is the moment captured by Tiepolo (1727–1804) in his drawing 'Aeneas recognising Venus as she disappears in a cloud'.[10] Finely armoured Aeneas stares in wonder as his youthful mother rises up, supported by Eros, smiling back beneficently. Tiepolo casts her largely in shadow, so that the radiance of Heaven falls mainly on Aeneas but not on Achates, who cowers behind. But that is not how Virgil wrote it. His Aeneas felt betrayed: why, he protested, do you mock me by appearing in disguise? 'May we never clasp hand in hand,' he protests, 'and hear and speak the words of truth?' This is the closest we come to learning how Aeneas really felt about having a largely absent goddess for a mother.

Directed by Aphrodite, Aeneas and Achates scaled a hill, and saw before them Carthage. Phoenicians from Tyre founded Qart-ḥadašt, their 'new city' that we call Carthage, on a promontory between salt lakes, several centuries after Aeneas's time. But Virgil imagined Aeneas watching men labouring like bees to raise their walls and towers, dredge their harbour and elect judges: 'O happy they,' Aeneas exclaimed, thinking of his own unfinished mission, 'whose walls are already rising.'

Aphrodite had explained to Aeneas the tale, already traditional by Virgil's day, of how Elissa, who was also called Dido, came here from Tyre and asked the native Libyans if she may purchase a piece of land as large as a bull's hide, and how she tricked them by cutting the hide into thin strips and laying them end to end, to encompass enough ground to build her city; hence the land's name, Byrsa, 'the hide'.

Once Rome won the Punic Wars, they razed Phoenician Carthage, so the ruins visitors are shown today, on the coast some 8 miles east of the centre of modern Tunis, are those of the Roman city which rose in its place. So our journey there, like Virgil's description of Aeneas's visit, can only be one of imagination.

28

Aeneas and Dido

As they approached Carthage, Aphrodite concealed Aeneas and Achates in mist, which allowed them to enter the city invisible and unmolested. They found the grove where Dido, soon after her arrival from Tyre, had dedicated a temple, says Virgil, to Hera. But the goddess whom the Carthaginians worshipped was called Tanit; she was their equivalent of Astarte, or Aphrodite, and was depicted in Carthage as a figure below a crescent moon.

Dido had decorated the temple's walls with scenes from the Trojan War. Thus, Aeneas became, like all the Greeks of Homer's time and beyond, and Virgil – and us – a spectator, experiencing the Trojan story through art. But unlike all later spectators, these flat, silent depictions of Troy's demise brought back living memories for Aeneas. He groaned at the sight of Hector's corpse; he even recognised himself, 'mingled in the mellay'. Yet these brutal images filled Aeneas with a strange hope that he had found a safe haven, because 'even here, virtue hath her rewards, and mortality her tears.' That is how Jackson translated Aeneas's words, but Virgil's phrase *lacrimae rerum*, which means literally, 'tears of things', is virtually untranslatable in this context: 'the world is a world of tears' is how Fagles rendered it. Aeneas continued, 'Even here, the woes of man touch the heart of man! Dispel thy fears,' he said to Achates: 'this fame of ours is herald to some salvation!'

Still invisible to others, Aeneas and Achates watched Dido arrive 'in radiant loveliness', like Artemis. She took her throne in the temple and began holding court. Suddenly, Aeneas saw some of his lost comrades approaching her. It turned out that when Poseidon calmed the seas, Triton and the Nereid Cymothoë helped him save all the Trojan ships except for that of Orontes, which was lost irrevocably. Aphrodite had already promised Aeneas that all were safe. Apart from Orontes's ship, 'all else tallies with your mother's word,' Achates commented, reminding us subtly that goddess's promises cannot always be taken at face value.

In Search of Aeneas

Antheus, Sergestus, Serestus, Cloanthus, Gyas and old Ilioneus approached Dido's throne. Ilioneus explained: 'There is a country that Greece styles Hesperia, an immemorial land, strong in battle and rich of soil. Oenotrians ['the people of the wine-land'] were they who held it: now, Fame tells, a new generation has named the country with the name of their leader – Italy.' These lines would later be used by Geoffrey of Monmouth as his model for the prophecy Artemis gives Aeneas's great grandson Brutus, when she directs him to Britain. Milton's translation of that is 'Brutus, far to the west, in th'ocean wide, beyond the realm of Gaul, a land there lies, seagirt it lies, where giants dwelt of old.' Both descriptions are pregnant with hope. But during their journey to their promised Italy, continued Ilioneus, they lost their pious leader, Aeneas, 'who matched skill at arms with justice and goodness'. Coming as they do in *Aeneid* 1, these lines herald Virgil's intention to portray Aeneas as a paragon of Augustan virtues or, at least, as one who strove to be so. Dido expressed her sympathy for the Trojans and offered the survivors a new home in Carthage. Now Aeneas revealed himself, dramatically, out of the mist. 'You alone have pitied the long ordeals of Troy,' Aeneas told Dido. 'If piety was still favoured in Heaven and justice and a sense of right and wrong still prevailed on Earth, may you have your reward.'

Dido remembers Teucer, a Greek survivor of the Trojan War, visiting Tyre when she was young. This Teucer was son of Telamon of Salamis, but his mother was Hesione, the captive sister of Priam, and he was named after her ancestor Teucer, the father-in-law of Dardanos. Teucer had praised the Trojans' valour, and Dido had never forgotten this.

Dido ordered a banquet for the Trojans. Aphrodite, having been duped by Hera into aiding her plot to thwart Aeneas's plans to go to Italy, made her son look even more handsome than normal. Virgil describes Aeneas and his men sitting on couches, draped in Phoenician purple. Servants brought water for rinsing their hands, linen napkins to spread on their laps, and bread in baskets. The silverware was engraved with scenes from Dido's family history. The Trojans were joined by Carthaginian courtiers, who admired the presents Aeneas gave Dido, including a veil with a woven border of yellow acanthuses that had once been a prized possession of Helen: a doomed token if ever there was one.

Aphrodite realised that Aeneas and his men were entirely in Dido's power, and feared what Hera, who had contrived this, might do next. She resolved to turn the tables by making Dido fall in love with Aeneas. Dido was still in mourning for her late husband Sychaeus, so, to soften her up, Aphrodite whisked Ascanius away temporarily to Idalion on Cyprus, and made her own son Eros take his form. Dido loved the boy so much that she cradled him in her breast, and Eros kindled there a long-dormant love, which he re-directed towards Aeneas himself.

The feast ended. The tables were cleared away; lamps were lit and out came the wine bowls, and the wine itself, 'crowned with wreaths'. Dido took her great golden bowl and toasted Zeus, Hera, Bacchus (Dionysos, the wine god) and the friendship of Troy and Carthage. The bard Iopas played his lyre and sang songs learned from Aeneas's ancestor Atlas; of the stars, moon and sun; the causes of storms and lightning; the origins of men and beasts. This magnificent account of the nature of the universe was an appropriate prelude to what came next, for Dido pressed Aeneas to tell his own, epochal story. It is now that we hear Aeneas's account of the fall of Troy and his journey thus far. His telling of it fills *Aeneid* 2 and *Aeneid* 3.

At the start of *Aeneid* 4, it was time for bed, but Dido was too moved by Aeneas's courage, lineage, looks and words to sleep. The Medieval *Roman d'Eneas* imagines Dido showing Aeneas to his chamber and then going to bed herself but being unable to sleep owing to her imaginings of him lying naked in her arms.[1] The next day, says Virgil, Dido realised that she loved Aeneas, and her sister Anna encouraged her with the prospect of Carthage being mightier for having the Trojans there, too. Love consumed Dido. She roamed the streets in a frenzy. The building of Carthage was neglected. As the months passed, she held banquets for Aeneas, and after he left she would throw herself longingly onto the couch where he had been sitting. In Nahum Tate's libretto for Purcell's 1689 opera, *Dido and Aeneas*, based on the *Aeneid*, Dido sings:

Whence could so much Virtue spring,
What Storms, What Battles did he sing?
Anchises Valour mixt with Venus' Charms,
How soft in Peace, and yet how fierce in Arms!

And Aeneas, falling in love too, yet fearing the consequences, replies prophetically:

Ah! make not in a hopeless Fire,
A Hero fall, and Troy once more Expire.

That is more than we hear from Virgil's Aeneas, who seems to have fallen in love unconsciously, but the cessation of building work in Carthage parallels the dulling of Aeneas's desire to leave and build a new city for himself. Now, Hera enlisted Aphrodite's help in engineering Aeneas and Dido's marriage. Aphrodite realised this would thwart the plan of Zeus, and Fate, but pretended to go along with it.

At dawn, the Massylian horsemen of Carthage and the flower of Trojan chivalry set out on a hunt. Dido herself appeared on a horse decked in gold and purple. Aeneas looked like Apollo. We can see the loving couple in the mosaics of Low Ham Roman Villa in Somerset, now in Taunton Museum. Aeneas gallops ahead on a dark horse; Dido follows eagerly behind on a white one. The horses' tails and their own cloaks stream behind them. Save for these, their boots and Aeneas's Phrygian cap, they are naked. Aeneas glances back to make sure Dido is following, seeming to anticipate what will come next.

In Search of Aeneas

A storm broke. The gullies along the north African coast surged with water; the huntsmen scattered and Aeneas and Dido sought refuge in a cave. Hera had planned it all. In 1822, John White Abbott drew the storm breaking and mounted huntsmen hurtling down the hillside, while in the foreground Aeneas escorted Dido towards the cave with gentlemanly calm.[2] Edward Francis Burney drew the couple like a pair of innocent sweethearts, he helping her down from her horse with the delicacy of a young lover.[3] A wall painting from Pompeii shows them together inside the cave; he burnt dark by the sun, she pale. Aeneas has his sword and is still a warrior, but Dido is dressed as a huntress, and leans towards Aeneas, toying with his chin. Eros hovers at Aeneas's shoulder, ensuring he will not resist.[4] An illustration for Heinrich von Veldecke's *Eeneide* shows them dressed much more decorously, in long robes and broad-brimmed hats, with horses sedate enough for Dido's lapdog to perch behind its mistress. But the result is the same, for lower down on the page we see the horses tethered to a tree, while the couple lock in passionate embrace.[5]

In Virgil, nymphs wailed wedding hymns from the mountain tops and Gaia and Hera made lightning flicker. For Aeneas, this was an erotic encounter in the countryside. But as far as Dido and Hera were concerned, it was a marriage, consummated in the presence of the primordial female deities of the Earth.

Rumour of Dido's marriage reached Iarbas, the native king of Libya beyond Dido's borders. He was the son of an African nymph by Zeus-Ammon. If anyone should marry Dido and rule in Carthage, Iarbas protested to his father, it should be him. Zeus agreed, but for different reasons, and sent Hermes down to remind Aeneas that his destiny lay in Italy. Hermes swooped down from Olympus to Mount Atlas and then flew 600 miles east along the coast to Carthage. He discovered Aeneas happily directing the building of new homes for his Trojans, clad too luxuriously in a cloak of Phoenician purple, his sword hilt studied gaudily with 'tawny jasper stars'.

William Blake captured in red chalk the moment when Hermes, all angular limbs and winged extremities, hurtles down from the sky. Aeneas has been asleep, naked. Startled, he raises himself up and stretches out his left arm. Hermes's wand is about to touch Aeneas's head.[6] He will impart the sort of divine inspiration for which Blake himself yearned: but in Aeneas's case, it is a bitter revelation. Aphrodite did not save you from death at Troy just for this, chided Virgil's Hermes. Your fate lies in Italy, where your progeny (the Romans) will bring the world under the rule of law. Even if you will not do this for yourself, will you deprive Ascanius of his Italian birthright?

Virgil had in mind the way that, further east along the north African coast, the equally exotic seductress Cleopatra had detained Caesar and later turned Mark Antony into a traitor, in Augustus's view at any rate, against Rome itself. As Aeneas listened to Hermes, 'his hair rose in horror, and his voice clove his throat' as he realised how things had gone wrong. Aeneas remembered, as all good Romans were supposed to remember, that personal feeling must come second to duty to the state – even if his re-assumption of his duty might destroy his beloved Dido altogether.

As Virgil's epic starts with Aeneas reaching Carthage, *Aeneid* 1 contains what R. D. Williams called one of the poem's 'great patriotic passages'.[7] Zeus told Aphrodite that Aeneas was destined by Fate to reach Italy, where he would win his war and become the ancestor of Romulus, the founder of Rome. 'I set no bounds to their fortunes,' Zeus assured her, 'nor any term of years: I have given them empire without end.' Even Hera would eventually be reconciled to this; the stock of Assaracus (Aeneas's grandfather, so a poetic way of saying Aeneas himself) would one day rule the whole world, even proud Greece. The gates of battle would be closed and wicked *furor*, Frenzy, would sit within, bound on a pile of weapons, raging through bloodstained lips; but her rage, says Zeus, would be in vain.

It is for this, in *Aeneid* 4, that stoic Aeneas instructed Mnestheus, Sergestus and Serestus to prepare the fleet in secret, while he tried to find the right time to break the news of his departure to Dido. But she had already heard of his plans and flew at him like a Maenad, one of those female worshippers of Dionysos, who abandoned themselves to uncontrolled emotions.

Aeneas tried to master his tormented heart: I shall never deny your kindnesses, he said, nor regret my memories of you. He had never considered any of their lovemaking, since that first passionate encounter in the cave, to constitute an official marriage. 'Did the fates suffer me to be captain of my own life, and at my own will to order my troubles,' he told Dido, 'before all I would dwell in the city of Troy amid the loved relics of my kindred [and] the lofty halls of Priam should yet stand.' But Fate, as revealed through Apollo's oracles, had sent him to Italy, so 'there is my love, there my country!' You have settled here in Carthage, he argued, so don't blame me for wanting to live in Italy. He revealed that at night, Anchises had been appearing in his dreams and chastising him for lingering in Carthage, and that Hermes had touched a raw nerve when he spoke of Ascanius's birthright, which was in Italy, not here in Dido's realm.

Dido's response was one of irrational fury: everything you say is false! You are not the son of a goddess, she screamed, nor the descendant of Dardanos. 'Rugged Caucasus begat you, and you were suckled by a Hyrcanian tigress.' You are no nobleman, but a savage from the eastern wilderness. Then she stormed off.

Virgil's story of Dido and Aeneas has been retold repeatedly, starting with Ovid's *Heriodes*, 'heroines', in which Dido asked of Aeneas, why do you turn your back upon all you have achieved, by always striving to achieve more? You have sought and gained this land, but now you think you must seek another, somewhere out there in the wide world. Though flung at him as an accusation, Aeneas may have agreed with this, but Dido's next attack was bitter: you never carried the sacred relics on your shoulders, nor even your father. 'You are false in everything,' she spits. Italy hides from your sight and will draw away in revulsion from your ships' keels. Dido offered him everything, and Aeneas rejected it, despite all the misery and death his decision would bring.

Virgil's Aeneas longed to run after and comfort Dido, but he was like an oak, shaken by the storm yet always holding its head towards Heaven. So, although his heart was pierced with sorrow, Aeneas returned to his ships. When he first saw Carthage, its people, labouring to build their city, were like bees: now, the Trojans were just as industrious, like ants. So keen were they to depart that they were cutting green, unseasoned wood for planks and oars.

Had Virgil ever been spurned by a lover, female or, more likely, male, who rejected his love in favour of duty? His focus is all on Dido's tormented mind. While he humours Augustus by showing his Roman audience how duty must be done, Virgil does not shy away from its awful, human consequences. 'Our eighteenth-century ancestors admired him for his national note, for his patriotic message,' wrote Williams, but 'the Victorians admired him for his tears for the lonely individual ... it is the many-sidedness of the poem that makes it great.'[8]

Virgil's public voice echoes Ennius, Cicero and the monumental Roman history, *Ab Urbe Condita*, of Livy (59 BC-AD 17). But Virgil's private voice echoes the young poet Catullus (*c*. 84-54 BC), who described the pathos of Ariadne standing on the lonely beach at Naxos, watching, incredulous, as her erstwhile lover Theseus sailed away with his shipmates; and, though Ariadne knew he had abandoned her entirely, she still felt love for Theseus tearing wildly at her breast.

Ariadne's lament is echoed consciously by Virgil, when Dido imagined how happy she would be now, if only the Trojan ships had never darkened her shore in the first place. She sent her sister Anna to reason with Aeneas, but he would not relent. Memories of Aeneas torment Dido's dreams. She told Anna to have a pyre built, topped with the bed in which she and Aeneas had so often made love, and with the clothes, armour and sword he had left behind. She pretended to want only to burn his memory, but as she sprinkled it with water, to simulate the rivers of Hades, Dido knew that her only release would be through death. Or should she go with him, a dispossessed queen sitting alongside Aeneas's sailors? Should she uproot her people and make them all follow her to Italy? No, the Trojans had been liars ever since Laomedon's reign; she had been tricked into loving Aeneas, into betraying the memory of her late husband Sychaeus. Death really was the only solution.

Meanwhile, Aeneas had been sleeping peacefully in his ship in Carthage's harbour. Suddenly, Hermes roused him: don't sleep in such a crisis! Women's minds are always changing, he warned. Before you know it, your ships will be set ablaze by angry Carthaginians. Terrified by the apparition, Aeneas leapt up, awakened his people and severed his ship's hawser with a sword.

Aeneas and Dido

Dido looked out at 'the first whitening glimmer of light' and saw the nineteen ships departing. Her lament 'when I am laid, am laid in earth' in Purcell's *Dido and Aeneas*, is one of the best-known pieces in English opera, with its heart-rending refrain 'remember me'. It lives on in the British psyche as one of the pieces played each year at the Remembrance Day service at the Cenotaph, where the focus is shifted from the jilted queen of Carthage to those who died in the World Wars, the pathos of whose fates would not have been lost on Virgil.

Dido considered pursuing the Trojans; regretted not having massacred them while she could; not having served up Ascanius's body, cooked, for his father to eat. She cursed Aeneas: may he find Italy plagued by war, never enjoy his new realm in peace and die and rot in the sand. May Carthage plague Aeneas's lineage for ever, she cried, anticipating, unknowingly, the Punic Wars, though not foreseeing their ultimate consequence: the destruction of Carthage itself. Now, she sought only to be rid of the loathed light of life. Dido impaled herself on Aeneas's sword and collapsed on their bed, and Hera sent down Iris to release her from the burdens of love and life.

As Aeneas looked back from his departing ship at the beginning of *Aeneid 5*, he saw smoke rising from Carthage, where Dido's death pyre was already ablaze. Ovid introduces a new and dreadful element to this already tragic tale: she may have been pregnant. As Dido burned, so too did his unborn child. But, like Cleopatra, the lives of both Dido and her child stood in the path of Rome's imperial destiny: death was the only possible outcome.

Aeneas turned his face towards Europe. A storm rose, and at his helmsman Palinurus's advice they diverted their course to seek a safe haven in Sicily. And thus they arrived back at Anchises's burial mound at Drepanum, exactly a year after they had departed.

29

Aeneas in Despair

Virgil's *Aeneid* does not tell Aeneas's story sequentially. It begins with Aeneas arriving on Dido's shore in *Aeneid* 1, and the story of his escape from Troy and voyage up to that point is told by Aeneas himself to Dido in *Aeneid* 2 and *Aeneid* 3. This makes the Carthaginian episode seem integral to Aeneas's whole story. But before Virgil had reworked the plot in this way, Carthage's role may have been far more ephemeral: Aeneas leaves Troy; reaches Sicily; buries Anchises; then he is swept off to Carthage where he falls in love with Dido, rejects her and makes it back to Drepanum *exactly* a year later. Then the main story of his journey resumes. It is as if the Carthaginian episode need never really have happened. Indeed, in Livy and Dionysius, it doesn't: Aeneas goes from Troy to Sicily, and Sicily to Rome: Carthage is never mentioned.

For his story of Dido, Virgil drew on a solely poetic source, which was so patently unhistorical that Livy and Dionysius ignored it: the *Bellum Punicum* of Gnaeus Naevius (*c.* 270-201 BC). This early Roman epic about the Punic Wars between Rome and Carthage survives only in fragments and seems to be the first Latin work that placed Aeneas at the heart of Rome's foundation myth. In it we hear, for the first time, how Aeneas was swept off course from Sicily to Carthage, where he met and fell in love with Dido, only to abandon her.

Before Naevius, Dido was known only as a princess from Tyre, the home-city of the Phoenicians, whose husband Sychaeus was murdered by her brother Pygmalion. Dido, whose name means 'wanderer', travelled west and founded Carthage. The neighbouring king Iarbas tried to force her to marry him, and the only way she could remain faithful to her dead husband was by committing suicide on a pyre. Naevius adapted this story, keeping Dido's suicide but attributing it to her grief at being abandoned by Aeneas. This in turn became Naevius's poetic explanation for the ancient enmity between Carthage and Rome.

Galinsky wondered whether the addition of Dido to Aeneas's story originated in Segesta, at the time when the city defected from Carthage to Rome in 263 BC, unless Naevius had invented it himself.[1] The latter seems more likely. Naevius's inspiration was probably Motya, the island off the Sicilian coast, 10 miles south of Eryx. Like Carthage, Motya was a Phoenician colony, founded a couple of hundred years after Aeneas's time. By Naevius's time, it was an ancient, crumbling city, with exotic north African walls and gravestones, the remains of which are still visible today. Thinking about Aeneas reaching Eryx, Naevius may have imagined him stopping on Motya and being delayed by a love affair with a Phoenician woman. Then, in a moment of inspiration, Naevius may have realised the dramatic potential of transferring Aeneas from Motya to Carthage itself and delivering him straight into the arms of its famous Phoenician queen, Dido.

Varro, writing shortly before Virgil, mentioned the story of Aeneas in Carthage but, according to Servius, he made the affair between Aeneas and Dido's sister, Anna.[2] Virgil returned to Naevius's idea and through the tragedy which he discovered in the story of doomed Dido, he made it, inadvertently, into the most famous episode in Aeneas's entire story.

As soon as Aeneas sets foot on Sicilian soil again at the start of *Aeneid* 5, the whole Carthaginian episode seems to fade like a dream. Aeneas was back where he was exactly a year before, and prepared to pay homage at Anchises' burial mound. As he did so, Acestes and his men came down from Mount Eryx with animals to sacrifice, hailing Aeneas and his people with fraternal greetings.

Delighted to meet them again, Aeneas put a wreath of his mother's myrtle on his brow and led the Trojans and Elymians to altars which had been raised in front of Anchises's tumulus. Aeneas poured on the soil 'two goblets of wine, two of fresh milk, and two of sacrificial blood' to feed his father's shade – echoing the way Odysseus attracted the shades of the dead in *Odyssey* 11 – 'and scattered bright-hued flowers and hailed his father'. As he did so, 'a serpent rolled forth from the holy base, smooth and huge with seven folds and seven coils peacefully encircling the tomb and gliding between the altars, his back streaked with blue, his lucent scales flaming with shot gold.' The serpent wound slowly among the bowls and goblets, 'tasted the feast, and vanished innocent beneath the mound'.

Was this a local deity, asks Virgil, or Anchises himself? It is tempting to make a connection of which Virgil was probably unaware – that Anchises, in death, had become Dumuzi the shepherd-king, who was indeed transformed into a serpent and whose affair with Inanna was the literary and ceremonial precursor to the story of Anchises's own encounter with Aphrodite. But that would venture, probably, beyond Virgil's intention. For him, the appearance of a snake behaving in this fashion was simply a sign that a spirit had accepted Aeneas's sacrifice.

Aeneas decided that after eight days' sacrificing, games would be held for the Trojans and Elymians; they would be a *parentalia*, a festival in honour of an ancestor – in this case, Anchises. The Romans' Parentalia festival ran for nine days from 13 February each year; here, Virgil invents (or confirms someone else's invention of) a Trojan origin for it. Aeneas's festival included a boat race, out to a rock that can still be seen from the beach. Acestes won the archery competition and the Trojan Dares wrestled Entellus, who wore the mighty gauntlets that Eryx had worn in his fatal bout against Hercules.

Thanks to her absorption of earlier manifestations of the Great Mother, such as Ishtar, Wanassa and Manuzza, and her consequent worship right across the central and eastern Mediterranean, Aphrodite accrued a panoply of genealogical connections. Her Olympian husband was Hephaestus, the lame god of metalworking, but she had many lovers, starting with Ares, the god of war, by whom she had Phobus (fear) and Deimos (terror), the constant companions of their father. By Hermes, Aphrodite had Hermaphroditos, who was both boy and girl. By Hermes, or Ares, or even Zeus, she had Eros or Cupid, a reincarnation of that earlier Eros, light, the ancestor of all the world. By Poseidon she had Rhodos, the female deity of Rhodes, and Herophilus; by Dionysos, or Apollo, she had Priapus, an ugly fertility god with a huge, permanent erection. By Adonis, her Cypriot lover, whom she loved more than all the rest together, and whose death from being gored by a boar she mourned deeply, she had both Golgos, founder of Golgi on Cyprus, and Beroë, the female eponym of Beirut, both places where Adonis's cult of death and rebirth were celebrated. Kadmos's wife Harmony was usually said to be the daughter of Zeus and Elektra of Samothraki, but occasionally we find her as a daughter of Ares and Aphrodite, fostered by Elektra. Aphrodite's last child, by Anchises, was Aeneas – the youngest and perhaps, judging by her constant involvement in his life, her favourite. Her penultimate offspring, by the Argonaut Butes, son of Poseidon, was Eryx.

Eryx's origins may have been similar to Aeneas's. Perhaps, in Elymian times, there had lived up on Eryx's peak a dynasty of priest-kings who, together with the *ierodules*, the sacred prostitutes, had re-enacted the sacred couplings of Aphrodite-Manuzza and her mortal lover, just as Anchises and a priestess of Kybele may have done on Mount Ida. Perhaps a real Elymian king called Eryx was born as a result; he was mythologised as having encountered Hercules, who was said to have come this far on his tenth labour, driving Geryon's cattle on their roundabout route to Greece. Hercules and Eryx argued over possession of a wandering bull and, like the meat-headed heroes they were, decided to fight to the death over it, and Hercules won.

These children of Aphrodite were all half-siblings of Aeneas, but he was younger than any of them by several human generations or more. In *Aeneid* 1 Aphrodite spoke to Eros of Aeneas as 'your brother' and he played a small part in Aeneas's story, impersonating Ascanius in Carthage, as we have seen, but they never knowingly met face to face. We can understand, therefore, Aeneas's fascination at seeing the gauntlets of his late half-brother, Eryx. They still had dried blood and spattered brains upon them, says Virgil. This was the closest to any of his mother's other children that Aeneas had ever come.

The next contest in the *parentalia* was a horseback contest for the boys, crowned with leaves, wearing golden necklaces and carrying spears made from of cornel shafts. They were in three groups of twelve, one led by Ascanius, the second by Atys who, writes Virgil, was Ascanius's 'boyish love', and the third by Priam, son of old king Priam's son Polites. Atys was one of many eponymous founding fathers of Roman dynasties Virgil wove into his story for, despite his youthful homosexuality, he was the mythological ancestor of the Gens Atii, the family of Augustus's mother. Young Priam, whose father had died in the Trojan War, would presumably have been the rightful heir to the Trojan throne, had it still existed. His presence never seems to challenge Aeneas's leadership of the Trojan exiles, and we do not hear of him again; perhaps he was claimed as the ancestor of a Roman *gens* too.

A whip cracked and the *Ludus Troiae*, the Troy Game, began.

> In equal troops they galloped apart and dissolved their array, three by three, into disjunct bands; and again, at summons, wheeled back and bore down with lances couched ... circle on alternate circle, and under arms evoked the semblance of battle ... As once, men tell, in high Crete, the labyrinth held a path threaded betwixt sunless walls ... even so the sons of Troy rode in their tangled course.

Virgil modelled this on the real Troy Games, which were held on special occasions in Rome, such as the dedication of the deified Julius Caesar's temple in 29 BC, an event Virgil had probably attended. In the Troy Games, young Romans galloped within a labyrinth, drawn out on the ground. It was said to resemble both the Cretan labyrinth and the complex fortifications of Troy, though archaeology shows that Troy's defences were not quite so labyrinthine as the Romans may have imagined. The game had probably been introduced to Rome by the Etruscans, the native people of Tyrrhenia or Etruria, the land north of Rome, which is now called Tuscany. A vase found at Tragliatella in Etruria, 13 miles north-west of Rome and dating from the mid-600s BC, shows boys on horseback approaching a labyrinth labelled, in Etruscan, 'TRUIA'. The Etruscans had probably learned this game from the horse-loving Euboean Greeks, who had started trading with them a century earlier.

While the vase, and even sometimes the game, is sometimes taken as evidence of a Trojan foundation myth in Etruria at this early date, *truia* in this context probably just meant 'palisaded camp', or, if it had anything to do with Troy itself, it was probably no more than an allusion to the city's 'labyrinthine' walls. By Virgil's time, however, the *Ludus Troiae* (sometimes also rendered *Lusus Troiae*) had been pressed into service by Roman antiquarians as evidence of Rome's Trojan origins. Virgil now confirmed this by making Aeneas the game's originator; every subsequent playing of it in Rome became, retrospectively, a replay of this first horse-race on the shingly shore of Drepanum. The *Ludus Troiae* had a long future ahead of it because Virgil's description was probably the inspiration for all the chivalric horseback tournaments of the Middle Ages.

While the Trojans and Elymians admired their sons' horsemanship, Hera tried again to doom Aeneas's journey, sending the rainbow goddess Iris to spread hysteria among the women, who attacked the ships with flaming torches. This is Virgil's reusing of those older foundation stories of the Magna Graecian towns in southern Italy, which involved the Trojan women burning ships so that they could settle down on dry land. In Virgil's version, Ascanius came galloping up, followed quickly by Aeneas and the others. This brought the women to their senses, but fire had already begun to devour the oak beams and pine planks of the ships.

Brought low by Anchises's death and his forced abandonment of Dido, Aeneas now ripped the tunic from his shoulders in despair. He had had enough. 'O Father,' he cried to his ancestor Zeus, let the fleet escape destruction for the sake of my people, but 'if so I have merited, fill thou the cup, and with hostile thunderbolt send me down to death and whelm me here under thy right hand!' We may imagine the clouds darkening, coal-black over Mount Eryx, their base lit lurid yellow by the crackling flames from the ships. A southerly wind whipped up the waves, lightning sizzled through the air and Zeus's thunder boomed. But instead of killing Aeneas with a thunderbolt, Zeus sent rain in 'tumultuous flood' to douse the flames. All the ships were saved except for four, whose steaming timbers had been reduced to charcoal.

Still, Aeneas felt like giving up and settling here in Sicily. But the aged priest Nautes was inspired to urge Aeneas to follow Fate's will and practise endurance, while Zeus sent an apparition of Anchises to urge him on to Italy. This was a turning-point for Aeneas. Inspired by these supernatural interventions, he resolved to press on.

First, though, Aeneas travelled 15 miles inland with Acestes, following a suggestion of Nautes's, to found the city of Segesta. Aeneas chose a hilltop within a broad valley amidst the Sicilian mountains. Segesta is best known today for its almost complete temple sitting on a low hill backed by a steep ravine, not far from the city's hilltop ruins. Though closely resembling a Classical Greek temple, it was built by the Elymians themselves, following techniques learned from their Greek neighbours. Some think it was dedicated to Aphrodite Urania, Aphrodite of the starry heavens, though the evidence is weak. We visited in April, when its thirty-six golden brown Doric columns, supporting a complete pediment, rose up from a sea of purple borage, yellow fennel and orange marigolds. According to Lycophron's *Alexandra*, Aeneas's friend Acestes, who, together with his mother, was the eponymous hero of the place, was said to have been the son of the god of a local river, the Crimisus (now called the Caltabellota). The river god took the form of a hound to impregnate Egesta;[3] and sure enough, on the temple's steps, we saw a large brown dog dozing in the spring sunshine.

Aeneas peopled Segesta with all those Trojan men who were too elderly or infirm to continue the journey, and all those women who wished no longer to travel. By doing so, Virgil provided a poetic confirmation of the Elymians' belief in their Trojan roots. Conveniently, too, it meant that once the Trojan men reached Latium, their lack of women of their own allowed them to choose local wives, thus explaining how the Trojan and Latin races would merge so rapidly into one.

Returning to Mount Eryx, Aeneas and Acestes climbed to the top and established 'a star-pointing fane to Idalian Venus', a temple to Aphrodite of Idalion in Cyprus. Dionysius attributes this same sanctuary at Eryx to Aeneas, too, and says it was dedicated to Aphrodite Aeneias.[4]

We approached Mount Eryx on a bright spring day, but as the long road wound up and up towards the summit, we were enveloped in dense fog. Wandering the streets of Eryx after dark, the fog remained so thick that we could imagine the hands of long-dead Trojans reaching out to us. It persisted through the night and was still there the following morning, as we explored the city's walls, which are still partly Phoenician. The real sanctuary, at the highest point, was Elymian, of course. Its ancient, rocky surface – including 'Venus's bath' – is mostly overlaid now by Phoenician, Classical Greek and Roman additions, and it is all enclosed within Medieval castle walls.

Suddenly, the fog began to billow away; blue sky appeared above and below there opened up a vista of the south-western coast of Sicily, dazzling green under the sun, with Motya a dark speck amidst the gleaming sea.

When evening came, new clouds bubbled up from the sea to form a soft white carpet just below us. As the sun started setting, this was transformed into a billowing ocean of rosy-gold. We felt as if we were on a sacred island of Aphrodite's, floating sublimely above the world. Then, as it grew dark, the star-pierced heavens – whose god was neutered Uranos, Aphrodite's progenitor – appeared as a sweeping arc overhead, so close that we felt we could reach up and brush the blackness of the firmament with our hands. No wonder so many generations had chosen to revere their goddesses here.

On the last night in Sicily, Aeneas and Acestes held a farewell feast. It was meant to be a celebration, but it must have been tinged with sadness, for Aeneas was leaving behind his father's bones. The Trojans were splitting up too, as they never thought they would, with Aeneas's men bidding sad farewells to those who had chosen to stay behind. When dawn came, Aeneas sacrificed three steers to the spirit of his late half-brother, Eryx, 'and a ewe-lamb to the Tempests'. He ordered his men to fling loose the hawsers of the fifteen remaining ships. 'A wind, rising from the stern, followed them on their way, and zealously the seamen smote the foam and swept the watery levels.'

Off the shore, says Virgil, and unnoticed by any mortals save Aeneas, Poseidon and his nautical court sat in their chariots, observing the Trojans' departure. And from her temple above the clouds, Aphrodite called across to Poseidon: not only had Hera caused the destruction of Troy, but she had also tried to drown the survivors with storms and derange the women so that they would burn some of the ships. No amount of sacrifices or prayers would change Hera's mind. But, says Aphrodite, I pray that you at least, Poseidon, will allow the Trojans safe passage over the waves to reach 'the Laurentine Tiber', where Fate had determined that Aeneas would found his eternal city. Poseidon reassured her: he had saved Aeneas's life twice already and would not drown him now.

His heart light, Aeneas 'commanded every mast to be reared with instant speed, and every sail to be stretched on its yard'. And away the Trojans sped, north, then west, towards Italy at last.

The night-time moon glinted on the lapping waves of the Tyrrhenian Sea, and lit the Calabrian mountains of southern Italy and the dark shores of the land the Greeks would later plant with vines and call Oenotria, 'the land of wine'. Wine-dark was the sea now, and the oarsmen, tired from the journey from Sicily, stretched out on their benches. Only the helmsmen were awake, making sure the fleet remained together. At their head, on the poop of Aeneas's own ship, sat faithful Palinurus, intent on keeping the ship parallel to the coast, eagle-eyed in case of rocks.

A Trojan called Phorbas came up quietly, says Virgil, and bade him sleep, for all was calm. But Palinurus replied that Poseidon had fooled him many times, and sometimes the calmest sea belied the greatest danger. Palinurus did not realise how right he was, for this was not Phorbas at all, but Poseidon in disguise. The god's promise to Aphrodite to grant safe passage for Aeneas had included a quick, but deadly proviso: 'One life shall be given for many!' So now Poseidon passed across Palinurus's brow a bough dipped in the Lethe, that river of Hades whose waters induced oblivion. Palinurus felt his eyelids grow heavy. Scarcely had he slumped down than impatient Poseidon flung him overboard, so violently that Palinurus's strong hand, still gripping the rudder, tore off both it and even part of the poop itself.

In *The Unquiet Grave*, Cyril Connolly constructed a tongue-in-cheek psychiatrist's report for Palinurus. Unsettled by traumas including Scylla and Charybdis, and the Cyclopses, Palinurus realised that the storm which arose after they left Carthage 'could not be ridden out because he knew it followed on Aeneas's betrayal of Dido'; he 'realised that Aeneas was guilty of hubris and impiety; he was "not the Messiah"'. Palinurus's falling from the ship was a subconscious attempt to escape; his tearing away of the tiller and part of the poop provided him 'not only with a raft but inflicts a kind of castration on Aeneas'.[5] As with Virgil's equivocal relationship with Augustus, in Connolly's analysis Palinurus's actions constituted a subconscious wish to destroy Aeneas.

Palinurus's cries went unheard as the sea's mood swung. Waves rose like mountains. We hear later, in *Aeneid* 6, that all Palinurus could think as he clung to the broken rudder was of the great danger in which he had left Aeneas and his rudderless ship. For three days Palinurus was tossed about. On the fourth dawn, he glimpsed a headland crowned with jagged rocks, embracing a little harbour to which, with the last of his energy, he swam. He struggled ashore to find dark-visaged people, waiting with sticks. There on the beach, they beat Palinurus to death.

30

The Posillipo Hill

When Virgil travelled south from Naples to Sicily, as many scholars believe he did, he must have passed the harbour of Palinuro, whose name, *palin ouros*, recalls its 'contrary winds', caused by the peninsula which protects it. In 36 BC, these winds wrecked an entire fleet of Augustus's, hence the sea there being called Mare Mortis: 'the sea of death'. Indeed, even during our brief visit there, we saw a drowned diver being carried out of a rescue boat while his grief-stricken family looked on.

Dionysius says Aeneas buried a pilot of his at Palinuro. In *Odyssey* 11, Odysseus encounters the shade of his erstwhile companion Elpenor, who had died falling off a roof in Circe's realm, which is just up the coast from here. Odysseus left the body unburied, so Elpenor's shade begged Odysseus to go back and bury him, with an oar to mark his grave so that he would be remembered, with honour, as a sailor. From these two sources came Virgil's story of Palinurus, whom Aeneas encounters later in the *Aeneid*, in Hades. There, Palinurus's shade begged him, likewise, to go back and bury him: but the Cumaean sibyl assured Palinurus that the natives (and not Aeneas), repenting their brutal deed, would raise a tomb for him on the headland, so he would never be forgotten.

We spent a lot of time on that headland, vainly seeking Palinurus's tomb, but found only a patch of scattered rocks so dense that even the white-flowering myrtles would not grow there. It is probably a natural outcrop but may have inspired a local myth of a hero being buried there. Palinuro remains proud of its connection to Aeneas's story and in a small square there is a large map made of glazed tiles showing the whole of Aeneas's journey from Troy to Rome, via that unfortunate passage past Cape Palinuro.

Why did Poseidon take Palinurus's life? Because if they do not seek to explain the random cruelty with which death seizes our friends, families and ultimately ourselves, then myths about the gods serve no useful purpose.

In Search of Aeneas

Aeneid 6 opens with Aeneas's rudderless ship drifting past Paestum, where the roses bloomed twice a year, and where the Greek temples are still impressive today. Then they approached the Sirenum Scopuli, whose cliffs were 'white with the bones of many men' killed by the Sirens. No Sirens were there now to trouble Aeneas: where they had gone, Virgil does not say, though one of their number, Parthenope, was credited with having founded the oldest part of Naples, not far from where Virgil lived. Maybe the cliffs were those of the Isola Licosa, where Dionysius says the Trojans stopped to bury Leucosia, 'a woman cousin of Aeneas who died at that place'.[1] Or maybe Virgil had in mind the towering cliffs of the Amalfi Peninsula and the channel between its westernmost tip and high-peaked Capri, through which Aeneas's fleet must have passed.

Only now did Aeneas awake and, finding Palinurus gone, 'with his own hand guided her [his ship] over the mighty flood'. Virgil never explains how this was possible without the rudder; it bothered John Dryden so much that, in his 1697 translation of the *Aeneid*, he inserted the line 'what the man forsook, the god supplies' by way of explanation.

Ahead was the broad sweep of the Gulf of Naples, like a crescent moon pitted with smaller semi-circular indents, for it is composed of a series of semi-intact volcanic craters. Above all looms Vesuvius, massive yet dormant, then as now. It awoke after Virgil's death, with its fearsome eruption of AD 79, and burning ash and lava engulfed Pompeii and Herculaneum, where Virgil had probably dined with friends less than a century before.

He was not from Naples, but from up north, from a place called Andes, which is probably modern Pietole, by a tributary of the Po called the Mincius. Mantua is 3 miles to the north, and 60 miles beyond rise the Alps, where the flocks were taken for summer grazing. The people there were a mixture of Etruscans and Gauls, all recently incorporated into Rome's rapidly expanding empire. He was born, smiling serenely says Suetonius in his *Life of Virgil*, on 15 October 70 BC, and they called him Publius Vergilius Maro. Suetonius adds, in his semi-apocryphal account that while pregnant, Virgil's mother had dreamed of giving birth to a laurel branch, which took root and sprouted 'fruits and flowers of various kinds'; as if, even before his birth, Virgil was destined to gather up all the fragmented myths of Aeneas and weave them into something new and immortal.

Virgil grew up, says Suetonius, 'tall and of full habit, with a dark complexion and a rustic appearance', in a golden world of shepherds, whom he would later idealise in his *Eclogues*, and of farmers, including probably his father, tending their corn, vines, bees and livestock, of whose arts he would sing in his *Georgics*. Both works were rooted in the Italian soil, and Virgil's love of this, above all else, is an important part of the second half of the *Aeneid*.

In his teens, Virgil left for Rome, eventually studying what he described in the fifth poem of his *Catalepton* as the 'empty tubs of rhetoricians, words inflated not with Attik [Greek] dew'. He may then have served a spell in the Roman army, before seeking out the philosopher Siro, who was teaching Epicureanism near Naples. Naples had been founded by Greeks and, although now under Roman rule, both the city and its hinterland, the Campania Felice, 'the happy country', retained a strongly Greek character, far removed, as Peter Levi wrote in his superb biography of Virgil, from the vicious practicality of Rome. Epicureanism was the philosophy of seeking happiness through knowledge and modest living. Enveloped in Siro's circle of poets and philosophers, it must have been like being submerged in the world of Greek mythology, a happy *secessus*, seclusion, 'from every care our life henceforward rendered free'.[2]

Virgil and his circle lived to the west of the old harbour in Naples, on the Posillipo Hill, whose name means 'freedom from worry'. It was the area of Naples most closely associated with the city's mythical founder, the Siren Parthenope, hence Virgil's nickname, Parthenias, whose double-meaning is simply 'the maiden'. When Siro died, he left his villa to Virgil, as is suggested by *Catalepton* 8. Here Virgil wrote his *Eclogues*, which were finally published in 38/9 BC, in which he developed his Epicurean view of the Golden Age, when Zeus's father Kronos had presided over an era of peaceful, natural bounty. 'Let Pallas [Athena] dwell by herself in the cities she has built,' he wrote in *Eclogues* 2, 'but let my chief delight be the woods.' Virgil lamented the loss of the Golden Age: back in 42 BC, Augustus, embroiled in civil war, needed to pay his army and did so with land confiscated from many Mantuan farmers, probably including Virgil's family. Thus, in *Eclogues* 1, the shepherd Tityrus laments how his 'humble cottage with its turf-clad roof' and fields of corn were now in the hands of 'a godless soldier'.

But Virgil's loss of income from these confiscated lands was soon made good by wealthy patrons in Rome, who grew misty-eyed as Virgil recited his pastoral love-songs about fair-skinned shepherd boys in their rustic neverland. These patrons included Asinius Pollio, poet, general and Roman consul, and Maecenas, Augustus's friend and advisor, who understood the political power of words and was keen to recruit promising young poets to his master's cause. Maecenas gave Virgil a house on the Esquiline Hill in Rome, but Naples remained his favourite home. Through Maecenas, Virgil came to know Augustus himself and found himself unable to dislike the younger man, so full of boyish energy, who showed such admiration for his poetry.

Next completed were the *Georgics*, modelled on Hesiod's *Works and Days*, and again harking back fondly to, and enlarging on, the Golden Age of Kronos. It was then that men were first seeded on Gaia, the fertile Earth. She fed them with leaves coated with honey; steams flowed with wine, and fire was available to all. It was only when Zeus overthrew his father that the world became what it is now, but he acted for a reason. It was only when our ancestors were forced to learn how to cultivate the earth, and to 'strike forth the spark hidden in veins of flint', that they learned skills and built civilisation. Virgil was careful to position Augustus's great uncle, Caesar, at the heart of his poetic vision. Caesar was now a god in Heaven, watching over Italy and the wider world. As Virgil wrote in *Georgics* 1, he was 'the giver of increase and lord of the seasons', and his brow was wreathed with 'the myrtle sacred to his mother' – in other words, of his mythological ancestress, Aphrodite.

In *Georgics* 3, Virgil even imagines for Caesar a temple on the banks of the Mincius, dominated by a statue of Augustus. 'And see,' Virgil wrote, thinking of the most recent people who had started paying tribute to Rome, 'how Britons raise the crimson curtain they are woven into.' Virgil peopled the temple with marble statues of 'the lineage of Assaracus [Aeneas's great grandfather] and the glorious names of Zeus's race, Tros, our ancestor, and Cynthian Apollo, architect of Troy'. Though a Mantuan, Virgil was also a Roman citizen, so could write 'our' with pride and sincerity.

Yet this temple, spun out of a few lines of poetry, was not enough. When Virgil read his *Georgics* to Augustus in 29 BC, 'his voice [so] sweet and wonderfully effective ... as to make other people's delivery of the same lines seem flat and toneless',[3] both he, Maecenas and Augustus himself were perhaps thinking the same thing: that Virgil's next work should be an even greater monument, in words, to the Caesars, laying emphasis on what they wanted to be regarded as their greatest virtue – piety. In 27 BC, as he recorded in his *Res Gestae Divi Augusti*, inscribed on the Monumentum Ancryanum in Anatolia, Augustus set up a golden shield in the Curia Iulia in Rome honouring his own virtue, clemency, justice and piety. In that same year, Virgil started work on the *Aeneid*.

They considered making the poem about Augustus's victory at Actium, but the truth about Augustus's victory was far from glorious. Maybe it should be about the Alban kings, whose genealogy was seen as a bridge from Rome's early rulers back to Aeneas. But at last they settled upon Aeneas himself. There were many versions of his life, and none of them, save for Homer's words, were considered canonical, so the scope for manipulating Aeneas's story into what the Augustan establishment wanted it to be was considerable. Actium would be described, but only as a flash-forward in Aeneas's own story.

Setting aside the loss of his own family property, Virgil had reason enough to love Augustus. Virgil was born not long after the end of the civil war between Marius and Sulla; he grew up during the sparring of Caesar and Pompey, and then came Augustus's civil war with Antony. These were dark days in which, as Horace wrote in his sixteenth *Epode*, Rome seemed determined to destroy itself. Virgil himself wrote in his first *Georgic* of the chaos of civil war, when ploughshares were beaten into swords, and Romans paid with their blood for 'the perjury of Laomedon's Troy' – Laomedon's faithless refusal to pay Apollo and Poseidon for building Troy's walls, or to repay Hercules for saving Hesione from the sea monster. Regardless of how culpable he had been in these conflicts, Augustus also ended the civil war decisively, ushering in peace and prosperity for the empire. So, in his *Eclogues*, instead of blaming Augustus personally for the loss of his family's land, Virgil condemned the civil dissention caused by Augustus's enemies that had engendered so many unhappy consequences. In similar vein, Virgil would later blame the civil war faced by Aeneas in Italy solely on the jealousy of those who opposed him.

Augustus sought, furthermore, to restore Rome to its ancient traditions and the high moral values which Virgil would later attribute to Aeneas: devoutness in religion; devotion to duty; loyalty to family and nation. For this, Virgil could love 'this young man', as he called Augustus in the first *Georgic*, for 'saving our [otherwise] ruined generation'. As Williams asserted, Virgil's Aeneas reflected Augustus's government policy because it accorded with Virgil's own beliefs: 'Both men saw things the same way; one acted by political power, the other by poetry.'[4] Augustus's aim in commissioning the *Aeneid* was to bolster his regime; Virgil's was to reinforce the resulting era of peace and good government. Yet these blessings had not been achieved, as Virgil realised, without 'great sacrifices, suffering and devotion'. Williams continued, 'and also disaster to those who stood in the way'. Thus, the destruction of Troy; the sufferings of the Trojans on their journey; the death of Palinurus, and the misfortunes which befell those who stood in Fate's path, from Dido to the countless Italians destined to die opposing Aeneas after he landed; all this was necessary, ironically, to achieve enduring peace.

'Arms I sing, and the man, who first from the shores of Troy came, Fate-exiled, to Italy and her Lavinian strand'. So, the *Aeneid* begins. But Suetonius tells us that Virgil had originally written that, having sung of shepherds' pipes and cultivated fields, he sang now of the 'dread deeds of the War God [Ares/Mars], arms I sing, and the man…' The edit was made by Varius, one of Virgil's literary executors, trying to improve what was already a masterpiece.

'His health was variable,' says Suetonius, 'for he very often suffered from stomach and throat troubles, as well as with headaches; and he also had frequent haemorrhages.' These worsened as Virgil laboured in his villa on Rome's Esquiline Hill, and perhaps in Sicily, but mainly on the Posillipo Hill in his beloved Naples. He worked not bent over a desk writing, but dictating to his slaves Cebes and Alexander, who were close friends and perhaps his lovers, too. For two years he worked out the story as a prose draft, dividing it into twelve books. Then, writes Suetonius, 'He proceeded [over nine years] to turn into verse one part after another, taking them up just as he fancied, in no particular order. And that he might not check the flow of his thought, he left some things unfinished, and, so to speak, bolstered others up with very slight words, which, as he jocosely used to say, were put in like props, to support the structure until the solid columns should arrive.'

As he walked on the Posillipo Hill with his philosopher friends, or with Cebes and Alexander, Virgil could gaze out across the Gulf of Naples and imagine Aeneas on his ship, grieving the loss of Palinurus, leading his fleet beneath the moon, their bow wakes still fresh in the timeless sea, whose plastic folds retain the memory of all that has passed across them, whether real or imagined.

From the Posillipo Hill, Virgil could also see on the western horizon the end of the bay sweeping south, dipping past Baiae and then rising to the sulphur-yellow cliffs of Cape Misenum, now called Cabo Miseno, bristling with holm oaks and pines. It was at the harbour there, around the point so just beyond Virgil's line of sight, that Aeneas's fleet came ashore. Dionysius tells us Aeneas named the cape after Misenus, who was said variously to have been Aeneas's new helmsman[5] or his trumpeter.[6] Misenus's story probably derives from a local tale, which was later co-opted into the Trojan myth. Famed for his shrill clarion, Misenus challenged Triton to produce as fine a sound on his mighty conch. The old sea god could not, so, jealous of Misenus, he dragged him off the rocks and drowned him. Virgil made Misenus into Aeneas's trumpeter, too, and tells how the grief-stricken Trojans fished his corpse out of the sea. In Florence *c.* AD 1540, Luca Penni drew the funeral procession, with Aeneas, his arms crossed across his chest, following the byre towards a pyre of tree trunks atop the promontory.[7] They built a tumulus over the ashes, crowned, following the traditional story given in *Pontifical Affairs*, by an oar and Misenus's trumpet. Maybe Virgil knew of such a shrine. When we climbed up the hill of Cabo Miseno at dusk one midsummer's evening, we saw stag beetles swarming about the trees and nightjars soaring out across the bay beneath the moon. There were remains of wartime fortifications there. Perhaps they were built over the last vestiges of Misenus's tumulus.

31

Aeneas in the Underworld

Another death followed quickly: the mother of Aeneas's comrade Euxinus succumbed to old age, says *Origo Gentis Romanae*, and when they buried her in a marsh between Misenum and Avernus, they heard that a sibyl lived at Cumae, a town perched on a hilltop above the long, straight coastline, 2 miles north of Misenum. It was founded by colonists from Kyme on Euboea in the 700s BC. Amidst a grove sacred to Trivia, the local name for Hecate, these incomers found a cavern and dedicated it as a shrine to Apollo, who was believed to deliver oracles there to pilgrims through the medium of a holy woman called a sibyl, just as he did at Delphi.

Virgil would have known Cumae well. From near his home, the Appian Way led past the crater of Lake Avernus and over the forested volcanic ridge of Monte Grillo (a route later improved by the new road running under the Arco Felice) and away north to Rome, and a turning off this road led the short distance west to Cumae. But even before he came to Naples, Virgil and all of Rome knew the story of Demerate, last of the Cumaean sibyls. She wanted the Roman king Tarquinius Priscus (d. 579 BC) to buy her nine books of prophecy, written on palm leaves. Tarquinius balked at the cost, so she burned three books and offered him the rest for the original price. He turned her down again, so she burned three more until, desperate to know at least a little of the future, the king paid the original price for the remaining three volumes. They were kept on the Capitoline Hill and were consulted by Apollo's priests whenever Rome was in need. They were destroyed by fire just before Virgil was born, but the priests recomposed them, with the help of the surviving oracles at Delphi and Dodona. These Sibylline Books still played an important role in the Roman psyche in Virgil's time, and consequently Augustus restored Apollo's temple at Cumae to its ancient glory.

Both Augustus and Virgil, therefore, wished to weave the oracle into Aeneas's story. So, back in Buthrotum, Virgil's Helenus had advised Aeneas to visit the Cumaean sibyl, even though her palm-leaf prophecies were too easily scattered by the breeze, resulting in confusing messages. As soon as the Trojans came ashore at Cape Misenum, and before Misenus died, Aeneas hurried with his companion Achates 'to the heights, wheresoever Apollo holds ward aloft, and to the cavern, vast and remote, that guards the secrecy of the dread Sibyl, on whom the seer of Delos [Apollo] breathes his great mind and soul, and unfolds the days to be'.

While Achates went off to fetch the sibyl, whose name was Deiphobe, Aeneas admired the mighty bronze doors of Apollo's temple. Fashioned by Daedalus, they depicted Minos's Cretan labyrinth and its Minotaur, both emblematic of the underworld. When the sibyl arrived, she shrieked in admonishment: why are you wasting time staring at doors when you should be sacrificing to the god? Aeneas did so, and she led Aeneas and Achates to her cavern, 'whither led a hundred broad avenues and a hundred gateways, alive with echoes'.

The whereabouts of this cavern was a mystery until 1932, when excavations revealed the tunnel now shown to visitors as the sibyl's grotto. It is at the base of the low cliff below the ruins of Apollo's temple, and next to a wooded ledge above a steep drop down to what are now coastal fields, but was then the sea. The tunnel runs parallel to the ledge, the seaward side pierced by periodic openings; these are scarcely 'a hundred gateways', but Virgil was presumably employing some poetic licence. The tunnel was carved about three hundred years before Virgil's time, probably for defensive purposes; originally low and narrow, the Romans later lowered the floor and cut the openings to allow shafts of light to pierce its length. At the end is a chamber that produces sonorous echoes, despite an opening in it leading to the woods outside. Through this opening had blown the dry leaves of holm oaks that provided us with the last whisperings of the long-departed sibyls.

As they approached this chamber, the sibyl shrieked 'it is the hour to inquire your fates! The god – behold the god!' 'Slothful Aeneas of Troy', as she called him, found his heart filled with longing and dread, but he resolved to enter. He prayed to Apollo, reminding him of all the hardships he had endured, and promised to build him a temple of white marble, and a solemn shrine 'in our realm': presumably, Virgil had in mind the place where the Sibylline Books were kept on the Capitoline Hill.

Deiphobe raved in 'limitless frenzy', trying to free herself from the god's demonic possession, babbling that Aeneas's journey was almost over. But, she prophesied, a new Trojan War awaited. A new foreign bride (Lavinia) would cause as much trouble as Helen had, and a new Achilles (Turnus) would yearn to destroy the Trojans. But never yield to your sufferings, she raved, however great they become: let them embolden you, for you are guided by Fate.

Until now, as Williams comments, Aeneas has been 'backward-looking, regretful, uncertain'.[1] Yet he seems more stoic now, with his feet on Italian rock. So Aeneas begged something new of the sibyl: that she guide him down into Hades, to confer one last time with his father. Both Theseus and

Aeneas in the Underworld

Hercules made such journeys and returned alive, Aeneas argued, and he had Zeus's blood in his veins, just as they did. The way down is easy, retorts the sibyl – it is coming back again that presents the problem. If he must make the dread journey, he must scour the woods for the golden bough, which alone guaranteed safe passage back.

It was now that, being a prophetess, she told Aeneas about Misenus's death. Aeneas hurried back to the camp. While he helped his men gather wood for the pyre, Aeneas's heart churned with anxiety, for the golden bough remained elusive. Then, his mother Aphrodite intervened, sending two doves to lead him to Lake Avernus. Here he found his golden bough, which was probably mistletoe. Though usually green, it can look golden in some lights, especially in the winter. Aphrodite was not an underworld deity, but in her earlier Mesopotamian incarnation as Inanna, she had entered the underworld. Now, by leading him to the golden bough, she helped her son do the same. Because he was fated to succeed, the bough came away easily in Aeneas's hand. A 1673 sketch-book of Claude Lorrain's in the British Museum shows the sibyl leading Aeneas towards dark woods, with Cape Misenum and Capri depicted accurately in the distance, and the blazing light of sunrise or sunset (both geographically impossible for the view is southward) beyond. In Virgil, she led Aeneas by Lake Avernus to 'a cavern ... abysmal and vast – jagged and guarded by its sunless lake and the midnight of its groves'. Having sacrificed to Hades, Persephone and Hecate, they began their *katabasis* – the Greek word for entering the underworld.

'Noisesome' Virgil calls Lake Avernus and 'loud' the woods that clothe the crater in which it lies. So pestilent was 'the breath steaming from its dark gorge' that birds shunned it, hence its name: *a-aves*, 'birdless'. It is neither noisy nor birdless now, but nearby, and only a couple of miles from Virgil's home, is the waterless crater of Solfatara. Here, we walked across a parched white crater-floor, dotted with rocks that are livid yellow and orange because of the arsenic they contain; a cautious stamp on the ground produced a hollow thud, revealing how thin the crust is and reminding us that not far below our feet was molten lava. Meanwhile, fumeroles of sulphurous gas, which Pliny called *spiracula*, sickened our nostrils. Had such fumes risen over Avernus in Virgil's time, which is perfectly possible, birds may well have given it a wide berth.

The Greeks called this whole area Phlegra, 'flaming', hence its modern name, Campi Flegrei, 'the fields of fire'. It was considered a twin of the Phlegran Peninsula in Thrace, below which lay the giants defeated by the Olympian gods, with the fumeroles of gas rising from their confined bodies as they broiled with frustrated rage. But Virgil did not create a myth here, because the volcanic vents really do lead straight down into the hellish world that exists beneath the Earth's surface. All Virgil had to do was find Aeneas an opening wide enough for him and the sibyl to walk into.

Such a cavern exists among the woods on Lake Avernus's southern shore. We found it guarded by friendly dogs, modern descendants, perhaps, of

In Search of Aeneas

Cerberus. In exchange for a few euros, a wonderfully ancient man called Carlo Santillo led us into the Stygian darkness, just as the sibyl led Aeneas, but slowly, the rubber end of his walking stick bumping softly on the tufa floor. It is a Roman military tunnel, perhaps built in Virgil's day, and it leads down to water, which Santillo identified confidently as the River Styx. This could hardly be the cavernous opening which Virgil described, unless this was an in-joke for his local friends – that the new military tunnels around Avernus were openings to Hell. A poet today might make a similar quip about the overcrowded London Underground.

Down they went through the vacant halls of Dis to the jaws of Hell, where dwelt Famine, Want, Death, Sleep, Strife and the Furies. In a great elm tree lurked Dreams. Out swarmed centaurs; Scyllas; Briareus; the Hydra; the Chimera; gorgons and harpies. Aeneas brandished his sword. The sibyl scolded him that these were mere shades, who used fear alone to stop souls making their way back to the world of the living. She later commented wryly that Aeneas was *pietate insignis et armis*, distinguished by both piety *and* weapons; however pious Aeneas might be, or Augustus might want him to be, he was and would always be an Homeric warrior, too.

Where the river Acheron flowed into the Cocytus, they found the banks crowded with the newly dead, begging Charon to ferry them across the marshes of the Styx. A print of about 1811 by Bartolommeo Pinelli shows Aeneas and the sibyl watching as a fearsome Charon refuses to allow aboard those whose bodies are unburied; they must wait a century before their passage. Their despair is palpable: one man buries his head in his hands. Another bearded figure holds his hands out to Charon in supplication.[2] This is Palinurus, but both his grief at being unburied, and Aeneas's anguish over this, were assuaged when the sibyl told them that the local people would soon be inspired by portents to raise him a tomb.

Charon was eventually persuaded to accept Aeneas and the sibyl as passengers. They passed the three-headed Hell-hound, Cerberus, barking ferociously in his cavern until the sibyl placated him with some drugged honey cake. Now they entered the realm ruled by Minos, who in life had been king of Minoan Crete. This underground realm was home to the souls of dead children. As they crossed the Mourning Plains, they saw it populated by women who died for love. Aeneas spied Dido, like 'the moon rising amid the clouds'. Aeneas said how riven he has been with guilt over her death. But she stood, motionless as marble, while he pleaded for forgiveness, and then turned silently away to join the shade of her original husband, Sychaeus. Dido had not forgiven Aeneas, but seeing her reunited with Sychaeus, he felt somewhat absolved of his guilt.

They entered meadows that were home to warriors. They came swarming towards Aeneas's bright armour. When the Greeks among them realised who Aeneas was, they fled whimpering in search of their long-lost ships. But the Trojans clustered around eagerly. Among them was Priam's son Deiphobus, who died when Troy fell. A drawing by Francis Cleyn (1582-1658), shows

Aeneas in the Underworld

Aeneas, aghast at the sight of Deiphobus's mutilated body, covered with wounds, one hand missing and the other dangling from his mutilated wrist.[3] Deiphobus reflected ruefully on Helen 'the Spartan whore', whom he had married in the last days of the war; she not only caused the war, but aided the Greeks in the sacking of the city. Aeneas had been feeling enormous guilt at having survived Troy when so many had died, but Deiphobus urged him forward, 'the glory of our race, towards a kindlier future'. His meetings with Palinurus, Dido and now Deiphobus enabled Aeneas to set a burden of guilt aside. He could, as Williams wrote, 'live for the future, not for the silent past'.[4]

Deiphobus guided them to a crossroads. One way led down to dismal Tartarus, ruled by Rhadamanthus, where flowed the flaming river Phlegethon. There lay the imprisoned Titans, and those who committed great wrongs on Earth, such as tyrants. They were scourged by Tisiphone, and suffered endless tortures, commensurate with the wrongs they perpetrated in life – a view which identifies Virgil's vision of the underworld as an Orphic one. Deiphobus pointed Aeneas to the other route, up past the palace of Dis and the Cyclops's workshops, to Elysium. Though still in Hades, Aeneas saw 'the pleasant lawns of the Happy Groves, and the Seats of the Blest'. Here dwelt those who led worthy lives, such as the 'loyal bards' who served Apollo, and who 'ennobled life by arts discovered'; these were led by Orpheus's follower Musaios, and perhaps Virgil counted on joining their number one day. Here, too, were those who died for their country, and many other worthies, including the shades of Aeneas's Trojan ancestors, right back to Dardanos, all arrayed in martial glory.

At last, Aeneas found his father. For Aeneas, for Virgil, for us all, the death of the man who gave us life reminds us of our own inescapable mortality, so who better to ask about death, to prepare oneself for what lies ahead? Anchises was sitting by the banks of the Lethe, watching the souls of generations yet unborn murmuring about like bees on a summer day. Aeneas asked, appalled: 'O father ... what unblest yearning for the light possesses their blind hearts?'

Anchises was eager to explain, and his explanation was an Orphic one: the entire material universe – sky, earth, sea, sun and stars – is animated by one great spirit, which the Orphics called Eros, he who was consumed by and reborn within his descendant, Zeus. The interaction of sky, earth and so forth brought to birth all life, and each living thing is animated by seeds of fire from that same divine origin, but each being is weighed down and dulled by mortal bodies. Those are the roots of our joys and sorrows. Even when we die, our souls are not free. In the underworld, they must be purged and purified, by the winds, waters and fires of Hades, of their Earthly evils – fear, desire, grief, pleasure – each for as long as is necessary. Some few souls, like Anchises's own, then dwell in these joyful fields of Elysium where, in the fullness of time, they are fully cleansed of all stain, and return to the state they had enjoyed before – 'the purified ethereal sense and the unsullied essential flame'. But the rest, after a thousand years, are summoned by Zeus to the River Lethe, to drink its waters and forget the life they had led before, so that they can be reborn into new bodies on Earth.

That may be what Virgil genuinely believed. Were it not for the advent of Christianity, it is probably what most Europeans would have been taught to believe for the next two thousand years. It enabled Anchises, standing on a low tumulus, to show Aeneas the shades of some of their more prestigious descendants, whose souls had yet to be born into the world above; the kings of Alba Longa, the ancient city up on the Alban Mount, to the south-east of Rome, who were destined to descend from Silvius, the son Aeneas would have by Lavinia; then those same kings' descendants, Romulus, who would found Rome, and Lucius Junius Brutus, who would instigate the Republic; and also Ascanius's descendants, the gens Julii, down to Caesar and all-conquering Augustus, the hero of Actium. Augustus, prophesied Anchises, would restore the Golden Age of Saturn in Latium and extend his rule further then even Dionysos or Hercules had roamed – even as far as the stars themselves.

Next appeared some of the earlier kings of Rome, including Numa, 'called from lowly Cures', the town on the Tiber where he had been born, whom Virgil admired for his civilised peace-making, in contrast to the violent king Tullus who followed. Then came 'the Greatest of the Fabii', Fabius Maximus, who, instead of rushing headlong into battle when Hannibal of Carthage attacked Rome, had the 'civilised' sense to hold back, thereby allowing the city to recover and eventually to overcome its foe.

Now, Virgil allows Anchises to summarise Rome's mission. Long before Virgil's time, as Livy tells us, an ancestor of the Caesars claimed to have seen a vision of Romulus, who told him 'The gods so wish it that my Rome should be the capital of the whole world. So let them foster the art of war.'[5] Virgil modified this speech, so Anchises proclaimed, let others (like the Greeks) breathe life into soft bronze; or charm forth images from marble; or exercise the orator's arts in court; or trace the course of the stars. But 'Roman, be this thy care, and these thine arts; to bear dominion over the nations and to impose the law of peace, to spare the humbled and to bring down the proud.' This, amidst so much glorifying of Augustus, was Virgil's vision of Rome's role in the world. It was an aspiration towards which the better of Rome's heirs in the modern world are still struggling, and it was one to which Aeneas, still shaking off his violent, Homeric past, would aspire for the rest of his life.

At the end of the parade of unborn heroes, Aeneas saw Marcellus, son of Augustus's sister Octavia. Marcellus was Augustus's heir-apparent until his death, aged eighteen, in 23 BC, while Virgil was composing the *Aeneid* – 'a sudden cloud of tragedy', as Williams wrote, 'when the sky seemed clear'.[6] Famously, having refused to allow Augustus to hear any of the *Aeneid* during its composition, Virgil relented and read to him and his court the only three books that he had finished by then, including this one. His apparition of Marcellus, reports Suetonius reports, caused poor Octavia to faint in shock.

Aeneas in the Underworld

This parade of heroes is one of the most important sequences in the *Aeneid*. It is anticipated in *Aeneid* 1, when Zeus assures Aphrodite that Aeneas will be the ancestor both of Romulus and Caesar, 'born of the fair stock of Troy, that shall bound his empire by ocean, his fame by the stars'. This and the parade's central message is also reiterated later in Virgil's description of the shield which Hephaestus makes for Aeneas. The three sequences bestow on Augustus's heavily mythologised ancestry the authority of Olympus, and of Anchises in Elysium. They are, as Hardie wrote, 'a way of claiming divine sanction for Augustus as the culmination of the historical process'.[7]

However, as W. H. Auden in his poem 'Secondary Epic' enquired, 'wouldn't Aeneas have asked – "What next?"' He was critical of Virgil for not endowing Anchises with yet longer foresight, but he ignored the fact that Virgil had explained that Elysium contained only the souls of those due to be reborn within the next thousand years or so (for those due to be reborn even later had not yet lived their previous lives). On Virgil and Anchises' behalf, Auden imagined the parade continuing down to the barbarian Alaric sacking Rome in revenge for Aeneas's slaying of Turnus. In Germany in 1768, the poet Neander continued the parade right down through the Holy Roman Empire, praising Charles V (d. 1558) as a new Augustus. Virgil could not foresee the way the Trojans would be claimed as ancestors by the newly Christianised Barbarian rulers of Dark Age Europe, or how, in Dark Age Wales, the name of Britain itself would be interpreted to create a founding hero called Britto. Britto was rapidly reimagined as Brutus of Troy, the founder of Britain and grandson of Aeneas's son Ascanius, and he was claimed as the ancestor of the princes of Dark Age Gwynedd. In AD 1135, Geoffrey of Monmouth penned for Brutus an heroic Virgilian voyage, guided by Artemis, from the Mediterranean to Britain, where he laid the foundations of London as Troy Novant, the new Troy in the West. In 1860, an anonymous poet called 'C.D.' published an epic about Brutus, in which the hero looks into a siren's mirror and sees the Virgilian parade of heroes extending through the Gwynedd princes to their descendants, the kings of Britain, culminating with Queen Victoria. In my book *Brutus of Troy*, I speculated how Brutus may then have seen the line continuing yet further, down to the birth of Prince George of Wales. Others will continue the story, I am sure, updating it constantly for their own times.

Having revealed all he could of the future, Anchises escorted Aeneas and the sibyl to the two gates of Sleep, one made of horn, through which prophetic dreams reached the upper world, the other of ivory, through which travelled false visions. He ushered them through the ivory gates – as if Virgil wanted us to question whether anything we had experienced through Aeneas had been true.

Virgil's vision of Hades, as Scherer wrote, 'lacks the clear plan of Dante's medieval Hell and Purgatory and Paradise',[8] but Virgil came first. On behalf of humanity, Virgil dared imagine how the afterlife might work, and on his foundations Christianity built the towering vision which Dante immortalised in his own epic.

Aeneas's mission would continue to be fraught with hardship and grief, but he learned in Hades that his world operated in the manner which the Greek Orphic thinkers imagined. Those who led bad lives must spend eternity in the misery of Tartarus; those whose lives were full of virtue could look forward to the congeniality of Elysium, while all those in between would wait a thousand years and then, having forgotten their past, would be born all over again. Ideas similar to the latter were adopted by many branches of early Christianity, such as the Gnostics, but they were eschewed by mainstream Catholicism and are only now making a comeback in the West through the influences of Hinduism and Buddhism.

Aeneas's visit to Hades absolved him of his guilt about the past and provided him with an understanding of the future. No longer would he merely obey Fate. Inspired by Deiphobus and his father, Aeneas returned to his fleet eager to fulfil his glorious destiny in Italy.

32

At Tiber's Mouth

The fleet set sail. Dionysius, following Naevius's *Bellum Punicum*, says that a Trojan woman died, so they stopped on the island nearest Cumae to bury her, which now bears her name, Procida. *Origo Gentis Romanae* claims that the sibyl had foretold this death, adding that Procida must not be buried on Italian soil, hence Aeneas's choice of the island.¹

As *Aeneid* 7 begins, they 'sailed unswervingly along the shore to Caieta's haven'. That is modern Gaeta, a small promontory just visible when looking north-west along the coast from Cumae, in the land Virgil sometimes calls Ausonia. *Origo Gentis Romanae* reports a story from *Pontifical Affairs* that Caieta's name was from the Greek *apo tou kaiein*, 'to burn', because this is where the Trojan women, tired of the journey, burned the ships. Virgil and Dionysius, however, claim that Caieta was Aeneas's nurse, who died on the voyage and was buried there. But the Homeric *Hymn to Aphrodite* says Aeneas was raised by nymphs, not nurses, so who was this Caieta? The next stop up the coast is the promontory now called San Felice de Circeo, where the Greeks located the magical realm of Odysseus's captor Circe. She customarily turned her prisoners into animals, so, as Virgil's Aeneas sailed past, he heard the clamour of lions, boars, bears and wolves, which had once been men. Circe is said in *Odyssey* 10 to have had a brother, Aeëtes, so maybe it was he who was imagined, originally, to have been buried on the Ausonian promontory. His name may have morphed into Caietes and then Caieta, and it was only later that the story was modified to become another piece of supporting evidence for the Trojan myth.

They sailed on north-west. 'Now the sea mirrored the orient red, and from her ethereal height the yellow Dawn shone in rosy chariot; when the winds were hushed and every breath suddenly fell, and the oars toiled slowly through sluggish waves. And now Aeneas, gazing forth from the flood, descried a mighty forest; and, in the midst, Tiber's pleasant stream.' Ahead lay war and unimaginable suffering. But for now, they rejoiced that their voyage was over.

That is how Virgil brought Aeneas to the Tiber's mouth. Dionysius says the journey took three years;[2] Virgil in *Aeneid* 1 says Aeneas spent seven summers at sea, i.e., six years, to reach Carthage, where he spent a year, so the total voyage was therefore seven years long. But how had the myth of Aeneas, a Trojan warrior in a Greek epic, really arrived on a shore so far from home, to be lauded by generations of Romans as their most pious founding ancestor? In the 1930s, when Mussolini was keenly seeking evidence that Rome really had Trojan origins, scholars in Europe, realising that the Mediterranean was aswarm with ships in Mycenaean times, wondered if Aeneas's myths might contain some genuine racial memory of Trojan settlement in Italy. In 1937, Knight wrote:

> The insistence, from the fifth century onwards, on a Greek or Trojan origin for elements at Lavinium and Rome strongly suggests some memory, however confused or misinterpreted, of foreign contacts at an early date. In Latium and elsewhere, movements and intercourse, not belonging strictly to Troy and Trojan times, may be expressed by the typical conception of Trojan dispersal.[3]

But even this perhaps goes too far. Greek mythmaking was more deliberate and literary and is unlikely to have been based on any central Italian 'racial memory' of earlier foreign contact at all. Despite Mussolini's aspirations, no archaeological evidence points to the arrival in Italy of any actual Trojans. An Italian in Homer's time is unlikely to have heard of Aeneas at all. But there is copious evidence to show how the story of Aeneas's arrival at the Tiber's mouth was invented and worked up over a period of centuries to satisfy a variety of political aspirations.

It did start, however, with the arrival of ships; not Aeneas's Trojan vessels, but those of Greek merchants, mainly from Euboea off the eastern coast of Greece, in the 700s BC. Having discovered Sicily, they ventured north to the island of Sardinia, where they were opposed by the fierce Ilian tribe. That name suggested 'Ilion' to the Greeks, who gave them a Trojan origin-myth similar to the Elymians'. Those other Sardinian tribes who sided with the Greeks became, by contrast, descendants of the forty boys who had been sired on the forty daughters of the king of Thespiae in Boetia by that most implacable of Troy's enemies, Hercules.

Euboean merchants also started colonising Ischia, off the coast of Naples, as Robin Lane Fox describes so finely in his book *Travelling Heroes*. From Ischia, the Greeks founded Cumae and started to trade further up the western, Tyrrhenian coast of mainland Italy, encountering the Latins at the mouth of the Tiber and also their northern neighbours, the Etruscans. As contact increased, Greek ships wound their way up the Tiber to the cattle market, the Forum Boarium, held regularly on a bend in the river among seven hills where, one day, Rome would rise. Here, contact between Greeks and proto-Romans began in earnest. These Greeks brought with them their myths, including the tales of Hercules's labours, the Trojan War and the *nostos* tales of the returning heroes. Thus, the Latins heard for the first time of Odysseus's tortuous journey home to Ithaka and of Aeneas's escape from burning Troy, and their stories began to take root in Italian soil as possible explanations for how peoples or cities there had come to be.

Five hundred years later, in the 200s BC, Rome had a flourishing Trojan foundation myth, but the evidence for precisely how this came about is difficult to interpret and has been the subject of fierce scholarly debate for centuries. It starts with two blind alleys. First, there is a suggestion that Italy had a native name, *Troia*.[4] According to Stephen of Byzantium, *troia* or *truia* meant 'palisaded camp'. While this was only coincidentally similar to the name of Troy, it might have given rise to ideas that the Italians came from Troy. However, evidence is lacking that *Troia* really was an old name for Italy at all, and so the notion should probably be discounted.

The second blind alley is on the tiny marble *Tabula Iliaca*, which sits in a dusty display cabinet in Rome's Capitoline Museum. It was made in Augustan times but claims to illustrate the work of Stesichorus (640-555 BC), a poet from the Greek colony of Himera in Sicily. The tablet shows Troy being beset by the Greeks and, in the bottom right-hand corner, Aeneas leading his people onto their ships. Above his head is inscribed: 'To the west? To Hesperia?' Hesperia was a Greek poetic term for 'the west', but by Roman times it had become a lyrical name for Italy, so some scholars have taken this as evidence that way back in the early 500s BC, Stesichorus thought Aeneas had come to Italy, so Rome's Trojan myth must go back that far. But there is no evidence that every last detail on the *Tabula* is a faithful rendering of Stesichorus's words, or that, if Stesichorus ever wrote 'Hesperia', he really meant Italy, as opposed to simply 'the west'. Stesichorus may have had in mind Aeneas's settlement in Thrace, or Greece, not necessarily Italy at all. Dionysius, who knew Stesichorus's work, never mentions the poet asserting that Aeneas ended up in Rome. The *Tabula* cannot, therefore, be taken as reliable evidence that Stesichorus ever imagined Aeneas reaching Italy.

The clearest evidence for what the Greeks in the 500s BC thought about Rome's origins comes from the concluding paragraphs of Hesiod's *Theogony*, which are believed to have been added at that time, long after Hesiod's death. Here, Latinus, the eponymous ancestor of the Latin race, is identified as a son of Circe by 'steadfast Odysseus' (who was believed to have roamed so far west), with no hint of a Trojan connection. Odysseus's myth was probably known to the Etruscans from at least the 600s BC, because a krater from that century, found at Caere in Etruria and probably bought from a Greek trader, shows Odysseus blinding Polyphemus. Odysseus's piety and intelligence, both emphasised by Homer, made him a desirable mythological founder, and the *Odyssey*'s geographical vagueness enabled Greek traders and Italians alike to imagine Odysseus sailing up the west coast of Italy, founding cities.

As we shall hear later, the Etruscans also developed an appetite for artefacts depicting Aeneas. Two of Rome's kings, Lucius Tarquinius Priscus (616-579 BC), and Lucius Tarquinius Superbus (535-509 BC), had at least some Etruscan blood; their names suggest origins in the Etruscan city of Tarquinia, 43 miles north-west of Rome. It is thought likely, therefore, that Rome was dominated by Etruria at the time. The story of the expulsion of Lucius Tarquinius Superbus in 509 BC, which heralded the start of the Roman Republic, might also echo Rome's rebellion against Etruscan supremacy. But across the river from Rome, the Etruscan Veiians held onto the Janiculum Hill until the Romans dislodged them in 484 BC. Dionysius claims that the original settlement on the hill had been founded by Remus, and was named Aeneia,[5] and Galinsky wondered whether this had been the Veiians' name for it.[6]

If Aeneas was seen as a great hero by the Etruscans, it seems unlikely that Rome would readily have embraced him as a founding hero at this period. In fact, when they built a temple in the Forum in 484 BC, they dedicated it to Pollux and Castor, the brothers of Helen, the Greek queen who had caused the downfall of Aeneas's Troy; a pair of well-matched brothers who contrasted sharply, moreover, with images of Aeneas carrying Anchises.

The first we hear of what the Greeks (as opposed to the Romans) thought about Rome's origins comes from Hellanikos of Lesvos (*c*. 490-*c*. 405 BC). According to Dionysius, Hellanikos wrote that 'Aeneas came into Italy from the land of the Molossians after Odysseus and became the founder of the city, which he named after Rome, one of the Trojan women. He says that this woman, growing weary with wandering, stirred up the other Trojan women and together with them set fire to the ships. And Damastes of Sigeum [*c*. 400 BC] and some others agree with him.'[7]

This story seems to contradict, or at least to build upon, another of Hellanikos's stories, that Aeneas had founded Aeneia on the Pallenê Peninsula in Thrace, as we heard earlier. For this new story, Hellanikos may have drawn on Lesches's story in the *Little Iliad*, in which Aeneas was enslaved by Neoptolemus. Perhaps Hellanikos imagined Aeneas being taken to Molossia in Epiros by Neoptolemus, then being freed and crossing to Italy. Hellanikos's story asserts that Odysseus arrived there first, and that Aeneas founded Rome only when his hand was forced by the Trojan women's boat-burning.

Hellanikos's story may have been influenced by the Etruscan fascination with Aeneas. Perhaps the Tarquin kings in Rome had come up with the idea of Aeneas founding the city, or, as Galinsky speculated, 'some elements in Rome with Etruscan sympathies' may have mooted the idea.[8] Etruscan vases show Aeneas escaping heroically from Troy with Anchises, but Hellanikos's version, with that echo of Aeneas's past slavery, his coming after Odysseus, and his being subject to the domineering will of Trojan women, not to mention the naming of the city after a mere woman, remove any hint of glory from the story. Unsurprisingly, therefore, there is no evidence from this period of Romans embracing such a shoddy foundation myth with any enthusiasm.

Having expelled the Tarquin kings, the newly founded Roman Republic began to turn the tables on its northern Etruscan neighbours. In 396 BC they besieged Veii, 10 miles to the north-west, which had once dominated Rome. Livy's account of the siege is clearly based on older accounts of the events, and turns the story into a mini Trojan War, with Rome in the role of the victorious Greeks and the Veiians as the vanquished Trojans.[9] If that reflects how Rome saw itself when that war was raging in the 300s BC, then it seems unlikely that the city would, at that stage, have embraced Hellanikos's idea of Aeneas as its founder.

Throughout the 300s, Greek mythographers, following Hellanikos and trying to piece together the past, toyed with the idea of Rome as a Trojan city. Dionysius reports a story told by Aristotle (384-322 BC), probably in his lost *Instituta Barbarica*, that some Greek ships with enslaved Trojan women aboard were blown off course on their return from the fall of Troy, and landed on the Latin shore. The Trojan women on board, exhausted by travelling, set fire to the boats and forced the whole party to settle there.[10] That gave Rome a mixed Greek and Trojan origin, but with no reference to Aeneas. By contrast, in the 340s BC, Alcimus related that Aeneas reached Italy and married Tyrrhenia, an eponym for Etruria, which, like Latium to the south, borders the Tyrrhenian Sea. Together, Aeneas and Tyrrhenia had a son, Romulus, whose daughter, Alba, had a son Rhomus, founder of Rome.[11] But Dionysius also quotes a story by the Sicilian historian Callias, who lived in the late 200s BC, which lacked Aeneas. 'Rhomê, one of the Trojan women who came into Italy with the other Trojans, said Callias, married Latinus, king of the Aborigines, by whom she had three sons, Romus, Romulus and Telegonus, and 'having built a city they gave it the name of their mother'.[12]

Later Roman historians tried to make sense of some of these conflicting stories in original ways. Servius, for example, heard that Roma was the wife of Aeneas and daughter of Odysseus.[13] At the start of his *Life of Romulus*, Plutarch listed many permutations, including Aeneas marrying Roma (daughter either of Italus and Leucaria, or of Hercules's son Telephus) and having a son, Romulus. Or, continues Plutarch, Romulus might have been a son of Ares and Aemilia, a daughter of Aeneas and Lavinia; or Romulus and Remus were sons of Aeneas and Dexithea, daughter of the Trojan Phorbas (and thus sister of Ilioneus). When the Trojans reached Italy, their fleet was destroyed by the swollen Tiber – and presumably Aeneas was drowned – but the infant brothers were saved and later founded Rome.

Such contradictory stories, all probably dating from the 300s and early 200s BC, show the mythmaking process in full swing, as the Greeks came to terms with the emerging power of Rome and tried to fit it into their world view, and the Romans, shaking themselves free of Etruscan domination, attempted in turn to make sense of the myths the Greeks were telling about them. These stories show that the emergence of Aeneas as Rome's founding hero was no foregone conclusion. They also help explain why, when Virgil wrote the *Aeneid*, he could not just let his hero turn up in a boat and found Rome; there were many contradictory myths to take into account. Thus the complexity, but also the resonant depth, of what follows.

In their camp at the mouth of the Tiber, Aeneas and his men rested beneath a tree and began eating food off flatbreads spread on the ground. They were so hungry that they proceeded to eat the bread itself – the first written evidence, as Peter Levi speculated, for pizzas – though *Origo Gentis Romanae* reports Domitius arguing that the 'tables' were not flatbreads, but beds of parsley.

Oh look, joked Aeneas's young son Ascanius: we have eaten our tables! At once, Aeneas remembered the prophecy that, once they had reached their destined home, they would eat their tables. Virgil makes a mistake here, attributing the prophecy to Anchises, whereas in *Aeneid* 3 it comes from the mouth of Celaeno. *Origo Gentis Romanae* says that the prophecy was given by Apollo on Delos, adding that Aeneas was at Tiber's mouth, between two pools of salt water, and remembered another prophecy, this time by Apollo, that his destined home lay 'between two seas'.

'Hail, land of destiny, promised to me!' cried Virgil's Aeneas. With his brow wreathed in leaves, he prayed to the *genius loci* of the place and to Mother Earth; the land's nymphs and rivers; Night; Zeus of Ida; Kybele, and to his parents, Anchises and Aphrodite. Zeus thundered on high in affirmation.

The next day, Aeneas began digging a trench as the boundary of his 'new Troy' or 'new Pergamos'. Virgil's location for Aeneas's new city was presumably Ostia, Rome's great sea port at the mouth of the Tiber. Bertha Tilly argued in 1947 that Virgil was inspired by Caesar's *castrum* at Ostia, as well as the temples of Zeus and Aphrodite there, and chose to make this the place where Aeneas came ashore.

Dionysius's version is different, stating that Aeneas's fleet stopped some 11 miles short of the Tiber and nosed instead up the Numicius, the mouth of which opened onto an inland lagoon that is now silted up. Here they rested near some springs which 'are no longer so full ... but there is just a little water collected in a hollow place'. Aeneas raised two Trojan altars and offered sacrifice in thanks for the water. They 'ate their tables' there, and Aeneas remembered the prophecy which, in Dionysius' version, came either from the oracle oak at Dodona, or from a sibyl on Mount Ida – probably the one said to have lived at Gergis, about 10 miles north-west of Palaiskepsis. Aeneas 'prepared pedestals and altars' for the statues of the household gods he had brought with him, 'and the women with shouts and dancing accompanied the images. And Aeneas with his companions, when a sacrifice had been made ready, stood round the altar with the customary garlands on their heads.'[14]

The sow they were about to sacrifice escaped, and Dionysius's Aeneas remembered the second part of the prophecy, that he should follow a four-footed animal and wherever it wearied, he should build a city. That was a deliberate echo of Aeneas's ancestor Ilos being led to the site of Troy by a cow. Aeneas followed the sow 24 stades, about 2½ miles, until she sank exhausted on a low hillock. Aeneas was not convinced that this was the best place for a city, but a disembodied voice from the trees assured him that, just as the sow would give birth to many young, so this new city would spawn many more. According to *Origo Gentis Romanae*, that story goes back to *The Origins of the Romans* by Cato the elder (234-139 BC), in whose version, reportedly, the prophecy came to Aeneas from his household gods in a dream. Satisfied, Aeneas sacrificed the sow and founded his city there, and called it Lavinium.

This is probably the scene depicted on the Belvedere Altar in the Vatican.[15] Created in Augustus's time, the altar depicts Aeneas as a muscular, middle-aged man, half-clad in a toga, leaning on a staff or spear, following a sow who is about to sink to the ground by a tree. In front of them sits a robed figure, reading from a scroll – perhaps the Scroll of Fate, telling of the cities destined to be founded from Lavinium, including Rome itself.

Whether Aeneas landed at Lavinium or just further north at Ostia, his landing spawned various spin-off myths. *Origo Gentis Romanae* quotes Marcus Octavius saying that while Aeneas made his sacrifice on the Italian shore, he saw Odysseus's fleet on the horizon, an occurrence not reported in any other version of the story. Fearing that Odysseus would recognise and disturb him before the solemn sacrifice was complete, Aeneas drew a veil over his head, and from this stemmed the Latin practice of making sacrifices *in capite velato*, 'with veiled head'. Another just-so story was told by the first Roman annalist, Cassius Hemina in about 146 BC:[16] Aeneas and 600 men reached Italy in the second summer after the fall of Troy and pitched a camp 'in the territory of Laurentum', which is between Ostia and Lavinium. Here, Aeneas dedicated a statue he had brought from Sicily. Servius says that Aeneas brought the Sicilian Venus (Aphrodite of Eryx) with him to Latium.[17] Two manuscript versions of Solinus say the statue Aeneas brought with him depicted Venus Ericis, while another version of Solinus says it was of 'Venus Frutis'. There was a temple of Venus Frutis at Lavinium. It seems likely that Frutis had been a native Latin goddess. As the Trojan myth took hold in the area in the 200s BC, Frutis was syncretised with Aphrodite-Venus, and particularly with Aphrodite of Eryx in Sicily. Thus, the foundation of the Frutis sanctuary came to be attributed, as with so much else in Latium and Rome, to Aeneas. And the Frutis sanctuary's very existence then became further evidence that Aeneas really had come to Italy.

In Search of Aeneas

As we have seen, Virgil deliberately ignored the existing tradition, as recorded by Dionysius, that Aeneas landed at Lavinium, and made his landing 11 miles north-east up the coast, at Ostia instead. For Virgil, the founding of Lavinium came later in Aeneas's life, beyond the end of the *Aeneid*. That is why we will find Virgil reusing the story of the sow later, in *Aeneid* 8, and not in connection with Lavinium. But Virgil, or his editors, gave a respectful nod to the Lavinian tradition in the opening lines of the *Aeneid*, in which we read – in contradiction to the story related in the poem – that Aeneas landed, not on the Ostian shore, but on the 'Lavinian strand'.

33

Aeneas in Latium

Until the early 200s BC, myths identifying Aeneas as Rome's founder, or at least as the originator of the dynasty which later founded the city, come to us from Greek writers, never from Roman ones. But then things change. Two major factors seem to have led to Rome adopting Aeneas's myth. The first was voiced by Hoffmann in his *Rom und die griechische Welt*,[1] and also by Momigliano and Galinsky.[2] During the Latin War of 340-338 BC, Rome consolidated her growing dominance over the Latin states immediately to the south, including Laurentum and Lavinium. By doing so, Rome assumed Etruria's role as the dominant power in the north. Thus Aeneas, who had been so beloved of the conquering Etrurians, may suddenly have seemed a more appropriate founding hero than Romulus or Rhomus (Remus), whose own myth may have had Latin roots. It was the second factor, however, which really thrust Aeneas's myth into the centre of Rome's mythological landscape. And that thrust came from the east – from Epiros.

In 355 BC, Olympias, daughter of king Neoptolemus I of Epiros, attended the annual summer festival of the sacred mysteries of the Great Gods on Samothraki. Also enjoying the festivities was the ruler of the land bordering Epiros to the east, Philip II of Macedon. And she caught his eye.

By the late 400s BC, as we heard earlier, the rulers of Epiros had established a myth claiming descent via the tribal kings of the Molossians from Achilles. That is why Olympias's father was named after Achilles' son Neoptolemus, the sacker of Troy. To match Epiros's conceit, Philip's forebears, the Argead dynasty of Macedonia, developed a similarly lofty origin myth for themselves. In the dark centuries following the fall of Troy and the collapse of Mycenae, the kings of the Dorian tribes sought legitimacy for their newly gained control of Greece, including Argos, by claiming descent from exiled sons of Hercules. In the 400s BC, the Argeads started claiming descent from the Dorian rulers of Argos, because the names sounded similar – and this, conveniently, handed them a ready-made boast of descent from Hercules.

Olympias and Philip married. Their son, reputedly conceived on Samothraki, was Alexander the Great (356-323 BC). He is essential to our story because like Caesar and Augustus after him, he placed implicit faith in his descent from heroes, in his case from both Hercules and Achilles, about whom he learned from his tutor, Aristotle. The 'school of Aristotle' has been rediscovered, just east of Naousa in Macedonia, next to a small river, where low cliffs have been carved out to create not only beam-sockets for porticos but also a fine Macedonian-style doorway, leading into a cave behind. In the centre of what would once have been the shaded yard between the riverbank and the carved cliff, a square stone block was carved out for the master to sit on; the boys, presumably including Alexander, would have sat on the ground before him. The school looks out east across the river, over the plain in the direction of the distant sea; when Aristotle spoke of ancient Troy, and of the present Persian menace, the boys had only to turn their heads in that direction for both to seem more real. Small wonder, when he grew up, east was the only direction in which Alexander wished to travel.

Each night, all his life, Alexander's pillow rested on a dagger and a copy of the *Iliad*, given him by his tutor, Aristotle. In his dreams, we may imagine, his ancestors Hercules and Achilles marched, each in his own generation, up to the walls of high-towered Troy, sacrificed to the eternal gods and fought with dust on their faces but ever-lasting glory on their brows. Such dreams were what must have helped inspire Alexander to muster his troops at Dion below Mount Olympus in 334 BC and to march away to battle the invading Persians back through Thrace, and all the way to Troy.

Instead of the great city known to Aeneas and Achilles, Alexander found at Troy a shepherds' village on an overgrown hillock with, perhaps, a few sanctuaries in which sacrifices were still offered to the heroes of the Trojan War. There was probably an awkward moment when Alexander asked the locals which of the barrows dotting the Troad was that of his ancestor, Achilles. Very likely they had no idea, but in typically Mediterranean fashion the matter would have been discussed at length, and eventually a conclusion was reached: that one over there! And so, at night, says Plutarch in his *Life of Alexander*, Alexander anointed the tumulus, which was probably Beşik Tepe, with oil, and 'ran a race by it with his companions, naked, as is the custom, and then crowned it with garlands, pronouncing the hero [Achilles] happy in having, while he lived, a faithful friend [Patroclus], and after death, a great herald of his fame [Homer]'.

The locals gave Alexander an old suit of armour, which they obligingly claimed had been Achilles'. Thus attired, Alexander marched east from Troy to meet the army of Darius III, Great King of Persia, which was camped at Zeleia. The armies clashed by the River Granicus. Brimming with confidence inspired by his ancestor Achilles, Alexander rocked the world by defeating Darius and making himself master of the entire Persian Empire. Marching through Afghanistan, Alexander entered India, determined now to reach the eastern coast of Asia and the shores of the all-embracing Ocean. When his

Aeneas in Latium

exhausted men begged him to turn back at the rain-swollen River Hyphasis in the Punjab, Alexander proclaimed, as Arrian reports in his *Anabasis of Alexander*, 'had our forefather Hercules remained in Tiryns or Argos, or gone no further than the Peloponnese, or Thebes, he would never have obtained enough glory to achieve the transition from man to god!' Inspired, the army continued to follow him; it was only later, and for other reasons, that they turned back. Wounded and sick, Alexander returned to Babylon, where he died in 323 BC.

Alexander's new empire was divided between his generals, who established new dynasties such as the Ptolemies in Egypt. General Lysimachos became ruler of Asia Minor and was succeeded later by another general, Seleucus. Under Lysimachos, Troy gained its new lease of life as the Greek city of Ilion, with new Classical temples rising over the ruins of Aeneas's city. The base of Lysimachos's temple to Athena is a dominant feature of the excavated Troy we see today.

Thanks to Alexander's brief blaze of glory, the bronze gates to the heroic past that had slammed shut with the Fall of Troy seemed to have flown open again. An Homeric hero had walked again among mankind, and an appetite for hero-ancestors from the story of Troy was revived across the Mediterranean, including in Rome, when otherwise, perhaps, civilisation's fascination with the *Iliad* might have faded away altogether.

In Epiros, Alexander's young cousin Pyrrhus (318-272 BC) shared Olympias's mythological descent from Achilles. He was the grandson of Olympias's uncle Arymbas and was named after Achilles' son, Neoptolemus, whose Homeric byname was Pyrrhus. Having established himself as the most powerful ruler in northern Greece, Pyrrhus of Epiros sought to emulate Alexander's victories in the east, by conquering the west. The steadily expanding Roman Republic was now in conflict with the Magna Graecian cities in southern Italy and Sicily, so Pyrrhus crossed the Straits of Otranto to intervene. In 280 BC, his army, which included twenty war elephants – an instrument of war discovered by Alexander in the east – scored a victory over the Roman forces near Heraclea, which is now called Policoro.

Among those siding with Rome against Pyrrhus were the Elymians of Sicily, who by now, thanks to their Greek neighbours, had adopted the myth of their foundation by Trojans. And Rome itself, the Greeks believed, had been founded either by Aeneas, or by Trojan women; Aristotle's views on the matter must have been well known to Pyrrhus because he had been Alexander's tutor. So, Pausanias tells us, when ambassadors from Taranto urged the king to help them against Rome, Pyrrhus 'remembered the sack of Troy, and he had the same hopes for his success in the war, as he, a descendant of Achilles, was waging war against a colony of the Trojans. So the proposal pleased him.'[3]

In Galinsky's interpretation, 'It was the Romans who started capitalising on the Trojan legend for political purposes' and Pyrrhus 'only responded to Roman initiative'.[4] But the evidence seems to point more the opposite way:

In Search of Aeneas

Pyrrhus saw this as his chance to bolster his status as Alexander's successor and Achilles' descendant by replaying the Trojan War in Italy, with Rome cast as his Trojan foe. Pyrrhus minted silver *didrachm* coins in southern Italy and Sicily showing Thetys and the shield she gave her son Achilles on one side, and Achilles' head, which was really an idealised portrait of Pyrrhus himself, on the other.

Buoyed up by the idea of himself as the new Achilles, Pyrrhus engaged his 'Trojan' foes, the Romans, at Asculum in 279 BC. He won, but this was the original 'Pyrrhic victory', for in winning the battle Pyrrhus lost so many of his generals and troops that he commented, as Plutarch relates, that another such victory 'would utterly undo him'. Later, Pyrrhus fought an indecisive battle against the Romans at Beneventum in 275 BC – and gave up. Withdrawing from Italy, he sought fresh glory in the Peloponnese. Three years later, he attacked Argos, an angry housewife flung a roof tile at his head, and that was the end of Pyrrhus.

Whether or not the Romans had really started to see themselves as Aeneas's heirs before these events, they certainly did so now. Astonished by their victory over the heir of Alexander and Achilles, Rome found that the Greek world had handed them a stunning piece of mythological propaganda. In this new Trojan War, mighty Achilles had been humbled and the Trojans had been victorious. The city's newly found – or at least, newly confirmed – descent from Aeneas obliterated any remaining notion that Rome was a mere nest of western barbarians. The Trojan myth now rooted Rome firmly within Greek civilisation, and at the heart of the Classical world. The reflected glory of Aeneas would stand the Romans in good stead as they began, inexorably, to extend their dominance across the Mediterranean.

Whether he landed at Ostia or Lavinium, Aeneas was now on Latin soil, and had to encounter the ruler of the Latin people, King Latinus. The *Origo Gentis Romanae*, reporting the words of Cato the elder (234-139 BC), tells how, as soon as he heard of the Trojan landing, Latinus sent his army to attack him with their primitive stones and clubs. Observing how well-ordered and technologically advanced the Trojans were, Latinus remembered a prophecy, delivered through entrails and dreams, that he should ally himself with a stranger. So Latinus entered into a treaty of friendship with Aeneas.

Virgil tells the story differently. While Aeneas traced the boundaries of his camp (at Ostia), he sent an embassy to Latinus, whose capital was at Laurentum. This was a real Roman town, perhaps the one whose ruins are now hidden in the Castel Fusano pine forest between Lavinium and Ostia, the location of the Villa di Plinio where Pliny the Younger lived a century after Virgil. Bases of the villa's walls, a brick arch and a mosaic floor can still be seen there, in a clearing among the flat-topped pine trees.

Virgil's Laurentum was 'royal and vast, sublime on a hundred columns', adorned with cedar statues of Latinus's ancestors. Virgil's heart was not in that 'vast urban agglomeration' of Rome, 'constantly increasing and inhabited largely by ex-slaves of mixed race',[5] as Levi put it, but rather in 'the landing of Aeneas on Italian earth and in the river winding through the trees and the noise of birds'.[6] Virgil looked back constantly in his poetry to the Age of Kronos, that golden age of innocence before the more sophisticated, yet crueller, rule of Zeus. Although Kronos had been overthrown, Virgil, following Ennius, imagined him living on as Saturnius, an Italian woodland deity, and made him father of Picus, whom that lustful local sorceress Circe turned into a magpie. Picus's son was Faunus. Dionysius makes Latinus a son of Faunus,[7] though he also repeats a story that Latinus was really a son of Faunus's Hyperborean mistress, by Hercules.[8] Virgil's Latinus is Faunus's son, and he thus continues Kronos's lineage and Golden Age down into Aeneas's time, concealed in the pine woods, amidst the hidden glories of Latium: for 'Latium' is from *latuit*, 'hidden', or 'latent'.[9]

Latinus received Aeneas's envoys kindly. They gave him gifts from Aeneas, including Priam's ill-omened robes and sceptre. Latinus recalled, 'though years have dimmed the tale', how Aeneas's ancestor Dardanos had come originally, not from Samothraki or Arcadia at all, but from 'Corythus's Tuscan home' in Italy.

Already, as Virgil tells us a little earlier, the arrival of Aeneas had been foreshadowed by omens. The great bay laurel growing at the heart of Latinus's palace had been invaded by a swarm of bees; his only child Lavinia's hair burst into flames, and Latinus recalled an oracle that a foreign prince would come; war would follow; the prince would marry Lavinia, and from their union would arise a people (the Romans) who would raise the name of Latium to the stars. Lavinia was already betrothed to Turnus, the prince of the Rutulians who lived south-east along the coast at Ardea, and whose father Daunas had come thence from Arcadia after the Trojan War. But now Latinus obeys Fate's will, and pledges Lavinia to the envoys as Aeneas's future bride.

Latinus was the eponymous king of the Latins, and his was a far more ancient tradition in Italy than Aeneas's. The growth of Aeneas's status entailed a subtle diminishing of Latinus's. Galinsky highlights two coins, first a gold stater from the Second Punic War, showing Latinus in a tunic, opposite Aeneas wearing armour, both about to sacrifice a sow. Latinus is stooping slightly through age, but if he stood upright he would be taller than Aeneas, and his spear is noticeably longer too. A later denarius, minted by Tiberius Veturius Barrus, shows the same scene, though this time Aeneas is the taller man, and his spear by far the longest.[10]

It was a joyous time. In AD 1765, when a new Grand Duke was welcomed into a previously leaderless Florence, the grateful citizens staged Baldassare Galuppi's new opera *The Arrival of Aeneas in Latium*, hoping that their new duke, like Aeneas, would usher in a new era of peace and prosperity.

While the Trojans and Latins celebrated their alliance, however, Hera fulminated on high. Aeneas had defied all her furious attempts to destroy him and was now set to fulfil his destiny in Italy. Hera knew she could not stand in Fate's way, but she could delay it, and inflict as much suffering on Aeneas as she could. Let the price of his success be blood, she cried; let Aphrodite discover that her son was a second Paris who, by stealing another man's woman, would cause a second Trojan War.

Hera sent down the female fury, Allecto, to unleash a storm of bloodshed. Allecto inspired Latinus's queen, Amata, to browbeat her husband into going back on his word by reasserting Lavinia's original betrothal to Turnus. Then Allecto stirred Turnus up against the incomer, until the Rutulians and Latins were united in hatred against the Trojans. Hera then caused Ascanius, who was out hunting, to kill a stag which had been tamed by the Latins. An altercation over this led to bloodshed, and the bodies of Latins killed by Trojans were borne back to Laurentum. Latinus, powerless in the face of his people's anger, allowed Turnus to pursue his plans for war. As with Hesione and Helen, it was now Lavinia's turn to be the cause of war. As with so much civil strife in ancient literature, *cherchez la femme*: 'look for the woman', or women who, in Virgil's view, were invariably the cause of so much trouble.

Virgil's *Aeneid* combines the themes of Homer's two great works, first an *Odyssey*, a perilous voyage, and now, on Italian soil, an *Iliad*, a tale of war. Virgil based the war in Latium on established sources. Livy relates that when Aeneas landed in Italy, he formed an alliance with Latinus, married his daughter Lavinia and founded Lavinium. Turnus of the Rutulians, Lavinia's jilted fiancé, attacked the combined Latins and Trojans, and although he was defeated, Latinus was killed, so Aeneas became king. Then a second war ensued, involving Mezentius of Caere. Dionysius, in similar fashion to Livy, relates how Aeneas married Lavinia and then led the Trojans and Latins in war against the invading Rutulians led by Tyrrhenus (the inspiration for Virgil's Turnus). Latinus and Tyrrhenus were killed, and Aeneas became king of Latium, after which came a second war, involving Mezentius.[11] But in Virgil's version, Mezentius's story became part of the single, world-changing war, with which the *Aeneid* ends.

In Livy and Dionysius, war is simply war. In the *Aeneid*, however, war is an evil which Aeneas wished to avoid, but which Fate dictated he must, nonetheless, undertake. In some ways, his engagement to Lavinia parallels Paris, who wilfully stole another man's wife; but in Virgil's telling Aeneas is far closer, as Hardie argued, to Odysseus, battling off the suitors who gathered around Penelope when they thought he was dead; fighting hard, in other words, to keep the woman Fate had designated, all along, to be his wife.[12]

Left alone, Aeneas and Latinus might perhaps have persuaded Amata and Turnus not to oppose Fate's will. But Hera's hatred of Troy made war inevitable. It would be a war in which Aeneas, though desirous of peace, would sometimes be provoked into furious slaughter, and during the course of which Virgil himself would try to work out how civilised Rome and its rulers should conduct themselves when provoked into conflict.

Now Virgil calls upon the Muses of Mount Helicon, who had inspired Homer and Hesiod, to help him in the monumental task of relating this second Trojan War. The rest of *Aeneid* 7 comprises an 'Homeric' style catalogue of the great forces of local peoples whom Turnus musters to help him exterminate the Trojans.

At the start of *Aeneid* 8, Aeneas lay awake in his camp (at Ostia), thinking thoughts so much more human than those of Homer's gilded heroes. Far from contemplating future glory, Aeneas knew, as Virgil reminds his Roman audience, that regardless of the righteousness of the cause, his pursuit of the war would cause countless deaths and untold misery and would wrong Turnus too (for Turnus was not to know that his engagement had gone against the will of Fate). But as these troubled thoughts filled Aeneas's mind, there rose before him amidst the poplar leaves the god of the River Tiber, his hair crowned with reeds. Tiber assured Aeneas, 'Here thy home is ... shrink not, nor dread the menace of war: the ire and menace of Heaven are spent.' Tiber advised Aeneas to ally himself with Evander, a king from Arcadia in Greece who led his people to Italy and now lived in antique simplicity but constant conflict with the Latins. It is here that Virgil uses the story of the sow, which belonged in previous versions of the myth to the founding of Lavinium. Tiber promised Aeneas that he would see a white sow and her piglets, and when he awoke, he did so. Aeneas killed these on Tiber's banks, on the river-god's advice, as a sacrifice to Hera, in an attempt to quell her anger with his 'suppliant prayers'. Virgil describes Aeneas's river voyage to Evander:

> The unwonted wood admired the heroes' far-flashing shields and the painted hulls that breasted the river. Through the night and the outworn day they rowed and ascended the spacious reaches, overshadowed by motley trees and glancing betwixt verdant woods over the tranquil tide. – The flaming sun had already scaled the mid arch of Heaven, when they discerned in the distance city-walls, and a tower, and scattered roofs – now exalted to the stars by Rome's empery, then Evander's scant domain! Quickly they swung their prows to land, and drew to the little town of Pallantium.

This was the settlement on the Palatine Hill that would one day be re-founded by Aeneas's descendant Romulus, as Rome.

34

Arrival in Rome

When the Romans learned that Pyrrhus of Epiros had left Italy, they rejoiced and embraced the idea that they, as descendants of the Trojans, had vanquished the heir of Achilles. But there was no time for them to bask in their new glory because in the vacuum created by Pyrrhus's absence, there began in Italy three periods of intense conflict with Carthage; the First (264-261 BC), Second (218-201) and Third (149-146) Punic Wars. On some of their coins, minted in occupied parts of Magna Graecia, Carthage showed their female founder, Dido. So Rome countered with coins depicting Roma – the Trojan mother of Romulus – who they probably imagined by then to have been the wife of Aeneas.

In 263 BC, during the first war, the Elymians of Segesta in western Sicily slaughtered their city's occupying Carthaginian garrison and renewed their alliance with Rome. The Segestans, too, had their myth of being founded due to Trojan women burning their boats; for the first time, the Segestans began to mint coins depicting Aeneas carrying Anchises. That suggests that they knew the Romans now attached some importance to myths which linked them, too, not just to any Trojan, but to Aeneas himself.

In 249 BC, between the First and Second Punic wars, Rome wrested Eryx out of Carthaginian control. This most famous holy place in Sicily, which had been the Carthaginians' main base in Sicily during the first war, became for the Romans an enduring symbol of hope for their ultimate victory over their foes. Eryx became a popular pilgrimage destination for Romans, not least because of all the sacred prostitutes at Aphrodite's temple there. Rome enforced its ties with western Sicily by giving Eryx's cosmopolitan Elymian, Phoenician and Greek goddess a new name, 'Venus Erycina' – Aphrodite of Eryx, the mother of Aeneas.

For perhaps the first and certainly not the last time, Romans claimed that a place where Aphrodite was worshipped had an intrinsic link to Rome because she was the mother of their founding hero. This identification was then back-dated, so that Aelian (d. *c*. AD 235) could attribute Carthage's defeat by the Greeks at Himera back in 480 BC to their lack of respect for the goddess of Eryx, who had always been, he claimed, an intrinsically *Roman* goddess.[1]

By the mid-200s BC, Rome's claim to Trojan roots had become, as Galinsky asserted, 'an important instrument in her eastern policy'.[2] Suetonius quotes the Roman senate writing to Seleucus Kallinikos (ruled 246-225 BC), promising their friendship if he would free their 'kinsfolk' in Troy from all taxation.[3] Justinus tells us that in about 237 BC, the Akarnanians in north-west Greece petitioned for Roman help on the grounds that they, alone of all Greek states, had not sent soldiers to the Trojan War.[4] And when Scipio went to Troy in 190 BC, Livy writes of 'the Trojans, by every act and expression of respect, showing themselves proud of the Romans being descended from them, and the Romans expressing their delight in their origin'.[5]

One myth, which probably arose in Pyrrhus of Epiros's aftermath, is related by Dionysius: besides Ascanius, who founded Alba Longa, Aeneas was father of Romulus and Remus.[6] This clearly adapted Alcimus's story from the 340s BC (as related earlier), in which Aeneas was father of Romulus, and Romulus's grandson was Rhomus, founder of Rome. The cities founded by Romulus in Dionysius's version are not recorded, but Remus founded Rome and also Aeneia (on the Janiculum Hill); Anchisa (whereabouts unknown) and Capua, which he named after his ancestor Capys, the father of Anchises. Capua was closely allied to Rome until it defected to Carthage in 216 BC, and Galinsky thought this myth dated from before that year, as a Roman method of endorsing Capua's ties to Rome.[7]

Aeneas's myth appears at the heart of Roman literary culture in Naevius's *Bellum Punicum* 'the Punic War', which was probably written sometime after 235 BC. Naevius's story included Aeneas and Anchises's voyage, in a ship built by Hermes, from Troy to Sicily. After Dido's death in Carthage, father and son landed in Italy and perhaps Aeneas founded Lavinium, though that is not clear from the surviving lines. Aeneas's daughter was the mother – perhaps by Amulius, king of Alba Longa – of Romulus, who, in this version, was Rome's founder. It was Naevius who, as we heard earlier, introduced the story of Aeneas's love affair with Dido. This had clearly been inspired by, and served as a literary justification for, the bitter enmity between the Rome and Carthage.

In the Second Punic War (218-201 BC), Hannibal's Carthaginian army famously crossed the Alps in 218 BC and defeated the Romans at the battle of Trebia at the end of that year, and again by Lake Trasimene in 217 BC. Though Rome lay largely undefended, Hannibal chose to march south instead, to seek allies among the Greek cities there. A further victory over Roman forces at Cannae in 216 BC led many of Rome's former allies, including Capua, to defect to the Carthaginian side, resulting in a decade-long struggle by Rome to regain supremacy in Italy.

In Search of Aeneas

In 217 BC, during this period of extreme crisis, Rome's acting dictator, Quintus Fabius Maximus, consulted the Sibylline Books and decided to dedicate a temple in Rome to Venus Erycina. The temple, on the south-western end of the Capitoline Hill, was finished and dedicated two years later, on 23 April 215 BC, the annual feast day of *Vinalia Priora*, when it was customary for Roman men to visit Aphrodite's sacred prostitutes. The feast's origins were of course unknown, but by Ovid's time they were believed to have originated in an oath sworn to Zeus by Aeneas before his duel with Mezentius[8] and perhaps this belief stemmed from the late 200s BC too. Once Rome's war against Carthage was won, the goddess on the Capitoline Hill became rightly associated with victory, so she became known as *Venus Victrix in Capitolio*. Aeneas's mother, therefore, was now enshrined at Rome's heart as the city's victory-bringing mother goddess.

In 181 BC, a second temple was dedicated to Venus Erycina. It stood by the Porta Collina, on the north-east of the Quirinal Hill, and was outside the *pomerium*, the sacred perimeter of Rome. The temple here probably had less to do with Aphrodite as the mother of Aeneas, and more to do with her as the goddess of love and patroness of sacred prostitutes. Each year, the goddess was brought out of the temple for a procession, during which roses were strewn in her path, just as Italian Catholics do to this day with statues of the Virgin Mary. The temple was circular, perhaps echoing the temple of Vesta, which was also linked to the Trojan myth. Nearby has been excavated the colossal head of a goddess, probably Aphrodite, and the 'Ludovisi Throne', which is now in the Museo Nazionale Romano. On it is a stunning relief, which appears to show Aphrodite rising out of the sea, aided by maidens who might be the Fates. Both were probably made in Attika about the 470s BC and had probably come to Rome via Aphrodite's temple on Eryx.

In Galinsky's analysis, the 'mobilisation' of Sicily's Trojan myth by the Romans during the Punic Wars was an essential factor in the rise of Aeneas's status in Rome. This, Galinsky argued, was in turn the reason why Aeneas's Sicilian sojourn played such a pivotal part in the *Aeneid*.[9] Just as Rome 'discovered' its Trojan roots, in part at least, through its dealings with Sicily, so had Virgil made Aeneas discover in Sicily the fresh resolve he had needed to press on with his mission, to lead his people to Italy.

In 204 BC, while the Second Punic War still raged, a prediction was found in the Sibylline Books that a foreign enemy threatening Rome would be defeated, as Livy reports, 'if the Idaean Mother should be brought from Pessinus to Rome'.[10] As a result, an embassy was sent in five quinqueremes to the east. The Delphic oracle advised them to go to Pergamon, 40 miles south of Mount Ida, and they went.

Pergamon's king, Attalus, conducted the Roman ambassadors 250 miles inland to Pessinus, deep in Phrygia. Although Kybele was worshipped on Mount Ida, Pessinus was her chief, acknowledged cult-centre in Anatolia. The Great Mother was worshipped on Samothraki in the form of magnetised

Arrival in Rome

rocks, and we have seen, she appears to have been worshipped in similar fashion at Palaiskepsis. It is thrilling, therefore, to hear from Livy that in Pessinus, the ambassadors were given 'a sacred stone, which the inhabitants said was the mother of the gods'. It was a black stone, perhaps a meteorite, as Mary Beard speculated or, dare one speculate, a rock that was partially magnetised. It was believed, for sure, to be the physical presence of Kybele, the eastern Aphrodite, the Great Mother, or *Magna Mater*, as she was now to be called in Latin.[11] And because Aphrodite was Aeneas's mother, the ambassadors could now regard this Anatolian rock as being firmly connected to Rome's origins.

The aim of the exercise was partly political, a symbolic strengthening of Rome's ties with Anatolia; partly too, perhaps, the patrician Romans who promoted the project were drawn from the *familiae Troianae* who had already started claiming descent from Trojan incomers, and who wished, by this grand gesture, to draw attention to themselves.

If so, it certainly worked. Magna Mater and her accompanying eunuch priests, the *galli*, whose noisy rites echoed those of the Corybantes, the traditional attendants of Kybele, were conveyed by sea via the Troad and Kythera in a ship which, says Ovid, was built specially using pines from Ida.[12] When the ship reached Ostia, it became grounded on a sandbank but was freed by a virgin using only her sash: so, even before she was carried reverently ashore, Magna Mater had already performed a miracle in Italy. The matrons of Rome handed the stone reverently, one to another, all the way from Ostia to the temple of Victory on the Palatine Hill, where it resided until a new temple was completed in 191 BC on the western slope of the same hill, close to what was said to have been Romulus's house. Magna Mater's temple was desecrated in AD 394 and the stone's whereabouts now is unknown. In 204 BC, however, the physical presence in Rome of Aeneas's mother helped harden the Romans' resolve to win the war.

Once the Second Punic War was won, Rome turned its attention to dominating Greece. Plutarch, in his *Parallel Lives*, tells how, during the Second Macedonian War (200-197 BC), the Roman general Flamininus (229-174 BC), having driven Philip V of Macedonia out of Greece, visited Delphi and made several dedications in which he described himself as 'a descendant of Aeneas' and 'the great leader of the children of Aeneas'. Maybe he was reminding the Macedonians that Rome fitted into the Greek world view. Or perhaps Flamininus was taunting them, that the descendants of the Trojans, whom the Macedonian kings' purported ancestors had vanquished in the Trojan War, were now in charge. Flamininus's gens, the Quinctii, were an old Alba Longan family, so perhaps they had developed a myth that Aeneas was their ancestor. It was about this time that the Roman poets started referring to Romans as *Aeneidae*, 'descendants of Aeneas' and coins started being minted there depicting Aphrodite or Venus wearing 'Phrygian' or Trojan headwear.

Aeneas's myth was working its way ever more closely into the heart of Rome's psyche.

Quintus Ennius (c. 239 BC-c. 169 BC) was a soldier from Rudiae in the heel of Italy, who was brought to Rome to write poetry by Cato the elder. Southern Italy was still soaked in Greek culture and, at the start of his *Annales*, Ennius relates a dream in which he climbed up Mount Helicon, near the home of Hesiod, and saw a peacock, its tail full of blind eyes. The peacock turned into Homer, who explained that he had been reincarnated like this, and that his future reincarnation would be Ennius himself.

Thus inspired, Ennius penned his *Annales* in stately Homeric hexameters, telling how Aphrodite floated 'swiftly, through rare wafts of mistiness' to find Anchises on Mount Ida, and Aeneas was born of their union. When Troy fell, Aphrodite persuaded Aeneas to obey his father by retreating to Mount Ida, but afterwards he embarked for Italy, where Kronos still ruled. Reaching Laurentum, Aeneas encountered the king of Alba Longa and presumably, though the surviving fragments of the poem do not include this, married his daughter. Aeneas's daughter Ilia encountered a man 'of beautiful looks', probably Ares, and gave birth to Romulus and Remus. Romulus founded Rome and, like Aeneas, he became a god. Thus, as Ennius put it in another poem called 'On the revival of Troy in Ilium', Troy was sacked but not captive; burned but not consumed; destined not to moulder on the 'Dardan plains', but to be reborn as Rome.

Ennius's *Annales* was the first Roman epic to be written in Homeric style. His work came to be held in the same respect with which we treat the work of Chaucer and Shakespeare. Later, when Virgil wanted to add authentically antique touches to the *Aeneid*, such as the speeches of Zeus or the sibyl, he copied the 'old-fashioned' way people spoke in Ennius's works.

The third Punic War was fought 149-6 BC and resulted in Rome's destruction of Carthage. Rome's attention could now focus wholly on the eastern Mediterranean, where the Trojan myth was pressed into continuing service as a political and diplomatic tool.

In about 82 BC, says Appian, when General Sulla (c. 139-78 BC) became dictator of Rome, the Delphic oracle bade him seek the favour of Aphrodite of Caria, because he belonged to the race of Aeneas. Caria is in Anatolia and contains the city of Aphrodisias, which is about 200 miles south-east of Troy. To the goddess's temple in Aphrodisias, Sulla sent a crown and double axe, both emblems associated with Venus Erycina, and the inscription 'The Imperator Sulla consecrated that one to you, Aphrodite, because I saw you in a dream exhorting my army and fighting with the arms of Ares.'[13] As with Kybele of Pessinus, the age-old worship of the goddess of Caria was converted, because of the Roman belief that her son Aeneas had come to Italy, into further evidence of Rome's ancient and enduring connection with Anatolia. Wherever in the world people worshipped Aphrodite, they

Arrival in Rome

worshipped the mother of Aeneas and – whether they liked it or not – the ancestral mother of Rome.

In 1675, Claude Lorrain painted the precise moment when Aeneas's ship reached the place which would become Rome. The picture, which is now in Anglesey Abbey, Cambridgeshire, shows the ship's sails being furled and the weary oarsmen pulling their final strokes to ease the ship up to the wooded bank. Soldiers with spears have come hurrying down from the city up on the Palatine Hill, which was then called Pallantium, and whose towers can be glimpsed through the trees. All is tranquil; men are fishing from a small boat in the background, and on the shore two Virgilian shepherds tend a flock. Young Ascanius, a man who is probably Achates, and Aeneas himself, resplendent in golden armour and a red cloak, stand in the ornate prow. They, too, have spears, but in his right hand Aeneas holds up an olive branch, signifying that he has come in peace.

This landing place below the Palatine Hill was the Forum Boarium, the old cattle market. Virgil's description differs to Claude's scene because, as Aeneas prepared to step ashore, he smelled the freshly shed blood of animal sacrifice and saw Evander and his people paying homage at the shrine of that great nemesis of Troy, Hercules. Today, traffic pours along the Forum Boarium's busy roads between the Tiber and the foot of the Palatine Hill, but in an oasis of greenery stands the circular temple of Hercules, with its elegant pillars and pointed terracotta roof. The magnificent golden statue of Hercules it used to contain is now in the Capitoline Museum.

Aeneas proffered his olive branch to Evander and utilised genealogy to further his diplomatic aims. Aeneas's ancestor Dardanos, he reminded Evander, was the son of Elektra, and her sister Maia was the mother of Hermes, who was Evander's own father. So the Greek habit of tracing everything back to the same genealogical origin was used here, as so often in real-life diplomacy, to justify an alliance. Evander, for his part, revealed that when Anchises and Priam tried to visit Hesione on Salamis many years ago, they had strayed into Arcadia. He, Evander, was a boy then and took an instant liking to Anchises, taking his hand and showing him eagerly around the fortifications of Pheneos, a city whose ruins lie, only partially excavated and generally ignored, in a peaceful valley immediately west of Mount Cyllene, which was sacred to Hermes. When Anchises left Arcadia, he gave Evander gifts, including two golden bridles. Thus, on two scores, the friendship of old Evander and Aeneas was ensured. Evander now explained how his realm had come to be.

When the first historical Greek merchants, whose memory would later be overshadowed by Aeneas's myth, first came to the Forum Boarium in the 700s BC, they encountered the Latin people who lived atop the steep cliffs of the Palatine Hill. The hill's name derives from Pales, goddess of farming, and the natives belonged to what archaeologists term the Villanovan Culture, which had spread south from Etruria a century before and was based on growing grain and rearing pigs. Before then, they had been less advanced, with roots going back, ultimately, to the pre-Neolithic lifestyle of hunting and gathering common to all of ancient Europeans. These people appear in Roman histories as 'Aboriginals' – a term applied much later to the indigenous peoples of Australia – and they were believed to have been *autochthonous*, born from Mother Earth herself. Dionysius thought they were identical with the Oenotrians, those early wine-making inhabitants of Italy. As a Greek, Dionysius claimed, rather outrageously, that even these 'native' Italians had come originally from the Peloponnese, and had driven the true natives, the Sicels, away to Sicily.

Evander's explanation of Rome's history is a Virgilian parallel to the foregoing. 'Once,' Evander told Aeneas, 'these woods were tenanted by Fauns and Nymphs, native-born, and by a generation of men sprung from boles of trees and the obdurate oak.' The first seeds of civilisation had been brought here, Evander claims – just as the real Greek merchants had speculated – by Hercules, who had passed this way while herding the cattle he had stolen from Geryon back to Greece, during his tenth labour. Reaching the Palatine Hill, Hercules had a nap, whereupon the local giant, Cacus, stole some of the cows and hid them in his cave on the nearby Aventine Hill. But Hercules heard them mooing, broke off the entire rock face in order to find them, and wrestled Cacus to death. Hercules then educated the locals in farming and religion, showing them how to build altars and make sacrifices. Then, Evander came from Arcadia and took this farming culture to a new level by building Pallantium. Evander showed Aeneas the original altar that Hercules had left there, and both men prayed together to 'our common deity'. Not for the first time, it was by absorbing Hercules's better qualities, and not by opposing them, that Aeneas assured his future success.

Rome today is a frenzy of crowded streets, but at its heart lies the Palatine Hill with the ruins of the forum at its foot. Away from the traffic, you can explore the forum's ruins, each one identified as something quite extraordinary – the temple of Saturn; the house of the Vestal Virgins; the temple of the divine Caesar, and so on. Paths lead you up, past cypresses and ivy-covered walls, to the hill itself, also strewn with ruins, mainly of the palaces of Augustus and Tiberius, but also much older structures, such as the Temple of Victory and the ruins whose massive stone blocks are identified as Romulus's house.

For Aeneas, the building of all these structures lay far in a future yet to be achieved. Evander now told Aeneas that the Etruscan city of Agylla, 21 miles to the north-west of Rome, had been ruled by Mezentius, who enjoyed tying living people to corpses and leaving them to die, just for his own amusement. Mezentius had lately been overthrown and had fled to join Turnus. The Etruscans, meanwhile, had rallied temporarily under Tarchon, but it has been prophesied that a foreign-born prince will come to lead them. Evander had been offered the leadership because he was from Greece, but he considered himself too old, and his son Pallas was born in

Italy, so did not qualify. So you, Evander said to Aeneas, must be the one decreed by Fate to lead us all.

Thunder boomed in divine confirmation. Aeneas sent most of his ships back to Ascanius in Ostia. He set off on horseback to find the Etruscans, clad, Herculaean style, in a lion's skin with gilded claws, to show that he meant business. By his side rode faithful Achates, and also young Pallas, bright like the morning star, with a cohort of Evander's Arcadians behind them. The drumming hooves were like thunder as they galloped towards Agylla, to seek out their new allies in the looming war against Turnus.

35

The Shield of Aeneas

Despite the colourful myths which they developed and which the Greeks cultivated for them, the Etruscans were, in essence, no different to their southern neighbours, the Latins and proto-Romans; descendants of the Villanovan farmers of central Italy. Contact with Greek and Phoenician merchants, the latter mostly from Carthage, stimulated trade. Etruria's copper and iron deposits started being mined intensively, making the Etruscans rich and powerful. When competition led to war between Greece and Carthage, the Etruscans allied themselves with the Carthaginians and won the decisive sea battle of Alalia, off the Corsican coast, in about 540 BC. That led to a decline in Greek power in the western Mediterranean, but it did not put a permanent stop to trade with Greece.

It was not Greek Odysseus, but Trojan Aeneas, who seems to have captured the Etruscans' imagination. Like them, Aeneas had stood up to the Greeks, and it was known from Poseidon's prophecy in *Iliad* 20 that he survived Troy's fall. In the 1960s, Galinsky analysed black-figure vases from the period 525-470 BC found in Italy, which seem to have been made in Athens specifically for the Italian market. Over fifty depictions of Aeneas survived, but the precise provenance of only twenty-seven was known for sure. Of these, five were from Sicily, three from Nola near Naples, and seventeen were from Etruria, suggesting that Aeneas's story had become especially popular there.

These vases often show Aeneas carrying Anchises on his shoulders. An Etruscan amphora from the 470s BC, for instance, shows Aeneas carrying Anchises, while in front of them walks Creusa, leading Ascanius by the hand and holding aloft a clay *dolium*, which probably contains the *sacra*, the gods, of Troy.[1] Aeneas's rescue of Anchises also appears on an Etruscan scarab ring, which shows just the two of them. Anchises holds a box, which may have been the *cista sacra*.[2]

These images, which imply that Troy's gods had been saved from the flames by Aeneas's actions, may have contributed to the peculiarly Italian idea of Aeneas as a figure of piety. Thus, in his 1951 book *Rom und Troia*, Franz Bömer argued that first the Etruscans, and then the Romans, adopted Aeneas as a founding hero because of his well-known piety, and in preference to the slyness of Odysseus. But we have seen that Rome did not blindly follow Etruria in adopting Aeneas as a founding hero: they did so much later, and for more pragmatic reasons. Likewise, Galinsky showed that while some vases cast Aeneas in a pious light, others show him helping Paris abduct Helen and, mainly, as a warrior – battling Diomedes, helping recover Troilus's body, and so on, as a hero often paired with Hector and equal to Achilles. Galinsky thought that the one found at Vulci, which shows Aeneas fighting Achilles, even 'borders on hero worship'.[3] Galinsky argued that emphasis on Aeneas's piety came much later, due to the Caesars. The archaeological evidence suggests that the Etruscans saw Aeneas more in the round; pious, for sure, but chiefly a brave warrior and a survivor. The presence of the household gods implied by the *dolium* and box was probably intended simply to identify Aeneas as a founder, for the real founders of cities often brought images of their homeland gods with them, so they were not a specific sign of piety in Aeneas's case.

The presence of so many depictions of Aeneas in Etruria opens up the possibility that one or more Etrurian city may have adopted Aeneas as a founding hero. Galinsky thought, on the basis of archaeological finds depicting Aeneas, that Vulci and Veii may have done so.[4] Galinsky dismissed Silvio Ferri's idea that Aeneas was the subject of one of the statues found at Portonaccio on the Veiian plateau, for the figure identified as such was simply a warrior, who was not depicted carrying Anchises or leading Ascanius. But in the mid-400s BC, votive statuettes were made in Veii showing Aeneas, beardless and naked save for a crested helmet, carrying a big shield and shouldering Anchises.[5] Although there are votive inscriptions at Veii invoking goddesses, however, no inscriptions have ever been found mentioning Aeneas. The idea that Aeneas was seen as a founding hero anywhere in Etruria at this time, therefore, can only be conjecture; his depictions there show that he was admired, but perhaps that was all.

Virgil's idea that Aeneas would find allies among the majority of Etruscans was most unusual. In most versions, such as Livy's Roman history, Mezentius was the leader of all the Etruscans, and all were Aeneas's foes. Virgil's alternative story had a precedent only in Lycophron's *Alexandra*, a pre-Virgilian work which is otherwise hopelessly undatable. This refers to Aeneas arriving in Etruria where, in places including Agylla, he would find 'the two sons of [Telephus] the King of the Mysians ... Tarchon and Tyrsenus [or Tyrrhenus], tawny wolves, sprung from the blood of Hercules', and implies that they become his allies. This, and Virgil (who may have had Etruscan blood himself), probably drew on the ancient Etruscans' fascination with Aeneas. Besides, both he and Augustus wished to promote Italian unity; so in the *Aeneid*, the majority of the Etruscans were set to become Aeneas's allies.

In Search of Aeneas

As Aeneas rode from nascent Rome into Etruria, hoping to be offered the leadership of the Etruscans in preference to their former tyrant, Mezentius, he rewrote Roman history. In Virgil's version, Aeneas belonged to Rome from the start, and the Etruscans would be his subservient followers.

Agylla, Aeneas's specific destination, is the Greek name for the city the Romans called Caere, and which is now Cerveteri. It stands, as Virgil describes it, on a rocky outcrop, or rather a rock plateau between two valleys, looking west over an agricultural plain to the Tyrrhenian coast, which was probably considerably closer then than it is now. Caere was founded about the 800s BC and became a flourishing trading city with a whole suburb of Greek merchants and artisans. Variously at war or in alliance with the Roman Republic, it was to Caere that, when Rome was sacked by the Gauls in 390 BC, the Vestal Virgins fled for safety. Caere is famous now for its big, round Etruscan tombs, some still finely decorated, in which were found some of the artefacts depicting Aeneas that are described in this book. The tombs are grouped in two necropolises, one on the southern edge of the city's plateau, where the steep cliffs of orange sandstone lead down into the wide valley of the River Vacchina, and the other, the best-preserved, on another plateau called Banditaccia, to the north of the town and separated from it by a much smaller valley, again edged with sandstone cliffs, called the Fossa di Manganello.

When Aeneas and his men reached Caere, he learned that Tarchon and his forces were camped down on the plain. But before he went down to announce himself, says Virgil, he and his men rested by Caere's 'cold stream', in a valley enclosed on all sides by hills clothed with pines, containing a grove sacred to Silvanus, the god of the countryside. Virgil does not say which of the two valleys, north or south, he had in mind. The woods are mainly now of holm oak, although a few flat-topped pines can still be seen. Both valleys have cool streams and their cliffs make them feel enclosed, the narrower Fossa di Manganello more so than the broader Vacchina valley, but the latter would be a more appropriate place for a hero and his army to make their camp, and it would have been less overlooked than the other, which is directly below the walls of Caere itself.

Aeneas had left his original armour behind in Carthage, so, to protect her son in the forthcoming war, Aphrodite asked her husband Hephaestus to order his Cyclopes to forge a new set, and a new shield, deep in the fiery heart of Etna, just as Thetys did for her son, Achilles, in *Iliad* 18. Aphrodite brought the finished armour and shield to the resting Aeneas, who saw them being laid by her unseen hand under an oak, presumably a holm oak like the ones that grow there now. The scene was painted on a wall of the Casa del Centauro in Pompeii, now lost, but known from a drawing made in 1829 by Marsigli, now in Naples Archaeological Museum. It probably meant a lot to the house's owners, as a prophecy of Rome's greatness. It shows Aphrodite on one side of a great tree-trunk, watching Aeneas and a companion, probably Achates, on the other. Aeneas, who is nude save for a short cloak and spear, has just found the armour and is holding up the helm to admire it. Later, in about 1635, Nicolas Poussin painted the scene. His painting shows rocky cliffs towering in the background, just like those at Caere, suggesting that Poussin had made the 20-mile journey from Rome to absorb the atmosphere for himself. In the foreground, Aphrodite stands in her ornate chariot, replete with cherubs and doves, pointing her son towards the glittering hoard.[6]

Aeneas's awestruck examination of his new arms allows Virgil to write an *ecphrasis*, a description of an imaginary work of art, paralleling Homer's description of Achilles' shield in the *Iliad*. Aeneas's shield depicts the great glories of Rome still to come, with an emphasis on Rome's civilisation and piety. It leads, like the parade of heroes which Aeneas witnessed in Hades, to Augustus. We see the gods of Rome drawn up on Augustus's side in his battle against Antony and Cleopatra, with her retinue of strange, animal-headed Egyptian deities. Here is Augustus at Actium, with flame shooting from his helm. There is Augustus celebrating his victory by adorning Rome with 300 temples and surveying a procession of conquered peoples from across the world. In Virgil's time, Britain paid Rome tribute, but remained unconquered, so it is not listed, but he does mention the Morini, the tribe who lived near Calais.

It is to frame such passages that the entire, grand edifice of the *Aeneid* exists. They also serve a dramatic function within the tale, reminding us, within the logic of the myth, that the success of Rome's mission to civilise the western world, including eventually even the British, hung on Aeneas's success. For his part, Aeneas marvelled at this future, our future. He did not understand it, but with great nobility, Aeneas nonetheless raised 'on to his shoulder the fame and destiny of his descendants'.

Aphrodite could have given her son his shield at any time, but Caere's artisan suburbs were famed for their metalworking, and this may have been why Virgil made it happen here. There is another possible reason. As we explored the Fossa di Manganello, we found a section along the top of the cliff on the southern side of Banditaccia into which several tombs had been carved. They were bare and empty, but others in Banditaccia itself, such as the Tomba dei Rilievi, are decorated with friezes of weapons. D. H. Lawrence, who was fascinated by the Etruscans, describes one tomb, the Grotta Bella, as being full of reliefs of 'shields, helmets, corselets, greaves for the legs, swords, spears', and he relates how, when the Regolini-Galassi tomb was opened in 1836, they found 'the remains of a warrior, with his bronze armour'.[7] Banditaccia has thousands of such tombs, which have been robbed long-since. Perhaps when Virgil came here he was shown rich hoards of recently exhumed golden armour and shields, and this was his inspiration for the miraculous appearance of Aeneas's, while the hero lay dozing in the vale.

Aeneid 8 ends with Aeneas admiring his new shield. *Aeneid* 9 is all about Turnus and his attack on the Trojan camp at Ostia, in Aeneas's absence. It is not until *Aeneid* 10 that we re-join Aeneas, riding down from Caere to the Etruscan camp, clad in his brilliant new armour, flanked by his Trojan generals and Evander's son Pallas, to meet Tarchon.

The Etruscans of the 500s and 400s BC may have idolised Aeneas to a certain extent, but their main foundation myth, which developed due to their contact with eastern Mediterranean traders, was that they came from Lydia, 200 miles south down the Anatolian coast from Troy. While the evidence points to Etruscan culture being mainly rooted in Italy, there is archaeological evidence of some immigration from the eastern Mediterranean, most likely by traders who established themselves in Etruria and never went home. Perhaps some of these really were from Lydia, or at least from Greek colonies on that part of the Anatolian coast.

Lydia, as Horsfall pointed out, had no significant heroes in Greek mythology from whom the Etruscans might claim descent. But Mysia, its neighbour to the north, did. When Hercules visited Tegea in Arcadia, he raped Auge and conceived Telephus. Telephus was abandoned on Mount Parthenius, to the north-east of Tegea, but was found and suckled by a doe. Later, Telephus was brought to King Corythus, a local ruler whose name was derived from Corytheis (modern Agiorgitika), a settlement within sight of Mount Parthenius. Auge later sailed to Mysia and married its king, and her son Telephus eventually inherited the Mysian throne.

The Etruscan foundation myth, which seems to have developed in parallel to Rome's Trojan myth, was that Telephus had a son, Tarchon, who sailed west and founded Etruria. By the 200s BC, Etruscan coins, urns and sarcophagi regularly depicted the doe suckling Telephus and, as we have heard, Lycophron's undatable *Alexandra* places Telephus's sons Tarchon and Tyrsenus in Etruria. Tarchon's name was in fact derived from the Etruscan city of Tarquinia, which is 24 miles north-west up the coast from Caere. That city also gave its name to the Tarquin kings of Rome, and the prominent Tarcra family of Caere. All this made Virgil's choice of the name Tarchon for his leader of the Etruscans highly appropriate.

Aeneas told Tarchon that Mezentius was mustering warriors, and Turnus was desperate for war. Tarchon agreed that Aeneas must be the one foretold by that most convenient and contrived of prophecies, that the Etruscans could only be led by a foreign-born prince, and he agreed to follow him.

In *Aeneid* 10, Aeneas led his new Etruscan allies south to join the war in Latium. But a line of Virgil's suggests a further adventure, for at the start of *Aeneid* 9, Iris goaded Turnus into attacking the Trojan camp by telling him that Aeneas had roamed 'as far as Corythus's most far-flung cities' to gather to his army 'Lydian' country-folk – in other words, Etruscans, who claimed descent from Lydians. There is no gap in Virgil's account of Aeneas's movements in which this recruiting expedition may have happened, but by now we are used to Aeneas's life being anything but strictly linear, so we may overlook this blip in Virgil's dramatic timeline and follow Aeneas to his ancestor Dardanos's birthplace in Etruria.

Just as the story of Aeneas's later life shifted west, so, too, did the myth of the early life of his ancestor Dardanos. Though originally a founding hero in Dardania, Dardanos's birthplace moved, as we have seen, to Samothraki. His connections to that sacred island were well established by Virgil's time, and were actively promoted in the eastern Aegean, but that did not stop other regions claiming him for their own political ends. We saw earlier how the myth arose that Dardanos had come from Arcadia and how Virgil then promoted the idea that he was in fact from Italy. This was why, when Aeneas's fleet left Crete in accordance with Apollo's prophecy on Delos to find 'the land that first bore you from the stock of your sires' they made for 'Italy ... Corythus and the Ausonian soil'; and why, when they arrived, Latinus confirmed that, 'though years have dimmed the tale', Dardanos was 'from Corythus's Tuscan home'.

Horsfall and others argued that Virgil was drawing here on an antiquarian tradition of Rome, or perhaps Etruria, albeit perhaps no more than a couple of generations old. In *Aeneid* 1, Aeneas tells Aphrodite, 'I seek my native Italy, and my forefathers, begotten by Zeus,' but Virgil does not explain that Dardanos was from Italy until *Aeneid* 7, so presumably he expected his learned Roman audience to know this already. Servius relates a variant of Dardanos's story, which could pre-date Virgil's, affirming that Dardanos was the son of Zeus and Elektra, but making his brother Iasion the son of Elektra by a hitherto unheard-of husband, Corythus, King of Italy.[8] That was surely an Italian invention. It may have been inspired, in part, by a story known to Diodorus Siculus, that Iasion had, by Kybele, a son called Corybas, the eponym of the Corybantes, the noisy worshippers of Kybele.[9] If Iasion's son was called Corybas, then one might deduce that Iasion's father was called Corythus. Corythus's name, as we saw earlier, was derived from Corytheis in Arcadia, and his transplanting to Italy was presumably a result of the Etruscans' appropriation of the myth of Telephus, who was Corythus's foster son. From this may have arisen the notion that Corythus had a kingdom, not Arcadia, but in Etruria.

Despite stretching even mythological credibility close to breaking-point, these stories may have helped loosen Dardanos's roots in the east and allowed for the final transplanting of his birthplace into Virgil's own Italian soil, so that Virgil, and perhaps antiquarians in the generations immediately preceding him, could claim that Dardanos was, by birth, an Italian. And this contrived mythmaking was important, because it allowed Aeneas's journey to Italy to become a *nostos*, or homecoming. As Buchheit argued, it rescued 'the Trojan ancestry of Augustus and Rome from the odium incurred by Troy as an Eastern city'[10] and succeeded, as Horsfall wrote, 'by a clever mythological stroke, to capture the whole glorious house of the Dardanidae for [Italy], given the secure place of both Aeneas and Telephus on Etruscan soil'.

In Search of Aeneas

Virgil's references to Corythus in Italy are perhaps deliberately ambiguous and it is not always clear whether he was referring to a realm of King Corythus in Italy, or to an actual place of that name. However, many writers have assumed that Virgil imagined a city in ancient Etruria called Corythus. Servius even repeats a story that, before he left Italy for Anatolia, Dardanos gave the name Corythus to a place where he fought a battle with the 'aboriginals', because he lost his helmet or *korus*, led a charge to regain it, and as a result won the battle.[11] But the consensus was that Corythus was the place where Dardanos was born.

Two locations for Corythus have been proposed. The first is Tarquinia, an archaeological site near the sea famous, like Caere, for its painted Etruscan tombs. The Medieval city near the site of the Etruscan one was called Cornetto, and Paul of Perugia (d. AD 1348) thought this was Corythus. Horsfall agreed, arguing that Virgil had changed the name from Tarquinia to Corythus to disguise the city's ancient enmity towards Rome, adding that Tarquinia was an important Etruscan city, yet Virgil did not mention it, so it must, ergo, be Corythus. However, Virgil does refer to Tarquinia obliquely, mentioning its port of Graviscae, so Horsfall's argument here is unconvincing.

The second and much more enduring candidate for Virgil's Corythus is Cortona, a city which spills down a dramatic outcrop of the Apennines, facing south-west onto the broad valley of the river Chiana, 100 miles north of Rome. Commanding an important overland route from Rome to the north-east coast of Italy, Cortona's original Villanovan settlement was greatly expanded by the Etruscans in the 600s BC, and its city walls stand to this day on imposing Etruscan foundations. While the idea that all Etruscans were descended from Lydian settlers is surely a myth, it probably is true that some easterners settled in Etruria, and the Tumulus Melone II, in the valley below Cortona, with its grand steps framed by sculptures of warriors having their heads almost swallowed by lions, is closely comparable to an altar on Cape Monodendri in Miletus, which is itself considered to be of Lydian inspiration.

If the story of Dardanos coming from Corythus dates back any further than Virgil, then so, too, might Cortona's claim to be Corythus, based perhaps on the vague similarity of the names. There are people in Cortona now who think the myth arose by at least the 100s BC, as a means of currying favour with Rome. The idea was certainly current in the generations immediately after Virgil: in his *Punica*, Silius (d. AD 103) refers twice to Corythus in a location that can only be Cortona.[12] Later, Cosimo I de Medici, whose Florentine grand duchy included Cortona, revived the story to try to upstage Rome. John Jackson was so convinced of this that, in his 1908 translation of the *Aeneid*, he actually translated Virgil's reference to Corythus in *Aeneid* 3 as 'Cortona'. Today, every Cortonan schoolchild is taught that, through Dardanos's birth there, Cortona was 'the mother of Troy and grandmother of Rome'.

The Shield of Aeneas

We walked up the narrow Medieval Via Dardano and later drove up to the Medieval Girifalco fortress on the hilltop above the town, that was once the *arx*, or acropolis, of Etruscan Cortona. Dark clouds enveloped us, and suddenly we were in the midst of a frenzied hailstorm, with the darkness pierced by bright lightning as thunder boomed. Was this Zeus, confirming that Cortona was indeed the Italian birthplace of his son Dardanos? Even if not, the storm underlined Cortona's grandeur, and enforced how appropriate it was as the imagined Italian birthplace of Aeneas's ancestor, Dardanos.

Thanks to his alliances with Evander and Tarchon, and his recruiting mission to 'the land of Corythus', Aeneas now had a considerable army at his command. *Aeneid* 10 includes a Homeric-style catalogue of his new Etruscan allies, from Clusium (Chiusi), a typical Etruscan hill-top city 18 miles due south of Cortona; Cosae (Cosa), 52 miles up the coast from Caere, which was in fact a Roman bastion that superseded the nearby Etruscan city of Vulci; Populonia, on the cliffs 53 miles further up the coast, famous for its Etruscan necropolis; Elba, an island lying just off Populonia, rich, as Virgil wrote, in iron; Pisa, 51 miles north along the coast from Populonia; Caere itself; Pyrgi (Santa Severa), 8 miles up the coast from Caere, whose recently excavated temples include one to Uni, the Etruscan version of Aphrodite; and fever-wracked Graviscae, Tarquinia's port. Aeneas's ranks were swelled, too, by chiefs from Liguria, which stretches along the coast north of Pisa as far as Gaul; and finally, Virgil's own Mantua, 100 miles north-east of Pisa, which he honoured by including it in his catalogue of Aeneas's allies.

Most of these places, save Clusium and Mantua, are on, or near, the Via Aurelia. Virgil ignored many other Etruscan cities, like Volterra, which are not. That suggests Virgil had travelled along that road but had not strayed far from it. But however he had created his list, Virgil supplied Aeneas with a formidable force with which to fight his much-anticipated war in Latium.

36

The Trojan War Replayed

Although Aeneas went north on horseback, he returned in *Aeneid* 10 from Caere to the Trojan camp at Ostia, by sea – and, surprisingly, in his own ship, with its carved lions snarling on the prow. How it had reached Caere, we are not told. Behind Aeneas followed the massed fleets of the Arcadians and Etruscans.

Whilst Aeneas had been busy raising his army, Turnus and his allies had surrounded the Trojan camp in Ostia. Young Ascanius, who was a mere child when his father saved him from the flames of old Troy, had been forced to step quickly into manhood as the defender of this new Troy. Ascanius was aided by forces from Evander, and by Etruscans. Virgil is vague on the details, but Aeneas might have despatched these earlier on from Caere, perhaps before his recruiting tour of the north. Ascanius's forces had so far held Turnus off, but a massed attack was due the following morning, and all the advantage lay with Troy's enemies.

Gazing down from Olympus, Zeus summoned a council. Hera asserted Turnus's right to defend his native land, but Aphrodite begged Zeus to turn Turnus back, or else allow her, at least, to spirit her grandson Ascanius away to safety in Cyprus. Zeus's reaction, when faced with these two opposed female forces, was inertia. This was no business of Heaven's, he argued. Fate, and the actions of Turnus and Aeneas, must decide the outcome.

Turnus's men discovered the remaining ships of the original Trojan fleet drawn up on the shore near Ostia. They tried to destroy them, but they, like those of Aeneas's own vessel, were made from the pines of Mount Ida. Kybele, the Great Mother of Ida, softened the ships' timbers and they melted into the forms of the nymphs from whose trees they had been hewn, and thus they escaped out to sea. They found Aeneas leading his fleet, his hand on the tiller beneath the starry heavens, and danced in the waves around him. I thought this scene sprang entirely from Virgil's imagination until my level-headed friend Dr Chris Farmer told me of his experiences sailing off the Italian coast at night, and seeing dolphins and fish swimming through plankton, causing it to phosphoresce and creating luminous blue streaks through the water which, he said, could easily be mistaken for mermaids – or nymphs. Virgil may have experienced the same thing.

'Wakest thou, Aeneas, scion of gods,' cried these Idean nymphs, 'wake, and fling loose the sheets of thy sails! Ascanius, thy child, is immured within moat and wall, amid the flying spears and Latium's fiery battle!' So saying, they sped Aeneas's fleet on its way, 'fleeter than a javelin or wind-swift arrow'.

On the shore, a cry went up. Dawn was breaking, 'rushing on in fullness of light, and dark was fled'. Trojans rubbed their eyes in disbelief, and Turnus and his men turned in alarm. The sea swarmed with ships and the rising sun's reflected light blazed from Aeneas's upheld shield, just as it would later shoot like flame, Virgil reminds us, from Augustus's helmet at Actium.

This is what gave Tolkien the idea of Gandalf leading the cavalry of Rohan to save Aragorn's beleaguered army from Sauron's forces in the last part of *The Lord of the Rings*. Like Aeneas, Gandalf came with the dawn. Tolkien has his hero charging out of the east, so that the orcs' eyes are blinded by the rising sun. Virgil was constrained by geography: he had to make Aeneas's ships' come out of the west, so made the sun blaze *in reflection* off Aeneas's helm.

Trumpets blasted and bronze weapons clashed. Turnus bore down upon the disembarking army, but Aeneas charged forward, killing all who stood against him, even the sons of Hercules's old comrade, Melampus. When all seven of Phorcas's sons attacked him, Aphrodite helped by flicking their spears aside. Turnus, like a ravaging lion, encountered and cut down young Pallas and then gloated over his corpse, wishing that Evander was there to witness his son's demise, and wrenched away the boy's precious sword-belt.

News of this cruelty drove Aeneas berserk. 'His constant efforts to control the irrational elements in himself here break down,' wrote Williams, 'he yields to fury,' to *furens*, and Virgil shows us both the glory of war and its bloody consequences.[1] First he captured eight enemy youths, to be sacrificed later at Pallas's funeral, just as Achilles made human sacrifices on Patroclus's tomb. Next he fell on an Italian called Magus, who hugged Aeneas's knees, and begged him in the name of Anchises and Ascanius to spare him, so as to save the grief of his own father and son. Turnus ended all prospect of bargaining when he slew Pallas, retorted Aeneas. So saying, Aeneas wrenched back Magus's head and plunged his sword into him, right up to the hilt. Like a whirlwind, Aeneas raged across the battlefield, cutting down all in his path, however much they pleaded for mercy: 'No kindest mother shall commit thee to earth,' he shouted, 'to the vultures shalt thou be left.' When he killed the second of two siblings, Aeneas even yelled sarcastically: 'Die and do not be separated from your brother.'

This is the violence that lies, thinly veiled, at the heart of all civilisation. Homer thought of it as the path to glory, but Virgil recognised war, and civilisation itself, as being soaked in *lacrimae rerum*, his famously untranslatable phrase meaning something like 'tears of things'. For Virgil, all glorious deeds come at a terrible price.

So determined was Aeneas to slay Pallas's killer that Hera, fearful for Turnus's safety, made a phantom Aeneas who lured Turnus away from the battlefield and onto a ship, where he was, for now, safe. In Turnus's absence, Mezentius, the evil king expelled from Etruscan Caere, took charge of the Rutulians. Mezentius was like a raging boar, with his young son Lausus at his side. Aeneas attacked and wounded Mezentius, but Lausus intervened. Aeneas warned the boy to stay back, not to attempt an unequal fight, but Lausus ignored him and Aeneas dealt him a mortal wound.

Seeing Lausus's dying face, pity returned to Aeneas. He remembered his love for his own father, Anchises. Aeneas promised not to strip Lausus of his armour, as Turnus had done to Pallas, and to return his body to his people for decent burial. Aeneas said, without arrogance, 'One thought shall solace thee for thy piteous doom: though fallest by great Aeneas's hand!'

Aeneas is the noble Roman again, not the wild Homeric hero. But, as Virgil knew, showing mercy in battle does not win wars, so there was the dilemma – for Mezentius was on the attack again.

In earlier Roman myth, before Aeneas came on the scene, this great battle was fought between Mezentius and Latinus, but the tradition which Virgil was adapting here had long-since replaced Latinus with Aeneas himself. In his *Fasti*, Ovid weaves a little story in here to explain the origins of the Roman feast of Vinalia Priora.[2] In order to secure Mezentius's aid in the battle, Turnus pledged him Latium's latest vintage. So, before he faced Mezentius in battle, Ovid's Aeneas prayed to Zeus, saying: 'The foe has pledged his vintage to the Tyrrhenian king; Jupiter, thou shalt have the new wine from the Latin vines.'

Eagerly, Virgil's Aeneas met his foe. Round him thrice rode Mezentius in his chariot, casting spears until Aeneas's shield bristled like a forest. Aeneas responded by killing the horse and bringing the chariot crashing down, crushing Mezentius beneath it. 'Where now is the fierce Mezentius and that wild savagery of soul?' railed Aeneas. A print by Abraham Bosse captures the moment, which he set beneath the towering walls of Laurentum, with the Alban Mount in the distance. The armies have withdrawn to a respectful distance: Mezentius kneels in supplication, but Aeneas's sword is ready.[3] I am ready to die, said Virgil's Mezentius, and beseeched Aeneas only to bury him with his son. Then, Aeneas slew him. 'The better vows prevailed,' commented Ovid, in his version of the tale, 'huge Mezentius fell, and with his breast indignant smote the ground. Autumn came round, stained with the trodden grapes; the wine that was his due was justly paid to Jupiter. Hence the day is called the Vinalia: Jupiter claims it for his own, and loves to be present at his own feast.'[4]

In *Aeneid* 11, in the aftermath of the great battle between the Trojans and the Rutulians, Aeneas set up a great oak trunk and hung on it the trophies stripped from Mezentius. Next, Aeneas proclaimed, we march on Latium; for Latinus, we must remember, had sided, against his better judgement, with Turnus. Aeneas visited the hut where Pallas's body lay, surrounded by Trojan women, 'their mourning tresses loosed'. Aeneas wept at the boy's death; at his own failure to protect him, and the fact that the lad would never know, as Aeneas had hoped, Ascanius's friendship. Aeneas shrouded the youthful body with robes given him by Dido – hinting, perhaps, at the true extent of his feelings for the boy.

An embassy arrived from Latium, asking for time to bury their dead, pleading that Troy was not at war with corpses. Aeneas agreed, adding that he had no wish to fight the living Latins either. His only quarrel was with Turnus, and if they could settle this through single combat, there would be no need for further war.

Virgil shows us the consequences of war now, as the stricken Latins bore home those bodies that could be identified, and also piled up a great mound 'of undistinguished carnage' to be burnt 'unnumbered and unhonoured'. By the third day of the truce, the fields were littered with mounds of ash.

Turnus sent an embassy to Diomedes, a survivor of the Trojan War and once one of Aeneas's greatest adversaries who, as we have heard, was now living in southern Italy. Age and experience had brought regret for war, so instead of relishing the prospect of a renewed fight with Aeneas, Diomedes reminded the envoys how many of the Greek captains who won the Trojan War suffered on their *nostoi*, or returns. Odysseus endured his long odyssey; Agamemnon was murdered by his wife when he returned to Mycenae; and he, Diomedes, who wounded Aphrodite on the battlefield of Troy, was punished by never being able to return to Greece, while his lost friends had been transformed into those nomadic birds called shearwaters, who roam the seas with plaintive cries. Aeneas was too formidable a foe, Diomedes advised the envoys: tell Turnus and Latinus to make peace with him.

On hearing this advice, Latinus longed for peace, but not so Turnus. To pre-empt another attack on Ostia, Aeneas marched on Laurentum. Turnus rushed out to meet him, like a stallion, says Virgil, released into a summer meadow. Aeneas fought only to end the war and usher in the new order; Turnus longed for the Homeric glory that can be gained only through combat. Virgil likens Turnus variously to lions, bulls, wolves, eagles and tigers, while the crest on his helmet was a chimera, whose belching flames grew ever hotter, in a very un-Roman manner, as the fierceness of battle increased. By Turnus's side charged Camilla, Queen of the Volscians, a warrior queen to mirror the Amazon Penthesilea in the Trojan War, and Messapus, the eponymous king of the Messapians of the heel of Italy, whom Virgil makes an Etrurian king.

It looks as if the Trojans are doomed; as if Rome would never be able to look back to Aeneas as their noble Trojan founder; as if the gens Julii would have no cause to claim him as their ancestor in the first place. But that is not, as we know, how things turned out.

37

Aeneas versus Turnus

By the mid-100s BC, Aeneas's myth was embedded irrevocably in Rome's mythological landscape and was being used for very real political ends. But although Lucretius (99-55 BC) wrote of Aphrodite as *Aeneadum genetrix*, 'mother of the [Roman] children of Aeneas', the Trojan myth had never been a strong vein of folklore handed down through countless generations of ordinary families. For the common Roman man, the most popular element of Aeneas's myth was probably his mother's temple of Venus Erycina at the Porta Collina, because of its multitude of prostitutes. Instead, the rise of Aeneas's myth, from at least the early 200s BC onwards, had been promoted consciously and knowingly by Rome's patricians, led perhaps by those who, like the gens Julii, believed in their own particular genealogical connection to Aeneas. It was such families who built Rome's temples of Venus Erycina and Magna Mater, all designed to harness Trojan mythology to clear, practical ends. Aeneas's myth bolstered Rome's self confidence in the city's struggles against Carthage and Greece. It aided Rome as a diplomatic and political tool in its dominance of the eastern Mediterranean, both in war and in the battle for the hearts and minds of the peoples they conquered. But, having achieved this, Aeneas's myth might have faded away. It was only due to the rise of the Caesars that Aeneas's story became the most dominant of all of Rome's myths. And it was thanks to the Caesars that we have the *Aeneid*.

By a process of cross-fertilisation, the rise in Aeneas's popularity in Rome encouraged individual families to believe they had Trojan descent, just as English families from the Tudor period onwards started laying claim to ancestors who had 'come over with William the Conqueror'. We have heard already of Flamininus (229-174 BC) claiming descent from Aeneas; his beliefs, and those of many other families (such as, probably, the Metelli, Fabia and Furia families), were enumerated in Varro's *De Familiis Troianis*. In this tragically lost equivalent of Britain's *Burke's Peerage*, Varro presumably recorded the claims of patrician families to be descended from heroes of the Trojan war named by Homer, particularly the Trojan ones; and doubtless Varro made a handsome living by doing so.

Varro's catalogue probably included the gens Julii. They were hereditary priests who tended a temple at Bovillae, on the Via Sacra between Rome and the sanctuary of *Jupiter Latiaris*, 'Zeus of the Latins', on the Alban Mount. The gens Julii seem to have known their ancestry back for sure to Numerius Julius Julus or Iulus, in the mid-400s BC. Before then, as with so many families, the records are unavailable or did not exist, but there must, they reasoned, have been a founding ancestor called 'Iulus'. That name was tantalisingly similar to 'Ilios', so almost inevitably, in the 200s BC if not before, a Trojan origin was imagined for him – and became yet another piece of false evidence of Rome's Trojan past. The histories of Troy did not mention this Iulus. But so powerful was the pull of Aeneas that, through a small but incredibly significant leap of imagination, it was decided that Iulus must have been a nickname for someone else, that reflected the name of Troy itself. Iulus must, the gens Julii decided, have been Aeneas's son Ascanius.

Within a few generations, this ludicrous conceit hardened into well-established family myth, and transformed the gens Julii from mere wayside priests into, in their own eyes at least, the descendants of a goddess. In 129 BC, one of the Julii minted coins depicting Aphrodite, symbolically invoking her power and authority as his divine ancestress. The myth was certainly ingrained in family tradition by the time of the birth of Gaius Julius Caesar (100-44 BC). Like Alexander the Great before him, Caesar grew up with a clear and unshakable belief in his descent from an Homeric hero with a divine parent. As Caesar progressed through his career, first as a priest and later as a politician and general, he carried with him the potent genealogical certainty that he had inherited a spark of divinity through Aeneas from Aphrodite, the Queen of Heaven. He said as much at a family funeral, as Suetonius's *Life of Julius Caesar* tells us: that while his grandmother Marcia was descended Rome's fourth king, Ancus Marcius, his father's side was sprung from Aphrodite, 'so then, in this stock there concur and meet the sanctity and majesty of kings, who among men are most powerful, and the religious supremacy of the gods, in whose power kings themselves are.'[1]

Caesar minted coins showing Aphrodite's head on one side and on the other, Aeneas as a naked warrior, striding along confidently, carrying Anchises. Instead of leading Ascanius, Aeneas brandishes the Palladium, the image of Athena armed for battle – an image reused later in the reign of the equally martial Trajan. Caesar's devotion to Aeneas's mother Aphrodite went so far, as Dio Cassius reported, as to make him 'anxious to persuade everybody that he had received from her a kind of bloom of youth. Accordingly, he used also to wear a carven image of her in full armour on his ring and he made her name his watchword in almost all the greatest dangers.'[2]

As Caesar's fame spread, those wishing to honour him held a mirror up to his self-belief. A near eastern inscription in *Sylloge Inscriptionum Graecarum* hails Caesar as 'the god-son of Ares and Aphrodite' (because Ares was

In Search of Aeneas

Aphrodite's lover).[3] A relief from Carthage shows what appears to be Caesar standing next to Eros, Aphrodite and her lover Ares,[4] a combination of the deities of love and war, conceived by Greek mythology and used now to glorify Caesar as Aphrodite's descendant.

As one military success followed another, Caesar probably imagined that Zeus was sitting on his throne on the Alban Mount, guiding his victories, and that Aeneas and Aphrodite were shielding him personally from harm. Just as Alexander had conquered the east, Caesar desired to subject the west to his power, conquering Gaul and invading Britain. Although he failed to establish a permanent Roman presence here, the southern British chieftains agreed to pay him tribute. He thus laid the foundations for Claudius's later, successful invasion. That led in turn, six centuries later, to Britain adopting its own version of the Trojan myth, which evolved into the story of Aeneas's Italian great grandson Brutus bringing Trojan settlers to cultivate Britain's fertile hills.

Caesar's failure to achieve a full conquest of Britain would have finished most generals, but, again, his implacable belief in his divine ancestry through Aeneas seems to have continued to fuel his ambition. Caesar crossed the Rubicon in 49 BC and used his army to make himself dictator of Rome in the face of opposition from the senate, and from Pompey, who fled east. Caesar forced the senate to elect him consul in 48 BC and set off to the Balkans and Greece to fight Pompey, using the watchword 'Victorious Venus'. In return, Pompey, perhaps sarcastically, adopted the watchword 'Invincible Hercules', as Appian notes in *The Civil Wars*.[5]

Despite being heavily outnumbered, Caesar defeated Pompey's army at Pharsalos in Thessaly. Pompey fled east again and Caesar followed him in a pursuit that led him to Troy. For a while, Caesar forgot about Pompey and became a tourist, seeking out the sites which, as Lucan (AD 39-65) says in his *Civil War*, owed much of their fame to poet-seers who preserved memories from being obliterated by fate, and bestowed a sort of immortality onto those mortals of whom they sang. Lucan describes Caesar finding Achilles' tomb and a plausible site for the Greek camp; but as to Troy itself, rotten tree trunks buried the halls where once the Trojan kings had feasted, and the temples were wrapped in thorns. Yet the locals, descendants of the Greek colonists of Ilion, were eager to show Caesar as many sites as possible: the rock on the coast to which Hesione was tied when she was offered to the sea monster; the exact spot from which Ganymede was abducted by Zeus; and Mount Ida where, they said, Paris judged the goddesses, and where Anchises and Aphrodite conceived Aeneas.

Every rock had some myth attached to it. Once, continues Lucan, Caesar walked into some tall grass and a peasant warned him to be careful, lest he trample on the ghost of Hector. Filled with reverence for Troy, which he believed was his ancestral homeland, Caesar built his own altars, lit incense and prayed to the gods of the ruins, the gods 'of my Aeneas', who settled his household gods at Lavinium, and whose Italian altars still blazed with

Phrygian fire. I, Caesar, 'the most illustrious grandson in Iulus's line', he said, offer pious incense on your altars, praying for success in my mission.[6]

Caesar then set sail again for Egypt, where Ptolemy handed him the blood-caked head of Pompey. Back in Rome, Caesar built the Basilica Julia in the Forum to honour his ancestors, and created a new part of the Forum itself, the Forum Iulium. Its centrepiece was a statue to Venus Genetrix, 'Mother Aphrodite'.

Before Caesar triumphed over Pompey and before all the vagaries and chances of history that led to Aeneas becoming Rome's pre-eminent founding hero, Virgil's mythical Trojans, massed in the field before Laurentum, faced annihilation. But Arruns, one of Aeneas's Etruscan allies, slew Camilla of the Volscians, and the tide of battle turned. The Volscians and their allies fled the field and the Trojans surged forward to Laurentum's walls.

In *Aeneid* 12, Turnus finally agreed to settle the conflict through single combat with Aeneas. Turnus was exultant. Aeneas is a mere woman, he bragged; I will tear his corselet and 'defile in dust his love-locks!' Aeneas, grim-faced, rejoiced only at the prospect of ending the war. At the first blush of dawn, both sides appeared before Laurentum's walls, the Trojan captains arrayed in gold and purple. Turnus seemed less confident now, feeling unequal to the task; his eyes were downcast, his cheeks pallid, as if Virgil himself was moved by compassion for his anti-hero. Hera, watching from the Alban Mount, urged Turnus's goddess-sister Juturna to stir up the Rutulians for battle, so as to save her Rutulian darling from harm. Bravely, Aeneas stood, weaponless and bare-headed, bidding the opposing hosts be calm, but an arrow shot from an unknown hand, probably Juturna's, pierced his knee. Aeneas staggered, clutching the agonising wound. Seeing his chance to defeat the Trojans without having to face Aeneas, Turnus goaded his men to battle and charged forward like the north wind.

Aeneas was enraged, but had to allow Achates, young Ascanius and Mnesthus, the eponymous ancestor of the gens Memmii, to help him back to the Trojan camp. A wall painting at Pompeii shows Aeneas standing bravely while his surgeon, Iapyx, removes the arrowhead from his thigh. Despite the pain, Aeneas comforts tearful Ascanius while Aphrodite looks on, concerned. In the background, soldiers hurry past. Across the millennia, Aeneas's agony is palpable as he clenches his spear; yet his expression is one of stoic Roman fortitude. Virgil tells us that Aphrodite sped away to Cretan Ida, picked some of the herb dittany, steeped it in spring-water, ambrosia and panacea, and returned to drop it into Iapyx's bowl. When this was applied to Aeneas's leg-wound, renewed strength surged through him. 'Learn valour and true endurance from me,' he told Ascanius, and 'fortune from others … while thy soul dwells on the example of thy kindred, let Aeneas and Hector – sire and uncle – wake thy prowess!'

With that paternal lecture, Aeneas thundered forth to battle. Many Rutulians died, but Aeneas sought only Turnus: the *furens* of battle was upon him again. Juturna, terrified for her brother's safety, pushed Turnus's charioteer aside and took the reins, so as to keep him away from Aeneas. Aphrodite bade Aeneas make a headlong onslaught on Laurentum. Within the ancient walls, Latinus tore his clothes in despair, and his wife Amata hanged herself. Outside, the battle raged until Aeneas spotted Turnus and, with, 'dread thunder on his arms', hurtled to meet him.

The battlefield fell silent. Trojans and Italians laid aside their arms; some even took off their armour. They were like herds of forest cattle, says Virgil, watching the clash of two mighty bulls. Aeneas and Turnus flung their spears at each other, then moved closer. The 'earth moaned; their swords showered recurrent blows'. Turnus, burning now with passion, brought down his sword to slay Aeneas. But due to an earlier mishap, the blade he thought was his father's was only that of his charioteer, and it shattered on contact with Aeneas's divinely wrought shield. Fearful again, Turnus leaped into his chariot and tried to flee, but found himself penned in by the men of Troy.

Despite his wounded knee, Aeneas pursued his quarry, like a hunter after a stag. Many times Turnus upbraided his Rutulians, demanding his true sword, but none dared brave the wrath of Aeneas by bringing it to him. Once, Achilles pursued Hector round the walls of Troy. Now Virgil's Aeneas chased Turnus around the bounds of Laurentum. Aeneas saw his spear sticking in the roots of a fallen olive tree sacred to Faunus. Pausing in his pursuit, he tried to pull it free, but Turnus prayed to Faunus to hold it fast. While Aeneas struggled, Juturna darted out and handed Turnus his sword at last.

A print by Wenceslaus Hollar, after Francis Cleyn, appeared in John Ogilby's 1654 *The Works of Publius Virgilius Maro*. As the armies watch, Turnus is handed his sword and seems about to bear down on Aeneas, who is helpless because his spear is stuck in the oak stump. Yet in a cloud next to Aeneas stands Aphrodite, pulling the spear free, just as Virgil described.[7] Hollar's print also show Zeus above the clouds berating Hera for having encouraged Juturna. Virgil describes this altercation in Heaven: Fate has decreed that Aeneas will succeed, and become a god, too, Zeus argued, so for how much longer will you prolong your destructive vendetta against him? Hera finally admitted defeat, but she made one last request. Once the Latins and Trojans were united as one people, let them retain the name, language and customs of Latium, not of Troy. Let the Trojans become Italians: 'Troy lies fallen, and fallen let her lie – herself and her name.' Zeus assented, thus providing a neat explanation for why the Romans of Virgil's day were not still called Trojans. Regardless of their name, Hera continued, they would surpass all other men, and even the gods, in their piety, and none would honour her more. At last, Hera laid aside her quarrel with Troy begun so long ago on Mount Ida, when Paris preferred Aphrodite's beauty to hers.

This was a joyful passage for Virgil's Roman readers, for now the future prosperity of Rome had been ensured. Arguably, it is a a joyful moment for any people who prospered under *pax Romanum*. It is that same peace politicians who are worth their salt strive to maintain to this very day.

Aeneas versus Turnus

It was necessary now only to enact Heaven's will. Zeus sent one of the serpent-tailed Furies hurtling down to Earth. It assumed the form of a nightingale, yet when it brushed past Turnus, it filled him with palsied fear. Juturna, perceiving what the bird really was, despaired for Turnus's life, shrouded her head in her grey robe and drowned herself in the river.

Aeneas challenged Turnus to fight. The Rutulian prince, brave in the face of doom, assented. Turnus raised a rock, which six ordinary men together could not lift, and hurled it at Aeneas. Yet even as Turnus did so, he felt paralysed, as in a dream, and saw the rock fall short of its target. Aeneas hurled his massive spear at Turnus. With the ear-splitting noise which follows a thunderbolt, it ripped through Turnus's shield and corselet and plunged deep into his thigh, and the groans of the observing Rutulians echoed through the pine woods.

Gazing up at all-conquering Aeneas, Turnus said nobly 'I have merited [this], I cry not mercy: use thy fortune to the full.' He made an appeal, however; that Aeneas remember old Anchises and spare his own father Daunus from the grief of hearing of his death – or at least, return his body to him. Aeneas was moved to pity, and so the *Aeneid* might now end with a noble gesture of conciliation. But throughout the *Aeneid*, Virgil has wrestled with the conflict between the pious spirit with which he and Augustus wished the Roman people to be imbued, and the *furens*, the rageful cruelty that they really possessed.

Thus, Aeneas looked down and saw that Turnus was still wearing the gleaming sword belt he had torn from Pallas's corpse and had kept as a trophy ever since. Like Achilles, who was roused to kill Hector by the death of Patroclus, this new Trojan War ends with Aeneas *furiis accensus et ira terribilis*: inflamed with fury and terrible wrath. War does not bring glory, then, as Homer thought: it reduces even the most pious of heroes to brute violence.

'And shalt thou,' cried Aeneas, 'clothed in the trophies of my friend, escape me hence? It is Pallas – Pallas immolates thee with this wound and exacts vengeance from thy guilty blood!' 'So saying,' wrote Virgil, Aeneas smote Turnus: 'Like fire he buried the steel full in his breast. The chilling limbs relaxed, and the indignant life fled moaning beneath the shades.' So ends Virgil's *Aeneid*.

38

The Unresolved Dilemma

It is victory, but at a price. Twice, once fighting Magus in *Aeneid* 10 and again, now, with Turnus, Aeneas's battle-rage caused him to forget the civilised dignity advocated by his father. How, asked Lactantius (*c.* AD 240-*c.* 320) in his *Divine Institutes*, could such a man be as pious as Virgil claimed?[1]

Robert Fagles, the great modern translator of the *Aeneid*, told *The New York Times*, 'If you depart from the civilized, then you become a murderer. The price of empire is very steep, but Virgil shows how it is to be earned, if it's to be earned at all. The poem can be read as an exhortation for us to behave ourselves'[2] – to learn, through Virgil, from Aeneas's shortcomings and from his strivings to be piously civilised, despite unbearable hardships that lead to uncontrollable emotions.

For centuries, the ending of the *Aeneid* so disturbed readers that other writers sought to resolve its tensions in their own works modelled upon it. In *Orlando Furioso*, Ludovico Ariosto (1474-1533) sets up similar duels but resolves them differently. When Zerbino is about to kill Medoro, he finds that he cannot, because he is overwhelmed with *pietade*. That marks the point in western civilisation, as Hardie writes, when 'Virgilian *pietas* evolves into the "pity" of the Romance languages'.[3] At the end of *Orlando Furioso*, Ruggiero fights the evil Rodomonte, in a direct echo of Aeneas fighting Turnus. But Ariosto makes sure that Rodomonte does more than Turnus to deserve his fate: Ruggiero offers him mercy, and Rodomonte responds by trying to stab him in the back, so when Ruggiero kills him, we feel none of the uneasiness inspired by Aeneas's furious slaying of Turnus. Hardie shows how this scene is replayed again in the *Gerusalemme Liberata* of Torquato Tasso (1544-1595). Tancredi defeats the pagan Argante and begs him to surrender, but the pagan tries to stab the hero in the heel.[4] That justifies Tancredi killing him, far more acceptably than Aeneas's killing of Turnus.

The Unresolved Dilemma

In the fifteenth century, Maffeo Vegio wrote out, in boldly Virgilian style, a *Supplementum* to the *Aeneid* itself. While he could not alter the circumstances of Turnus's death, Vegio reminded his readers how, instead of obeying the gods' will by allowing the Trojans to settle peacefully in Latium, Turnus had bred up 'hateful broyles of warres' and emphasised the positive outcomes of his death: immediately, both sides lost any desire of further war and craved only peace and rest. Aeneas made a speech laying the blame squarely not on his own, but on Turnus's 'furie great'. Aeneas returned Turnus's corpse to his people, just as Achilles ultimately gave Hector's body back to Priam, and he sent Pallas's sword belt back to Evander. I swear by the stars, says Vegio's Aeneas, that I never willingly pursued war.

Virgil, however, eschewed such easy ways out of moral dilemmas and leaves us with the shock of Aeneas's abandonment of Dido and wrathful killing of Turnus, and unresolved questions: should we put duty to the state, or to our loved ones, first? Should we seek peace at all costs, or pursue just wars, with all the violence they entail? Virgil does not provide answers because, having wrestled with these dilemmas through his crafting of Aeneas's personality, he had none.

Eleven years after Virgil had started writing the *Aeneid*, when his work was nearing completion and Aeneas stood at last, gazing down at the dead body of Turnus, Augustus set out for Anatolia. Augustus's purpose was to assert himself as Aeneas's rightful heir in the face of the territorial ambitions of the Parthian Empire to the east. In his *Civil War*, Lucan tells us that when Julius Caesar visited Troy in pursuit of Pompey, he promised to build a new Roman Troy on the site of the old one.[5] But it was left to Augustus to put this aspiration into action. He declared Troy a 'free and federate city' of the Roman Empire, and among the rebuilding work he commissioned was probably a shrine of Aeneas, which according to Bülent Erdemoğlu is believed, from an inscription, to have existed in Troy, but whose exact location is unknown.[6] Augustus also enlarged the city's theatre and may even, as Manfred Korfmann suggested, have had the completed parts of the *Aeneid* recited there. Thanks to Augustus, the Roman city of Ilium flourished, much visited by Roman tourists, until its decay (along with so much else) from the AD 400s onward.

Having for so many years imagined Troy from his garden in Naples, Virgil could not resist following Augustus east. He bade his slaves, Cebes and Alexander, pack up the papyrus rolls on which his drafts of the *Aeneid* were inscribed, and they set off, probably bumping along the Appian Way over the Apennines by mule-carriage. Virgil most likely made a detour to visit Castrum (Castro Marina), so that he could describe Aeneas's landing there. Then he crossed the Straits of Otranto, tracing the journey of Aeneas in reverse, to Buthrotum probably, and thence Greece. As Virgil travelled, Aeneas's world unfolded before him: the centuries fell away and he was back in the Age of Heroes, and all the time he revised and improved his poem. But

In Search of Aeneas

at Megara near Athena 'in a very hot sun,' says Suetonius, 'he was taken with a fever.'[7]

Augustus had reached Athens on his way back from the east and brought the ailing poet back home with him. Perhaps it was during the voyage back across the Straits of Otranto that Virgil added to his poem the sense of hope experienced by the Trojans when they first saw Italy: '*Italy*, Achates cried the foremost: *Italy*, the crews shouted in joyful acclaim.'

At the opening of his novel *The Death of Virgil*, Hermann Broch imagined the returning fleet with its deccaremes and duodeccaremes, 'of an ornate structure in keeping with the Augustan imperial rank'. Augustus's own ship was 'the most sumptuous, its bronze-mounted bow gilded ... under purple sails, festive and grand'. And, on the ship which followed was 'the poet of the Aeneid and death's signet was graved upon his brow'.[8]

They reached Brindisium (Brindisi) and Broch describes, minutely, how they bore Virgil and the precious scrolls of the *Aeneid* up the steps, which Mussolini rebuilt in 1933, to the Piazzetta Colonne, where there are two Roman columns and the house in which Virgil is said to have been lodged. Here, Virgil made his last alterations to the poem. The plaque there, purportedly from 1900, but actually erected later by Mussolini, reads:

> Here, at the end of the Appian Way, Virgil, the greatest singer of the fields and the empire, returned two thousand years ago from Greece, and was for the last time greeted by the Saturnian land [of Italy], and the immortal spirits sung by him gathered around his dazzling light, guarding the renewing power of Rome.

So flawed did Virgil regard both humanity and his own work, that he decided, as he lay dying in Brindisium, to burn it all. 'All but twice in the flames unhappy Pergamon perished,' wrote Sulpicius of Carthage. 'Troy on a second pyre narrowly failed of her doom.'[9]

In *The Death of Virgil*, Augustus comes to Virgil's sick-bed, plumping himself down on a stool without any of Aeneas's dignity, to reason with his poet. Augustus sees in the *Aeneid* proof of Anchises's words in Hades, that Rome's destiny is to rule nations, maintain peace and spread the rule of law. This, says Augustus, after he has read the passage back to Virgil 'is the very spirit of Rome, and it is magnificent'. He has no time for Virgil's finer concerns, that the dilemmas remain unfulfilled, that the poem only scratches the surface of humanity's true nature. When Virgil argues that the unfinished poem is his to destroy, Augustus disagrees. It belongs already to the Roman people, who have encouraged its composition, for the poem proclaims and comprehends Rome, its gods, glory and piety, from its Trojan origins right through to the afterlife. It comes closer than any other work of art to encompassing all life and death 'in a single work, in a single glance'. It may be flawed, but so are all the works of man, and the *Aeneid* is less imperfect than any other. And so Virgil has no choice but to agree not to destroy it.

The Unresolved Dilemma

On 21 September 19 BC, soon after that imagined encounter, Virgil died. His body was taken back to Naples and buried at Piedigrotta, in the city's western suburbs. His tomb can still be seen there, in the Parco Virgiliano. The trees there include pines and oaks brought specially from the Troad. It is a chamber carved out of the rock; inside, we found that someone had left, reverently, a bronze tripod and a wreath of olive leaves.

In Medieval Naples, Virgil became regarded as a sort of patron saint cum magician, whose bones were believed to protect the city from invasion, and whose magical creations, such as a mechanical golden fly he is said to have fashioned, kept the plague at bay.

Virgil bequeathed his writings to Varius and Tucca, 'with the stipulation', says Suetonius, 'that they should publish nothing which he himself would not have given to the world'. Suetonius then quotes Propertius praising the *Aeneid*'s first appearance: 'Yield, ye Roman writers; yield, ye Greeks; a [poem] greater than the *Iliad* is born.'[10]

Cicero's friend Attikus was the first to lecture on Virgil at school. Quintilian (AD 35-100) paired Virgil with Homer as the two texts which Roman schoolboys should study first. Thus the books that told the two halves of Aeneas's life became the core of an educational model that remained little altered in many schools until the mid-twentieth century, albeit that, in the Middle Ages, the Trojan histories of Dares and Dictys tended to be substituted for the *Iliad*. The *Aeneid* is still taught now, because 'the history of European literature is real and still an urgent subject. You cannot arrive at Ibsen or Pushkin without going back through Byron to the ancient writers and Virgil; and without mastering those writers you will not advance to an understanding of the modern world.' So wrote Peter Levi.[11]

Though the *Aeneid* was an epic poem and not an historical account, it forged a coherent narrative out of the many strands of Aeneas's complex mythological life. It resolved many of the contradictions found in the myths collected by Dionysius, or admitted by Livy; and this new Virgilian orthodoxy then propelled Aeneas's story, with the Imperial stamp of approval, across the expanding empire with more force than any invading army. Aeneas's struggles could be read in quiet atriums by Roman gentlemen, or be declaimed during banquets, and be recalled as a ripping adventure story by soldiers from the Parthian frontier to Hadrian's Wall. When Aeneas is seen in Roman art from Augustus's time onwards, from the wall paintings of Pompeii to the mosaic floor of Low Ham Roman villa in Somerset, he is invariably the Aeneas conjured up for us by Virgil.

The myth of Aeneas as either the founder of Rome, or at least of the realm out of which Rome would later rise, grew up slowly, almost tentatively, from the 700s BC onwards, and only took proper root in Rome itself in the 200s BC, thanks to the exploits of Pyrrhus of Epiros, who claimed descent from Achilles and hoped to gain glory by defeating the Roman 'Trojans', but ended up reflecting glory back on Rome through his own failure. Even so, it did not become the dominant foundation myth in Rome until the rise to power of the gens Julii, first Julius Caesar and then his great-nephew and adopted son, Augustus, who saw themselves as Aeneas's descendants and heirs.

It was Augustus who really pushed Aeneas to prominence and promoted him as a pious hero. Until then, Aeneas was seen more in the round, as the Greeks and Etruscans had depicted him, as a mighty warrior battling Diomedes and Achilles, or fighting over Patroclus's body; as a jealous man, even as a foolhardy participant in the disastrous abduction of Helen. Aeneas was pious towards the gods for sure, but no more so than other heroes such as Odysseus; Pliny's list of famously pious characters omits him altogether. But under Augustus, piety was emphasised at the expense of all other aspects of Aeneas's character, in order to remind Rome, as Galinsky wrote, that the emperor was at once 'the object of pietas from his subjects, and an example to them of pietas towards the gods'.[12]

After Augustus, therefore, Seneca's *De Beneficis* cites Aeneas, staggering under Anchises's weight, as an example of piety, whereas before, being able to carry his own father was a feat more macho than holy. The very idea of linking this act to piety may have come, as Galinsky suggested, from a story of two Sicilian brothers, Amphinomus and Anapias, who were lauded for their piety by carrying their parents to safety when Etna erupted. In about 100 BC, a member of the gens Herennii minted a coin with the goddess Pietas on one side and a man carrying a parent on the other; regardless of whether this man was Amphinomus, Anapias or Aeneas, the coin may have served as Augustus's inspiration for turning the image into an instantly recognisable emblem of piety. Unlike the macho Aeneas shown on Caesar's coins, Augustus's coinage copied the Herennii coins, making him less martial, more elegant and, arguably, more pious.[13]

We heard earlier how, in his *Georgics* 3, Virgil had imagined a temple of Caesar on the banks of the Mincius, centred on a statue of Augustus. That temple of words found its physical manifestation in the new Forum of Augustus, whose gleaming marble pillars rose to dominate the age-old Roman Forum, facing the Palatine Hill. Visitors after its inauguration in 2 BC, seventeen years after Virgil's death, found its courtyard dominated, as Ovid described in his fifth *Fasti*, by an imposing statue of Augustus. Beyond, loomed a temple of Mars Ultor – Ares the avenger, god of war – built to commemorate Augustus's victories, not least over Mark Antony at Actium. Within the temple, stood a statue of Mars, flanked by his lover Venus Genetrix, 'Mother Aphrodite', and her descendant, the now divine Julius Caesar, transmogrified effectively into Mars's stepson.

On either side of the temple were two colonnaded bays. In one of these were statues of Rome's past rulers, clustered around Romulus, son of Ares and Rhea Silvia, who was descended via the Alban kings from Aeneas. In the opposite bay stood the leading members of the gens Julii, who were now also seen as Aeneas's descendants. They were grouped, Ovid tells us, around their mythological ancestor, Aeneas himself, grasping the hand of his son Ascanius, now mythologised as Iulus, the progenitor of the Julii. Aeneas carried on his shoulders old Anchises, *in capite velato*, with veiled head, who himself bore in his sinewy arms the *cista sacra*, containing the Penantes, the household gods of Troy.

That Augustan statue of Aeneas was probably, as the Italian scholar M. Camaggio suggested, the direct model for many of the other depictions of him found all across the Empire, from the forum at Pompeii[14] to pottery lamps showing the same family group fleeing past a temple and a palm tree, with the inscription 'Aeneas Anchises Ascanius Rex Pie', 'pious king'.[15] Though dressed as a Roman general, Aeneas lacks weapons in these scenes, because piety, not martial prowess, was what was being emphasised.

Aeneas's myth was also promoted in Augustus's time through the *Tabulae Iliacae*. Twenty-two survive; there must once have been many more. *Tabulae Iliacae* are stone tablets, engraved with tiny scenes from the Trojan War, each carefully labelled. They seem to have come from one or two Roman workshops and were for both private enjoyment and the education of children. They may date from just before the *Aeneid* appeared, because they illustrate different versions of the story, showing Aeneas as both warrior and pious hero, fighting the Greeks and also piously rescuing his father and the household gods. The version in the Capitoline Museum, which purports to illustrate Stesichorus's retelling of the Trojan War, depicts Aeneas twice. First, at the very centre of the tablet, Aeneas is led out of the Scaean Gate by Hermes, carrying his father, who holds the *cista sacra*, presumably containing the Penantes, leading Ascanius, and with a woman, probably Creusa, following. Secondly, we see Aeneas, still carrying Anchises and leading Ascanius, accompanied by trumpet-bearing Misenus, boarding their ship and about to embark for *Hesperia*, 'the west'.

Little survives today of the Forum of Augustus except for its foundations and its high back wall, but another Augustan edifice, the Ara Pacis Augustae, survives almost intact. Built by Augustus in the Campus Martius, it was buried by mud, excavated by Mussolini in 1938 and reassembled next to Augustus's Mausoleum by the Tiber, where it is now housed within a glass-walled museum, flooded with light.

The Ara Pacis comprises a hollow box of pale marble, 38 by 34 feet square and 20 feet high, surrounding a central altar. Its walls are adorned, inside and out, with reliefs of powerful elegance and peaceful dignity, showing scenes from Rome's ancient history, including Romulus and Remus being suckled by the wolf on one of the two panels on the west side. The other panel seems to show Aeneas, *in capite velato*, in very similar guise to the scene shown on the Belvedere Altar, described earlier. He is about to make a sacrifice. Before him stands the sow, and two boys, perhaps his sons Ascanius and Silvius (of whom we shall hear soon), crowned with olive wreaths, who will assist him in his sacred work. Behind them, in a miniature temple, stand the Penantes, the household gods of Troy. Galinsky described this as 'a most felicitous and lasting expression' of Rome's Trojan myth, largely inspired by the *Aeneid*, and 'the artistic counterpart of what Horace and Virgil did in poetry'.[16] But while the mood seems Virgilian, the scene does not illustrate a single, identifiable scene from the *Aeneid*, and if it comes from Virgil at all, it can only be a composite of Aeneas's sacrifice when he landed at Ostia, and his later sacrifice of the sow by the Tiber, in *Aeneid* 7 and 8 respectively. So ambiguous is the scene that some scholars, such as Paul Rehak, have argued that the man sacrificing the sow was not Aeneas at all, but Numa Pompilius, a later king of Rome strongly associated with peace.

Similar problems beset the identification of the eastern side of the Ara Pacis. This also has two panels, one showing what is probably Roma, a goddess invented to personify Rome itself, sitting on a pile of weapons, and the other, the so-called 'Tellus panel', showing three goddesses, or perhaps the same goddess depicted three times. Galinsky, convinced that the whole Ara Pacis was based on the Trojan myth, argued that this could only be Aphrodite in the form of Venus Erycina, whose coins sometimes showed her fully clothed and enthroned like the goddess(es) here. One coin of Venus Erycina shows her being offered flowers by Eros, just as the goddess on the 'Tellus panel' has two children in her lap, one of whom is offering her an apple, which was an emblem of Aphrodite. But others disagree, suggesting that the goddess(es) are, variously, Italia, Roma, Gaia (Tellus) or Magna Mater. Galinsky's answer to this was that, where the imagery suggested other goddesses, this was because Augustus wanted to see them all as aspects of his ancestress Aphrodite. Galinsky argued that warlike Aeneas and Venus Erycina, who had symbolised Rome's determination to win the Punic Wars, had both been tamed and brought in line with Augustus's desire to promote peace.[17]

Ultimately, all we can say is that the Ara Pacis *might* depict Aphrodite and Aeneas. But even if it does not, it is still in keeping with the mood of the times; one in which Horace could write in his fourth *Ode* of the way Augustus had brought order and plenty to the civilised world. And how the grateful Romans could now offer prayers of thanks to Heaven and to their Trojan sires, Anchises and the son of Aphrodite.

39

The Marriage of Aeneas and Lavinia

On a circular altar from c. 40 BC unearthed at Città Castellana about 35 miles north of Rome, is depicted what must surely be the immediate aftermath of Aeneas's victory over Turnus. Aeneas stands, bearded and wearing a tunic, clenching his spear and wearing a Phrygian helmet, sacrificing in the presence of Aphrodite, Hephaestus and Ares – Aeneas's mother, her husband and her lover. Behind Aeneas stands Victory, holding a laurel wreath over his head.[1]

Virgil differs from his sources on the order of events of these turbulent times. Livy relates that Aeneas married Lavinia soon after he had arrived in Italy. Turnus, king of the Rutulians, had been betrothed to Lavinia and was angered by this, so he attacked the combined Trojans and Latins. The Rutulians were defeated, Turnus survived to fight another day, Latinus was killed, and Aeneas became king of the Latins.

Dionysius says that once Aeneas reached Latium and married Lavinia, the Rutulians revolted against Latinus because he had allowed his daughter and heiress to marry a foreigner. A rebel called Tyrrhenus – Turnus under a different spelling – became the Rutulians' leader. War ensued, Latinus and Tyrrhenus were killed, and Aeneas became king of the Latins.[2] This is the version followed most closely by *Origo Gentis Romanae*, which agrees that Latinus was killed during the war between Aeneas and Turnus, but Turnus, hearing of Latinus's death, committed suicide, leaving Aeneas as the undisputed king. This war is the one which Virgil embellished in his *Aeneid*. His major changes were that Aeneas's *betrothal* alone led to the war, and that Latinus sided with Turnus in the conflict. In the *Aeneid*, Aeneas's final peace with Latinus and his marriage to Lavinia lie in the future, as all educated Romans would have understood.

In Vegio's *Supplementum*, Aeneas, having won the war, could have proclaimed himself king, but instead he chose to honour his old agreement with Latinus. Let him enjoy his sceptre, said Aeneas to the Latins, but learn from me the art of warfare. Having grieved over the body of Turnus, Latinus embraced Ascanius and gave Aeneas the hand of his Lavinia, 'so sad of look, so fresh of face'.

The cover of the *cista Pasinati*, which is probably an Augustan work made in deliberately archaic style, shows Latinus, centre stage and almost god-like, with one arm raised, standing on the spoils of war. To Latinus's right, and holding his other hand, is armoured Aeneas. Beyond him are two soldiers who, guided by winged Eros, are carrying off the body of Turnus. One of them offers Aeneas a nuptial wreath. To Latinus's left is his daughter Lavinia, who gazes at Aeneas. Behind her is winged Eros again, and two women, one very agitated, probably her mother Amata, who by now in the *Aeneid* is already dead. Below are a satyr, a despairing Juturna and the reed-bearing god of the Tiber.[3]

For Virgil, Aeneas's betrothal to Lavinia was a mere necessity, devoid of emotion. But the Medieval poets discovered in it a love story. Heinrich von Veldecke's AD 1100s *Eneide* imagines a chaste Lavinia, before the war is over, gazing on Aeneas from the high towers of Laurentum and writing a love letter to him. Von Veldecke emphasised, as Scherer wrote, that Lavinia's love, 'though ardent, is a gentle, wholesome affection, unlike that of Dido, which he regarded as ungoverned and ill-omened'.[4] A 1200s German manuscript of von Veldecke's work shows Lavinia handing her letter to an archer, who shoots it into the Trojan camp. Here, Aeneas finds it and his desire for the princess is duly awakened.[5]

The *Roman d'Eneas* of the 1160s tells how␣Aeneas and Lavinia fell in love as soon as they met. Lavinia was keen to establish that Aeneas loved her truly, in contrast to his earlier, lustful desire for Dido, or indeed for boys, an allegation levelled at him by her mother Amata, probably because of his great affection for Pallas. But the love of Lavinia and Aeneas proved true, and furnished Aeneas with the courage he needed to win his war.

In Vegio's *Supplementum*, Aeneas gave Lavinia rich garments and a collar set with precious gems, which Andromache had given him in Buthrotum. They married during nine days of banqueting and dancing in Laurentum, at which the Trojans and Italians 'comixed, in joyful sight'. That was the beginning of the mixing of the two peoples into one. A panel on an AD 1400s marriage chest in the Musée de Cluny, Paris, sets the scene in the brilliance of a Medieval court. Aeneas wears a pleated coat and elegantly high boots, and Lavinia has a flowing robe and high headdress, with the veil pulled back. We see them as they touch hands, almost hesitantly, for the first time.[6]

In Ursula Le Guin's novel *Lavinia*, Aeneas waited nine days after the end of the war before coming to Laurentum to claim his bride. He had to sit down during his audience with Latinus because of the wound in his thigh. As a marriage pledge, Aeneas gave Lavinia a red clay vessel containing his household gods: her role, as wife and queen, would be to cherish these. They married at Lavinium, amidst the Trojans' tents and palisades. Lavinia wore a robe of rusty orange, her hair was braided with wool, and she told him,

The Marriage of Aeneas and Lavinia

Roman-style, 'Where you are Gaius, I am Gaia.' Lavinia found Aeneas 'all muscle and sinew and bone and scar', full of that force from his mother 'that moves the stars and the waves of the sea and couples the animals in the fields in spring, the power of passion, the light of the morning star'. Around them, Lavinium arose; the land was cultivated; Trojans married Latins, and mixed-race children were born, including their own son, Silvius.

After his wedding, wrote Vegio, whilst Aeneas traced out the walls of Lavinium with a plough, 'a mighty flame bright-shining' flashed down from Heaven and flickered over Lavinia's head. Aeneas prayed to Zeus, 'by whatever else remains to do, or is behind, with happy soothsay bring us quiet rest.' As Aeneas spoke, he turned and saw his mother standing nearby. Do not fear, Aphrodite told him: the flame is Zeus's blessing on your new city, and a promise that your progeny will one day rule the world; and some of your descendants – by which she meant the deified Caesar and Augustus – will one day ascend to Heaven itself.

The great marble frieze of the Basilica Aemilia in Rome's Forum, designed in line with Augustan dogma, includes a lively scene of Lavinium's walls being built by toiling men, while Lavinia looks on. Aside from overseeing such practical work, Le Guin's Aeneas became absorbed in preserving his Trojan rituals and learning the Latin ones, 'working in every way he could for the wellbeing of his people, his family, himself'. He remained troubled by his lapse into battle-rage which had led to his murder, as he saw it, of Turnus: 'unquestionably a vice, an abuse of skill, *nefas* [unspeakable wrong]'. It overshadowed all Aeneas was trying to achieve. Lavinia tried to console him, arguing that he had been justified in killing Turnus, but later realised she had been wrong to say this. It was better for Aeneas to see his killing of Turnus as a terrible deviation from the true order of the universe. For otherwise, the order of the universe must include such wild battle-rage, and that was not the sort of ordered, Roman world that Aeneas was striving to create.

The ruins of Lavinium, the city said to have been built by Aeneas and named after his new Latin wife, lie below and around the village of Pratica di Mare, 15 miles south of Rome, and date back to at least the 600s BC. In a field just south of the city stand its Thirteen Altars, now excavated. The location's sacred nature probably had a long pedigree and was a place of pilgrimage for many Latins, Romans included, long before Aeneas's myth appeared. The close connection between Rome and Lavinium resulted from the expansion of Rome's territory when, in 338 BC, the two cities signed a treaty. Though a new alliance, Roman writers came to see this as a revival of a more ancient one, made variously by Ascanius, Romulus or Numa Pompilius, while Livy claimed it was a renewal of the ancient agreement between Latinus and Aeneas themselves.[7] From 338 BC onwards, Lavinium became an important cult centre for the expanding Roman Republic. It became customary for generals about to depart for the provinces to come first to Lavinium, and for Roman consuls, dictators and praetors to pay annual visits here, to sacrifice to the Penantes and Vesta. The century that followed saw Aeneas's myth taking root in Rome, and it developed in Lavinium as well. The myth affected the way visiting Romans saw Lavinium. The Aeneas myth in Lavinium, in turn, helped the myth gain strength in Rome itself.

In the older myths, Rome was founded either by Aeneas or by a character called Romulus (or similar), but by the time Aeneas's myth was adopted fully by Rome in the 200s BC, the tradition of Romulus as Rome's founder had become fixed too firmly to be dislodged. As a founding hero, Aeneas had to build a city, and if this could not be Rome, it had, as Galinsky wrote, 'to be elsewhere'.[8]

Initially, both Alba Longa and Lavinium, it seems, were in the frame. In the late 200s BC, Rome's first historian, Fabius Pictor, linked the sow and piglet story not to Aeneas founding Lavinium but to Ascanius founding Alba Longa, and this shows how fluid these myths were at the time.[9] In the late first century BC, the Greek mythographer Conon heard the echo of a story that Aeneas had founded Alba Longa.[10] But in the end, Lavinium won out. A connection between Aeneas and Lavinium is implied in the 200s BC by Timaeus's reference to a Trojan vessel there, as reported by Dionysius.[11] Later, Varro's *On the Latin Language* stated clearly that Lavinium, home of the Penantes, was 'the first town of the Roman line which was founded in Latium [and was] named from the daughter of Latinus who was wedded to Aeneas, Lavinia'.[12]

Among the local gods worshipped at Lavinium were the Penantes, or *patrôoi*, as Dionysius called them, 'the gods of the race'.[13] They were hidden from profane sight, though Dionysius reports Timaeus in the 200s BC claiming to have seen them. They were, claimed Timaeus, 'iron and bronze *caduceii*', heraldic rods entwined with snakes – as borne most familiarly by Hermes – and there was also 'a Trojan earthenware vessel'. But you could see public images of the Penantes in the Roman Forum, in a 'small shrine ... darkened by the height of the adjacent buildings', according to Dionysius, and here the Penantes were depicted as two seated youths holding spears. Perhaps these were originally two local gods, like the pair Clusems and Selvans, dug up at Cortona and now in that city's museum; deities respectively of the civilised world within the city walls, and of the wild fields beyond. Otherwise, maybe they were the Dioscuri, the semi-divine twins Pollux and Castor. When the Gauls attacked Rome in 390 BC, says Livy, the *sacra*, probably these same Roman Penantes, were hidden in a *doliola* or earthen jar,[14] probably akin to the 'Trojan' one Timaeus saw at Lavinium. Similar clay vessels were associated with the Dioscuri; at Sparta and Tarentum, for instance, their statues lived in two amphorae. The suggestion that the Lavinian Penantes were originally Pollux and Castor is given weight by the discovery of an inscription found near the Thirteen Altars there, dating from the early 500s BC: *Castorei Podlouqueique qurois*, 'to Castor and Pollux, the Dioscuri'.

Perhaps, therefore, the Greeks introduced the worship of the Dioscuri to Lavinium and it spread to Rome where, it will be recalled, a temple to them was built in 484 BC. Whatever Timaeus thought he saw, the Lavinian Penantes were probably originally a pair of youths. Rome recognised Lavinium's cult of these two youths as being the same as theirs. This may have facilitated the treaty between the two cities in 338 BC, and from then on, what was believed about one pair applied to the other.

Once the Trojan myth took hold in Rome in the 200s BC, a notion began to develop that Aeneas had brought the Lavinian Penantes with him. Timaeus's identification of their earthenware container as 'Trojan' is from this century and probably reflects the emergence of this belief. The early Etruscan images of Aeneas, on amphorae and scarab rings, include the *cista* (box) or *dolia* (clay vessels), which must have contained the household gods of Troy. It was an easy step for the Romans to assert that the Penantes in Lavinium were identical with the Trojan household gods, not least, as Galinsky pointed out, because they both happened to be associated with *dolia*.[15] Part of Aeneas's importance in Roman mythology was that he brought the Penantes to Lavinium. Lycophron's *Alexandra* says that Aeneas set up (it is implied at Lavinium) 'the images of his fathers' gods'. In *Aeneid* 1, Aeneas refers to himself as having brought his household gods from Troy, and Ovid, in his *Metamorphoses*, calls him 'Penatiger'.[16] This role probably underlies the peculiarly Italian view of Aeneas as a figure of piety. So, although the Penantes were not originally Trojan at all, the way the myth developed meant that their very presence at Lavinium ended up as further proof of Aeneas's presence there, and that link to Aeneas then helped keep current the idea that he founded Lavinium before Rome.

If the Romans ended up believing that the Penantes had been brought to Lavinium by Aeneas, then where did they think they originated? One Roman view was that their origins lay on Samothraki – an idea doubtless encouraged by the priests in both places, Lavinium's priests wishing to arrogate to themselves the sacred aura of Samothraki, and Samothraki's priests hoping to gain the practical good will of Rome. On Samothraki, the *Kabeiroi*, Dardanos and Iasion, the island's local pair of youthful deities, had already been syncretised with Pollux and Castor, while another Samothrakian deity, Kadmilos, was often identified with Hermes, whose emblem was the caduceus, reminding us of Timeus's description of the Lavinian Penantes. In the 400s BC, Hellanikos's *Troika* referred to Aeneas rescuing the statues of his country's gods from burning Troy, without saying that they were from Samothraki, or destined for Italy. But later, lines in Lycophron's *Alexandra* describe Aeneas negotiating bravely with the Greeks to take both his father *and* his household gods away (ultimately, to Italy), and because of this he is described as *ensevestatos*, 'pious', a term used specifically for Samothrakian initiates. Critolaus (d. 118 BC) believed that 'Saon from Samothraki ... brought over the household deities with Aeneas', and Lucius Cassius Hemina's *Annals* (*c.* 146 BC) assert likewise that the Lavinian Penantes originated on Samothraki. Servius tells us that Varro (116-27 BC), who was himself a Samothrakian initiate, believed that the Lavinian Penantes represented some of the *Magnis Dis* – the Great Gods of Samothraki, which Dardanos had taken from Samothraki to the Troad, and which Aeneas then brought from Troy to Italy.[17]

Following these stories, Dionysius repeats a tale that, when Dardanos married his first wife Chryse in Arcadia, her dowry included 'the sacred symbols of the Great Gods, in whose mysteries she had been initiated'. Dardanos took these to Samothraki and established a mystery cult of the Great Gods there, and when he left for the Troad he brought their images with him, so that 'the holy objects brought [from Troy] into Italy by Aeneas were the images of the Great Gods, to whom the Samothrakians, of all the Greeks, pay the greatest worship.'[18] From this developed the further idea, found in Titus Pomponius Attikus (d. 32 BC),[19] but not taken up by Virgil himself, that Aeneas collected the Penantes personally from Samothraki at the start of his voyage to Italy.

The Lavinian Penantes, therefore, appear to have been two ancient statues of boys, perhaps local deities or else Pollux and Castor which, during the 200s BC, and due to the rise of Rome's Trojan myth, came to be viewed as the household gods of Troy that Aeneas had brought with him, and whose origins lay ultimately on Samothraki.

Mythmaking around Rome's Palladium was no less complex. It lived in the Temple of Vesta in the Forum and was probably a very old wooden statue of Pallas Athena, the patroness of cities. But once it was believed that Rome's origins lay in the east, this statue became identified with the Palladion, a great wooden statue which Athena created of her childhood girlfriend Pallas, whom she had killed by accident – and thus became known as the Palladium.

Dionysius, following Callistratus and Arctinus, makes the Palladium (or Palladia, in some version) another part of the dowry given to Dardanos on his marriage to his first wife Chryse. Her father was an Arcadian king called Pallas, so this story may have arisen due to a confusion of two different Pallases. Dardanos took the Palladium with him to Samothraki and thence to the city that he built in the Troad, which we know was Palaiskepsis. Dardanos's descendant Ilos took the Palladium with him when he built Troy, placing it in the Temple of Athena on the acropolis there.[20] Pseudo-Apollodorus's *Bibliotheka* relates, differently, that while the Palladium was still in Arcadia, Elektra fled to it when she was raped (by Zeus, presumably). Because it had been thus sullied, Zeus flung it out of Arcadia and it landed on the Hill of Ate, where Ilos was about to build Troy.[21]

The scholiast on Euripides' *Phoenissae*, on the other hand, asserted that Elektra took the Palladium to the Troad and presented it personally to her son Dardanos. In any event, the Palladium ended up in the Temple of Athena in Troy. During the Trojan War, Odysseus and Diomedes stole either it, or a copy of it, made intentionally to fool thieves. In Cassius Hemina's account of Aeneas's arrival at Lavinium, he claimed that having founded Venus Frutis's temple, Aeneas 'received the Palladium from Diomedes'. Presumably, in that version, Diomedes was believed to have stolen the true Palladium. But in

The Marriage of Aeneas and Lavinia

another version, Diomedes must have stolen the copy, because Dionysius says that Aeneas rescued the true Palladium from the flames of Troy. Thus, coins of Antandros, and also some minted by Julius Caesar himself, show Aeneas carrying Anchises aboard ship at Antandros with Anchises holding the Palladium.

Thanks to this mythmaking, Rome's old statue of Athena became known as the Palladium and, as with the Lavinian Penates, it became further evidence of Rome's Trojan origins. We do not know what became of the Penates; maybe they underwent a further reinterpretation and are now in a church somewhere, labelled as ancient statues of saints. The Palladium is said to have been taken by Constantine to Constantinople and was buried beneath the Column of Constantine there. Maybe it is still there now.

40

The Shrine by the Numicius

In Dionysius and Livy's accounts, Latinus was killed in the war. We do not know precisely when, in Virgil's imagined world, Latinus died, but die he surely would, after the *Aeneid* was over, leaving Aeneas as the sole ruler of the Trojans and Latins, with Lavinia at his side.

After the war, says Dionysius, Aeneas ruled over the combined Trojans and Latins for three full years. Livy speaks of Lavinia giving birth to a son and of Aeneas conferring the name of Latins upon the Trojans, starting thus to weld his two peoples into one.

Ursula Le Guin fills in some details of this precious period of (relative) peace. She relates how Aeneas saw off an army of Rutulians and Volscians led by Camers of Ardea, but Lavinia realised that greater trouble was brewing. 'He looked at me with the eyes that had seen his city burn' and reassured her 'I will keep as much of it from happening as I can.' Aeneas strengthened his alliances with old Evander and Tarchon of Etruria, and even visited Diomedes in the south, where they reminisced about the Trojan War. To channel Ascanius's boisterous energies, Aeneas sent him off to found Alba Longa in the hills above Lavinium. But when Ascanius's belligerence caused friction with the Rutulians, Aeneas ordered him back again. Instead of the blind pursuit of glory in war, which had availed their Trojan ancestors nothing, Aeneas hoped to open his son's eyes to the virtues of farming, good government and the careful worship of the gods. But Ascanius continued to be wayward, and Aeneas derived more pleasure from his new, younger son by Lavinia, whom he taught to ride. How far you have travelled, Lavinia muses. 'How far I came to come home,' Aeneas replies.

But war was imminent. Le Guin describes a squabble over some strayed cattle, which led to fresh, armed conflict with the Rutulians. While in Virgil Mezentius was killed in Aeneas's first Latin war, Dionysius says that when the Rutulians revolted on this occasion, they joined forces with Mezentius of the Tyrrhenians – the Etruscans – in a new war with Aeneas. Livy, similarly,

The Shrine by the Numicius

says that Mezentius, who ruled the Etruscans from Caere, joined forces with the Rutulians under Turnus who, like Mezentius, had survived the first war.

Despite their variations, these stories all lead Aeneas back, inexorably, to exactly where he never wanted to be again – the battlefield. The battle by the Numicius is shown in a frieze in the family tomb of T. Statilius Taurus on the Esquiline Hill, Rome. Dating from the mid to late first century BC, it is now in the Museo Nazionale Romano in the Palazzo Massimo, Rome. The frieze illustrates Roman history through the building of Lavinium, Alba Longa and Rome. On one panel, Trojans in sophisticated, Greek-style armour battle semi-naked, burnt-umber Rutulians with tall white shields, in a scene reminiscent of depictions of the uniformed British battling 'savage' Zulus in nineteenth-century Africa.

Le Guin describes a fight with the Rutulians, which Aeneas won, but when he was about to slay one young man he remembered the guilt he felt over killing Turnus, so spared him. But the youth, escaping, picked up a spear and threw it at Aeneas, piercing him through the chest. Aeneas fell face down in the Numicius. They bore him back to Lavinium, still just alive, and his last words, spoken to Lavinia, were 'go on'.

In Livy, Aeneas's army was victorious, but he himself was slain. In Dionysius's version, 'a severe battle took place not far from Lavinium and many were slain on both sides … when night came on the armies separated,' and the body of Aeneas was nowhere to be seen.

In about AD 380, *Origo Gentis Romanae* retold these old stories of Aeneas's death, but in more detail than before. Although defeated when Aeneas first came to Italy, the Rutulians rallied themselves and encouraged Mezentius of the Etruscans to invade Aeneas's realm. Aeneas, despite having fewer men, had no choice but to march out to meet his foes on the banks of the Numicius. As battle commenced, the skies darkened; a whirlwind whipped across the fields; a great deluge of rain crashed down, and thunder boomed. The soldiers, already disorientated, were blinded by fiery flashes of lightning. Neither side had an appetite for battle any more. As the Trojans and Latins wandered about, dazed, they realised Aeneas had vanished, 'carried off in the tumult of the sudden storm'. 'It is handed down,' adds the *Origo*'s writer, that Aeneas had fallen into the river and drowned.

'He lies buried on the river Numicius,' wrote Livy. Dionysius wrote 'the Latins built a heroon or hero-shrine to him,' though he added, with typical scholarly thoroughness, that some said the shrine concerned was erected by Aeneas in honour of his father Anchises. 'It is a small mound, around which have been set out in regular rows trees that are well worth seeing.'[1]

In the fields between Lavinium and the sea, not far from the Numicius, are the excavated remains of a tumulus. Though controversial – and Cornell, for one, disagrees – it is believed widely to be the place identified by Livy and Dionysius as Aeneas's heroon. The site is on private land and it required a special arrangement with the local superintendent archaeologist to visit it. It was a mild, sunny February morning when we did, and skylarks were singing

In Search of Aeneas

as we were led over the green fields, with the Tyrrhenian coast to the left and to our right, the pale blue peaks of the mountains around Alba Longa.

We found the tumulus to contain a rectangular stone grave, with a large boulder for a pillow. The bones were no longer there: they were probably taken long-since, as hero-relics for the temples of Rome, and perhaps they are still in a church there, misidentified as a saint's relics. But when the bones were still there, the hero would have lain looking back towards the sea, whence, presumably, he had come. The grave goods are from the 600s BC and are now housed in the museum up the road at Pratica di Mare, on the site of Lavinium, and which proudly declares 'Hic Domus Aeneas' – 'here lives Aeneas'.

Nobody knows the true identity of the 600s BC man for whom the heroon was really built. He was probably one of the Greek merchant-adventurers who had come to trade with the Latins, and who helped spread the tales of Aeneas and Hercules in Italy in the first place. He was presumably an important figure in the early history of Lavinium; maybe he had some Elymian blood, suggestive of Trojan ancestry. Perhaps he intervened in local tribal wars between the Latins and Rutulians and his story fed, in some now indefinable way, into the development of Aeneas's story.

In his 1963 book *Early Rome*, Andreas Alföldi argued that the Etruscans' fascination with Aeneas in the 500s BC fed directly into some sort of cult worship of Aeneas at Lavinium, based on this tumulus, from that time onwards. But, as we have seen, it took until the 200s BC for Aeneas's myth to take root in the patrician and religious circles of Rome and Latium. It was only then that the worship of the Penates at Lavinium was reinterpreted as evidence of Aeneas's arrival there, so it was probably then, too, that this tumulus was drawn into the Trojan nexus. Dionysius's uncertainty as to whether the tomb was Aeneas's or Anchises' is an echo, perhaps, of mythmakers considering different options. In the 200s BC, as part of the Trojanising process, part of the tumulus's mound was cut away and a set of false stone doors and an antechamber were added. Pilgrims could now come and see the bones of the hero buried there, just as, today, Catholic pilgrims visiting churches are shown relics that are supposedly of saints. From the 200s BC onwards, the Lavinians would have left pilgrims in no doubt that the bones they were being shown were those of Aeneas himself.

After Aeneas's death, says Livy, his widow Lavinia ruled in Lavinium as regent for her son by Aeneas, until he was old enough to rule Latium himself. In Virgil, Dionysius and most other Roman sources, this son of Aeneas and Lavinia is called Silvius. But Livy, admitting that 'no one can pretend to certainty on something so deeply buried in the mists of time,' calls the boy Ascanius, the same name as his older half-brother, the son of Aeneas and Creusa, and gives this second Ascanius a son called Silvius.

Generally, it seems to have been accepted from at least the 100s BC onwards that the son of Aeneas and Lavinia, whether called Silvius or Ascanius (mark two), was the ancestor of Romulus, the brother of Remus and founder of Rome, while the older Ascanius, the son of Aeneas and Creusa who had come with his father from Troy, was also known as Iulus, and was the ancestor of the gens Julii, the line that led down to Caesar and Augustus. Late in Roman history, the *Origo Gentis Romanae* tells a charming story, based on that of the *Vinalia Priora* that we heard earlier, to explain the change of name from Ascanius (mark one) to Iulus. In a further conflict with the Etruscans, the older Ascanius was besieged in Lavinium by Mezentius's son Lausus, who offered to end the war in return for all the Latins' wine already made and the vintages of several years to come. That was too much for Ascanius, who publicly consecrated all Latium's wine to Zeus. He burst forth from the city, killed Lausus and put his enemies to flight. Because of this and his descent via Dardanos from Zeus, whom the Latins called Jove or Iove, Ascanius became known as Iolus or Iulus, and 'from him the Julian family originated.'

We do not know whether the gens Julii ever made up the names of ancestors to fill the gap between their earliest certain forebear, Numerius Julius Julus in the mid-400s BC, and Aeneas's son. But Rome certainly needed a catalogue of rulers to fill the space between the inception of the Roman Republic in 508/9 BC, and the time of Aeneas. Initially, this desire was met by the names of seven kings; Lucius Tarquinius Superbus, whose overthrow started the Republic, was preceded by Servius Tullus; Lucius Tarquinius Priscus; Ancus Marcius; Tullus Hostilius; Numa Pompilius and, earliest of all, Romulus. The date for Rome's founding, counting back through the reigns of those seven kings, was fixed at 753 BC. The last six kings may well have been historical characters, but the first, Romulus, is clearly derived from the name of Rome itself.

It seems to have been agreed quite early on, perhaps as early as the 600s BC, that Rome's eponymous founder hero must have been called either Romus, Rhomê, Rhemus or Romulus. The idea, voiced in the 400s BC by Hellanikos of Lesvos, that Rome's founder was Aeneas, was a purely Greek one, probably echoing the earlier domination of Rome by Etruria, and this did not catch on. As we heard earlier, different foundation myths were proposed whereby Romus (or similar) founded Rome and was associated in various ways with either Aeneas or Odysseus. Eventually, they settled on Romulus as the name for Rome's founder. One story, reported by Dionysius with the preface 'others say', even suggested that Aeneas had sons called Ascanius, Romulus, and Remus, and the latter was Rome's founder, and Ennius (*c.* 239 BC-*c.* 169 BC) seems to have identified Romulus as Aeneas's grandson.[2]

In about the late 200s or early 100s BC, however, some sober-minded Roman historian must have realised that if Rome was indeed founded in 753 BC, then almost four hundred years had elapsed since, according to the Greeks, the Trojan War was fought. Aeneas may have been Romulus's ancestor but, if so, many more generations must have come between the two than were admitted by the myths. Some more names had to be found to plug this gap.

During his wars with the neighbouring Latins, Tullus Hostilius, the third of Rome's kings, conquered the mountain stronghold of Alba Longa. Now called Castel Gandolfo, it is a settlement strung along part of the crater of an extinct volcano, below the Alban Mount (itself another, taller, extinct volcano). The crater below Alba Longa is filled by the cold, clear waters of the Alban Lake. The settlement commands inspiring views, east into the Apennines, south-west over Lavinium to the Tyrrhenian Sea, and north-west to Rome, 13 miles distant. Alba Longa had a dynasty of kings who were contemporaries of the kings of Rome, and whose line continued for a while after Tullus's conquest, as sub-kings, until the start of the Republic.

In the 200s BC, the pedigree of the Alba Longa kings was known in Rome, but it did not lead anywhere, except perhaps to a few patrician families who fancied themselves as descendants, so it was rather redundant. However, it was of enough antiquity to be credible, and of about the right length to plug the gap between Aeneas and Romulus. A bold Roman historian, therefore, shifted it bodily back in time. Aeneas's son by Lavinia became the founder of Alba Longa, with Aeneas Silvius as his son and Latinus Silvius as his grandson. Then the first legendary king of Alba Longa, whose name was of course Alba, was grafted in, as Latinus Silvius's son. The pedigree of the Alba Longa kings then ran down to Numitor, who became father of Rhea Silvia, who was raped by Ares to become, neatly, the mother of Romulus.

Galinsky regarded the use of the Alban kings' genealogy to plug the gap as 'the triumph of the indigenous Latin tradition' which resulted in 'the relegation of Aeneas to the background'.[3] But once the Romans had become aware of the gap between 753 BC and the Trojan War, this temporal 'relegation' was essential to maintain Aeneas as a credible progenitor for the Roman people. By grafting in the pedigree of the Alba Longa kings, Aeneas was cemented far more realistically into Roman mythological history as the progenitor of all the luminaries in Roman history who came thereafter, probably including the founders of some of the great patrician *gens*, or clans, of Rome, too.

The clearest result of this entire mythmaking process is found in Livy's *Ab Urbe Condita*. Livy was concerned mainly with the traceable history of Rome, not with the earlier origins of its people, which he considered to be too caught up in 'the charm of poetry' to be properly discernible. In order to maintain Augustus's favour, however, he focussed obligingly on the Trojan myth, stating that before the Trojans came, the area around Rome had been ruled by the native king, Latinus. Aeneas tried to end to the Trojan War by offering to negotiate the return of Helen. Aeneas's efforts to make peace failed, but when the Greeks took the city they spared his life and allowed him to leave. Aeneas sailed to Greece, then Sicily, reached Latinus's realm, married his daughter Lavinia and named his new city after her. From Aeneas and Lavinia's son (whom he calls Ascanius) descended the kings of Alba

The Shrine by the Numicius

Longa, whom Livy enumerated down to Numitor, whose daughter Rhea Sylvia became pregnant by Ares and give birth to Remus and his brother Romulus, the founder of Rome. Dionysius tells a similar story, in much greater detail. It is to this tale that the *Aeneid* looks forward, particularly through the parade of heroes seen by Aeneas in Hades.

Rome's magnificent Trojan pedigree was destined to produce offshoots, particularly the one that led to Britain. Nennius's *Historia Brittonum*, which was written in the AD 800s in Gwynedd, north Wales, reproduces several contradictory versions of Aeneas's pedigree, as re-imagined from the AD 600s onwards. These include Aeneas and Lavinia having a son Ascanius, father of Silvius, who has a son called Britto, an eponym for Britain, whose name is also rendered, in more Latin style, Brutus, while another of Nennius's pedigrees makes Brutus son (not grandson) of Ascanius. When Geoffrey of Monmouth wrote his account of Brutus in about AD 1135, he decided that Brutus was son of Silvius, son of the Ascanius who had come with his father Aeneas from Troy (and whose mother, therefore, was Priam's daughter Creusa).

This Brutus grew up in Alba Longa, but accidentally killed his father Silvius while hunting and was exiled. After many adventures and tribulations, 'Brutus of Troy', as he was known, was guided by Artemis to an island 'far to the west, in the wide ocean', where he founded Britain. The Welsh pedigrees made Brutus the ancestor of all the later British kings, including Leir and 'Old King' Coel, and the rulers of Gwynedd. The Gwynedd dynasty included Llewellyn the Great (1173-1240) and Owain Glyndŵr (*c.* 1359-*c.* 1415), who were both well aware of their Trojan ancestry, and from their children's intermarriages with English royal and noble families innumerable genealogical lines can be traced right down to the present. The descendants concerned include the present British royal family. The Princess of Wales's father, Michael Middleton, also has a line going back to this nexus of English and Welsh royal blood; his grandmother was an eighth cousin of my grandmother's, so I share that same connection back, through the Gwynedd dynasty, to Brutus and Aeneas. None of us are really descended from Aeneas's great grandson Brutus, because he never existed. But we are descended from many, many generations of ancestors who believed they were; ancestors who, just like the Caesars, allowed their belief in their descent from Aeneas to inform the very real acts and deeds that shaped their lives, and their countries' histories.

41

Aeneas Indiges

If there was a real Aeneas, he lived one life and died one death, probably all within sight of Mount Ida in the Troad. But as the mythological hero he became, Aeneas lived many lives and died many times, and his story does not end even with his ultimate death by the River Numicius. In some versions of his myth, Aeneas's body mouldered away in its tumulus at Lavinium. But the *Origo Gentis Romanae* relates how, after Aeneas's battle with Mezentius was over, the storm clouds cleared away and the sun appeared. Aeneas' body could not be found, so 'it was believed that he had been taken up to Heaven alive,' and they dedicated a temple to him there as *Patrem Indigetem*.

That story is based on earlier ones. A surviving fragment of the *Antiquitates Rerum Divinarum* of Varro (116 BC-27 BC) mentions 'Aeneas Indiges'.[1] Dionysius tells the story that Aeneas's body could not be found after his battle with Mezentius; some thought he had 'perished in the river beside which the battle was fought', but others concluded that his body 'had been translated to the gods'. The hero shrine dedicated to Aeneas, Dionysius continues, was inscribed 'To *pater deus indiges*, who presides over the waters of the river Numicius'.[2] Livy, while reporting that Aeneas died and was buried, adds, 'Was he man or god? However it be, men call him *Iovem Indigitem*'.[3] And Pliny adds, in his *Natural History*, that the deity worshipped in a 'grove' near the Numicius was called *Sol Indiges*.[4]

Pater of course means 'father'; *Deus* and *Iovem* are names for Zeus, while *Sol* was the god of the sun. *Indiges* seems to have been the original name for the local, 'native' deity worshipped at the tumulus before it, along with Lavinium's Penantes, was 'Trojanised'. Where once Indiges was worshipped in his own right, and later in association with Zeus, or the sun, he came to be seen, by the 100s BC at least, as the deified Aeneas.

The Statilius tomb referred to earlier, which shows the battle by the Numicius, also depicts an imposing, armoured figure departing the fight towards a winged figure, generally held to be Victory – though it may be

Aeneas Indiges

Aphrodite – who is handing him a wreath. This armed figure is thought to represent Aeneas, about to be apotheosed into the heavens. This is in line with *Aeneid* 1, in which Zeus assures Aphrodite that 'thou shalt bear aloft thy great-hearted Aeneas to the stars,' and *Aeneid* 12, when Zeus tells Hera that 'the skies [would] claim Aeneas, as hero made divine, and the Fates exalt him to the stars.'

It was Virgil's younger contemporary, Ovid (43 BC-AD 17/18), who undertook to describe Aeneas's actual transformation from man into god, in a sequence near the end of his *Metamorphoses*, which he composed between about AD 2 and AD 8. Rushing up to Zeus, who was probably seated on this throne on Mount Olympus, Aphrodite threw her arms around his neck and pleaded: you've never been harsh to me, dear father, so please be kind now. Aeneas is your grandson, with divine blood in his veins, so please make him into a god, no matter how humble. He has already been down into Hades and crossed the river Styx, and once is enough.

All the gods agreed with Aphrodite. Even Hera smiled, for her feud with the Trojans, which had caused most of Aeneas's troubles, was now over. Both you and you son deserve what you are asking, Zeus assured Aphrodite; have that which you desire. Aphrodite thanked her father joyfully. She hurried to her chariot, which was drawn by doves, and wafted down on the gentle breezes until she saw below her the Numicius, winding through the reed beds towards the Laurentine shore. There lay Aeneas's body, just as it had fallen in battle. She instructed the horned god of the river to wash away all those parts of Aeneas which were mortal, until all the corrupt matter was cleansed away. What was left was 'all that was best'; the purified body of a god. Aeneas's mother anointed him gently with divine fragrance, and placed ambrosia mingled with nectar on his lips. Thus, Aeneas became a deity, says Ovid, and the Romans called him Indiges.

Aeneas was never more, however, than a minor deity. There was no official cult of Aeneas in Rome. 'None of the numerous festivals,' asserted Galinsky, 'and none of the public games commemorated him.'[5] While he speculated that a cult of Aeneas may have been practised by 'one or more of Rome's numerous *familiae Troianae*',[6] such as the Julii, Galinsky admitted there was no evidence. Of Augustus's contemporary poets, Horace's catalogue of deified mortals omits Aeneas altogether. Virgil only alludes to it. Ovid's lines stand alone as the only full description of Aeneas becoming a god, and these were written, clearly, to keep his poem in line with imperial dogma.

There is, however, some archaeological evidence suggesting that a belief in Aeneas as a god may have seeped beyond Imperial propaganda and into the credence of at least a few ordinary Romans. A handful of private Roman funerary monuments, found from Turkey to the Rhineland and dating from the first and second centuries AD, include depictions of Aeneas carrying Ascanius. Two, in Cologne, Germany, and Pannonia (modern Hungary), show Aeneas in armour; perhaps these were graves of soldiers.[7] The fact that these images appeared on gravestones suggest some spiritual element. Maybe his deification, and Virgil's description of him navigating his way successfully in and out of Hades, are what inspired the soldiers' families to invoke Aeneas on these funerary monuments.

Also, the Veronese scholiast on the *Aeneid* alleges that, besides the Penantes and Vesta, sacrifices were made at Lavinium to *Aeneas Indigeti*, so at least a few people there were praying to Aeneas as a god.[8] A small piece of archaeological evidence that is suggestive of this is a dedicatory inscription on a *cippus*, a small pillar used perhaps as a landmark, found at Tor Tignosa, about 5 miles inland from Lavinium and a third of a mile from the River Numicius. Of uncertain date, this pillar is now displayed in the Diocletian Baths in Rome. It is inscribed *Lare Aineia D[onum]*, 'Dedication to Lar Aeneas'. The Latin word *lar* may have denoted a field god, a fertility demon or a deified ancestor, so this dedication was probably connected to Aeneas's tumulus by the Numicius and the healing cult at Lavinium. Although never seen as a major god, Aeneas was treated as a minor one, and a belief in him may have brought comfort to at least a few citizens of Rome's empire.

Aeneas's ascent into Heaven, as imagined in the last two centuries BC and the start of the first century AD, was not unique. In the late 100s BC, Ennius refers to Romulus becoming a god, too. Livy describes him being surrounded by a dark cloud on the Campus Martius, and when the cloud lifted, he was gone. Some said he had been torn to pieces by his senators, but one of them, Proculus Julius, presumably a mythological ancestor of the gens Julii, claimed to have seen Romulus in a vision at dawn, saying 'the gods so wish it that my Rome should be the capital of the whole world. So let them foster the art of war.'[9]

Latinus, too, was deified. Festus relates a tradition that it was Latinus who fought Mezentius and then disappeared after the battle, to become Jupiter Latiaris,[10] the god worshipped on the Alban Mount, where massive, dark blocks of stone from his temple's base can still be seen today. Once Aeneas's myth was woven into the fabric of Roman history, he became the one who fought Mezentius, so it followed that, like Latinus, he, too, should become a god, though obviously not the same one. Lavinium's cult of Aeneas as Indiges seems, therefore, to have been a Trojan counterpart of the Latin cult of Jupiter Latiaris up on the Alban Mount. It seems likely from all this that the belief in Latinus becoming a god predates the belief in the deification of Aeneas.

These deifications belonged to a wider belief across the eastern Mediterranean that kings, when they died, became gods; indeed, for Hittite kings, 'became a god' appears to have been the equivalent of 'passed away'. This was not a culture shared by Republican Rome, and it was probably regarded with the same lofty disdain with which patrician Romans viewed many aspects of the east. But then came the *Sidus Iulium*, 'the Julian star', the comet which blazed above Rome in 44 BC during the funeral games for

Aeneas Indiges

Julius Caesar. Without this, Aeneas's story might never have been any more than a curiosity of Roman mythological history. But, like the magnetic stones of Samothraki, Ida and Pessinus, and the meteor which probably gave rise to the myth of Aphrodite's foaming maritime birth, the *Sidus Iulium* comet was an actual, natural phenomena, its active presence in the real world helping to convince our ancestors of the existence of divinity. It was taken in Rome, albeit after considerable encouragement by Augustus, as confirmation of Caesar's translation into Heaven. And this reflected interest back onto the deification of his ancestor Aeneas, which assumed far great prominence than before, as a precedent for Caesar's.

These assumed apotheoses of Aeneas and Caesar gained even greater importance during Augustus's reign as precedents for his own eventual translation into Heaven. At the end of his *Metamorphoses*, Ovid describes Julius Caesar's ascent into Heaven, praises the peace-giving reign of Augustus and then concludes with a prayer to 'the gods who attended Aeneas through fire and sword', to ensure that, when Augustus died, long after Ovid's death, he would rise up to Heaven likewise, where he might answer the prayers of his adoring worshippers below.

In fact, Augustus died before Ovid, in AD 14. Ovid's words helped speed him up into Heaven. The Great Cameo, now in the Bibliothèque Nationale in Paris, shows the Imperial family in the time of Claudius; above them is Augustus, *in capite velato*, being born up to Heaven by a figure carrying a globe.[11] Some scholars suggest that this globe-bearer is Alexander, but as he wears a Phrygian cap, his identification as Aeneas is far more likely. If so, this is the only image of Aeneas as a god from Julio-Claudian times, and it is appropriate that this image is associated with the deification of the greatest promoter of his myth, Augustus himself.

One might assume, now that Aeneas had been set up as Rome's primary founding hero and accepted by some as a god, that his popularity would remain unsurpassed, at least until the demise of the last Julio-Claudian emperor, Nero, in AD 68. Roman Troy honoured Livilla, wife of Augustus's grandson Drusus and, though her mother, a great great niece of Caesar's, as 'Goddess Aphrodite Anchiseias',[12] but such invocations of Aeneas are in fact few and far between.

Beyond the villas and temples of those patrician families who considered themselves to be of Trojan origin, most ordinary Romans were probably more engaged by Romulus and Remus than by Augustus's poster-boy, Aeneas. Further afield, wall paintings preserved by Vesuvius's ashes at Pompeii show that, while Aeneas was undoubtedly well-known, the imperial dogma of him as a pious founding hero had perhaps not sunk in fully. Aeneas appears on Pompeiian walls seven times, four as warrior or lover, and only thrice saving Anchises from Troy. Of these three, the first is a very conventional scene of Aeneas, Ascanius and Anchises leaving Troy. Paired with a depiction of Romulus, it is on the outside wall of the shop of Fabius Multitremulus on Via dell'Abbondanza.[13] It was clearly, as Galinsky wrote, 'an outward documentation of [the shopkeeper's] patriotism' but perhaps not a true reflection of what the shopkeeper really believed.[14] Second is a fragment of a mural in the 'Homeric House', in which Hermes guides Aeneas and his family away from burning Troy.[15] But this is only one of many scenes on the house's walls showing the Trojan myth and, as it appears by the street-door, it may have been little more than an elaborate 'exit' sign. Thirdly, in the depths of a private house, Aeneas and his family are shown, not as noble humans, but as composite monkeys with dog heads and large phalluses. Instead of the *cista sacra* containing the Penates, Anchises, who is perched jauntily on Aeneas's shoulders, holds a dice box, alluding to a favourite pastime of Caesar's.[16] That suggests what most Pompeiians really thought of Aeneas and the all-powerful heirs of Augustus, lording it up in Rome.

The emperors who followed the Julio-Claudians did not share the Julii's fabled descent from Aeneas via Iulus. But the man who supplanted Nero, the Emperor Galba, struck a coin showing the veiled figure of the goddess Pietas standing by an altar, and Aeneas carrying Anchises and leading Ascanius, under the legend 'Pietas Augusti', indicating his wish to restore the piety of Augustus's reign. The mother of the Emperor Trajan (d. AD 117) belonged to the gens Marcii, who traced themselves back to Numa Pompilius, and on that basis Trajan's adopted son the Emperor Hadrian (d. AD 138) seems to have fudged a descent for Numa back to Aeneas. In the British Museum is a medallion showing Hadrian on one side, and Aphrodite on the other, resting on a shield depicting Aeneas with Anchises and Ascanius;[17] and an altar in Carthage from Hadrian's time, dedicated to the gens Julii, also shows the latter three. Aeneas is depicted in a general's garb but unarmed and, Galinsky thought, pious.[18] 'When Aeneas's *pietas* is singled out in official imperial sculpture,' wrote Galinsky, 'it exalts, above all, the *pietas* of the emperor himself.'[19] Hadrian's adopted son, the Emperor Antoninus Pius (d. AD 161) made even more effort to bolster his position by copying the prestigious piety of Augustus, depicting Aeneas, in Augustan style, on some of his bronze sesterii.[20] When Antoninus's grandson the Emperor Commodius (d. AD 192) went mad in later life, however, he roamed the Imperial Palace in a lion skin and claiming to be a reincarnation, not of Aeneas, but of Hercules.

Many of the later emperors lacked the patrician blood necessary to make any plausible claims to descent, via blood or adoption, from the exalted stock of Aeneas. But Aeneas did not fall out of favour entirely. The British Museum has coins of emperors Severus Alexander (d. AD 235)[21] and Gallienus (d. AD 268)[22] depicting the now age-old image of Aeneas carrying his father and leading his son. Later rulers of Rome, from the Popes to Mussolini, made use of Aeneas where it suited them in their efforts to reassert their city's former glories. And Aeneas survives in Rome to this day, in Bernini's marble statue in the Galleria Borghese, for instance, and the fine modern bronze in the Via C. Battisti, both depicting him carrying his father and leading his son. Aeneas is less visible in Rome, though, than his mythological descendants

Aeneas Indiges

Romulus and Remus, or his mother, Aphrodite. Her popularity in Rome was due entirely to her having been Aeneas's mother, yet now you see dozens of images of her in Rome for every one of him. Very few Romans or tourists, one suspects, appreciate that Aeneas is the main reason why Aphrodite is there at all.

Aeneas's real afterlife was not in such imagery, or imperial propaganda, or even as a god, but in literature. Even after Rome itself succumbed to the barbarians, Aeneas's story lived on in Livy, Dionysius and, most of all, in Virgil. Thanks to the *Aeneid*'s forward-looking, nation-building ethos, Aeneas's story remained at the heart of European culture long after Rome's collapse. Indeed, when Christianity started to 'civilise' the barbarian tribes who had invaded the empire and caused its collapse, the *Aeneid*'s tale of a pious king leading his people in a westward quest to build a new realm sanctioned by Fate, provided a role model for the establishment of the new kingdoms of Europe. And when the princes of Gwynedd secured their north-western Welsh realm against some of those encroaching barbarians, the Saxons, they, too, looked back to Virgil's hero, fighting his wars against Mezentius and Turnus to establish his kingdom in Italy, and laid claim to Aeneas as their ancestor, as we have seen, via his mythical great grandson, Brutus of Troy.

42

Apotheosis

About twenty years after Augustus's death and, in Roman belief, his ascension into Heaven, another man, far less well-known in his lifetime, followed suit. Jesus of Nazareth was born in the Roman province of Judea during Augustus's reign, and his crucifixion at Jerusalem was in the reign of Augustus's successor, Tiberius.

The story that Jesus came back from the dead and then ascended into Heaven helped spread his cult throughout the Roman world. Christianity eventually overwhelmed the worship of the Olympian gods and the Classical belief-system, through which Aeneas's myth had run its dazzling course. But Christianity did not emerge fully developed out of a vacuum. It drew heavily on Jesus's Jewish heritage, identifying him as the Jews' much-awaited Messiah, and using the Jewish Old Testament to replace Hesiod's *Theogony* as the authoritative account of the origin of the world. But Christianity also owed a great deal to the Hellenised, Roman world in which Jesus and his followers lived.

The accounts of Jesus's conception, by the Holy Spirit and the mortal Mary, seem to echo the way Zeus conceived a host of heroes, from Hercules to Aeneas's ancestor Dardanos. The *Sidus Iulium*, which was taken as a sign of Caesar's ascent into Heaven, was echoed by the eastern star which blazed over the infant Jesus's crib in Bethlehem. Jesus's greatest supporter was his mother Mary, just as Aeneas's was his mother, Aphrodite. Indeed, under Christianity, Mary acquired those of Aphrodite's attributes that were not directly connected with sex: doves and roses; patronage of mariners as the Star of the Sea; and the robes and starry crown of Aphrodite Ourania, Queen of Heaven.

Jesus's early life in rural obscurity has some parallels with Aeneas's early childhood in the wilds of Ida. Jesus came into his own when he reached Jerusalem, just as Aeneas's career began in earnest when he arrived at Troy. Jesus wandered in the desert, just as Aeneas roamed the seas. Jesus shouldered the weight of the cross, just as Aeneas bore the 'dear burden' of old Anchises. Jesus died and came back to life, just as Aeneas visited Hades but returned alive. Jesus ascended into Heaven just as Aeneas and his descendants, the Caesars, had done already. Rome, the seat of Aeneas's heirs, became the seat of St Peter's successors, the Popes. We may speculate to what extent Jesus and his followers knew Aeneas's story, and how many of them had read the *Aeneid*; they may well have done so – and may have drawn ideas of piety and divine providence directly from it.

There were early Christians, particularly St Augustine and his pupil Orosius, who condemned Aeneas for 'the strifes he aroused', but on the whole, early Christianity tended to embrace Virgil and his *Aeneid*. In his fourth *Eclogue*, written in about 40 BC, Virgil used 'oracular language', as Hardie wrote, 'to express hopes for future political and social stability after years of Roman civil war'.[1] It heralded 'the last age of Cumaean song; the great line of the centuries begins anew. Now the Virgin returns, the reign of Saturn returns; now a new generation descends from Heaven on high ... a golden race spring up throughout the world!' This eclogue looked forward to the birth of a son and heir; it is not entirely clear who, but whoever it was, the hope was that this heir would succeed Augustus and continue his reign of peace. As this heir grew up, signs of the returning Golden Age would appear. A replay of history would ensue, in which the Argonauts would set sail again and Achilles would embark once more to destroy Troy; but after that purging, the child would become a man, and the Golden Age of peace would burgeon in full. Virgil's lines were intended to praise Augustus and his successor, but many early Church Fathers, from Lactantius (*c.* 240-*c.* 320), author of *Divine Institutes*,[2] and his patron Constantine I (d. AD 337) onwards, turned this around, praising Virgil as a sort of prophet, who anticipated, albeit unknowingly, the great suffering of Christ, akin to that second Trojan War, which came before the Resurrection.

Hardie suggests that Virgil had drawn inspiration from existing Messianic hopes among the Hellenised Jews in Egypt and, perhaps, in Rome.[3] But who knows how direct an influence Virgil's fourth *Eclogue* may have had on those who first hailed Jesus as being something more than a mere prophet in the first place? Similarly, Virgil's view of Elysium, and the condition of human souls there, influenced the Christian view of Heaven. Virgil's praise of piety and peace; his clear aversion to the cruelty and barbarism of war, and Anchises's injunction in *Aeneid* 6 to 'spare the humbled and to bring down the proud' might have had a direct influence on the mind-sets of Jesus' followers.

The *Aeneid* was even taken, as Hardie argues, to reveal a grand plan of God's.[4] Aeneas's divinely inspired mission led to the founding of Rome, whose empire spread across the known world. Therefore, when Christianity appeared, it could spread easily and effectively through the empire, which owed its origins to Aeneas. Zeus's prophetic line 'I have given them empire without end' was intended to refer to the Roman people. But under Christianity, it was reinterpreted as a prophecy of Aeneas's ultimate successors in Rome, the Popes.

The *Aeneid* itself contained the oracular words of Apollo, Helenus, Cumaean Sibyl and the gods, so it acquired a prophetic aura. It became commonplace, from the time of Hadrian onwards, to practise *sortes Virgilianae*, dipping into the *Aeneid* and reading a line at random, in order to divine the future. Early Christians, trying to avoid persecution, composed *centos*, sentences made up of short phrases from Virgil's works, recombined to affirm Christian truths; the fact that this was even possible was a sign, they thought, that Virgil's work was an active anticipation of Christianity. Thus, an apocryphal story, related by Paul de Metz in 1245 in his *Image du Monde*, relates how, when St Paul reached Italy, he found Virgil's body in its tomb and said 'Ah, if I had found you [alive], I would have given you [by baptising you] to God!'

In the *Divine Comedy* (1300), the Florentine poet Dante Alighieri imagined himself wandering through the murmuring woods around Lake Avernus, where the sibyl had once led Aeneas down into Hades and encountering the ghost of Virgil, he who had 'made Anchises's upright son the subject of [his] song'. Virgil had been in Limbo, the highest of the nine circles of Hell, the place reserved for those who led blameless lives on Earth, yet who died before Christ, so had not had the opportunity of being baptised and saved. Limbo was the same as Elysium, where Aeneas had discovered Anchises living contentedly, but that was before the world knew of Christian salvation. So now, says Virgil bleakly, 'we live [in Elysium], desiring [but] without hope' of ever reaching Heaven.

Just as Virgil had imagined the sibyl guiding Aeneas into the underworld, so Virgil now showed Dante the way, right down through the circles of Hell, past the feet of colossal Satan himself and then out through a tunnel to the other side of the world. Here, they saw a ship gliding across the seas, with an angel in its prow, using his outspread wings as sails, bearing souls of the newly dead to the foot of Mount Purgatory. Together, Virgil and Dante climbed Mount Purgatory. Beyond, lay Paradise, but that was as far as the unbaptized Virgil could go – and he vanished.

The Romans, inspired in part by their myths of Aeneas, had ushered in an unprecedented era of order and peace across the Mediterranean world, in which a freshly optimistic view of the afterlife could take shape. Aeneas and his Imperial descendants might ascend gaily into Heaven, but for everyone else, Virgil's description of the souls of the dead which Aeneas saw in Hades highlighted the question: 'where next for *us*?' – a question we continue to ask to this very day. The old Mesopotamian view, that humanity existed only to serve the gods, required a meek acceptance that death was necessary to stop the world becoming overpopulated. It suggested no happy afterlife. Nor did Homer's view of death: when Odysseus conferred with Achilles' shade, the dead hero told him he would rather be a slave on Earth than a king in Hades.

Apotheosis

Yet even in Homer's time, if not before, philosophies were developing around Greece to try to ameliorate this stark view. Over the centuries between Homer and Virgil – during the entire time, in fact, that Aeneas's own mythological story developed – the Orphics, Pythagoreans and other mystery cults philosophised about the possibility of finding happiness after death. The mystery cult of Demeter at Eleusis's aim, as we learn at the end of the Homeric *Hymn to Demeter*, was to offer the initiate a better lot 'down in the musty dark when he is dead'. The mystery cult which Aeneas's ancestor Dardanos was believed to have founded on Samothraki, entailed initiates making a night-time journey through the Sanctuary of the Great Gods, which was designed to prepare them for death and to enable them to retain their purified personalities in the afterlife. Piecing together fragments of the Orphic hymns in his 'Instructions to the Orphic Adept', Robert Graves thought that Samothrakian initiates believed that they were destined to become 'lords of the uninitiated', enjoying an afterlife being fed honeyed water by nymphs.

All these cults and philosophies were human imaginings of how our souls might enjoy a happier afterlife. What Anchises told Aeneas in Hades, that after being purged of their Earthly stains, souls would either live on in blissful Elysium or be reborn in a cleansed state on Earth again, was a great step forward from Homer's bleak view that even the greatest of the dead heroes were submerged in the eternal greyness of Hades. Anchises' words were, in fact, the best the Roman world could offer. Virgil had set out, as Broch wrote in *The Death of Virgil*, to understand death, but he had succeeded only in 'hemming in death by metaphor', sending Aeneas down into Hades, only to have him return empty-handed, through the gate of dreams. But it was arguably on these Virgilian ideas that the followers of Christ built their hopes, that Jesus, improving on Aeneas, had come back from the dead with the more optimistic promise of salvation, bodily resurrection and eternity spent in Heaven – for those, at least, who deserved it.

There are ways, therefore, of seeing Christianity not as a jarring break with Aeneas's era, but as an almost inevitable, if unexpected, result of it. Jesus's triumph over the hearts and minds of the Roman world was achieved through his purported resurrection from the dead. The Jews had their own tradition of ascents into Heaven, such as Elijah in his fiery chariot, but Elijah lay far back in their history. The supposed apotheoses of Caesar and Augustus, Virgil's anticipation of Aeneas' ascent into Heaven and Ovid's lively description of it, all came only a few decades before the widely believed ascent into Heaven of Jesus. It is beyond question that the apostles, as citizens of the Empire, were well aware of the claims of Imperial apotheoses, and it would seem extraordinary if they were unaware of Virgil and Ovid. It seems likely, therefore, that all these Roman ideas influenced the apostles.

But Jesus did not rise up into Heaven having simply died; he did so having died and then come back to life again. That much had not been claimed even by the advocates of the apotheoses of Caesar and Augustus, but Aeneas was one of the few Classical heroes who descended into Hades and came back to tell the tale; true, he had to die properly, later on, before he rose up into Heaven, but his triumph over death was still an improvement on what had come before. Caesar and Augustus were recent political figures, whom the Jews had no reason to love. But Aeneas, so long in the past, so pious, so victorious over death – his was not a bad precedent to follow. When Christian mythology spirited Jesus up to Heaven, he followed where Aeneas had gone before.

Aeneas's parallels with Christ come together most sharply in *Origo Gentis Romanae*, written in about AD 380, towards the end of the Classical world, as Christianity took hold even of Zeus's chosen city of Rome. The darkness and thunder which dominated Aeneas's last battle by the Numicius may echo the earthquake in Matthew, and the darkness which covered the Earth in both Mark and Luke, that accompanied Jesus's death on the cross.[5] Jesus lay in his tomb for three days and then rose from the dead, being seen first by Mary Magdalene and then by the rest of his followers. So, by a process of cross-fertilisation of stories, the *Origo* reports that Aeneas's corpse was never found, but it is 'affirmed that he was seen later by Ascanius and certain others above the bank of the Numicius with the same garb and weapons in which he had advanced to battle. This event confirmed the rumour of his immortality.' Maybe this was, as Banchich thought, 'a sort of inside joke for the amusement of ... learned readers'; or, perhaps, there were those in Rome who, though unwilling to give up their Classical beliefs, had developed an appetite for Christianity's promises of an afterlife that included bodily resurrection. In this version, Aeneas, like Jesus, died, but did not die; when he rose up into Heaven he did so as a living man, who had overcome death. Had history turned out only slightly differently, maybe Christianity would have withered away, and the promises of resurrection and eternal life for all may have become the province of Aeneas alone.

Today, Aeneas really does dwell in the heavens. When, in the early twentieth century, German astronomers were discovering the asteroids which orbit the sun on the same plane as Jupiter, they found that they fell into two groups, on opposite sides of the Solar System. Jupiter is the Roman name for Zeus, so they named one group of these asteroids after Greek heroes of the Trojan War, and the other after Trojans. One of the latter group of asteroids, some 88 miles across and discovered by Carl Rijnmut in 1930, is called Aeneas.

Aeneas's voyage from Antandros, his battles in Italy and his ultimately Christ-like apotheosis into Heaven exist only in literature and in our imaginations. So, too, does quite a lot, though surely not all, of what we know about Aeneas's earlier life. It results from layer upon layer of mythologizing, which this biography has attempted to chronicle and understand. Yet, during our journey, we have encountered surprisingly hard, physical evidence at the root of Aeneas's myths. The myths about the Great Mother, which fed into the story of Dardanos's mother Elektra, go back to an actual rock, around which the Sanctuary of the Great Gods on Samothraki grew up. Using a magnet, we have felt the pull from the patch of this sacred stone that was struck, long ago, by lightning. The myths of Aeneas's birth on Mount Ida appear to go back to similarly magnetised rocks on Büyük, next to a plausible site for Palaiskepsis. We have witnessed the effect of pieces of magnetised rock from the same hill on the needle of a compass. Magna Mater, another Anatolian manifestation of the same deity, was taken to Rome in the form of a rock which very likely possessed a similar, actual, magnetic force. The birth of Aeneas's mother, Aphrodite, was said to have been caused by the severed penis of Uranos dropping into the foaming sea. We have touched the actual meteorite, in the museum on the site of Aphrodite's temple at Palaipaphos on Cyprus, that appears to have caused the myth. The myth of Julius Caesar's ascension into Heaven was caused by a real comet which passed over Rome at the time of his funeral games. The interpretations placed on rocks struck by lightning, and rocks hurtling through the heavens or falling to Earth, exist only in human minds, but their actual, physical power is anything but imaginary.

We have seen, time and again on our journey, how geography seems to invite mythological interpretation and then support its conclusions. The Drepanum peninsula near Eryx, Sicily and the Drepanum peninsula near Palaipaphos, Cyprus look like the giant sickle which Kronos used to sever Uranos's penis. Büyük and Küçük together look like the twin breasts of the Great Mother. Mounts Eryx on Sicily, and Vikles behind Amathous on Cyprus, resemble single breasts, again inspiring thoughts of goddess-worship. The adjacent islands of Rheneia and Delos look, from across the sea, like the recumbent Titaness Asteria, from whose body they were imagined to have been formed. And it is almost impossible to gaze up at Olympus, whose peaks seem to rise up and up for ever until they pierce the sky, without willingly suspending any disbelief that, right up there in the golden clouds, live the Olympian gods.

The ruins on Küçük which Professor Cook identified as Aeneas's home city of Palaiskepsis are tangible and real, albeit frustratingly unexcavated. But the ruins of Troy have been studied intensively, both the acropolis (also called the Pergamos), and also, increasingly, the lower city, with its double-ditched defences. Around Troy, many of the landmarks identified in Homer's *Iliad*, from the ford in the Skamander to the burial mounds of the Trojan and Greek heroes, can be identified. The Greek camp's great defensive ditch, now called the 'Kesik Canal', remains impressive in scale, over 3,000 years after it was used to halt the chariots of Aeneas and his compatriots. These physical survivals make it ever more likely that there was a real Agamemnon, a real Achilles, a real Aeneas, however much their stories were embellished after their deaths.

It was the interaction of human minds with the physical world that ignited our ancestors' imaginations and inspired them to create myths about deities and heroes. Tales about real events and wars went into the mix to generate complex, multi-layered mythological careers for heroes such as Aeneas. These myths still speak to us today of human aspirations for glory; for love; for a safe home; for a happy afterlife. This same human imagination, once ignited, continued to burn long after belief in these myths had started to wane; it led to the birth of scientific enquiry and of our modern, scientific understanding of the universe. Yet, as long as science cannot stop us dying, we continue to look for solace. And at the pivotal point between Christianity and the myths of the Classical world, we find Aeneas, holding the golden bough he found by Lake Avernus, that allowed him to unlock the secrets of the afterlife. Aeneas, whose piety, loyalty, endurance, fortitude and determination in the face of adversity, can still serve as an inspiration to us all.

Ovid described how Aeneas was transformed into a god, but even he did not presume to follow him on his ascent into Heaven. Later artists, however, did. Peter Candid (c. 1548-1628) depicted Aeneas, naked save for a green drape, late middle-aged but still muscular, his bearded head just a little Christ-like, stepping up out of Numicius's waters. His mother Aphrodite, virtually nude save for a few gold adornments and a scrap of casually draped pink cloth, leans forward from her golden chariot to anoint him. Above the clouds, we see a great circle of distant, golden deities, including Poseidon, pointing down to Aeneas, and in their number is a figure in Imperial armour, perhaps Aeneas, depicted again, translated into Heaven. Above all, amidst rainbow colours, sits Zeus, enthroned in glory.

Giovanni Battista Tiepolo (1696-1770) pictured Aeneas clad in red, being borne aloft by winged Victory towards the gods, particularly Hera and Aphrodite, seated on clouds, while Zeus is half veiled from our sight in the background. Francois Boucher (1703-1770) depicted Aeneas in a sumptuous blue robe. Bare-breasted Aphrodite, partly clothed in pale blue and white, holds her son's gleaming helm behind his head. She is young and beautiful and Aeneas also is restored to the bloom of youth. Aeneas stares, wonderstruck, up past the naked gods to the Olympian throne, where Zeus glances fondly at his sister-wife Hera, who in turn gazes down on Aeneas, without any remaining trace of animosity.

Such apotheosis scenes were adapted, many times over, in Western art. The ceiling of the Banqueting House in Whitehall depicts the apotheosis of James I, who united England and Scotland under his rule. The rotunda ceiling in the United States Capitol building in Washington D.C. shows, likewise, the apotheosis of the republic's founder, George Washington. There are many more examples. Each sought to arrogate to their patrons the nation-building kudos of Aeneas.

Another depiction of Aeneas's apotheosis appears in a print in the British Museum by Nicolas Tardieu, after a picture by Marc Nattier (1642-1705).[6] It shows Hades, seated on a dark cloud, watching Aphrodite stepping out of her chariot and presenting her son to the other Olympian gods. Eros and two other cherubs bear Aeneas's sword and helm. Aeneas himself, in full armour, kneels on the dark cloud on which he is ascending, his arms outspread in reverence as he draws ever closer to the pantheon, seated on pale clouds that swirl around Zeus enthroned on his eagle. What thoughts fill a newly immortal mind? Perhaps, remembering his early childhood, he is content simply to bask in the loving presence of his divine mother.

In the drawing, we can see beyond Zeus to what Aeneas sees, as his eyes adjust, and as he discovers what it feels like to be immortal, eternal. For at this moment Aeneas perceives that which defines the gods, and which also came before, and lies beyond them; that first-born essence of the universe, of existence, of everything: Light.

Aeneas's family tree

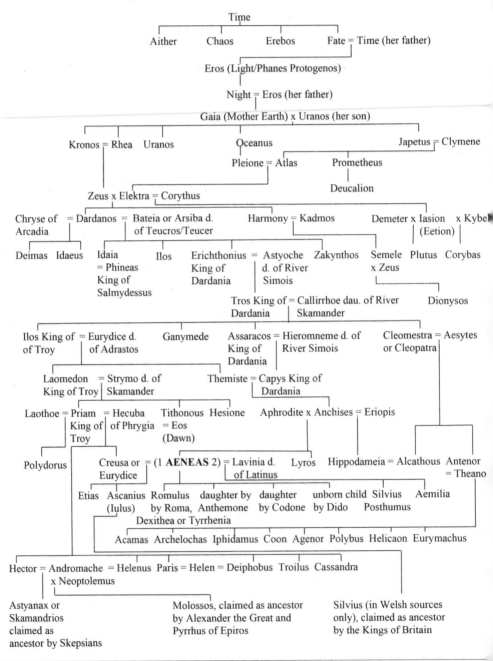

Aeneas and the rulers of Rome

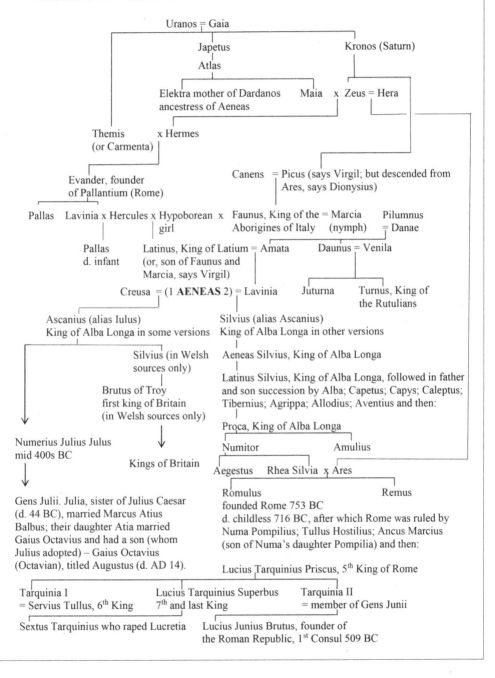

Select Timeline

BC	
3500	Troy 0
c. 3100	First cuneiform writing in Uruk, the city of Gilgamesh
2920-2550	Troy I
2550-2250	Troy II
2250-2200	Troy III
2200-1730	Troy IV/V
c. 1750	Collapse of Minoan civilisation on Crete and rise of Mycenaean (Achaean) power on mainland Greece
1730-1250	Troy VI
1360-1344	Reign of Tudhalija III, Hittite Great King
1344-1322	Reign of Suppiluliuma I, Hittite Great King
1322-1321	Reign of Arunwanda II, Hittite Great King
1321-1295	Reign of Mursili II, Hittite Great King
1295-1272	Reign of Muwatalli II, Hittite Great King
1274/5	Dardanians served in the Hittite army at the Battle of Qadesh
1272-1267	Reign of Mursili III, Hittite Great King
1267-1237	Reign of Hattusili III, Hittite Great King
c. 1250	Likely date of the Trojan War according to modern scholarship (as opposed to the more traditional estimate of 1194-1184 by Eratosthenes, *et al*)
1250-1140	Troy VIIa: last occupation of Troy by Trojans
c. 1175	Sack of Hattusa, end of Hittite Empire
1140-950	Troy VIIb: Troy occupied by Balkan peoples
753 BC	Traditional date for founding of Rome
c. 735	Homer's *Iliad*, by Janko's dating (but Herodotus thought c. 850, and some think as late as c. 670)
c. 725	Homer's Odyssey, by Janko's dating

Select Timeline

c. 700	Hesiod's *Theogony* (c. 780 is also suggested; the last lines, mentioning Aeneas, were added by another hand c. 680-650)
700-785	Troy VIII: Greek Ilion
700s	Euboean Greeks settling in southern Italy and visiting Rome
580-520	*Catalogue of Women* (by West's dating)
555	Death of Stesichorus
540-525	Aeneas on vases found in Etruria, especially Vulci
509	Expulsion of last Tarquin king and start of Roman Republic
499-449	Persian Wars; Trojans start being depicted in Greek art as effeminate easterners
c. 490-405	Hellanikos of Lesvos, first writer to claim that Aeneas founded Rome
484	Temple to Pollux and Castor in Rome
400s	Votive statuettes of Aeneas and Anchises in Veii, Etruria
338	Treaty between Rome and Lavinium
396	Rome captures Veii
356-323	Alexander the Great
c. 300s	Menecrates writes of Aeneas as traitor to Troy
318-272	Pyrrhus of Epiros
c. 270s	Likely adoption of Aeneas myth in Rome
264-1	First Punic War
c. 270-201	Naevius, author of *Bellum Punicum*
c. 239-169	Ennius, author of *Annales*
218-201	Second Punic War (Hannibal)
217	Cult of Venus Erycina introduced to Rome.
204	Magna Mater (Kybele) brought to Rome
c. 200	Pseudo-Apollodorus's *Bibliotheka*
200-197	Second Macedonian War
149-6	Third Punic War
146	Rome annexes Macedonia, with protectorate extending over the rest of Greece (which was formally incorporated into the Empire in 27 BC)
116-27	Varro
85	Start of Troy IX: Roman Ilium
70 (15 October)	Birth of Virgil
64	Birth of Strabo (d. AD 24)
c. 60-30	Diodorus Siculus writes his *Bibliotheka Historia*
58	Caesar invades Gaul
55 and 54	Caesar's two failed invasions of Britain
c. 54	Birth of Dionysius of Halicarnassus (died post 7 BC)
59	Birth of Livy (died AD 17)

44	Caesar assassinated
43	Birth of Ovid (died AD 17/8)
31	Augustus defeats Antony and Cleopatra at Actium
19 (21 September)	Death of Virgil

AD

14	Death of Augustus
33/34	Crucifixion of Jesus
c. 500	Start of Troy X: Byzantine Ilium
600s	Brutus of Troy's myth begins in Britain
820s	Nennius's *Historia Brittonum*, makes Brutus into a great-grandson of Aeneas
c. 1135	Geoffrey of Monmouth's *History of the Kings of Britain* develops Brutus's story
1810	Byron visits Troy
1868	Heinrich Schliemann starts excavating Troy
1998	Troy becomes a UNESCO Cultural Heritage of the World site
2004	*Troy* movie released in cinemas
2015	Publication of my book *Brutus of Troy*
2023	Publication of my book *In Search of Aeneas*

Acknowledgements

I am deeply indebted to Scott Crowley, who accompanied me on all my journeys, and to the many people who have encouraged and helped me, including the following: Michael Alcock; Mustafa Aşkin (the Troy Guide); Sabina Basile (Lavinium Museum); Tanmoy Bhattacharya; Professor Mary Beard; Mark Bonthrone; Dean Bubier; Uğur Candar (Antandros); Sheila Cohen (Friends of Troy); Professor James E. Crimmins; Nick Crowe; Mr Erhan (Zeytinbagi Hotel); James Essinger; John Galani; Eleanor Ghey (British Museum); Dr Harry Gouvas (Preveza); Francesco Graziani of the Soprintendenza per i beni Archeologici del Lazio; Alistair Hogarth; Mirka Konstantirides; Raimond Kola director of Butrint; Petros Koutoupis; Andrew Lownie; George Logothetys; Trevor McCallum; John D. McLaughlin; Dr Stuart Needham, British Museum; Guglielmo Parisani (Brindisi); Susan Payne; Jeff Saward (Labyrinthos); Andrew Shapland (British Museum); Miles Stephenson; John Townsend; Ann Walsh (Reef TV); Professor Calvert Watkins (Harvard); Dr Konstantina Zidrou, University of Ionannina, and many other people, some mentioned in the text, some not. I am grateful to you all. Thank you also to Richard Sutton, Shaun Barrington, Alex Bennett and Connor Stait of Amberley Publishing for their enthusiasm for, and care of, the manuscript in its journey to publication.

Endnotes

Introduction
1. Hardie, p. 78

1 Love Story on Mount Ida
1. British Museum, item 1814,0704.916

2 Anchises' City
1. Strabo, 13.1.51
2. Strabo, 13.1.52
3. Cook, p. 301
4. Cook, p. 302

3 The Great Mother
1. Joseph of Exeter, lines 510-11
2. Frymer-Kensky, p. 52
3. Frymer-Kensky, p. 52
4. Hughes (2005/2013), pp. 78-9
5. Gurney, p. 149
6. Vermaseren, p. 14
7. Cook, p. 300

4 Lightning on Rock
1. Bates et al.
2. Vermaseren, p. 30

5 The Sons of Dardanos
1. West, 1985, p. 136
2. Gurney, pp. 27, 47
3. Servius, *ad Aeneid*, 3.167
4. Pseudo-Apollodorus, *Bibliotheka*, 3.12
5. Aristotle, *De Anima*, 2. 405.20: Reeve (2017), p. 12
6. Pseudo-Apollodorus, *Bibliotheka*, 3.12
7. Strabo, 13.1.48
8. Dion. Hal. 1.61
9. Leaf (1912), p. 143
10. Pseudo-Apollodorus, *Bibliotheka*, 3.12.2

6 The Hill of Ate
1. Joseph of Exeter, lines 519-522
2. Pseudo-Apollodorus, *Bibliotheka*, 3.12.3
3. Plato, *Laws*, 3.677-8

7 Searching for Troy
1. Marchand, pp. 8.21-2

8 The Centaur's Cave
1. Gurney, p. 53
2. Pseudo-Apollodorus, *Bibliotheka*, 3.12.2
3. Luce, p.131
4. Scherer, figure 29
5. Joseph of Exeter, lines 72-5
6. Pausanias, 10.26.1

9 Journey to Sparta
1. As quoted in West, *Epic Fragments*, p. 65
2. Strabo, 9.5.13
3. Carl Blegen, quoted in Wood, M., p. 119
4. Wood, M., p. 120

10 The Rape of Helen
1. Herodotus, 6.61
2. Pausanias, 13.9.9
3. Galinsky, plate 108, in Berlin
4. Galinsky, plate 36, in the Bibliothèque Nationale, Paris
5. Hampe and Simon, p. 42
6. As quoted in Guthrie, pp. 74-5
7. Calasso, p. 100
8. Galinsky, plate 37, in Boston, Massachusetts
9. Galinsky, p. 41
10. Galinsky, plate 37, in Berlin
11. Galinsky, plate 109
12. Galinsky, p. 129
13. Hughes (2005/2013), p. 155
14. Pausanias, 3.22.1-2

11 The Princes at Large
1. Herodotus, 1.105
2. Xenophon, *Hellenika*, 4.8.7.
3. Pausanias, 3.23.1
4. Scherer, figure 24 B, in Metropolitan Museum of Art, New York
5. Scherer, figure 34, in Walters Art Gallery, Baltimore
6. Scherer, figure 3, in Metropolitan Museum of Art, New York
7. Pseudo-Apollodorus, *Bibliotheka*, epitome, 3.13.1
8. Herodotus, 1.105
9. Hughes (2019), p. 30
10. Herodotus, 2. 112-120
11. Herodotus 2. 113
12. Earl of Sandwich, p. 435
13. Herodotus 2. 115

12 The War Begins
1. Giorgos Serefis, 'Helen', 1953'.
2. Tzetzes, *ad Lycophron*, 467, as quoted by Hornblower, p. 227
3. *Iliad* 15, 18 and 23
4. Luce, p. 144
5. Hughes (2005/2013), p. 192

13 The Blind Poet
1. Latacz, p. 205
2. Apollonius of Rhodes, *Argonautica*, 1, 936, ff.
3. Wood, M., p. 246

14 Musters and Raids
1. Latacz, pp. 244-5
2. Strabo 13.1.7
3. Leaf (1912) pp. 198-252
4. Leaf (1912), p. 270
5. Leaf (1912), pp. 217-8
6. Cook, p. 305
7. In *Iliad* 6, 9 and 23 respectively
8. Leaf (1912), p. 245
9. Strabo, 13.1.61
10. Leaf (1912), p. 219

15 'Men that Strove with Gods'
1. Strabo, 13.1.48
2. Galinsky, pp. 36-7
3. Galinsky, p. 37
4. Pausanias, 5.22.3
5. Galinsky, plate 102; in Boston
6. Galinsky, plate 105; in Wurzburg
7. Galinksy, plate 33
8. British Museum, item 1916,0411.68
9. British Museum, item 1864,1007.1685: Galinsky plate 9
10. Galinsky, p. 15
11. Galinsky, plate 104, in Thorvaldsen Museum, Copenhagen

16 Aeneas and Cressida
1. Galinsky, plate 14, in the Louvre
2. Galinsky, plate 97, in Munich
3. British Museum, item 1837,0609.69
4. Galinsky, plate 98, in Florence

5. Dares, 21-22
6. Luce, p. 115
7. Luce, p. 134
8. Luce, p. 125
9. Thornton, p. 150
10. Schliemann, *Ilios*, p. 93
11. Leaf (1912), p. 12
12. Luce, p. 19

17 The Battle by the Ships

1. Galinsky, plate 32, third line from the bottom of the *Tabula Iliaca*
2. Galinsky, plate 32, bottom line of the *Tabula Iliaca*
3. Galinsky, plate 106, in the Vatican
4. Galinsky, pp. 17-8
5. Galinsky, plate 103, in Berlin
6. Galinsky, plate 12

18 Aeneas Faces Achilles

1. Cook, p. 169
2. Galinsky, plate 99, in Copenhagen
3. Galinsky, p. 127
4. Galinsky, plate 22
5. Scherer, p. 182
6. Reinhardt, p. 380
7. British Museum, item 1867,0508.1333: Galinsky plate 42
8. Hild, p. 48
9. Cook, p. 145
10. Days numbered according to Latacz's system (p. 193)

19 Defender or Traitor?

1. Galinsky, plate 95, now in Munich
2. Galinsky, plate 97, now lost
3. Dion. Hal., 1.48
4. Scherer, plate 87
5. Joseph of Exeter, lines 674-7
6. Joseph of Exeter, lines 694-7, 710

20 The Fall of Troy

1. Calasso, p. 22

2. Veronese scholiast on the A*eneid*, 2.717, as quoted in Peter, 1.96
3. Dion. Hal., 1.46
4. According to Tzetzes' commentary on Lycophron's *Alexandra*, as quoted in West (2003), p. p 139-141 (and confirmed also in Simmias of Rhodes).
5. Dion. Hal., 1.46
6. Veronese scholiast on the A*eneid*, 2.717; see Peter, 1.96
7. Aelian, *Varia Historia*, 3.22, quoted in Galinsky, p. 57
8. Vatican *Epitome* to pseudo-Apollodorus, *Bibliotheka*, 21.19
9. Dictys, 5
10. Scherer, plate 167

21 Of Fire and Flood

1. Williams, p. 36
2. *Pall Mall Budget*, 28 June 1878, p. 21.
3. Shakespeare, *Hamlet*, 2.2
4. British Library, Harley MS 2472f. 19b, 2.567-588, in the cited by Hughes (2005/1013), p. 275
5. Fagles, introduction to his translation of the *Aeneid*, p. 12
6. British Museum, item 1865,1111.226
7. Hardie, p. 78
8. Galinsky, plate 388, in Boston, Massachusetts
9. Galinsky, plate 91, in the Vatican
10. Galinsky, plate 41c, from the Navarra collection in Gela, Sicily
11. Galinsky plate 92
12. British Museum, item 1836,0224.137
13. Galinsky, plate 94, now at Syracuse
14. Galinsky, plate 90, once in Munich
15. Galinsky, plates 41a and 41b, now in the Acropolis Museum, Athens
16. Tiberius Claudius Donatus, ed. H. Georgii, Leipzig, 1905-6, quoted in Galinsky p. 51
17. British Museum, 1877,0609.1731
18. Galinsky, plate 93

Endnotes

19. British Museum, item 1836,0224.138
20. Pausanias, 10.25-6
21. Kazantzakis, p. 392
22. Calasso, pp. 358-9
23. Fragmenta Historicorum Graecorum (FHG) 2 F 39, quoted by Galinsky p. 46
24. Genesis, 6.1–4

22 Aeneas, King of Troy?

1. Joseph of Exeter, lines 886-8
2. Strabo, 13.1.53
3. Dion. Hal., 1.53
4. Latacz, pp. 112-3
5. Quoted by Leaf (1912), p. 195
6. Dion. Hal., 1.47
7. Dion. Hal., 1.47-8
8. Strabo, 13.1.52
9. Dionysios of Chalkis, quoted in the scholion on Eurypides's *Andromache* 10, as quoted in turn by Smith (1981), p. 36 note 22
10. Smith (1981), p. 397.
11. Cook, p. 274

23 'I Fared Forth to the Deep'

1. Coin code: Triton XI. 478
2. Dion. Hal., 1.47-8
3. Joseph of Exeter, lines 889-894
4. Williams, p. 28
5. Williams, p. 31
6. In *Aeneid* 4, 5 and 12 respectively.
7. Galinsky, plates 106, 14, 392, 97
8. Galinsky, plate 103, from Vulci
9. Galinsky, plate 37
10. Galinsky, plate 36a
11. Berlin Staatsbibliothek Preussucher Kulturbesitz, ms germ. F. 282, sheet LIIIr.
12. British Museum, item 1946,0713.282
13. Critolaus, as reported by Festus
14. As reported by the Veronese scholiast on *Aeneid* 2.717: see Peter, 1.96
15. Servius, *ad. Aeneid* 7.207
16. Servius, *ad. Aeneid* 8.679
17. Servius, *ad. Aeneid* 3.287
18. Perret, pp. 24-31
19. Dion. Hal., 1.61
20. Diodorus Siculus, 5.47
21. *Aeneid* 2.

24 'Seek ye Your Mother of Old'

1. Fragmenta Historicorum Graecorum (FHG) 4 F 31, cited by Galinsky p. 111
2. Galinsky, plate 87
3. British Museum, item 1840,0921.260
4. Dion. Hal., 1.49
5. Dion. Hal., 1.49
6. Strabo, 13.1.54
7. Dion. Hal., 1.50
8. Dion. Hal., 1.50
9. Pausanias, 3.22.11-13
10. Dion. Hal., 1.50
11. Dion. Hal., 1.49
12. Pausanias, 8.12.8-9
13. Pausanias, 8.36.3
14. Dion. Hal., 1.61
15. Galinsky, p. 110
16. Pausanias, 6.2.4
17. Pausanias, 7.19.7
18. Dion. Hal., 1.50

25 Encounter at Buthrotum

1. Dion. Hal., 1.50
2. Appian, *The Civil Wars*, 2.16
3. Dion Hal., 1.50
4. Dion. Hal., 1.51

26 Via Enea

1. Dion. Hal., 1.51
2. Strabo, 6.3.5
3. Scherer, plate 168, in the Metropolitan Museum of Art, New York
4. *La Repubblica*, 26 April 2007, national report p. 37
5. Strabo, 6.1.14

6. Strabo, 6.1.13
7. Galinsky, plate 24
8. Galinsky, p. 30

27 Landfall in Africa
1. Galinsky, p. 93 ff
2. Galinsky, pp. 96-7
3. Pindar, *Pythian Odes*, 5. 82
4. Herodotus, 4.191.1
5. Dion. Hal., 1.22
6. Thucydides, *History of the Peloponnesian War*, 6.2.3
7. Galinsky, p. 89, ff
8. Levi, p. 149
9. British Museum, item 1957,1214.186
10. In Yale University Art Gallery

28 Aeneas and Dido
1. *Roman d'Eneas*, lines 1200-1235
2. British Museum, item 1880,0313.21
3. British Museum, item 1859,0709.12
4. Galinsky, plate 26, from house Regio IX, Pompeii
5. Scherer, plate 171
6. British Museum, item 1874,1212.111
7. Williams, p. 17
8. Williams, p. 62

29 Aeneas in Despair
1. Galinsky, p. 189
2. Servius, *ad Aeneid*, 4.682; 5.4
3. Lycophron, *Alexandra*, 951-78
4. Dion. Hal., 1.53
5. Connolly, pp. 126-138

30 The Posillipo Hill
1. Dion. Hal. 1.53
2. *Catalepton 5*
3. Suetonius, *Life of Virgil*
4. Williams, 16-17
5. Dion. Hal., 1.53

6. *Origo Gentis Romanae*, quoting *Pontifical Affairs*
7. British Museum, item SL,5237.55

31 Aeneas in the Underworld
1. Williams, p. 45
2. British Museum, item 1949,1008.219
3. British Museum, item 1968,1012.22
4. Williams, p. 48
5. Livy, 1.16
6. Williams, p. 68
7. Hardie, p. 27
8. Scherer, p. 205

32 At Tiber's Mouth
1. Dion. Hal 1.53
2. Dion. Hal. 1.64
3. Knight, p. 73
4. Stehle, p. 587
5. Dion. Hal., 1.73
6. Galinsky, p. 139
7. Dion. Hal., 1.71
8. Galinsky, p. 139
9. Livy, 5.1-25
10. Dion. Hal., 1.72
11. *Fragmenta Historicorum Graecorum* (FHG) 560 F 4
12. Dion. Hal., 1.72
13. Servius, *ad Aeneid*, 1.273
14. Dion. Hal., 1.55
15. Galinsky, plate 18
16. As retold by Solinus, 2.14, in the AD 200s, and quoted by Galinsky, p. 115
17. Servius, *ad Aeneid*, 1.720

33 Aeneas in Latium
1. Hoffmann, pp. 123-6
2. Galinsky, p. 160
3. Pausanias, 1.21.1
4. Galinsky, p. 171-2
5. Levi, pp. 186-7
6. Levi, p. 197
7. Dion. Hal., 1.31

8. Dion. Hal., 1.43
9. Levi, p. 208
10. Galinsky, plates 122 and 123
11. Dion. Hal., 1.64
12. Hardie, p. 66

34 Arrival in Rome

1. Aelian, *de Natura Animalium*, 10.50, quoted in Galinsky, p. 174
2. Galinsky, p. 187
3. Suetonius, *Life of Claudius*, 25.3
4. Justinus, *Epitome of the Philippic History of Pompeius Trogus*, 28.1
5. Livy, 37.37.3
6. Dion. Hal., 1.73
7. Galinsky, p. 170
8. Ovid, *Fasti*, 4.893-4
9. Galinsky, p. 190
10. Livy, 29.10.4-6, 11, 8-9
11. Beard, p. 44
12. Ovid, *Fasti* 4, 247, ff
13. Appian, *The Civil Wars*, 1.97

35 The Shield of Aeneas

1. Galinsky, plate 45, in Munich
2. Galinsky, plate 44
3. Galinsky, p. 127 and plate 99
4. Galinsky, pp. 131-9
5. Galinsky, plate 111.
6. Scherer, plate 183, in the Art Gallery of Toronto
7. D.H. Lawrence, p. 34
8. Servius, *ad Aeneid*, 7.207
9. Diodorus Siculus, 5.49.2
10. Buchheit, p. 166
11. Servius, *ad Aeneid*, 3.170
12. Silius, *Punica*, 4.718, 5.122

36 The Trojan War Replayed

1. Williams, p. 54
2. Ovid, *Fasti*, 4.893-4
3. British Museum, item 1858,0417.1517
4. Ovid, *Fasti*, 4.893-4

37 Aeneas versus Turnus

1. Suetonius, *Life of Julius* Caesar, 6.1
2. Dio Cassius, *Roman History*, 43.43.3
3. In *Sylloge Inscriptionum Graecarum*, 760, as quoted by Galinsky, p. 233
4. Galinsky plates 162, 163, in the Louvre
5. Appian, *The Civil Wars*, 2.76
6. Lucan, *Civil War*, 9: 1176-1243
7. By Wenceslaus Hollar, after Francis Cleyn: British Museum, print Q,4.180

38 The Unresolved Dilemma

1. Lactantius, *Divine Institutes*, 5.10
2. Robert Faggles, quoted in Charles McGrath, 'Translating Virgil's Epic Poem of Empire', *New York Times*, 30 October 2006
3. Hardie, p. 83
4. Hardie, p. 84
5. Lucan, *Civil War*, 9: 1237
6. Erdemoğlu, p. 60
7. Seutonius, *Life of Virgil*
8. Broch, pp. 11-12
9. As quoted by Seutonius, *Life of Virgil*
10. Seutonius, *Life of Virgil*
11. Levi, p. 1
12. Galinsky, p. 153
13. For example, British Museum items R.9140; 1864,1128.23, etc
14. Galinsky, plate 6
15. British Museum, item 1978,0603.1. An almost identical one is in the Kestner Museum, Hanover; Galinsky plate 5
16. Galinsky, pp. 190, 192
17. Galinsky, p. 241

39 The Marriage of Aeneas and Lavinia

1. Galinsky plate 16, in Città Castellana Cathedral
2. Dion. Hal., 1.64

3. Galinsky, plate 121
4. Scherer, p. 215
5. Berlin's state library, cod.germ. fol.282, 69: Scherer, plate 184
6. By 'the Master of the Tournament of Santa Croce', Musée de Cluny, Paris, item 1710: Scherer plate 185
7. Livy 8.11.15 (see Galinsky p. 147)
8. Galinsky, p. 143
9. Galinsky, p. 141
10. *Fragmenta Historicorum Graecorum* (FHG) 26 F1
11. Dion. Hal., 1.67
12. Varro, in *On the Latin Language*, 5.144
13. Dion. Hal., 1.67-8
14. Livy, 5.40.7-8
15. Galinsky, p. 156
16. Ovid, *Metamorphoses*, 15.450
17. Servius, *ad Aeneid*, 3.12
18. Dion. Hal., 1.68
19. As quoted by the Veronese scholiast on *Aeneid* 2.717
20. Dion. Hal., 1.68-9
21. Pseudo-Apollodorus, *Bibliotheka*, 3.12

40 The Shrine by the Numicius

1. Dion. Hal., 1.64
2. Dion. Hal., 1.73
3. Galinsky, p. 142

41 Aeneas Indiges

1. Varro, *Antiquitates Rerum Divinarum*, 15, fr. 12

2. Dion. Hal., 1.64
3. Livy 1.2
4. Pliny, *Natural History*, 3.5.56, as quoted in Galinsky, p. 150
5. Galinsky, p. 166
6. Galinsky, p. 165
7. Galinsky, plates 125 and 128
8. Veronese scholiast on the *Aeneid*, 1.259, as quoted in Galinsky, p. 147
9. Livy, 1.16
10. Festus, 212 L, quoted by Galinsky, p. 144
11. Galinsky, plate 124
12. Galinsky, p. 66
13. Galinsky, plate 27
14. Galinsky, p. 31
15. Galinsky, plate 28
16. Galinsky, plate 30
17. British Museum, item 1844,1008.22
18. Galinsky, plate 7
19. Galinsky, p. 10
20. British Museum, items R.13472; 1896,0608.26; 1847,0709.1
21. British Museum, item CGR5620
22. British Museum, item 1911,1010.17

42 Apotheosis

1. Hardie, p. 128
2. Lactantius, *Divine Institutes*, 1.5.11
3. Hardie, p. 129
4. Hardie, pp. 127-8
5. Matthew 27:51; Mark, 15:33; Luke, 3:44
6. British Museum, item 1917,1208.2013

Bibliography

Ancient sources in translation
Apollonius Rhodius, *Argonautica*, Seaton (1912)
Appian, *The Civil Wars*: White (1899)
Arctinus of Miletus, *Aethiopis*: West (2003)
Aristotle, *De Anima* Reeve (2017)
Byron's letters: Marchand (1978)
Catalogue of Women: West (1985)
Colluthus of Lycopolis, *The Rape of Helen*: Mair (1928)
Cypria: West (2003)
Dares: Laurén (2012)
Dictys: Laurén (2012)
Dionysius of Halicarnassus, *Rhōmaikē archaiologia*: Cary (1937)
Dio Cassius, *Roman History*: Cary (1914-27)
Ennius, 'On the revival of Troy in Ilium' (trans. Dunlop, J.C.): Peter (1847)
Ennius, *Annales*: Warmington (1935)
Euripides, *Andromache*: Morwood (2000)
Excidium Troiae: Fadhlurrahman (n.d.).
Festus: Peter (1870)
Geoffrey of Monmouth, *De Gestis Britonum*: Reeve & Wright (2007)
Gilgamesh: Campbell Thompson (1928)
Hesiod's *Theogony*: Evelyn-White (1914)
Homer, *Iliad*: Butler (1898)
Homer, *Odyssey*: Rieu (1946)
Herodotus, *Histories*: Rawlinson (1996)
Hymn to Aphrodite, Evelyn-White (1914)
Hymns about Inanna: Frymer-Kensky (1992)
Inanna's descent into the nether world: Black et al (1998)
Joseph of Exeter, *Daretis PhrygiiIlias*: Rigg (2005)
Justinus, *Epitome of the Philippic History of Pompeius Trogus*: Yardley (1994)
Lactantius, *Divine Institutes*: Bowen (2003)

Lesches of Miletus, *Little Iliad*: West (2003)
Livy, *Ab Urbe Condita Libri*: Sélincourt (1960)
Lucan, *Bellum Civile*: Fox (2012)
Lycophron, *Alexandra*: Mair (1921) and Hornblower (2015)
Nonnos, *Dionysiaca*: Rouse (1940)
Origo Gentis Romanae: Haniszewski et al, 2004
Ovid, *Fasti*: Frazer (1931)
Ovid, *Heriodes*: Showerman (1914)
Ovid, *Metamorphoses*: Raeburn (2004)
Pindar, Pythian Odes: Gildersleeve (2010)
Pausanias, *Description of Greece*: Jones (2014)
Plato, *Laws*: Bury (1926)
Proclus, *Chrestomathy*: West (2003)
Pseudo-Apollodorus, *Bibliotheka*: Hard (1997)
Quintus Smyrnaeus, *The Fall of Troy*: Way (1913)
Roman d'Eneas: Yunck (1974)
Servius, *ad Aeneid*: Lion (1826)
Strabo: Jones (1917-1932)
Suetonius, *Lives of Julius Caesar; Claudius; Virgil*: Thomson (1889)
Thucydides, *History of the Peloponnesian War*: Hobbes (1843)
Varro, *On the Latin language*: Kent (1938).
Vegio, Maffeo, *Supplementum*, Twyne's 1584 translation: Brinton (1930)
Veronese scholiast on *Aeneid*: Peter (1870, 1906)
Virgil, *Aeneid*: Jackson (1908)
Virgil, *Catalepton*: Mooney (1916)
Virgil, *Eclogues* and *Georgics*: Fairclough (1916)
Xenophon, *Hellankia*: Brownson (1918-21)

Modern works

Adolph, Anthony, *Brutus of Troy, and the Quest for the Ancestry of the British* (Barnsley: Pen and Sword, 2015).
Allen, Thomas W., *The Homeric Catalogue of Ships* (Oxford: Clarendon Press, 1921).
Askin, Mustafa, *Troy: a revised edition* (Istanbul: Keskin Color Kartpostalcilik Ltd, 2007).
Auden, W.H., 'Secondary Epic' (1959), in Edward Mendleson, ed., *Collected Poems* (London: Random House, 1996).
Bates, C.R., Bates, M, Ganey, C., Ganey, V., and Raub, T.D., 'Geophysical Investigation of the Neolithic Calanais Landscape', *Remote Sensing*, 11 December 2019.
Beard, Mary; North, John; Price, Simon, *The Religions of Rome, Volume 2. A Sourcebook* (Cambridge: Cambridge University Press, 1998).
Bird, H.M., *Suetonius, Lives of the Twelve Caesars* (Ware: Wordsworth Classics of World Literature, 1997 (1930)).
Black, J.A., Cunningham, G., Ebeling, J., Flückiger-Hawker, E., Robson, E., Taylor, J., and Zólyomi, G., *The Electronic Text Corpus of Sumerian Literature* http://etcsl.orinst.ox.ac.uk/, Oxford (1998-).

Bibliography

Bowen, A and Garnsey, P., *Lactantius, Divine Institutes* (Liverpool: Liverpool University Press, 2003)

Bradford, Ernle, *Ulysses Found* (London: Century Publishing, 1985 (1964). Brinton, A.C., *Maphaeus Vegius and his Thirteenth Book of the Aeneid: A Chapter on Virgil in the Renaissance* (Stanford: Stanford University Press, 1930).

Broch, Hermann (trans. Jean Starr Untermeyer), *The Death of Virgil* (New York: Vintage International, 1945/1995).

Brownson, C.L., *Xenophon in Seven Volumes* (London: William Heinemann, 1918-21).

Bruschetti, Paolo and Giulierini, Paolo, *Museo ell'Accademia Etrusca e della Città di Cotona: a guide to the collections* (Cortona: MAEC, 2011).

Bruto, M.L., *Il Museo Archeologico Lavinium* (Rome: Forma Urbis. Itinerari Nascosti di Roma Antica, 2008).

Bruto, M.L., *Lavinium* (Rome: Forma Urbis. Itinerari Nascosti di Roma Antica, 2006).

Buchheit, V., *Vergil über die Sendung Roms. Untersuchungen zum Bellum Poenicum und zur Aeneis. Gymnasium Beihefte* 3 (Heidelberg, 1963).

Bury, R.G., *Plato. Laws*, Loeb Classical Library (Cambridge, MA: Harvard University Press, 1926).

Butler, Robert, *The Iliad of Homer, Rendered into English Prose for the use of those who cannot read the original* (London: Longmans, Green and Co., 1898): see also Fagles (1990).

C.D., *Brutus the Trojan, A Poem. Cantos I, II, III & IV* (London: Hamilton, Adams and Co., 1860).

Calasso, Roberto (Parks, Tim, trans.), *The Marriage of Cadmus and Harmony* (London: Vintage, 1994 (1988)).

Campbell Thompson, R. (trans.) *The Epic of Gilgamish* (sic) (Oxford: Clarendon Press, 1930).

Cary, E., (trans.), *Dio's Roman History*, Loeb Classical Library (London: William Heinemann, 1914-1927).

Cary, E. (trans.), *The Roman Antiquities of Dionysius of Halicarnassus*, Loeb Classical Library (London: William Heinemann, 1937).

Cary, H.F., Dante Alighieri, *The Divine Comedy* (Ware: Wordsworth Classics, 2009).

Castellan, Antoine-Laurent, *Lettres sur la Morée et les iles de Cérigo, Hydra et Zante* (Paris, 1820).

Ceka, Neritan (Xhelo, Pranvera, trans.), *Buthrotum, its history and monuments*, (Tiranë: Migjeni, n.d.).

Ceram, C.W. (trans. Garside, E.B. and Wilkins, S.), *Gods, Graves & Scholars, The story of archaeology* (London: Book Club Associates, 1971, 1949).

Coldstream, J.N. and Huxley, G.L. (eds), *Kythera, Excavations and Studies* (London: Faber and Faber Limited, 1972).

Conington, J., and Nettleship. H, *The Works of Virgil* (London: Whittaker & Co., 1858-71).

Connolly, C., *The Unquiet Grave* (London: Hamish Hamilton, 1973 (1944)).

Cook, J.M., *The Troad, an archaeological and topographical study* (Oxford: Oxford University Press, 1999 (1973)).

Cornell, T.J., *The Beginnings of Rome: Italy and Rome from the Bronze Age to the Punic Wars (c. 1000-264 BC)* (London and New York: Routledge, 1995).

Cornell, T.J. (ed), *The Fragments of the Roman Historians*, vol. 3 (Oxford: Oxford University Press, 2013).

Cotterill, H.B., *Ancient Greece, Myth & History* (New Lanark: Geddes & Grosset 2004 (1913)).

Eliot, T.S., 'What is a Classic?' (address to the founding meeting of the Virgil Society, 1944) (London: Faber, 1944).

Erdemoğlu, Bülent, *Troy and Surrounding Areas* (Uranos Travel Guide, 2015).

Ergen, Yüksel (trans. Ender Gürol), *The Ancient City of Troy: the past and the present* (Istanbul: Mas Matbaacilik Sanayi ve Ticaret A.S., 2014).

Evelyn-White, H.G. (trans.), *Hesiod, Homeric Hymns, Epic Cycle, Homerica*, Loeb Classical Library (1914) (Cambridge MA: Harvard University Press, 1995) (see also West (1988 and 2003)

Fadhlurrahman, M.S., (trans.), *Excidium Troiae or Destruction of Troy* (n.d.) on us.archive.org.

Fagles, R. (trans.), *Virgil, The Aeneid* (London: Penguin Books, 2006)

Fagles, Robert (trans.) *Homer: The Iliad* (London: Viking Penguin, 1990).

Fairclough, H. R., *Virgil. Eclogues. Georgics. Aeneid: Books 1-6.*, Loeb Classical Library (London: William Heinemann, 1916).

Farnell, L.R., *The Cults of the Greek States*, vol. 2 (Oxford: Clarendon Press, 1896).

Fowler, W. Warde, *Aeneas at the site of Rome* (Oxford: Basil Blackwell, 1931).

Fox, M. (trans.), *Lucan, Civil War* (New York: Penguin Books, 2012).

Frazer, J.G., *Ovid. Fasti*, Loeb Classical Library (London: William Heinemann, 1931).

Frymer-Kensky, T., *In the Wake of the Goddesses: women, culture and biblical transformations of pagan myth* (New York: Fawcet Columbine, 1992).

Galinsky, G.K., *Aeneas, Sicily, and Rome* (Princeton, NJ: Princeton Univerisity Press, 1969).

George, A., (trans), *The Epic of Gilgamesh* (London: Penguin Books, 1999).

Ghali-Kahil, L., *Les enlèvements et le retour d'Hélène* (Paris: École française d'Athènes, 1955).

Gildersleeve, B.L., *Pindar: Olympian and Pythian Odes* (London: Macmillan, 1890, repr. Cambridge University Press, 2010).

Graves, Robert, *The poems of Robert Graves: chosen by himself* (New York: Doubleday, 1958).

Gurney, Oliver. R., *The Hittites* (London: Penguin, 1952).

Guthrie, W.K.C., *Orpheus and Greek Religion* (London: Methuen, 1935).

Hamilton, H.C., and Falconer, W., *The Geography of Strabo, literally translated, with notes, the first six books* (Henry G. Bohn, 1856).

Hampe, R., *Frühe griechische Sagenbilder in Böotien* (Athens: Deutsches Archaeologisches Institut, 1936).

Hampe, R., and Simon, E., *Griechische Sagen in der fruhen etruskischen Kunst* (Mainz, 1964).

Haniszewski, K., Karas, L., Koch, K., Parobek, E., Pratt, C and Serwicki, B., (translators), Banchich, T.M. (into.), *The Origin of the Roman Race [Origo Gentis Romanae]* (New York, Canisius College Translated Texts 3, 2004).

Hard, Robin (ed.), *Apollodorus, The Library of Greek Mythology* (Oxford: Oxford University Press, 1997).

Hardie, P., *The Last Trojan Hero: A cultural history of Virgil's Aeneid* (London: I.B. Tauris, 2014).

Bibliography

Hercher, R., *Claudii Aeliani de natura animalium libri xvii, varia historia, epistolae, fragmenta*, vol. 2 (Leipzig: in Aedibus B.G. Teubneri, 1866).

Hild, J.A., *La Legende d'Enée avant Virgil* (Paris: Librairie E. Leroux, 1884).

Hobbes, Thomas (trans.), *Thucydides*, in *The English works of Thomas Hobbes of Malmesbury* (London: John Bohn, 1843).

Holliday, Peter J., 'The rhetoric of "*Romanitas*": the "Tomb of the Statilii" frescoes reconsidered', *Memoirs of the American Academy in Rome*, 50, 2005, pp. 89-129).

Homer, *Odyssey*: Rieu, E.V. (trans.), *The Odyssey* (Harmondsworth: Penguin Books, 1946).

Hope-Simpson, R, and Lazenby, J.F., 'The Kingdom of Peleus and Achilles', *Antiquity*, 33 (1959, pp 102-105).

Hornblower, S. (trans.), *Lykophron, Alexandra* (Oxford: Oxford University Press, 2015).

Horsfall, N., 'Corythus re-examined', *Bulletin of the Institute of Classical Studies* suppl. 52 (1987, pp. 89-104) (developing his earlier 'Corythus: the return of Aeneas in Virgil and his sources', *JRS* 63, 1973).

Horsfall, N.M., 'The Aeneas-legend from Homer to Virgil', Bremmer, J.N., and Horsfall, N.M., *No. 52, Roman Myth and Mythography* (Bulletin Supplement, University of London, Institute of Classical Studies, 1987, pp. 12-24).

Hughes, Bettany, *Helen of Troy: goddess, princess, whore* (Cape, 2005/London: Pimlico 2013).

Hughes, Bettany, *Venus & Aphrodite: history of a goddess* (London: Weidenfeld & Nicolson, 2019).

Jackson, J. (trans.), *Virgil, The Aeneid* (Oxford: Clarendon Press, 1908). See also Fagles (2006).

Jones, H.L. (trans.), *The Geography of Strabo*, Loeb Classical Library (London: William Heinemann, 8 vo., 1917-1932).

Jones, W.H.S., *Pausanias, Complete Works* (Delphi Classics, 2014).

Kalamboukidou-Paschali, E., *Samothrace: History – Archaeology – Touring* (Nea Beltiomehi Ekdosi, 2002).

Kamptz, H. von, *Homerische Personennamen* (Göttingen: Vandenhoeck & Ruprecht, 1982 (1958)).

Kazantzakis, N., *Report to Greco* (London: Faber & Faber, 1973 (1965)).

Kent, R.G., *On the Latin language*, by Marcus Terentius Varro (London: William Heinemann, 1938).

Kirk, G., *The Iliad: a commentary* (Cambridge: Cambridge University Press, 1985).

Knight, W.F.J., 'Aeneas and History', *Greece & Rome*, 6.17 (Feb. 1937, pp. 70-77).

Korfmann, M. O. (trans trans. Carpenter Efe, J.D., *Troia/Wilusa: General Background and Guided Tour* (Çanakkale: Yayinlari, rev. ed., 2005).

Lane Fox, R., *Travelling Heroes* (London: Penguin, 2009).

Larence, D.H., *Etruscan Places: travels through forgotten Italy* (New York: Tauris Parke Paperbacks, 2011 (1932)).

Latacz, J., (trans. Windle, K. and Ireland, R.), *Troy and Homer: Towards a Solution of an Old Mystery* (Oxford: Oxford University Press, 2004).

Laurén, G. (ed.), *The Other Trojan War: Dictys & Dares. Parallel texts* (Sophron, 2012).

Leaf, W., *Homer and History* (London: Macmillan, 1915).

Leaf, W., *Troy, a study in Homeric Geography* (London: Macmillan, 1912).

Le Guin, Uusula K., *Lavinia* (London: Phoenix, 2010 (2008)).
Lehman, K., *Samothrace: A Guide to the Excavations and the Museum*, 5th ed., (Institute of Fine Arts, New York University, 1983).
Lesky, A., *History of Greek Literature* (London: Methuen, 1966).
Levi, P., *Virgil: a life* (London: Tauris Parke Paperbacks, 2012 (1997)).
Lion, H.A., *Commentarii in Virgilium Serviani; Sive Commentarii in Virgilium, Qui Mauro Servio Honorato Tribuuntur* (Göttingen: Vandenhoeck et Ruprecht, 1826).
Luce, J.V., *Celebrating Homer's Landscapes: Troy and Ithaca Revisited* (New Haven and London: Yale University Press, 1998).
Mair, A.W. (trans.), *Oppian, Colluthus and Tryphiodoros*, Loeb Classical Library (London: William Heinemann, 1928).
Mair, A. W. & G. R., (trans.) *Callimachus, Hymns and Epigrams. Lycophron. Aratus*, Loeb Classical Library (London: William Heinemann, 1921).
Marchand, L.A., (ed.), *Byron's Letters and Journals* (London: John Murray, 1978).
Matsas, D., Poularakis, I., and Mantzana, E., *Preservation and Presentation of the Eastern Region of the Sanctuary of the Great Gods, Samothrace* (Thessaloniki, 2015).
Matthiae, A., *Animadversiones in Hymnos Homericos* (Leipzig, 1800).
Mayor, A., *The First Fossil Hunters: Dinosaurs, Mammoths, and Myth in Greek and Roman Times* (Princeton and Oxford: Princeton University Press, 2011).
McGilchrist, N., *Kythera with Antikythera & Elafonisos* (London: Genius Loci Publications, 2010).
Mieroop, M. van de, *A History of the Ancient Near East c. 3000-323 BC* (Oxford: Blackwell Publishing, 2004).
Mooney, J.J., (trans.) *The Minor Poems of Vergil* (Birmingham: Cornish Brothers, 1916).
Morwood, J., (trans.), *The Trojan Women and other plays* (Oxford: Oxford University Press, 2000).
Olalla, P. and Priego, A., *Mythological Atlas of Greece* (Athens: Road Editions, 2002).
Page, D.L., *History and the Homeric Iliad* (Berkeley: University of California Press, 1959).
Pandermalis, Dimitrios, *Dion: the archaeological site and museum* (Katsimicha: Adam Editions, 1997).
Penglase, Charles, *Greek Myths and Mesopotamia: Parallels and Influence in the Homeric Hymns and Hesiod* (London: Routledge, 1994).
Perret, J., *Les origines de la legende troyenne de Rome* (Paris, 1942).
Peter, Hermann, *Historicorum Romanorum Reliquiae*, 2 vols (Leipzig, 1870, 1906); see also Cornell (2013).
Peter, W. (ed.), *Specimens of the Poets and Poetry of Greece and Rome by Various Translators* (Philadelphia: Carey and Hart, 1847).
Plommer, H., 'Kythera: the Doric fragments preserved in Ayios Kosmas', chapter in Coldstream & Huxley (see above).
Pound, E., *ABC of Reading* (New Haven: Yale University Press, 1934).
Raeburn, D (trans.), *Ovid, Metamorphoses* (London: Penguin Books, 2004).
Rawlinson, G., *Herodotus, Histories* (Ware: Wordsworth Classics, 1996).
Reade, J., *Mesopotamia* (London: British Museum, 1991).
Reeve, C.D.C., *Aristotle, De Anima* (Indianapolis: Hackett, 2017).

Bibliography

Reeve, M.D. (ed) and Wright, N (trans.), *Geoffrey of Monmouth, The History of the Kings of Britain* (Woodbridge: The Boydell Press, 2007).

Reinhardt, K., *Die Ilias und ihr Dichter* (Gottingen: Vandenhoeck & Ruprecht, 1961).

Renault, M., *The Nature of Alexander* (Harmondsworth: Penguin, 1975).

Rigg, A.G. (trans), *Joseph of Exeter, Daretis PhrygiiIlias* (Centre for Medieval Studies, University of Toronto, 2005).

Rose, C.B., *The Archaeology of Greek and Roman Troy* (Cambridge: Cambridge University Press, 2013).

Rose, H.J., 'Anchises and Aphrodite', *The Classical Quarterly* (18.1.11-16, January 1924).

Rouse, W.H.D., Nonnus: *Dionysiaca* (books 1-15), Loeb Classical Library (London: William Heniemann, 1940, 1955-6).

Rubens, B. and Taplin, O., *An Odyssey round Odysseus: the man & his story traced through time and place* (London: BBC Books, 1989).

Rutherford, I., 'Theoria and Theatre at Samothrace: The Dardanos by Dymas of Iasos', in Wilson P. (ed.) *The Greek Theatre and Festivals Documentary Studies* (Oxford: Oxford University Press, 2007, pp 279-293).

Ryan, W. and Pitman, W., *Noah's Flood* (New York: Simon & Schuster, 1998).

Samivel, *The Glory of Greece* (Thames and Hudson, 1979).

Sandwich, Earl of, *A Voyage Performed by the Late Earl of Sandwich round the Mediterranean in the years 1738 and 1739* (London, 1799).

Scherer, Margaret R., *The Legends of Troy in art and literature* (New York: Phaidon Press, 1963).

Schliemann, Heinrich, *Ilios, City and Country of the Trojans* (London: John Murray, 1880).

Seaton, R.C. (trans.) *Apollonius Rhodius. Argonautica*, Loeb Classical Library (London: William Heinemann, 1912).

Sélincourt, Aubrey de, *Livy, The Early History of Rome* (London: Penguin Books (1960 (2002)).

Serafis, Giorgos, 'Helen', Keeley, E., and Sherrard, S., *Four Greek Poets* (Harmondsworth: Penguin Books, 1966).

Showerman, G., *Ovid: Heriodes and Amores*, Loeb Classic Library (New York: Macmillan, 1914).

Smith, Peter M., 'The Aineiadai as patrons of *Iliad* XX and the Homeric *Hymn to Aphrodite*', *Harvard Studies in Classical Philology* (vol. 85, 1981, pp. 17-58).

Smith, W., *Dictionary of Greek and Roman Geography* (London: Little, Brown & Co., 1854).

Stehle, E., 'Dii Penantes a Samothracia sublati', *Latomus*, T. 50, Fasc. 3 (July-Sept. 1991, pp. 581-601).

Stoneman, R., *A Traveller's History of Turkey* (Moreton-in-Marsh: Windrush Press, 1993).

Thomson, A. (trans.) and Reed, E. (ed.), *The Lives of the Twelve Caesars; An English Translation, Augmented with the Biographies of Contemporary Statesmen, Orators, Poets [including Virgil], and Other Associates* (Philadelphia, Gebbie & Co., 1889). See also Bird (1997).

Thornton, A., *Homer's Iliad: Its Composition and the Motif of Supplication* (Göttingen: Vandenhoeck & Ruprecht, 1984).

Tilly, Bertha, *Vergil's Latium* (Oxford: Blackwell, 1947).
Van Seters, J., *Prologue to History: the Yahwist as Historian in Genesis* (Louisville: Westminster/John Knox Press, 1992).
Vaux, W., *Greek Cities and Islands of Asia Minor* (London, S.P.C.K., 1877).
Vermaseren, Maarten J. (trans. A.M.H. Lemmers), *Cybele and Attis, the myth and the cult* (London: Thames and Hudson, 1997).
Von Gunten, Ruth (Negroni, Cristina, trans.), *Segesta* (Marsala: La Medusa Editrice, 2006).
Warmington, E.H. (trans), *Remains of Old Latin I: Ennius and Caecilius*, Loeb Classical Library (London: William Heinemann, 1935).
Way, A.S. (trans.), *Quintus Smyrnaeus. The Fall of Troy*, Loeb Classical Library (Cambridge, MA: Harvard University Press, 1913).
West, M. L., *Homeric Hymns, Homeric Apocrypha, Lives of Homer*, Loeb Classical Library (Cambridge, MA: Harvard University Press, 2003).
West, M.L. (trans.), *Hesiod, Theogony and Works and Days* (Oxford: Oxford University Press, 1988).
West, M.L., *Greek Epic Fragments: from the seventh to the fifth centuries BC* (Cambridge, MA: Harvard University Press, 2003).
West, M.L., *The Hesiodic Catalogue of Women. Its nature, structure and origin* (Oxford: Clarendon Press, 1985).
West, M.L., *The Orphic Poems* (Westbury: The Prometheus Trust, 2016 (1983)).
White, H., *The Civil Wars. Appian* (London: Macmillan, 1899).
Williams, R.D., *Aeneas and the Roman Hero* (London: Bristol Classical Press, 2002 ((1973))).
Wolf, C., *Cassandra* (trans. Heurck, J. van) (London: Daunt Books (2013 (1973)).
Wood, M., *In Search of the Trojan War* (London: BBC, 1985).
Wood, R., *An Essay on the original genius of Homer* (London, 1769).
Yardley, J.C. (trans.) *Justin: Epitome of the Philippic History of Pompeius Trogus*, Classical Resources Series, no. 3 (Society for Classical Studies, 1994).
Yunck, J.A. and Baswell, C (trans.), *Eneas: A Twelfth-Century French Romance* (New York and London: Columbia University Press, 1974).
Zangger, Eberhardt, *The Flood from Heaven: Deciphering the Atlantis Legend* (Sidgwick & Jackson, 1992).

Index

Apaliunas, 100
Abas, 175, 192
Abbott, John White, 216
Aborigines, 245, 262, 270, 317
Aboukir (Abu Qir), 88
Abu Simbel, 89
Abydos, 107, 174
Acamas, 106, 108, 118, 126, 316
Acestes, 210, 212, 221-2, 224-5
Achaea, Achaeans, 63, 72, 99, 103, 130, 150, 186
Achaemenides, 202–203
Achates, 175, 211–213, 234, 261, 263, 267, 279, 284
Acheron, 193, 200, 236
Achilles, 15, 35, 42, 49, 54, 62-3, 66-7, 69–70, 77, 80, 91–2, 96–7, 99, 105, 109–114, 120, 122, 124, 127 & passim, 174, 181, 194–195, 206, 234, 249–252, 256, 265-7, 273, 278, 280–1, 283, 285-6, 309–310, 313
Aci Trezza, 202
Aciris, 200
Acragas, 204
Acropolis, Athens, 155
Actium, 189–193, 195, 230, 238, 267, 273, 286
Ad Urbe Condita, 218, 300
Adonis, 88, 222
Adramyttium, 20, 67, 108, 110-1, 176
Adrasteia, 52, 79
Adrastos, 52, 107
Adresteia, 107
Aecae, 199
Aeëtes, 241
Aegestus, 210, 317

Aegialea, 72
Aegina, 67, 69, 71
Aelian, 66, 150, 257
Aemilia, daughter of Aeneas, 245, 316
Aenea, 163
Aeneadum genetrix (Aphrodite), 276
Aeneia, 177, 180–182, 244, 257
Aeneid, 4, 32, 64, 68, 136 & passim
Aeneidae, 166–168, 176, 259
Aeolian, Aeolians, 34–35, 165
Aeschylus, 206
Aesopus, 20, 26–27, 51
Aesytes, 61, 105, 137, 316
Aethicus, 140
Aetolia, 186
Agamemnon, 35, 57, 60, 91–92, 94, 99, 112–114, 118, 120–121, 124, 126–129, 131, 139–140, 145, 150, 160, 174, 183, 275, 313
Agathyllus, 186, 188
Agenor, 91, 122, 126, 128–129, 136, 316
Agrigento, 204
Agrippa, 191, 317
Agylla, 262–263, 265–266
Ahhijawa, 99, 103
Aineus, 103, 180
Aither, 79, 318
Ajax (unspecified), 122, 129, 175, 206
Ajax of Lochris, 123, 128, 130, 140, 144, 153
Ajax, Telamonian, 75, 121, 123, 126, 128, 130, 140
Akamas, 166
Akarnania, 192-3, 257

Aktios, 192
Akusilaus, 158
Alaksandu, 100, 102–103
Alalia, Battle of, 264
Alaric, 239
Alba Longa, 238, 245, 257, 259–260, 292, 296–298, 300–301, 317
Alban Mount, 169–170, 230, 238, 274, 277–279, 300, 304
Alcathous, 61, 64–65, 96, 127–128, 131, 316
Alcimedon, 130, 143
Alcimus, 245, 257
Alcmene, 79
Aletes, 175
Alexander (Paris), 67, 88, 102-104
Alexander the Great, 37, 53, 57, 161, 166, 168, 178, 181, 250–252, 277–278, 305, 316
Alexandra, 224, 265, 268, 293
Alexandreia, Mount, 67, 172
Alexandria Troas, 53, 61
Alexandria, Egypt, 88
Alföldi, Andreas, 298
Algeria, 207
Allecto, 254
Alope, 70
Alos, 70
Alpheus, River, 203
Altes, 108
Altinoluk, 172
Alybe (Tirebolu), 108
Amata, 254, 280, 290, 317
Amathous, 98, 210, 313
Amazons, 105, 139, 275
Ambracian Gulf, 189-193
Amenhotep, 99

337

Amphimachus, 108, 124, 127, 145
Amphinomus, 286
Amulius, 257, 317
Amyclas, Amykles, 74, 76, 83, 100
Amycus, 175
Amydon, 108
Anabasis of Alexander, 251
anagóghia, 209
Ananke, 79–80
Anapias, 286
Anchisa, 257
Anchises, 19 & passim
Anchisia, Mount, 186, 188
Ancus Marcius, 277, 299, 317
Andes, 228
Andria, Francesco, 199
Andromache, 69, 110, 120, 149, 165, 194–196, 290, 316
Andromachus, 142
Andros, Island of, 182
Anglesey Abbey, 261
Anius, King of Delos, 182–183
Anna, sister of Dido 215, 218, 221
Antalya, 108
Antandros, 67, 172, 174–175, 295, 312
Antenor, 61, 69–73, 91, 106, 121–122, 126–127, 136, 142, 144–147, 150–151, 155, 163–164, 173–174, 207, 316
Anthemonê, 186, 316
Antheus, 175, 214
Anticlus, 148
Antikythera, 185
Antilochus, 118, 139
Antiphus, 108, 111
Antiquitates Rerum Divinarum, 302
Antoninus Pius, 306
Antony (Marcus Antonius), 170, 191–192, 216, 230, 267, 286
aoidoi, 98
Aphnitis, Lake, 166
Aphrodisias, 23, 185, 260
Aphrodite Aeneias, 176-177, 189–190, 192–193, 225
Aphrodite Anchiseias, 305

Aphrodite (Venus), 13 & passim
Apis, 88
Apollo, 49–50, 63, 68, 74, 77, 79, 92 & passim, 203, 209 & passim, 237, 246, 269, 310
Apollodorus, 43, 45, 66, 85, 90, 94, 150
Apollon Smintheion, 113
apotheosis, 14, 170, 183, 192, 303, 305, 311-312, 314
Appian, 191, 233, 260, 278, 283–284
Apulia, 198
Ara Pacis Augustae, 287–288
Aragorn, 273
Arakthos, 193
Arcadia, Arcadians, 78, 149, 179, 184, 186–188, 203–204, 253, 255, 261–263, 268–269, 272, 294, 316
Archelochus, 106, 126, 316
Arco Felice, 233
Arctinus of Miletus, 139, 147–148, 151, 163, 294
Arcturus, 197
Ardea, 253, 296
Ares (Mars), 79, 84, 117–118, 120, 128–129, 132, 136, 142–143, 161, 170, 192, 222, 231, 245, 260, 277–278, 286, 289, 300–301, 317
Arethusa, 203
Aretus, 130
Argante, 282
Argives, 99–100
Argonauts, 66, 68, 77, 95, 222, 309
Argos, 70, 91, 95, 100, 115, 143, 160, 207, 249, 251–252
Ariadne, 184, 218
Ariaethus, 186, 188
Ariosto, Ludovico, 282
Arisbe, 107, 165
Aristolochus, 140
Aristotle, 35, 44, 245, 250–251
Arne, Fountain of, 187
Arrian, 251
Arruns, 279
Arsiba, 45–46, 316

Arsinoë, Rotunda of, 37
Artemis (Diana), 31, 63, 79, 92, 118, 136, 161, 175, 182–183, 203, 213–214, 239, 301
Artemisio, 186
Arymbas, 251
Arzawa Lands, 102, 109
Ascalaphus, 128
Ascania, 108, 165–166
Asclepios, 204
Ascra, 78, 87
Asculum, 252
Ashtoreth, 30, 87
Asinius Pollio, 229
Asius, 107
Askalon, 50, 87
Aşkin, Mustafa, 54–55
Assaracus, 42, 46, 49, 51–52, 103, 107, 217, 230, 316
Assos, 100, 108, 112
Assuwa, 100, 110
Astarte, 30–31, 83, 87, 209–210, 213
Asteria, 182, 313
Astyanax, 120, 165, 195, 316
Astyoche, 46, 316
Ate, Hill of, 49, 51-2, 56, 68, 182, 294
Athena (Minerva), 26, 31, 50, 57, 64, 67–68, 79, 84, 111–112, 114–115, 117–118, 120, 124–125, 131–132, 135–137, 143–144, 147, 152, 154, 161, 198–200, 203, 207, 251, 277, 284, 294–295
Athens, Athenians, 26, 46, 59, 63, 71, 80, 86, 91, 128, 155, 157, 160, 166, 194, 201, 207, 264, 284
Athos, Mount, 180
Atii, gens, 223
Atlantis, 207
Atlas, 44, 78–79, 187, 215–216, 316-317
Atreus, 99
Attalos, 23
Attalus, 258
Attikus, 177, 285, 294
Attis, 31
Atys, 223
Auden, W.H., 239

Index

Auge, 268
Augusta, Gulf of, 203
Augustine, St, 309
Augustus, 13–14, 19, 136, 156, 161, 170, 190–193, 196, 216, 218, 223, 226–227, 229–231, 233, 236, 238–239, 247, 250, 262, 265, 267, 269, 273, 281, 283–288, 291, 299–300, 303, 305–306, 308–309, 311–312, 317
Aulis, 91–92, 106
Aurelia, Via, 271
Ausonia, 178, 184, 241, 269
Automedon, 130
Avebury, 39
Aventine Hill, 169, 262
Avernus, Lake, 233, 235–236, 310, 314
Avgo, 86
Avilcar, 172
Avlemonas, 82–83
Axieros, 37–38, 45
Ayazma, 48
Azmak stream, 93

Babylon, 50, 159, 251
bacchantes, 184
Bacchus (Dionysos), 184, 214
Badisco, Porto, 198
Baiae, 232
Balkans, 34, 63, 165, 278
Balli Dağ, 48–49, 53–55, 138, 142, 163
Banchich, T.M., 312
Banditaccia, 266–267
Baphyras, River, 181
Barrus, Tiberius Veturius, 253
Basilica Aemilia, 291
Basilica Julia, 169, 279
Bateia, daughter of Teucer, 45, 316
Batieia, the, 105–6, 109, 114
Baur, J.W., 182–183
Bayramiç, 26, 48
Beard, Mary, 259
Behramkale, 108
Beirut, 85, 222
Bellonius, 53
Bellum Punicum, 220, 241, 257

Belos, 207
Belvedere Altar, 247, 287
Beneventum, 252
Bergama, 91, 100, 108
Bernini, Gian Lorenzo, 306
Beşik Tepe, 56, 140, 250
Beşika Burnu, 92–93
Bethlehem, 308
Bible, 32, 85, 159
Bibliotheka, 43, 45–46, 51, 60, 66, 85, 90, 150, 294
Bithynia, 108
Blegen, Carl, 72, 164–165
Bodrum, 34, 45, 108
Boetia, 78, 106, 141, 242
Bogazkale, 33
Boiai, 185
Bömer, Franz, 265
Bosch, Hieronymus, 151
Bosporus, 20, 179
Bosse, Abraham, 274
Botticelli, Sandro, 86–87
Bovillae, 277
Bozcaada, 47
Bremon, 142
Briareus, 114, 236
Brindisi, Brindisium, 284
Briseida, 121
Briseis, 112, 114, 121, 131
Briseus, 114
Britain, the British, 13, 14, 26, 48, 54, 56, 117, 122, 134–135, 149, 153, 157, 161, 176, 214, 219, 230, 235, 239, 267-268, 276, 278, 301, 306, 314, 316-317
Britto, 239, 301
Broch, Hermann, 284, 311
Brückner, Alfred, 93
Brutus of Troy, 13–14, 42, 121, 134, 161, 176, 214, 238–239, 278, 301, 307, 317
Brutus, Lucius Junius, 238, 317
Bryant, Jacob, 53–54, 58
Buchheit, V., 269
Buddhism, 240
Butes, 222
Buthrotum, 16, 194-296, 201, 233, 283, 290
Butrint, 194, 196
Büyük, 27, 35, 38–41, 43–44, 313

Byblos, 50
Byron, George, 6th Baron, 53–54, 285
Byrsa, 212
Byzantium, 49, 53, 165, 193, 198-199, 243

Cacus, 262
Cadmus, 80
caduceii, 292-293
Caere, 128, 243, 254, 266–268, 270–272, 274, 297
Caesar, Gaius Julius, 13–14, 19, 169–170, 183, 190–191, 196, 216, 223, 229–230, 238–239, 246, 250, 262, 277–279, 283, 286, 291, 295, 299, 305–306, 308, 311–313, 317
Caesars, the 13, 42, 134, 230, 238, 265, 276, 301, 309
Caicus, 175
Caieta, Caietes 241
Cairo, 89
Calabria, 200, 226
Calanais, Lewis, 38
Calasso, Roberto, 80, 91, 148, 157–158
Calchas, 92, 114, 156
Callias, 245
Callinus, 45
Callirrhoe, 46, 49, 316
Callistratus, 294
Calpurnius, 209
Caltabellota, 224
Calvert, Frank, 26, 54–55
Calydonian boar, 66
Camaggio, M., 287
Camarina, 157, 204
Cambiaso, Luca, 176
Camers, 296
Camilla, 275, 279
Campania, 229
Campi Flegrei, 235
Campus Martius, 287, 304
Canaan, 85
Çanakkale, 107, 168
Candid, Peter, 314
Cannae, 257
Canup, Canupians, 88–89
Capetus, King of Alba Longa, 317

339

Caphiae, 186
Capitol, Washington D.C., 314
Capitoline Hill, 169, 233-234, 258
Capri, 228, 235
Capua, 257
Capys, 42, 46, 52, 103, 175, 186, 257
Caracci, Annibale, 154
Caria, 108–109, 124, 260
Carthage, Carthaginians, 15, 174, 204, 210–222, 226, 238, 242, 256–258, 260, 264, 266, 276, 278, 284, 306
Cassandra, 60, 64–65, 68, 73, 90–91, 94, 96, 113, 141, 147–148, 152–153, 316
Cassope, 193
Castello Gandolfo, 300
Castelvetere, 201
Castor, 72, 76, 244, 292–294
Castro Marina, 198–199, 283
Castrum Minervae, 198-199, 283
Catalepton, 228–229
Çatalhöyük, 27, 30
Catalogue of Women, 43–45, 77, 158–159
Catholics, Catholicism, 240, 258, 298
Cato, 247, 252, 260
Catullus, 218
Caulon, Caulonia, 201
Cebes, slave of Virgil, 231, 283
Cecrops, 160
Celaeno, 188, 246
centaurs, 62, 63, 150, 236
Cephalon, 181
Ceraunian Mountains, 196–197
Cerberus, 236
Cerveteri, 266-7
Chalcidia, 140
Chalkidiki, 180
Chalkis, 166–167
Chaonia, 193-195
Chaos, 78–79, 316
Charon, 236
Charybdis, 201–202, 226
Chasm, 52, 78, 160
Chaucer, Geoffrey, 121, 260
Chersonese, 20, 163

cherubs, 267, 315
chimeras, 236, 275
Chios, 34, 97-98
Chiron, 62–64, 66–67, 69, 72, 150
Chiusi, 271
Choiseul-Gouffier, Count, 48, 167
Chrestomathy, 66, 139
Chromis, 108
Chromius, 115, 130
Chronos, 79
Chryse, 187, 294, 316
Chryseis, 110, 112–114
Cicero, 177, 218, 285
Ciclopi, Isola, 202
Cilicians, 108
Cimmerians, 206
Ciplak Ridge, 49, 61, 105
Circe, 201, 227, 241, 243, 253
Cista Pasinati, 290
Cista sacra, 264, 287, 290-293, 306
Civita Castellan, 83
Claudius, 156, 278, 305
Cleomestra, 46, 61, 142, 316
Cleopatra Marina, Epiros, 192
Cleopatra, 46, 61, 170, 191–192, 216, 219, 267, 316
Cleyn, Francis, 236, 280
Cloanthus, 175, 214
Clusems, 292
Clusium, 271
Clymene, 316
Clytius, 42
Cocytus, 236
Codex Oxoniensis, 150
Codonê, 186, 316
Colchis, 95
Colluthus, 67, 73–74, 76–77, 80, 85, 91
Colonna, 201
comets, 190–191, 304–305, 313
Commodius, 306
Constantine, 295, 309
Cook, Professor J.M., 26–28, 35, 38, 49, 107, 110, 123–124, 132, 137, 140, 167–168, 313
Corcyra, 173
Corfu, 88, 173, 193, 195–197

Corinth, 72, 78, 129, 180
Cornell, T.J., 297
Cornetto, 270
Coroebus, 152
Corsica, 264
Cortona, 270–271, 292
Corybantes, 259, 269
Corybas, 269, 316
Corythus, 184, 253, 268–271, 316
Cosae, 271
Cosway, Maria, 156
Cotylus, 20, 27, 78
Cranae, 80–81
Cressida, 76, 114, 121-122
Crete, Cretans, 30, 45, 50, 61, 63, 71, 76, 78, 82–83, 98, 127–129, 140, 142, 157, 183–185, 187–188, 199, 204, 209, 223, 234, 236, 269, 279
Crethon, 118
Creusa, 15, 60, 65, 151, 154–157, 162, 181, 195, 264, 287, 298–299, 301, 316-317
Crimisus, River, 224
Criseyde, 121
Critolaus, 177, 293
Crociera Virgiliana, 195
Crotone, 200–201
Cumae, 227, 233, 241–242, 309–310
cuneiform, 97–99, 102–104, 107, 159, 165
Cunningham, Michael, 15
Cupid, 86, 222
Cures, 238
Curia Iulia, 230
Cychreus, 71
Cyclades, 182, 184
Cyclopses, 16, 78, 153, 202–204, 226, 237, 266
Cyllene, 261
Cymothoë, 213
Cynegeticus, 62, 150
Cynossema, 'the tomb of the bitch', 174
Cynthian, 230
Cypria, the, 65–66, 73, 77, 96–97, 122

Index

Cyprus, 19–20, 30–31, 33, 83, 85–88, 98, 165, 209–210, 214, 222, 225, 272, 313
Cyrene, 207, 208

Daedalus, 209, 234
Damastes of Segeum, 244
Danaans, 99–100
Danaus, 91
Dante Alighieri, 239–240, 310
Dardanelles, 20, 26, 50–51, 56, 73, 91, 93, 108, 163, 174, 176, 179
Dardania, Dardanians, 21, 25–27, 29, 39-40, 42–44, 46-48, 50–52, 57, 60-61, 65, 77, 89, 96, 100, 102, 104, 106-7, 109, 111–114, 122, 129, 137, 146, 148–150, 163, 166–168, 172–173, 178-179, 260, 269, 316
Dardanidae, 269
Dardanos, 20–22, 25–26, 36, 32–46, 49, 52, 60, 74, 77, 79, 91, 104, 110, 113, 133–134, 156, 159–160, 167, 174–175, 178–179, 183–184, 187–188, 206–208, 214, 217, 237, 253, 261, 269–271, 293–294, 299, 308, 311, 313, 316
Dares Phrygius, 59, 61, 64, 69–70, 72–73, 82–84, 90, 96, 121, 123, 139, 145–148, 173–174, 185, 222, 285
Darius, 250
Dascylitis, 165-6
Daskalopetra, 97
Daskyleion, 166
Daunas, 253
Daunus, 281, 317
Dawn, goddess of, 22, 241, 316
De Beneficis, 286
De Familiis Troianis, 276
Deicoon, 118
deification, 223, 291, 302–305
Deimas, 187, 316
Deimos (terror), 222
Deiphobe (sibyl), 234
Deiphobus, 60–61, 122, 126–128, 137, 140, 142,
144, 148, 160, 236–237, 240, 316
Delos, 45, 182–184, 203, 234, 246, 269, 313
Delphi, 70, 87, 129, 157, 159, 194, 233, 258-260
Demerate, 233
Demeter (Ceres), 31, 43, 79, 155–156, 162, 311, 316
Demetrius of Skepsis, 26, 166–167
Demodokos, 97, 99
Deucalion, 159-161, 179, 316
Devren Hill, 172
Dexithea, 245, 316
Diana (Artemis), 161
Dias, 195
Dictys Cretensis, 61, 85, 91–92, 94–96, 109, 122–123, 127, 139, 142, 144–148, 151, 163, 173, 285
Dido, 14, 23, 64, 152–153, 162, 172, 174, 188, 204, 211–221, 224, 226, 231, 236–237, 256–257, 275, 283, 290, 316
Dio Cassius, 277
Dio Chrysostom, 173
Diocletian, 304
Diodorus Siculus, 179, 269
Diogenes, 23
Diomedes, 62, 107, 115–118, 120–122, 124, 142, 144–145, 199, 211, 265, 275, 286, 294–296
Dion, 181, 250
Dione, 30, 86, 117, 181, 195
Dionysica, 178
Dionysios of Chalkis, 166–167
Dionysius of Halicarnassus, 45, 145, 149, 151, 163, 165–167, 173, 177, 179–181, 184–190, 192–193, 195–196, 198, 200, 208, 220, 225, 227–228, 232, 241–248, 253–254, 257, 262, 285, 289, 292, 294–299, 301–302, 307, 317
Dionysos (Bacchus), 79, 183-184, 188, 214, 217, 222, 238, 316
Dioryctus, 189
Dioscuri, 72, 292
Dis, 236–237, 294
Divine Comedy, 310
Divine Institutes, 282, 309
Dodekatheon, the, 21
Dodona, 195, 233, 246
doliums, 181, 264–265, 292-3
Dolon the herald, 123–124, 145
Domitius, 246
Donatus, Tiberius Claudius, 156
Dorians, 34, 75, 165, 249
Dorion, 106
Dorpfeld, Wilhelm, 55–57
Drapanon, 210
Drdny, 43, 89, 100, 104
Drepanum, 88, 204, 209–210, 219–220, 224, 313
Drusus, 305
Dryden, John, 228
Dubrovnik, 173
Dulichium, 188
Dumrek Su, 49
Dumuzi, 32, 40, 74, 221
Dymas, 152, 178

eannas, 32–33, 40
earthquakes, 27, 34, 63, 75, 164, 312
Ebe Tepe, 167
Echemmon, 115
Echepolus, 60
Eclogues, 228–230
Eden, 32
Edremit, 108, 110–111, 172
Eeneide, 216
Eetion, 43, 110–111, 316
Egesta, 210, 224
Egypt, Egyptians, 43, 50, 56, 63, 67, 71, 88–90, 95, 99-100, 102, 104, 165, 175, 191–192, 207-208, 251, 267, 279, 309
Eileithyia, 23, 31, 79
Either, 98, 173
Elafonisos, 185
Elba, 271
Elektra, 43–44, 74, 79, 87, 91, 159, 177–178, 187, 222, 261, 269, 294, 313, 316-317

341

In Search of Aeneas

Eleon, 106
Eleusis, 311
Elimo, 210
Elis, 100
Elissa, 212
Elizabeth I, 121
Elpenor, 227
Elsheimer, Adam, 151
Elymians, 204, 208, 210, 221-222, 225, 242, 251, 256, 298
Elysium, 237, 239–240, 309–311
Empedocles, 211
Enea's Tomb, 167
Eneide, 176, 290
Enetae, 108
Enez, 180–181
England, the English, 13, 28, 110, 176, 219, 276, 301, 314
Enki, 31
Ennius, 149, 218, 253, 260, 299, 304
Enoch, Alfred, 64
ensevestatos, 293
Entella, 210
Entellus, 222
Enyalios, 101
Enyo, 142
Epaphos, 88
Epeios, 146–147
Ephesus, 34, 150, 175
Ephyra, 194
Epic poetry, 66, 97-99, 102
Epicureanism, 229
Epiros, 34, 149, 190, 193-196, 244, 249, 251, 256-257, 285
Epistrophus, 108
Epitome (to *Bibliotheka*), 150
Epytus, 130, 152
Erdemog, Bülent, 283
Erebos, 79, 316
Ereshkigal, 31
Ergen, Yüksel, 50, 156
Erichthonius, 42, 46, 316
Eriopis, 60, 316
Eros, 19, 76, 78–80, 86, 92, 135, 212, 214, 216, 222, 237, 278, 288, 290, 314, 316
Erymanthus, 72

Erys, 67, 80, 92
Eryx (Erice), 189, 204, 208–210, 221–222, 224–225, 247, 256–258, 313
Eski Skisepje, 27
Esquiline Hill, Rome, 229, 231, 297
Ethiopia, 50, 139, 175
Etias, 185, 316
Etna, Mount, 16, 202–203, 266, 286
Etruria, Etrurians, 76, 80, 116, 122, 139, 175, 223, 243–245, 249, 261, 264–266, 268–270, 275, 296, 299
Etruscan, Etruscans, 80, 223, 228, 242–246, 262-272, 264–266, 268–271, 274, 279, 286, 296–299
Euboea, 70, 182, 223, 233, 242
Eunoë, 60
Euphemus, 108
Euphrates, 30
Euratos, 76, 80
Euripides, 69, 77, 92, 158, 194, 294
Europa, 95
Eurotas Valley, 73–75, 77, 160, 186
Eurydice, 52, 65, 316
Eurymachus, 142, 316
Eurymenes, 141
Eurypylus, 108, 127, 140–142
Euxine (Black Sea), 108, 166
Euxinus, 233
Evander, 175, 255, 261–263, 268, 271–273, 283, 296, 317
Evans, Sir Arthur, 63
Excidium Troiae, 162
Exeter, Joseph of, 32, 47, 64, 145, 163, 173
Ezine, 48, 167

Fabia, gens, 238, 276
Fabius Multitremulus, 305
Fabius Pictor, 292
Fagles, Robert, 153, 213, 282
familiae Troianae, 259, 303
Farnell, L.R., 176–177
Farsala, 69
Farmer, Dr Chris, 272

Fasti, 274, 286
Fate, 15, 77, 79–80, 86, 135, 137-138, 140, 142-143, 148, 154, 156-157, 183, 191, 215, 217, 224, 226, 231, 234, 240, 247, 253–255, 263, 272, 280, 307, 316
Faunus, 253, 280, 317
Faustus, 92
Fengari, Mount, 36
Ferri, Silvio, 265
Festus, 149, 304
Fitzgerald, Frankie, 64
Flamininus, 259, 276
floods, 152–153, 155–157, 159–161, 178–179, 183, 187, 203, 224, 228, 241
Florence, 86, 232, 253, 270, 310
Fokia, 208
Forum Boarium, 169, 242, 261
Frutis, 247, 294
furens, 273, 279, 281
Furia, gens 276
Furies, 188, 236, 281
Fusano, Castell, 252

Gaeta, 241
Gaia, 30, 78–79, 86, 216, 229, 288, 291, 316, 317
Galinsky, Karl, 76, 80, 115, 117, 129, 134, 136, 188, 202, 206–208, 220, 244, 249, 251, 253, 257–258, 264–265, 286, 288, 292–293, 300, 303, 306
Gallienus, 306
Gallipoli, 20, 163, 176
Galuppi, Baldassare, 253
Gandalf, 273
Ganymede, 22, 42, 46, 95, 107, 278, 316
Gargarus, 20, 39–40, 47–48, 110, 112, 123, 125, 128
Garlic Bridge, 48, 167
Gaul, Gauls, 214, 228, 266, 271, 278, 292
Gela, 155, 204
genealogy, 13, 16, 43, 61, 66, 78-79, 91, 133, 159-160, 167, 187, 191, 207, 222,

Index

230, 261, 276–277, 300-301
Genesis, Book of, 159
Genoa, 176
Geographia, 26
Georgics, 191, 228–231, 286
Gergis, 181, 246
Gerusalemme Liberata, 282
Geryon, 222, 262
Geshtinanna, 32
Ghali-Kahil, L., 76
Ghar el Melh, 211
Gilgamesh, 159
Giza, 89
Gla, 63
Glauce, 71–72
Glaucus, 109, 126, 128–129
Glyndŵr, Owen, 301
Gnostics, 240
Gökçeada, 36
golden bough, 235, 314
Golgos, 222
Gondor, 151
Granicus, River, 20, 51, 107, 250
Graves, Robert, 311
Graviscae, 270–271
Great Foray, the, 110, 112
Great Mother, 30-31, 37-40, 43-44, 65, 86, 104, 157, 175-177, 195, 205, 222, 258-259, 272, 312-313
Grillo, Monte, 233
Grotta Bella, 267
Grüninger, Erasmus, 198
Gulf of Megara, 203
Guzelyali, 50, 168
Gwynedd, 42, 239, 301, 307
Gyas, 175, 214
Gythio, 80–81

Haballa, 109
habiru, 165
Hades (Pluto), 34, 78, 129, 134, 157, 193, 200, 218, 226–227, 234–235, 237, 239–240, 267, 284, 301, 303–304, 309–312, 314
Hadrian, 140, 285, 306, 310
Halicarnassus (Bodrum) 34
Halizonians, 108
Hampe, R., 76

Hanay Tepe, 49
Hannibal, 238, 257
Hardie, Philip, 14, 154, 239, 254, 282, 309
Harmony, 80, 178, 222, 316
Harpies, 188, 236
Hattusa, 33, 165
Hattusili(s), 33, 103
Heaven, 14, 31–32, 38, 67, 87, 122, 130, 132, 136, 140, 143, 154, 161, 181, 191, 197, 212, 214, 218, 229, 255, 272, 277, 280–281, 288, 291, 302, 304–305, 308–314
Hebe, 79
Hebrews, 32, 158-159
Hebros, River, 180
Hecate, 233, 235
Hector, 48, 60, 80, 92–94, 104–107, 109–110, 114, 118–130, 134, 136–139, 141–142, 149, 152, 157, 165–167, 173, 194, 206, 213, 265, 278–281, 283, 316
Hecuba, 60, 65, 67, 108, 120, 153, 173–174, 316
Hegasianax of Alexandria, 145, 149
Hegemon of Alexandria Troas, 178
Hegesippus, 181
Heiromene, 316
Helea, 82–83
Helen of Sparta (Helen of Troy), 33, 63, 67–69, 73–77, 79–85, 89–92, 94–96, 99, 114, 118, 122–123, 138, 142, 144–145, 148, 153–154, 157, 160–161, 163, 173, 175, 201, 214, 234, 237, 244, 254, 265, 286, 300, 316
Helenus, 60, 73, 120, 126, 141–142, 145, 194–196, 199, 201, 233, 310, 316
Helicaon, 316
Helicon, Mount, 78, 255, 260
Hell, 151, 236, 239, 310
Hellanikos, 43, 145, 149, 165, 180, 208, 244–245, 293, 299

Hellê, 20
Hellenika, 83
Hellespont, 20, 26, 93, 105, 108
Helorus, 203
Helymus, 210
Hemina, Lucius Cassius, 247, 293–294
Hephaestus (Vulcan), 59, 87, 131, 133, 136, 188, 191, 202, 222, 239, 266, 289
Hera (Juno), 23, 27, 30, 67–68, 78, 101, 114, 120, 124, 128, 132, 135–136, 154, 182, 199–201, 204, 210–211, 213–217, 219, 224–225, 253–255, 272, 274, 279–280, 303, 314, 317
Heraclea, 200, 251
Heracleum, 88
Herakliad, 192
heraldry, 176, 292
Herculaneum, 62, 228
Hercules, 23, 64, 66, 68–69, 72–73, 79, 88–89, 92, 132, 141, 143–144, 154, 176, 191, 199, 210, 222, 230, 235, 238, 242–243, 245, 249–251, 253, 261–262, 265, 268, 273, 278, 298, 306, 308, 317
Herculeum, 89
Herennii, gens, 286
*Heriode*s, 23, 77, 217
Hermaphroditos, 222
Hermes (Mercury), 21, 79, 90, 132, 216–218, 222, 257, 261, 287, 292–293, 306, 317
Hermione, 194
Herodes of Priene, 178
Herodotus, 35, 69, 75, 82–83, 86, 88–89, 97, 185, 208
Heroicus, 119
Herophilus, 222
Hesiod, 19, 43, 78–79, 83, 86–87, 97–98, 160, 229, 243, 255, 260, 308
Hesione, 68–69, 71–74, 80, 82, 90–91, 95, 127, 145, 157, 173, 214, 230, 254, 261, 278, 316

343

In Search of Aeneas

Hesperia, 214, 243, 287
Hestia (Vesta), 31, 153
Hesychius of Alexandria, 60
Hieromneme, 46
Hiketaon, 42
Hild, J.A., 135
Himera, 243, 257
Himilco, 204
Hippasus, 129
Hippocrates, 35
Hippodameia, 60–61, 127, 316
Hippothous, 107
Hişarlik, 54–55, 58
Historia Brittonum, 301
Hittites, 33, 43, 59, 89, 94, 99–100, 102–104, 107, 109–110, 164–165, 304
Hobhouse, John Cam, 53
Hoffmann, Wilhelm, 249
Hogarth, William, 117
Hollar, Wenceslaus, 280
Homer, 14 & passim
Homeric hymns, 21, 86, 97, 166-167, 175, 241
Homeridae, 98
Hope-Simpson, R., 70
Horace, 76, 230, 288, 303
Horsfall, Nicholas, 268–270
Huxley, G.L., 84
Hyacinthos, 74
Hyads, 197
Hydra, 141, 143, 236
Hyginus, 32
Hyle, 106
Hyllus, 141
Hypanis, 152
Hyperboreans, 253, 317
Hyphasis, 251
Hypolympidia, Aphrodite, 181
Hyrtacus, 107

Iamids, 188
Iapygia, 198
Iapyx, 279
Iarbas, 216, 220
Iasion, 43, 45, 175, 187, 269, 293, 316
Ibsen, Henrik, 285
Ida, Mount, 18 & passim, 199, 222, 246, 258–260, 272-273, 278–280, 302, 305, 308, 313

Idaeus, 45, 123, 187, 316
Idaia, daughter of Dardanos, 45, 316
Idalian Venus, 225
Idalion, 214, 225
Idean cave, 184
Idomeneus, 61, 127–128, 140, 183, 199
ierodules, 209, 222
Ikizce, 27
Ilia, daughter of Aeneas, 260
Iliad, 14 & passim, 183, 209, 244, 250–251, 254, 264, 266–267, 285, 313
Ilian Plain, 49
Ilians of Sardinia, 242
Ilion (Greek Troy), 35, 53, 101, 178, 209, 242, 251, 278
Ilioneus, 175, 214, 245
Ilios (Homer's Troy), 51, 85, 100-101, 103, 208, 277
Ilium (Roman Troy), 53–54, 67, 101, 103, 260, 283
Iliupersis, 135, 155
Ilos, King of Troy, 42, 46, 51–53, 56, 65, 101, 103, 107, 124, 126, 164, 182, 247, 294, 316
Image du Monde, 310
Inachids, 160
Inanna, 30–33, 38, 221, 235
Inbu-Hedj (Memphis), 89
Indiges, 302-304
Innana, 33, 87
Inopus, 182
Instituta Barbarica, 245
Io, 88
Ioannina, 71
Iolkos Cycle, 66
Iolus, 299
Ionian, Ionians, 34-35, 97, 101, 192–193, 197
Iopas, 215
Iovem Indigitem, 302
Iphidamas, 126, 316
Iphigeneia, 92
Iris Hotel, 50, 156,
Iris, 105, 117, 219, 224, 268
Ischia, 242
Ishtar, 30–31, 34, 87, 222
Isin, 33
Ismarian Lake, 73

Isola Licosa, 228
Isola San Pantaleo (Mozia), 210
Isole Cyclopi, 202
Isos, 111
Istanbul, 20
Italus, 245
Ithaka, 91, 97, 161, 188, 243
Iulus, 170, 277, 279, 287, 299, 306, 316-317
Izmir, 34, 47, 59, 91, 96, 108

Jackson, John, 213, 270
Janiculum Hill, Rome, 169, 244, 257
Janko, Richard, 97
Jason of Iolkos, 66
Jericho, 56
Jerusalem, 85, 308
Jesus, 14, 308–309, 311–312
Jews, 308–309, 311–312
Jove (Zeus), 299
Judah, 85
Judea, 308
Julia, Caesar's sister, 190, 317
Julian star (see Sidus Iulium), 191, 304
Julii, gens, 170, 238, 275–277, 286–287, 299, 303–304, 306, 317
Julio-Claudians, 23, 305–306
Jupiter (Zeus), 178, 274, 277, 304, 312
Jupiter Latiaris, 277, 304
Justinus, 257
Juturna, 279–281, 290, 317

Kabeiroi, 45, 293
Kadesh, Battle of, 43, 89, 100, 102
Kadmilos, 45, 293
Kadmos, 98, 178, 222, 316
Kalafat, 92, 124, 156
Kalidbahir, 174
Kalivo, Hill of, 195
Kallicolonê, Hill of, 132, 134
Kamariotissa, 36
Kamptz, H. von, 103
Kara Tepe, 132
Karabel Pass, 59
Karaburun Peninsula, 197
Kaskalkur, 100
Kastania, 62, 186

Index

katagóghia, 209
Kato Rematiaris, 182
Kaukones, 124, 135
Kaz Daği, 20, 110, 123
Kazantzakis, Nikos, 157
Kebren, 27, 35, 67
Keiler, Alexander, 39
Kemer Su, 49
Kerkyra, 173, 193
Keryneia, 72
Kesik Canal, 68, 93–94, 123, 126, 132, 140, 313
Khonsou son of Amun, 88
Kikkuli, 107
Kikones, 108, 124
Kirk Goz, 'forty eyes', 49
Kirk, G., 106
Knight, W.F.J., 206, 208, 242
Knossos, 63, 142, 184
Koca Kaya, 123
Korcula, 173
Korfmann, Manfred Osman, 55, 57, 98, 100, 165, 178, 283
Kouklia, 86
Kronos, 52, 62, 78, 86–88, 187, 202, 209, 229, 253, 260, 313, 316-317
Kubeleya, 31
Küçük, 27–29, 35, 40, 42, 313
Küçukkuyu, 123
Kukkuni, 102-103
Kulaba, plain of 32
Kum Kale, 50, 56
Kum Tepe, 56
Kursak, River, 29, 48
Kurşunlu, 26, 27
Kuş Gölü, 166
Kybele, 30-31, 33, 35, 37–40, 45, 97, 168, 175, 222, 246, 258–260, 269, 272, 316
Kyme, 97, 233
Kynthos, Mount, 182–184
Kythera, 62, 82–86, 88, 92, 100, 185, 259
Kyzikos, 103

labyrinths, 63, 223, 234
Lacedaemon, 74, 80
Lacedaemonia, 74–75, 100, 145, 185
Lacinia, Hera, 201
Laconia, 73-74, 80, 82
Lacrimae rerum, 213, 274
Lactantius, 282, 309
Lane Fox, Robin, 87, 98, 242
Laocoön, 147–148, 152
Laogonus, 129
Laomedon, 42, 46, 52, 68, 73, 103, 107, 144, 210, 218, 230, 316
Laothoe, 108
Lapiths, 62
Lar Aeneas, 304
Larisa, 107
Larissa Kremaste, 70
Larme, Cape, 201
Latacz, Jachim, 98–99, 101
Latinus, 184, 243, 245, 252–254, 269, 274–275, 280, 289–292, 296, 300, 304, 316-317
Latium, 184, 204, 225, 238 & passim, 299, 317
Laurentum, 226, 247, 249, 252, 254, 260, 274–275, 279-280, 290, 303
Lausus, 274, 299
Lavinia, 24–25, 157, 184, 234, 238, 245, 253–254, 289–292, 298, 300–301, 316-317
Lavinium, 200, 231, 242, 247–249, 252, 254–255, 257, 278, 290–300, 302, 304
Lawrence, D.H., 267
Lazba (Lesvos), 100, 103
Lazenby, J.F., 70
Le Guin, Ursula K., 24, 290–291, 296–297
Leaf, Walter, 46, 55, 107–112, 125
Lebanon, 83, 85
Lecce, 199
Lechevalier, Jean Baptiste, 48, 53
Leda, 76, 91
Lefkada, 188–191
Lehman, K., 37
Leiocritus, 130
Leir, King 301
Lëkursit hill, 196
Leleges, 108, 111, 124, 159, 172

Lemba, 86
Lemnos, 106, 142
Lerna, 143
Lesbos, 100, 103, 149, 165
Lesches, 65–66, 140–142, 147, 149, 165, 244
Lesvos, 34–37, 43–44, 100, 112, 145, 149, 165, 176–177, 180, 244, 299
Lethe, 226, 237–238
Lethus, 107
Leto, 79, 118, 182
Leuca, 199
Leucosia, 228
Levant, 63, 83, 85, 89, 104, 109
Levi, Peter, 211, 229, 246, 253, 285
Levidi, 187
Lewis, Isle of, 38
Libya, Libyans, 50, 207-208, 211-212, 216
lightning, 34, 38, 40, 43–44, 87, 128, 142-143, 187, 200, 204, 215–216, 224m 271, 297, 313
Liguria, 271
Lilybaeum, 204
Liman Tepe, 107
Limbo, 310
Linear A, 98
Linear B, 34, 73, 98, 106, 149, 352
lions, lionesses, 19, 21, 23, 31, 37, 62, 65, 76, 79, 115–116, 122, 129, 132, 140, 142, 154, 175–176, 241, 263, 270, 272-273, 275, 306
Litochoro, 181
Livilla, 305
Livy, 218, 220, 238, 245, 254, 257–259, 265, 285, 289, 291–292, 296–298, 300–302, 304, 307
Llewellyn the Great, 301
Lochris, 69–71, 123, 143
lodestones, 37–38
Lolos, Yiannis, 71
London, 13, 58, 64, 236, 239
Lord of the Rings, the, 273
Lorrain, Claude, 211, 235, 261
Louvre, the, 36
Lucan, 52, 278, 283

Lucanian Apennines, 200
Lucatius Catulus, 151
Luce, J.V., 36, 55, 61, 68, 93–94, 97–98, 105, 114, 123–126, 132, 136–137, 147, 164
Lucretius, 276
Ludovisi Throne, 258
Ludus Troiae, 223–224
Luke, St, 312
Lukka, 109
Luwian, 100–101, 103–104
Lycaon, 107, 115
Lycia, Lycians, 107–109, 114-115, 118, 121, 123-124, 129, 175
Lycophron, 90, 224, 265, 268, 293
Lydia, Lydians, 50, 108, 268, 270
Lykaon, son of Priam, 131–132
Lykios, 107

Macedonia, 50, 178, 249–250, 259
machlosýne, 77, 99
Maclaren, Charles, 54–55
Maecenas, 229–230
Maeonia, Maeonians, 100, 108, 124, 141
Maera, 186
Maghreb, 207–208
Magna Graecia, 199-201, 208, 251, 256
Magna Mater, 259, 276, 288, 313
Magnesia, 44, 69–70
magnets, 37–40, 43-44, 57, 258–259, 313
Magnis Dis, 294
Magnisi Peninsula, 203
Magus, 273, 282
Maia, 79, 261, 317
Mainalo, 78, 186
Makron, 80, 175
Maleas, Cape, 62–64, 72–73, 88
Malian Gulf, 70
Manatabarhunta of Seha, 100
Manganello, Fossa di, 266-267
Mantineia, 187

Mantua, 228-230, 271
Manuzza, 204, 209, 222
Marcellus, 238
Marcia, 277, 317
Marcii, gens 306
Marcus Octavius, 247
Marius, 230
Marlowe, Christopher, 92
Marmara, Sea of, 20, 51, 91, 103, 107, 109, 166, 179
Maron, Anton von, 162
Mars (Ares), 161, 170, 231, 286
Marsala (Marsa Allah), 204
Marsic War, 150
Mary Magdalene, 312
Mary, Virgin, 258, 308
Masa (Mysia), 102, 109
Massimo, Palazzo, Rome, 297
Massyli (Maxyans), 208, 215
Matthew, St, 312
Matthiae, August, 166
Medea, 95
Medici, Cosmo I de, 270
Medon, 128, 143
Medusa, 84
Megara, Greece, 284
Melampus, 273
Melesigines (Homer), 96
Meliboeans, 106
Mellaart, James, 27
Memmii, gens, 279
Memnon, 139
Memphis, Egypt, 88–89
Mendere (Skamander), River, 20
Menecrates of Xanthus, 145–146, 149, 187
Menelaion, the, 75, 160
Menelaus, 33, 72, 74–76, 80, 82, 85, 89–91, 94–95, 99, 109, 114–115, 118–119, 123, 129–130, 134, 140, 142, 144–145, 148, 160–161, 163
Menestheus, 71, 201
Meonia, 109
Meriones, 101, 129
Merops, 107
Meshwesh, 208
Mesopotamia, 30–33, 56, 87, 97–99, 159, 235, 310

Messana, 100
Messapians, 199, 275
Messiah, 226, 308-309
Messina, Straits of, 201
Mesthles, 108
Metamorphoses, 161, 174, 182–183, 191, 201, 293, 303, 305
Metaponto, 200
Metelli, gens, 276
meteors, 34, 87, 259, 313, 305
Metis, 79
Metz, Paul de, 310
Mey, Oscar, 93
Mezentius, 254, 258, 262, 265–266, 268, 274–275, 296–297, 299, 302, 304, 307
Middleton, Michael, 301
Migonitis, Aphrodite 81
Miletus (Milawata), 34, 44, 90, 108, 139, 163, 165, 270
Millawanda, 164
Milton, John, 214
Mincius, 228, 230, 286
Minerva (Athena), 198–199
Minervae, Castrum vel Arx, 198
Minoans, 36, 45, 63, 82–83, 184, 236
Minos, 127, 209, 234, 236
Minotaur, 63, 234
Minyan ware, 57
Mira, 59, 109
Misenus, 175, 232, 234–235, 287
Mithymna, 35, 112
Mit-Rahineh, 89
Mitrikou, Lake, 73
Mnestheus, 175, 217, 279
Molossia, 153, 194, 244, 249
Molossos, 194, 316
Molus, 129
Momigliano, Arnaldo, 249
Mommsen, Theodor, 206
Monmouth, Geoffrey of, 161, 176, 214, 239, 301
Monumentum Ancryanum, Anatolia, 230
Mordtmann, Andreas 27
Morini tribe, 267

Index

Motya (Mozia), Sicily, 209–210, 221, 225
Mursili II, 102
Musaios, 79, 237
Muses, 97, 255, 296
Mussolini, Benito, 195, 203, 205, 242, 284, 287, 306
Muwatalli, 100, 102–103
Mycenae, 30, 33-34, 51, 55 & passim, 107, 110, 143, 153, 158-160, 165, 186-7, 208, 242, 249, 275
Mynes of Lyrnessus, 112
Myrine, 105
Myrmidons, 69, 92, 110–111, 129-130, 142
Mysia, 51, 91, 108–110, 124, 140, 165, 268
Mysteries, Samothrakian, 45, 249, 294

Naevius, Gnaeus, 220–221, 241, 257
Naousa, 250
Naples, 16, 76, 227–229, 231, 233, 242, 264, 266, 283, 285
Naplion, 100
Nastes, Carian warrior, 108
Nattier, Marc, 314
Natufians, 56, 63
Nau, Capo, 201
Nautes, 175, 224
Navarino, 72
Naxos, 184, 218
Nea Michaniona, 180
Neaethus, River, 200
Neander, 239
Neapolis, 185
Necessity, goddess, 79
Nemean Odes, 194
Nemesis, 76, 79
Nennius, 301
Neolithic, 38–39, 50, 52, 56–57, 86, 140, 199, 209, 262
Neoptolemus, 69, 140–143, 149–150, 153, 165, 173–174, 190, 194, 244, 249, 251, 316
Neptune (Poseidon), 191
Nereids, 213

Nereus, 76
Neritus, 188
Nero (or Uva) di Troia, 199
Nero, 199, 305–306
Nestor, 62, 72–73, 118, 124, 139, 200
Neto, River, 200
New York Times, 282
Newton, Charles, 124
Neïth, goddess of Saïs, 207
Nicea, 108
Night, 19, 24, 76, 79, 246, 316
Nike, 36
Nikopolis, 193
Nile, River, 88–89, 203, 207
Ninshubur, 33, 40
Nireus, 124
Noah, 159, 161, 179
Nola, Italy, 76, 264
Nonnus, 43, 178–179
nostos stories, 160-161, 184, 206, 243, 269, 275
Nova Siri, 200
Numa Pompilius, King of Rome, 238, 288, 291, 299, 306, 317
Numerius Julius Julus, 277, 299, 317
Numicius (also called Numicus), River, 246, 297, 304, 312, 314
Numidia, 208
Numitor, King of Alba Longa, 300–301, 317
nymphs, 15, 17–18, 23–25, 45, 47, 49, 60, 62, 67, 78, 193, 203, 211, 216, 241, 246, 272–273, 292, 311

Ocean(os), 44, 78, 91, 250, 316
Octavia, 238
Odius, Halizonian leader, 108
Odysseus, 62, 66, 91, 94–97, 99, 109, 124, 133, 136, 140–141, 144–146, 148, 161, 188, 201–202, 207, 221, 227, 241, 243–245, 247, 254, 264–265, 275, 286, 294, 299, 310
Odyssey 72, 89, 97, 99, 125, 136, 146, 148, 160–161,
201–202, 221, 227, 241, 243, 254
Oedipus, 66
Oenomaus, 128
Oenone, 67
Oenotrians, 214, 226, 262
Oeta, Mount, 141
Ogilby, John, 280
Olearos, 184
Oltos, 116–117, 122, 129, 175
Olympia, 14, 31, 116, 192, 203
Olympiai, 159
Olympias, 249–251
Olympus, 19, 21, 65, 77–79, 114–115, 117, 131, 157, 161, 170, 178, 181, 216, 239, 250, 272, 303, 313
Onchesmus (Sarandë), 196
Onetor, priest of Zeus, 129
Ophryneion, 149
Orchomenos, 63, 186
Orestes, 35, 77
Origo Gentis Romanae, 150–151, 183, 233, 241, 246–247, 252, 289, 297, 299, 302, 312
Orion, 184, 197
Orlando Furioso, 282
Orontes, 175, 211, 213
Orosius, 309
Orpheus, Orphism, 19, 65, 79, 96, 135, 237, 240, 311
Orthrys, Mount, 70
Ortygia, 182, 203
Ostia, 246–248, 252, 255, 259, 263, 267, 272, 275, 288
Otranto Straits of, 196, 251, 283–284
Otreus, 21
Ourania, Aphrodite, 308
Ovid, 23, 77, 161, 174, 182–183, 191, 195, 201, 217, 219, 258–259, 274, 286–287, 293, 303, 305, 311, 314

Pachynus (Cape Passero,), 203
Paeonians, 108, 124
Paestum, 228
Pagasitikos Gulf, 69–70
Page, Denys L., 106
Palaikastro, 82–83, 185

Palaiopoli, 36
Palaiopyrgos, 186
Palaipaphos, 86–88, 209, 313
Palaiskepsis, 26–29, 35, 39–40, 42, 45, 47–49, 56, 110, 163, 166–168, 246, 259, 294, 313
Palatine Hill, Rome, 169, 255, 259, 261–262, 286
Palazzola Acreide, 203
Paleopolis, 82
Pales, goddess, 261
Paliaskepsis, 40
Palinodia, 90
Palinuro, Cape, 227
Palinurus, 175, 197–198, 219, 226–228, 231, 236–237
Palladion, 294
Palladium, 52, 172, 174, 277, 294–295
Pallantium, 200, 255, 261–262, 317
Pallas (Athena), 229, 294
Pallas, son of Evander, 262-3, 268, 273–275, 281, 283, 290, 317
Pallenê Peninsula, 180–181, 244
Pammon, 140
Panagitsa, 186
Pandarus, 107, 114–116, 121, 123
Pantagia, 203
Pantokrator, Mount, Corfu, 196
Paphlagonia, 108-109, 118, 140
Paphos, Cyprus, 86
Paradise, 239, 310
Parco Virgiliana, Naples, 285
Parentalia, festival, 221, 223
Parian Marble, the, 160
Paris, 48 & passim, 199, 254, 265, 278, 280, 290, 305, 316
Pariya-muwasi, 103
Parnassos, Mount, 70, 159
Paros, 184
Parthenias (Virgil), 229
Parthenius, Mount, 268
Parthenon, the, 155
Parthenope, 228–229

Parthians, 170, 283, 285
Paşa Tepe, 105
Passero, Cape, 203
Pater deus indiges, 302
Patras, 188
Patrem Indigetem, 302
Patroclus, 127, 129–131, 137–138, 140, 147, 250, 273, 281, 286
Paul, St, 310
Pausanias, 65, 75, 81, 83–84, 116, 157, 185–188, 251
Pavlopetri, 185
pax Romanum, 280
Pedasos, 108, 111-112
pedigrees, 42-43, 45–46, 52, 56, 79, 103–104, 167, 207, 291, 300–301
Peirous, 108
Pelasgia, Pelasgians, 69- 70, 107, 124
Pelasgic Argos, 70
Peleus, 67, 69–71, 77, 80, 130–131, 133–134, 138
Pelion Peninsula, 62, 65–67, 69–70, 141
Pelodes, Lake of, 193
Peloponnese, 34, 62–63, 72–73, 82, 88, 116, 118, 149, 185–186, 188, 251–252, 262
Penates, 36, 170, 174, 178, 287–288, 291–295, 298, 302, 304, 306
Penatiger, (Aeneas), 293
Penglase, Charles, 31
Penni, Luca, 232
Penthesilea, 139, 275
Penthilus, 35
Perama, 184
Percote, 107
Pergamea, 184
Pergamon, 50, 258
Pergamos (Pergamum), (Troy) 50, 57, 118, 122, 184, 194, 246, 284, 313
Periphas, 130
Perret, Jean, 177, 189
Persephone, 31, 79, 235
Persia, 71, 181, 206, 250
Perugia, Paul of, 270
Pessinus, 258–260, 305
Peteon, 106

Petra Tou Romiou, 87
Phanes Protogonos, 19, 79, 316
Pharsalia, 70, 149
Pharsalos, 69–70, 278
Pheneos, 261
Phereclus, 73
Philoctetes, 69, 106, 141–144
Philostratus, 119
Philyra, 62
Phineas of Salmydessus, 45, 316
Phlegethon, 237
Phlegra, Naples, 235
Phlegran Peninsula, Thrace, 235
Phobus, 222
Phocus, 69, 71
Phoenicia, Phoenicians, 30, 82-83, 85, 87, 98, 185, 207–210, 212, 214, 216, 220–221, 225, 256, 264
Phoenissae, 294
Phoenix, 207
Phoinikous, 83
Phorbas, 226, 245
Phorcas, 273
Phorcys, 108
Phrygia, Phrygians, 21, 23, 51, 59, 80, 108, 124, 155, 166, 173, 175, 199, 215, 258-259, 279, 289, 305
Phthia, 69–70, 73, 149, 194
Phylace, 92
Piazzetta Colonne, Brindisi, 284
Picus, 253, 317
Piedigrotta, Naples, 285
Pietas, goddess, 286, 306
Pietole, 228
piety, *pietas*, 37, 63, 136, 150, 154, 161, 174, 214, 230, 236, 243, 265, 267, 280, 282, 284, 286–287, 293, 306, 309, 314
pigs, piglets, 255, 261, 292
Pijamaradu, 102–103
Pilos, 72
Pinarbaşi, 49, 137
Pindar, 159, 194, 207
Pinelli, Bartolommeo, 236
Piraeus, 71

Index

Pisa, 271
Pizzolungo, 205
Pla, 109
Plantagenets, 176
Plato, 52, 56, 157, 207
Pleiades, 44, 74
Pleione, 44, 91, 316
Plemmirio, Plemmyrium, 203
Pliny, 235, 252, 286, 302
Plommer, H., 83
Plough my Vulva, 33
Podarces, 68, 103
Polichna, 27
Policoro, 200, 251
Polis, Cyprus, 88
Polites, 60, 105, 137, 153, 223
Pollux, 72, 76, 244, 292–294
Polybus, 126, 316
Polydamas, 126, 128–129, 140–141, 145
Polydorus, 60, 94–95, 182, 316
Polygnotos, 157
Polymestor, 142
Polyphemus, 202, 243
Polyxena, 94, 139, 173–174
Pompeii, 135, 191, 202, 216, 228, 230, 266, 278–279, 283, 285, 287, 305-306
Pontifical Affairs, 232, 241
Popes, 306, 309–310
Populonia, 271
Porta Collina, 258, 276
Portonaccio, 265
Poseidon (Neptune), 34, 36, 68, 71–72, 77–78, 94, 114, 123–124, 127–128, 131–132, 134–136, 148, 154, 161, 163, 166, 183, 187, 191–192, 199, 211, 213, 222, 225–227, 230, 264, 314
Posillipo Hill, Naples, 229, 231–232
Pound, Ezra, 136
Poussin, Nicholas, 267
Pratica di Mare, 291, 298
Preveza, 192
Priam, 15 & passim, 194–195, 210, 214, 217, 223, 236, 253, 261, 283, 301, 316
Priapus, 222

Priscus, Lucius Tarquinius, 233, 244, 299, 317
Procida, 241
Proclus, 66, 85, 92, 94, 96, 139
Proculus, 304
proditor, Aeneas, 145, 151
Prometheus, 316
Propertius, 285
prophecy, prophecies, 22, 54, 65, 119, 135, 142, 147-148, 152-153, 163, 166–167, 178, 183, 195, 198, 214-215, 233, 235, 239, 246–247, 252, 264, 266, 268-269, 309-310
prostitutes, prostitution, 32, 209, 222, 256, 258, 276
Protesilaus, 69, 92, 96, 106, 109
Proteus, 89
Protogonos, Phanes, 19, 79, 316
proxenos, 194
Pseudo-Apollodorus, 43, 45, 66, 85, 90, 150, 294
Pseudo-Servius, 32
Pseudo-Xenophon, 3, 62-3, 72, 83, 150
ptolemoio gephurai, the 'bridges of war', 124
Ptolemys, 251, 279
Punic Wars, 212, 219–220, 253, 256–260, 288
Punica, 270
Purcell, Henry, 14, 215, 219
Purgatory, 239, 310
Pygmalion, 220
Pylaemanes, 108, 118
Pylaeus, 107
Pylos, 63, 72, 82, 149, 200
Pyraechmes, 108
pyramids, 75, 89
Pyrgi, 271
Pyrrhus II of Epiros, 153, 251–252, 256–257, 285, 316
Pythagoras, Pythagoreans, 200, 311
Pythian Odes, 207
Pythocles, 155

Qart-ḥadašt (Carthage), 212
Quinctii, gens, 259

Quintilian, 285
Quintus Fabius Maximus, 238, 258
Quintus Smyrnaeus, 140–144, 146, 156, 258, 260
Quirinal Hill, 258

Ramesses II, 43, 89, 102
Raphael Sanzio da Urbino, 84
Rehak, Paul, 288
Reinhardt, K., 135
Remus, 244–245, 249, 257, 260, 287, 299, 301, 305, 307, 317
Report to Greco, 157
Repubblica, La, 199
Res Gestae Divi Augusti, 230
Resurrection, 309, 311–312
Rhadamanthus, 237
Rhamnous, 76
Rhea Silvia, 161, 170, 286, 300-301, 317
Rhea, 30, 78, 187, 316
Rheneia, 182, 313
Rhipeus, 152
Rhodes, 50, 117, 204, 222
Rhomê, 245, 299
R(h)omus, 245, 249, 257, 299
Rijnmut, Carl, 312
Roma, 245, 256, 288, 316
Roman d'Eneas, 215, 290
Roman de Troie, 121
Romulus, 161–162, 170, 217, 238–239, 245, 249, 255–257, 259–260, 262, 286–287, 291–292, 299–301, 304–305, 307, 316-317
Rubicon, 278
Rudiae, 260
Rusuca, 211
Rutherford, I., 178
Rutulians, 253–254, 274, 279–281, 289, 296–298, 317

Sahara Desert, 89
Saint-Marie, Benoit de, 121
Salamis, 68–69, 71–72, 214, 261
Salentine Peninsula, 198–199
Salerno, 47

Salmydessus, 45
Sâme, 188
Samothraki (Samothrace), 36–38, 40, 43–45, 87, 174, 176–180, 184, 187–188, 190, 222, 249–250, 253, 258, 269, 293–294, 305, 311, 313
Samuha, Ishtar of, 34
Sandwich, Earl of, 88
Santa Severa, 189, 271
Santillo, Carlo, 236
Saon from Samothraki, 177, 293
Saos, Mount, Samothraki, 36–37, 177, 179
Sarandë, 196–198
Sardinia, 242
Saronic Gulf, 69, 71
Sarpedon, 109, 118, 126–129
Satan, 310
Saturn, 169, 238, 262, 284, 309, 317
Saturnius, 253
Savran Tepe, 167–168
Saïs, 207–208
Scaean Gate, 57, 61, 114, 120, 136, 139, 146–147, 194, 196, 287
Scherer, Margaret R., 135, 239, 290
Schliemann, Heinrich, 54–57, 61, 63, 83–84, 93, 102, 105, 123, 125
Schliemann, Sophia, 55
Scholia on *Iliad*, 60
Scipio, 257
Scylaceum (Squillace), 201
Scylla, 201–202, 226, 236
Scythia, 50, 206
Sebasteion, Aphrodisias, 23
Seferis, Giorgos, 90
Segesta, 208, 210, 220, 224, 256
Segrais, Jean Renaud de, 211
Seha (Maeonia), 100, 109
Selçuk, 34
Seleucus I Nicator, 251,
Seleucus Kallinikos, 257
Selinus (Selinunte), 204, 208, 210

Selvans, 292
Semele, 316
Seneca, 286
Serestus, 175, 214, 217
Sergestus, 175, 214, 217
serpents, 19, 32, 127, 147–148, 153, 175, 188, 221, 281
Servius Tullus, 299
Servius, 43, 153, 177, 211, 221, 245, 247, 269–270, 293
sesterii, 306
Sestos, 107
Severus Alexander, Roman emperor, 172, 306
Sextus Pompey, 191
Shahhat (Saïs), 207
Shakespeare, William, 24, 76, 114, 121–122, 153, 260
shearwaters, 275
Shulgi hymns, 33
Sibylline Books, 233–234, 258
sibyls, 227, 233–236, 239, 241, 246, 260, 310
Sicanians, 203, 208
Sicels, 208, 262
Sicily, Sicilians, 15, 32, 88, 155, 157, 199–204, 206, 208–212, 219–221, 224–227, 231, 242–243, 245, 247, 251–252, 256–258, 262, 264, 286, 300, 313
sickles, 78, 87–88, 196, 209, 313
Sicyon, 60
Side, near Neapolis, 185
Sidon, 50, 85, 89, 92, 95
Sidus Iulium, 191, 304–305, 308
Sigeum Ridge, 50–51, 68, 93, 109, 112, 126, 132, 140, 176
Silius, 270
Silvanus, 266
Silvius, 238, 287, 291, 298, 300–301, 316-317
Simois, River, 46, 49–50, 54, 125, 132, 194, 316
Simon, E., 76
Sinon, 149

Sinop, 108
Siphnian Treasury, Delphi, 129
Sirens, 228–229, 239
Sirenum Scopuli, 228
Siris, 200
Siro, 229
Sivri Tepe, 140
Skamander, River, 18, 20–21, 26–27, 29, 39, 45–46, 48–50, 54, 60, 67, 92–93, 103, 105, 124–125, 128, 136–137, 156, 163, 167, 313, 316
Skamandrios, 164–166, 195, 316
Skandeia, 82–83
Skepsis, 25–29, 35, 48, 135, 161, 166–168, 176, 316
Skiathos, Island of, 69
Skipping Myrine's Tump, 105
Skyros, Island of, 141
Smyrna, 34, 96–97, 125
snakes, 32, 48, 79, 122, 130, 141, 155, 221, 292
Socrates, 157
Sol Indiges, 302
Solfatara, 235
Solinus, 247
Solon of Athens, 207
Sortes Virgilianae, 310
Sounion, Cape, 71
Sparta, 33, 72-74, 80, 85, 90, 184–186, 194, 199, 237, 292
Sperchios, River, 70
Squillace, 201
Starke, Franz, 100
Statilius Taurus, T., 297, 302
Stavros, Ithaka, 97
Stele Virgiliana 205
Stephen of Byzantium, 49, 165, 243
Stesichorus, 90, 243, 287
Sthenelus, 115–116
Strabo, 26–27, 35, 45, 54, 61, 67, 70, 93, 107–108, 111, 113, 163, 166–167, 183, 198, 200
Strife, goddess, 126, 236
Strophades, 188
Strymo, 60

Index

Styx, River, 139, 236, 303
Suetonius, 228, 231, 238, 257, 277, 284–285
Sulla, 230, 260
Sulpicius, 284
Sumerians, 56
Superbus, Locius Tarquinius, 244, 299, 317
Suppiluliuma I, 102
Suppiluliuma II, 165
Supplementum to the *Aeneid*, 283, 289–290
Sybaris, 200
Sychaeus, 214, 218, 220, 236
Sylloge Inscriptionum Graecarum 277
Symi, Island of, 124
Syracusa, 203–204
Syria, 33, 87, 165
Syrtes reefs, 211

Ta Dardanika, 178
Tabula Iliaca, 116, 127–128, 135, 243, 287
Tancredi, 282
Tanit, goddess of Carthage 213
Taranto, 199–201, 251
Tarchon, 262, 265–266, 268, 271, 296
Tardieu, Nicolas, 314
Tarentum, 292
Tarhunna, 43–44, 59
Tarkasnawa of Mira, 59
Tarquins, 244–245, 268, 317
Tarquinia, 244, 268, 270–271
Tartarus, 78, 237, 240
Tasso, Torquato, 282
Tavole Palatine, Metaponto, 200
Tawagalawa Letter, 103
Taxiarhis chapel, Pelion, 67
Taygetus, River, 73–75, 161
Tegea, 268
Telamon, 68–69, 71–72, 90–91, 121, 123, 214
Telegonus, 245
Telephus, 92, 108, 140, 245, 265, 268–269
Tellus (Gaia), 288
Tenedos, 47, 90, 92–93, 141, 147, 176

Tennes, son of Apollo, 92
Tennyson, Alfred, Lord, 115, 117
Tereia Mount, 107
Testament, Old, 85, 159, 308
Tešup, 43
Tethys, 128
Teucer, 45, 52, 68, 113, 126, 140, 183–184, 207, 214, 316
Teucrians (Trojans), 45
Teukria, 207, 208
Teuthrania, 91
Tevfikiye, 55
Thales of Miletus, 44
Thapsus, 203
Thaumasion Mount, 78, 186–187
Theban cycle, 66
Thebe in the Troad, 108, 110–112, 141, 194
Thebes, Boetia, 100, 106, 149, 163, 184, 194, 251
Themis, 77, 317
Themiste, 52, 68, 164
Theocritus, 209
Theogony, 78, 86, 243, 308
Theoi Megaloi (the Great Gods), 36
Theoroi, 37, 177–178
Thera, Mount, 63
Therapne, 74–76, 94, 160, 186
Thermaic Gulf, 180–181
Thersander, 141
Thersites, 114
Theseus, 63, 66, 184, 218, 234
Thespiae, 242
Thessaloniki, 108, 180
Thessaly, 34, 92, 182, 194, 278
Thetys, 67, 70, 77, 80, 92, 114, 131–133, 139, 143, 194, 252, 266
Thirteen Altars, Lavinium, 291–292
Thonis, 89
Thornton, Agathe, 125
Thrace, Thracians, 36–37, 45, 50, 65, 73, 79, 108–109, 118, 124, 139, 174,
176–177, 180–182, 235, 243–244, 250
Thronos Dios, 181
Throsmos (on the Plain of Troy), 126
Thucydides, 99, 208
Thymbra, 49, 124, 183
Thymbraeus, 175
Thymbrian Apollo, 122, 127, 139
Tiber, River, 156–157, 162, 169, 179, 226, 238, 241–242, 245–246, 255, 261, 287–288, 290
Tiberius, Emperor, 308
Tiepolo, Giovanni Battista, 212, 314
Tigris, River, 30
Tilly, Bertha, 246
Timaeus, 207, 292–293
Timandra, 80
Time, 79, 135, 158, 160, 178, 316
Timeus, 293
Tinos, 182
Tirebolu, 108
Tiryns, 63, 73, 251
Tisiphone, 237
Titans, 44, 67, 70, 77–78, 86, 118, 182, 187, 237, 313
Tithonus, 22, 42, 52, 139, 316
Titus Pomponius Attikus, 294
Tityrus, 229
Tmolus, Mount, 108
Tolkien, J.R.R., 151, 273
Tongurlu, 27–28
Tor Tignosa, 304
Toxaechmes, 144
Trachi, Mount, 186
Trachis, 70
Tragliatella, 223
Tragos Valley, 186
Trajan, Emperor, 277, 306
Trambelus, 68, 90
Trapani, 88, 204–205, 209
Trebia, Battle of, 257
Triton, 213, 232
Trivia, 233
Troad, 20 & passim, 199, 250, 259, 285, 294, 302
Troezenus, 108

351

Troia (Aecae), 199
Troia Projekt, 55
Troika, 43, 149, 180, 293
Troilus and Cressida/Troilus and Criseyde, 76, 114, 212
Troilus, 76, 114, 121–122, 265, 316
Tros, 42, 46, 51, 61, 103, 107, 149, 230, 316
Troy Novant (London), 13, 239
Tucca, 153, 285
Tudhalija I, 100, 102
Tudhaliya IV, 164-165
Tudors, 13, 42, 276
Tullus Hostilius, 238, 299–300, 317
Turnus, 234, 239, 253 & passim, 291, 297, 307, 317
Tuscany, 223, 253, 269
Tydeus, 115
Tyndareus, 33, 76
Typhon, 202
Tyre, 91, 212–214, 220
Tyrrhenia, 223, 245, 296, 316
Tyrrhenian Sea and coast, 201, 226, 242, 245, 266, 298, 300
Tyrrhenus, 254, 265, 289
Tyrsenus, 265, 268
Tzetzes, 90

Ucalegon, 145
Ugolini, Manfred, 195–196
Uluburun Peninsula, 51
Ulysses (Odysseus), 188
Ulysses, 115, 117
Uni, goddess, 271
United States of America, 314
Unquiet Grave, The, 226
Urania (Aphrodite), 224
Uranos, 52, 78–79, 86–87, 196, 209, 225, 313, 316-317
Urhi-Teshub, 34
Uruk, 33, 97, 159
Uta-napishtim, 159, 161, 179

Vacchina, River, 266
Varia Historia, 150

Varius, 153, 231, 285
Varro, 149–150, 181, 221, 276–277, 292–293, 302
Vatican Museum, 148, 150, 247
Vaux, W., 27
Véa, 185
Vegio, Maffeo, 283, 289–291
Veii, 244-245, 265
Veldecke, Heinrich von, 176, 216, 290
Venus (Aphrodite), 15, 30, 86, 122, 162, 181, 212, 215, 225, 276, 278, 288, 294
Venus Ericis/Erycina, 247, 256, 258, 260, 276, 288
Venus Genetrix, 170, 279, 286
Venus Victrix in Capitolio, 258
Vermaseren, Maarten J., 35, 39
Veronese scholiast on *Aeneid*, 150, 304
Vesta (Hestia), 258, 291, 294, 304
Vestal Virgins, 262, 266
Vesuvius, Mount, 228, 305
Via Sacra, 169, 277
Victoria, Queen, 239
Victorians, 218
Victory, 36, 259, 262, 289, 302, 314
Villa Borghese, 162, 306
Villanovan culture, 261, 264, 270
Vinalia Priora (Vinalia Prima), 258, 274, 299
Vines, vineyards, 32, 47, 49, 149, 226, 228, 274
Virgil, 14–15, 19, 32, 45, 64–65, 68–69, 87, 122, 136, 151 & passim
Vivarini, Antonio, 84
Volscians, 275, 279, 296
Volterra, 80, 271
Vothonos, 82
Vrina, 193–196
Vulci, 116, 122, 129, 134, 140, 155, 157, 175, 265, 271

Vytina, 187

Wadi al Natuf, 56
Waggon-road, at Troy, 49, 136
Wales, 13, 42, 121, 239, 307
Wales, Catherine, Princess of, 301
Walmu, King of Wilusa, 164
Wanassa, goddess, 30–31, 86–87, 209–210, 222
Washington, George, 314
waterspouts, 73, 87
West, Martin, 43, 46, 66, 96, 139
Wilamowitz-Moellendorff, Enno von, 166, 206–207
Williams, 152, 174, 217–218, 231, 234, 237–238, 273
Wilusa, Wilusija, 100–103, 109, 164
wine, 47, 51, 65, 76, 80, 125, 131, 141, 155, 183–184, 188, 195, 197, 199, 202, 204, 210, 212, 214, 221, 226, 229, 262, 274, 299
Wolf, Christa, 64–65, 68, 90, 96, 113, 141, 148, 153
Wood, Michael, 72–73, 104
Wood, Robert, 166
Wooden horse, 56, 146-7

Xanthus, River, 20, 103, 156, 194

Yahweh, 159–160
Yaphio, 74
Yassi Tepe, 93
Yeats, W.B., 136
Yenice, 110–111
Yesilyurt, 123

Zakynthos, 188, 192, 316
Zangger, Eberhard, 207
Zeitünlü, 111
Zeleia, 107, 250
Zeus (Jupiter), 19 & passim
Zeus Altari, 123
Zeus Ammon, 216
Zeytinli, 111–112
Zidrou, Dr Konstantina, 193